THE CAMBRIDGE COMPANION TO NINETEENTH-CENTURY AMERICAN LITERATURE AND POLITICS

The Cambridge Companion to Nineteenth-Century American Literature and Politics addresses the political contexts in which nineteenth-century American literature was conceived, consumed, and criticized. Individual chapters examine how US literature from this period engaged with broad political concepts and urgent political issues, such as liberalism, conservatism, radicalism, nationalism, communitarianism, sovereignty, religious liberty, partisanship and factionalism, slavery, segregation, immigration, territorial disputes, voting rights, gendered spheres, and urban/rural tensions. Chapters on literary genres and forms show how poetry, drama, fiction, oratory, and nonfiction participated in political debate. The volume's Introduction situates these chapters in relation to two larger disciplines, the history of political thought and literary history. This Companion provides a valuable resource for students and instructors interested in nineteenth-century American literature and politics.

JOHN D. KERKERING is Professor of English at Loyola University Chicago. His first book, *The Poetics of National and Racial Identity in Nineteenth-Century American Literature* (2003), was a *Choice* Outstanding Academic Title. He has published essays in *American Literature, Studies in Romanticism,* and *Victorian Poetry*. His latest book is *Racial Rhapsody: The Aesthetics of Contemporary U.S. Identity* (2019).

THE CAMBRIDGE COMPANION TO NINETEENTH-CENTURY AMERICAN LITERATURE AND POLITICS

JOHN D. KERKERING
Loyola University Chicago

Shaftesbury Road, Cambridge CB2 8EA, United Kingdom

One Liberty Plaza, 20th Floor, New York, NY 10006, USA

477 Williamstown Road, Port Melbourne, VIC 3207, Australia

314–321, 3rd Floor, Plot 3, Splendor Forum, Jasola District Centre, New Delhi – 110025, India

103 Penang Road, #05-06/07, Visioncrest Commercial, Singapore 238467

Cambridge University Press is part of Cambridge University Press & Assessment, a department of the University of Cambridge.

We share the University's mission to contribute to society through the pursuit of education, learning, and research at the highest international levels of excellence.

www.cambridge.org
Information on this title: www.cambridge.org/9781108841894

DOI: 10.1017/9781108895095

© Cambridge University Press 2024

This publication is in copyright. Subject to statutory exception and to the provisions of relevant collective licensing agreements, no reproduction of any part may take place without the written permission of Cambridge University Press & Assessment.

First published 2024

A catalogue record for this publication is available from the British Library

A Cataloging-in-Publication data record for this book is available from the Library of Congress

ISBN 978-1-108-84189-4 Hardback
ISBN 978-1-108-81526-0 Paperback

Cambridge University Press & Assessment has no responsibility for the persistence or accuracy of URLs for external or third-party internet websites referred to in this publication and does not guarantee that any content on such websites is, or will remain, accurate or appropriate.

In memory of
Carol Jean Murphy
1941–2013

Contents

List of Figures	*page* ix
List of Contributors	x
Acknowledgments	xiv
Chronology of Major Works and Events	xv

    Introduction: Politics and Literary History   1
    John D. Kerkering

PART I CONCEPTS

1   The Liberal Tradition and Slavery   19
    Arthur Riss

2   Conservatism: Tradition, Hierarchy, and Fictions of Social Change   35
    Edward Whitley

3   The Literature of Radicalism   51
    J. Michelle Coghlan

4   Nationalism: Character, Identity, and Hyphenated Selfhood   67
    John D. Kerkering

5   Communitarianism and Its Literary Contexts   93
    David Faflik

6   Constructing Sovereignty through Legal and Religious Discourses   107
    Rochelle Raineri Zuck

7   Religious Reestablishment from Pulpit to Page   125
    Ashley Reed

8   Competing Views of Partisanship and Factionalism   143
    Sandra M. Gustafson

PART II ISSUES

9 Slavery: African American Vigilance in Slave Narratives of the 1820s and 1830s — 161
Kelly Ross

10 Disfranchisement, Segregation, and the Rise of African American Literature — 178
Kenneth W. Warren

11 Immigration: "The Chinese Question" in Economics, Law, and Literature — 190
Spencer Tricker

12 Territoriality: The Possessive Logics of American Placemaking — 205
Kathryn Walkiewicz

13 Voting Rights: "The Most Salient and Peculiar Point in Our Social Life" — 221
Leslie Petty

14 Defining and Defying a Woman's Sphere — 238
Monika M. Elbert

15 Beyond the City and the Country: Rural Scarcity and Indigenous Survivance — 253
John Funchion

PART III GENRES

16 Political Poetics: Intercrossing Discourses and American Belonging — 271
Shira Wolosky

17 Staging Debate in American Drama: Cheeses and Politics and Pigs — 289
Heather S. Nathans

18 The Evolving Modalities of Fiction and Politics — 304
D. Berton Emerson

19 Oratory: Persuasion in Performance — 319
Angela G. Ray

20 Authors on the Campaign Trail: "We Are Politicians Now" — 332
John Hay

Index — 348

Figures

4.1 *Southern Chivalry*, John L. Magee, lithograph, 1856.   *page* 69
Division of Home and Community Life, National
Museum of American History, Smithsonian Institution,
Catalog Number 60.3451.
4.2 *Walt Whitman, 1819–1892*, Samuel Hollyer, steel engraving,   71
1854. www.loc.gov/pictures/item/2002710162/.
4.3 *The Laying of the Cable*, Baker & Godwin Printers,   73
New York, woodcut, 1858. https://lccn.loc.gov/2004665357.
4.4 *The Stride of a Century*, Currier & Ives, New York,   75
lithograph, 1876. https://lccn.loc.gov/93506699.
4.5 *I Become a Transparent Eyeball*, Christopher Pearse Cranch,   90
manuscript drawing (recto), undated. https://digital.tcl.sc.e
du/digital/collection/myerson/id/566/.

Contributors

J. MICHELLE COGHLAN is Senior Lecturer in American Literature and Programme Director for American Studies at the University of Manchester. She is the author of *Sensational Internationalism: The Paris Commune and the Remapping of American Memory in the Long Nineteenth Century* (Edinburgh, 2016), which won the 2017 Arthur Miller Centre First Book Prize in American Studies, and editor of *The Cambridge Companion to Literature and Food* (Cambridge, 2020). Her new project is *Louise Michel in America*.

MONIKA M. ELBERT is Professor of English and Distinguished University Scholar at Montclair State University. She edits the *Nathaniel Hawthorne Review* and has published widely on the Gothic and on such nineteenth-century writers as Louisa May Alcott, Margaret Fuller, and Nathaniel Hawthorne. She is the editor of *Hawthorne in Context* (Cambridge, 2018) and coeditor of *American Women's Regionalist Fiction: Mapping the Gothic* (Palgrave, 2021).

D. BERTON EMERSON is Associate Professor of English at Whitworth University. His work has appeared in *American Literature*, *ESQ*, *Nineteenth-Century Literature*, and the *Los Angeles Review of Books*. With Gregory Laski, he edited *Democracies in America* (Oxford, 2023). His monograph titled *American Literary Misfits: The Alternative Democracies of Mid-Nineteenth-Century Print Cultures* is in press (North Carolina).

DAVID FAFLIK is Professor of English at the University of Rhode Island. A specialist in nineteenth-century American literature and culture, he is the author, most recently, of *Transcendental Heresies: Harvard and the Modern American Practice of Unbelief* (Massachusetts, 2020) and *Urban Formalism: The Work of City Reading* (Fordham, 2020).

JOHN FUNCHION is Associate Professor of English at the University of Miami. He is the author of *Novel Nostalgias: The Aesthetics of Antagonism in Nineteenth-Century US Literature* (Ohio State, 2015) and coeditor with Edward Watts and Keri Holt of *Mapping Region in Early American Writing* (Georgia, 2015). His essays have appeared in *Early American Literature*, *ESQ*, and *Modern Language Quarterly*, and his next book is entitled "Insurgent Fictions: Partisan Mythology and the War State in Nineteenth-Century US Literature."

SANDRA M. GUSTAFSON is William R. Kenan Jr. Professor of English at the University of Notre Dame and is the author of *Imagining Deliberative Democracy in the Early American Republic* (Chicago, 2011) and *Peace in the US Republic of Letters, 1840–1900* (Oxford, 2023) as well as the coeditor, with Robert S. Levine, of *Reimagining the Republic: Race, Citizenship, and Nation in the Literary Work of Albion W. Tourgée* (Fordham, 2023).

JOHN HAY is Associate Professor of English at the University of Nevada, Las Vegas, where he specializes in nineteenth-century American literature. He is the author of *Postapocalyptic Fantasies in Antebellum American Literature* (Cambridge, 2017) and the editor of *Apocalypse in American Literature and Culture* (Cambridge, 2020).

JOHN D. KERKERING is Professor of English at Loyola University Chicago. He is the author of *The Poetics of National and Racial Identity in Nineteenth-Century American Literature* (Cambridge, 2003) and *Racial Rhapsody: The Aesthetics of Contemporary U.S. Identity* (Routledge, 2019). His essays have appeared in *American Literature*, *Victorian Poetry*, *The Cambridge Companion to Nineteenth-Century American Poetry*, and *The Cambridge History of American Poetry*.

HEATHER S. NATHANS is Professor in the Tufts University Department of Theatre, Dance, and Performance Studies and is also the Nathan and Alice Gantcher Professor in Judaic Studies. Her publications include *Early American Theatre from the Revolution to Thomas Jefferson* (Cambridge, 2003), *Slavery and Sentiment on the American Stage, 1787–1861* (Cambridge, 2009), and *Hideous Characters and Beautiful Pagans: Performing Jewish Identity on the Antebellum American Stage* (Michigan, 2017). She is the recipient of Guggenheim, Mellon, National Endowment for the Humanities (NEH), and Katz Center fellowships.

LESLIE PETTY is Professor of English and T. K. Young Chair of English Literature at Rhodes College. Her research focuses on first-wave feminism and American literature. She has published essays in *Legacy*, *Studies in the American Short Story*, and *Women's Studies* and is currently writing a book entitled "Feminism, Modern Fiction, and American Literature Culture."

ANGELA G. RAY is Associate Professor of Communication Studies and Associate Dean for Graduate Education in the School of Communication at Northwestern University. She is the author of *The Lyceum and Public Culture in the Nineteenth-Century United States* (Michigan State, 2005) and coeditor, with Paul Stob, of *Thinking Together: Lecturing, Learning, and Difference in the Long Nineteenth Century* (Penn State, 2018). She recently has contributed chapters to *The Oxford Handbook of Rhetorical Studies* (Oxford, 2017) and *Nineteenth-Century American Activist Rhetorics* (MLA, 2021).

ASHLEY REED is Associate Professor of English at Virginia Tech and author of *Heaven's Interpreters: Women Writers and Religious Agency in Nineteenth-Century America* (Cornell, 2020). Her articles have appeared in *J19*, *ESQ*, and *Religion Compass*.

ARTHUR RISS is Associate Professor of English at Salem State University. He has published *Race, Slavery, and Liberalism in Nineteenth-Century American Literature* (Cambridge, 2006) and is currently working on a project that examines the question of "When did slavery end in the United States?"

KELLY ROSS, Associate Professor of English at Rider University, is the author of *Slavery, Surveillance, and Genre in Antebellum United States Literature* (Oxford, 2022). Her work has appeared in *PMLA*, the *Oxford Handbook of Edgar Allan Poe* (Oxford, 2019), and *American Literature in Transition: 1820–1860* (Cambridge, 2022). She coedits, with Emron Esplin, the journal *Poe Studies: History, Theory, Interpretation*.

SPENCER TRICKER is Assistant Professor of English at Clark University. His book manuscript in progress is titled "Imminent Communities: Liberal Cosmopolitanism and Empire in Transpacific Literature." He has published essays in *Studies in American Fiction*, *American Literary Realism*, and the edited volume *Crossings in Nineteenth-Century American Culture* (Edinburgh, 2022).

List of Contributors   xiii

KATHRYN WALKIEWICZ (walk-uh-wits) is an enrolled citizen of Cherokee Nation and Associate Professor of Literature at the University of California – San Diego. Walkiewicz is the author of *Reading Territory: Indigenous and Black Freedom, Removal, and the Nineteenth-Century State* (North Carolina, 2023).

KENNETH W. WARREN is Fairfax M. Cone Distinguished Service Professor at the University of Chicago. His books include *Black and White Strangers: Race and American Literary Realism* (Chicago, 1993), *So Black and Blue: Ralph Ellison and the Occasion of Criticism* (Chicago, 2003), and *What Was African American Literature?* (Harvard, 2010).

EDWARD WHITLEY is Professor and Chair of English at Lehigh University. He is the author of *American Bards: Walt Whitman and Other Unlikely Candidates for National Poet* (North Carolina, 2010) and the co-editor, with Joanna Levin, of both *Whitman among the Bohemians* (Iowa, 2014) and *Walt Whitman in Context* (Cambridge, 2018).

SHIRA WOLOSKY is Professor Emerita of the Hebrew University. Her books include *Emily Dickinson: A Voice of War* (Illinois, 1984), *Language Mysticism* (Stanford, 1995), *The Art of Poetry* (Oxford, 2001), *Poetry and Public Discourse* (Palgrave Macmillan, 2010), *Feminist Theory across Disciplines* (Routledge, 2013), and *The Bible in American Poetic Culture* (Palgrave Macmillan, 2023). Her foundation fellowships include Guggenheim, American Council of Learned Societies (ACLS), Fulbright, Princeton's Institute for Advanced Study, Israel Institute for Advanced Studies, Tikvah Center, Katz Center, Hadassah-Brandeis Institute, and Oxford's Drue Heinz Professorship.

ROCHELLE RAINERI ZUCK is Associate Professor of English at Iowa State University. Her publications include *Divided Sovereignties: Race, Nationhood, and Citizenship in Nineteenth-Century America* (Georgia, 2016) and articles in scholarly journals such as *Eighteenth-Century Studies*, *ELH*, *American Periodicals*, *Studies in American Indian Literatures*, and *Journal of American Studies*.

Acknowledgments

I have many people to thank for their various contributions to bringing this volume to fruition. I am grateful to Ray Ryan for inviting me to submit an initial proposal and to readers of that proposal for helpful suggestions. I thank the Syndics of Cambridge University Press for approving that proposal and the various contributors to this volume for agreeing to write the chapters appearing here. The contributors have all been graciously receptive to my feedback, and I thank them for that as well as for their patience with me and with each other as we have all faced the challenges of pandemic-altered schedules and lives. I thank Anthony Shoplik for creating this volume's chronology and helping select the suggestions for further reading. My students at Loyola University Chicago have been a tremendous asset to me as I taught courses exploring the issues addressed in this volume; of notable help were extended conversations with graduate students Daniel Cheung, Emma Horst, Jack O'Briant, and Anthony Shoplik. I received helpful critical feedback on my Introduction and Chapter 4 on nationalism from Daniel Cheung, Jake Fournier, Leslie Petty, and Anthony Shoplik, and I thank all of them for their thoughtful comments and suggestions. Adam Maze challenged me to think better about how to place Abraham Lincoln within the history of political thought, which greatly assisted me in writing this volume's Introduction. Finally, I am grateful to my wife, Jennifer, and my stepchildren, Alexandra, Anna, Audrey, Amelina, and Andrew, for their support and patience as we all lived with this project much longer than any of us anticipated.

Chronology of Major Works and Events

1620	Mayflower Compact drafted and signed by English settlers
1648	Peace of Westphalia ends the Thirty Years' War
1669	John Locke coauthors *The Fundamental Constitutions of North Carolina*
1682	Mary Rowlandson, *The Soveraignty and Goodness of God* (published that year in London as *A True History of the Captivity and Restoration of Mrs. Mary Rowlandson*)
1689	John Locke, *The Second Treatise of Civil Government*
1730	Beginning of the First Great Awakening, lasting roughly three decades
1732	Ephrata Cloister (1732–1813) founded by German Pietists
1775	The American Revolutionary War (1775–1783)
	Society for the Relief of Free Negroes Unlawfully Held in Bondage (1775–1784) founded
1776	Declaration of Independence
1777	Articles of Confederation adopted by states
1783	Treaty of Paris ends the Revolutionary War
1784	Pennsylvania Society for the Abolition of Slavery (1784 to present) founded
1786	Shays' Rebellion in Western Massachusetts (1786–1787)
1787	*The Federalist Papers* published
	US Constitution signed in Philadelphia
1788	Anti-Federalist riot in Carlisle, Pennsylvania
1789	George Washington elected president
	The French Revolution begins
1790	US population at first census: 3,929,000
	Naturalization Act
	The Second Great Awakening spreads across the United States, lasting roughly the next forty years

	Chronology of Major Works and Events
	Edmund Burke, *Reflections on the Revolution in France*
1791	Congress ratifies the Bill of Rights
	Whiskey Rebellion (1791–1794)
1792	Democratic-Republican Party (1792–1834) founded
	Hugh Henry Brackenridge publishes the first volume of *Modern Chivalry* (the fourth and final is published in 1815)
1793	First fugitive slave law passed
1798	Alien and Sedition Acts
	Charles Brockden Brown, *Wieland, or the Transformation*
1800	Census: 5,308,000
	Thomas Jefferson elected president
	US capital moves from Philadelphia to Washington, DC
1803	Louisiana Purchase
1805	Thomas Morton, *The School of Reform*
1808	US Shakers publish *The Testimony of Christ's Second Appearing*
1810	Census: 7,240,000
1812	War of 1812 (1812–1815)
	General Land Office established
1815	David Humphreys, *The Yankey in England*
1816	African Methodist Episcopal Church (1816 to present) founded
	American Bible Society (1816 to present) founded
	American Colonization Society (1816–1964) founded
1817	The *New Harmony Gazette* (1825–1828) founded
1819	Spain cedes Florida to the United States
	Washington Irving, "Rip Van Winkle"
	Mordecai Noah, *She Would Be a Soldier*
1820	Census: 9,634,000
	Missouri Compromise
1821	African Methodist Episcopal Church Zion (1821 to present) founded
1822	American colony of Liberia (1822–1846) established in Africa
	Catharine Maria Sedgwick, *A New England Tale*
1823	James Monroe promulgates the Monroe Doctrine in his State of the Union Address
	James Fenimore Cooper publishes *The Pioneers*, the first of his five The Leatherstocking Tales
	Johnson v. *McIntosh*, the first of three Supreme Court decisions on federal Indian law, known collectively as the Marshall Trilogy (the other cases being *Cherokee Nation* v. *Georgia* [1831], *Worcester* v. *Georgia* [1832])

Chronology of Major Works and Events xvii

1824 Lydia Maria Child, *Hobomok*
John Eaton, *The Life of Andrew Jackson*
1825 New Harmony settlement founded in Indiana by the British socialist Robert Owen
American Tract Society (1825 to present) founded
Solomon Bayley, *A Narrative of Some Remarkable Incidents in the Life of Solomon Bayley*
William Grimes, *Life of William Grimes, the Runaway Slave*
1826 General Colored Association (1826–1833) founded
James Fenimore Cooper, *The Last of the Mohicans*
1827 Constitution of the Cherokee Nation
James Fenimore Cooper, *The Prairie*
Catharine Maria Sedgwick, *Hope Leslie*
First African American newspaper *Freedom's Journal* (1827–1829) founded
Baltimore Society for the Protection of Free People of Color (1827–1829) founded
1828 Andrew Jackson elected president
Beginning of the era of the Second Party System
Democratic Party founded by Martin Van Buren and Andrew Jackson
John C. Calhoun's *South Carolina Exposition and Protest* defends state nullification of federal legislation
Principal Chief of the Cherokee John Ross (Guwi Sguwi) takes office (1828–1866)
Robert Montgomery Bird, *The City Looking Glass*
Free Enquirer (1828–1835) founded (previously the *New Harmony Gazette*)
1829 William Apess, *A Son of the Forest*
Lydia Maria Child, *The American Frugal Housewife*
Robert Voorhis, *Life and Adventures of Robert, the Hermit of Massachusetts*
David Walker, *Appeal to the Colored Citizens of the World*
1830 Census: 12,866,000
Indian Removal Act
Joseph Smith founds the Mormon Church
Black Conventions movement begins
French intellectuals organizing the July Revolution draw inspiration from the utopian socialist Charles Fourier and his concept of the communitarian *phalanstère*

Chronology of Major Works and Events

1831　Nat Turner leads slave rebellion in Virginia
Cherokee Nation v. *Georgia* decided, rendering all Indigenous nations "domestic, dependent nations"
Samuel Francis Smith writes the words of "My Country 'Tis of Thee"
Robert Montgomery Bird, *The Gladiator*
Lydia Maria Child, *The Mother's Book*
The Liberator (1831–1865) founded by William Lloyd Garrison and Isaac Knapp
Angelina Grimké incorporates threats from a violent mob into her antislavery speech in Philadelphia

1832　Andrew Jackson reelected president
South Carolina's Ordinance of Nullification and federal responses to it: President Andrew Jackson's Nullification Proclamation and Congress's Force Act (1833)
New England Anti-Slavery Society (1832–1835) founded

1833　Whig Party founded by Henry Clay
Mashpee Revolt
American Anti-Slavery Society (1833–1870) founded

1834　John Greenleaf Whittier, "Hymn"
George Bancroft publishes the first volume of his *History of the United States of America*

1835　Massachusetts Anti-Slavery Society (1832–1835) founded
New York Committee of Vigilance founded
Alexis de Tocqueville, *Democracy in America*
William Gilmore Simms, *The Yemassee*

1836　Charles Ball, *Slavery in the United States*
Ralph Waldo Emerson, *Nature*
Angelina Grimké, *An Appeal to the Christian Women of the South*
Richard Hildreth, *The Slave; or, Memoirs of Archy Moore*
Maria Monk, *Awful Disclosures of the Hotel Dieu Nunnery in Montreal*
John Greenleaf Whittier, "Clerical Oppressors"

1837　*The United States Magazine and Democratic Review* (1837–1859) founded
Robert Montgomery Bird, *Nick of the Woods; or, The Jibbenainesay*
John Lloyd Stephens, *Incidents of Travel in Egypt, Arabia Petraea, and the Holy Land*

1838	The Cherokee Trail of Tears Underground Railroad organized Ralph Waldo Emerson delivers his "Divinity School Address" at Harvard James Fenimore Cooper, *The American Democrat* William Harper, *Memoir on Slavery* Lydia Sigourney, *Letters to Mothers* James Williams, *Narrative of James Williams* Unitarian minister William Ellery Channing delivers lecture entitled "Self-Culture" in Boston
1839	First Opium War (1839–1842) Fourier Society founded in New York Nathaniel Hawthorne starts working at the Boston Custom House Sarah Josepha Hale, *The Lecturess* Theodore Weld, *American Slavery As It Is*
1840	Census: 17,000,000 The popularity of Charles Fourier's communitarianism in the United States results in thirty communities or phalanxes established in this decade across the country Albert Brisbane, *Social Destiny of Man* Richard Hildreth, *The People's Presidential Candidate; or, The Life of William Henry Harrison, of Ohio*
1841	Brook Farm founded in West Roxbury, Massachusetts by George Ripley Lydia Maria Child begins publishing a weekly column, "Letters from New-York," during her stint as editor of *National Anti-Slavery Standard*; the letters are later collected and published as *Letters from New-York* in two volumes Ralph Waldo Emerson, *Essays* John Lloyd Stephens, *Incidents of Travel in Central America, Chiapas, and Yucatán*
1842	Catharine Beecher, *A Treatise on Domestic Economy for the Use of Young Ladies at Home and at School*
1843	Abby Kelley becomes the first woman to speak at a national political convention at the Liberty Party meeting in Buffalo, New York Nathaniel Hawthorne, "The Celestial Rail-Road" Fourierist journal *The Phalanx* (1843–1845) founded

1844	Know Nothing Party (1844–1860) founded
	Ralph Waldo Emerson, "Politics"
	Nathaniel Hawthorne, "Earth's Holocaust"
	Epes Sargent, *The Life and Public Services of Henry Clay*
1845	Annexation of Texas
	The journalist John O'Sullivan first uses the term "Manifest Destiny"
	Beginning of the Irish Potato Blight
	Frederick Douglass, *Narrative of the Life of Frederick Douglass, an American Slave, Written by Himself*
	Margaret Fuller, *Woman in the Nineteenth Century*
	Johnson Jones Hooper, *Adventures of Captain Simon Suggs*
	Anna Cora Mowatt, *Fashion*
	The Harbinger (1845–1849) founded at Brook Farm
1846	US-Mexican War (1846–1848)
	American Union of Associationists founded in New York
1848	Treaty of Guadalupe Hidalgo requires Mexico to cede more than half of its prewar territory to the United States
	Gold discovered at Sutter's Mill in California, prompting the Gold Rush (1848–1855)
	Seneca Falls Convention for women's rights
	Karl Marx and Friedrich Engels, *The Communist Manifesto*
	James Fenimore Cooper, *Oak Openings; or, The Bee-Hunter*
	Elizabeth Cady Stanton and Lucretia Mott, *Declaration of Sentiments*
1849	Astor Place Riot
	Henry David Thoreau, "Resistance to Civil Government"
1850	Census: 23,192,000
	The Fugitive Slave Act is passed by Congress
	Nathaniel Hawthorne, *The Scarlet Letter*
	Edgar Allan Poe, "The Poetic Principle"
	Susan Warner, *The Wide, Wide World*
	Harper's New Monthly Magazine (1850 to present) founded
1851	Nathaniel Hawthorne, *The House of the Seven Gables*
	Herman Melville, *Moby-Dick*
	Henry David Thoreau delivers lecture entitled "Walking" at the Concord Lyceum
	Sojourner Truth delivers "Ain't I a Woman" at the Women's Rights Conference in Ohio

Chronology of Major Works and Events xxi

1852　Martin Delany, *The Condition, Elevation, Emigration and Destiny of the Colored People of the United States, Politically Considered*
Frederick Douglass, *The Heroic Slave*
Nathaniel Hawthorne, *The Blithedale Romance*
Nathaniel Hawthorne, *The Life of Franklin Pierce*
Mary Ann Shadd, *A Plea for Emigration; or, Notes of Canada West*
William Gilmore Simms, *The Sword and the Distaff*
Harriet Beecher Stowe, *Uncle Tom's Cabin*
Frederick Douglass delivers his speech "What to the Slave Is the Fourth of July?" in Rochester, New York
Uncle Tom's Cabin first adapted to the stage

1853　Solomon Northup, *Twelve Years a Slave*
William Wells Brown, *Clotel; or, The President's Daughter*
Sarah Josepha Hale, *Liberia; or, Mr. Peyton's Experiments*
First issue of *The Provincial Freeman* published (1853–1857) by Mary Ann Shadd

1854　Kansas–Nebraska Act
Republican Party founded, bringing together antislavery parties
Fanny Fern, *Ruth Hall*
Frances Ellen Watkins Harper, "Bible Defence of Slavery"
Caroline Lee Hentz, *The Planter's Northern Bride*
John Beauchamp Jones, *The Adventures of Col. Gracchus Vanderbomb*
Herman Melville, *The Encantadas, or Enchanted Isles*
John Rollin Ridge, *The Life and Adventures of Joaquín Murieta: The Celebrated California Bandit*

1855　Herman Melville, *Israel Potter: His Fifty Years of Exile*
James Pollock, the Whig Governor of Pennsylvania, delivers his inaugural address in Harrisburg
Walt Whitman, *Leaves of Grass*
James Russell Lowell delivers a lecture titled "The Ballads" at the Lowell Institute
Mary Ann Shadd delivers a speech promoting emigration to Canada at the Colored National Convention in Philadelphia
Jacob C. White delivers his "Address Read on the Reception of Governor Pollock at the Institute for Col'd Youth" in Philadelphia

1856	Second Opium War (1856–1860) Laura Bullard, *Christine; or, Woman's Trials and Triumphs* Harriet Beecher Stowe, *Dred: A Tale of the Great Dismal Swamp* Walt Whitman, *Leaves of Grass* (2nd ed.) includes correspondence with Ralph Waldo Emerson
1857	Dred Scott decision denies citizenship to African Americans Edward G. Parker, *The Golden Age of American Oratory* Frank J. Webb, *The Garies and Their Friends* *The Atlantic Monthly* (2004 to present titled *The Atlantic*) founded Spiritualist journal *Banner of Light* (1857–1907) founded
1858	The first of seven Lincoln–Douglas debates occurs in Ottawa, Illinois on August 21; the final takes place in Alton, Illinois on October 15 John Brown and members of the Chatham Convention write the Provisional Constitution and Declaration of Liberty First transatlantic telegraph cable Frances Ellen Watkins Harper, "Bury Me in a Free Land" William Wells Brown, *The Escape; or, A Leap for Freedom*
1859	John Brown carries out his raid on Harpers Ferry in October; Brown is executed for treason against the Commonwealth of Virginia in December Charles Darwin, *On the Origin of Species* R. M. DeWitt, *The Life, Trial, and Execution of Captain John Brown, Known as "Old Brown of Ossawatomie," with a Full Account of the Attempted Insurrection at Harper's Ferry: Compiled from Official and Authentic Sources* Kate Edwards Swayze, *Ossawattomie Brown* Henry David Thoreau delivers his lecture "A Plea for Captain John Brown" in Concord, Massachusetts Harriet Wilson, *Our Nig*
1860	Census: 31,443,000 Abraham Lincoln delivers his Cooper Union Speech in New York City Abraham Lincoln elected president South Carolina secedes from the Union Jane Johnston Schoolcraft (Bamewawagezhikaquay) of the Anishinaabe community at Bawating (currently Sault Ste. Marie, MI), "Invocation" (written 1823) William Dean Howells, *Life of Abraham Lincoln*

Chronology of Major Works and Events xxiii

James Parton, *Life of Andrew Jackson*
Walt Whitman, *Leaves of Grass* (3rd ed.)
Walt Whitman, "Facing West from California's Shores"
First series of Beadle's Dime Novels published

1861 American Civil War (1861–1865)
The American Bible Society distributes more than 3 million Bibles to both North and South
The Rebellion Record (1861–1868) publishes the first of twelve volumes
Harriet Jacobs, *Incidents in the Life of a Slave Girl*
Henry Timrod, "Ethnogenesis"
William Dean Howells serves as US Consul to Venice (1861–1865)

1862 Lincoln issues Emancipation Proclamation
The Homestead Act
Emily Dickinson contacts Thomas Wentworth Higginson, sharing four poems
Nathaniel Hawthorne, "Chiefly about War Matters, by a Peaceable Man"
Oliver Wendell Holmes Sr., "Never or Now"
Henry Timrod, "Spring"

1863 Lincoln delivers his "Gettysburg Address"
Construction begins on the first transcontinental railroad (1863–1869)
Nathaniel Hawthorne, *Our Old Home*
William M. Thayer, *The Pioneer Boy, and How He Became President*

1864 International Workingmen's Association (1864–1876) founded
Henry J. Raymond, *The Life of Abraham Lincoln, of Illinois*

1865 Robert E. Lee surrenders to Ulysses S. Grant at Appomattox Courthouse
Lincoln assassinated
Thirteenth Amendment abolishes slavery
The Nation (still publishing) founded as a successor to *The Liberator* (1831–1865)
Central Pacific begins hiring Chinese workers in large numbers

1866 American Equal Rights Association (1866–1869) founded
William Dean Howells, *Venetian Life*
Herman Melville, *Battle-Pieces and Aspects of the War*
Andrew Johnson's infamous "Swing Around the Circle" speaking tour (August–September)

1867	Reconstruction Acts grant African American men the right to vote
	The Granger movement (1867 to present) founded by Oliver Hudson Kelley
	Augustin Daly, *Under the Gaslight*
	John W. De Forest, *Miss Ravenel's Conversion from Secession to Loyalty*
	Charles Sumner, "Are We a Nation?" address
1868	Burlingame–Seward Treaty
	Fourteenth Amendment ratified
	William Taylor Adams, *Our Standard-Bearer; or, The Life of General Ulysses S. Grant*
	Louisa May Alcott, *Little Women*
	John W. De Forest, "The Great American Novel"
	Elizabeth Stuart Phelps, *The Gates Ajar*
	Harriet Beecher Stowe, "Ulysses S. Grant"
1869	Central Pacific and Union Pacific railroad lines join at Promontory Point
	Prohibition Party (1869 to present) founded
	American Woman Suffrage Association (1869–1890) founded
	National Woman Suffrage Association (1869–1890) founded
	Frances Ellen Watkins Harper, *Minnie's Sacrifice*
	Catharine Beecher and Harriet Beecher Stowe, *The American Woman's Home*
	Mark Twain, *The Innocents Abroad*
1870	Census: 38,553,000
	Fifteenth Amendment ratified
	Bret Harte, "Plain Language from Truthful James"
	Julia Ward Howe, "Mother's Day Proclamation"
1871	The Paris Commune established (lasting two months)
	Los Angeles Chinese massacre
	Ambrose Bierce, "The Haunted Valley"
	Elizabeth Boynton Harbert, *Out of Her Sphere*
	Frances Ellen Watkins Harper, "The Freedom Bell"
	Charles Foster, *Bertha the Sewing Machine Girl*
	Helen Potter, *Manual of Reading, in Four Parts: Orthophony, Class Methods, Gesture, and Elocution*
1872	Mark Twain, *Roughing It*

1873	Panic of 1873 begins the Long Depression
	Susan B. Anthony courtroom speech during her trial for casting a vote in the 1872 presidential election
	Friedrich Nietzsche, "On Truth and Lies in a Nonmoral Sense"
1874	Bon Homme Hutterite Colony founded in South Dakota
	Women's Christian Temperance Union founded
	Mark Twain and Charles Dudley Warner, *The Gilded Age*
1875	Page Act passed by Congress
	Civil Rights Act of 1875
1876	Socialistic Labor Party founded
	William Dean Howells, *A Sketch of the Life and Character of Rutherford B. Hayes*
1877	Great Railroad Strike of 1877 begins in West Virginia in July and spreads to cities across the country (duration of approximately two months)
	Compromise of 1877 effectively ends Reconstruction
	Farmers' Alliance (1877–1890) founded
	Workingmen's Party of California founded by Denis Kearney
	Elizabeth Stuart Phelps, *The Story of Avis*
	Mark Twain and Bret Harte, *Ah Sin*
1879	Horatio Alger, *The Young Miner*
	Edward Harrigan and Tony Hart, *The Mulligan Guard Ball*
	Albion Tourgée, *A Fool's Errand*
1880	Census: 50,156,000
	Henry Adams, *Democracy: An American Novel*
	Joel Chandler Harris, *Uncle Remus, His Songs and His Sayings*
	James R. Gilmore, *Life of James A. Garfield*
	Albion Tourgée, *Bricks without Straw*
	Lew Wallace, *Ben-Hur*
	Constance Fenimore Woolson, "Miss Grief"
1881	Elizabeth Cady Stanton and Susan B. Anthony publish the first volume of *History of Woman Suffrage*
	Henry James, *Portrait of a Lady*
	Sarah Orne Jewett, "From a Mournful Villager"
1882	Chinese Exclusion Act
	Emma Lazarus, "The New Colossus"
1883	Russian Jewish immigrants establish New Odessa co-op in Oregon
	Pendleton Civil Service Reform Act
	Ella Thayer Cheever, *Lords of Creation*

	William Graham Sumner, *What Social Classes Owe to Each Other*
	Albion Tourgée, *Hot Plowshares*
	Mark Twain, *Life on the Mississippi*
1884	Laurence Gronlund, *The Cooperative Commonwealth*
	Sarah Winnemucca Hopkins, *Life Among the Paiutes: Their Wrongs and Claims*
1885	George Washington Cable, "The Freedman's Case in Equity"
	María Amparo Ruiz de Burton, *The Squatter and the Don*
	Mark Twain, *Adventures of Huckleberry Finn*
1886	The Haymarket Affair, which results in the conviction of eight anarchists, including Albert Parsons
	Lucy Parsons embarks on a lecture tour after the arrest of her husband, Albert Parsons, who was accused of conspiracy in the Haymarket Affair
	Henry George, *Progress and Poverty: An Inquiry into the Cause of Industrial Depressions, and of Increase of Want with Increase of Wealth*
	Henry James, *The Bostonians*
	Henry James, *The Princess Casamassima*
1887	Albert Parsons and three other anarchists are hanged
	Charles Chesnutt publishes "The Goophered Grapevine," the first of his "conjure tales," in *The Atlantic Monthly*
	Wong Chin Foo, "Why Am I a Heathen?"
	Yan Phou Lee, "Why I Am Not a Heathen: A Rejoinder to Wong Chin Foo"
	Celia B. Whitehead publishes an alternative ending to Henry James's *The Bostonians* under the pseudonym Henrietta James
1888	Edward Bellamy, *Looking Backward*
	Lew Wallace, *Life of Gen. Ben Harrison*
1889	Bronson Howard, *Shenandoah*
	Mark Twain, *A Connecticut Yankee in King Arthur's Court*
1890	Census: 62,948,000
	William Dean Howells, *A Hazard of New Fortunes*
	Jacob Riis, *How the Other Half Lives*
1891	Mary Wilkins Freeman, "A New England Nun"
	Hamlin Garland, *Main-Travelled Roads*
	William Dean Howells, *An Imperative Duty*
1892	Geary Act of 1892 extends the Chinese Exclusion Act
	The People's Party (1892–1909) founded

Anna Julia Cooper, *A Voice from the South*
Frances Ellen Watkins Harper, *Iola Leroy*
Helen Hamilton Gardener, *Pray You Sir, Whose Daughter?*
Charlotte Perkins Gilman, "The Yellow Wall-Paper"
Thomas Nelson Page, *The Old South: Essays Social and Political*

1893 World's Columbian Exposition
Frederick Jackson Turner presents his essay "The Significance of the Frontier in American History" to the American Historical Association in Chicago
US military overthrows the Hawaiian Kingdom
Panic of 1893
Charlotte Perkins Gilman, "The Holy Stove," "Homes: A Sestina," "Nationalism"

1894 William Dean Howells, *A Traveler from Altruria*
Hamlin Garland, *Crumbling Idols*

1895 J. McHenry Jones, *Hearts of Gold*
Adeline Knapp, "The Ways That Are Dark"
Margaret Murray Washington, "The New Negro Woman"
Booker T. Washington delivers his Atlanta Exposition address (also known as "The Atlanta Compromise")
Zitkála-Šá (Yankton Dakota) delivers her address "Side by Side" at Earlham College

1896 *Plessy* v. *Ferguson* rules segregation by race to be constitutional
Theatrical Syndicate founded
Abraham Cahan, *Yekl: A Tale of the New York Ghetto*
Paul Laurence Dunbar, "An Ante-bellum Sermon"
Julia Ward Howe delivers "Why Are Women the Natural Guardians of Social Morals" at the annual congress of the Association for the Advancement of Women

1897 Hamlin Garland, *A Spoil of Office*
Charles Sheldon, *In His Steps: What Would Jesus Do?*
W. E. B. Du Bois, "Strivings of the Negro People"

1898 Spanish-American War results in US military occupation of Cuba until 1902
Treaty of Paris goes into effect and Spain cedes sovereignty over Puerto Rico, Guam, and the Philippines
White supremacists carry out insurrection in Wilmington, North Carolina
Home Colony founded on Puget Sound in Washington State
Charlotte Perkins Gilman, *Women and Economics*

	Thomas Nelson Page, *Red Rock*
	Frank Norris, *Moran of the Lady Letty*
	Will Marion Cook and Paul Laurence Dunbar collaborate to create and stage *Clorindy: The Origin of the Cakewalk*, the first show with an all-black cast
1899	Kate Chopin, *The Awakening*
	Sutton E. Griggs, *Imperium in Imperio*
	Simon Pokagon (Potawatomi), *Ogimawkwe Mitigwaki (Queen of the Woods: A Novel)*
1900	Census: 76,304,000
	Eugene V. Debs campaigns for the presidency for the first of five consecutive times
1901	The first of the Insular Cases decided, creating the US doctrine of incorporation
	Charles Chesnutt, *The Marrow of Tradition*
	Booker T. Washington, *Up from Slavery*
	Frances Ellen Watkins Harper, "Deliverance"
	Zitkála-Šá (Yankton Dakota), *Old Indian Legends*
1902	Cuba becomes an independent country
	Zitkála-Šá (Yankton Dakota), "Why I Am a Pagan"
1903	Charlotte Perkins Gilman, *The Home: Its Work and Influence*
	W. E. B. Du Bois, *The Souls of Black Folk*
1904	Charlotte Perkins Gilman, "The Purpose"
	Jacob Riis, *Theodore Roosevelt, the Citizen*
1905	Industrial Workers of the World (1905 to present) founded
	Sutton E. Griggs, *The Hindered Hand*
1906	Lodge Act replaces patronage-based diplomatic appointments with a merit-based system
1911	Charlotte Perkins Gilman, *Our Androcentric Culture; or, the Man-Made World*, "Turned," "Making a Change"
1912	Little Theater movement
	Sui Sin Far, *Mrs. Spring Fragrance*
1914	Charlotte Perkins Gilman, "His Mother," "Matriatism"
1915	Stone–Flood Act
	Charlotte Perkins Gilman, *Herland*
	Upton Sinclair, *The Cry for Justice*
1916	Charlotte Perkins Gilman, "The Unnatural Mother"
1917	Immigration Act of 1917 creates "Asiatic Barred Zone"
1920	Nineteenth Amendment ratified
1921	Zitkála-Šá (Yankton Dakota), *American Indian Stories*

1923	Hamlin Garland, *The Book of the American Indian*
1924	Johnson–Reed Act restricts immigration based on national origin
1925	Manuel Gomez, *Poems for Workers*
1931	Emma Goldman, *Living My Life*
1943	Magnuson Act repeals Chinese Exclusion
1954	*Brown* v. *Board of Education* rules racial segregation unconstitutional
1965	Hart–Celler Act of 1965 ends national origin quotas on immigration and instead prioritizes family reunification and attracting educated workers

INTRODUCTION

Politics and Literary History
John D. Kerkering

In order to prepare readers of this *Cambridge Companion to Nineteenth-Century American Literature and Politics* to recognize and appreciate the mode of literary history practiced across the twenty chapters assembled here, this Introduction examines a key moment from a well-known sequence of events in nineteenth-century US political history, the seven debates staged across the state of Illinois in the fall of 1858 between Abraham Lincoln and Stephen A. Douglas as Lincoln sought to unseat the incumbent Douglas as an Illinois US senator. Though Douglas won reelection (with the state's legislators, not the people, casting the votes), media attention to the debates gave Lincoln a notoriety that launched his successful bid for the presidency two years later. The key moment I examine, taken from the first of these Lincoln–Douglas debates, which was held in Ottawa, Illinois on August 21, 1858, will provide the occasion to consider competing approaches to politics and rival understandings of how – and indeed whether – we might convincingly account for literature's relationship to such historical moments, political or otherwise. My discussion will yield a set of terms that specify the approach to politics and the mode of literary history that the chapters in this volume employ.

One of these terms is the "history of political thought" (also termed "political theory"), which I will distinguish from both "political philosophy" and "political science." Another term is "pragmatism," which I will distinguish not only from foundationalism (which is sometimes called positivism or objectivism, in association with the "hard" sciences) but also from two modes of analysis that purport to be, as does pragmatism, committed to antifoundationalism. The first of these is a "discourse" mode whose structuralist assumptions and commitments extend principles first outlined in the linguistics of Ferdinand de Saussure. The second is the mode of "standpoint epistemology," which adapts Marxist accounts of class consciousness in order to learn from the experiences and perspectives of marginalized groups situated in delimited material and social locations.

I will suggest that both the discourse and the standpoint epistemology modes of analysis founder due to the incompleteness of their antifoundationalism – that is, due to their sense that foundationalism, or objectivity, is simultaneously unavailable to those who would make truth claims about, for instance, US literary and political history and, at the same time, essential to the validity of those truth claims. This combination – embracing objectivity's impossibility and its necessity – commits both the discourse and the standpoint epistemology modes of literary history to an antifoundationalism that, in depriving them ("anti-") of necessary support ("foundations"), undermines, in the minds of these modes' practitioners, any and all pretensions that either mode may have to offer true statements about literary history. Pragmatism, by contrast, understands antifoundationalism differently, seeing foundations or objectivity as neither available *nor necessary* in order for literary historians (or, for that matter, anyone else) to offer claims that are convincing, persuasive, and warrant believing. By distinguishing in this way among approaches to politics and modes of literary history, this Introduction sets the stage for readers of this volume to be persuaded by each of its chapters' convincing accounts of literature's consequential participation in the history of political thought.

***

During the first of his now-classic debates with incumbent Illinois US senator Stephen A. Douglas, Abraham Lincoln chooses an unusual method – reading aloud – to rebut Douglas's accusation that Lincoln and his allies in the new "Black Republican party" support an "abolition platform."[1] To contest being labeled an abolitionist, Lincoln offers to "read a part of a printed speech" that he had delivered four years earlier, in Peoria, Illinois, in which he had condemned "the monstrous injustice of slavery itself" but had stopped short of endorsing full equality for enslaved persons once they have been freed.[2] "Now, gentlemen," Lincoln states to the crowd assembled for the debate,

> I hate to waste my time on such things, but in regard to that general Abolition tilt that Judge Douglas makes, when he says that I was engaged at that time in selling out and Abolitionizing the Old Whig party, I hope you will permit me to read a part of a printed speech that I made then at Peoria, which will show altogether a different view of the position I took in the contest of 1854.
> [*Voice from the Crowd*:] Put on your specs.
> [*Lincoln's Reply*:] Yes, sir, I am obliged to do so. I am no longer a young man.

---

[1] *The Lincoln–Douglas Debates*, ed. Rodney O. Davis and Douglas L. Wilson (University of Illinois Press, 2008), 8.
[2] *The Lincoln–Douglas Debates*, 18, 19.

Introduction: Politics and Literary History

[*Lincoln Reading:*] ... If all earthly power were given me, I should not know what to do, as to the existing institution [of slavery]. My first impulse would be to free all of the slaves, and send them to Liberia, – to their own native land. But ... [this plan's] sudden execution is impossible ... What then? Free them all, and keep them among us as underlings? Is it quite certain that this betters their condition? ... What next? Free them, and make them politically and socially, our equals?

[*Lincoln here breaks from reading to address Douglas:*] Let the Judge note this. I am now among men who have some abolition tendencies.

[*Lincoln resumes reading:*] Free them, and make them politically and socially, our equals? My own feelings will not admit of this; and if mine would, we well know that those of the great mass of white people will not. Whether this feeling accords with justice and sound judgment, is not the sole question, if indeed, it is any part of it. A universal feeling, whether well or ill-founded, can not be safely disregarded. We can not, then, make them equals ...

[*Lincoln, having finished reading, now addressing the crowd:*] Now, gentlemen, I don't want to read at any great length, but this is the true complexion of all I have ever said in regard to the institution of slavery and the black race. This is the whole of it, and anything that argues me into his idea of perfect social and political equality with the negro is but a specious and fantastic arrangement of words, by which a man can prove a horse-chestnut to be a chestnut horse. [*Laughter, applause*][3]

As debate practice, this rebuttal is remarkable for its evasiveness as a rhetorical maneuver (since Lincoln replaces the question of abolition with the question of political and social equality) and for its weakness as a counter to Douglas's charge of abolitionism (since the section of his Peoria speech that Lincoln reads aloud calls slavery a "monstrous injustice"). As a historical event, this rebuttal is remarkable for its challenge to viewing Lincoln as having been, at least at this early stage of his political career, the "Great Emancipator" (since Lincoln clearly demonstrates "feelings" against making freed slaves his political and social equals). For our purposes here, however, in this Introduction to *The Cambridge Companion to Nineteenth-Century American Literature and Politics*, this passage is most notable for its potential to shed light on two of the volume's central concerns: understanding what Lincoln and his contemporaries understood politics, itself, to entail and understanding whether, how, and to what effect literature participates in politics.

The answer to the first question is implicit in the question being addressed: whether or not a current state of politics, or "the social exercise of power," ought to be altered such that some persons currently held in bondage would

---

[3] *The Lincoln–Douglas Debates*, 19–20.

instead be set free.[4] Taking this understanding of politics for granted, Lincoln makes explicit a further question about how proposed changes in the social exercise of power ought to be assessed, whether by reference to "justice and sound judgment" or to "universal feeling, whether well or ill-founded," and his clear answer to this question is to reject sound judgment in favor of universal feeling. Regarded from our own historical moment, Lincoln's distinction between sound judgment and universal feeling as modes of assessing proposed changes in the social exercise of power aligns with a boundary between what are now independent fields of study, political philosophy and political science: Political philosophy engages in normative debates about how people ought to formulate and institute social policy (Lincoln's "accord[ance] with justice and sound judgment"), while political science provides empirical descriptions of what people actually do when they produce and enact such policy (Lincoln's regard for "universal feeling").[5] And again, from our contemporary vantage, since he describes "justice" as "not the sole question, if indeed, it is any part of it," siding instead with regard for "universal feeling" (including his own), Lincoln's speech might appear to be best explained by the discipline of political science, its concern with describing political activity within social contexts being better suited than political philosophy for the study of Lincoln's practical effort to win a US Senate seat for the state of Illinois in the nineteenth-century United States.

While this disciplinary choice (political science rather than political philosophy) may seem clear as a way of understanding Lincoln's performance in the Ottawa, Illinois debate, the fact that Lincoln's own views – not only his feeling but also his decision to privilege it over a sense of justice – seem to us in retrospect to be deeply flawed and indeed unjust might give us pause in favoring the descriptive project of political science over the normative project of political philosophy in accounting for Lincoln's approach to politics. Shouldn't we condemn him morally in addition to, or in preference to, merely describing

---

[4] This definition of politics as "the social exercise of power" appears in Nigel A. Jackson and Stephen D. Tansey, *Politics: The Basics*, 5th ed. (Routledge, 2015), 6. Offering a similar definition, Adrian Leftwich argues that "There is one overriding concern of those who study politics and that is a concern with *power*, political power – and its effects"; see Adrian Leftwich, "Thinking Politically: On the Politics of Politics," in Adrian Leftwich, ed., *What Is Politics? The Activity and Its Study*, new ed. (Polity, 2004), 1–22, 19. Adam Swift's "Introduction," in *Political Philosophy: A Beginner's Guide for Students and Politicians*, 4th ed. (Polity, 2019), similarly argues that "what politics really is . . . is a process by which some people get the state to back up, with its coercive apparatus, their preferred ways of doing things – to compel obedience from those who might not want to do things that way" (4).

[5] According to Adam Swift, "The fact that it asks – and answers – moral questions makes political philosophy a different kind of enterprise from political science. Political scientists tell us what happens and why it does. Political philosophers tell us what ought to happen and why it should"; see Adam Swift, "Political Philosophy and Politics," in Leftwich, *What Is Politics?*, 135–146, 139.

him factually? According to scholars who study yet another discipline, the history of political thought, we ought to do neither, since to read him in terms of our present disciplinary modalities like political science or political philosophy is to risk practicing what Richard Whatmore calls "presentism" and "prolepsis":

> The history of political thought as an academic discipline ... emerged in the 1960s as a rebellion against what might be termed hero and villain studies. Historians of political thought were critical of "presentism," the reading into the past of contemporary debates on the assumption that the same questions were being studied over and over through history. They equally sought to avoid "prolepsis," the anachronistic reading of historic books as if they were taking a stand on issues that in fact would have made no sense to their authors ... In rejecting such approaches, the history of political thought provides an account of past ideas that is more accurate and more revealing because it is less judgmental.[6]

While it is inevitable that we all have our own present judgments of Lincoln and his nineteenth-century contemporaries for their participation in abuses and atrocities like slavery, genocide, imperialism, sexism, racism, and a host of other exploitative social and political practices, Whatmore asserts that "Historians of political thought interrogate the social lives of historic communities in their own terms, studying their cultural practices, languages, and discourse to recover as far as possible people's own conversations about their lives," and they do so "by looking at what was said, either directly in written form or through significant artefacts from surviving art and buildings to objects of everyday life."[7] This volume features literary works as "significant artefacts" enabling us to recover the political life and thought of the nineteenth-century United States; it presents the history of political thought, revealed via the analysis of literature, rather than either political philosophy or political science.[8] Whatmore's emphasis

---

[6] Richard Whatmore, *The History of Political Thought: A Very Short Introduction* (Oxford University Press, 2021), 15. Using the label "political theory" rather than "the history of political thought," John S. Dryzek, Bonnie Honig, and Anne Phillips similarly distinguish this approach to politics from both political science and political philosophy: "Political theory is located at one remove from this quantitative vs. qualitative debate, sitting somewhere between the distanced universals of normative philosophy and the empirical world of politics"; see their "Introduction" in John S. Dryzek, Bonnie Honig, and Anne Phillips, eds., *The Oxford Handbook of Political Theory* (Oxford University Press), 2006, 3–41, 5.
[7] Whatmore, *The History of Political Thought*, 19.
[8] For thorough accounts of each of these approaches to politics, see, for the history of political thought (here termed "political theory"), Dryzek, Honig, and Phillips, *The Oxford Handbook of Political Theory*; for political philosophy, George Klosko, ed., *The Oxford Handbook of the History of Political Philosophy* (Oxford University Press, 2011); and for political science, Robert E. Goodin and Hans-Dieter Klingemann, eds., *A New Handbook of Political Science* (Oxford University Press, 1996).

here on "the social lives of historic communities" gestures, further, to an expansion of the history of political thought beyond a focus on institutions like Congress or the presidency and events like elections and impeachments, which remain the focus of political science. Political historians, by contrast, as Frank Towers observes, have been "redefining the subject matter of political history beyond the confines of voters, parties, and legislatures. Building on work already underway in the 1980s, historians have developed a much more complete understanding of how disenfranchised Americans acted politically and how their history redefines the boundaries of the political."[9]

But if politics embraces social as well as political history, involving poems and plays as well as debates and elections, what is its relation to literary history – and indeed, recalling the second question prompted by the above-cited Lincoln passage, what is and is not political in literature? One way of thinking about this, again in light of Lincoln's debate performance, is to consider the mixed media of that event – oratory, drama between antagonists (Lincoln and Douglas) on a stage, and reading from a prepared and indeed printed text. Literature is irreducible to any of these modes, so we should not hastily distinguish the oratory from the plot of the political horserace or the language that is, unlike either, "printed" on a page and then try to privilege any one mode as emphatically literary. Indeed, in Lincoln's speech, the language in print is serving an evidentiary function more than a literary one, using the institution of printing to affirm, as Allen Grossman asserts, his "rational style of discourse of unfailing adequacy and persuasiveness. He was a *novus homo*, a man impersonated by his language."[10] At the same time, this ethos of consistency underscored by the material continuity of print (even more than the material continuity of his own body across that same space of time since the 1854 Peoria speech) is something Lincoln can resist in this live event, the printed speech serving as a kind of theatrical prop enabling a back-and-forth between his prior printed self as a persistent entity (one constructed by print) and a present, embodied self who can break from that print self to offer spontaneous, unscripted asides – as in the playful banter with the crowd

---

[9] Frank Towers, "Party Politics and the Sectional Crisis: A Twenty-Year Renaissance in the Study of Antebellum Political History," in Jonathan Daniel Wells, ed., *The Routledge History of Nineteenth-Century America* (Taylor & Francis, 2018), 109–130, 116. For a related discussion concerning political history and gender, see Jean Harvey Baker, "Public Women and Partisan Politics, 1840–1860," in Gary W. Gallagher and Rachel A. Shelden, eds., *A Political Nation: New Directions in Mid-Nineteenth-Century American Political History* (University of Virginia Press, 2012), 64–81.
[10] Allen Grossman, "The Poetics of Union in Whitman and Lincoln: An Inquiry toward the Relationship of Art and Policy," in *The Long Schoolroom: Lessons in the Bitter Logic of the Poetic Principle* (University of Michigan Press, 1997), 60.

Introduction: Politics and Literary History

about needing his "specs," or his later turn away from the printed speech to address the Judge (Douglas) directly, as if the two of them could not be overheard by those very "abolitionists" referenced in the audience, or finally, once he has finished reading aloud from the print, offering a summary dismissal of clever wordplay as the "specious and fantastic arrangement of words" only, then, to indulge fully in precisely such wordplay himself – "by which a man can prove a horse-chestnut to be a chestnut horse" – to the effect of generating laughter and applause, which respond as much if not more to his actual use of wordplay than to his dismissal of it – or perhaps to the enactment of the one by means of the other. Politics is thus, here, fully imbricated in the modalities (oratory, drama, and print) of literature, its techniques both of revealing character – both as continuous in its commitments and as charismatically spontaneous in context – and of "arrangement of words" for comedic support of his persuasive effort: As Horace writes of poetry, Lincoln's purpose and effect are both to instruct and to delight.

If the passage from Lincoln's first senate debate with Douglas invites us to view literature and politics in these terms, as mutually imbricated or intertwined, that mutual involvement might in turn invite us to approach the literature of the nineteenth century in the manner outlined by Jacques Rancière, who has written extensively and influentially on aesthetics and politics, most notably *The Politics of Aesthetics*. As Rancière's translator, Gabriel Rockhill, observes,

> Rancière has forcefully argued that the emergence of literature in the nineteenth century as distinct from *les belles-lettres* was a central catalyst in the development of the aesthetic regime of art. By rejecting the representative regime's poetics of *mimêsis*, modern literature contributed to a general reconfiguration of the sensible order linked to the contradiction inherent in what Rancière calls *literarity*, i.e. the status of a written word that freely circulates outside any system of legitimation. On the one hand, literarity is a necessary condition for the appearance of modern literature as such and its emancipation from the representative regime of art. However, it simultaneously acts as the contradictory limit at which the specificity of literature itself disappears due to the fact that it no longer has [as it did in the prior, representative regime of art] any clearly identifiable characteristics that would distinguish it from any other mode of discourse. This partially explains the other major form of writing that has been in constant struggle with democratic literarity throughout the modern age: the idea of a "true writing" that would incorporate language in such a way as to exclude the free-floating, disembodied discourse of literarity.[11]

---

[11] Gabriel Rockhill, "Editor's Introduction: Jacques Rancière's Politics of Perception," in Jacques Rancière, *The Politics of Aesthetics: The Distribution of the Sensible*, ed. Gabriel Rockhill (Bloomsbury Academic, 2004), viii–xvii, xvi.

Rockhill continues that it is in this "constant struggle" that Rancière's "central argument is discernible: ... the contradictory relationship between elements of the representative and aesthetic regimes of art" produces "the historical conditions of possibility for the appearances of these practices" – that is, for "the appearance of modern literature as such" in the nineteenth century.[12] Lincoln, in Rancière's view, might then be understood as setting "true writing," the print record of his 1854 speech in Peoria, which he reads aloud to the assembled crowd, against the accusations of Douglas (that Lincoln is an abolitionist), which Lincoln reduces to mere "literarity" – that is, to Rancière's aesthetics rather than to mimetic representation – in an effort to align himself with the earlier, representative regime of mimesis and conformity to rules while relegating Douglas to an artist's role of producing the "free-floating, disembodied discourse of literarity," which Lincoln then mocks in his line about proving a horse-chestnut to be a chestnut horse.

While Rancière's approach, as outlined by Rockhill, appears to favor the kind of engagement between literature and politics that I have associated with the discipline of the history of political thought, it also has liabilities that are apparent in prioritizing what Rockhill calls "a *necessary condition* for the appearance" or "the historical *conditions of possibility* for the appearance": By giving priority to a historical sequence of aesthetic "regimes" (the "ethical" and "representative" regimes dominating in Western antiquity and pre-modernity until, Rancière argues, the "aesthetic" regime of modernity rose to dominance in the nineteenth century), Rancière proposes a mode of analysis in which legibility of the world as such is itself *made possible* only by reference to, and only in terms of, a prior, necessary, and *enabling system* of intelligibility, which Rancière calls "the distribution of the sensible."[13] While initially abstract, this notion becomes clear when we recognize its indebtedness to the linguistics of Ferdinand de Saussure, who asserted the conditions of possibility for the legibility of any given instance of speech, or *parole*, to be its prior implication in a broader system, or *langue*.[14] Just as, for Saussure, only speakers competent in that *langue* or system at a given synchronic moment can make legible an instance of that synchronic moment's *parole* or speech (i.e. only those

---

[12] Rockhill, "Editor's Introduction," xvii, xvi.
[13] For Rancière's definition of this idea, see his *The Politics of Aesthetics*, 7–8; see also Rockhill's note that the distribution of the sensible should be understood as "what *makes or produces* a community and not simply an attribute shared by all of its members" (109n5; my italics).
[14] For a thorough exposition of Saussure's distinction between *langue* and *parole*, see Jonathan Culler, *Ferdinand de Saussure*, rev. ed. (Cornell University Press, 1986), 39–45.

who already know medieval or Elizabethan *English* can interpret instances of medieval or Elizabethan *speech*), so too, for Rancière, only the competency of historical perceivers in an era's given "distribution of the sensible," or its enabling conceptual system of rending the sensible world intelligible, makes it possible for the broader world to become legible to those perceivers, a legibility that changes with time as the larger system of intelligibility (Rancière's "distribution of the sensible") undergoes – as do languages, for Saussure (medieval and Elizabethan English becoming modern English) – alterations in its grammar and structure.

This orientation's structuralist priorities would shift us away from studying individual instances of expression and toward, instead, studying the systemic conditions of possibility for those instances being rendered intelligible at all, a shift at the heart of Jonathan Culler's Saussure-inspired promotion of "poetics" over "hermeneutics" in an effort to understand "literary competence" by analogy to the Saussurean linguist's effort to understand "linguistic competence."[15] This same privileging of the study of enabling systems of intelligibility over the various objects that those systems are necessary to render intelligible is apparent in the similarly Saussure-inspired efforts of theorists like Michel Foucault and Judith Butler to view persons (described as "subjects") as intelligible to themselves and each other only by means of mediating "discourses" that together, again like Saussure's *langue*, confer intelligibility to those "subjects" in the way, and only in the way, that these reigning discursive systems prescribe

---

[15] See Jonathan Culler's "Preface to the Routledge Classics Edition" of *Structuralist Poetics: Structuralism, Linguistics and the Study of Literature* (Cornell University Press, 1975), vii–viii, and the chapter "Literary Competence." While Culler employs linguistic competence as an analogy for literary competence, a further extension of Saussure's linguistics beyond literature to social life in general, an extension that equates social life with linguistic competence rather than merely drawing an analogy between them, is apparent in Jacques Rancière's claim about "literature as such" as it functions within – and indeed produces – what he calls the aesthetic regime of modernity: "It's not a matter here of the influence of this author on that. It's a matter of a poetic and metaphorical model put in place by literature as such and to which our human and social sciences largely owe their modes of interpretation," these human and social sciences corresponding to the "discourses" central to the work of Rancière's contemporary, Michel Foucault; see Rancière's "The Politics of Literature," in *The Politics of Literature*, trans. Julie Rose (Polity Press, 2011), 22. This consistent approach across word, work, and world is enabled by the structuralist transformation of word into sign (Saussure), work into text (Culler [following Roland Barthes]), and self into subject (Rancière and Foucault), a transformation that enables each level – language, literature, and politics – to imagine the individual entity of central concern to it – a sign, text, or subject – to be, as Saussure writes of signs, "emanating from a linguistic system"; see Saussure's *Course in General Linguistics* (1916), trans. Roy Harris, ed. Charles Bally, Albert Sechehaye, and Albert Riedlinger (Open Court, 1972), 115. The result is a signomorphism of selves as political "subjects": Just as signs, for Saussure, emanate from the system that is *langue*, and texts, for Culler, emanate from a system that is poetics, subjects (for Rancière, Foucault, and as we will see, Judith Butler) emanate from a system that is "language as such" or "discourse."

for them.[16] If this volume, following in this structuralist tradition, were to prioritize descriptions of the enabling system of intelligibility (Rancière's "distribution of the sensible," Culler's "poetics," or Foucault's and Butler's "discourse") over particular instances rendered legible by it, it would look more like Rancière's recent *Aisthesis*, which devotes just one chapter to nineteenth-century US literature and politics in an effort to illustrate an artistic modernity enabled by an "aesthetic regime" that governs modern literary expression in Western capitals ranging from Moscow to Berlin to Paris to London to New York and finally Hollywood.[17] The priority in this volume, however, is less a social-scientific accounting of the enabling conditions of possibility for literature being legible to those competent in applying its systemic rules than it is a demonstration of literary practice in action, featuring events like Lincoln's speech and its use of many types of mediating strategies to effect the practical result of defeating the incumbent US senator from Illinois.

If the mix of politics and literature in the Lincoln example is not, as it will be in this volume, a priority for Rancière's structuralist approach to the politics of aesthetics, it is an opportune target for a competing approach to literary history, standpoint epistemology. This approach would urge us to observe two key features of Lincoln's speech: first, his acknowledgment that competing standpoints exist and are present – which he does in his aside to Douglas to note that "I am now among men who have some abolition tendencies" even as he is about to deny (disingenuously) being one of them – and second, Lincoln's failure to acknowledge that other relevant standpoints, in particular that of the black race, are absent – no black "voice" speaks from Lincoln's and Douglas's shared podium, so it is

---

[16] Judith Butler invokes Saussure's linguistics in her assertion that "to understand identity as a *practice*, and as a signifying practice, is to understand culturally intelligible subjects as the resulting effects of a rule-bound discourse that inserts itself in the pervasive and mundane signifying acts of linguistic life. Abstractly considered, language refers to an open system of signs by which intelligibility is insistently created and contested," and "discourses" are "historically specific organizations of language" understood in these same Saussurean terms; see Judith Butler, *Gender Trouble: Feminism and the Subversion of Identity* (Routledge, 1990), 145. Butler underscores the antifoundationalism of her account by rejecting "the foundationalist reasoning of identity politics [which] tends to assume that an identity must first be in place in order for political interest to be elaborated and, subsequently, political action to be taken. My argument is that there need not be a 'doer behind the deed,' but that the 'doer' is variably constructed in and through the deed" (142). On Saussurean linguistics as the "first step" toward this "culture as semiosis" mode of literary history, a mode that tends to yield "debilitating methodological practices," see Lee Patterson, "Literary History," in Frank Lentricchia and Thomas McLaughlin, eds., *Critical Terms for Literary Study*, 2nd ed. (University of Chicago Press, 1995), 250–262, 256, 261.

[17] See Jacques Rancière, *Aisthesis: Scenes from the Aesthetic Regime of Art*, trans. Zakir Paul (Verso, 2013); only the fourth chapter considers literature from the nineteenth-century United States.

a space of whiteness, a narrow and partial vantage by comparison to the effort of standpoint epistemology to be inclusive and respectful of multiple perspectives whose diverse experiences generate correspondingly variant yet – standpoint epistemologists claim – no less accurate knowledges of the world. For a standpoint-epistemology approach, Lincoln's recognition of a competing perspective – of the abolitionists with whom he supposedly disagrees – registers the power and need of such insights in our study of literature and politics, suggesting that the debate here – which goes so terribly wrong in endorsing racism – would have gone much better if black as well as white voices had been part of the conversation. Indeed, Lincoln can privilege feelings over justice and sound judgment precisely because, a standpoint epistemologist might argue, there are no black or other minority voices sharing those perspectives' different experiences of the harms his feelings inflict. And that exclusion might in turn call for a volume like this to expand Lincoln's partial acknowledgment of multiple standpoints (abolitionists and their opponents) in order to extend beyond it so as to correct his exclusionary practice (and racist judgment) by organizing itself oppositionally, refusing such past exclusions of voices and, on the contrary, multiplying and amplifying such formerly silenced perspectives.[18] To do so would, on this account, provide a fuller, truer, and

---

[18] My use of the term "standpoint" to describe both being an abolitionist and being black may seem odd since abolitionism appears to be a revisable belief about policy while many understand blackness to be an inescapable condition of the body. But such a distinction misunderstands both abolition as a political movement and standpoint epistemology as an account of identity. Regarding abolition, Corey M. Brooks has characterized it as not so much an opinion about policy as "among the more impressive examples in American history of a social movement that found itself shut out from national policymaking and thus moved into political activism to bring its issues before the nation"; see Corey M. Brooks, *Liberty Power: Antislavery Third Parties and the Transformation of American Politics* (University of Chicago Press, 2016), 13. Indeed, the title of Albion Tourgée's 1893 novel *Hot Plowshares* references the abolitionist commitment to undergo the medieval ordeal of trial by fire, walking barefoot across "hot plowshares," rather than compromise a principled commitment to human liberty. By contrast, the titular "fool" in Tourgée's 1879 novel *A Fool's Errand* is foolish precisely because, unlike the abolitionists, he questions his principles: "was there any absolute standard of right, or were religion and morality merely relative and incidental terms? Was that right in Georgia which was wrong in Maine? ... He could not tell" (317), but he soon "felt he was learning wisdom" when, after having moved from the North to the South, "he had come almost to believe that what are termed 'principles' are only ingrained habits of thought, and hereditary systems of belief" (339) specific to a regional or local standpoint, an idea that Tourgée's "fool" considers "following the paths of wisdom" (344) but that Tourgée himself presents as genuine foolishness – an abandonment of principle that the abolitionists rightly refused; see Albion Tourgée, *A Fool's Errand*, ed. John Hope Franklin (Harvard University Press, 1961). This very alienation from principle is, however, essential as a matter of principle to racial identity (at least as standpoint epistemology understands it): It is rooted in the truth not of principle but of experience that is itself situated within a local perspective that one comes to understand as one's identity, and just one among many others, only as a consequence of having become alienated from it – precisely the alienation that the abolitionists refused on their path toward political success. Thus to characterize abolition as revisable

more genuine picture of the various knowledges, epistemologies, or what we now call identities than Lincoln himself could have known of his own world, a picture that our vantage from the present – and our use of literature as the privileged vehicle for expressing such experiences and knowledges – can make possible.[19]

While this political and epistemic optimism explains standpoint epistemology's appeal to many as a methodological and disciplinary roadmap for correcting injustices both past and present, it has met important challenges as an approach to social and literary history in the work of Dick Pels and Stanley Fish. Pels observes that "Critical intellectuals" – those who speak from and advocate on behalf of marginalized perspectives associated with race, class, and gender – "indeed find themselves in a contradictory social location, because they identify with the oppressed but simultaneously take their distance from their unmediated experiences of oppression. Marginal standpoints by themselves do not suffice; they must be intellectualized, pass through theory," but what this essential and distancing passage through theory implies, Pels continues, is that

> theory also *liberates* from standpoints; the correct consciousness opens up the correct standpoint, even if one "naturally" occupies the incorrect one. Theory provides an alienative methodology, a procedural code of distanciation, which is in principle accessible for all subjects of rational or emancipatory goodwill. Once again we are returning to the methodological voluntarism that standpoint theory started out to combat.[20]

---

opinion sells short the movement's persistent convictions, and to see blackness as an inescapable identity misunderstands standpoint epistemology's requirement of estrangement from one's locally derived experience and knowledge as a necessary condition of knowing this location as one's own, just one local identity among many others. Abolitionism thus proved to be more of an identity in committed practice than blackness – when it is understood in terms of standpoint epistemology's requirement of principled alienation from local practice in order to discern what local practice is properly one's own – can ever be.

[19] "Strong objectivity," Sandra Harding argues, "requires that the subject of knowledge be placed on the same critical, causal plane as the objects of knowledge. Thus, strong objectivity requires what we can think of as 'strong reflexivity,'" which means, in turn, that "[t]he subject of knowledge – the individual and the historically located social community whose unexamined beliefs its members are likely to hold 'unknowingly,' so to speak – must be considered as part of the object of knowledge from the perspective of scientific method"; see Sandra Harding, "Rethinking Standpoint Epistemology: What Is 'Strong Objectivity'?," in Sandra Harding, ed., *The Feminist Standpoint Epistemology Reader: Intellectual and Political Controversies* (Routledge, 2004), 127–140, 136. On challenges to objectivity within the sciences and social sciences, see "The Scientific Self" in Lorraine Daston and Peter Galison's *Objectivity* (Zone Books, 2010), 191–251; and "The Rise and Fall of Objectivity," in Sarah Maza's *Thinking about History* (University of Chicago Press, 2017), 199–208.

[20] Dick Pels, "Strange Standpoints, or How to Define the Situation for Situated Knowledge," in Harding, *The Feminist Standpoint*, 273–289, 281, 283–284. A different approach to challenging standpoint epistemology appears in Tony Hilfer's "Visible Saints: The Politics of Standpoint Epistemology," in *The New Hegemony in Literary Studies: Contradictions in Theory* (Northwestern

Introduction: Politics and Literary History

What Pels calls "the methodological voluntarism" of "subjects of rational or emancipatory goodwill" Stanley Fish labels "antifoundationalist-theory-hope," and just as Pels finds standpoint epistemologists to be "in a contradictory social location," so too Fish asserts that antifoundationalist-theory-hope's

> radical culture ... cannot be lived ... [because] it demands from the wholly situated creature a mode of action or thought (or writing) that is free from the entanglements of situations and the lines of demarcation they declare; it demands that a consciousness that has shape only by virtue of the distinctions and boundary lines that are its content float free of those lines and boundaries and remain forever unsettled.[21]

Fish makes this general observation against antifoundationalist-theory-hope as part of a more specific challenge to the claim made by the New Historicism that such antifoundationalist-theory-hope makes its historicist methodology different and better:

> The methodological difference claimed by New Historicism is the difference of not being constrained in its gestures by narrow disciplinary and professional boundaries. The reasoning is that since New Historicists are aware of those boundaries and are aware, too, of their source in ultimately revisable societal (and even global) structures, they can angle their actions (or interventions as they prefer to call them) in such a way as to put pressure on those structures and so perform politically both in the little world of their institutional situation and the larger world of POLITICS.[22]

University Press, 2003), 39–54, which criticizes an ethos of "demonstrating personal perfection through identification with an ascriptively righteous group" (53), an ethos that Hilfer compares to the similarly righteous conviction among Puritan "visible saints" that they are among God's chosen few, the "saved" "elect" (50). For Pels, by contrast, the problem with standpoint epistemology is not its ethos but its logos, not self-righteous certainty but logical incoherence: "theories about situated knowledges are prone to suffer from a vicious circularity which results from their efforts to derive objectivity claims from ontological situations which must first be 'defined as real' before such claims can be contextually situated"; see Dick Pels, *The Intellectual As Stranger: Studies in Spokespersonship* (Routledge, 2000), xvii–xviii. My own analysis of this logical problem has cast it in aesthetic terms, rendering its logical circularity as aesthetic cycle, with the racial self oscillating between, on the one hand, a "scientific" mode of objectivity that enables enumerating the possibilities for experiencing an object – either oneself or others as racial bodies – and, on the other hand, rhapsodic immersion in the immediate experience of that object (which is only possible, for a raced body, if that body is one's own). In this aesthetic account (itself parallel, I argue, to northern New Critical aesthetic formalism), the objective distance of the "scientific" mode corresponds to Pels's estrangement of the spokesperson, and the rhapsodic immersion aligns with Pels's contextual situation where immediate experience produces situated perspectival knowledge; see my *Racial Rhapsody: The Aesthetics of Contemporary U.S. Identity* (Routledge, 2019).

[21] Stanley Fish, "Commentary: The Young and the Restless," in H. Aram Veeser, ed., *The New Historicism* (Routledge, 1989), 303–316, 307, 311.

[22] Fish, "Commentary," 313.

This reasoning, however, Fish pointedly questions: "Can one grasp the political constructedness and relatedness of all things in order to do one thing in a different and more capacious way? ... The answer," Fish concludes, "is 'no,'" continuing:

> In short, there is no road, royal or otherwise, from the insight that all activities are political to a special or different way of engaging in any particular activity, no politics that derives from the truth that everything is politically embedded. Interrelatedness may be a fact about disciplines and enterprises as seen from a vantage point uninvolved in any one of them (the vantage point of another, philosophical, enterprise), but it cannot be the motor of one's performance. Practices may *be* interrelated but you cannot *do* interrelatedness – simultaneously stand within a practice and reflectively survey the supports you stand on.[23]

For the project of doing literary history, which is the project of this volume, the alternative to the impossible antifoundationalist-theory-hope method of historicism central to the New Historicism is a necessary and inevitable return to the conventions of the historicism it sought to transcend or surpass: "The only way the New or any other kind of historicism could be new," Fish claims,

> is by asserting a new truth about something in opposition to, or correction of, or modification of, a truth previously asserted by someone else; but that newness – always a possible achievement – will not be *methodologically* new, will not be a new (non-allegorical, non-excluding, non-forgetting, non-boundary-drawing) way of doing history, but merely another move in the practice of history as it has always been done.[24]

This is not, to be sure, a foundationalist (as in positivist or objectivist) history; in rejecting "antifoundationalist-theory-hope" as its method, this volume is not therefore rejecting antifoundationalism; it is, instead, properly understanding antifoundationalism, which, when it is properly understood, recognizes two points about foundations: not only that we do not have them but also that we do not need them. As Fish put it in his earlier essay "Consequences," "the lesson of antifoundationalism is not only that external and independent guides will never be found but that it is unnecessary to seek them," which is almost as succinctly put as the more recent account of it in *Pragmatism: A Guide for the Perplexed*: "*Antifoundationalism*: Knowledge neither has nor requires foundations."[25] Pragmatism's version of antifoundationalism is strongly indebted to

---

[23] Fish, "Commentary," 314 (emphasis in original).   [24] Fish, "Commentary," 313.
[25] Stanley Fish, "Consequences," in W. J. T. Mitchell, ed., *Against Theory: Literary Studies and the New Pragmatism* (University of Chicago Press, 1985), 106–131, 113; Robert B. Talisse and Scott F. Aikin, *Pragmatism: A Guide for the Perplexed* (Continuum, 2008), 39.

the work of nineteenth-century US philosophers such as C. S. Peirce and William James, but as I have suggested, it is not the Americanness but rather the correctness of its account of antifoundationalism that makes pragmatism a more suitable method for producing literary history than the linguist analogy of discourse analysis or the spatial metaphor of standpoint epistemology.[26] Underscoring this connection between pragmatism and literary history, Fish asserts, "If you set out to determine what happened in 1649, you will look to the materials that recommend themselves to you as the likely repositories of historical knowledge and go from there. In short, you and those who dispute your findings (a word precisely intended) will be engaged in empirical work," and it is empirical work of just this sort that has generated the several chapters collected in this volume.[27]

Having provided this methodological overview for the chapters that follow, I will forego the conventional practice for such introductions of summarizing each chapter, instead directing readers to the chapters themselves, which are organized in three parts, the first devoted to general political concepts like liberalism and conservatism, the second to broad political issues like slavery and territoriality, and the third to a variety of genres or modes of presentation such as poetry and drama.

---

[26] On the emergence of pragmatism in the nineteenth-century United States, see Louis Menand, *The Metaphysical Club: A Story of Ideas in America* (Farrar, Straus and Giroux, 2001).

[27] Fish, "Commentary," 313. Regarding pragmatism's antifoundationalist empiricism, Fish later underscores that "If pragmatism is true it has nothing to say to us; no politics follows from it or is blocked by it; no morality attaches to it or is enjoined by it," continuing, "If I am a pragmatist and hold that beliefs are internal to practices and cannot be justified by independent and general criteria, *this* belief will not lead me to lose confidence in my other beliefs or inhabit them more loosely than would be the case if I had another account of them"; see Fish's "Afterword: Truth and Toilets: Pragmatism and the Practices of Life," in Morris Dickstein, ed., *The Revival of Pragmatism: New Essays on Social Thought, Law, and Culture* (Duke University Press, 1999), 418–433, 419, 420.

PART I
Concepts

CHAPTER I

The Liberal Tradition and Slavery
Arthur Riss

Liberalism has long loomed large in any interpretation of the United States. Formulated most notoriously by Louis Hartz in his deeply influential *The Liberal Tradition in America* (1955), the argument has been that the United States is essentially and inherently liberal, a nation where "an absolute and irrational attachment" to liberal ideals – individual liberty, self-determination, a minimal state, the free marketplace, and innate natural rights – is so deeply hegemonic that those ideals exist not in any specific political party or social program but as the basis of US politics itself. Liberalism, according to this argument, circulates at an almost preconscious level, fully present at the birth of this nation, operating as "the master assumption of American political thought."[1] But, of course, any claim for the absolute dominance of liberal thought in the United States immediately faces a conspicuous problem. How does a monolithically liberal society – a nation that declares it "self-evident" that "all men are created equal" and promises all "life, liberty, and the pursuit of happiness" – not simply sanction but entrench slavery, the ultimate institution of unfreedom? Dominick Losurdo neatly encapsulates the problem: "[H]ow should we situate" John Calhoun, who "burst into an impassioned ode to individual liberty," private property, and the free market in order to "brand abolitionists as 'blind fanatics'" and to declare slavery "a positive good," the foundation of our free, civilized society?[2] Is Calhoun's implacable devotion to an individual's freedom to own slaves quintessentially liberal?

The problem of how to understand the historical nexus of liberal values and slavery has become an abiding problem in any discussion of the United States, one formulaically rehearsed in discussions about Thomas Jefferson (the slave owner who wrote the Declaration of Independence) and the patron saint of liberalism, John Locke himself, who authored the *Second*

---

[1] Louis Hartz, *The Liberal Tradition in America* (Harcourt Brace, 1955), 6, 62.
[2] Domenico Losurdo, *Liberalism: A Counter History* (Verso, 2014), 1.

Treatise of Government (1689), often taken to be the prototypical expression of liberalism's commitment to individual rights and freedom, yet also wrote *The Fundamental Constitutions of Carolina* (1669), a document that explicitly promoted slavery, as well as owned stock in the Royal African Company, the mercantile company that administered the African slave trade for England. Indeed, the question of how the United States could imagine itself as a beacon of individual liberty while so many were held in chains and, even more troublingly, how so many Americans could, as Calhoun did, summon liberal values (such as autonomy and the individual's right to own property) in order to champion slavery, has come to be called the "American Dilemma," the "central paradox of American history."[3]

This "promethean contradiction," as David Brion Davis terms it, has, for the most part, been explained in one of three ways.[4] For some, liberal ideals and slavery are presumed to be fundamentally opposed and therefore the existence of slavery is, most straightforwardly, an example of patent hypocrisy or, more politely, an example of ideological misprision, the coexistence of slavery and liberal thought merely demonstrating that liberal ideals can in practice be distorted by racism, sexism, or capitalism (thus liberalism in itself is pure). In such an account, the historical conjunction of the practice of slavery and liberal ideals is not explained as much as explained away, dismissed as an anomaly, a mistake about what liberalism truly is.[5] As Judith N. Shklar argued, "until the Civil War amendments, America was neither a liberal nor a democratic country, whatever its citizens might have believed."[6] Liberalism, in this view, remains an ideal worth pursuing.

In response to the claim that liberal ideals in and of themselves remain pure and categorically opposed to slavery, some have explained slavery's flourishing under nineteenth-century liberalism in a second way, arguing that the coincidence of liberalism and slavery is not an oxymoron but an insight, one proving, once and for all, that the idea that "liberalism is

---

[3] Gunnar Myrdal, *An American Dilemma* (Harper, 1944); Edmund S. Morgan, *American Slavery, American Freedom* (Norton, 1975), 4.
[4] David Brion Davis, *Challenging the Boundaries of Slavery* (Harvard University Press, 2003), 67.
[5] Hartz himself exemplifies this line of thought; see *The Liberal Tradition in America*, especially 145–177. Rogers Smith's "multiple traditions" thesis of US political thought – liberalism competing against republicanism, as well as various hierarchical systems – also inoculates liberalism from its historical conjunction with slavery by contrasting liberalism to these other traditions. Rogers M. Smith, "Beyond Tocqueville, Myrdal, and Hartz: The Multiple Traditions in America," *The American Political Science Review* 87:3 (September 1993), 549–566.
[6] Judith N. Shklar, "Redeeming American Political Theory," *The American Political Science Review* 85:1 (1991), 3–15, 4.

synonymous with liberty and the defense of liberty doesn't hold water."[7] According to this line of argument, liberalism might promise individual liberty and equality, but it delivers only inequality and exclusion. In this account, liberalism cannot be purified from extraneous, irrational elements (racism or sexism) because liberalism and oppressive hierarchies are essentially imbricated. In Richard Delgado's formulation, "liberal democracy and racial subordination go hand in hand, like the sun, moon, and stars."[8] In such arguments, slavery is not an exception to but a consequence of liberalism, inseparable from the logic of liberalism. In Saidiya Hartman's influential account, for example, not only does individual freedom emerge because of the unfreedom of others, but the promise of freedom to the unfree is fundamentally false, working only to compel the disenfranchised to endorse the very structures that enforce their oppression.[9]

The third position has been to conclude that the maddening malleability of liberal practices (the fact that possessive individualism, for example, has both powerfully opposed and effectively defended slavery) demonstrates that liberalism ultimately exceeds any definition. Frustrated by the open-endedness of liberal thought, such accounts foreground the "protean character of American liberalism" and characterize liberalism as "radically plastic."[10] For example, Eric Voegelin has asked "whether there is even such a thing as liberalism as a clearly definable subject and whether this subject, should it not be clearly definable, can have a history."[11] In such accounts, the fact that most US political arguments have circulated within the liberal tradition stands as proof that liberalism possesses no authentic essence. This approach renders fundamentally unproductive the effort to answer the question whether the compatibility of liberalism and slavery is a glitch in it or a feature of it.

Although the historical flexibility of liberal thought has doubtlessly thwarted efforts to distill the pure essence of liberalism and to distinguish authentic liberals from liberals manqué, this does not mean that instances

---

[7] Domenico Losurdo, "The Tangled Paradox of Liberalism," *International Socialist Review* 84 (2012), 22–26, 22.
[8] Richard Delgado, *The Rodrigo Chronicles* (New York University Press, 1995), 144.
[9] See Saidiya Hartman's *Scenes of Subjection: Terror, Slavery, and Self-Making in Nineteenth-Century America* (Oxford University Press, 1997), especially 152–157.
[10] Gary Gerstle, "The Protean Character of American Liberalism," *The American Historical Review* 99:4 (October 1994), 1043–1073; Carol A. Horton, *Race and the Making of American Liberalism* (Oxford University Press, 2005), 232n5.
[11] Eric Voegelin, "Liberalism and Its History," *The Review of Politics* 36:4 (October 1974), 504–520, 504. For similar arguments, see Duncan Bell, "What Is Liberalism?," *Political Theory* 42:6 (December 2014), 682–715, and Edmund Fawcett, *Liberalism: The Life of an Idea* (Princeton, 2014).

of liberal thought share no discernible family features. Thus, one might conclude with Jeremy Waldron that "[t]o say ... that a commitment to *freedom* is the foundation of liberalism is ... too vague and abstract to be helpful."[12] But liberalism's abiding understanding of freedom and slavery as mutually exclusive categories, nonetheless, reveals something crucial. One needs to ask: How can liberalism be theoretically structured by the binary opposition between slavery and liberty yet historically constitute this opposition in such fundamentally different ways? Or to put it another way, how can the same liberal ideal of individual freedom be summoned so effectively both by slavery's opponents and by its champions? As Abraham Lincoln explained in the midst of a war that had finally become a war over who deserves freedom, "We all declare for liberty; but in using the same *word* we do not all mean the same *thing*."[13] Liberal thought, thus, provokes us to find what allows liberals to be haunted by the threat of the enslavement of some but not necessarily oppose the slavery of certain others.[14] The historical fluidity of liberal political theory compels us to ask exactly whose enslavement does a liberal oppose? Who at any particular historical moment possesses – and does not possess – the right to have natural, equal, and universal rights?[15]

To ask this question is to bring forward the conceptual category grounding liberal thought: the "person." Liberalism condemns slavery, but only the slavery of "persons."[16] The "person" stands as the relay

[12] Jeremy Waldron, "Theoretical Foundations of Liberalism," *The Philosophical Quarterly* 37:147 (1987), 127–150, 131.
[13] "Address at Sanitary Fair, Baltimore, Maryland, April 18, 1864," in Roy P. Basler, ed., *The Collected Works of Abraham Lincoln*, Vol. 7 (Rutgers University Press, 1953), 302–303 (emphasis in original).
[14] One might think of how many Founding Fathers claimed to be motivated by the threat of their enslavement even as they themselves owned slaves, or one might productively be reminded of arguments that foreground the fact that there are more than 40 million slaves in the world today and simultaneously acknowledge that little political will exists to abolish such slavery.
[15] Arendt discusses "the right to have rights" when examining how little the recognition of being "human" in and of itself guarantees. See Hannah Arendt, *The Origins of Totalitarianism* (Houghton Mifflin, 1973), especially chap. 9. See also Walter Johnson, "To Remake the World: Slavery, Racial Capitalism, and Justice," *Boston Review* [online forum] (February 1, 2017), www.bostonreview.net/forum/walter-johnson-to-remake-the-world/.
[16] My attempt to name the conceptual category that a liberal society imagines itself as committed to protecting and nourishing underwrites my use of the term "person." I have put this conceptual category under quotation, however, to accent this term as a site of struggle and to provoke uncertainty about the way that the term is traditionally deployed. To convey the sense of the identity that liberalism imagines as existing in a "state of nature," before and outside the structures of the law and society, I have chosen the term "person," rather than "subject" or "citizen." And I have chosen this term over "individual," "human being," or "Man" to move beyond masculinist, modernist, and biological categories and to foreground the theoretical open-endedness of the term. At some historical moments the "person" is more restricted than the "human being," while at others it wildly exceeds the category of the human (corporations, rocks and trees, and synthetic

point of liberal thought, both naming the subject of liberal rights and designating – by virtue of their exclusion from the category of "person" – those for whom such rights can be legitimately refused. The term "person" (for lack of a better word) occupies what Jacques Derrida would call the *center* of liberal thought.[17] This figure names the conceptual category that orients liberalism, that functions as the self-evident point of departure for any emancipatory project, but, as we will see, one that liberalism simultaneously keeps beyond scrutiny, maintaining it as liberal thought's governing identity, something deployed *and* never examined. Liberal theory, in other words, calls forth the "person" as its privileged and primary object – as that which must be accurately reflected in and absolutely protected by the formal institutions of a liberal polity – at the same time that it inaugurates the question of who is a "person" as liberalism's inescapable interpretive problem. The "person," in this sense, is both inside and outside any liberal argument, a center, as Derrida would say, that is not a center.

The *centrality* of the conceptual category of the person to liberalism explains why the persistence of slavery in the United States neither unmasks the inequality implanted at the core of liberal thought nor violates the true principles of liberalism. Since liberalism is not necessarily allied with some historically inevitable, in-built definition of who is a "person," the powerful defense of the natural, inherent rights of "persons" embedded in liberal political theory can either convincingly defend or forcefully repudiate slavery, providing a justification for it when the enslaved is understood not to be a "person" and a condemnation of it when the enslaved is understood to be a "person": both arguments are fully and equally liberal.[18]

---

life-forms have all been argued to possess the right to have rights). Arguments for attributing "personhood" to nature, for example, have become increasingly commonplace; see the chapter "Legal Personhood for Wildlife: US and Foreign Domestic Judicial Developments," in Randall S. Abate's *Climate Change and the Voiceless: Protecting Future Generations, Wildlife, and Natural Resources* (Cambridge University Press, 2019), 97–119.

[17] Perhaps the most cited sources for Derrida's account of the "center" are "Structure, Sign, and Play in the Discourse of the Human Sciences," in Jacques Derrida, *Writing and Difference*, trans. Alan Bass (University of Chicago Press, 1978), 278–293; and "White Mythology: Metaphor in the Text of Philosophy," in Jacques Derrida, *Margins of Philosophy*, trans. Alan Bass (University of Chicago Press, 1982), 207–272.

[18] Although the term "person" has long been discussed in the history of law, I am deploying the term "person" to designate a conceptual category distinct from its juridical usage. For this alternative use, see, for example, essays by Jeannine Marie DeLombard, Aaron Ritzenberg, and Susana Blumenthal in Nan Goodman and Simon Stern, eds., *The Routledge Research Companion to Law and the Humanities in Nineteenth-Century America*, Routledge, 2017. In contrast to such discussions of the person as a precise legal term – accounts distinguishing "natural persons" from the fictive, purely juristic persons (i.e. corporations) and debating the mixed legal character of the slave (as both natural

During the antebellum period, the moment when slavery becomes the focus of increasingly intense national debate, it becomes especially clear how the conflict over slavery pivots on debates over the absoluteness of the "person." The debate over slavery was, for all intents and purposes, a debate over who is *obviously* included within and who is excluded from "personhood." As Lincoln clarifies, the question of who is a Man (his term for the conceptual center of liberal thought) lies at the heart of the liberal debate over slavery:

> If we admit that a negro is not a man, then it is right for the Government to own him and trade in the race, and it is right to allow the South to take their peculiar institution with them and plant it upon the virgin soil of Kansas and Nebraska. If the negro is not a man, it is consistent to apply the sacred right of popular sovereignty to the question as to whether the people of the territories shall or shall not have slavery; but if the negro ... *is* a man, then there is not even the shadow of popular sovereignty in allowing the first settlers upon such soil to decide whether it shall be right in all future time to hold men in bondage there.[19]

What Lincoln makes clear is the extent to which liberalism absolutely condemns slavery only if those being enslaved immanently possess the right to liberty. The point is not the specific word Lincoln is using ("man") but the conceptual category he is invoking ("person"). Lincoln, in short, articulates the problem that he and his opponents – all committed liberals – relentlessly debate: the question of who unconditionally deserves liberty.

The invocation of the words "all men are created equal" as if these words could resolve the slavery question is perhaps the clearest symptom of the competing yet equally absolute accounts of the "person" circulating within antebellum culture. Beginning from the same liberal premise that "persons" can never be legitimately held as slaves, both anti- and proslavery thinkers understood the words famously announced in the Declaration of Independence as possessing diametrically opposed but nonetheless unequivocally transparent meanings. Thus, antislavery thinkers, like an exasperated David Walker, quoted the "self-evident" truth that "all men are created equal" and asked whether "the American people ... understand your own language?"[20] In contrast, William Harper accused antislavery advocates of misunderstanding what these words *literally* mean.

---

person and property) – I am using the term to foreground the logic of liberal thought, to make a theoretical claim about the structure of liberal thought.

[19] "Speech at Bloomington, Illinois, Sept. 26th, 1854," in *The Collected Works of Abraham Lincoln*, Vol. 2, ed. Roy P. Basler (Rutgers University Press, 1953), 239.

[20] David Walker, *Walker's Appeal* (David Walker, 1830), 85.

Opponents of slavery, he argues, regularly "quote from our Declaration of Independence" words that are "palpably false" for "no two men were ever born equal." Indeed, Harper continues, since it is "palpably nearer to the truth to say that no man was ever born free" or equal, the literal "substance" of the Declaration of Independence verges on being "false, sophistical or unmeaning."[21] Similarly, the proslavery thinker R. B. Mays asks dismissively, "Are all men created equal in size, weight, health, strength, beauty, worldly circumstances and expectancies?" – concluding, almost identically, that since Men are not "born free from natural laws" and cannot "do as they like," abolitionists must be interpreting the Declaration of Independence in a purely "political sense," as what they fancy the document "*ought to be.*"[22] Thus, it is far from surprising that Chief Justice Taney cites the words "all men are created equal" as "conclusive" evidence that the Founders never considered the Negro to be "part of the people" who deserve freedom.[23]

The literal meaning of the Declaration of Independence may be self-evident, but it clearly has not been self-evident to all in the same way. Any *literal* reading of these words is ultimately a political interpretation, one that reveals any understanding of the "person" to be inevitably interested, inescapably dependent upon a set of partisan assumptions. The liberal premise is that the "person" in and of itself should ground and govern politics, but these words – "all men are created equal" – recapitulate rather than decide the slavery question precisely because the "person" is what is in dispute. Thus, it is simultaneously quintessentially liberal and fundamentally unproductive to claim that the Declaration simply needs to be allowed to speak for itself, to be liberated from any political bias, in order to resolve the contradiction of American slavery. And it is ultimately gratuitous to lament that its glaringly comprehensible emancipatory meaning has still

---

[21] William Harper, *Memoir on Slavery* (James S. Burges, 1838), 6. Ralph Waldo Emerson similarly makes clear that the debate over these words is always a debate over what they *literally* mean: "I believe that nobody now regards the maxim 'that all men are born equal,' as any thing more than a convenient hypothesis or an extravagant declamation. For (all) the reverse is true," "Nov. 8, 1822," in *The Journals and Miscellaneous Notebooks of Ralph Waldo Emerson*, Vol. 2, ed. William H. Gilman, Alfred R. Ferguson, and Merrell R. Davis (Harvard University Press, 1961), 42.

[22] R. B. Mays, "The Divine Legation of Thomas Jefferson – Are All Men Created Free! – Are All Men Created White," *DeBow's Review* 30:5 (May–June 1861), 521–532, 524, 525 (original emphasis). Massachusetts US Senator Rufus Choate similarly dismissed "the glittering and sounding generalities of natural rights which make up the Declaration of Independence." *The Works of Rufus Choate*, Vol. 1 (Little, Brown, 1862), 215.

[23] *Dred Scott v. Sandford*, 60 US (19 How.) 410.

not been realized.[24] These words never speak for themselves. The former slave Solomon Northup effectively crystallizes the political impasse that this supposedly definitive document inevitably provokes when he describes an argument between the antislavery Samuel Bass and Northup's master, Edwin Epps:

> "Look here, Epps," continued his companion [Bass]; "you can't laugh me down in that way. Some men are witty, and some ain't so witty as they think they are.
> Now let me ask you a question. Are all men created free and equal as the Declaration of Independence hold they are?" "Yes," responded Epps, "but all men, niggers, and monkeys ain't."

Precisely to the extent that the self-evident meaning of these words inevitably depends upon an interpretation of who is a "person," the Declaration of Independence simultaneously solidifies the foundational nature of the "person" and foregrounds how this foundational term is what is always in question in liberal thought. What is striking is not the historically different ways the "person" has been or can be specified but the degree to which this conceptual category nonetheless continues to be summoned as if it could determine political interpretation, treated as if it could function simply as, to put it in Derridean terms, a transcendental signified.

Once we approach the antebellum controversy over slavery as a debate over the "person," we can easily see this debate being waged in multiple arenas, contested not only in the political and legal spheres but also in scientific, religious, philosophical, and aesthetic discourse. This nation's most influential scientists were exploring the question of whether the Negro constituted a separate species, while biblical scholars were heatedly debating whether there were multiple Creations.[25] In this sense, the problem of the "person" exceeded legal debates over the mixed character of the slave (part property, part human); it constellated moral and biological, metaphysical and empirical, aesthetic, political, and ethnological concerns. Thus, the influence of a sentimental literary text like Harriet Beecher Stowe's *Uncle Tom's Cabin* extends far beyond the literary sphere precisely because of its spectacular effectiveness in representing slaves as "persons" unjustly deprived of their innate "personhood." Originally

---

[24] One of the clearest instances of how political these words always are: Today we take the word "men" obviously to mean Men and Women and (to many) the nonbinary even though in 1848 Elizabeth Cady Stanton and Lucretia Mott felt compelled to rewrite the Declaration to assert "that all men and women are created equal; that they are endowed by their Creator with certain inalienable rights"; see their "Declaration of Sentiments, Seneca Falls Conference, 1848."
[25] See, for example, John S. Haller, *Outcasts from Evolution* (University of Illinois Press, 1971).

subtitled *The Man Who Was a Thing, Uncle Tom's Cabin* intervened so powerfully in the antebellum culture's argument over the "personhood" of the slave that it was regularly recognized as the single most powerful instrument for destroying slavery.[26]

In contrast to Stowe, Nathaniel Hawthorne, probably the period's most canonical author, may seem singularly unconcerned with the question of the "personhood" of the slave, a position perhaps particularly surprising since his short stories and Romances repeatedly return to the problem of one character's psychological bondage to another, a form of inhumane mastery that he calls the "Unpardonable Sin."[27] It is precisely such unconcern for *actual* slaves that has led modern scholars to regard Hawthorne's use of the master–slave relationship as merely metaphorical, an aesthetic flourish that shows him to be not only indifferent to their plight but exploiting it.[28]

When we see Hawthorne's concern with slavery as simply figurative, however, we ignore the authenticity of the very question being interrogated during the antebellum period (is "Negro slavery" wrong?), and we instead substitute our modern certainty about "Negro slavery" (slavery obviously violates the slave's "personhood"). To the extent that we indict Hawthorne for representing middle-class problems of white people as if a form of literal enslavement and assert that in doing so Hawthorne diminishes the *real* humiliations and *real* pain suffered by *real* slaves, we leave unexplored how Hawthorne's literary preoccupations do not sidestep but actively participate in the antebellum debate over who is a "person," what counts as slavery, and which actions unconscionably violate the sanctity of "persons." By not concerning himself with "Negro slavery," Hawthorne is aggressively arguing that slaves are not "persons."

Although antebellum debate over slavery may seem to reveal how "personhood" is historically granted, politically petitioned for, or culturally produced, it is crucial to restate that, according to the logic of liberal thought (both then and now), the "person" is never imagined as socially

---

[26] This understanding is best captured by Lincoln's famous yet most likely apocryphal comment upon meeting Stowe: "so you're the little woman who wrote the book that made this great war." See Daniel R. Vollaro, "Lincoln, Stowe, and the 'Little Woman/Great War' Story: The Making, and Breaking, of a Great American Anecdote," *Journal of the Abraham Lincoln Association* 30:1 (Winter 2009), 18–34.

[27] Critics have often used this concept to establish Hawthorne's ethical stance. For the definition so often cited, see *The American Notebooks in the Centenary Edition of the Works of Nathaniel Hawthorne*, Vol. 8, ed. Claude M. Simpson (Ohio University Press, 1972), 251.

[28] See, for example, Eric Cheyfitz, "The Irresistibleness of Great Literature: Reconstructing Hawthorne's Politics," *American Literary History* 6:3 (Autumn 1994), 539–558.

constructed. "Personhood" simply exists. It is made known, not made. Hawthorne's and Stowe's works represent different figures as "persons," but both authors' works operate within the liberal framework because neither author sees literary, legal, or political representations as constructing "personhood." Rather, these authors are liberal because they imagine literary, legal, and political representation as ethical only if these forms of representation accurately reflect this preexisting conceptual category. Former slaves do not write slave narratives or speak powerfully to plead for or to earn "personhood."[29] They know themselves already to be "persons," a conviction that makes them liberal. Stowe does not imagine herself producing more and more "persons" – to her, slaves were always already "persons" whose "personhood" slavery unjustly denied; nor does Hawthorne formulate his project as an effort to restrict "personhood" (since to him, the "Negro slave" always already was not a "person"). Both are liberal to the extent that they claim to be representing an identity that exists beyond and before literary, legal, or political interpretation. They are liberal precisely because they engage the relentless subject of antebellum political debate (the question of who is a "person") and simultaneously assert that the question possesses an objective answer, one beyond politics that can thus serve to orient social justice. Antebellum society may look to modern readers as if it is socially constructing – restricting or expanding – who is a "person," but antebellum liberalism understands itself as simply representing the "person" properly.

Because both pro- and antislavery thinkers each claim simply to be representing the unmediated, self-evident Truth about who is a "person," the antebellum argument over slavery may seem to us fundamentally intractable: The category of the "person" is summoned to resolve the argument over slavery but it ultimately only reproduces it. Each side cites the identity under debate as if it were the definitive means to end all debate. The argument thus exposes the fulcrum of liberal thought as embedded in contingency and politics, revealing that liberalism's central concept, the identity appealed to as the unequivocal arbiter of social justice, is not the firm and permanent foundation that the structure of liberal

---

[29] Frederick Douglass in "What to the Slave Is the Fourth of July?" thus refuses to argue the question:

> Must I undertake to prove that the slave is a man? That point is conceded already. Nobody doubts it. . . . When the dogs in your streets, when the fowls of the air, when the cattle on your hills, when the fish of the sea, and the reptiles that crawl, shall be unable to distinguish the slave from a brute, then will I argue with you that the slave is a man!

In *The Frederick Douglass Papers, Series 1: Speeches, Debates, and Interviews, Vol. 2: 1847–1854*, ed. John W. Blassingame, Richard G. Carlson, and Clarence L. Mohr (Yale University Press, 1982), 508.

thought demands. Those who opposed slavery always already assumed that the slave was a "person" from whom freedom was unjustly withheld, while those who thought slavery was, at worst, legal, or, at best, a positive good, assumed that the slave was patently not a "person."

The argument over slavery became irresolvable, in short, precisely to the degree that the argument remained essentially liberal. Thus, Frederick Douglass declares, the "whole defence [sic] of the slave system" depends upon the "*denial* of the negro's manhood," while, in contrast, any encroachment on an enslaver's property is called, as Albert T. Bledsoe asserts, an obvious "*denial* of the constitutional right of the master."[30] The conclusion to be drawn is not that the "person" is an ambiguous or vague identity. Rather, the problem is that liberal thought permits competing, historically specific definitions without offering any way to adjudicate among competing accounts. Axiomatically opposed to slavery, liberalism claims simply to remain subordinate to the irreducibly prior "person" at the same time as it establishes this identity as the primary object of political and social dispute. The "person" remains both the fundamental interpretative problem incited by liberalism and the unexamined foundation of any liberal understanding of freedom and slavery.[31]

Seeing how clearly antebellum arguments over slavery are arguments over "personhood," one might think scholars would approach the conceptual category of the "person" as historically contingent knowledge and that we could finally move beyond "the central paradox of American history," no longer trying to resolve the contradiction between slavery and liberalism, a contradiction that only emerges if we presume that the slave (or anyone) intrinsically possesses a fixed, transhistorical identity as a "person." If we truly did begin from the premise that the "person" is a historically contestable identity, we would no longer lament how slaves were dehumanized, wonder why enslavers denied the "personhood" of their slaves, or affirm that nobody could have held slaves without discomfort, denial, and self-delusion.

What is significant, however, is the degree to which we have continued to remove the "person" from history, to immunize the "person" from

---

[30] Frederick Douglass, "The Claims of the Negro Ethnologically Considered: An Address Delivered in Hudson, Ohio, on 12 July 1854," in *The Frederick Douglass Papers*, 508. Albert T. Bledsoe, *Liberty and Slavery* (J. B. Lippincott & Co., 1856), 368. Bledsoe's tract was reprinted in E. N. Elliott's influential collection of proslavery arguments *Cotton Is King* (1860). (Emphasis added to both quotations.)

[31] In this sense, the crucial innovation of liberal thought is for the "person" to lose its traditional relationship to a dramatic mask (persona). See, for example, Hannah Arendt, *On Revolution* (Penguin, 1963), especially 106–109.

context. Instead of abandoning the logic of liberalism, we remain unswervingly within its thrall. As clearly as we may see the "personhood" of the slave being debated, we more relentlessly disavow such debate. Modern scholars continue to approach slavery as a violation of the slave's "personhood," to discuss slavery as evidence of how "persons" can be "commodified," be incorrectly treated as things or property. Thus, slavery is regularly discussed as a form of "obscene blindness," a deliberate refusal to see the incontestable "personhood" of those enslaved.[32] Indeed, so powerful is the presumption that it is fundamentally unethical ever to see slaves as anything but "persons" that Edward Baptist and Nikole Hannah-Jones, far from idiosyncratically, substitute the phrase "enslaved people" for the word *slave*. Seeking to distinguish an essential identity from a circumstance, scholars transform the political problem intrinsic to liberal thought (how anyone becomes a "person") into an inescapable, self-evident truth (slaves always already *are* "persons").[33] To discuss the slave as anything but a "person" has become so outrageous that it has been enthusiastically preempted.

To the extent that we continue to emphasize the denial of "personhood" as the inaugural and defining act of slavery, we proceed as if slaves simply and absolutely are not commodities, not chattel personal, not animated things. The stability and solidity of such knowledge, however, are precisely what the antebellum debates over who is a "person" should compel us to question. When we imagine such knowledge as something that could never really be in doubt, we both perpetuate and mark ourselves as fully embedded in the logic of liberal thought. In other words, even though antebellum debates over slavery reveal the degree to which the "person" does not

---

[32] Hortense J. Spillers has indicted the "inveterate obscene blindness" of slavery, a practice of such monumental inhumanity that it "might be denied, point blank, as a possibility for *anyone*, except that we know it happened"; Hortense J. Spillers, "Mama's Baby, Papa's Maybe: An American Grammar Book," in *Black, White, and in Color* (University of Chicago Press, 2003), 210.

[33] See Edward Baptist, *The Half Has Never Been Told: Slavery and the Making of American Capitalism* (Basic Books, 2014) and Nikole Hannah-Jones's opening essay in the *New York Times*'s "The 1619 Project," "Our Democracy's Founding Ideals Were False When They Were Written. Black Americans Have Fought to Make Them True" (August 14, 2019), www.nytimes.com/interactive/2019/08/14/magazine/black-history-american-democracy.html. The historian Joseph Yannielli has neatly summarized the argument: "the term 'slave' is reductive and static and does not accurately reflect reality. Enslaved individuals are dynamic and complex human beings – they are more than mere slaves." See "Re: use of 'enslaved'," on the H-Net Discussion Networks, https://lists.h-net.org/cgi-bin/logbrowse.pl?trx=vx&list=H-Slavery&month=1002&msg=ipxCJim5wkqJnnd2syl8%2BQ. See also Nicholas T. Rinehart, "The Man That Was a Thing: Reconsidering Human Commodification in Slavery," *The Journal of Social History* 50:1 (2016), 28–50; and Gregory O'Malley, *Final Passages: The Intercolonial Slave Trade of British America, 1619–1807* (University of North Carolina Press, 2014).

accomplish what liberal thought asks of it – that is, stand beyond debate and thus serve as the universal guarantor of social justice, the absolute means to prevent brutality – we, nonetheless, treat the historical debate over "personhood" as if it were always already an inauthentic debate – one rooted in either a shameful ignorance of the truth or a willful, self-interested disregard for it.

Perhaps the clearest example of how deeply we continue to operate within a liberal framework is that it has become completely unremarkable for scholars to cite racism to explain how slavery was justified. The notion of inherent racial difference is imagined as the ideological construct that allowed "large classes of human beings" to be "denied recognition as equal legal and moral persons – treated as property or objects or as otherwise less-than-persons."[34] Such a line of argument understands race as brought into existence to "systematically explain" an "anomaly apparent to even the least observant and reflective members" of liberal society: why "some people [i.e. slaves] could rightly be denied what others took for granted."[35]

To explain slavery with or through racism, however, is to make at least two assumptions. First, the linking of slavery and racism too quickly suggests that we already know the institution of slavery to be a fundamentally unethical and unjust violation of "persons." Racism, after all, remains a rhetorically incendiary and notoriously shapeless term precisely because it simply names a practice that we want to classify as an indisputably invidious account of the "person." It is an evaluative term masquerading as a constative one. Our certainty that slaves are "persons," in other words, has allowed us to redescribe the historical difference between antebellum and modern interpretations of slavery as an unconditional difference between antebellum mystification and modern demystification, inflating our present knowledge into an incontestable universal. We announce ourselves as liberal to the extent that we see "personhood" as prior to its distortion by racism.

Secondly, if we try to be a bit more precise and specify that racism is wrong because it attributes essential, biological differences to "persons" – rather than seeing such differences as contingent, politically charged attributions – then we again transform a particular, historical argument about the "person" into something that is beyond argument and history. We assume that fixed, innate racial essences always already violate "personhood" and treat our knowledge of "personhood" as if it has escaped being

---

[34] Cristin Ellis, *Antebellum Posthuman* (Fordham University Press, 2018), 4.
[35] Karen E. Fields and Barbara J. Fields, *Racecraft* (Verso, 2014), 141.

distorted by prejudice, misled by ignorance, or swayed by irrationality. We, in short, presume an abstract model of personhood – a disembodied, formal equality – and then conflate all accounts of racial difference as inevitably and equally destructive of "personhood." The problem created by treating "personhood" as an identity untouched by race or racism becomes particularly apparent when we try to understand how some of the most powerful antebellum arguments against the institution of slavery were in fact inseparable from arguments for innate racial differences. Abraham Lincoln, Harriet Beecher Stowe, and Martin Delany, for example, have all been attacked for being "ensnared by the fallacy of race even as they sought to refute racism's insult against ... humanity [i.e. they oppose slavery]."[36] Scholars, thus, have consistently been troubled by the fact that Stowe's argument against slavery depended on giving the "Negro" an essentially Christian disposition, claiming that Stowe's dependence on racial essentialism automatically undermines her unequivocal antislavery message. Similar claims have been made about Lincoln's effort to attack slavery but maintain racial difference and Delany's efforts to enforce racial nationalism.[37] Scholars have expected any repudiation of the slave system to be accompanied by a correspondingly powerful repudiation of racial essentialism precisely because they assume that both deny what a "person" *truly* is.

The possibility that, at least during the antebellum period, essentialist ideas constituted rather than blocked or distorted "personhood" is rarely explored. Only if "personhood" is no longer decontextualized, no longer assumed to be an abstract transhistorical given, will we ever study the historical possibility that the "personhood" of slaves (or anybody) was formulated in terms of, rather than in opposition to, racial essences. If we did not presume that "personhood" must be formulated in antagonism to material or physical difference (i.e. that some are excluded from "personhood" because they are the ultimate "bearers of the bodily"), we would no longer conflate racism and racial essentialism and, most crucially, we would no longer be confused by the fact that notions of racial difference could both underwrite and oppose the institution of slavery. We would no

---

[36] Mia Bay, *The White Image in the Black Mind* (Oxford University Press, 2000), 224.
[37] See, for example, Tunde Adeleke, *Without Regard to Race* (University Press of Mississippi, 2003), a text committed to denying the conventional charge that Delany is a racial nationalist. A cottage industry has sprung up around the question of Lincoln's racism; see, for example, George Fredrickson, *Big Enough to Be Inconsistent: Abraham Lincoln Confronts Slavery and Race* (Harvard University Press, 2008).

longer dismiss any conjunction of racial essentialism and freedom as "contradictory," as an example of an "inchoate politics."[38] That we continue to condemn, be embarrassed by, or feel the need to excuse Lincoln's, Stowe's, or Delany's investment in racial difference suggests how vigorously we keep the "person" – the center of liberal theory – outside examination at the very moment when this identity most clearly is being historically contested.

Modern interpretations of the antebellum argument over slavery, in short, reveal how liberal we remain: The "person" continues to function as the unexamined center of our readings of debates over slavery. Thus, one might say that the central problem for US political history ought to be how the conjunction of slavery and freedom ever became paradoxical. And although it would be impossible, as Derrida argues, to imagine any structure without a conceptual center, perhaps we need to think about what it would mean to imagine a politics of freedom that is no longer a liberal one. What kind of monstrous birth, we might ask, would be required for something other than the "person" to be the center of emancipatory thought?

Further Reading

Arendt, Hannah. *The Origins of Totalitarianism.* Houghton Mifflin, 1973.
Armstrong, Tim. *The Logic of Slavery: Debt, Technology, and Pain in American Literature.* Cambridge University Press, 2012.
Berlin, Isaiah. *Four Essays on Liberty.* Oxford University Press, 1969.
Caney, Simon. "Egalitarian Liberalism and Universalism." In Anthony Simon Laden and David Owen, eds., *Multiculturalism and Political Theory.* Cambridge University Press, 2007, 151–172.
Chambers, Simone and Will Kymlicka, eds. *Alternative Conceptions of Civil Society.* Princeton University Press, 2002.
Dillon, Elizabeth Maddock. *The Gender of Freedom: Fictions of Liberalism and the Literary Public Sphere.* Stanford University Press, 2004.
Feidelson, Charles. *Symbolism and American Literature.* University of Chicago Press, 1953.
Hartz, Louis. *The Liberal Tradition in America.* Harcourt Brace, 1955.
Henry, Katherine. *Liberalism and the Culture of Security: The Nineteenth-Century Rhetoric of Reform.* University of Alabama Press, 2012.

---

[38] Robert S. Levine, *Martin Delany, Frederick Douglass, and the Politics of Representative Identity*, University of North Carolina Press, 1997, 146; Joan Hedrick, *Harriet Beecher Stowe*, Oxford University Press, 1994, 216.

Losurdo, Domenico. *Liberalism: A Counter History*. Verso, 2014.
Morgan, Edmund S. *American Slavery, American Freedom*. W. W. Norton, 1975.
Myrdal, Gunnar. *An American Dilemma*. Harper, 1944.
Rawls, John. *Political Liberalism*. Expanded edition. Columbia University Press, 2005.
Sandel, Michael J. *Liberalism and the Limits of Justice*. Second edition. Cambridge University Press, 1998.

CHAPTER 2

Conservatism: Tradition, Hierarchy, and Fictions of Social Change

Edward Whitley

William F. Buckley, Jr., is responsible for one of the most memorable definitions of modern conservatism. In his 1955 mission statement for the then new political magazine *National Review*, Buckley writes that the goal of the conservative intellectual is to stand "athwart history, yelling Stop, at a time when no one is inclined to do so, or to have much patience with those who so urge it."[1] A similar opposition to the rapid pace of social change could have been expressed a century earlier by Nathaniel Hawthorne, whose fiction also includes cautionary tales about the excesses of social progress. One of these tales, "Earth's Holocaust" (1844), is as perfect an allegory of American conservatism as any middle-aged, white, male Protestant could ever hope to write.[2] "Earth's Holocaust" satirizes the radical reformers whose method of ushering in a new era of human history is to pitch the emblems and artifacts of the past into a giant bonfire. Bibles, crowns, and constitutions are all burned to a crisp in pursuit of a utopian future unburdened by the relics of outdated tradition. While Hawthorne's narrator never explicitly yells "Stop!" as he stands athwart the blaze, he does note that all of the problems that the reformers seek to solve have their origins not in the Bibles, crowns, and constitutions of human society but in the frailty of the human heart. The moral of the story is clear: The traditions of the past, however imperfect they may be, are a defense against deeper ills plaguing the soul. We dismiss these traditions at our peril.

The conservatism of both Buckley and Hawthorne emerged from a set of interrelated assumptions about human nature, civil society, and historical progress that have their origins in Anglo-American opposition to the French Revolution and its radical theories of social change. The starting

---

[1] William F. Buckley Jr., "Our Mission Statement," *National Review* (November 19, 1955), www.nationalreview.com/1955/11/our-mission-statement-william-f-buckley-jr/.
[2] Nathaniel Hawthorne, *Nathaniel Hawthorne's Tales*, 2nd ed., ed. James McIntosh (Norton, 2013), 181–197.

assumption of conservatism is that human beings are inherently flawed, either as a result of original sin or from a moral insufficiency born of our imperfect biological origins. Following closely from this assumption is the notion that the best way to govern flawed beings is through adherence to precisely what the French Revolution overthrew: time-tested traditions rooted in the culture and heritage of communities where social hierarchies preside over both public institutions and the private domain of the home. Finally, conservatives acknowledge that when social change *is* necessary – when traditions must be modified or discarded for one reason or another – such changes should be gradual and incremental, not radical or revolutionary, and should be grounded in the lived experience of generations rather than the theoretical speculation of ambitious reformers.[3] Original sin (or, for the secular conservative, a profoundly imperfect human nature) persists in and pervades the world to such an extent that constraints and restrictions of an institutional, hierarchical sort have been established and ought to be maintained if we are to survive, let alone flourish, as a species.

These conservative assumptions were everywhere in the nineteenth-century United States, even, and perhaps especially, when they were poorly defined and unsystematically deployed. In Abraham Lincoln's 1860 speech at the Cooper Union, for example, he notes that claiming to be conservative resides less in one's actual policies than in the rhetorical gesture of connecting those policies to some aspect of cultural tradition. Arguing against advocates for the expansion of slavery in federal territories, Lincoln asks, "you say you are conservative – eminently conservative – while we are revolutionary, destructive, or something of the sort. What is conservatism? Is it not adherence to the old and tried, against the new and untried?"[4] Lincoln made the terms of the debate perfectly clear: Conservatism is "adherence to the old and tried," as opposed to "revolutionary" theories that, by virtue of their being "new and untried," are bound to be "destructive" to the social order. But, according to Lincoln, the proslavery policies that his opponents claimed under the rubric of conservatism – from reviving the foreign slave trade to granting authority over slavery in the territories either to Congress or to the judiciary – lacked any discernible connection to time-tested traditions from "the century within which our Government originated." Lincoln then pointedly asked "whether your

---

[3] Patrick Allitt, *The Conservatives: Ideas and Personalities throughout American History* (Yale University Press, 2010); Roger Scruton, *Conservatism: An Invitation to the Great Tradition* (All Points Books, 2018); Charles W. Dunn and J. David Woodard, *The Conservative Tradition in America* (Rowman and Littlefield, 1996).

[4] Abraham Lincoln, *The Portable Abraham Lincoln*, ed. Andrew Delbanco (Penguin, 2009), 208.

claim of conservatism for yourselves, and your charge of destructiveness against us, are based on the most clear and stable foundations."[5]

Proslavery advocates were not the only ones whose conservatism lacked "clear and stable foundations." Before the 1950s, there was no ideologically coherent conservative movement in the United States to speak of, and no single party up to that point had, according to the historian Patrick Allitt, "monopolized the political expression of conservatism."[6] Conservatism as a movement emerged only when post–World War II writers such as Buckley, Russell Kirk, and Clinton Rossiter pieced together a conservative intellectual heritage out of Edmund Burke's critique of the French Revolution, John Adams's contributions to the Federalist Party, and John C. Calhoun's defense of southern regionalism, among other sources.[7] Even then, writes Allitt, conservatism has functioned less as an *argument* against precipitous social change and more as "an *attitude* to social and political change that looks for support to the ideas, beliefs, and habits of the past and puts more faith in the lessons of history than in the abstractions of political philosophy."[8] Because it privileges those traditional institutions whose leaders have already secured positions of power and authority, conservatism is susceptible to being characterized as what Allitt calls "the defense of privilege by the holders of privilege," rendering its argument against precipitous social change "vulnerable to the accusation that it is really just the self-interested special pleading of men who have a lot to lose."[9]

The tension Allitt notes between conservativism's *attitude* in favor of social and institutional hierarchy and its *argument* against precipitous change animates the three novels that I survey in this chapter. Nathaniel Hawthorne's *The Scarlet Letter* (1850), Harriet Beecher Stowe's *Uncle Tom's Cabin* (1852), and Frank J. Webb's *The Garies and Their Friends* (1857) all test arguments for social change – women's rights, abolition, and interracial marriage, respectively – against attitudes in support of hierarchy. Hawthorne follows what would become the prevailing wisdom of post–World War II conservatism by suggesting that change should happen gradually, rather than precipitously, based on the reasoning that social institutions are gifts bestowed upon the present generation by wise

---

[5] Lincoln, *Portable*, 208.   [6] Allitt, *The Conservatives*, 2.
[7] William F. Buckley, Jr., *God and Man at Yale* (Regnery, 1951); Russell Kirk, *The Conservative Mind from Burke to Santayana* (Regnery, 1953); and Clinton Rossiter, *Conservatism in America* (Knopf, 1955). See also David Brooks, "What Happened to American Conservatism?," *The Atlantic* (December 8, 2021).
[8] Allitt, *The Conservatives*, 2 (emphasis in original).   [9] Allitt, *The Conservatives*, 5.

ancestors. For Stowe, social ills as grievous as slavery demand total and immediate change. But in the world of *Uncle Tom's Cabin* hierarchy is consistently depicted as both valuable and necessary, and as such the novel argues (radically) in favor of immediate abolition of slavery by condemning slavery's affront to attitudes that value (conservatively) existing social hierarchies of gender, class, and race. Finally, Webb brings conservatism into a reckoning with its own fundamental assumptions by taking a successful argument for gradual social change – his novel depicts mixed-race families who move quietly into middle-class life without agitating for radical change – and subjecting it to the hierarchical attitude of white supremacist violence.

***

A little more than halfway through Hawthorne's *The Scarlet Letter*, the novel's protagonist, Hester Prynne, quietly asks herself how women in seventeenth-century Massachusetts could possibly endure life under patriarchy: "Was existence worth accepting, even to the happiest among them? As concerned her own individual existence, she had long ago decided in the negative, and dismissed the point as settled."[10] Hester had famously been ordered to wear a scarlet letter "A" on her breast as a badge of shame for having committed the sin of adultery, and at this point of the novel she begins to attribute her suffering under this punishment to an oppressive hierarchy that affects *all* women, not only those who violate social and religious mores. Upon having this thought, Hester concludes that gradually reforming the world to better the condition of women would be insufficient, and that revolution is the only real alternative: "As a first step, the whole system of society is to be torn down, and built up anew." During this complete overhaul of society, "the very nature of the opposite sex" – including long-held beliefs about gender sustained by "hereditary habit" – would need to be "essentially modified, before woman can be allowed to assume what seems a fair and suitable position."[11]

This is a stirring moment in the novel, one that could have led to a much different conclusion than the one Hawthorne ultimately decided upon. Instead, Hawthorne's narrator steps in to yell some version of Buckley's "Stop!" by explaining that the impulse to revolt against the centuries of tradition that bolster the collective social world had emerged from a speculative "sphere of theory" that had worked its way into "the dark labyrinth of [Hester's] mind" during the days of "Shame, Despair,

---

[10] Nathaniel Hawthorne, *The Scarlet Letter*, ed. Thomas E. Connolly (Penguin, 2003), 144.
[11] Hawthorne, *Scarlet Letter*, 144.

Solitude!" that had "taught her much amiss."[12] Left to this state of theoretical contemplation as an isolated individual, the radical idea to tear down society and build it up anew comes into Hester's troubled mind as she (anachronistically) falls prey to Enlightenment thinking from the still-distant Age of Revolutions: "Men of the sword had overthrown nobles and kings. Men bolder than these had overthrown and rearranged – not actually, but within the sphere of theory, which was their most real abode – the whole system of ancient prejudice, wherewith was linked much of ancient principle. Hester Prynne imbibed this spirit."[13] The men whose spirit Hester imbibed a full century before they had put revolutionary theories ahead of the traditions of the ages are the same men against whom Edmund Burke laid the foundation for Anglo-American conservatism in texts such as *Reflections on the Revolution in France* (1790).

Burke had used similar terms as Hawthorne – rejecting bold "theory" in favor of "ancient principle" and "ancient prejudice" – to oppose projects for radical change, advocating instead for those traditions and hierarchies that had served human society well. These traditions, Burke wrote, emerge from "a deliberate election of ages and of generations ... made by the peculiar circumstances, occasions, tempers, dispositions, and moral, civil, and social habitudes of the people, which disclose themselves only in a long space of time."[14] For Burke and those who followed him, the laws and customs that have been refined and perfected across the generations are preferable to the well-intentioned idealism of individuals whose hubris prevents them – as it prevents Hawthorne's Hester – from acknowledging the collective wisdom of the ages. As Yuval Levin writes, "Burke believes that what we owe the future above all is not freedom but rather the accumulated wisdom and work of the past.... Society exists not to facilitate individual choice but to meet the needs of the people, and to do so it must draw on the wisdom of the past."[15] Burke himself is more succinct: "The individual is foolish," he wrote, "but the species is wise."[16]

Burke would have been pleased with Hawthorne's decision to place a scarlet letter upon the breast of a character in need of her species' wisdom, as he called such generational wisdom "a vestment, which accommodates itself to the body."[17] The architects of twentieth-century US conservatism who followed in Burke's footsteps similarly read *The Scarlet Letter* as an expression of a conservative disposition. Following Henry James, who

[12] Hawthorne, *Scarlet Letter*, 145, 174.   [13] Hawthorne, *Scarlet Letter*, 145.
[14] Edmund Burke, *The Portable Edmund Burke*, ed. Isaac Kramnick (Penguin, 1999), 176–177.
[15] Yuval Levin, *The Great Debate* (Basic Books, 2014), 214–215.   [16] Burke, *Portable*, 177.
[17] Burke, *Portable*, 177.

wrote in 1879 that "Hawthorne cast his lot with the party of conservatism, the party opposed to change and freshness," Russell Kirk argued in the 1950s that "very few other Americans have been so congenitally conservative as Hawthorne, so steeped in tradition and suspicious of alteration."[18] It was "Hawthorne's resolute conviction," Kirk wrote, "that progress is a delusion, except for the infinitely slow progress of conscience."[19] Unsurprisingly, Kirk and other conservative thinkers prefer Hester Prynne's advocacy for slow and gradual change at the conclusion of *The Scarlet Letter* – along with the implication that change of *any* kind emerges from the moral guidelines of the community – over her proposal at the novel's midpoint to tear down "the whole system of society" and build it up anew. In the final pages of the novel, Hester is seen offering advice to women who ask for "the remedy" to the challenges of life under patriarchy, and the narrator assures us that Hester has come to the "firm belief, that, at some brighter period, when the world should have grown ripe for it, in Heaven's own time, a new truth would be revealed, in order to establish the whole relation between man and woman on a surer ground of mutual happiness."[20]

The gradual approach to reform at the conclusion of *The Scarlet Letter* appears in Hawthorne's political writing on slavery as well. In his 1852 campaign biography for Franklin Pierce, Hawthorne claimed that calls for abolition and emancipation were unnecessary because slavery is "one of those evils ... which, in its own good time, by some means impossible to be anticipated, but of the simplest and easiest operation, when all its uses shall have been fulfilled, [Providence] causes to vanish like a dream."[21] Not only did Hawthorne say that slavery would eventually disappear without the need of intervention from government or agitation from abolitionists but he also said that *all* attempts at social engineering ultimately do more harm than good: "No human effort, on a grand scale, has ever yet resulted according to the purpose of its projectors," he wrote in the *Atlantic* in

---

[18] Henry James, *Hawthorne*, ed. Dan E. McCall (Cornell University Press, 1997), 56; Kirk, *Conservative Mind*, 251.

[19] Kirk, *Conservative Mind*, 259.

[20] Hawthorne, *Scarlet Letter*, 227–228. See also Lee Trepanier, "The Need for Renewal: Nathaniel Hawthorne's Conservatism," *Modern Age* 45:4 (2003), 315–323, and Kathleen Colgan, *The Influence of Political Events and Ideologies on Nathaniel Hawthorne's Political Vision and Writings* (Edwin Mellen, 2001).

[21] Nathaniel Hawthorne, *The Life of Franklin Pierce* (Ticknor, Reed, and Fields, 1853), 113. See Jonathan Arac, "The Politics of *The Scarlet Letter*," in Sacvan Bercovitch and Myra Jehlen, eds., *Ideology and Classic American Literature* (Cambridge University Press, 1986), 247–266.

1862. "We miss the good we sought and do the good we little cared for."[22] Twentieth- and twenty-first-century conservatives have given this phenomenon names like "the law of unintended consequences," "the jeopardy thesis," or "the change principle," arguing that because the complex and interlocking pieces that make up a society have gradually settled into place over the course of many generations, removing one offensive element (even something as "vile, unjust or violent" as chattel slavery) could trigger a chain reaction causing unforeseen damage to blameless people and institutions.[23] As such, Kieron O'Hara writes that the duty of the conservative is "to distinguish between beneficial and costly changes, and then to allow the former to happen while preventing too much damage being done to existing institutions and wider society by the latter."[24]

This willingness "to allow" for "beneficial changes" sounds very much like the mission statement for *Uncle Tom's Cabin*, which argues for radically changing society through the immediate emancipation of millions of enslaved human beings while also remaining deeply committed to endorsing attitudes in favor of preserving traditional social hierarchies. Specifically, Stowe's novel fully embraces the conservative notion of "right relations" for gender (men preside while women nurture) and social status (the elite provide leadership and administer resources for those of lower status), arguing that the dominion of men over women and the elite over the masses is as beneficial to society as would be the abolition of slavery. Angela D. Dillard explains this conservative attitude as follows: "These 'right relations' are, more often than not, unequal and hierarchical. But this is acceptable precisely because inequality is, in this understanding of conservatism, a positive good."[25] *Uncle Tom's Cabin* is sincere in its desire for the abolition of slavery, but this desire does not extend to the abolition of established hierarchies. *Uncle Tom's Cabin* laments that the system of slavery has not only devastated the lives of Africans and African Americans but also weakened the traditional hierarchies of gender and status among

---

[22] Nathaniel Hawthorne, "Chiefly about War Matters," *Atlantic* (July 1862), www.theatlantic.com/magazine/archive/1862/07/chiefly-about-war-matters/306159/.
[23] Kieron O' Hara writes, "Even when a society is clearly vile, unjust or violent, one should be cautious about wishing it away." Kieron O'Hara, *Conservatism* (Reaktion Books, 2011), 70–71. On the law of unintended consequences, the jeopardy thesis, and the change principle, see O'Hara, *Conservatism*, 55, 88, and Albert O. Hirschman, *The Rhetoric of Reaction: Perversity, Futility, Jeopardy* (Harvard University Press, 1991).
[24] O'Hara, *Conservatism*, 17.
[25] Angela D. Dillard, "Conservatism," in Glen Hendler and Bruce Burgett, eds., *Keywords for American Cultural Studies*, 3rd ed. (New York University Press, 2020), 61–65, 62.

white Americans that conservatives would count as a "positive good" necessary for the existence of a harmonious society.[26]

The opening pages of *Uncle Tom's Cabin* depict a challenge to the "right relations" of social status when a lower-class white southerner who has been successful in the slave trade rises above his station to gain a financial upper hand over the plantation gentry. The novel's first image is of "two gentlemen" sitting together "in a well-furnished dining parlor ... discussing some subject with great earnestness."[27] Immediately upon presenting readers with this scene (we are all of fifty words into the narrative proper), Stowe qualifies that the word "gentleman" carries specific meanings regarding social hierarchies that readers should not overlook: "For convenience sake, we have said, hitherto, two *gentlemen*. One of the parties, however, when critically examined, did not seem, strictly speaking, to come under the species."[28] Italicizing the word "*gentlemen*" is Stowe's way of raising her eyebrows and tilting her head disapprovingly toward Mr. Haley, a man who has weaseled his way into the ranks of the aristocracy through a tear in the social fabric – a tear, we later learn, opened by the easy profit to be made from the traffic in human bodies: "If any of our refined and Christian readers object to the society into which this scene introduces them," Stowe writes, they should brace themselves for when "the trader and catcher may yet be among our aristocracy."[29] We know that this faux gentleman does not belong here because the "swaggering air of pretension" he has acquired from his wealth and success cannot compensate for the unrefined sense of fashion that betrays his lower-class origins: "He was much over-dressed, in a gaudy vest of many colors, a blue neckerchief, bedropped gayly with yellow spots, and arranged with a flaunting tie." The narrator's gaze fixates on this ostentatious display of new money as a sign of "a low man who is trying to elbow his way upward in the world." Stowe writes, "His hands, large and coarse, were plentifully bedecked with rings; and he wore a heavy gold watch-chain, with a bundle of seals of portentous size, and a great variety of colors, attached to it – which, in the ardor of conversation, he was in the habit of flourishing and jingling with evident satisfaction."[30] All of this contrasts with the very brief description the narrator provides of an *actual* gentleman, the plantation-owning Mr. Shelby, who "had the appearance of a gentleman; and the

---

[26] See Jane Tompkins, *Sensational Designs: The Cultural Work of American Fiction, 1790–1850* (Oxford University Press, 1985), 145.
[27] Harriet Beecher Stowe, *Uncle Tom's Cabin*, ed. Elizabeth Ammons (Norton, 1994), 1.
[28] Stowe, *Uncle Tom's Cabin*, 1. [29] Stowe, *Uncle Tom's Cabin*, 62.
[30] Stowe, *Uncle Tom's Cabin*, 1.

arrangements of the house, and the general air of the housekeeping, indicated easy, and even opulent circumstances."[31] Mr. Shelby exhibits neither affectation nor a conspicuous display of wealth; he clearly belongs to the "species" of gentleman.

It is important to Stowe that her readers understand how the status distinction between these two white men is significant enough to categorize them as different species of humans, but it is also ironic. Only a few paragraphs later, Stowe expects her readers to gasp when the slave-trading Mr. Haley insinuates that African American mothers are of a different species than their white counterparts, saying that they are incapable of the kind of grief that a white mother would experience upon being separated from her children: "These critters ain't like white folks, you know; they gets over things."[32] Stowe wants readers to reject the idea that African Americans are subhuman "critters," but she also wants readers to accept that there are different "species" of white gentlemen. This is part of her larger strategy to use accepted social hierarchies as a position from which to advocate for the abolition of slavery. By putting the severe racism of calling African American women "critters" in the mouth of someone whom readers should reject as a false gentleman, Stowe presents a choice over which white gentleman they should endorse, hoping that they will choose Shelby's less virulent racism (he is still, after all, a slaveholder) because it is more benevolently patriarchal. Stowe's primary concern in this first chapter is to present status hierarchies as vulnerable to, and in need of protection against, the economic and market volatility that enables speculators in slaves to force the hands of their betters. Indeed, one of the arguments *against* the slave system in these first paragraphs of the novel is that the market for slaves has made it possible for a lower-class man like Haley "to elbow his way upward in the world." According to the internal logic of *Uncle Tom's Cabin*, one of the evils of slavery has been the overturning of "right relations" in the social hierarchy. It is here that Stowe takes her turn to yell Buckley's "Stop!"

Stowe's attitude in favor of gender hierarchy follows her attitude in favor of social hierarchy, in that slavery interferes with the beneficial hierarchy of traditional gender roles where men preside over women in patriarchal homes. The early chapters of the novel feature men and women from different backgrounds who all fulfill the expected duties of their gender.[33]

---

[31] Stowe, *Uncle Tom's Cabin*, 1. [32] Stowe, *Uncle Tom's Cabin*, 5.
[33] Arthur and Emily Shelby (white slaveholders from Kentucky), Uncle Tom and Aunt Chloe (enslaved African Americans on the Shelby plantation), George and Eliza Harris (enslaved African

In every instance, the husbands in these heterosexual relationships are strong, presiding figures whose authority, while unquestioned, is nevertheless responsive to the entreaties of compassionate wives who provide a spiritually nurturing influence. (One example of this pattern takes place in chapter nine, where an Ohio senator's insistence on obeying the Fugitive Slave Law is tempered by his wife's compassion toward a runaway who shows up at their door.)[34] After introducing these traditional families as successes, the novel presents readers with two Louisiana plantations where slave labor has interfered with the expectation for women to nurture their own families and tend to their own households. On the plantation of Augustine and Marie St. Clare, enslaved African Americans run all of the affairs of the household, effectively removing Marie from the sphere of influence that would allow her to nurture her family. Because of this, Marie is an ineffectual matriarch, and Augustine, left without her nurturing presence, becomes a feckless leader who is undermined by an enslaved man who takes his clothing and parades throughout the house playacting as the patriarch.[35] Similar to the breakdown in the hierarchy of gender roles at the St. Clare home is the plantation of Simon Legree, where there is no matriarchal authority whatsoever as the unmarried Legree forces a series of enslaved women to be his sexual partners and the managers of his household. Without the compassionate nurturing of a lawfully married wife, Legree's masculinity has created a toxic environment of both sexual and physical abuse.[36] According to the conservative logic of the novel, Legree's excesses demonstrate why the structured hierarchies of heterosexual marriage are necessary checks against corrupt human nature.

In preserving these hierarchies of gender and status, *Uncle Tom's Cabin* ends up making the case for the tradition of southern conservatism that would outlive both the abolition of slavery and the Reconstruction of the Union, enduring into the late twentieth century as what Eugene Genovese called a society that "accepts hierarchy and stratification as natural,

---

Americans escaping to the North), Senator and Mrs. Bird (white Ohioans), and Simeon and Rachel Halliday (white Quaker abolitionists).

[34] Stowe, *Uncle Tom's Cabin*, 67–80.

[35] See chapter 16 of Stowe, *Uncle Tom's Cabin*, especially 152–153. See also Gillian Brown, "Getting in the Kitchen with Dinah: Domestic Politics in *Uncle Tom's Cabin*," *American Quarterly* 36:4 (1984), 503–523; and Michael Borgstrom, "Passing Over: Setting the Record Straight in *Uncle Tom's Cabin*," *PMLA* 118:5 (2003), 1290–1304.

[36] See chapter 35 of Stowe, *Uncle Tom's Cabin*, especially 321. See also Carolyn Vellenga Berman, "Creole Family Politics in *Uncle Tom's Cabin* and *Incidents in the Life of a Slave Girl*," *NOVEL: A Forum on Fiction* 33:3 (2000), 328–352.

necessary, and proper."[37] Such a society is not merely southern, however, since it is consistent with Edmund Burke's attitude that hierarchical relationships are necessary to "regulate and hold together the community by a chain of subordination."[38] No one advocated for a hierarchical society built on subordination more emphatically than Stowe's sister, Catharine Beecher, who wrote in *A Treatise on Domestic Economy for the Use of Young Ladies at Home and at School* (1842) about "the duties of subordination." Subordination, for Beecher, is not an injustice to be remedied (in the gradual manner that Hawthorne used Hester to endorse) but a necessary condition of human existence to be embraced:

> There must be the magistrate and the subject, one of whom is the superior, and the other the inferior. There must be the relations of husband and wife, parent and child, teacher and pupil, employer and employed, each involving the relative duties of subordination. The superior, in certain particulars, is to direct, and the inferior is to yield obedience. Society could never go forward, harmoniously, nor could any craft or profession be successfully pursued, unless these superior and subordinate relations be instituted and sustained.[39]

It is this exercise of regulatory power – this insistence that "subordination" is both a social and a moral good – that fuels many critiques of conservatism. Corey Robin, for one, has claimed that conservatism is fundamentally a practice of social control, writing that "a wariness of change, a belief in evolutionary reform, or a politics of virtue ... may be the byproducts of conservatism," but the "animating purpose" of the conservative movement is "the opposition to the liberation of men and women from the fetters of their superiors."[40] The regulatory aspect of conservatism – understood not as an argument against precipitous change but as an attitude in favor of hierarchy – is on full display in Frank J. Webb's *The Garies and Their Friends*, a novel that pits (racial) hierarchy against (national) tradition as the defining attitude of American conservatism before ultimately agreeing with Robin that Burke's "chain of subordination" animates conservatives more than an argument for gradual change ever could.

The Garies and Their Friends centers on two families who want nothing more than to live lives of middle-class respectability in comfortable homes

---

[37] Eugene Genovese, *The Southern Tradition: The Achievement and Limitations of an American Conservatism* (Harvard University Press, 1994), 29.
[38] Burke, *Portable*, 414.
[39] Catharine E. Beecher, *A Treatise on Domestic Economy, for the Use of Young Ladies at Home, and at School* (T. H. Webb, 1842), 26.
[40] Corey Robin, *The Reactionary Mind: Conservatism from Edmund Burke to Sarah Palin* (Oxford University Press, 2013), 16.

surrounded by the people they love – fully embodying the "politics of virtue" that Robin associates with at least a surface-level display of conservatism. The Garies are a mixed-race family (Clarence is white and Emily is African American) who move from Georgia to Philadelphia hoping that their interracial marriage will be better received in the thriving African American community that is home to Charles and Ellen Ellis, both of whom are black. This seemingly mundane premise for a novel – along with its detailed descriptions of domestic life – has led scholars to call *The Garies* a "thoroughly bourgeois novel,"[41] "the *Poor Richard's Almanack* of the black middle class,"[42] and a novel whose "blind faith in the American Dream"[43] makes it less compelling than contemporary texts like William Wells Brown's *Clotel* (1851) or Harriet Wilson's *Our Nig* (1859). *The Garies and Their Friends* touches on the same issues of interracial sex and northern racism that appear in both *Clotel* and *Our Nig*, and it even features a horrifying scene of white supremacist violence that not only kills Clarence and Emily but decimates the African American neighborhoods of Philadelphia. Nevertheless, as Gregg Crane notes, Webb's readers have been "troubled or embarrassed by what they see as a distasteful capitulation to the cultural standards of the white middle class," largely because the characters in the novel do not so much want to change the status quo as they simply want to participate in it.[44] But it is this assent to capitalism and patriarchal domesticity that allows *The Garies* to respond to white supremacy from inside the prevailing attitudes of conservatism.

It is precisely the novel's refusal to be revolutionary in its argument that enables its forceful challenge to conservative attitudes. By associating interracial marriage with a general endorsement of other existing institutions (such as the family and capitalist meritocracy), the novel presents a conservative argument for gradual change – that formerly enslaved populations can gradually move into the middle class just as dark-skinned populations can gradually intermarry – as running up against a conservative attitude that values racial hierarchy. In the process, *The Garies and Their Friends* precipitates a conservative reckoning with itself.

---

[41] Werner Sollors, "Introduction," in *Frank J. Webb: Fiction, Essays, and Poetry*, ed. Werner Sollors (Toby, 2004), 4.

[42] Addison Gayle, Jr., *The Way of the New World: The Black Novel in America* (Doubleday, 1975), 13.

[43] Bernard W. Bell, *The Afro-American Novel and Its Tradition* (University of Massachusetts Press, 1987), 43.

[44] Gregg Crane, *The Cambridge Introduction to the Nineteenth-Century American Novel* (Cambridge University Press, 2007), 44. For the history and literature of African American conservatism, see Angela D. Dillard, *Guess Who's Coming to Dinner Now? Multicultural Conservatism in America* (New York University Press, 2001).

As Webb places his African American characters within the hierarchies and traditions of the mid-nineteenth-century United States, he shows that even their good faith efforts to embrace tradition run afoul of the "chain of subordination" that structures white supremacy. The group of white Philadelphians who lead the attack on the city's black neighborhoods do so on the grounds that the Garies' interracial marriage in particular and the prosperity of black Philadelphians in general had disrupted the social order, leading to "the absolute necessity for inflicting some general chastisement, to convince them that they were still negroes, and to teach them to remain in their proper place in the body politic."[45]

While the white mob ends up destroying the homes of any property-owning African American family aspiring to middle-class status, they focus their violence on mixed-race families like the Garies, hoping that the attack will "convince them that they were still negroes." The mob is outraged that a white man married to a light-skinned woman, whose children are light-skinned as well, would want a place for himself and his family in the American middle-class, chanting, "Down with the Abolitionist – down with the Amalgamationist!"[46] But the Garies aren't abolitionists. They don't actively call for the elimination of slavery and thereby pose no threat to the system of wealth generated from a slave economy, either southerners' direct investment in slavery or northerners' indirect benefit from the profits of slave labor. Nevertheless, it is their willingness to marry across racial boundaries as "amalgamationists" that the white mob considers an intolerable affront to the "chain of subordination" undergirding a white supremacist society: "they have n[egro] blood in them," says one white terrorist of Emily and her children, "and they are, therefore, as much n[egroe]s as the blackest."[47] Social hierarchies depend upon rigid boundaries to maintain everyone's "proper place in the body politic," and the hierarchy of white supremacy is no different.

What *is* different, however, is how the novel presents white Philadelphians' moving up the social ladder without arousing the kind of suspicion that Stowe directs toward undeserving white gentlemen in *Uncle Tom's Cabin*. In *The Garies and Their Friends*, we meet a white woman named Mrs. Thomas who hosts "grand dinners and large evening parties" for middle-class white families who, only a few generations earlier, were part of the working class (they are a scant "two or three

---

[45] Frank J. Webb, *The Garies and Their Friends*, ed. Robert Reid-Pharr (Johns Hopkins University Press, 1997), 175–176.
[46] Webb, *Garies*, 221.   [47] Webb, *Garies*, 157.

removes from the class whose members occupy the cobbler's bench or the huckster's stall"). When these families gather, there is an unspoken rule never to mention ancestry or bloodlines: "At these social gatherings the conversation never turned upon pedigree, and if any of the guests chanced by accident to allude to their ancestors, they spoke of them as members of the family, who, at an early period of their lives, were engaged in mercantile pursuits."[48] The members of the white middle class conspire to misrepresent themselves to each other out of a shared allegiance to an American tradition of meritocratic progress, while denying black and mixed-race families like the Garies and the Ellises the same opportunity for social advancement.

Webb's novel underscores the hypocrisy of such attitudes toward upward mobility by inviting us to contrast the social climbing of the white middle-class with Emily Garies's cousin, George Winston, who is light enough to pass for white and is even able to hide his African American heritage from a white man who "prides himself on being able to detect evidences of the least drop of African blood in any one."[49] This white man believes that "the existence of 'a gentleman' with African blood in his veins, is a moral and physical impossibility," even though the narrator has assured us that George is a "fine-looking gentleman" who could hold his own with any member of Georgia's plantation gentility.[50] Despite having been enslaved only fifteen years prior to the events of the novel, George's "polished manners and irreproachable appearance might have led you to suppose him descended from a long line of illustrious ancestors," when the reality is that he is "the offspring of a mulatto field-hand by her master."[51] The contrast between these two scenarios is clear: White Philadelphians have access to an American tradition of meritocratic progress but black and mixed-race Philadelphians do not.

One of the core Burkean principles of conservative thought is the idea that "we owe an implicit reverence to all the institutions of our ancestors."[52] The cruel paradox facing the characters in Webb's novel is that the ancestors who determine their place in society (those who have bestowed upon them "the least drop of African blood") have no relation to the institutions of American culture that they have chosen to adopt. Despite having "African blood," no one in the novel speaks an African language, practices an African religion, eats an African diet, or celebrates African holidays. They have, instead, chosen to embrace American traditions, including those that permit social

[48] Webb, *Garies*, 73. [49] Webb, *Garies*, 4. [50] Webb, *Garies*, 4, 8. [51] Webb, *Garies*, 8.
[52] Burke, *Portable*, 34.

climbing on the basis of individual merit. But the hierarchies of white supremacy take precedence over these traditions, effectively erasing the claims of black and mixed-race Philadelphians to participate in the American meritocracy. This is true both in the novel and in history as actual mobs of white Philadelphians burned black homes to the ground in 1834, 1838, 1842, and 1849.[53]

For colonized and enslaved peoples, everything depends upon where one puts the emphasis in Burke's maxim to "owe an implicit reverence to all the institutions of our ancestors." If the emphasis is on *institutions*, there should be no reason for white Philadelphians to oppose African American and biracial citizens from participating in the traditions established by earlier generations of Americans that lead to commercial prosperity and domestic stability. If the emphasis is on *our ancestors*, however, and if *ancestors* are a family's biological progenitors rather than a nation's historical predecessors, then it is obvious that the blood purity of white supremacy wins the day. The nineteenth-century novel is particularly adept at staging such tensions in the social world, given Dorothy Hale's argument that novels "give form to society" and Elaine Hadley's contention that novels allow us "to imagine inhabiting it."[54] It is here, then, that Webb's novel goes one step further than Hawthorne's and Stowe's in forcing conservatism to reckon with its own fundamental assumptions about social hierarchy and social change. Both *The Scarlet Letter* and *Uncle Tom's Cabin* navigate the space created between a conservative argument that allows for incremental change to the boundaries set by traditional institutions and a conservative attitude committed to preserving the power and authority of those who preside over such institutions. *The Garies and Their Friends* identifies a crisis point between these two conservatisms that is violently resolved in bonfires exponentially more real than those set by the out-of-control revolutionaries Hawthorne can only fantasize about in "Earth's Holocaust" as he watches the tradition and heritage of the Anglo-American past metaphorically burn to the ground. In *The Garies and Their Friends*, those fires are no mere allegory for the death of tradition; they are the force by which hierarchy is strengthened and power retained.

---

[53] Patrick Grubbs, "Riots (1830s and 1840s)," in *The Encyclopedia of Greater Philadelphia* (Rutgers University, 2015), https://philadelphiaencyclopedia.org/archive/riots-1830s-and-1840s/.

[54] See James Vernon's review of Dorothy Hale's *Social Formalism: The Novel in Theory from Henry James to the Present* (Stanford University Press, 1998) and Elaine Hadley's *Living Liberalism: Practical Citizenship in Mid-Victorian Britain* (University of Chicago Press, 2010) in "What Was Liberalism, and Who Was Its Subject? Or, Will the Real Liberal Subject Please Stand Up?" *Victorian Studies* 53:2 (2011), 303–310, 306.

Further Reading

Allen, William B. *Rethinking Uncle Tom: The Political Thought of Harriet Beecher Stowe*. Lexington Books, 2009.

Allitt, Patrick. *The Conservatives: Ideas and Personalities throughout American History*. Yale University Press, 2010.

Alvis, John E. *Nathaniel Hawthorne As Political Philosopher: Revolutionary Principles Domesticated and Personalized*. Transaction Publishers, 2014.

Dillard, Angela D. *Guess Who's Coming to Dinner Now? Multicultural Conservatism in America*. New York University Press, 2001.

Dunn, Charles W. and David J. Woodard, *The Conservative Tradition in America*. Rowman and Littlefield, 1996.

Genovese, Eugene. *The Southern Tradition: The Achievement and Limitations of an American Conservatism*. Harvard University Press, 1994.

Hirschman, Albert O. *The Rhetoric of Reaction: Perversity, Futility, Jeopardy*. Harvard University Press, 1991.

Levin, Yuval. *The Great Debate: Edmund Burke, Thomas Paine, and the Birth of Right and Left*. Basic Books, 2014.

Reynolds, Larry J. *Devils and Rebels: The Making of Hawthorne's Damned Politics*. University of Michigan Press, 2010.

Robin, Corey. *The Reactionary Mind: Conservatism from Edmund Burke to Donald Trump*, 2nd ed. Oxford University Press, 2017.

CHAPTER 3

The Literature of Radicalism

J. Michelle Coghlan

In her 1931 memoir *Living My Life*, the anarchist writer, publisher, and activist Emma Goldman candidly reflects on the difficulty of writing an account of her life – and of the late nineteenth- and early twentieth-century US radical scene of which she was so famously part – without access to her personal archive: "Almost everything in the way of books, correspondence, and similar material that I had accumulated during the thirty-five years of my life in the United States had been confiscated by the Department of Justice raiders and never returned. I lacked even my personal set of the *Mother Earth* magazine, which I had published for twelve years."[1] Yet Goldman's radical paper trail was not the only one to suffer such state-sponsored erasure. The African American anarchist activist, orator, and Haymarket biographer Lucy Parsons, whom Chicago police once described as "more dangerous than a thousand rioters" and whom the historian Robin D. G. Kelley identifies as "the most prominent black woman radical of the nineteenth century,"[2] similarly amassed a personal library of some 3,000 books and newspapers on the topics of "sex, socialism and anarchy" over the course of her long life of activism, in addition to her collection of personal papers – all of which were seized by Chicago police and promptly disappeared by the FBI following her death in a house fire in 1942.[3] And even those communal nineteenth-century radical collections that evaded outright seizure were nevertheless prone to evanescence because, unlike traditional membership libraries or Carnegie-sponsored free public libraries, they operated under police repression, without philanthropic funding, and

---

[1] Emma Goldman, "In Appreciation," in *Living My Life*, Vol. 1 (Alfred A. Knopf, 1931), 3. Goldman tells readers she pieces together the story of her life through the letters she exchanged with friends and fellow activists that were returned to her as she began writing the memoir – thus crucially marking it as, at least in part, a communal archival project.
[2] Robin D. G. Kelley, *Freedom Dreams: The Black Radical Tradition* (Beacon Press, 2002), 41.
[3] Carolyn Ashbaugh, *Lucy Parsons: American Revolutionary* (Charles H. Kerr, 1976), 266; and Jacqueline Jones, *Goddess of Anarchy: The Life and Times of Lucy Parsons, American Radical* (Basic Books, 2017), 343.

out of subversive reading spaces. Take, for example, Justus Schwab's radical basement saloon, which opened in the Lower East Side of New York City in the late 1870s and served as a second home to political refugees from across Europe as well as a vital meeting space for radical New Yorkers. The saloon offered its patrons a convivial space for political discussions and equally importantly a radical lending library of "no less than 600 volumes" – a bar reading room that weathered near-constant police raids for nearly three decades and a vital community resource that was lost when the pub foundered following Schwab's death.[4]

In light of such police raids, forced disappearances, and de facto forms of censorship, Shelley Streeby has powerfully pointed to what she aptly terms "the *limits* of print as an archive of radical memory," and, so too, the limits within American literary studies in so far recognizing the various and voluminous genres of nineteenth-century radical print culture – from fiery speeches and satirical strike songs to political pamphlets, worker song-poems, insurgent novels, and experimental biography – as literature.[5] As she observes, much of what nineteenth-century radicals wrote and read would be unlikely to turn up on a syllabus of nineteenth-century American literature.[6] To consider the questions of how US literature engaged with nineteenth-century American radical politics and in what ways nineteenth-century American radicals themselves drew on literature to sustain their activism and mobilize support for their movements, then, is always to wrestle first with how much has been lost and how much remains to be recovered. But it is also to begin to recognize the nineteenth century as far more radical than we might otherwise recall and American radicalism as far less marginal to the fabric of everyday nineteenth-century life than it so far has been to the study of nineteenth-century American literature.

Given the gaps in the nineteenth-century US radical archive and the fact that few of the hundreds of radical periodicals that emerged in the nineteenth-century United States have so far been digitized, an unexpectedly rich alternate vehicle for indexing the reach of nineteenth-century American radicalism and the footprint American radicals occupied in the nineteenth-century US

---

[4] Tom Goyens, *Beer and Revolution: The German Anarchist Movement in New York City, 1880–1914* (University of Illinois Press, 2007), 44.
[5] Shelley Streeby, "Labor, Memory, and the Boundaries of Print Culture: From Haymarket to the Mexican Revolution," *American Literary History* 19:2 (2007), 406–433, 414 (emphasis mine); and Streeby, "Doing Justice to the Archive: Beyond Literature," in Dana Luciano and Ivy G. Wilson, eds., *Unsettled States: Nineteenth-Century American Literary Studies* (New York University Press, 2014), 103–118, 104.
[6] Streeby, "Doing Justice to the Archive," 104.

The Literature of Radicalism 53

cultural imaginary is to track how often their words and accounts of the meetings they spoke at appeared in print cultural venues altogether antithetical to their political projects: namely, mainstream US newspapers that otherwise decried their politics and altogether vilified their movements.[7] Take, for example, the simultaneous alarm and widespread coverage provoked by Lucy Parsons's 1886 lecture tour on behalf of her Haymarket-martyr husband. As Parsons crisscrossed the country, speaking to crowds ranging from several hundred to several thousand people in cities across Ohio, Kentucky, New York, New Jersey, Pennsylvania, Connecticut, Maryland, Missouri, Nebraska, and Kansas, reporters for major metropolitan US newspapers were everywhere in attendance, telegraphing back at times lengthy transcripts of her speeches and equally detailed accounts of her performance, her dress, and her reception that were in turn immediately reprinted in smaller newspapers across the country. As *The Galveston Daily News* acidly reported in September 1886, "All her utterances, and especially her speeches at the anarchist gatherings, are wired throughout the country as though she were ... a Petroleuse of the Paris Commune."[8] Attention to the intersections of mainstream and radical nineteenth-century US print culture thus helps us begin to recover the fascination radicalism held for even those Americans least poised to agree with its politics, thereby challenging the continuing tendency among scholars to read nineteenth-century radical culture in isolation or treat it as a minor subplot to the study of American literature.

Another way to register radical culture's ripples across nineteenth-century American culture is to turn to the way that it resurfaces, often – though not always – in satirical form, in "canonical" American literature of this period, in literary works written by authors who did not themselves identify with radical causes or in any way directly espouse radical politics. For example, traces of the Brook Farm utopian community – and with it the more than 100 other utopian settlements that emerged across the United States over the course of the nineteenth century – are archived in Nathaniel Hawthorne's representation of a radical utopian community and its ultimate combustion in *The Blithedale Romance* (1852).[9] Later in the

---

[7] For more on mainstream coverage of late nineteenth-century US radical culture, see J. Michelle Coghlan, *Sensational Internationalism: The Paris Commune and the Remapping of American Memory in the Long Nineteenth Century* (Edinburgh University Press, 2016), 79–104.
[8] "A Parsons Family Affair," *The Galveston Daily News*, September 19, 1886. For more on the circulation of this article in US newspapers, see Jones, *Goddess of Anarchy*, 158.
[9] On radical possibilities in *The Blithedale Romance*, see Nina Baym, "*The Blithedale Romance*: A Radical Reading," *Journal of English and Germanic Philology* 67:4 (1968), 545–569; and Robert S. Levine, "Sympathy and Reform in *The Blithedale Romance*," in Richard H. Millington, ed., *The Cambridge Companion to Nathaniel Hawthorne* (Cambridge University Press, 2004), 207–229.

century, a taste of the some 36,757 strikes that occurred across a variety of US industries between 1881 and 1905 flashes up in William Dean Howells's impassioned representation of a New York City streetcar strike in *A Hazard of New Fortunes* (1890).[10] In the mid-1880s, Howells's contemporary, and the by then expatriate American writer, Henry James, began work on his most avowedly political novels, turning his attention to two different late nineteenth-century radical scenes: *The Bostonians*, set in Boston, focused on the question of women's suffrage at a moment of increasing agitation for (and anxiety about the possibility of) American women getting the vote, and *The Princess Casamassima*, set in London, explored the anarchist movement at precisely the moment when the British capital was rocked by a series of Fenian bombings and bomb threats that had left the city reeling.[11] Serialized in 1885 in the *Century* and the *Atlantic Monthly*, respectively, and published the following year in complete form, neither novel was, at the time, a commercial or critical success, and James famously gave up on "social problem fiction" altogether in the wake of this double disappointment.

Recent work by Michaela Bronstein has nevertheless helped to recover the importance of *The Princess Casamassima* for later American radicals, in particular mid-twentieth-century African American writers such as James Baldwin, Ralph Ellison, and Richard Wright who, as Bronstein observes, embraced its "representations of the psychology of an oppressive society and [its] fierce skepticism about the motives and practices of revolutionary groups."[12] By contrast, *The Bostonians* might seem, on the face of it, at once far less politically charged and far less primed to speak to us about American radicalism, past or present. The novel's depiction of the stolidly bourgeois feminist spinster Olive Chancellor, backdated to the Boston of the 1870s rather than the 1880s, might seem altogether removed from both the international underground radical scene that James unfolded in *The Princess Casamassima* and the anxiety surrounding domestic anarchist agitation that would have been fresh on the minds of so many of James's

---

[10] David Montgomery, "Strikes in Nineteenth-Century America," *Social Science History* 4:1 (1980), 86. On Haymarket and Howells's radicalization, see Timothy L. Parrish, "Haymarket and *Hazard*: The Lonely Politics of William Dean Howells," *The Journal of Popular American Culture* 17:4 (1994), 23–32; and Sophia Forster, "Americanist Literary Realism: Howells, Historicism, and American Exceptionalism," *Modern Fiction Studies* 55:2 (2009), 216–241.

[11] On the Fenian bombing campaigns that are displaced in the novel, see Jeffory A. Clymer, *America's Culture of Terrorism: Violence, Capitalism and the Written Word* (University of North Carolina Press, 2003), 69–99.

[12] Michaela Bronstein, "*The Princess* among the Polemicists: Aesthetics and Politics at Midcentury," *American Literary History* 29:1 (2017), 28.

American readers because of the Haymarket bombing in Chicago in the spring of 1886, the ongoing coverage of the anarchists' trial that summer, and their execution the following autumn. At the time of *The Bostonians*'s publication, James was soundly critiqued for satirizing the genteel humanitarian aspirations of Boston's lingering, but seemingly not quite effectual postbellum reform movement culture. Writing in the *Atlantic* in 1886, Horace E. Scudder noted that James's Olive Chancellor had "cast in her lot with a set of reformers much the worse for wear," while Lucia T. Ames's bristling review of the novel that same year in the respected Boston suffrage periodical *Woman's Journal* opined that "the book is evidently intended as a tremendous satire on the whole 'woman question'" and would have been more fittingly titled "*The Cranks.*"[13] Certainly, Basil Ransom, the ex-Confederate soldier who moves to Boston and eventually wins the heart of the budding suffragist activist Verena Tarrant, is savagely skeptical of the ragtag bunch of Bostonian non-conformists that he meets through his cousin Olive: "He had a general idea they were mediums, communists and vegetarians."[14] And despite the fact that Olive is branded in the novel's opening as not just a "radical," in the words of her skeptical sister, Mrs. Luna, but indeed "a female Jacobin" and "nihilist" who would "reform the solar system if she could get hold of it," *The Bostonians* seems to suggest the highpoint of American radicalism has by then already passed, with Olive and her protégé Verena already nostalgic for the heady pre–Civil War radicalism figured in the person of their aging hero Miss Birdseye, "one of the earliest, one of the most passionate, of the old Abolitionists."[15]

Little wonder, then, that so much later criticism of the novel would point to its seemingly regressive politics and disconnection from the radical history – or rather, radical near-present – by which it seemed ostensibly most transfixed and which James himself claimed so much to want to register. (In his notebooks, he famously suggested that he had aimed in *The Bostonians* "to write a very *American* tale, a tale very characteristic of our social conditions, and I had asked myself what was the most salient and peculiar point in our social life. The answer was: the situation of women ... the agitation on their behalf.")[16] Influential mid-twentieth-

---

[13] Horace E. Scudder, Review of *The Bostonians*, *The Atlantic* (June 1886), 851–853, reprinted in *Henry James: The Contemporary Reviews*, ed. Kevin J. Hayes (Cambridge University Press, 1996), 168; and Lucia T. Ames, "The Bostonians," *Woman's Journal* (March 13, 1886), 82, 83.
[14] Henry James, *The Bostonians* (Penguin, [1886] 2000), 26.   [15] James, *The Bostonians*, 7, 18.
[16] *The Complete Notebooks of Henry James*, ed. Leon Edel and Lyall H. Powers (Oxford University Press, 1987), 20.

century Jamesian scholars largely sidestepped the novel's representation of the US feminist movement of the 1870s and 1880s, as Sara deSaussure Davis pointed out in her germinal 1979 study of the feminist sources of *The Bostonians*, in which she describes critics such as Granville Hicks claiming that "James knew nothing at all of the fight for women's rights."[17] And as Jennifer Fleissner has pointed out, later Jamesian scholars have too often similarly discounted the novel's connection to its time and the movement it seems most focused upon, with some of those scholars suggesting, as Howard Kerr does, that the spiritualist movement of the 1850s was James's real focus while others argue that, as Fleissner aptly summarizes them, "the topical concerns of *The Bostonians* [are] mostly window dressing for a story of less time-bound human relations."[18] Most recently, Sharon Cameron has disconnected the novel in this way from its radical political context by arguing that while "the achievements of women activists like Elizabeth Cady Stanton, Susan B. Anthony, and Julia Ward Howe were palpable [at the time of the novel's conception and writing] ... James was not interested in depicting a political movement that had substance. Rather, the savage comedy of the novel arises from his skewering of fringe types: failed utopians, quacks, and media celebrities."[19]

And yet, as deSaussure Davis's work did so much to recover, James was far from unfamiliar with the women's movement of his day, both by personal acquaintance and by way of his attendance at various "demonstrations, meetings, seances, and speeches by reformers" as he hunted for "fictional subject matter" in Cambridge in the spring of 1872.[20] And as deSaussure Davis argues, he drew on this knowledge both by crucially reworking in the novel key details and personalities of the feminist movement of the 1870s, in particular the figure of the charismatic suffrage speaker Anna Dickinson, and by embedding its key political positions into the fabric of the novel, as when Verena explains to Basil Ransom that their aims are "equal rights, equal opportunities, equal privileges."[21] Building on deSaussure's suggestion that "in *The Bostonians*, [James] left more of a picture 'of [his] time'" than he has typically been given credit for, and more recently John Funchion's work to draw attention to the never totally foreclosed upon radical energy of the novel by way of Verena's

---

[17] Sara deSaussure Davis, "Feminist Sources in *The Bostonians*," *American Literature* 50:4 (1979), 570.
[18] Jennifer L. Fleissner, *Women, Compulsion, Modernity: The Moment of American Naturalism* (University of Chicago Press, 2004), 126.
[19] Sharon Cameron, "The Hole in the Carpet: Henry James's *The Bostonians*," *Daedalus* 150:1 (Winter 2021), 93.
[20] DeSaussure Davis, "Feminist Sources in *The Bostonians*," 574.   [21] James, *The Bostonians*, 178.

ability to "draw up dream-like memories of what could have been" in her orations so that "the form of her speech does not transcend its historical moment but instead immanently redefines how her audience apprehends the present and its consequential future,"[22] this chapter reconsiders the portrait James paints of nineteenth-century American radicals and, by extension, how best to read and recognize the literature of American radicalism in this period.

What can Henry James tell us about American radicalism that we might otherwise be likely to overlook? Critics have often described Olive and her circle of fellow activists as "reformers" – a term that might suggest, particularly from our later vantage point, a desire to make only modest alterations to the structure of their society, thus obscuring not only the radical charge that the "Woman Question" actually held in this period but also the lingering anxiety that a woman speaking on a platform simultaneously occupied a none-too-metaphorical barricade.[23] And yet James himself, in an 1883 letter to his publisher J. R. Osgood, described his characters as "for the most part persons of the radical reforming type who are especially interested in the emancipation of women,"[24] and he opens his novel with the explicit suggestion that the scene that Olive inhabits is that of "roaring radicals."[25] It is worth pausing for a moment over James's choice of terms. The term "radical" comes into wide circulation to connote, as the *Oxford English Dictionary* puts it, "advocating thorough and far-reaching political or social reform; representing or supporting an extreme section of a party" in the United States in the lead-up to and directly following the Civil War with the emergence of the Radical faction of the Republican party, which called for both an immediate end to slavery in the United States and a post–Civil War Reconstruction program in the South aimed at guaranteeing the civil rights of formerly enslaved people and the voting rights of African American men. But the term was already in use by the Garrisonian wing of the antislavery movement in the 1850s, and the term would come to be embraced by – and used by critics to provoke anxiety about the changes advocated by – a number of later left-wing movements in the United States in the nineteenth century (and beyond),

---

[22] DeSaussure Davis, "Feminist Sources in *The Bostonians*," 587; John Funchion, "Critical Oversights: The Aesthetics and Politics of Reading *The Bostonians*," *The Henry James Review* 34:3 (2013), 281.

[23] On the links between American women radicals and the figure of the Parisian pétroleuse, see Coghlan, "Framing the Pétroleuse: Postbellum Poetry and the Visual Culture of Gender Panic," in Coghlan, *Sensational Internationalism*, 23–51; and David A. Zimmerman's chapter on "Panic and the Pétroleuse" in Zimmerman, *Panic! Markets, Crises, and Crowds in American Fiction* (University of North Carolina Press, 2006), 39–80.

[24] *The Complete Notebooks of Henry James*, 18. [25] James, *The Bostonians*, 7.

among them those who identified as socialists, communists, and anarchists, as well as those who agitated for greater social and sexual freedoms, access to birth control, and the like.[26]

Ransom's dismissal of Boston's postbellum activists for their commitment to seemingly incongruous radical causes – women's rights, dietary reform, alternative forms of spirituality, and the overturning of capitalism – echoes the novel's at times similarly dismissive tone toward the aging Miss Birdseye and her long life of activism. The narrator describes her, for example, as having "belonged to any and every league that has been founded for almost any purpose whatsoever," and we learn over the course of the novel that her commitment to the abolition of slavery took her down South, where she faced hostile crowds and weathered "a month in a Georgia jail," but equally involved her in the temperance crusade, the campaign for women's rights, and tireless work on behalf of impoverished urban children and international political refugees. But while the novel at times pokes fun at Miss Birdseye's seemingly inexhaustible altruism and enthusiasm for radical causes – her sense of "charity [which] began at home and ended nowhere"[27] – I would argue that it is exactly that impulse which most draws into relief an important aspect of nineteenth-century American radicalism, particularly in the decades leading up to the Civil War. That is, the fight for the immediate abolition of slavery led radical abolitionists to question every aspect of American life and, in turn, work to champion a variety of seemingly disparate causes, from prison abolition and free speech to dress and dietary reform, the fight for an eight-hour workday, access to birth control, and Native American rights. But where Ransom sees in Miss Birdseye's activism only a hodgepodge of *cri de cœur*, antebellum radicals saw deeply interconnected social ills in need of fundamental redress. For as Holly Jackson observes in her important recent book *American Radicals: How Nineteenth-Century Protest Shaped the Nation*,

> Drawn into one flash-point issue, they would soon find that it was inextricable from other oppressive systems ... As Wendell Phillips reflected after thirty years agitating for abolition, universal suffrage, and labor rights, he had been awakened as a young man to the fact that slavery "had poisoned everything it touched." It was not a single institution but the invisible, toxic framework of the entire society.[28]

---

[26] My thanks to Holly Jackson for drawing my attention to the circulation of the term "radicals" in William Lloyd Garrison's antislavery newspaper *The Liberator* in the 1850s.
[27] James, *The Bostonians*, 23.
[28] Holly Jackson, *American Radicals: How Nineteenth-Century Protest Shaped the Nation* (Crown, 2019), xiii.

Over the past four decades, American literary studies has devoted increasing attention to the literary wing of abolitionism – the slave narratives, sentimental novels, poetry, performances, and political pamphlets – that shaped and sustained the movement by countering proslavery propaganda and the scientific racism often underpinning it, converting transatlantic audiences to the antislavery cause, and equally crucially raising funds for the fight.[29] But, until recently, far less attention has been paid to the radicality of the most militant wing of that movement, and to the fact that they – like later nineteenth-century radicals – often called for nothing short of the upending of society and capitalism by any means necessary, as Jackson's recent work has done so much to remind us.[30] And the legacy of that radical abolitionism – whether in the form of its tactics, its textual forms, its commitment to manifold social change, or the ongoing activism of key voices of its movement – has so far received comparatively short shrift.

Such a gap in the story of nineteenth-century American radicalism and its literature highlights the way that labor studies – and with it the study of the cultural forms of American radicalism – continues to be what Dana Luciano and Ivy Wilson have rightly identified as a "minor field" in nineteenth-century American literary studies.[31] It also bears remarking that such a gap exists despite or perhaps because so much recent work to recover the literary forms of nineteenth-century US radicalism has focused on the post–Civil War/post-Reconstruction period.[32] This renewed critical attention to the final decades of the nineteenth century makes sense given the unparalleled levels of labor unrest and organization in the United States

---

[29] See, for example, Teresa A. Goddu, *Selling Antislavery: Abolition and Mass Media in Antebellum America* (University of Pennsylvania Press, 2020); Britt Rusert, *Fugitive Science: Empiricism and Freedom in Early African American Culture* (New York University Press, 2017); Martha Schoolman, *Abolitionist Geographies* (University of Minnesota Press, 2014); and Shelly Jarenski, "'Delighted and Instructed': Panoramic Aesthetics and African-American Challenges in J. P. Ball, Kara Walker, and Frederick Douglass," *American Quarterly* 65:1 (2013), 119–155.

[30] See, for example, Jackson, *American Radicals*; Michael Bennett, *Democratic Discourses: The Radical Abolition Movement and Antebellum American Literature* (Rutgers University Press, 2005); Mary Kelley, "'Talents Committed to Your Care': Reading and Writing Radical Abolitionism in Antebellum America," *New England Quarterly* 88:1 (2015), 37–72; and John Stauffer, *The Black Hearts of Men: Radical Abolitionists and the Transformation of Race* (Harvard University Press, 2001).

[31] Luciano and Wilson, *Unsettled States*, 7.

[32] See, for example, Kristin Boudreau, "Elegies for the Haymarket Anarchists," *American Literature* 77:2 (2005), 319–347; Shelley Streeby, *Radical Sensations: World Movements, Violence, and Visual Culture* (Duke University Press, 2013); John Funchion, *Novel Nostalgias: The Aesthetics of Antagonism in Nineteenth-Century U.S. Literature* (Ohio State University Press, 2015), 134–172; Coghlan, *Sensational Internationalism*; and the historian Clark D. Halker's *For Democracy, Workers, and God: Labor Song-Poems and Labor Protest, 1865–95* (University of Illinois Press, 1991).

in this period and increasing interest in alternatives to capitalism as people then knew and lived it, an interest that manifested in both a craze for utopian fiction and a surge in the membership of radical organizations. And as John Funchion has pointed out, "Cheap paper prices drove an unprecedented rise in the number of radical publications across the nation at the end of the nineteenth century,"[33] a boom in radical print culture that went hand in hand with a burgeoning Red Scare and, as discussed, the equally intense recirculation of radical speeches and coverage of radical gatherings in mainstream US newspapers. These turbulent decades also famously witnessed the formation of the International Workingmen's Association in 1864; the short-lived emergence of the Paris Commune, the first successful worker uprising, in 1871; the founding of the first Socialistic Labor Party (later the Socialist Labor Party) in the United States in 1876 and, the following year, both the abandonment of Reconstruction and the failure of the Great Strike of 1877, the first and still among the largest nationwide railroad strike in US history; and the rise of the movement for an eight-hour workday and the 1886 Haymarket bombing in Chicago, whose aftermath saw seven anarchist speakers sentenced to death for radical beliefs they held and the words they had said on the day of the bombing though they played no role in the bombing itself, a cause célèbre that served to radicalize a generation of American activists.[34]

Yet the ongoing critical disjunction between antebellum and postbellum US activism grows, too, from a long-standing lapse of memory regarding American radicalism – the lingering sense that its highpoint has always already passed and that its failures are imagined to leave few resources for later movements while its successes are too often forgotten as soon as they become – like the eight-hour workday – simply part of the fabric of everyday life.[35] As the historian Lewis Perry put it in his groundbreaking reevaluation of William Lloyd Garrison's wing of the antislavery

---

[33] Funchion, *Novel Nostalgias*, 139.

[34] Although only four of the defendants would ultimately be executed, seven anarchists received a capital sentence at the Haymarket trial and all seven – Albert Parsons, Samuel Fielden, Auguste Spies, Louis Lingg, Adolphe Fischer, Michael Schwab, and George Engel – were routinely depicted together in illustrated newspapers and radical periodicals, both in 1887 and for decades after. After two failed appeals and a last-ditch clemency campaign involving William Dean Howells (Oscar Wilde also signed), two of these defendants, Samuel Fielden and Michael Schwab, the only ones to write and ask for clemency from the Governor of Illinois, something the others refused to do on grounds of their innocence – belatedly received commuted sentences two days before they were due to be executed. Only four were executed on November 11, 1887, because another of the defendants, Louis Lingg, committed suicide in prison the day before he was due to die by hanging.

[35] For more on the "declension narrative" of American radicalism, see Coghlan, *Sensational Internationalism*, 153–159.

movement in *Radical Abolitionism: Anarchy and the Government of God in Anti-Slavery Thought*, notably published in the wake of the 1960s civil rights, antiwar, and liberation struggles (another highpoint of American radicalism): "Radical antislavery is more valuable for the clues it holds for an understanding of the time in which it occurred than for delineating a tradition of American radicalism. If any tradition was involved, it was one that *scarcely survived its own era*."[36]

What interests me about *The Bostonians*, then, is the way it helps us to begin to tell a different story about nineteenth-century American radicalism, crucially highlighting the legacy of radical abolition and antebellum activist networks in the movements that both overlapped with and followed them. Critics such as Daniel Heaton have suggested that the aging Miss Birdseye is "unquestionably a relic of a past age who has lost touch with the present," noting that as the novel progresses (and Miss Birdseye's health seems ever more on the wane) the narrator describes her as increasingly aware that "her uses were ended."[37] Her ongoing activism might be a matter of merely going through the motions, or, as the novel puts it, "still pretending to go about the business of unpopular causes."[38] And yet, the activism the novel describes her as continuing daily to perform – signing petitions, attending conventions, wearing "short stuff dresses" and agitating for dress reform, organizing gatherings at her home on behalf of women's suffrage and other issues – nevertheless very directly connects her to the novel's present moment and the feminist movement on which it centers. And even as both Basil Ransom and the novel's narrative voice alternate between biting satire and begrudging respect for Miss Birdseye's "eighty years of innocence" and activism, the novel registers both her sustained involvement across various nineteenth-century movements and her commitment to various radical causes – among them abolition, temperance, dress reform, political refugees, and women's suffrage – and even more crucially her role in supporting and sustaining a younger generation of US women activists.[39] In this way, she echoes the Transcendentalist reformer Elizabeth Palmer Peabody, a James-family friend who worked tirelessly on behalf of the cause of educational reform, spearheading the kindergarten movement in the United States in addition to agitating in support of the antislavery movement and advocating for greater religious

---

[36] Lewis Perry, *Radical Abolitionism: Anarchy and the Government of God in Anti-Slavery Thought* (Cornell University Press, 1973), 297 (emphasis mine).
[37] Daniel H. Heaton, "The Altered Characterization of Miss Birdseye in Henry James's *The Bostonians*," *American Literature* 50:4 (1979), 594.
[38] James, *The Bostonians*, 138.   [39] James, *The Bostonians*, 140.

freedom, and whom James was immediately critiqued for satirizing by way of his, at times less than flattering, characterization of Miss Birdseye. And though James strenuously denied, in a letter to his brother William, that he had had Peabody in mind as he crafted the character of Miss Birdseye, he nevertheless suggests in that same missive that "she is ... the best figure in the book ... every virtue of heroism [and] disinterestedness is attributed to her," later insisting that "[*The Bostonians*] will remain longer than Miss P's name or fame, [and] I don't hold that it will be an obloquy or ground of complaint for her."[40] (As Bruce A. Ronda points out, however, when *The Bostonians* first began to appear in the pages of the *Century*, Peabody herself seemed to take little notice of either its publication or her parallels in its pages, for "the eighty-one-year-old [Peabody] was recovering from an extended lecture circuit in support of the Paiute people and their spokesperson, Sarah Winemucca.")[41]

But if *The Bostonians* archives the way that antebellum radicalism lives on in and overlaps with later movements, it also illuminates the often underappreciated reverence that many later US radicals held for the abolitionist movement, as well as the inspiration they often explicitly suggested they drew from it. The veneration that Olive Chancellor and Verena Tarrant – and, by extension, the feminist movement of which they are representatives – hold for Miss Birdseye is palpable across the novel, always jostling against the views of her rendered by the unreconstructed Southerner Ransom and the novel's at times biting characterizations of her. James suggests that the "perennial freshness of [Miss Birdseye's] faith" is part of the "contagion" she holds for the next generation of Bostonian activists.[42] However, her appeal is also rooted in Olive's sense of her as representing a radical past otherwise – or soon to be – beyond their reach: "this frumpy little missionary was the last link in a tradition, and ... when she should be called away the heroic age of New England life – the age of plain living and high thinking, of pure ideals and earnest effort, of moral passion and noble experiment – would effectually be closed."[43] The dawning sense of belatedness overhanging the ostensible vanguards of American radicalism in the novel and their desire again and again to hear about Miss Birdseye's abolitionist past have led critics such as Heaton to argue

---

[40] Henry James, letter to William James, February 14, 1885, in *The Complete Letters of Henry James, 1884–6*, Vol. 1, ed. Michael Anesko and Greg W. Zacharias (University of Nebraska Press, 2020), 113; James, letter to William James, February 15, 1885, in *The Complete Letters of Henry James*, 116.
[41] Bruce A. Ronda, *The Fate of Transcendentalism: Secularity, Materiality, and Human Flourishing* (University of Georgia Press, 2017), 63.
[42] James, *The Bostonians*, 139.   [43] James, *The Bostonians*, 139.

that there is something deeply "anachronistic" about the backward-looking younger activists in her thrall.⁴⁴ And yet, as John Funchion has done so much to remind us, late nineteenth-century radical activists, intellectuals, and writers saw the recent radical past and otherwise "estranged histories" as vital resources in the work to agitate for radical causes and radical futures, an insurgent affective relationship to the past that Funchion aptly terms "left nostalgia."⁴⁵ Put a little differently, Olive and Verena's interest in connecting with the not-yet closed recent radical past makes them emblems of their contemporary radical moment rather than outliers or relics from some other time. And the particular radical past with which they seem so taken – the impassioned abolitionism represented by Miss Birdseye – at once marks them as deeply entwined with the memory culture of late nineteenth-century US radicalism even as it archives the prominent place that radical abolitionists held for a variety of American radicals going about "the business of unpopular causes."

To appreciate James's Olive and Verena as emblems of late nineteenth-century radicalism, take, for example, the American labor organizer Eugene V. Debs, who helped to found the Industrial Workers of the World in 1905, ran for the US presidency five times on the Socialist ticket between 1900 and 1920 (attracting nearly a million votes in the 1912 election), and throughout his career returned to the topic of abolition to remind readers and would-be voters both of the infamy that once surrounded that movement's calls for immediate emancipation and of the courage shown by radical abolitionist agitators such as William Lloyd Garrison and Wendell Phillips.⁴⁶ As Debs put it in the September 1900 speech, "Cooperation vs. Competition," which launched his first run for the US presidency: "They didn't ask, 'Is it popular, can I afford it, does it pay?' They simply asked: 'Is it right?' and satisfied that it was right, they stood by it without fear of consequences."⁴⁷ Or consider the anarchist orator and essayist Voltairine de Cleyre's attention to John Brown's violent tactics and her own grandfather's work for the underground railroad in her 1912 essay for *Mother Earth* on "Direct Action," and her return to the subject of abolition in the pages of that magazine later that year in "The Commune Is Risen." This latter essay looks back to the Paris Commune's

---

⁴⁴ Heaton, "The Altered Characterization of Miss Birdseye," 594.
⁴⁵ Funchion, *Novel Nostalgias*, 135.
⁴⁶ See, for example, Eugene V. Debs, "Abolitionists," *Locomotive Fireman's Magazine* 11:2 (1887), 67–68; Debs, "William Lloyd Garrison," *Locomotive Fireman's Magazine* 16:6 (1892), 491–493; and Debs, "John Brown: History's Greatest Hero," in *Debs: His Life, Writings and Speeches* (Charles H. Kerr & Company, 1908), 272.
⁴⁷ Eugene V. Debs, "Competition vs. Cooperation," *Appeal to Reason* (October 13, 1900), 3.

legacy for US radicals and forward to the promise of "world-wide" revolt that she sees taking hold in Europe, China, and Mexico to describe how the anarchists of her generation "have listened with curious fascination to our elders' stories of the abolition movement" with as much attention as they "welcomed the Russian revolutionists, and enviously listened to their accounts of deeds done or undone."[48] Two years later, the Czech American anarchist Hippolyte Havel's introduction to the posthumously published collection of de Cleyre's *Selected Writings* would point out that though most Americans continue to refuse to hear it, "the tocsin of revolt resounds in the writings of Emerson, Thoreau, Hawthorne, Whitman, Garrison, Wendell Phillips, and other seers of America."[49]

That radical abolitionists such as Garrison and Phillips would appear alongside contemporary American authors such as Emerson, Thoreau, Hawthorne, and Whitman as equal "seers" sounding the "tocsin of revolt" in the biographical sketch of a militant turn-of-the-century American anarchist suggests not just the unexpectedly vital role that the recent radical abolitionist past continued to play in the story of US radicalism but also the surprisingly expansive shape of the nineteenth-century radical canon as defined by nineteenth- and early twentieth-century radicals themselves. Labor song-poems and elegies were perhaps the most ubiquitous genre of nineteenth-century American radicalism – the historian Clark D. Halker suggests that several thousand of them appeared in US labor periodicals between 1865 and 1895 alone and points out that they bolstered solidarity in labor organizing and on picket lines in strikes but were also a key part of the cultural apparatus of US labor organizing in this period, part and parcel with "parades, picnics, lectures, reading rooms, singing groups, raffles, concerts, balls, potluck suppers, newspapers, broadsides, banners, auxiliaries and marching bands."[50] But the late nineteenth-century anarchist and socialist periodicals notably worked to cultivate their readers' interest in a wide range of radical texts and genres by figures such as Karl Marx, Eugene V. Debs, James Connolly, William Morris, Edward Bellamy, Victor Hugo, and others, many of which did not originate in the United States and some of which were authored by writers who did not themselves identify as radical.[51] This perhaps begins to explain why the first anthology

---

[48] Voltairine de Cleyre, "The Commune Is Risen," *Mother Earth* (March 1912), 13.
[49] Hippolyte Havel, "Introduction," in *Selected Works of Voltairine de Cleyre*, ed. Alexander Berkman (Mother Earth Publishing, 1914), 6.
[50] Halker, *For Democracy, Workers, and God*, 2, 5.
[51] Funchion, "Reading Cultural Capital in Radical Periodicals," biennial meeting of the British Association of Nineteenth-Century Americanists, University of Nottingham, December 2019.

of "social protest" literature in the English language, Upton Sinclair's *The Cry for Justice* (1915), contained essays and speeches by socialists such as Debs and William Morris and anarchists such as Emma Goldman, Joe Hill, Peter Kropotkin, and Francisco Ferrer alongside poems by Walt Whitman and English poets such as William Cowper and William Wordsworth, extracts from the writings of the Russian novelist Leo Tolstoy, the Bengali writer Rabindranath Tagore, and the African American sociologist and socialist W. E. B. Dubois (among others), though examples of labor song-poems were notably absent from its pages, much as they would be from Manual Gomez's groundbreaking 1925 *Poems for Workers* anthology for the Little Red Library. But while such absences speak to the ephemerality and erasure of much nineteenth-century US radical writing and the ongoing limits of print as an archive for US radicalism, these anthologies nevertheless also help to point to the capacious reach of nineteenth-century US literary radicalism and the ways that radical and mainstream US print culture so often crisscrossed in this period.

Further Reading

Boase, Paul H., ed. *The Rhetoric of Protest and Reform: 1878–1898*. Ohio University Press, 1980.

Castronovo, Russ. *Beautiful Democracy: Aesthetics and Anarchy in a Global Era*. University of Chicago Press, 2009.

Coghlan, J. Michelle. *Sensational Internationalism: The Paris Commune and the Remapping of American Memory in the Long Nineteenth Century*. Edinburgh University Press, 2016.

Darsey, James. *The Prophetic Tradition and Radical Rhetoric in America*. New York University Press, 1997.

DeLamotte, Eugenia C. *Gates of Freedom: Voltairine de Cleyre and the Revolution of the Mind*. University of Michigan Press, 2010.

Funchion, John. "Critical Oversights: The Aesthetics and Politics of Reading *The Bostonians*." *The Henry James Review* 34:3 (2013), 279–284.

Funchion, John. *Novel Nostalgias: The Aesthetics of Antagonism in Nineteenth-Century U.S. Literature*. Ohio State University Press, 2015.

Halker, Clark D. *For Democracy, Workers, and God: Labor Song-Poems and Labor Protest, 1865–95*. University of Illinois Press, 1991.

Jackson, Holly. *American Radicals: How Nineteenth-Century Protest Shaped the Nation*. Crown, 2019.

Kowal, Donna M. *Tongue of Fire: Emma Goldman, Public Womanhood, and the Sex Question*. State University of New York Press, 2016.

Packer, Barbara L. "The Hope of Reform." In Sacvan Bercovitch, ed., *The Cambridge History of American Literature, Vol. 2: Prose Writings, 1820–1865*. Cambridge University Press, 1995, 459–494.

Richards, Juno Jill. *The Fury Archives: Female Citizenship, Human Rights, and the International Avant-Gardes*. Columbia University Press, 2020.

Sartwell, Crispin. "Anarchism and Nineteenth-Century American Political Thought." In Nathan J. Jun, ed., *Brill's Companion to Anarchism and Philosophy*. Brill, 2018, 454–483.

Streeby, Shelley. "Looking at State Violence: Lucy Parsons, José Marti, and Haymarket." In Russ Castronovo, ed., *The Oxford Handbook of Nineteenth-Century American Literature*. Russ Castronovo. Oxford University Press, 2014, 115–136.

Streeby, Shelley. *Radical Sensations: World Movements, Violence, and Visual Culture*. Duke University Press, 2013.

CHAPTER 4

Nationalism: Character, Identity, and Hyphenated Selfhood

John D. Kerkering

Nationalism, as Raymond Williams has observed, is typically associated with an existing nation or "people" seeking to establish governing institutions (a "state") to sustain and protect that people's distinctive character, with success in that effort yielding a "nation-state" recognized as such within an international political order.[1] Yet precisely the opposite project was underway in the nineteenth-century United States, where writers eagerly sought a nationality to accompany their existing state institutions and thereby legitimize those institutions as indeed sustaining and protecting the interests of an American "people."[2] This national legitimacy would extend beyond the legitimacy already conferred by the United States' democratic processes, which failed, in the eyes of many nationalists, to provide the kind of legitimacy conferred upon the state by a parallel and distinct idea of nationality, the central legitimizing concept of which was nativity, or corporeal "birth," implying bodily unity, integrity, and vitality – in short, identity.[3] This concern over nationality's absence from the United States animates an open "Letter to Ralph Waldo Emerson," published as an appendix to the second (1856) edition of *Leaves of Grass*, in which Walt Whitman confidently asserts, "Of course, we shall have a national character, an identity. As it ought to be, and as

---

[1] Raymond Williams, "Nationalist," in *Keywords: A Vocabulary of Culture and Society* (Oxford University Press, 2014), 159–161.
[2] On the standard narrative of nations preceding their states, see Andrew W. Orridge, "Varieties of Nationalism," in Leonard Tivey, ed., *The Nation-State: The Formation of Modern Politics* (Martin Robertson, 1981), 39–58, 55. On the US reversal of that sequence, see Susan-Mary Grant, "State-Building and Nationalism in Nineteenth-Century USA," in John Breuilly, ed., *The Oxford Handbook of the History of Nationalism* (Oxford University Press, 2013), 395–413, 397–398.
[3] On the distinction between legitimate democratic institutions practicing majority rule and the unified national will of a people, see Pierre Rosanvallon, *Democratic Legitimacy: Impartiality, Reflexivity, Proximity*, trans. Arthur Goldhammer, Princeton University Press, 2011, 1–2.

soon as it ought to be, it will be."⁴ I argue in this chapter that while Whitman is entirely correct in his conviction that, by 1856, "a national character, an identity" had not yet emerged in the United States, his confident nationalist prediction that either would "soon" emerge was and remains profoundly mistaken.

Nationalist discourse was prominent in Whitman's historical moment, emanating forcefully from European countries whose failed nations (Germany and Italy) and successful ones (England and France) were widely discussed in the United States either as cautionary tales or as positive models.⁵ While Whitman's 1856 prediction that the United States "shall have a national character, an identity" exemplifies just such a nationalist disposition, this nationalism served the distinctively American political purpose, I argue, of permitting nineteenth-century Americans like Whitman to imagine and represent themselves, both domestically and abroad, in the positive (although still prospective) guise of a nation-state rather than in the more accurate yet more sinister terms of empire. This tension between nation-state and empire would lead, by the century's end, to the sought-after hyphenation of the nation-state being displaced onto the bodies, and ultimately within the consciousnesses, of US imperial subjects, producing a divided or hyphenated self: The American adjudicating international tensions within the self by regulating relations among its distinct inner nations emerged from nineteenth-century nationalist discourse to become the enduring paradigm of the hyphenated American.⁶

Nation or Empire?

Whitman made his prediction that the United States "shall have a national character, and identity" in the same year (1856) that the South Carolina representative Preston Brooks caned the Massachusetts senator Charles

---

⁴ Walt Whitman, "Letter to Ralph Waldo Emerson," *Leaves of Grass*, 1856, 358, https://whitmanarchive.org/published/LG/1856/whole.html.

⁵ For contemporary references to these models, see Charles Sumner, "Are We a Nation?" Address before the New York Men's Republican Union at the Cooper Institute, Tuesday evening, November 19, 1867 (New York Young Men's Republican Union, 1867), 1–36, 8–11; and David Dowling, "Reporting the Revolution: Margaret Fuller, Herman Melville, and the Italian Risorgimento," *American Journalism* 31:1 (2014), 26–48.

⁶ The normative status of hyphenation in the United States is evidenced by the 2017 "Hyphen-Nation" project jointly produced by the PBS documentary film project *POV* and the *New York Times*: www.nytimes.com/interactive/projects/storywall/hyphen-nation.

Figure 4.1 *Southern Chivalry*, John L. Magee, lithograph, 1856. Division of Home and Community Life, National Museum of American History, Smithsonian Institution, Catalog Number 60.3451.

Sumner on the US Senate floor (see Figure 4.1).[7] Concern over national unity's absence would intensify immediately after the Civil War for writers like the Union soldier turned novelist John W. De Forest who, in an essay published in *The Nation* (formerly the abolitionist *The Liberator*) titled "The Great American Novel," writes that, perhaps with the exception of Stowe's *Uncle Tom's Cabin*, the great American novel, which would be a "portrait" of "the American soul," has yet to be written because "We are a nation of provinces, and each province claims to be the court," the term "province" implying an overarching imperial power.[8] Likewise, in 1867, US Senator Charles Sumner, the target of Brooks's notorious Senate caning, delivered a speech called "Are We a Nation?" in which he answers his title's question in the affirmative: "Surely we are not ... an empire

---

[7] Scholars have repeatedly shown this absence of national unity to be a preoccupation of US writers in the antebellum period; for a thorough recent account, see J. Gerald Kennedy, *Strange Nation: Literary Nationalism and Cultural Conflict in the Age of Poe* (Oxford University Press, 2016).
[8] John William De Forest, "The Great American Novel," *The Nation* 6 (January 9, 1868), 27–29, 27, 29.

cemented by conquest, like that of later Rome, or like that of Charlemagne"; instead, the US nation is evident in the "one authentic voice ... swelling in that majestic utterance of the people, the Declaration of Independence ... [and] the constitution of the United States." "Call it imperialism, if you please," Sumner goes on to state; "it is simply the imperialism of the Declaration of Independence, with all its promises fulfilled."[9] Calling it imperialism is precisely what James Russell Lowell had done two years earlier in the poem he recited at Harvard University's commemoration of its Civil War dead: "A people rise / Up to a noble anger's height, / ... And certify to earth a new imperial race."[10] This triumphal imperialism confirms the worst fears of a defeated Confederacy whose institutions of state had formed to sustain and protect the seceded South's distinctive national interests – its "peculiar institution" of slavery – against the external encroachment of abolitionism, and a similar anti-imperialism would become the explicit southern rationale for foiling Reconstruction and replacing it with Redemption.[11]

The formidable challenge to claiming for the United States a genuinely *national* legitimacy becomes apparent in figural gymnastics that Whitman must perform in his 1856 letter to Emerson, which anthropomorphizes the American continent as if it were a bodily person – the kind of thing we easily accept as having been born (hence "nativity," the root meaning of nation) and thus might genuinely have or claim a "national character, an identity."[12] But Whitman's figurations also invert that vector, not just anthropomorphizing the continental terrain but also terra-morphizing bodies – a move implicit in his infamous hubris in offering his own body as the ideal reference and equivalent for a national body. This equation appears not just in his poetry (for instance, his first poem in this second, 1856 edition of *Leaves of Grass* is titled "Poem of Walt Whitman, an American") but also in the bold frontispiece to this edition of *Leaves of Grass* that, identically to the first edition, in lieu of naming him as the

---

[9] Sumner, "Are We a Nation?," 11, 34.
[10] James Russell Lowell, "Ode Recited at the Harvard Commemoration," quoted in Jennifer Rae Greeson's *Our South: Geographic Fantasy and the Rise of National Literature* (Harvard University Press, 2010), 227.
[11] On Redemption, see Henry Louis Gates, Jr., *Stony the Road: Reconstruction, White Supremacy, and the Rise of Jim Crow* (Penguin, 2019); on the anti-imperialism of postbellum southern writing, see Walter Benn Michaels, "Anti-imperial Americanism," in Amy Kaplan and Donald E. Pease, eds., *Cultures of United States Imperialism* (Duke University Press, 1993), 365–391.
[12] Katherine Verdery notes that "Nation is ... an aspect of the political and symbolic/ideological order" whose "root meaning, 'to be born' – [is] an idea crucial to making any system of categories appear natural"; see "Whither 'Nation' and 'Nationalism'?," *Daedalus* 122:3 (Summer 1993), 37–46, 37.

Nationalism: Character, Identity, and Hyphenation 71

Figure 4.2 *Walt Whitman, 1819–1892*, Samuel Hollyer, steel engraving, 1854. www.loc.gov/pictures/item/2002710162/.

book's author, features a daguerreotype of himself as embodied American nationality (see Figure 4.2). Seemingly despite but in fact, as we will see, because of this hubristic pretension to national embodiment, Whitman addresses Emerson repeatedly in his 1856 open letter as "Master," writing to him and all readers of this edition as follows:

> Of course, we shall have a national character, an identity. As it ought to be, and as soon as it ought to be, it will be. That, with much else, takes care of itself, is a result, and the cause of greater results. With Ohio, Illinois, Missouri, Oregon – with the states around the Mexican sea – with cheerfully welcomed Hampshire, Rhode Island – with all varied interests, facts, beliefs, parties, genesis – there is being fused a determined character, fit for the broadest use for the freewomen and freemen of The States, accomplished and to be accomplished, without any exception whatever – each indeed free, each idiomatic, as becomes live states and men, but each adhering to one enclosing general form of politics, manners, talk, personal style, as the plenteous varieties of the race adhere to one physical form. Such character is the brain and spine to all, including literature, including poems. Such character, strong, limber, just, open-mouthed, American-blooded, full of pride, full of ease, of passionate friendliness, is to stand compact upon that vast basis of the supremacy of Individuality – that new moral American continent without which, I see, the physical continent remained

incomplete, may-be a carcass, a bloat – that newer America, answering face to face with The States, with ever-satisfying and ever-unsurveyable seas and shores.

Those shores you found. I say you have led The States there – have led Me there.[13]

Whitman's catalogue of individual states ("Ohio, Illinois, Missouri, Oregon" and the rest) anthropomorphizes them (equating "live states and men") as at once unique ("each indeed free, each idiomatic") but also typical ("but each adhering to one enclosing general form"). Yet this "enclosing general form" achieves such enclosure only by enlisting the metaphor of anatomical classification of human bodies ("as the plenteous varieties of the race adhere to one physical form"): Different states are like different races (as well as like individual "men"), but just as all races (and all persons) are, despite their physical variations, ultimately human in "physical form" or species (*Homo sapiens*), so all states are, despite local diversity ("with all varied interests, facts, beliefs, parties, genesis"), ultimately American, sharing traits that are, here, not physical and anatomical but behavioral and thus characterological ("politics, manners, talk, personal style"), these behavioral traits constituting (like the anatomical traits that constitute the "one physical form" of "the [human] race") the "determined character" that "is being fused" among and across "The States." Whitman's sequence of metaphors casts him as a national character on par with allegorical figures of nationality that were prominent early in the century, as in the British John Bull and the American Brother Jonathan, each assigned to a distinct (because enclosed by an ocean barrier) swath of land (see Figure 4.3).[14]

But Whitman anticipates attaining not just "a national character" but also (and as a foundation for this character) what he calls, appositionally, "an identity," and introducing this separate but related term complicates his corporeal metaphor, shifting it away from the categorical taxonomy in which the "plenteous varieties of the race" are subsumed within "one physical form" (human) and toward the internal anatomy of a particular individual ("brain and spine"), a single body that, as a site of individual "identity," confers singularity upon the nation (*this* nation) as a particular

---

[13] Whitman, "Letter to Ralph Waldo Emerson," 357–358.
[14] On the concept of national character in nineteenth-century literature, see Susan Manning, *Poetics of Character: Transatlantic Encounters 1700–1900* (Cambridge University Press, 2013), viii–ix; and Marjorie Garber, *Character: The History of a Cultural Obsession* (Farrar, Straus and Giroux, 2020), 131–194.

Nationalism: Character, Identity, and Hyphenation 73

Figure 4.3 *The Laying of the Cable*, Baker & Godwin Printers, New York, woodcut, 1858. https://lccn.loc.gov/2004665357.

body, unique in itself.[15] Whitman, that is, recasts this body-*like* shared national "character" as *itself* the nation's *physical* body – "Such character is the brain and spine to all" – so as to make this now corporealized ("brain and spine") "character" responsible for physically constituting the "identity" of a single nation made up of the various states. But having thus been conflated with the national body ("brain and spine to all") and thus "identity," national "character" can then, via Whitman's vertiginous figurations, once again separate from that bodily identity to become, instead, that *physical* ("identity") body's *moral* ("character") counterpart: This "new moral American continent" stands in apposition to, and thus distinguishes itself from (as irreducible to), America's continental geographic terrain, its mere brain and spine of a physical body, making that physical site of "identity" coincident with but also separable from such "moral"

---

[15] The 1853 edition of Noah Webster's *An American Dictionary of the English Language* defines "identity" as "Sameness, as distinguished from similitude and diversity" (512): https://archive.org/details/americandictionaoowe/page/n9/mode/2up.

"character" traits as "politics, manners, talk, personal style."[16] The "new *moral* American continent" of "character" claims this "*physical* continent" as its body (brain and spine) and thus its "identity," revealing that the "physical continent remained incomplete, may-be a carcass, a bloat [US slang for a dead body]" without the copresence of this vital principle of national character. In tasking this now separate "moral" element of character to supplement and infuse with vitality the otherwise "incomplete" "carcass" of the merely "physical" continent of identity (the brain and spine as mere "bloat"), Whitman distinguishes national character from that "physical continent" such that it might itself stage an encounter with the now mere physical body of those states subsumed under the "American continent": "that newer America, *answering face to face* with The States." This shift in the corporeal metaphor from the abstract physical form of a biological species (which yielded an enclosed national character across several states) to an individual's unique physical body (which yields a natal or born site of corporeal "identity" where that character might locally dwell) demonstrates Whitman's ambition of US ethnogenesis, the production (through a kind of in-person-nation) of an autochthonous "people," one whose distinctive and continentally embodied national character affirms "the supremacy of Individuality" for men, states, and the US nation alike, with corporeal personhood, the born (natal) body, being central, literally or metaphorically, to each "individual" up and down this scale of both characterized and embodied selves: "a national character, an identity." Writing ("including literature, including poems") will express the character of this American "Individuality": "Such character, strong, limber, just, open-mouthed, American-blooded, full of pride, full of ease, of passionate friendliness" – precisely what the casual pose of Whitman's frontispiece image is intended to evoke: a national body as suitable substitute for Brother Jonathan. (See Figure 4.4 of the body of Brother Jonathan, the precursor to Uncle Sam [and parallel to Whitman's vision for himself], spanning the continent.) Whitman expects the nation to love its poets, just as Emerson loved him (that love – "I greet you at the beginning of a great

---

[16] Whitman's association of identity with corporeality is apparent in the poem that this 1856 edition of *Leaves of Grass* titles "Poem of Walt Whitman, and American" and later editions will call "Song of Myself," which asks, "Is this then a touch? .... quivering me to a new identity," where "villain touch" makes identity "new" through a treacherous corporeality whose betrayal is figured metaphorically in terms of international relations among nation-states: "I am given up by traitors"; see Walt Whitman, *Leaves of Grass: The First (1855) Edition*, ed. Malcolm Cowley (Penguin Books, 1986), 53–54.

Nationalism: Character, Identity, and Hyphenation 75

Figure 4.4 *The Stride of a Century*, Currier & Ives, New York, lithograph, 1876. https://lccn.loc.gov/93506699.

career" – having been announced in Emerson's private letter to Whitman, which is printed just prior to Whitman's public reply).

Yet, much as Emerson greets Whitman at the beginning of a great career, so too Whitman's account of national character betrays the nation's own career ambitions: America's achievement of nationality "is a result, and the cause of greater results," these "greater results" suggesting an expansionist potential and ambition. Just as Emerson, whom, again, Whitman addresses throughout this letter as "Master," had written about a Transcendentalist "Over-Soul," so too, for Whitman, the "one enclosing general form" of the national character cannot contain the moral principle (the "supremacy of Individuality") that is supposedly local to, while also being irreducible to, the continental United States: That face turned toward its own bodily identity, "face to face with The States," can also turn itself abroad – indeed, has already done so by referencing the "American continent" (much of which had recently been acquired by a war of conquest with Mexico) without distinguishing Canada, Indigenous nations, or the various nations of Central and South

America from a nationality enclosed (fused, and determined) within those states comprising the United States. This is the imperialist implication of the phrase "with ever-satisfying and ever-unsurveyable seas and shores," where an openness of geographic "survey" confirms that US national character – as "the supremacy of Individuality" embodied by Whitman – might both be local to the nation-continent's physical terrain, its identity, but also reach outward to other seas and shores yet to be surveyed, and this extension would amount to imperial expansion, spreading the American "supremacy of Individuality" abroad as an imposition upon other continents likewise understood as distinct national characters and identities, although that imposition is benevolently imagined by Whitman as what Sumner would call "simply the imperialism of the Declaration of Independence, with all its promises fulfilled," precisely what had just been imposed on the rebellious Confederacy. Defending "America" as a national name for the United States, Sumner writes, "Names . . . grow out of the soil. They are autochthonous," but both he and Whitman envision the autochthonous (chthonian) *genius loci* turned mobile (Olympian) *Genius Mundi*, an expansionist sense of American character and identity that, on the political level of the metaphor, makes the United States look not like an enclosed nation but like an expanding empire and casts Whitman as the prototype of all selves everywhere.[17] This is indeed the principle of Whitman's own "omnivorous lines," each individual line of his catalogues fused to the whole of a poem that admits no principle of delimitation or formal enclosure.[18] Whitman's phrase "These shores you found" ultimately defers to Emerson, casting him less as a "founding father" than as a colonial explorer akin to Columbus, whose discovery of the American continent prompted the imperial principle of the doctrine of discovery.[19] What Whitman's nationalism ultimately celebrates, then, is an imperial "Master" of the Transcendentalist "Over-Soul" whose vision he espouses and to whom he seeks espousal, offering his allegiance and service as solicitous poet-disciple and agent.[20]

---

[17] Sumner, "Are We a Nation?," 27, 26.
[18] Prior to the 1867 edition, this phrase from section 42 of "Song of Myself" read "omnivorous words."
[19] See Robert J. Miller, "The Doctrine of Discovery," in Robert J. Miller, Jacinta Ruru, Larissa Behrendt, and Tracey Lindberg, eds., *Discovering Indigenous Lands: The Doctrine of Discovery in the English Colonies* (Oxford University Press, 2010), 1–25, 11–12.
[20] On Emerson teaching Whitman "lessons from the Master," see Kerry Larson, *Whitman's Drama of Consensus* (University of Chicago Press, 1988), 30–55. On what she calls "Walt Whitman's Poetess poetics," see Virginia Jackson, *Before Modernism* (Princeton University Press, 2023), 193.

Bodily Metaphors, Expressions, and Affections

In Whitman's handling of it, the metaphor of nation as embodied person (having both a moral "character" and a corporeal "identity") enables a version of nationalism that turns out – given the expansionist ambition of that national character's turn toward other seas and shores – to be a barely disguised form of imperialism. Properly understood, nationalism must resist such imperialism, affirming national autonomy rather than permitting "the supremacy of Individuality" to rationalize subsuming all other nations within this overarching imperial framework. Nationalism affirms the dignity of all individual nations as pseudo-selves warranting recognition and deference as autonomous, particular, discrete, and unique collectives or "peoples." Indeed, the physically embodied, and thus actually born, person (with brain and spine) had functioned for centuries, as it does in Whitman's open letter to Emerson, as the metaphor for such national dignity and autonomy.[21] This long-standing strategy of attributing the bodily nativity of persons to nations as similarly discrete, autonomous entities would become highly politically consequential, as Ben Holland has argued, at the dawn of the nation-state era: "Kant," Holland writes,

> described the state as a moral person, and he did so when dealing with the subject of interstate relations or the right of nations. In *Perpetual Peace*, he wrote that the state, like "a trunk, ... has its own roots; and to annex it to another state as a graft is to do away with its existence as a moral person and to make a moral person into a thing."[22]

This anthropomorphic model and metaphor reside, furthermore, at the core of the historical invention of the nation-state as a remedy against precisely such imperialist threats: Legitimized by the nation they serve, itself understood as a moral person, state institutions have, under the international law of nations, a dignity that external imperial aggressors can be held bound to respect, both by treaties between such nation-states and imperial powers and by solidarity among such (mutually acknowledging) nation-states themselves.[23] By attributing the moral dignity and bodily

---

[21] Katherine Verdery notes "the homology between the nation and the individual" in which "Nations, like individuals, are thought to have identities, often based in so-called national characters"; see her "Whither 'Nation' and 'Nationalism'?," 40. For a broader discussion of this nation–person homology, see Patrick Colm Hogan, *Understanding Nationalism: On Narrative, Cognitive Science, and Identity* (Ohio State University Press, 2009), 72, 124–166.

[22] See Ben Holland, "The Perpetual Peace Problem: Kant on Persons and States," *Philosophy and Social Criticism* 46:6 (2017), 599–620, 601–602.

[23] Ben Holland, *The Moral Person of the State: Pufendorf, Sovereignty and Composite Polities* (Cambridge University Press, 2017), chap. 3.

autonomy of persons to nations, this corporeal and anthropomorphic metaphor underwrites an international order with the nation-state at its heart, an era that, according to George W. White, begins when the 1648 Treaty of Westphalia inaugurated the "Westphalian system" whose ongoing viability as a model for geopolitical order scholars continue to assess.[24]

Of course, while all people are in fact born, "peoples" are born only metaphorically (or their claims to it are just that, claims that anthropomorphize peoples as a person), and some scholars of nationalism, seeking to curb what they view as nationalism's excesses, attack this metaphor as incoherent, preferring – if they retain the term "nationalism" at all – to qualify it as ethnic or civic nationalism. Both alternatives, however, are contradictions in terms that, in so being, help make the critical point: Members of a collective, whether ethnic or civic, are not the literal limbs or members of a physical, natal body.[25] Other scholars, trying to rescue nationalism from such attacks, likewise sideline bodily nativity (despite its centrality, etymologically, to nationalism) and, while affirming nationality as made rather than begotten, also resist, as Bernard Yack has phrased it, throwing out the affective baby with nationalism's nativity bathwater.[26] However worthwhile these projects may be (i.e. to resist nationalism by challenging nativity's centrality to it, or to defend nationalism by sidelining nativity as a requirement of it), I seek to do something different with nativity and corporeality here. Focusing on this exclusiveness of the born body that we saw Whitman taking such pains to claim (if only metaphorically) for the American continent so as then to be able to offer it up to the state (much like, as Whitman plays to Emerson, a legitimizing, willing bride to that state), I want to ask, what is the result, politically, for nationalism if one remains committed to it in precisely Whitman's terms of corporeal nativity (a physical "identity" with a distinct "national character"), rather than either dismissing nationalism for its reliance on those natal terms or else committing to nationalism in non-natal terms (each of

---

[24] George W. White, *Nation, State, and Territory: Origins, Evolutions, and Relationships*, Vol. 2 (Rowman and Littlefield, 2004), 123. For a more extended discussion, see Jennifer L. Beard, "The Peace of Westphalia: Words, Writings, and Outrageous Actions," in *The Political Economy of Desire: International Law, Development and the Nation State* (Routledge, 2007), 124–156.

[25] Skeptics of the distinction between civic and ethnic nationalism include Rogers Brubaker, "'Civic' and 'Ethnic' Nationalisms," in *Ethnicity without Groups* (Harvard University Press, 2004), 132–146; Erika Harris, *Nationalism: Theories and Cases* (Edinburgh University Press, 2009), 28–34; and Bernard Yack, "The Myth of the Civic Nation," in *Nationalism and the Moral Psychology of Community* (University of Chicago Press, 2012), 23–43.

[26] See Yack, *Nationalism and the Moral Psychology of Community*, 4.

which denude nationalism of its anthropomorphic moral force as the ethical unit of the person)? What are the results of embracing – as Whitman does – nationalism with natal birth and bodily individuality ("brain and spine to all") at its core?

Such a nationalism encounters an initial pair of representational obstacles that, however, the natal–body metaphor quite promptly ends up solving. Efforts to represent the "character" specific to that natal bodily "identity" must either specify the proper content of that body's national expression or identify the proper objects of that body's national affection. Expressions that represent the national body are what Whitman claims literature, including poems (and especially his own poems), can do, and Emerson, as we have seen, heartily agrees; this is the familiar romantic nationalism of Herder's spirit or *Geist* of the people or *Volk*.[27] But if one does not agree with Emerson that Whitman is the proper expression of American national character – some might consider Emily Dickinson or Phillis Wheatley, for instance, to be a better way of representing it – then uncertainty arises about what the continental bodily identity's proper expression actually is, about what accurately represents it, and this precipitates debate about the true content of that continental body's character. Similarly, efforts to identify the corporeal nation's proper expressions can produce exactly the opposite problem for natal nationalism: not the embarrassment-of-riches dilemma of choosing among competing expressive options (Whitman or Dickinson or Wheatley?) but an embarrassment of impoverishment, the problem of a fledgling nation not yet having produced any expressions at all, or any yet of any value. Hence the uproar prompted by Sydney Smith's impertinent question, "In the four quarters of the globe, who reads an American book?"[28] Such skepticism prompts efforts to induce the American continental terrain, as national identity, to express its character as a corporeal "voice" whose thematic content or message remains yet to be disclosed – the very problem to which Whitman presented himself as the solution.

Just as identifying the national body's represented expressions poses a challenge for the nativity model (whether it be choosing coherently

---

[27] Marlon Ross, "Romancing the Nation-State: The Poetics of Romantic Nationalism," in Jonathan Arac and Harriet Ritvo, eds., *Macropolitics of Nineteenth-Century Literature: Nationalism, Exoticism, Imperialism* (Duke University Press, 1995), 56–85. For a discussion of Herder with reference to US accounts of both nation and race, see Kwame Anthony Appiah, "Ancestral Voices," *Salmagundi* 188/189 (Fall/Winter 2015), 295–308.
[28] Quoted in Robert Weisbuch, *Atlantic Double-Cross: American Literature and British Influence in the Age of Emerson* (University of Chicago Press, 1986), 12.

among them or discovering any trace of them), so too this body's proper objects of affection are likewise difficult to catalogue in a consistently delimited way. In an 1855 lecture titled "The Ballads," for instance, James Russell Lowell proposes English-language ballads as objects of affection for Americans, but cherishing these as the British do deprives Americans of national autonomy (a challenge to British distinctiveness that Lowell clearly intends).[29] In his 1867 speech "Are We a Nation?," Charles Sumner supports his answer "yes" by listing four "tokens of nationality" as objects of shared affection: the flag, the nation's motto, its name, and its geographic unity; but what about Frederick Douglass's potent question in a speech of 1852 titled "What to the Slave Is the Fourth of July?"[30] Perhaps July 4, 1776, isn't a proper object of affection for Americans – not just for "the Slave" but for anyone who sympathizes with the enslaved, as should all Americans – because the Declaration's and thus the nation's founding promise stands unfulfilled under slavery, and empty promises are not proper objects of affection. Uncertainty about the proper objects of the bodily nation's affection, then, poses a similar problem for representing the national body as its effusive or elusive expressions: As representations of that body that emanate from that body, they are not themselves identical or reducible to that body, so they can lead us away from – even as they pretend to index – the nation "itself" whose bodily "identity" consists of geographical-corporeal physicality.[31]

These problems of sorting among the corporeal nation's various expressions and fugitive affections nevertheless each contain, as I have suggested, the seeds of a solution, what Whitman calls "identity": the corporality to which each approach to representing the nation separately points; the physical body as expression's source and affection's seat. Treating an actual body itself as the point of origin for both expression and affection is the solution that John W. De Forest devises to locate and affirm national continuity in his own attempt to write what his 1868 essay in *The Nation* called "the great American novel," his 1867 novel *Miss Ravenel's Conversion from Secession to Loyalty*. If Whitman treats the nation as a body (his own),

---

[29] See James Russell Lowell, "The Ballads," *Lectures on English Poets* (The Rowfant Club, 1897), 59–75.
[30] Sumner, "Are We a Nation?," 23–29.
[31] This failure of representations to constitute what they represent is helpfully elaborated, with respect to racial rather than national identity, in Walter Benn Michaels's "Autobiography of an Ex-White Man: Why Race Is Not a Social Construction," *No Politics but Class Politics* (Columbia University Press, 2023), 115–130. On the particular relevance of this point to national as well as racial identities, see Paul Gilroy, "Between Camps: Modernity and Infrahumanity," in Philip Spencer and Howard Wollman, eds., *Nations and Nationalism: A Reader* (Rutgers University Press, 2005), 149–162.

De Forest treats a body, Miss Ravenel's, as the nation, and her bodily continuity across the Civil War, which entails shifting both the content of her expressions (from secessionism to loyalty) and the objects of her affections (from men of the South to men of the North), confirms national identity in and through her nationalized physical body's persistence across these expressive and affective changes.[32] Lillie Ravenel's continuity as an expressive source and affective seat is central to the novel: "Baby was for the first time the whole thought, the whole life, of this girl, who a little previous existed through her husband, and before that through her father. Each passion had been stronger than its predecessor; but now she had reached the culminating point of her womanhood: higher than Baby it was impossible for her to go."[33] National continuity, despite the Civil War, is thus to be found in Lillie's bodily continuity across its self-representations in distinct expressions (secession and loyalty) and distinct objects of affection (father, first husband, second husband, and son). Her second husband marvels at how "the two great incidents of maternity and widowhood" have left her "so little changed," and this continuity across change is what, as we have seen, "identity" meant in Whitman – the very continuity across change that a born, physical, natal body guarantees.[34]

Lillie's physical body thus becomes the continuous element of corporeal nationality in De Forest's innovative, postwar account of Union – not, as in Whitman's letter to Emerson, a federal union of the several states but, instead, a marriage of her body as nation with the proper husband as governing state (the very marriage Whitman implies with his "Master," Emerson). No longer subject to her father, Dr. Ravenel (like the American nation under British colonial rule), and no longer married to her first husband, Carter (like the American nation under the Articles of Confederation, which allowed loose fidelity comparable to Carter's extramarital affairs), but now married to a second husband, Colburne (a northerner and thus supporter of the Constitution and Union), Lillie provides De Forest with an identity that these various male characters can encounter (as Whitman did "The States") "face to face," an encounter that produces a hyphenated identity of nation-state as conjugal union, corporeal wife

---

[32] In a hostile contemporary review of De Forest's novel, William Gilmore Simms wrote that "The heroine (Miss Ravenel) ... is converted from secession to loyalty, by appetite rather than argument"; see his "John William De Forest's *Miss Ravenel's Conversion from Secession to Loyalty*," in *William Gilmore Simms's Selected Reviews on Literature and Civilization*, ed. James Everett Kibler, Jr., and David Moltke-Hansen (University of South Carolina, 2015), 176.

[33] John W. De Forest, *Miss Ravenel's Conversion from Secession to Loyalty* (Penguin Books, 2000), 363.

[34] De Forest, *Miss Ravenel's Conversion*, 436.

(Lillie) and rational husband (Colburne). Lillie's body as physical national identity represents the whole continent (including its comprising states – her native South and her adopted North) while her husband, across the conjugal hyphen, serves as the proper character (no longer residually Confederate, as was Carter, and thus more progressively evolved) to govern, as state, Lillie's national affective body as continental corporeality.[35] Here, the nation as the born body of Miss Ravenel can, despite – and indeed because of – her shifting expressions of loyalty and her shifting objects of affection, serve as the corporeal core of a national "identity" on Whitman's (continentally) corporeal model. Though Lillie is female rather than male, domestic rather than public, she is loved by the husband-state as Whitman is loved by the Emerson he calls Master, and her physical fertility stands in for literary poesis, each making Americans in their respective media. As with Whitman, the nation as body is the "identity" ultimately indexed, if variously represented, by Miss Ravenel's inconsistent expressions and shifting objects of affection (not unlike Whitman's own "Do I contradict myself; very well then . . . I contradict myself").[36] De Forest would have Miss Ravenel be the bodily identity for a national character (her second husband, Colburne, the defender of the Union and Constitution) that Whitman likewise offers to Emerson in his letter of espousal of – and simultaneous espousal to – the Transcendentalist principle of "the supremacy of Individuality."

Interracial Corporeality As Imperialist Assimilation

De Forest's postbellum vision of American conjugal union as the hyphenated Lillie-Colburne, bodily national identity plus institutional state character, replicates the Whitman-Emerson combination we saw in the section "Nation or Empire?," and it could seem comparably imperialist for its extension of Colburne's character dominance over Lillie's once-secessionist southern bodily identity. There is a crucial sense, however, in which De Forest's novel – and both Lillie and Colburne – are expressly antiimperialist: They refuse to extend their identity-character union over foreign soil. That soil is the African bodies of those liberated from slavery

---

[35] My sense of "conjugal union" here builds upon Robert Reid-Pharr's use of the term (which he takes from Martin Delany), but while Reid-Pharr associates it with a heteronormativity that "steers us away from . . . homoeroticism" (126), my own example of Whitman soliciting such a union with Emerson belies this constraint; see Robert Reid-Pharr, *Conjugal Union: The Body, the House, and the Black American* (Oxford University Press, 1999). See also the chapter "The Marriage of Nation and State," in Terry H. Pickkett, *Inventing Nations: Justifications of Authority in the Modern World* (Greenwood Press, 1996), 65–77.
[36] Whitman, *Leaves of Grass (1855)*, 85.

by Union troops, people for whom Lillie's father, a medical doctor but also a student of minerology and thus of soil types and qualities, hatches "plans, agricultural and humanitarian," plans requiring that he "make himself analytically acquainted, not only with the elements and possibilities of the soil, but with those of the negro soul."[37] Ravenel's effort to organize freed slaves to till the southern soil is inseparable from a project to seed the "negro soul" with a different crop, that of character: Ravenel "delivered them a lecture on the universal application of the law of honesty," saying "It is your great business, your great duty toward yourselves, to establish a character for perfect honesty and harmlessness."[38] And it is clear to Dr. Ravenel, at least, that cultivating this soil of the "negro soul" will require centuries to counteract their "immemorial degradation, first as savages and then as slaves."[39] Colburne – figure for the Constitution – is thus "too impatient" in expecting more from them: "What right has Captain Colburne to demand roses or potatoes of land which has been sown for centuries with nothing but thistles? We ought to be thankful if it merely lies barren for a while."[40] With the black body thus declared barren, Lillie's fertile body provides continuity across this sequence of men (Colonization, Confederation, Constitution) who each represent the state's character, the result being, for De Forest, two racial tiers of Americanness: Lillie's affective and expressive body is conjoined with Colburne's ideal character to yield an American nation-state via conjugal union; and black bodies (like Whitman's American continent as mere brain and spine – a carcass, a bloat) have identity without a corresponding character and are thus excluded from De Forest's vison of a postwar Union. The result is segregation along bodily-continental and thus racial lines, an American continental body plus character (Lillie-Colburne) and an African-southern continental body (displaced from Africa to the US South) devoid of character for centuries to come.

If De Forest's postbellum Lillie Ravenel presents an anti-imperialist (because racially-continentally segregationist) version of national embodiment, a post-Reconstruction rejoinder to his view, one that is both imperialist and assimilationist, emerges in the tragic mulatta Rhoda Aldgate, featured in William Dean Howells's 1891 novel *An Imperative Duty*. By contrast to De Forest's racial segregation of Lillie, as an expressive and affective US body, from a bodily blackness barren of character (Whitman's continental carcass), Howells includes blackness within the

---

[37] De Forest, *Miss Ravenel's Conversion*, 227. [38] De Forest, *Miss Ravenel's Conversion*, 236.
[39] De Forest, *Miss Ravenel's Conversion*, 235. [40] De Forest, *Miss Ravenel's Conversion*, 244.

individual physical body of his protagonist, who becomes convinced that she *is* black ("I am a negress!") through her aunt's revelation that Rhoda's mother had been an "octoroon."[41] The question this revelation poses is whether black bodies – which were, for De Forest's Dr. Ravenel, the characterless, soulless soil of the continent of Africa – can become part of the continental corporeality of the United States, serving as locations or "identities" for an American "character" like Whitman had imagined, whose "brain and spine" was the American soil. Howells uses Rhoda's aunt, Caroline Meredith, to stage De Forest's segregationist and anti-imperialist nationalism. In terms of "heredity" (57), Aunt Meredith asserts that Rhoda can't have an American character because of potential "atavism," or "the reversion to the inferior race type in the child of parents of mixed blood": "I think that in some occult, dreadful way she feels her affinity with them ... It's her race *calling* her! ... It is the race instinct! It must assert itself sooner or later."[42] Further, given this hereditary tendency, Aunt Meredith believes that she and Rhoda are ethically bound – hence the "imperative duty" of the novel's title – to disclose Rhoda's blackness to a white suitor who, unaware of its bodily presence in her, seeks Rhoda's hand in marriage ("Those ancestral traits, those tendencies, may die out," Aunt Meredith admits, "but I can't let anyone take the risk of their recurrence unknowingly").[43] Arguing against Aunt Meredith, and thus against De Forest's Dr. Ravenel, Howells's presents his own medical doctor, Dr. Olney, who refutes both Aunt Meredith's account of heredity and her judgment of moral duty. "The chances of atavism, or reversion to the black great-great-great-grandfather are so remote that they may be said hardly to exist at all," so the duty to disclose an essentially nonexistent threat essentially dissolves.[44] The more difficult misguided imperative for Olney to challenge is Rhoda's sense that, because "I *am* one," she must also become one: "Oughtn't I to go down there and help them; try to educate them, and elevate them; give my life to them?"[45] Olney replies that had Rhoda "voluntarily chosen" or "ever consented to be of their kind," then "to desert them ... would be a treason of the vilest sort," but since she hadn't, and since her black family relations had never tried to find her, then she is under no moral obligation (except under the foolish, romance-novel-induced extreme of "dutiolatry") to secede from her Americanness – both as character and as

---

[41] William Dean Howells, *An Imperative Duty*, ed. Paul R. Petrie (Broadview Editions, 2010), 115, 63.
[42] Howells, *An Imperative Duty*, 57, 67, 69.   [43] Howells, *An Imperative Duty*, 60.
[44] Howells, *An Imperative Duty*, 58.   [45] Howells, *An Imperative Duty*, 117, 118.

identity – and devote her loyalties to black people as a site of affective intensity (as she had initially intended to do: "I can endure them if I can love them, and I shall love them if I try to help them").⁴⁶ Indeed, her expressions and affections are contradictory, but as with De Forest's convert, Lillie Ravenel, the body provides contradiction with underlying consistency (as it had Whitman: "Do I contradict myself? / Very well then ... I contradict myself"). By enabling Olney to prevent Rhoda's planned secession from whiteness and conversion to black uplift, Howells gives her continuity both as a body (which is white save for "an infinitesimal part") and as a character (in whom "the remote taint of her servile and savage origin gave her a kind of fascination").⁴⁷ Replacing Lillie with Rhoda undoes the racial segregation of De Forest's novel and defies the segregationist Lamarckism of his Dr. Ravenel, who had affirmed "hard Lamarckism" for former slaves (who would need centuries to establish a character for their continentally African bodies) and "soft Lamarckism" for whites (including Lillie's son Ravi who, despite having two southerners for parents, will become, due to being raised by his northern, unionist, and constitutionalist stepfather Colburne, a loyal American in the course of his individual lifetime rather than centuries in the future).⁴⁸

Instead, then, of becoming a traitor to the only corporeal identity and associated character she has ever known, Americanness, Rhoda marries Dr. Olney himself. Her doing so affirms the novel's larger assimilationist vision both in terms of bodily physicality (Olney asserts, "The tame man, the civilized man, is stronger than the wild man; and ... where there are very strong ancestral proclivities ... toward evil, they will die out ... because vice is savage and virtue is civilized") and in terms of moral character (Olney says to Rhoda, "You belong incomparably more to the oppressors than to the oppressed").⁴⁹ Howells's vision of national identity and character, then, locates continuity in a bodily identity that is racially-continentally-corporeally mixed rather than (as was the case with Miss Ravenel) racially-continentally-corporeally pure (though continent-spanning, as Lillie moves from South to North), the mixture advancing imperialism and the purity, nationalism. Like the feminized Whitmanian bride exchanging love letters with an Emersonian "Master," and like Lillie coming to espouse the views of, and coming to be espoused to, Colburne and the Constitution, Rhoda is made a bodily locus of expression and

---

⁴⁶ Howells, *An Imperative Duty*, 117, 114, 111, 91. ⁴⁷ Howells, *An Imperative Duty*, 118, 111.
⁴⁸ On the distinction between hard and soft Lamarckism, see George Stocking, "The Turn-of-the-Century Concept of Race," *Modernism/modernity* 1:1 (1994), 4–16, 16.
⁴⁹ Howells, *An Imperative Duty*, 58, 118.

affection that is itself governed by a rational male character as state such that the hyphenation of conjugal union, Rhoda-Olney, nation-state, once again conjoins identity-character. Rhoda's transcontinental corporeality (including both Africa and America) underscores Howells's ultimately assimilationist and imperialist vision for Rhoda-Olney. Olney observes of the recently arrived Irish, "We can predicate of a brother Teuton that this will please him, and that will vex him, but we can't of an Irishman," adding that "the Irish ... seem more foreign to our intelligence, our way of thinking, than the Jews – or the negroes, even," but if "the transition from the Old World to the New, as represented in them, was painful," Olney nevertheless considers the Irish to be "adoptive citizens."[50] Though slow to assimilate, they will do so eventually, catching up to the more assimilated, though currently segregated, "colored people" – an inversion of Dr. Ravenel's use of hard Lamarckism for former slaves and soft Lamarckism for German and Irish immigrants.[51] Yet Whitman's "supremacy of Individuality" will ultimately apply to both and, by implication, all. Indeed, Rhoda and Olney live abroad, in Italy, exporting as a couple their American dyad of moral character married to transcontinental corporeal identity and thus demonstrating this national conjunction of American body-American character, or Rhoda-Olney, to look toward other seas and shores, in the same assimilationist and imperialist manner as had Whitman's Emerson-induced and Emerson-endorsed imperialism of the "supremacy of Individuality."

Internationalism Within: Intra-natalism As Hyphenated Selfhood

Howells's integrationist and cosmopolitan answer to De Forest's segregationist vision for the postbellum US nation faced resistance in terms expressed three years later by W. E. B. Du Bois in "The Afro-American": "The majority of us," Du Bois writes, "are not of pure Negro blood, and therefore, as a people, cannot be described as Negroes; neither we nor our ancestors for generations were born in Africa and thus we are not African. We describe ourselves by the perhaps awkward, but certainly more accurate term of Afro-American."[52] This term's hyphen marks a "fissure into a white and black hemisphere. These two halves ... are adjacent and not superimposed spheres," echoing what De Forest, in his 1867 essay "The Great

---

[50] Howells, *An Imperative Duty*, 50, 36, 37.   [51] Howells, *An Imperative Duty*, 38.
[52] W. E. B. Du Bois, "The Afro-American" (c.1894), *The Problem of the Color Line at the Turn of the Twentieth Century: The Essential Early Essays*, ed. Nahum Dimitri Chandler (Fordham University Press, 2015), 33–50, 34.

Nationalism: Character, Identity, and Hyphenation 87

American Novel," had called "provinces."⁵³ The overtly spatial and geographic elements of Du Bois's phrasing here ("adjacent," "hemispheres") disappear from his subsequent account of this hyphenation, "double-consciousness," which first appears three years later in an essay published in *The Atlantic Monthly*. And while the 1894 version had cast this hyphenation in terms of deficit (hence an Afro-American is neither fully a Negro nor fully an African), Du Bois's 1897 formulation presents "double-consciousness" not as deficit but as surplus: "One ever feels his two-ness – an American, a Negro, two souls, two thoughts, two unreconciled strivings; two warring ideals in one dark body, whose dogged strength alone keeps it from being torn asunder."⁵⁴ In contrast to Howells's Rhoda, to whom Howells's narrator attributes "the double consciousness of trouble" in which "the world of misery within her" confronts an emotionally neutral external world "about her" (87), Du Bois's doubleness involves two circumstances that are both within: "two warring ideals in one dark body."⁵⁵ Yet in "ever feel[ing] his two-ness," Du Bois implies that he observes each of his consciousnesses – "an American, a Negro" – from a vantage distinct from both, suggesting a third space ultimately resembling a "third" self that Howells's narrator attributes to Rhoda: "There seemed two selves of her, one that had lived before that awful knowledge, and one that had lived as long since, and again a third that knew and pitied them both."⁵⁶ This "third" self in Rhoda observes two distinct temporal moments (one "before" and the other "long since" she gained "that awful knowledge" of her distant African ancestry), whereas the self who, for Du Bois, "ever feels his two-ness" observes what are not different times of knowing but different places of being: a white soul and a black one, each consciousness inhabiting a distinct continental-corporeal soil and doing battle with its corporeally geopolitical neighbor: "two unreconciled strivings; two warring ideals." From his third position above the fray, however, Du Bois can offer advice for managing the internalized race relations of "double-consciousness": the Negro "does not wish to Africanize America, for America has too much to teach the world and Africa; he does not wish to bleach his Negro blood in a flood of white Americanism, for he believes – foolishly, perhaps, but fervently – that Negro blood has yet a message for the world."⁵⁷

---

[53] Du Bois, "The Afro-American," 35.
[54] W. E. B. Du Bois, "Strivings of the Negro People" (1897), in *The Problem of the Color Line*, 67–75, 68.
[55] Howells, *An Imperative Duty*, 87.   [56] Howells, *An Imperative Duty*, 86.
[57] Du Bois, "Strivings of the Negro People," 69.

While Du Bois casts the dilemma of "double consciousness" in terms of race rather than nation, I have tried to suggest, instead, that it is better understood as a matter of two or more nations seeking state recognition and protection in a corporeally and cognitively interiorized international arena, the individual "consciousness."[58] The individual body that was long supposed, due to its inviolable natal singularity, to figure a privileged entity, a nation, the autonomy of which should be preserved by post-Westphalian international law, has here in effect swallowed whole that very international order so as to stage that order's geopolitical conflicts of competing national interests as internal conflicts between rival hemispheres within the multiracial self, a self whose consciousness adjudicates conflicts between the nations-races internal to it.[59] The ethical dilemma faced by such a self will be whether it will act as an evolved, post-Westphalian internationalist, respecting the nationality-as-personhood of its distinct interior nations (as Du Bois does by urging black Americans to conserve their Africanness as double-consciousness), or else as an atavistic pre-Westphalian imperialist, imposing one nation's sway over others (as Whitman is disposed to do in espousing Emerson's "supremacy of Individuality" for all).[60] The corporeal-natal comparison of nations to persons gives the post-Westphalian position of Du Bois the ethical upper hand: One's imperative duty is to allow nations or races to be themselves, as Du Bois himself does with respect to his blackness, checking his Americanness rather than imperially imposing it upon the Africa within him, thus permitting time for the barren soil of his Negro hemisphere to cultivate and harvest its "message for the world."[61]

This win for internationalism – the insistence on being hyphenated rather than not – is also, however, a win for Whitman in his espousal of and espousal to Emerson, and in several ways. One way is that in adopting Whitman's model of an American national character and identity, which is one of the key concepts in Du Bois's internalized internationalism (and

---

[58] As Raymond Williams observes, race and nation were interchangeable terms for much of the nineteenth century; see Williams, "Nationalist," 160.

[59] Raymond Williams notes that "internationalism, which refers to relations between nation-states, is not the opposite of nationalism in the context of a subordinate political group seeking its own distinct identity; it is only the opposite of selfish and competitive policies between existing political nations" (Williams, "Nationalist," 160–161); Williams associates these selfish and competitive policies with "Imperialism" in his *Keywords*, 112–113.

[60] Du Bois advocates conserving racial groups against their dissolution by atomized individualism in "The Conservation of Races" (1897), in *The Problem of the Color Line*, 51–65, 53.

[61] Du Bois, "Strivings of the Negro People," 69. This essay, retitled "Of Our Spiritual Strivings," became the first chapter of Du Bois's *The Souls of Black Folk* (1903).

that of every hyphenated American), double-consciousness grants Whitman's model of continental nationality more broadly: The character and identity of America as Whitman imagines it (i.e. as himself) have their counterpart in each continent (the character and identity of Africa, the character and identity of Asia, the character and identity of Europe, much like Britain had its John Bull and America its Brother Jonathan). Another win for the Whitmanian espousal to Emerson is that this international-interracial order governed by and within the individual self elevates the self to a position of supranational oversight of its multiple internal continents and their relationships. This oversight requires an over-soul superintending relationships between the "two souls" potentially warring within the self, which promotes the self above each of those competing continental races to the position of international arbiter, or imperial "rector," responsible for overseeing both and adjudicating their disputes.[62] This self-promotion to proconsular governance of autonomous internal provinces or hemispheres of the self thus affirms – as Whitman affirmed of Emerson as his "Master" – the ultimate Americanness of his and Emerson's "supremacy of Individuality," which becomes an exportable American exceptionalism at the site of – and as the governing and enabling condition of – selfhood understood as a stable international order located within the hyphenated American.[63] At the core of every hyphenated self, then, is the espoused Transcendentalist Emerson, author of "The Over-Soul" (1841), whom Whitman called "Master" and whose first published work, *Nature* (1836), infamously imagined the self as a "transparent eye-ball": "Standing on the bare ground, – my head bathed by the blithe air, and uplifted into infinite space, – all mean egotism vanishes. I become a transparent eye-ball; I am nothing; I see all; the currents of the Universal Being circulate through me; I am part or particle of God" (see Figure 4.5).[64] It is this

---

[62] Eighteenth-century theories of international law similarly envision, as Ben Holland observes in *The Moral Person of the State*, "a person of international standing, a *rector*" (118) whose "authority" the "moral personae of the individual states must accept" as they form a "composite polity" that is itself modeled, Holland argues, on "the German Empire" (120), the very same imperial entity for which Du Bois, according to Kenneth Barkin, had a "lifelong affection"; see Kenneth Barkin, "W. E. B. Du Bois' Love Affair with Imperial Germany," *German Studies Review* 28:2 (2005), 285–302, 285.
[63] For a related account that calls Du Bois's work "transnational cosmopolitanism," see Inés Valdez, *Transnational Cosmopolitanism: Kant, Du Bois, and Justice As a Political Craft* (Cambridge University Press, 2019), 102. See also Vilashini Cooppan's discussion of what she calls Du Bois's "psychic politics of place" in *Worlds Within: National Narratives and Global Connections in Postcolonial Writing* (Stanford University Press, 2009), 98–139.
[64] Ralph Waldo Emerson, *Nature*, in *Essays and Lectures* (Library of America, 1983), 10.

Figure 4.5 *I Become a Transparent Eyeball*, Christopher Pearse Cranch, manuscript drawing (recto), undated. https://digital.tcl.sc.edu/digital/collection/myerson/id/566/.

ultimately Emersonian, Transcendentalist vantage that authorizes an interiorized internationalism of hyphenated selfhood sufficient to resist the "mean egotism" of colonialist imperialism and guarantee the autonomy and bodily integrity of each of the continental-racial nations located within the corporeal/continental self. This is the self whose dissemination across the United States and export abroad provides the rationale for twentieth- and twenty-first-century selves to believe that their stories of Whitman's American identity-character line are stories of the racial color line and that their commitments to interiorized multinationalism/multiracialism are an alternative to, rather than evidence of, embracing an exceptionalist nineteenth-century American imperialism.

Further Reading

Baker, Anne. *Heartless Immensity: Literature, Culture, and Geography in Antebellum America*. University of Michigan Press, 2006.
Berthold, Dennis. *American Risorgimento: Herman Melville and the Cultural Politics of Italy*. Ohio State University Press, 2009.
Breuilly, John. "Introduction: Concepts, Approaches, Theories." In John Breuilly, ed., *The Oxford Handbook of the History of Nationalism*. Oxford University Press, 2013, 1–18.
Breuilly, John. *Nationalism and the State*, 2nd ed. University of Chicago Press, 1994.
Breuilly, John. "On the Principle of Nationality." In Gareth Stedman Jones and Gregory Claeys, eds., *The Cambridge History of Nineteenth-Century Political Thought*. Cambridge University Press, 2011, 77–109.
Fleche, Andre M. *The Revolution of 1861: The American Civil War in the Age of Nationalist Conflict*. University of North Carolina Press, 2012.
Gado, Frank. "Asserting a National Voice." In Alfred Bendixen and Stephen Burt, eds., *The Cambridge History of American Poetry*. Cambridge University Press, 2014, 155–176.
Gellner, Ernest. *Nations and Nationalism*. 2nd ed. Cornell University Press, 2009.
Grant, Susan-Mary. "Making History: Myth and the Construction of American Nationhood." In Geoffrey Hosking and George Schöpflin, eds., *Myths and Nationhood*. Routledge, 1997, 88–106.
Gross, Robert A. "Building a National Literature: The United States 1800–1890." In Simon Eliot and Jonathan Roses, eds., *A Companion to the History of the Book*. Blackwell Publishing, 2007, 315–328.
Harris, William C. *E Pluribus Unum: Nineteenth-Century American Literature and the Constitutional Paradox*. University of Iowa Press, 2005.
Havard, John C. *Hispanicism and Early US Literature: Spain, Mexico, Cuba, and the Origins of US National Identity*. University of Alabama Press, 2018.
Immerwahr, Daniel. *How to Hide an Empire: A Short History of the Greater United States*. Farrar, Straus and Giroux, 2019.
Laitin, David D. *Nations, States, and Violence*. Oxford University Press, 2007.
Leoussi, Athena S., ed. *Encyclopaedia of Nationalism*. Transaction Publishers, 2001.
Levander, Caroline F. *Voices of the Nation: Women and Public Speech in Nineteenth-Century American Literature and Culture*. Cambridge University Press, 1998.
Levine, Robert. *Dislocating Race and Nation: Episodes in Nineteenth-Century American Literary Nationalism*. University of North Carolina Press, 2008.

Matt, Michael. "A Political Theory of Nationalism and Its Excesses." In Sukumar Periwal, ed., *Notions of Nationalism*. Central European University Press, 1995, 44–64.

Pollard, Finn. *The Literary Quest for an American National Character*. Routledge, 2009.

Ross, Dorothy. "'Are We a Nation?': The Conjuncture of Nationhood and Race in the United States, 1850–1876." *Modern Intellectual History* 2:3 (2005), 327–360.

Schmidt, Peter. *Sitting in Darkness: New South Fiction, Education, and the Rise of Jim Crow Colonialism, 1865–1920*. University Press of Mississippi, 2010.

Unger, Frank. "Are We Dreaming? Exceptional Myths and Myths of Exceptionalism in the United States." In Sima Godfrey and Frank Unger, eds., *The Shifting Foundations of Modern Nation-States: Realignments of Belonging*. University of Toronto Press, 2004, 82–99.

Walker, Cheryl. *Indian Nation: Native American Literature and Nineteenth-Century Nationalisms*. Duke University Press, 1997.

Wells, Jeremy. *Romances of the White Man's Burden: Race, Empire, and the Plantation in American Literature, 1880–1936*. Vanderbilt University Press, 2011.

Woodard, Colin. *American Nations: A History of the Eleven Rival Regional Cultures of North America*. Viking, 2011.

CHAPTER 5

Communitarianism and Its Literary Contexts
David Faflik

However much the American nineteenth century can be associated with the emergence of a nationally distinctive brand of individualism, the historical period extending from the Revolution to the First World War was equally an era of the collective. This was more than a matter of Americans belatedly acknowledging in these years the political implications that came from regarding themselves as a totality en masse. As Michael Walzer reminds us, the politics of any time or place is only ever concerned with "the connection of constituted selves, the pattern of social relations."[1] Rather, Americans' interest in a *communitarian* ethos grew pronounced enough in the nineteenth century that they adopted a corresponding –ism to distinguish a particular strain of their socially minded sentiments from a more traditional politics. For several generations of Americans, this spirit of communitarianism was to apply a collectivist logic to everything from housing conditions to labor relations to the habits of family organization, the better to help the citizens of the United States make sense of the sweeping transformations that attended the specific local instantiations of urbanization, industrialization, and the changing dynamics of group association in a modern age.

Less well appreciated than the self's general orientation toward society are the *literary* ramifications that communitarianism carried for Americans in that day. As a hallmark of communitarian complaint, for example, the critique of liberal society that Karl Marx and Friedrich Engels advanced in *The Communist Manifesto* (1848) has long been a touchstone for many a subsequent indictment of the fragmentation of modern intellectual and cultural life. Meanwhile the comparative "coherence" and "connection" that Walzer again says accrue to the concept (and lived reality) of community in its "narrative capacity" have more quietly come to function as a corelative, relationally oriented foil for any storytelling practice that would insist on rendering an individualistic account of a self that had

[1] Michael Walzer, "The Communitarian Critique of Liberalism," *Political Theory* 18:1 (1990), 6–23, 21.

somehow been severed from society.² "The narrative of any one life is part of an interlocking set of narratives," Alasdair MacIntyre explains.³ And, as a sizable number of US authors demonstrated, any such story was relatable precisely because it was *relational*, which is to say attuned to the self's necessary ties to the community in which it figured as a constituent part.

This is not to conflate literary communitarianism with the loosely affiliated notion of the "imagined community," any more than it is to suggest that the topical or rhetorical use of a community for storytelling purposes must qualify as the type of communitarianism under examination here.⁴ For readers and writers of the nineteenth century, *communitarianism* referred at once to a unique social, political, religious, and literary form. As was the case with the self's relation to society, those forms overlapped, adding to the mutual complexities of each. But not even the blurring of such formal categories would have led the original creators or consumers of "the commune" to think they were partaking of anything but the singular experiment in socio-literary engineering that was signaled to them by the communitarian name. By the standards of the nineteenth century, communitarianism can be defined as the voluntary attempt by a like-minded people to establish a local model community that would then be emulated, and perhaps duplicated, by society at large. The men and women who enlisted in such an enterprise typically cohabited together in some communal domestic arrangement, with or without dividing the attendant labors of the community between them on a basis of something other than sex. Such work as the members of the settlement did undertake (agriculture, handicrafts, light manufactures, etc.) was frequently intended to be not only profitable enough to allow the community to sustain itself over time; it would serve as proof, too, of how a more equitable, life-affirming alternative to the corrosive competition and deadening routines of "free" market capitalism could operate in an industrial age.

Communitarianism in America had deep colonial roots, beginning with the model religious societies founded in the early eighteenth century by German pietist sects at places like Ephrata (in what is now Lancaster County, Pennsylvania) and continuing thereafter with a series of Shaker settlements in New York, Pennsylvania, and surrounding territories.

---

² Walzer, "The Communitarian Critique," 9.
³ Alasdair MacIntyre, *After Virtue: A Study in Moral Theory* (1981; rept. Bloomsbury, 2013), 253.
⁴ On the "imagined community," see Benedict Anderson, *Imagined Communities: Reflections on the Origin and Spread of Nationalism* (Verso, 1983). On the use of the boardinghouse as a communal narrative device, refer to David Faflik, *Boarding Out: Inhabiting the American Urban Literary Imagination, 1840–1860* (Northwestern University Press, 2012).

Many, if not all, of these early American religious communities were raised on the millenarian expectations of their founders, as residents either announced or anticipated with their respective perfectionist ventures the arrival of a veritable kingdom of heaven on earth. Even outside of this cataclysmic, world-changing context – throughout its history, the American commune has reflected a native impulse for reform instead of revolution – communitarianism in America has, to a certain extent, recalled a Protestant Christian communitarian tradition exemplified by the egalitarian principles and collectivist practices of the apostles in the New Testament.[5] Yet, beginning with the national attention that was afforded the founding, in 1825, of the New Harmony settlement in Indiana, the brainchild of the British philanthropist, reformer, and socialist Robert Owen, communitarianism in America began to take on a more explicitly secular utopian cast. American socialism was no more synonymous with communitarianism in the nineteenth century than any of the other political ideologies that were then available in the United States. The communitarian worldview that took hold in the country nevertheless proved especially amenable to the socialist program, dedicated as it was to effecting wholesale social and institutional change through collective action. Whether sectarian or secular, communitarianism in America achieved a broad enough appeal to enjoy what can only be viewed in retrospect as a golden age of nearly a century's duration.

Not only did communitarianism depend for its appeal on a promotional literature that was normally composed and distributed at communitarians' expense; the very idea of the commune began to reappear as an informing subject matter, image, and plot device inside a diverse body of contemporary American fiction and nonfiction. As early as 1808, US Shakers would publish the first complete work to expound their communitarian body of principles, *The Testimony of Christ's Second Appearing*. Having been brought before the public, as indicated by its title page, in accordance with the communal ideal of "union," this "Shaker Bible," as it was widely known, in fact initiated a forty-year period in which a continuing transatlantic fascination with the Shakers developed into a more comprehensive vision of communitarian social reform.[6] Authors from Alexis de Tocqueville and Charles Dickens to the Americans Nathaniel Hawthorne and Herman Melville thought about

---

[5] Yaacov Oved, *Two Hundred Years of American Communes* (Transaction Books, 1988), 370–371.
[6] *The Testimony of Christ's Second Appearing, Containing a General Statement of All Things Pertaining to the Faith and Practice of the Church of God in this Latter-Day. Published in Union. By Order of the Ministry* (From the Press of John McLean, Office of The Western Star, 1808).

and sometimes wrote about the Shakers whom they traveled out of their accustomed paths to visit.[7] That they should have done so suggests they regarded communitarianism, as did many observers, not merely as a fad but as an elusive symbol of certain "American" tendencies that traced back into the nation's past. Already with the drafting of the Mayflower Compact, for example, the English settlers at Plymouth had set an important New World precedent when they revealed their readiness to organize freely into groups. By the close of the colonial period, moreover, the founders would devise a federalist system of governance under the US Constitution that apportioned political responsibilities between a central government and the states. They thereby reinforced in such accompanying publications as *The Federalist Papers* (1788) what Arthur Bestor describes as an American proclivity for "political experiment on a small scale," or what he calls a "counterpart of the communitarian philosophy, with its conception of the community as an insulate laboratory for testing social measures."[8]

Still, Americans prepared for their reception of communitarianism as much by looking forward as backward. The prior experiences of both the religious communities and colonial patriots might have been instructive, in other words, in displaying the benefits of the close-knit community. But it was the present-day tensions that had begun to appear between capital and labor in the 1820s, most notably over the introduction of workplace measures that eroded long-standing artisanal traditions, that helped to foster an environment in which more and more Americans would indicate a willingness to entertain communitarian solutions to a set of problems pertaining to their crafts. These responses could be as reactionary as they were progressive, meaning that the "politics" of communitarianism did not rule out the possibility that the subscribers to communitarian views in this period might occasionally take up what can only be characterized as

---

[7] Tocqueville never mentions the Shakers by name in *Democracy in America* (1835), but his reflections there on religious extremism stem from his attendance at a Shaker meeting outside Albany, New York. Dickens later visited a nearby Shaker settlement in the same state, leaving a record of his impressions in *American Notes for General Circulation* (1842). Hawthorne, for his part, published a pair of Shaker tales in the gift book annual *The Token*: "The Shaker Bridal" (1833) and "The Canterbury Pilgrims" (1838). And Melville, having toured the Shaker settlement near his Arrowhead estate in Pittsfield, Massachusetts, featured a deranged Shaker character in a chapter, "The Jeroboam's Story," from his romance *Moby-Dick* (1851).

[8] Arthur Bestor, *Backwoods Utopias: The Sectarian Origins and the Owenite Phase of Communitarian Socialism in America, 1663–1829* (University of Pennsylvania Press, 1950), 18–19. Bestor claims that communitarian writers sometimes argued from the example of US federalism, as did Robert Owen's New Harmony associate William Maclure in his multivolume *Opinions on Various Subjects* (1830–).

a conservative political position.⁹ The moralist, nationalist campaigns of agrarian reformers against what they perceived to be the runaway commerce and political corruption of the age are telling in this respect. On the whole, however, Americans were attracted to communitarianism not despite but because of the radicalism that attached to it. Not a few of them were thus inclined to greet with favor the likes of Robert Owen's experimental ideas relating to family and community formation when these began to appear inside the United States as early as 1817, by means of the nationwide circulation of the British weeklies. They were no less receptive to Owen's US newspaper, the *New Harmony Gazette*, which, from the time of its establishment, in 1825, increased the American readership for communitarianism enough to afford it the status of a legitimate discursive community.¹⁰

The national audience for a politics of the communitarian persuasion enjoyed its earliest support among the labor advocates and trade unionists who comprised the rank-and-file members of next-generation communities like New Harmony, as well as the short-lived imitations of this model factory town that sprang up in the vicinity of New York, Philadelphia, Pittsburgh, and Cincinnati. But the form of communitarianism (and its literary equivalent) would enter a new phase with the expansion of this audience into the American middle classes. Leading the way in this development was the French utopian socialist Charles Fourier. By the end of the second decade of the nineteenth century, Fourier, who is credited today as a pioneer of the modern social sciences, had already composed two dense and difficult volumes that expounded the "scientific" basis of his communitarian philosophy. Like so many of his brethren, the Frenchman attributed the ills of modern life to the unhealthy competition of the liberal marketplace. Unlike his fellow communitarians, Fourier propounded an oddly detailed solution to what he had decided was rotten in the nineteenth-century West. The lynchpin in his plan was the archetypal community he named the phalanx. Here, a population of 1,620 inhabitants from varied backgrounds and social strata would rotate through such occupations as were afforded them by the surrounding fields, workshops, and cultural institutions that would exist on site at any given

---

⁹ Craig Calhoun, *The Roots of Radicalism: Tradition, the Public Sphere, and Early Nineteenth-Century Social Movements* (University of Chicago Press, 2012), 21, 30.
¹⁰ The *New Harmony Gazette* appeared under that title from 1825 to 1828, at which time it was reconstituted as the *Free Enquirer*. Beginning in 1829, Owen's son, Robert Dale Owen, and the labor reformer Frances Wright removed the paper from Indiana to New York, where they continued publishing it until 1835.

phalanx. Fourier's underlying analysis of the variable "passions" that he associated with different types of human personalities determined when, where, and whether any given individual worked within his community. Not only was the embrace of this flexible organizational principle meant to counteract the stultifying effects of heightened workplace regimentation; it also applied to the living arrangements inside the phalanx's dormitory-style housing facility, or phalanstery, where the nuclear family would be replaced by a social system in which children were to be raised in common and sexual relationships between consenting adults were to be nonpermanent and nonbinding. Neglected in his home country until the July Revolution of 1830, when a circle of French intellectuals took inspiration from Fourier's work in launching a movement for humanitarian reform, Fourier did not quite live to see a redacted (and morally sanitized) version of his writings undergo a renaissance in the United States beginning in the early 1840s. The introduction of his ideas to a more inclusive American readership nevertheless raised the commune to its peak position of US influence during the decade that followed. Within that same ten-year period, some thirty phalanxes would be founded over a geographic area that stretched from New England as far west as Iowa. Such was the fanfare greeting Fourierism that the publicity it generated helped to elevate communitarianism from being a minority culture in the antebellum United States to a culture of and for the mass of Americans.

Fourier's communitarian plan would be broadcast domestically through an array of different outlets. Some of these were in accord with the Frenchman's "science," while others were not. Among the leading evangelists of Fourierism in the United States was Albert Brisbane, who, after studying under the master himself in France during the 1830s, returned to his native New York to found the Fourier Society there in 1839 ahead of publishing his popular distillation of "Associationist" (as the American iteration of Fourierism was known) ideas in his first and most celebrated book, *Social Destiny of Man* (1840).[11] The impact of that work was great enough to see Brisbane receive, in short order, an invitation to contribute a regular column on Associationism to the editor Horace Greeley's high-profile *New-York Tribune* newspaper. Although Greeley was an outspoken proponent of a range of socialist reforms, his politics were anything but "countercultural," as Adam-Max Tuchinsky claims.[12] Indeed, another

---

[11] Also see Brisbane's follow-up work, *Association; or, A Concise Exposition of the Practical Part of Fourier's Social Science* (1843).
[12] Adam-Max Tuchinsky, *Horace Greeley's "New-York Tribune": Civil War-Era Socialism and the Crisis of Free Labor* (Cornell University Press, 2009), 10–11.

member of the *Tribune*'s stable of writers, its German-born European correspondent Karl Marx, later dismissed the broadsheet of his sometime employer by saying it had been published "under the guise of ... philanthropic socialistic anti-industrialism," when in fact, and in Marx's estimation, it was the voice of the "industrial bourgeoisie."[13] Compromised or not, Greeley's *Tribune* provided an important forum for Associationism in the United States, and the nineteen months during which the paper carried Brisbane's column represented a pivotal moment in the lifespan of the communitarian cause. Before long, enthusiasts in some two dozen American cities and towns had launched Associationist "unions" dedicated to the dissemination of the utopian socialist point of view. To this end, they met regularly to discuss Fourier's ideas, held public lectures for the same purpose, and launched such modified Associationist ventures as cooperative stores and urban communes. By 1846, when an assortment of the country's related clubs federated as the American Union of Associationists, headquartered in New York, Fourier's American disciples could count as many as 100,000 supporters. Together they heralded what they announced was a "New Industrial World." More to the point, from the participating phalanxes and the American Union there flowed forth a steady stream of some seventy Associationist pamphlets and books that ensured communitarianism's distinction as a nineteenth-century literary phenomenon.[14]

A fair index of this literary output is provided by the example of Brook Farm. Founded in West Roxbury, Massachusetts in 1841 by the Unitarian minister turned transcendentalist reformer George Ripley, this particular utopian settlement, situated on 170 rural acres fifteen miles southwest of Boston, attracted attention up and down the eastern seaboard of the United States, not least because of the quality and comparative conspicuousness of its writerly activities. Ripley, for his part, set a lyrical tone for his joint-stock project in the letter he penned to his friend Ralph Waldo Emerson on November 9, 1840, outlining the scope of the community he planned. Of Brook Farm, Ripley wrote, "If wisely executed, it will be a light over this country and this age. If not the sunrise, it will be the morning star."[15] Emerson himself of course was a writer of no mean reputation at this time, on the eve of the publication of his first series of *Essays* (1841). He was, accordingly, quick to recognize the literary

---

[13] Tuchinsky, *Horace Greeley*, 11.
[14] Carl J. Guarneri, *The Utopian Alternative: Fourierism in Nineteenth-Century America* (Cornell University Press, 1991), 3.
[15] From *Emerson: Political Writings*, ed. Kenneth S. Sacks (Cambridge University Press, 2008), 95.

implications of communitarianism in a way that perhaps others were not. Barely a week before Emerson had received Ripley's letter, a statement that effectively reinforced the private pressure the leading spokesperson for New England transcendentalism was under to join Brook Farm, he had informed his own correspondent, the British author Thomas Carlyle, of the flurry of words being written on behalf of projects not unlike the one at West Roxbury. "We are all a little wild here with numberless projects of social reform," Emerson declared. "Not a reading man but has the draft of a new Community in his waistcoat pocket."[16] As it turned out, Emerson would resist the offer to remove his family to Brook Farm, wrapped up as he was in his own struggles to reconcile his views on the self's relation to society.[17] His hesitation did not prevent him from airing his views on the matter at hand in his journal, where he memorably captures Brook Farm on the page as a paradox of modern rootlessness:

> I wished to be convinced, to be thawed, to be made nobly mad by the kindlings before my eye of a new dawn of human piety. But this scheme was arithmetic and comfort: this was a hint borrowed from the Tremont House and United States Hotel; a rage in our poverty and politics to live rich and gentlemanlike, an anchor leeward against a change of weather; a prudent forecast on the probable issue of the great questions of Pauperism and Poverty. And not once could I be inflamed, but sat aloof and thoughtless; my voice faltered and fell. It was not the cave of persecution which is the palace of spiritual power, but only a room in the Astor House hired for Transcendentalists.[18]

Emerson's occasional Concord, Massachusetts, neighbor Nathaniel Hawthorne hewed to a similar skepticism in his more famous writing on Brook Farm, the *roman-à-clef The Blithedale Romance* (1852). If Hawthorne's *Blithedale* cannot lay claim to being the first communitarian novel (a likelier candidate would be Étienne Cabet's *Voyage en Icarie*, from 1840, the motive force behind a French-based utopian "Icarian" socialist movement that established a series of egalitarian communes in the states of Texas, Illinois,

---

[16] Letter from Ralph Waldo Emerson, in Cambridge, Massachusetts, to Thomas Carlyle, October 30, 1840, in *The Correspondence of Thomas Carlyle and Ralph Waldo Emerson, 1834–1872*, Vol. 1 (Chatto & Windus, Piccadilly, 1883), 308.
[17] Sam McGuire Worley, *Emerson, Thoreau, and the Role of the Cultural Critic* (State University of New York Press, 2001), xi–xii; and Stanley Cavell, *Conditions Handsome and Unhandsome: The Constitution of Emersonian Perfectionism. The Carus Lectures, 1988* (University of Chicago Press, 1990), 4, 37.
[18] See Emerson's journal entry for October 17, 1840. From *Journals and Miscellaneous Notebooks of Ralph Waldo Emerson, Vol. 7: 1838–1842*, ed. A. W. Plumstead and Harrison Hayford (The Belknap Press of Harvard University Press, 1969), 407–408.

Iowa, Missouri, and California), his six months' residence as a joint stockholder at Brook Farm did enable him to do more than idly speculate about a communitarian future.

As it turned out, the commune in its mid-century phase would lend itself more to a serial form of literary representation than book-length treatment. On the one hand, Fourierist-inspired communities in the United States would seldom endure for more than a few years' time. This was as much the result of poor planning by the founders and members of American communes as it was what Carl Guarneri calls the Fourierists' "ambiguous blend of capitalist means with communitarian ends."[19] On the other hand, one of the communitarians' usual moves was to establish an in-house printing press and journal, with the interrelated aim of turning a profit from any printing job they might perform while also positioning themselves to foster the spread of their Associationist beliefs. Whether profitable or political (or both), the communitarian periodical thus tended to facilitate more of a short form of writing in keeping with the restrictions of its limited length and format. Surely the most influential literary organ of this kind was Brook Farm's *The Harbinger*, which, in its run from 1845 to 1849, functioned as an immediate replacement for Albert Brisbane's comparable periodical *The Phalanx* (1843–1845) as well as John Allen's *The Social Reformer and Herald of Universal Health* (1844–1845). Practically speaking, *The Harbinger* added emphasis – in public and in print – to Brook Farm's transition to Fourierism in 1843–1844. It would, in addition to supplying a reliable source of income for the Association (an annual subscription cost two dollars), provide a platform for the further championing of the commune in all its many shapes and sizes.

Artistically, *The Harbinger* was no less at the cutting edge of the latest developments in nineteenth-century letters. In George Ripley, Charles Dana, and John Sullivan Dwight, it boasted coeditors and primary contributors who would later go on, respectively, to work as the chief literary reviewer of Greeley's *Tribune*, rise to become the managing editor of the same, or else emerge as the leading music critic in the United States. This eminent triumvirate might have failed to secure contributions from their "friends" in the Associationist cause (Emerson, for one, objected to involving himself with a journal that he said was "desperately sectarian"), but this did not prevent *The Harbinger*'s management team from compiling an

---

[19] Guarneri, *Utopian Alternative*, 161.

edifying mix of content for their readers.[20] "Art" was accorded the reverence it was due, as is evidenced by the 350 literary reviews (covering contemporary American, British, and Continental authors) and 100 art and music reviews that appeared in the periodical's pages over the course of its lifetime. There were translations of extracts from Fourier. There were socialist-leaning essays and editorials on Associationism. And there were even two rare occasions when *The Harbinger* included fiction between its covers, when it published serial installments from a pair of novels by the controversial French writer George Sand, *Consuelo* (1842) and *The Countess of Rudolstadt* (1843). In the words of one recent commentator, *The Harbinger* was as "daring and courageous" in its literary tastes as it was with its politics.[21]

Of the recurring conflict between "individual interest" and "collective interest," Albert Brisbane wrote, "This is one of the shameful results of civilized politics, which, in practice, is always in contradiction with theory."[22] Neither the theory nor the practice of American communitarianism was able to escape a comparative state of neglect during the embattled years of the US Civil War and Reconstruction, when sectional politics overrode what remained of the domestic interest in socialist reform.[23] And what with the passing, in 1856, of the last remaining Fourierist community in the United States (the North American Phalanx, near Red Bank, New Jersey), not even the residual treatment that Associationism received by the likes of the Swedish writer Fredrika Bremer, whose travel narrative *The Homes of the New World: Impressions of America* (1853) recounted her visit to the abovementioned North American Phalanx in September 1851, could restore the commune to its previous place of privilege in the modern consciousness. But as in her novels (which sold well with Americans in their English translation), where Bremer took pains to portray the exigencies of everyday life, the commune, too, managed to politicize the affairs of

---

[20] Emerson passed this judgment in a letter (that has not survived) to *The Harbinger* editor John Sullivan Dwight. The Brook Farmer George William Curtis quotes from this letter at length in his biography *John Sullivan Dwight, Brook-Farmer, Editor, and Critic of Music* (Small, Maynard, 1898), 103–105.

[21] Sterling F. Delano, *Brook Farm: The Dark Side of Utopia* (The Belknap Press of Harvard University Press, 2004), 227–228.

[22] Albert Brisbane, *Social Destiny of Man* (C. F. Stollmeyer, 1840), 19.

[23] Before the war, many of the US members of non-Fourierist communities tended to be northern abolitionists, pacifists, and vegetarians. A limited number of southern planters nonetheless regarded Fourier's phalanstery as a workable paternalist plan for American society. From Guarneri, *Utopian Alternative*, 4–5.

the pedestrian day-to-day in a way that continued to resonate with those who had ever taken communitarian principles and practices seriously.

With the passage, then, of the Homestead Act in 1862, the utopian energies of the United States began to shift more and more to the American West, as did the manifold literary expressions of the aspirational community. Religious groups like the Mormons, of the Church of Jesus Christ of Latter-Day Saints, headed westward in their ongoing search for a garden utopia of spiritual proportions. Secularists and technologists, meanwhile, increasingly came to regard the vast American landscape west of the Mississippi as a veritable workshop for the wholesale application of the latest advances in science, industry, and invention.[24] From the perspective of these true believers, America's communitarian future seemed bright. Further impetus for this upsurge in communitarian hopefulness during the 1870s and 1880s came from a fresh wave of recent arrivals from Europe. These included both socialists of a fervent reformist bent and additional religious groups like the Hutterites in the Dakotas and the new Odessa community of Russian Jewish immigrants in Oregon. Many of these groups undertook to establish some variety of collective experiment in their new American home. There were historical forces tempering their reasons for optimism, however. The economic dislocations and industrialist expansion of the 1880s and 1890s prompted the recurrent domestic tensions between capital and labor to return to levels not seen since the aftermath of the Panic of 1837. In response, a native tradition of what had been, during the preceding decades, a relatively dormant communitarianism among a US-born citizenry reawakened throughout the country to launch an excited round of groundbreaking on dozens of new communes. Taken in tandem, these two communitarian tides – one imported, one internal – combined to ensure that there were more communes in the United States by the end of the nineteenth century than there had been even during the halcyon days of the 1840s.[25]

Communitarian journalism and literature blossomed under these late-century conditions. Under the influence of ideologically aligned newspapers and periodicals, committed socialist and anarchist groups from Maine to Georgia established colonies (mostly in the South and West) in an attempt to resist a rising national rate of unemployment while also imposing their reformist plans upon what must have seemed, in the face of

[24] Otto F. Kraushaar, "America: Symbol of a Fresh Start," in Gairdner B. Moment and Otto F. Kraushaar, eds., *Utopias, the American Experience* (Scarecrow Press, 1980), 11–29.
[25] Oved, *Two Hundred Years*, 12.

the grassroots efforts of the Populists, anarchists, and trade unionists, an unsettled American political scene. It was no coincidence that a number of these communes nurtured a climate conducive to literature and the arts. To begin, the artistic opportunities they afforded residents comprised many a community's cultural life, not least inside the well-stocked libraries that most communes maintained (in rural communities, these were often superior to any other in their respective regions) for the use of members. At the same time, those communities that produced their own journals positioned themselves to convey their ideas to a broad public.[26] That an anarchist community such as the "Home" settlement, located amid a cluster of socialist communes in Puget Sound County, in Washington State, oversaw the publication of no less than three anarchist periodicals – *New Era*, *The Agitator*, and *Discontent* – underscores the mutually constitutive relation of American communal and literary culture. That Home became a "Mecca" for such celebrity itinerant anarchists as Emma Goldman and Alexander Berkman illustrates that "art" for its own sake was never an end to which most communitarians would subscribe. As was true with a majority in the US socialist community, communitarians by and large rated art and literature to the extent that these activities furthered the greater cause.

There were, too, "mainstream" writers of communitarian leanings who testified to the benefits of social experimentation in their work without necessarily advocating for the creation of any specific planned community. Noteworthy among these is Laurence Gronlund, whose well-received book *The Cooperative Commonwealth* (1884) read as a primer for nonspecialists in Marx's labor theory of value. More memorably, Edward Bellamy's science fiction utopian novel *Looking Backward* (1888) launched a full-fledged Bellamyite movement on the strength of the author's call for the rational, planned management of America's human and natural resources. And, perhaps most lastingly, the author, editor, and literary tastemaker William Dean Howells produced a body of reform-inflected writings that describe an entire arc of communitarian politics for a mass audience of Americans that, like Howells himself, was ready to count the costs of the nation's transition from seeming agrarian simplicity to urban industrial complexity.[27] The Ohio native would revisit the subject of the Shakers

---

[26] Oved, *Two Hundred Years*, 405; and Donald Drew Egbert, "Socialism and American Art," in Donald Drew Egbert and Stow Persons, eds., *Socialism and American Life*, 2 vols. (Princeton University Press, 1952), 1: 621–751, 631.

[27] Michael Fellman, *The Unbounded Frame: Freedom and Community in Nineteenth Century American Utopianism* (Greenwood Press, 1973), 143.

and their communities in no less than four of his novels, but it was with his fictional fantasy *A Traveler from Altruria* (1894) that he engaged in the representational work of proposing a voluntarist, Christian communitarian model of the United States to replace the secular Progressive state that was then in the ascendance.[28] By this late stage, a full roster of writers would likewise continue to urge upon their readers the need for deep-seated social reform on a massive scale, while making the American future that Howells predicted seem parochial by comparison. Mark Twain, in his Arthurian novel *A Connecticut Yankee in King Arthur's Court* (1889), laid bare the dystopian risks involved in putting communitarian principles into even hypothetical practice. The turn-of-the-century feminist Charlotte Perkins Gilman, in her study *Women and Economics* (1898), restored women to their rightful place in a conversation on community spearheaded by Fourier nearly a century earlier. And the muckraking photojournalist Jacob Riis, in his sensational exposé *How the Other Half Lives* (1890), offered visual literary evidence of the urban slum community as social pathology.

The tenor of the politics of cooperation that was behind the work of these writers remained strong, even if their investment in the technical programs of communitarianism per se was negligible. Much the same can be said for other authors from the nineteenth century. Although they might have had their imaginations captured by an accommodating communal ideal, they were liable to conceive of community less according to the voluntarist terms of the commune than the involuntary terms of such identitarian categories-cum-causes as gender, ethnicity, aesthetics, or species. Antebellum women writers wrote of the conventions of a feminine community in the representative texts of literary domesticity. Herman Melville assessed the prospects of human and animal communities in books like *Moby-Dick* (1851) and *The Encantadas* (1854).[29] And the writer Henry James, son and namesake of a father who pledged his faith in Associationism, dramatized the stakes of his instinctive need to prefer a community of artists to a community of activists in his novel *The Bostonians* (1886).[30] Communitarianism hardly expired at the turn of the

---

[28] Howells's Shaker novels include *The Undiscovered Country* (1880); *The Day of Their Wedding* (1896); *A Parting and a Meeting* (1896); and *The Vacation of the Kelwyns* (1920). He also included an essay on Shirley, a Shaker community in Massachusetts, in his collection *Three Villages* (1894).

[29] Michael Jonik, *Herman Melville and the Politics of the Inhuman* (Cambridge University Press, 2018), 17, 156.

[30] Kristin Boudreau, *Henry James' Narrative Technique: Consciousness, Perception, and Cognition* (Palgrave Macmillan, 2010), 31.

twentieth century, but it did recede into a less visible position in the literatures, and politics, of the modern period that followed.

Further Reading

Baker, Jean Harvey. "Women in Utopia: The Nineteenth-Century Experience." In Gairdner B. Moment and Otto F. Kraushaar, eds., *Utopias, the American Experience*. Scarecrow Press, 1980, 56–71.

Bestor, Arthur. *Backwoods Utopias: The Sectarian Origins and the Owenite Phase of Communitarian Socialism in America, 1663–1829*. University of Pennsylvania Press, 1950.

Delano, Sterling F. *"The Harbinger" and New England Transcendentalism: A Portrait of Associationism in America*. Associated University Presses, 1983.

Engeman, Thomas S. "Religion and Politics the American Way: The Exemplary William Dean Howells." *The Review of Politics* 63:1 (Winter 2001), 107–127.

Jenco, Leigh Kathryn. "Thoreau's Critique of Democracy." In Jack Turner, ed., *A Political Companion to Henry David Thoreau*. University Press of Kentucky, 2009, 68–96.

Jennings, Chris. *Paradise Now: The Story of American Utopianism*. Deckle Edge, 2016.

Kanter, Rosabeth Moss. *Commitment and Community: Communes and Utopias in Sociological Perspective*. Harvard University Press, 1972.

Kytle, Ethan J. *Romantic Reformers and the Antislavery Struggle in the Civil War Era*. Cambridge University Press, 2014.

McKanan, Dan. "Making Sense of Failure: From Death to Resurrection in Nineteenth-Century American Communitarianism." *Utopian Studies* 18:2 (2007), 159–192.

Persons, Stow. "Christian Communitarianism in America." In Donald Drew Egbert and Stow Persons, eds., *Socialism and American Life*, 2 vols. Princeton University Press, 1952, 1: 127–151.

Pfaelzer, Jean. *The Utopian Novel in America, 1886–1896: The Politics of Form*. University of Pittsburgh Press, 1985.

Phillips, Derek L. *Looking Backward: A Critical Appraisal of Communitarian Thought*. Princeton University Press, 1993.

Roemer, Kenneth M. *The Obsolete Necessity: America in Utopian Writings, 1888–1900*. Kent State University Press, 1976.

Taylor, Charles. *Sources of the Self: The Making of the Modern Identity*. Cambridge University Press, 1989.

CHAPTER 6

Constructing Sovereignty through Legal and Religious Discourses
Rochelle Raineri Zuck

In 1682, Mary Rowlandson published *The Soveraignty and Goodness of God*, a captivity narrative whose four printings that year made it "one of the first American best sellers."[1] Or rather, that was the American title of the work. London readers received Rowlandson's narrative that same year under a different title: *A True History of the Captivity and Restoration of Mrs. Mary Rowlandson*. As Teresa Toulouse argues, the emphasis on "sovereignty" in the colonies and its noted absence in London editions suggest the term's significance in broader political conversations of its day. She characterizes Rowlandson's narrative, which was edited by and circulated under the auspices of a group of New England ministers (including Increase Mather), as "an indirect rhetorical salvo in an emerging cultural battle involving beliefs about 'new' English versus 'royal' English sovereignty in the New World."[2] In highlighting the "sovereignty" of God in a covenantal relationship with Massachusetts, the American title implicitly frames God, more immediately than the crown, as a sovereign power who could aid colonial individuals and, by extension, the colonies themselves as they opposed a range of external threats to the sovereignty of the colonies. These perceived threats included not only those posed by American Indian peoples like Rowlandson's captors and by European competitors for New World colonial holdings like France and Spain but also – and this is the implication that the altered London title tried to suppress – those posed by "'royal' English sovereignty" to the colonists' "'new' English" sovereignty in America, where colonists were increasingly imagining their own sovereignty deriving directly from/by direct relation to God, without "'royal' English" mediation.

---

[1] Katheryn Zabelle Derounian [Stodola], "The Publication, Promotion, and Distribution of Mary Rowlandson's Indian Captivity Narrative in the Seventeenth Century," *Early American Literature* 23:3 (1998), 239–261, 239.
[2] Teresa Toulouse, "The Sovereignty and Goodness of God in 1682: Royal Authority, Female Captivity, and 'Creole' Male Identity," *ELH* 67:4 (2000), 925–949, 926.

Rowlandson's text, an important work of early American literature and an early example of the captivity narrative genre, gestures toward key attributes of sovereignty: its theological underpinnings, which lingered well into the nineteenth century, and what David Carlson calls its "oppositional pedigree." Carlson discusses the emergence of the term "sovereignty" in a historical and political context in which early modern European rulers sought to break away from the "respublica Christiana" and the authority of the Catholic Church.[3] The interplay between religion and law continued to shape discussions of sovereignty throughout the British Empire well into the eighteenth century, argues J. C. D. Clark, who notes that "[l]aw and religion dominated men's understanding of the public realm."[4] Underscoring this point, Rowlandson's London title, by retreating from the American title's contentious implication that the divine sovereignty in America need not derive from the divine sovereignty of English royalty, reveals that the contested, oppositional nature of sovereignty became particularly acute in the context of empire. As Ken MacMillan asserts, English expressions of "New World sovereignty" were articulated in opposition to both "the rights of native peoples" and "the competing claims of other European colonizing powers."[5] But Rowlandson's title change reveals such opposition likewise to be occurring within a single European colonizing power – between England and its colonies – and, in so doing, demonstrates that such conceptions of sovereignty were not only articulated and debated on the pages of legal treatises but also embedded within the stories told by and for English subjects on both sides of the Atlantic.

This chapter considers literary expressions of sovereignty in the nineteenth-century United States that underscore sovereignty's oppositional nature and its productive potential, and it demonstrates how these literary expressions were, like public argument about sovereignty, constructed through the interplay between law and religion. Religious discourse provided a set of terms, examples, and motifs that shaped the nineteenth-century debate over political autonomy as it ranged across matters of territorial possession and the individual conscience. In what follows, I first briefly address ideas of sovereignty that circulated in the long nineteenth century and informed US literature and public argument. Then I turn to competing visions of sovereignty expressed by the

---

[3] David Carlson, *Imagining Sovereignty: Self-Determination in American Indian Law and Literature* (University of Oklahoma Press, 2016), 17.
[4] J. C. D. Clark, *The Language of Liberty, 1660–1832* (Cambridge University Press, 1993), 1.
[5] Ken MacMillan, *Sovereignty and Possession in the English New World: The Legal Foundations of Empire, 1576–1640* (Cambridge University Press, 2006), 8.

Cherokee Nation, the state of Georgia, the US federal government, and the US Supreme Court during what Maureen Konkle has called "the most heated years of their [Cherokee Nation's] struggle against removal, from about 1826 to 1837."[6] In the final section, I briefly turn to the figure of John Brown who, in linking the vision of American Indian sovereignty expressed by the Cherokee Nation to the sovereign individuality espoused by Henry David Thoreau and the Transcendentalists, serves as a harbinger of the contests over political sovereignty that ultimately led to the US Civil War.[7]

Sovereignty: A Brief Overview

Sovereignty is and has been a contested term with a number of possible meanings that have evolved over time and across political and cultural formations. As Carlson notes, "Sovereignty has always been a fluid concept, capable of dialectical transformation, whose definitions and applications have been shaped by real-world political interests and power struggles."[8] It can refer to political and legal autonomy, a vision of sovereignty that is often, but not always, linked to a particular territory. This understanding of sovereignty addresses the exercise of political authority and legal jurisdiction across a particular space and over individuals living within that space. Yet sovereignty can also refer to cultural and economic self-determination, the right to dictate one's own mode of living, speak one's own language, and tell one's own stories.[9] As noted, Anglo-European conceptions of sovereignty in the medieval and early modern eras were infused with a theological understanding of God's supreme

---

[6] Maureen Konkle, *Writing Indian Nations: Native Intellectuals and the Politics of Historiography, 1827–1863* (University of North Carolina Press, 2004), 43.
[7] See "The Portent," in *The Battle-Pieces of Herman Melville*, ed. Hennig Cohen (Yoseloff, 1963), 35, line 14.
[8] Carlson, *Imagining Sovereignty*, 17.
[9] Space does not permit an exhaustive list of sources related to sovereignty. On sovereignty in the context of empire, see Clark, *The Language of Liberty*; MacMillan, *Sovereignty and Possession*; and Jonathan Elmer, *On Lingering and Being Last: Race and Sovereignty in the New World* (Fordham University Press, 2008). On Indigenous sovereignty, see Chickasaw scholar Amanda Cobb, "Understanding Tribal Sovereignty: Definitions, Conceptualizations, Interpretations," *American Studies* 46:3–4 (2005), 115–132. On arguments against applying the concept of sovereignty in Indigenous contexts, see Mohawk scholar Gerald Taiaiake Alfred's *Peace, Power, and Righteousness: An Indigenous Manifesto* (Oxford University Press, 2008), 55–72. Creek/Cherokee scholar Craig Womack asserts, however, that "Sovereignty is inherent as an intellectual idea in Native cultures, a political practice, and a theme of oral traditions; and the concept, as the practice, predates European contact." See Craig Womack, *Red on Red: Native American Literary Separatism* (University of Minnesota Press, 1999), 51.

authority, and they located earthly sovereignty within a single figure (the sovereign monarch ruling by divine right) who exercised authority over those born into what James Kettner has called a "community of allegiance."[10] Scholars often point to the end of the Thirty Years' War and the 1648 Peace of Westphalia as a turning point in the development of sovereignty, marking, in the words of Daniel Philpott, a "shift in Europe from the medieval world to the modern international system."[11] A hallmark of this shift was a growing emphasis on territory, with sovereignty understood to be operative within a particular bounded geopolitical space and on the bodies of individuals within that space. European and American ideas of sovereignty were informed by numerous theological and historical sources, including the Bible, the ancient republics of Greece and Rome, and works by theorists such as Thomas Hobbes, Jean Bodin, William Blackstone, John Locke, and others.[12] As MacMillan's work suggests, European and American ideas of sovereignty were also shaped by imperial ambitions as European colonial powers competed with one another to build transatlantic empires. Shifting to meet these new political, economic, and cultural exigencies, conceptions of sovereignty moved away from locating power's authorization in the body of a single figure, the sovereign monarch, and became more concerned with authorizing power's exercise across a particular geopolitical space.

And yet, the eighteenth-century project of consolidating a far-flung empire challenged what had become central tenets of state sovereignty: that it referred to indivisible political and legal authority exercised within a state's geographic boundaries. To have multiple sovereign powers existing within the same geopolitical space of the state was, according to the English jurist William Blackstone, a political impossibility.[13] Indeed, in the 1760s, supporters of British Parliamentary sovereignty over its North American colonies extended Blackstone's dismissal of divided sovereignty to challenge American colonists' complaints about

[10] James Kettner, *The Development of American Citizenship, 1608–1870* (University of North Carolina Press, 1978). On the community of allegiance, see especially, "Part 1: The English Background."
[11] Daniel Philpott, *Revolutions in Sovereignty: How Ideas Shaped Modern International Relations* (Princeton University Press, 2010), 4.
[12] On the development of American ideas of sovereignty, see Rochelle Raineri Zuck, *Divided Sovereignties: Race, Nationhood, and Citizenship in Nineteenth-Century America* (University of Georgia Press, 2016). On the influence of Thomas Hobbes, see Paul Downes, *Hobbes, Sovereignty, and Early American Literature* (Cambridge University Press, 2015).
[13] William Blackstone, *Commentaries on the Laws of England, 1765–1769*, 4 vols. (University of Chicago Press, 1979); see especially 1: 49. On Blackstone's conceptions of sovereignty, see Howard L. Lubert, "Sovereignty and Liberty in William Blackstone's *Commentaries on the Laws of England*," *Review of Politics* 72:2 (2010), 271–297.

their lack of representation in Parliament and calls for colonial legislatures to exercise greater control in some matters. They argued that dividing political authority between Parliament and various colonial bodies, as some of these colonists demanded, would produce the very divided sovereignty that Blackstone deemed impossible.[14] However, the lived realities of people within a transatlantic empire reaffirmed what Carlson has called the "fluid" nature of sovereignty by suggesting that sovereignty could be divided, and indeed almost had to be divided, but that not all approaches to structuring divided sovereignty were acceptable to the state – hence, again, the removal of "sovereignty" from Rowlandson's London title.[15] The Framers of the US Constitution inherited these concerns about the ramifications of divided sovereignty (particularly those that had become apparent under the existing Articles of Confederation) and sought to manage its implementation through the creation of a new federal system in which sovereignty was distributed between state and federal authorities but ultimately located in a single/undivided source, "the people," whose will was framed as the supreme and incontrovertible authority within a democracy.[16] Arguments grounded in popular sovereignty, however, raised thorny questions about who comprised "the people."

Questions about who was considered to be part of the body politic speak to what scholars call the "paradox of sovereignty," summarized by Adam Dahl as the idea that "any constitutional order rests on forms of exclusion that are beyond the realm of legal legitimacy," and thus "law and sovereignty always rest on violence and exclusion." As Dahl elaborates, "many contemporary democratic theorists see the paradox of sovereignty as an enabling dilemma that generates a productive politics of conflict and contestation. By exposing the contingency of modern rule, the paradox of sovereignty produces sites of contestation that allow political actors to challenge unjust legal exclusions and produce new political possibilities."[17] Dahl's emphasis on "contestation" brings us back to Carlson's discussion

---

[14] See Kettner's chapter on "The Pre-Revolutionary Debate," in *The Development of American Citizenship, 1608–1870* (University of North Carolina Press, 1978), 131–172.

[15] As Kettner notes, American colonists pointed to the example of England and Scotland prior to the Acts of Union – two separate states (each with their own legislature) under the authority of a single monarch – as proof that sovereignty could be successfully divided within the empire. See Ketner, "The Pre-Revolutionary Debate," 158–164.

[16] See Zuck, *Divided Sovereignties*, 3, 20–25. Robert L. Tsai observes, "In establishing the American republic, the Framers unleashed a pair of seductive ideas: popular sovereignty and written constitutionalism." See Tsai, *America's Forgotten Constitutions: Defiant Visions of Power and Community* (Harvard University Press, 2014), 2.

[17] Adam Dahl, *Empire of the People: Settler Colonialism and the Foundations of Modern Democratic Thought* (University Press of Kansas, 2018), 157.

of sovereignty's "oppositional pedigree." One key feature of sovereignty as it operated in the nineteenth-century United States was that it created such "sites of contestation" that allowed for both violent demonstrations of state sovereignty (e.g. Indian Removal) and efforts to forge new political futures (e.g. the Cherokee Constitution of 1827). As the following section will show, critics of Cherokee nationhood framed American Indian sovereignty, particularly territorial sovereignty, as a dangerous political monstrosity threatening the territorial sovereignty of the state of Georgia, while the Cherokees and their advocates proposed a different vision of Cherokee sovereignty that articulated an alternative relationship between the Cherokee Nation and the United States, a relationship between sovereign equals that shifted the US state seeking to exert jurisdiction over them – Georgia – from a superior to a subordinate role, one lacking the sovereign authority that only the Cherokee Nation and the United States as a whole could rightfully exercise.

Contested Sovereignty: *Cherokee Nation* v. *Georgia* and Its Literary Legacy

Conceptions of European and later US sovereignty in North America were informed by engagements with American Indian nations in ways that produced both conflict and the possibility of new political futures.[18] Cherokee political leaders began to express their political identity in terms of nationhood and sovereignty in the nineteenth century as a means of forcefully asserting their political autonomy and territorial claims in language that would be understood by US state and federal authorities.[19] Cherokee leaders in fact "defined their nation ... as the product of a partnership with white Americans."[20] Konkle describes the arguments of those advocating Cherokee nationhood thusly: "they claimed

---

[18] On the development of English and American ideas of sovereignty through engagements with American Indians, see MacMillan, *Sovereignty and Possession*; Elmer, *On Lingering*; Lisa Ford, *Settler Sovereignty: Jurisdiction and Indigenous People in America and Australia, 1788–1836* (Harvard University Press, 2010); and Zuck, *Divided Sovereignties*.

[19] On Cherokee political and social organization before and after the formation of the Cherokee Nation, see Joshua B. Nelson, *Progressive Traditions: Identity in Cherokee Literature and Culture* (University of Oklahoma Press, 2014), 137–164; Andrew Denson, *Demanding the Cherokee Nation: Indian Autonomy and American Nationhood, 1830–1900* (University of Nebraska Press, 2015), 19–20; and William G. McLoughlin, *Cherokee Renascence in the New Republic* (Princeton University Press, 1986). On the diversity of political and cultural perspectives among the Cherokee, see Daniel Heath Justice, *Our Fire Survives the Storm: A Cherokee Literary History* (University of Minnesota Press, 2006), 55–88; and Nelson, *Progressive Traditions*, 165–200.

[20] Denson, *Demanding the Cherokee Nation*, 15–16.

Constructing Sovereignty through Law and Religion 113

to form a modern Indian nation, one that could not be characterized as representing a timeless prepolitical state of nature, but one that existed in time, as European nations did."[21] In the 1827 Constitution of the Cherokee Nation, Cherokee leaders characterized the nation as existing in and exercising sovereignty over a bounded geographic space. What followed the ratification of the 1827 Constitution set the stage for the legal battles to follow. This and other assertions of Cherokee sovereignty – when coupled with the discovery of gold in Cherokee territory in the 1820s and the election of Andrew Jackson as president of the United States in 1828, among other events – emboldened advocates of Indian Removal, particularly those aligned with the state of Georgia. Cherokee scholar Daniel Heath Justice offers the following summary of events: "Georgia's response was to extend its authority over Cherokee lands and political affairs, thus defying both U.S. claims of exclusive control over Indian affairs as well as Cherokee social and political sovereignty."[22] Congress passed the Indian Removal Act in May of 1830, which aimed to remove tribes east of the Mississippi and relocate them to lands in the West to both free up lands for white settlement and resolve the tensions between state and federal authorities over claims of authority over American Indian peoples. The Cherokee Nation then challenged Georgia's actions in court, thus becoming embroiled in a larger struggle over the division of sovereignty between the US federal government and individual states, a debate as old as the US nation itself that contributed to the Civil War and continues, in various forms, to this day. The Cherokee Nation's expressions of sovereignty in their 1827 Constitution and the arguments in *Cherokee Nation v. Georgia* (1831) captured public attention, reverberated in popular literature, and demonstrated how the interplay between legal and religious discourse, including the widely circulated "lost tribes" theory of American Indian origins (i.e. the idea that Indigenous Americans were descendants of the ten lost tribes of Israel), informed nineteenth-century debates over US federal, state, and American Indian sovereignty.[23]

The Cherokee Constitution of 1827 stands as the first written constitution ratified by an American Indian nation, and the Cherokees became a model not only for other American Indian nations but also for non-Native groups including, as I will discuss in the following section, the

---

[21] Konkle, *Writing Indian Nations*, 44. [22] Justice, *Our Fire Survives the Storm*, 75.
[23] See Elizabeth Fenton, *Old Canaan in a New World: Native Americans and the Lost Tribes of Israel* (New York University Press, 2020).

antislavery activists led by John Brown.[24] Jill Norgren observes that this document "was in many ways modeled after the constitutions of neighboring American states and that of the United States" but also "maintained the core values of their [Cherokees'] culture."[25] Demonstrating the oppositional and generative nature of sovereignty, the Cherokee Constitution reconfigured the 1798 constitution of the state of Georgia, which established the current boundaries of the state and projected "an extension of settlement and extinguishment of Indian claims in and to the vacant territory of this State to the east and north of the said river Chatahoochee."[26] While the 1798 Georgia Constitution imagines a future in which it can claim all American Indian lands within its putative borders, the 1827 Cherokee Constitution asserts competing sovereign claims to that same land, which, the document contends, is "reserved forever to the Cherokee Nation by the Treaties concluded with the United States." Like the Cherokee Constitution, the writings and speeches of Principal Chief John Ross (Guwi Sguwi), who led the Cherokee Nation from 1828 to 1866, position the Cherokee Nation as a sovereign state vis-à-vis the United States and relegate the state of Georgia to the political and geographic margins of the story. Ross was careful in his address to the Cherokee Nation on October 13, 1828, to distinguish between the "new character" the Cherokee Nation had taken on "under a constitutional form" and its claims to sovereignty, which, he goes on to argue, are not new at all but in fact predate those of both the state of Georgia and the United States.[27] He thereby disputes Georgia's claim that the Cherokees have only recently asserted their sovereignty and created a dangerous, new instance of divided sovereignty within the borders of the state of Georgia. As Justice notes, in Ross's message, published in both English and Cherokee, "[t]here is no attempt to mediate or negotiate with the state of Georgia or the United States on this point [sovereign equality between the Cherokee Nation and the United States]: reason, justice, and common sense alike reveal the truth

---

[24] See, for example, the Choctaw Constitution of 1847, the Chickasaw Constitution of 1860, and the Muscogee Nation's Constitution of 1868.
[25] Jill Norgren, *The Cherokee Cases: Two Landmark Federal Decisions in the Fight for Sovereignty*, 1996 reprint (University of Oklahoma Press, 2004), 43. On issues of federal versus state sovereignty and definitions of personhood in US law and culture, and *Cherokee Nation* v. *Georgia*, see Priscilla Wald, *Constituting Americans: Cultural Anxieties and Narrative Form* (Duke University Press, 1995), 20–40.
[26] On the 1827 Cherokee Constitution's reworking of Georgia's territorial claims in its 1798 Constitution, see Zuck, *Divided Sovereignties*, 39.
[27] "Annual Message" (October 13, 1828), in *The Papers of Chief John Ross, 1807–1839*, ed. Gary Moulton, 2 vols (University of Oklahoma Press, 1985), 1: 142–143.

of Cherokee sovereignty."[28] Elsewhere, Ross positioned the Cherokee Nation as "placed in the heart of so powerful a Nation" (the United States) in a reciprocal relationship in which the Cherokee Nation "surrendered a portion of our sovereignty, as a security for our protection."[29] Ross contends that the Cherokee Nation maintains a close and "reciprocal" relationship with the United States, thus still maintaining, despite surrendering a portion of its sovereignty in exchange for security (against, for instance, threats like that posed by the state of Georgia), its status as a sovereign nation-state.

The Cherokee Nation's struggles with the state of Georgia over issues of political and territorial sovereignty went all the way to the US Supreme Court in *Cherokee Nation* v. *Georgia* (1831) and demonstrated how religious discourse, including the "lost tribes" theory of American Indian origins, played a role in shaping legal thought.[30] The Supreme Court's decision in this case hinged not only on whether the Cherokee Nation could be considered a *state* and, if so, what kind of state it was but also on *where* the Cherokee Nation was located. The term state can be understood as a "defined and delimited territory, with a permanent population, under the authority of a government," and at issue in the case was whether the Cherokee Nation could legally make such claims to territorial authority.[31] Arguing on behalf of the Cherokees, their lawyers, William Wirt and John Sergeant, repeated Ross's insistence on Cherokee sovereignty's ancient sources, claiming "that, from time immemorial, the Cherokee nation have composed a sovereign and independent state" recognized as such by the United States and other nations as part of treaty negotiations.[32] The Cherokees and their lawyers disputed the characterization of the Cherokee Nation as a new sovereign state that emerged from *within* the territorial boundaries of the state of Georgia. Rather, they argued that the Cherokee Nation had recently developed a new political form – the democratic nation-state – but had existed contiguous with and enjoyed a relationship of sovereign equality with the United States since the US founding.[33] Put simply, the Cherokee Nation was a foreign state that was not subject to the jurisdiction of the state of

---

[28] Justice, *Our Fire Survives the Storm*, 76.
[29] Ross, "Annual Message" (October 24, 1831), in *Papers of Chief John Ross*, 1: 229.
[30] On the three cases involving the Cherokee Nation and the state of Georgia – *State* v. *Tassels* (1830), *Cherokee Nation* v. *Georgia* (1831), and *Worcester* v. *Georgia* (1832) – see Norgren, *The Cherokee Cases*.
[31] See Robert Jackson, *Sovereignty: Evolution of an Idea* (Polity Press, 2007), 5–6.
[32] *Cherokee Nation* v. *Georgia*, 30 U.S. (5 Peters 1) (1831), 2.
[33] See Zuck, *Divided Sovereignties*, 32–68.

Georgia. Convinced by part of this argument, Chief Justice John Marshall argued that American Indian peoples possess an "unquestionable ... right to the lands they occupy, until that right shall be extinguished by a voluntary cessation to our government." Even as he acknowledged their territorial rights, Marshall dismissed the Cherokees' claim to be a foreign state that could seek redress through the US Supreme Court. Instead, he framed the Cherokee Nation, and all American Indian nations, as "domestic, dependent nations," a phrase that undercuts the Cherokee's assertion of sovereign autonomy and characterizes them as existing in a state of perpetual wardship.[34] Marshall writes that the United States and other nations see American Indian peoples as "completely under the sovereignty and dominion of the United States" and not as foreign, sovereign states in their own right.[35] As such, Marshall concludes that the Supreme Court "is not the tribunal which can redress the past or prevent the future" for the Cherokee Nation, a conclusion that gestures toward two (unwritten) possibilities for the Cherokees – "voluntary cessation" or Removal.[36]

In his concurring opinion, Justice William Johnson offered a vision of American Indian political autonomy divorced from the territorial sovereignty that Marshall was willing to grant to American Indian peoples – until, that is, what Marshall calls their "voluntary cessation" of those lands. Johnson denies Cherokee sovereignty and claims to statehood, arguing that "[t]hey never have been recognized as holding sovereignty over the territory they occupy." What they have instead, he suggests, is a kind of political autonomy that could only be demonstrated to him and to the broader "family of nations" through the collective political act of ceding their territory.[37] To elaborate this point, Johnson evoked the long-standing connection between American Indian and ancient Israelites (the "lost tribes" theory) to assert that the Cherokees could be considered "a state, though not a sovereign state" in the sense that they, like the Israelites before they reached the so-called promised land, maintain what he calls a "right of personal self government" without claims to any particular territory (and here I quote at some length because of its importance to later discussions of popular literature):

> because I believe, in one view and in one only, if at all, they are or may be deemed a state, though not a sovereign state, at least while they occupy a country within our limits. Their condition is something like that of the

[34] *Cherokee Nation* v. *Georgia*, 17.
[35] *Cherokee Nation* v. *Georgia*, 17.
[36] *Cherokee Nation* v. *Georgia*, 20.
[37] *Cherokee Nation* v. *Georgia*, 22.

Israelites, when inhabiting the deserts. Though without land that they can call theirs in the sense of property, their right of personal self government has never been taken from them; and such a form of government may exist though the land occupied be in fact that of another. The right to expel them may exist in that other, but the alternative of departing and retaining the right of self government may exist in them. And such they certainly do possess.[38]

By comparing them with the ancient Israelites, Johnson frames the Cherokees, and by extension, all American Indian polities, as displaceable in ways that furthered the project of Removal by denying even the possibility of American Indian territorial sovereignty. In an era in which sovereignty was increasingly linked with territorial possession, Johnson argues that Cherokees can only demonstrate proof of their political capacity through voluntary departure, an act that then confirms a view of them as a non-sovereign state devoid of "property." The emphasis on *departure* as proof of political autonomy also worked to promote a narrative of American Indian consent to the ceding of their lands and to obscure how that "consent" was the result of legal, political, and economic forces and, ultimately, forcible dispossession.

Such debates about sovereignty, land, and jurisdiction were also taken up in the pages of nineteenth-century US popular literature.[39] The nineteenth-century "frontier romances" of James Fenimore Cooper, Catharine Maria Sedgwick, and Lydia Maria Child have been read either as endorsing settler colonialism and perpetuating the myth of the "Vanishing Indian" or as critiquing the violence and cost, both to human beings and to the environment, of European and Anglo-American imperial aims.[40] Both readings – whether endorsement or critique – reveal the centrality of issues of sovereignty to some of the most well-known nineteenth-century US writers and texts. *Oak Openings* (1848), the last of Cooper's "frontier romances," offers a sustained engagement with issues related to sovereignty and the "lost tribes" theory. Set in Michigan Territory during the War of

---

[38] *Cherokee Nation* v. *Georgia*, 27.
[39] See, for example, Jillian J. Sayre, *Mourning the Nation to Come: Creole Nativism in Nineteenth-Century American Literature* (Louisiana State University Press, 2019); Fenton, *Old Canaan*; and Edward Watts, *Colonizing the Past: Mythmaking and Pre-Columbian Whites in Nineteenth-Century American Writing* (University of Virginia Press, 2020).
[40] On discussions of race in the "frontier romance," see Ezra Tawil, *The Making of Racial Sentiment: Slavery and the Birth of the Frontier Romance* (Cambridge University Press, 2006). On Cooper's positions on race and empire, see Robert S. Levine, "Temporality, Race, and Empire in Cooper's *The Deerslayer*: The Beginning of the End," in Russ Castronovo, ed., *The Oxford Handbook of Nineteenth-Century American Literature* (Oxford University Press, 2012), 163–178.

1812, this novel dramatizes conflicts not only between the United States and Great Britain but also between the United States and Ojibwe, Odawa, Potawatomi, and Wyandot (Huron) peoples. It features a charismatic leader, Onoah (or "Scalping Peter"), whose tribal affiliation is never revealed and who tries to create a pan-Indian confederacy to challenge American and European settler colonialism. The "oppositional" nature of sovereignty is dramatized in a series of debates between Onoah, his followers, and Parson Amen, a Methodist preacher and devoted adherent to the "lost tribes" theory. At various points in the novel, Amen insists that American Indian people are lost Israelites who should return to their homeland, thereby rendering their lands in North America available for white settlement. The promised land, says the Parson, "was given to the children of Israel, for a possession forever; and though you have been carried away from it for a time, there the land still is, open to receive you, and waiting the return of its ancient masters. In good season that return must come; for we have the word of God for it, in our Christian Bible."[41] Amen extends Johnson's figurative comparison of American Indian peoples to the ancient Israelites, arguing that they are *actually* descendants of the lost tribes whose voluntary "return" to their imagined homeland can fulfill biblical prophecy and, it is implied, further the secular project of freeing up lands in North America for white settlement. As Edward Watts notes, by "reiterating settler colonialism's grounding in land acquisition and white sovereignty, Amen imagines both Palestine and precontact North America as intrinsically empty and therefore available for legal inhabitation."[42] Onoah and others vigorously deny that they are descended from the lost tribes in terms that expose and resist the territorial ambitions bound up with this theory. Onoah asserts:

> We never saw the place where the sun rises. We do not wish to see it. Our hunting-grounds are nearer to the place where he sets. If the pale-faces believe we have a right to that distant land, which is so rich in good things, we will give it to them and keep these Openings, and prairies, and woods.[43]

Onoah echoes the Cherokee Nation's arguments that their sovereignty predates the claims of white settlers, who, he notes, arrived later than

---

[41] James Fenimore Cooper, *Oak Openings; or, The Bee-Hunter*, 2 vols (Burgess & Stringer, 1848), 2: 31.
[42] Watts, *Colonizing the Past*, 90. Fenton, *Old Canaan*, also highlights the issue of sovereignty in the novel but reads *Oak Openings* as dismissive of the "lost tribes" argument and those who hold it, suggesting that the novel "configures the American frontier as a space hostile to both the Native peoples who challenge white settlement and the white Christians whose theological positions might buttress Native claims to sovereignty" (142).
[43] Cooper, *Oak Openings*, 2: 31.

American Indian peoples. Playing on the idea that American Indian capacity for "self government" can be recognized by white Americans only through an act of collective departure (as Johnson had argued in *Cherokee Nation* v. *Georgia*), Onoah deploys that same logic against the white Christians by offering, on behalf of the American Indian peoples he leads, to give up any claims upon the promised land to white settlers and facilitate *their* collective departure from the "Openings, and prairies, and woods" claimed by American Indian peoples. In a rhetorical move that resonates with Johnson's statements but circumvents his denial of American Indian sovereignty, Onoah demonstrates, in the very terms Johnson had imagined ("the alternative of departing and retaining the right of self government"), American Indian people's capacity for self-governance by voluntarily and collectively "departing" – if only figuratively – from the biblical homeland that has been assigned to them. What results is a "Removal" in which what Marshall had called "voluntary cessation to our government" – but in this case cessation of land in the Middle East rather than Georgia – enacts Johnson's "alternative of departing and retaining the right of self government," but it does so in a way that, rather than according Native peoples self-government without land (like "the Israelites, when inhabiting the deserts," as Johnson had asserted), instead maintains their connection to the lands that they currently occupy. By thus recasting the US Supreme Court's logic in *Cherokee Nation* v. *Georgia*, Cooper's Onoah offers a fictional reworking of the Marshall Court's characterization of American Indian sovereignty and extends Johnson's use of the "lost tribes" theory in order to further rather than subvert the territorial claims of American Indian peoples and to achieve a kind of fictional redress that the Cherokee Nation was denied in *Cherokee Nation* v. *Georgia*.[44]

By the end of the novel, Onoah and his followers have killed the Parson, but the pan-Indian confederacy is unable to stop the forces of settler colonialism. Onoah converts to Christianity, and the novel ends with what reads like a sales pitch to settle the newly formed state of Michigan where, it turns out, Cooper held substantial economic investments.[45] Yet, even as the ending of *Oak Openings* can be seen to problematize Onoah's

---

[44] As Norgren notes in *The Cherokee Cases*, in *Worcester* v. *Georgia* (1832), the Marshall Court sided with the Cherokee Nation and "concluded that Georgia's jurisdiction laws were 'repugnant to the constitution, laws, and treaties of the United States' and had violated the political rights of the Cherokee Republic" (5).

[45] Alan Axelrad reads the final chapter of *Oak Openings* as a piece of "promotion literature" in *History and Utopia: A Study of the Worldview of James Fenimore Cooper* (Norwood Editions, 1978), 104. On Cooper's financial investments in Michigan, see Wayne Franklin, *James Fenimore Cooper: The Later Years* (Yale University Press, 2017), 172–174, 426–450.

vision of American Indian sovereignty, the debates between American Indian characters and the Parson create a space in which alternative futures (and histories) can be considered. In the debates between the Parson and Onoah and his followers, the contested nature of sovereignty comes into sharp relief. The Parson advocates a religio-historical theory that, as much in this novel as in the decisions of the US Supreme Court, worked to displace American Indian peoples by erasing their claims to lands in North American and, in the Parson's plan, by "returning" them to a biblically ordained homeland (figured to be empty and waiting for settlement). The American Indian peoples, led by Onoah, expose the colonialist ambitions of the "lost tribes" theory and imagine an alternative future in which Americans and Europeans are removed from North America to claim the "open land" offered to them in the Middle East. This discussion is given significant space in the novel and allows Onoah and his followers to assert, in the very terms provided by those who seek to remove them, that they are neither lost nor vanishing, enabling them to enact a form of American Indian sovereignty that creatively reworks the logic of the Marshall Court in *Cherokee Nation* v. *Georgia*.

"A Transcendentalist Above All": John Brown's Vision of Sovereignty

The Cherokee Constitution of 1827 had wide-ranging implications for subsequent nineteenth-century discussions of sovereignty. It inspired the constitutional efforts of other American Indian nations and, according to Martin Delany, inspired the Provisional Constitution and "Declaration of Liberty" created by John Brown and the members of the Chatham Convention in May of 1858.[46] Brown and those in attendance "strove to create a 'provisional' or virtual antislavery nation within the larger United States but outside of any particular state jurisdiction."[47] The Provisional Constitution and "Declaration of Liberty" outlined a temporary national government, grounded in a radical form of popular sovereignty and predicated on an opposition to slavery. These documents, Brown and his

---

[46] Delany discussed the Chatham Convention with his biographer, Frances Rollin, and compared the provisional government he, Brown, and others sought to create with the Cherokee Nation. See Frank [Frances] A. Rollin, *Life and Public Services of Martin R. Delany*, quoted in *Martin R. Delany: A Documentary Reader*, ed. Robert S. Levine (North Carolina Press, 2003), 331.

[47] Zuck, *Divided Sovereignties*, 104. On Brown and his Provisional Constitution, see Zuck, *Divided Sovereignties*, 113–120; Tsai, *America's Forgotten Constitutions*, 83–117; and David S. Reynolds, *John Brown, Abolitionist: The Man Who Killed Slavery, Sparked the Civil War, and Seeded Civil Rights* (Vintage, 2005), 249–255.

followers hoped, would help the United States become a different kind of nation, one characterized not by slavery and racism but by the idea, as expressed in the "Declaration of Liberty," "that the Slaves are, and of right ought to be as free and independent as the unchangeable Law of God, requires that all men Shall be."[48] Here Brown invokes the "Law of God" in arguing that enslaved people owe no "allegiance" to those who hold them in bondage. The sovereignty of God becomes for Brown a means of refuting the secular legal claims of slaveholders over the people they claimed as property and over others who, through laws such as the Fugitive Slave Act of 1850, were legally compelled to support the system of slavery, much as it had been a means for Rowlandson's *The Sovereignty and Goodness of God* (1682) to refute the English crown's claims over New World colonies. The Provisional Constitution claims not to be an effort to "overthrow" the US federal government or the government of individual states. Rather, its stated goal was "amendment and repeal" of US state and federal laws that supported slavery, including the US Constitution. Article XLVI of the Provisional Constitution concludes with the assertion, "[O]ur flag shall be the same that our fathers fought under in the Revolution."[49] Brown and his followers thus represented themselves as continuing the efforts of the US founders to form "a more perfect Union," not as traitors threatening the survival of that union. In addition to the US founding documents, Brown and his followers looked to the Cherokee Nation as a model of how to create a state that could relate to the US government on a nation-to-nation basis, an alternative version of the US government that would rewrite the nation's political future.

The Commonwealth of Virginia, however, saw things quite differently. After Brown's raid on Harpers Ferry, he was tried by the state of Virginia for treason, and the Provisional Constitution and other documents were cited by the prosecution as evidence that Brown and his followers were animated by the "aim of overthrowing and abolishing the Constitution and laws of said Commonwealth."[50] Despite his lawyer's arguments that Brown, who had attacked a US federal armory at Harpers Ferry, should not be tried by the state of Virginia because he had committed no crime against

---

[48] "Declaration of Liberty," in *The Tribunal: Responses to John Brown and the Harpers Ferry Raid*, ed. John Stauffer and Zoe Trodd (Harvard University Press, 2012), 43. See also Zuck, *Divided Sovereignties*, 114.

[49] Brown, "Provisional Constitution," 15.

[50] *The Life, Trial, and Execution of Captain John Brown, Known as "Old Brown of Ossawatomie," with a Full Account of the Attempted Insurrection at Harper's Ferry: Compiled from Official and Authentic Sources* (R. M. DeWitt, 1859), 59. On the role that the Provisional Constitution played in Brown's trial, see Tsai, *America's Forgotten Constitutions*, 103.

that state, he was convicted of treason and executed. Brown's efforts to forge a provisional government, aligned with the United States and dedicated to remaking it from within (through the creation of something like Marshall's conception of American Indian nations as "domestic [and] dependent" polities), were refigured as acts of treason by Virginia authorities, a move echoing Georgia's characterization of the Cherokee Nation as violating Georgia's sovereignty.

The significance of this moment and of the competing claims to sovereignty that it generated were noted by several well-known nineteenth-century writers, including Herman Melville, Ralph Waldo Emerson, and Henry David Thoreau. Melville's poem "The Portent," which serves as a kind of epigraph to his *Battle Pieces and Aspects of the War* (1866), dramatizes poignantly the contestation between viewing Brown's execution as an operation of earthly sovereign power ("such the law") and viewing Brown himself as a prophet of the higher law/power, the latter view positioning Brown, "The Portent" implies, as a harbinger of the looming sectional crisis: The poem's final line dubs Brown "the meteor of the war."[51] Brown had described himself as "an avenging angel of the Lord," and his efforts to refigure US sovereignty through a Provisional Constitution that abolishes slavery and recognizes African American natural rights (in contrast to Justice Taney's famous denial of such rights in the 1857 Supreme Court case *Dred Scott* v. *Sandford*) demonstrate the interplay between his sense of religious mission and his views on the law.[52] Both Emerson and Thoreau penned defenses of Brown that captured this aspect of Brown's life and work, with Emerson speaking of him as a "*Saint*, whose fate yet hangs in suspense, but whose martyrdom, if it shall be perfected, will make the gallows as glorious as the cross."[53] Thoreau's "A Plea for Captain John Brown" (1859), a lecture delivered prior to Brown's execution, extends this assignment of sovereign religious authority to Brown by characterizing Brown as the consummate Transcendentalist because of his enactment of

---

[51] Melville, "The Portent," 35. On how questions of sovereignty informed antebellum debates over nullification and secession, see Neil H. Cogan, ed. *Union and States' Rights: A History and Interpretation of Interposition, Nullification, and Secession, 150 Years after Sumter* (University of Akron Press, 2013) and Kyle Scott, *Federalism: A Normative Theory and Its Practical Relevance* (Continuum, 2011). On nineteenth-century law and literature, particularly as they relate to shifts in thinking about slavery, sovereignty, and the law that led to the creation of the Fourteenth Amendment, see Deak Nabers, *Victory of Law: The Fourteenth Amendment, the Civil War, and American Literature, 1852–1867* (Johns Hopkins University Press, 2006).
[52] Quoted in Kent Ljungquist, "'Meteor of the War': Melville, Thoreau, and Whitman Respond to John Brown," *American Literature* 61:4 (1989), 674–680, 678.
[53] Quoted in Ljungquist, "Meteor of the War," 676.

a kind of self-sovereignty akin to Emersonian "Self-Reliance."[54] Thoreau writes of Brown, "No man in America has ever stood up so persistently and effectively for the dignity of human nature, knowing himself for a man, and the equal of any and all governments. In that sense he was the most American of us all."[55] Brown was, Thoreau suggests, a government unto himself and in this sense unlike the mass of Americans because they did not yet recognize the same capacity for self-sovereignty in themselves. Thoreau's praise of Brown, which functioned as a rejoinder to popular conceptions of Brown as "crazy," extends the work of "Resistance to Civil Government" (1849), a key work of both US literature and US political philosophy, by suggesting that not only should the principled individual withdraw from an unjust government but, in so doing, that individual *becomes* a kind of government, a sovereign body of one. This kind of sovereign self-reliance, which Thoreau attributes to Brown just one year before the outbreak of the Civil War, points to ongoing efforts to craft new political futures by invoking sovereignty in both collective and individual terms, not only through the act of nation (re)formation at stake in the Civil War but also (such is the oppositional pedigree of sovereignty) through the ascendency of a kind of modern liberal subjectivity of the sovereign self, governed by individual "conscience."[56]

Further Reading

Carlson, David. *Imagining Sovereignty: Self-Determination in American Indian Law and Literature*. University of Oklahoma Press, 2016.
Downes, Paul. *Hobbes, Sovereignty, and Early American Literature*. Cambridge University Press, 2015.

---

[54] Emerson refers to an "aboriginal Self, on which a universal reliance can be grounded," and the search for this "aboriginal self" can be seen as an exploration of self-sovereignty that links this concept with ideas of both Indigeneity and divinity (through the capital "S" in Self) at once. See Ralph Waldo Emerson, "Self-Reliance," in *Essays and Lectures*, ed. Joel Porte (Literary Classics of the United States, 1983), 268–269. Moreover, in an 1838 letter to Martin Van Buren, Emerson suggests that the forced Removal of the Cherokees disfranchises not only the Cherokees themselves but also white New Englanders who support them, leaving the latter with no alternative but a kind of moral exercise of self-sovereignty. He writes, "For how could we call the conspiracy that should crush these poor Indians our Government, or the land that was cursed by their parting and dying imprecations our country, any more?" See "Letter to Martin Van Buren," in *Emerson's Antislavery Writings*, ed. Joel Myerson and Len Gougeon (Yale University Press, 1995), 1–5, 3.
[55] Henry David Thoreau, "A Plea for Captain John Brown," in *The Tribunal*, 107.
[56] On Thoreau and the idea of the sovereign individual following the dictates of conscience, see his "Resistance to Civil Government," in *The American Transcendentalists: Essential Writings*, ed. Lawrence Buell (Modern Library, 2006), 257–277; 259.

Elmer, Jonathan. *On Lingering and Being Last: Race and Sovereignty in the New World*. Fordham University Press, 2008.

Konkle, Maureen. *Writing Indian Nations: Native Intellectuals and the Politics of Historiography, 1827–1863*. University of North Carolina Press, 2004.

MacMillan, Ken. *Sovereignty and Possession in the English New World: The Legal Foundations of Empire, 1576–1640*. Cambridge University Press, 2006.

Tsai, Robert L. *America's Forgotten Constitutions: Defiant Visions of Power and Community*. Harvard University Press, 2014.

Zuck, Rochelle Raineri. *Divided Sovereignties: Race, Nationhood, and Citizenship in Nineteenth-Century America*. University of Georgia Press, 2016.

CHAPTER 7

Religious Reestablishment from Pulpit to Page

Ashley Reed

On April 1, 1804, Catharine Maria Sedgwick, then fourteen years old, wrote to her father Theodore that at the most recent "town-meeting" in their home of Stockbridge, Massachusetts, the "Jacobins ha[d] carried the day" and that "their most diabolical act was endeavoring to lessen Dr. West's salary," an attempt at which they "fortunately ... did not succeed."[1] Catharine Sedgwick would grow up to become the first internationally famous female author born in the United States. Her father Theodore had made the professional and social climb from backwoods lawyer to prominent Federalist politician; when Catharine wrote this letter to him, he was sitting on the Massachusetts Supreme Judicial Court. "Dr. West" was the Congregationalist pastor in Stockbridge; he was uncle to Theodore's wife Pamela – herself descended from a celebrated old Connecticut family – and thus Catharine's great-uncle.[2] Stephen West had taken up Stockbridge's clerical post when Jonathan Edwards – the famed Congregationalist minister and theologian whose preaching had sparked the first Great Awakening in 1735 – vacated the post to become president of Princeton University.

Stockbridge was originally founded as a missionary village, a "praying town" for the Stockbridge Indians, Housatonic and Mahican converts to Christianity. By the time Theodore Sedgwick moved there with his law practice, however, the town's Indigenous residents, already uprooted from their original lands, had been further dispossessed by white settlers – including Pamela Sedgwick's antecedents – who gobbled up the town's real estate. Theodore had participated in the "final land grab" that drove the remaining Stockbridge Indians out of town, so that by the time Catharine wrote to her father in 1804, Stockbridge was only periodically

---

[1] Catharine Maria Sedgwick, *Life and Letters of Catharine M. Sedgwick*, ed. Mary Dewey (Harper & Brothers, 1871), 80.
[2] Catharine Maria Sedgwick, *The Power of Her Sympathy: The Autobiography and Journal of Catharine Maria Sedgwick*, ed. Mary Kelley (Massachusetts Historical Society, 1993).

125

visited by its founding Native population, who returned every winter to tend their ancestors' graves.³

I begin with this anecdote about the Sedgwick family because it opens out on topics essential to any discussion of the relationship between religion, literature, and politics in the nineteenth-century United States even as it undermines whatever notions we might have about fundamental distinctions between those terms. That Catharine Sedgwick, at only fourteen, had so imbibed her father's Federalist political loyalties as to share his disdainful view of Democrats (the "Jacobins" she derides) belies the old canard of nineteenth-century "separate spheres" in which women, confined to the home and domestic subjects, were shut out from political and economic concerns. That Stephen West's clerical salary as head of Stockbridge's Congregational Church was decided by the town's elected officials reminds us that Thomas Jefferson's proposed "wall of separation between Church & State" was then (and remains) more aspirational than actual.⁴ And that the Sedgwick home, from which Theodore and his children launched their careers as lawyers, politicians, authors, and homemakers, stood – and still stands – on stolen Housatonic and Mahican land reminds us that the United States' religious, political, and literary history is inextricable from the ongoing march of settler colonialism and empire.

In this chapter I triangulate religion, politics, and literature to demonstrate their entanglement over the course of the nineteenth century. While secularization theory would assert that religion is becoming less salient in western cultures over time or that literature and other arts have replaced religion in modern lives, the complicated history of nineteenth-century religion belies such master narratives.⁵ There were likely as many configurations of religious identification, belief, and practice in nineteenth-century

---

³ Karen Woods Weierman, "Reading and Writing *Hope Leslie*: Catharine Maria Sedgwick's Indian 'Connections,'" *The New England Quarterly* 75:3 (2002), 415–443, 427. For further discussion of the Stockbridge Indian mission, see Patrick Frazier, *The Mohicans of Stockbridge* (University of Nebraska Press, 1992); and James Axtell, "The Rise and Fall of the Stockbridge Indian Schools," *Massachusetts Review* (1986), 367–378.
⁴ Thomas Jefferson, "Jefferson's Letter to the Danbury Baptists: The Final Letter, As Sent," *The Library of Congress Information Bulletin*, 57:6 (1998), www.loc.gov/loc/lcib/9806/danpre.html.
⁵ On the secularization thesis and its problems for the study of American literature, see, among others, Elizabeth Fenton, "The Secularization Narrative and Nineteenth-Century American Literature," in Robert S. Levine and Caroline F. Levander, eds., *A Companion to American Literary Studies* (Wiley-Blackwell, 2011), 61–76; Tracy Fessenden, *Culture and Redemption: Religion, the Secular, and American Literature* (Princeton University Press, 2007); and Michael W. Kaufmann, "The Religious, the Secular, and Literary Studies: Rethinking the Secularization Narrative in Histories of the Profession," *New Literary History* 38:4 (2007), 607–627. On the recent "spiritual turn" in American literary studies, see Harold K. Bush, "Above the American Renaissance: Tracking and Theorizing the Spiritual Turn in American Literary Studies," in Harold K. Bush and Brian Yothers,

America as there were nineteenth-century Americans – and the category "American" was itself unstable. Even the culturally dominant Protestant Christian religion came in countless varieties and was perpetually reshaped by internal forces (theological innovation, schisms over slavery) and external ones (immigration, territorial expansion). What held constant throughout the century, however, was religion's centrality to cultural and political life in the United States.

The Long Disestablishment

At the beginning of the nineteenth century, religion and politics were not separable legally, practically, or discursively. When Catharine Sedgwick wrote to her father in 1804, several of the new US states still supported established churches through mandatory taxation. Jefferson's Virginia had been the first state to jettison its established church in 1786; the Sedgwicks' Massachusetts was the last, in 1833. As Michael Warner has noted, formal disestablishment was a messy endeavor, since established churches were entangled with nearly every aspect of private and public life.[6] The legal scholar Steven K. Green has argued that disestablishment, rather than a one-time event initiated with the ratification of the Constitution and Bill of Rights, has been an ongoing process in American civil society, with the elimination of state-supported churches marking the first of three stages. The nineteenth century, Green suggests, saw a long "second disestablishment" in which tasks formerly handled by established churches were divvied up between the state (elections, civil marriage, laws regarding labor and time), denominational organizations (choosing ministers, maintaining church property), and moral reform societies (missionary activities, community care, and anti-poverty and anti-vice initiatives). Determining which matters were public and which were private – which "religious" and which "secular" – was particularly contentious when it came to law and public education.[7]

---

eds., *Above the American Renaissance: David S. Reynolds and the Spiritual Imagination in American Literary Studies* (University of Massachusetts Press, 2018), 1–17.

[6] This could include "levying taxes for clerical salaries, choosing ministers, allotting land and labor for meetinghouses, compelling attendance, dividing time through sabbath laws, [...] organizing government functions such as elections and meetings, recognizing legitimate forms of private life through personal and family law, monopolizing public ritual discourse, maintaining a joint church/state monopoly of consecrations for marriage and other functions, joint keeping of birth/death records, [and] delivering care." Michael Warner, "Was Antebellum America Secular?," *The Immanent Frame* (October 2, 2012), http://tif.ssrc.org/2012/10/02/was-antebellum-america-secular/.

[7] Steven K. Green, *The Second Disestablishment: Church and State in Nineteenth-Century America* (Oxford University Press, 2010).

The formal disestablishments that began this process in the early nineteenth century were met with prophecies of doom from Protestant authorities – particularly those whose denominations benefited from the establishment system. The influential Presbyterian minister Lyman Beecher warned that, without established churches, the young, presumptively Protestant nation would be overrun by foreign forces. Since new European immigrants were increasingly arriving from Ireland and Italy rather than England and Germany, the new United States, and particularly its western frontiers, was filling up with Catholic adherents. Beecher feared that, goaded by a "priesthood educated under the despotic governments of Catholic Europe," these new arrivals would form "the union of church and state in the midst of us ... the Greek in the midst of Troy."[8] The anti-Catholic rhetoric spread by Beecher and others produced widespread discrimination and even violence against Catholic adherents. Because "the Catholic often appear[ed] in this era as a threat not only to Protestant religious practice but also to democratic governance," discrimination could be framed as patriotism and violence as self-defense.[9] One of anti-Catholicism's more pervasive literary manifestations was the convent escape narrative that flourished in the 1830s through 1850s; texts like Maria Monk's *Awful Disclosures of the Hotel Dieu Nunnery in Montreal* (1836) fanned the flames of prejudice – flames that had taken literal form just two years earlier when a mob set fire to an Ursuline convent in Charlestown, Massachusetts.[10]

Contrary to Beecher's warnings, formal disestablishment proved a spur rather than a hindrance to religious adherence in the nineteenth-century United States. A growing population, increasing literacy, fervent evangelization, and competition for members produced an explosion of new religious movements and major realignments among existing Protestant sects. Voluntary religious association made the laity rather than the clergy the driving force in American Christianity "[b]y allowing the people to become the final arbiters of religious taste," with the result that "evangelical Christianity not only successfully survived the transition from colonial to post-revolutionary society, but even enhanced its image and

---

[8] Lyman Beecher, *A Plea for the West* (Truman & Smith, 1835), 57, 59.
[9] Elizabeth Fenton, *Religious Liberties: Anti-Catholicism and Liberal Democracy in Nineteenth-Century US Literature and Culture* (Oxford University Press, 2011), 5.
[10] On anti-Catholicism and its literary manifestations in nineteenth-century America, see Jenny Franchot, *Roads to Rome: The Antebellum Protestant Encounter with Catholicism* (University of California Press, 1994) and Susan M. Griffin, *Anti-Catholicism and Nineteenth-Century Fiction* (Cambridge University Press, 2004).

appeal."[11] Between 1776 and 1840, church membership in America doubled, and the number of people involved in religious activities – whether they claimed membership in a denomination or not – skyrocketed.[12] This transatlantic phenomenon, known among historians as the Second Great Awakening, prompted explosive growth among some Protestant religious denominations, particularly the Methodists and Baptists, sapped others like the Congregationalists and Episcopalians (formerly Anglicans), and gave rise to new religious movements that included Joseph Smith's Church of Jesus Christ of Latter-Day Saints (the Mormons) and William Miller's eponymous Millerites, who coalesced around their leader's 1831 prediction that the world would end in 1843.

A Literary Awakening

On-the-ground evangelizing activities like large outdoor revivals and Methodist circuit riding were a major cause of the meteoric rise in religious adherence that marked the early nineteenth century. But increasing religiosity was also propelled, as Candy Gunther Brown has shown, by an unprecedented mobilization of print.[13] In the decades before the Civil War the American Tract Society, American Bible Society, and other Protestant publishing ventures distributed millions of books and pamphlets, including Bibles, Sunday School primers, and tracts, to Americans of all ages and in every geographic region. The eighteenth-century Puritan ministers who oversaw the first Great Awakening had been suspicious of fiction as a medium for spurring Christian conversion and had stuck to true stories of minds persuaded and souls saved. But antebellum Protestant evangelizers came to regard fiction as an important tool for both religious and social reform.[14] Catharine Maria Sedgwick began her first novel, *A New England Tale* (1822), as a short religious tract, but it soon expanded beyond her original outline.[15] Nevertheless, its goal as a vehicle for religious persuasion remained clear in its final form.

---

[11] John H. Wigger, *Taking Heaven by Storm: Methodism and the Rise of Popular Christianity in America* (Oxford University Press, 1998).
[12] On the rise in church membership during the early national and antebellum period – particularly the meteoric rise of Methodism – see Roger Finke and Rodney Stark, *The Churching of America, 1776–1990: Winners and Losers in Our Religious Economy* (Rutgers University Press, 2005).
[13] Candy Gunther Brown, *The Word in the World: Evangelical Writing, Publishing, and Reading in America, 1789–1880* (University of North Carolina Press, 2004).
[14] See David S. Reynolds, *Faith in Fiction: The Emergence of Religious Literature in America* (Harvard University Press, 1981).
[15] Sedgwick, *Life and Letters*, 153.

While British productions still dominated the US publishing market in the early nineteenth century, a rising intellectual elite insisted that an independent nation needed a unique literary culture. Foremost among these proponents was the Unitarian minister William Ellery Channing, who surveyed the paltry reputation held by US letters and put out a call in the *North American Review* for authors who would "venture to give [their] days and [their] nights, to the labours of the mind, that [they] may do something toward the literature of [their] country."[16] For Unitarians and other liberal thinkers, religion, literature, and progressive politics were mutually reinforcing endeavors: A robust and enlightened literary culture would spread Christianity's blessings far and wide, while a literate, broad-minded, and pious populace would ensure the nation's future health. When Channing (and others) called for a uniquely American literary culture, many authors responded by adopting and modifying a Scottish model: Walter Scott's historical romances. Catharine Sedgwick, James Fenimore Cooper, Lydia Maria Child, Harriet Vaughan Cheney, John Neal, and others drew on their country's "native peculiarities" and "national language"[17] to spin tales of settlement and revolution that enshrined America's founding narratives, promulgated ideals of religious pluralism, and justified the violent displacement of Indigenous peoples in the name of white Christian progress.[18]

Unitarianism, as a short-lived but influential theological insurgency within New England Congregationalism, made its most lasting cultural imprint by spawning the Transcendentalist movement. As K. P. Van Anglen has noted, the exact role that religion played in Transcendentalism has been debated by scholars for at least a hundred years,[19] but it is certainly true that both the Transcendentalists themselves and the public who encountered their writings and lectures apprehended the movement as one with immense religious implications. A reaction against Unitarianism's dry theologizing, Transcendentalism combined a reverence for English and

---

[16] William Ellery Channing, "Reflections on the Literary Delinquency of America," *The North American Review* 2 (1815), 33–43, 34.

[17] William Ellery Channing, "Essay on American Language and Literature," *The North American Review* 1 (1815), 307–314, 308.

[18] On the relationship between nineteenth-century Unitarianism and the early national historical novel, see Dan McKanan, *Identifying the Image of God: Radical Christians and Nonviolent Power in the Antebellum United States* (Oxford University Press, 2002).

[19] As Van Anglen notes, historians and critics in the early twentieth century approached Transcendentalism through the lens of Protestant institutional change, while those of the late twentieth century hailed it as a signal achievement in America's supposed march toward secularization. See K. P. Van Anglen, "Transcendentalism and Religion: The State of Play," *Literature Compass* 5:6 (2008), 1010–1024.

German Romanticism with philosophical borrowings from Eastern spirituality. Its core belief in the fundamental divinity of the self struck some observers as liberating and many others as rank apostasy. Ralph Waldo Emerson's resignation of his pulpit and his 1838 Divinity School Address – so controversial that it outraged even Unitarian Harvard – marked him in the public mind as a religious renegade. Theodore Parker's abolitionism and Bronson Alcott's education reform – including his decision to admit a mixed-race child to his experimental Temple School – struck moderate observers as dangerously radical. Henry David Thoreau's nascent anti-capitalism and Margaret Fuller's full-throated insistence on women's social, intellectual, professional, and sexual equality with men suggested a movement intent on undermining every decree of both God and nature. And Orestes Brownson's conversion to and advocacy for Roman Catholicism confirmed even for many liberal Protestants that Transcendentalism was a byway to hell.

And yet, despite critique and even ridicule, Transcendentalism became one of the most influential religious, philosophical, political, and literary movements of the century. Over his long career, Emerson would emerge as the nation's premier public intellectual, and Transcendentalist thought would inspire reformers and writers including, most explicitly, Walt Whitman. In answering Emerson's call for a poetic "genius [who] with tyrannous eye" would detail "[o]ur logrolling, our stumps and their politics, our fisheries, ... the northern trade, the southern planting, the western clearing, Oregon, and Texas,"[20] Whitman engaged in "The Great Construction of the New Bible," composing "Song of Myself" in fifty-two sections that could be parceled out and studied in the manner of a weekly devotional manual.[21] *Leaves of Grass*, Herbert J. Levine has argued, is a "scriptural poem" that enabled Whitman to become "his own religious tradition, devoting his first volume and six subsequent editions to exegesis, drawing out its fundamental beliefs and images into new poems."[22]

Not every poet was interested in rewriting or replacing the Bible, however, and neither the form nor the content of Whitman's verse typifies nineteenth-century poetic practice. Far more popular and influential – at

---

[20] Ralph Waldo Emerson, "The Poet," in *Essays, Second Series* (James Munroe and Co., 1844), 3–48, 41, HathiTrust Digital Library, https://hdl.handle.net/2027/hvd.hnu3qj.

[21] "The Great Construction of the New Bible" appears in a manuscript note written by Whitman and dated June 1857. See Walt Whitman, *Notebooks and Unpublished Prose Manuscripts, Vol. 1: Family Notes and Autobiography, Brooklyn and New York*, ed. Edward F. Grier (New York University Press, 1984), 353.

[22] Herbert J. Levine, "'Song of Myself' As Whitman's American Bible," *Modern Language Quarterly: A Journal of Literary History* 48:2 (1987), 145–161, 146.

least until modernism's appearance in the twentieth century – were the Fireside Poets: Henry Wadsworth Longfellow, William Cullen Bryant, John Greenleaf Whittier, Oliver Wendell Holmes, and James Russell Lowell. These poets, as Claudia Stokes has discussed, built their reputations on a "ministerial self-presentation" as guardians and transmitters of culture. Instead of painting as-yet-unseen democratic vistas, they most often affirmed the unity of mainstream Protestant religious values with patriotic American virtues, and much of their poetry has come to seem quaint or quietist as a result.[23] But the ubiquity and variety of nineteenth-century poetry meant that it could be turned to nearly any religious or political purpose: private devotion and speculation (manuscript poetry – like Emily Dickinson's – written in diaries and letters and never circulated), public worship (the hymns that, as Stokes notes, the Fireside Poets transformed from a "suspect and even vulgar" form to "a conventional feature of congregational worship"),[24] parental mourning (innumerable odes to deceased children), moral uplift (abolitionist and temperance verse), and historical commemoration (Emerson's "Concord Hymn," Whitman's "O Captain! My Captain!," and thousands of similar works). In public or in private, as thundering prophet or humble suppliant, nineteenth-century poets addressed every issue and occasion available to language, and religious issues and occasions figured prominently here.

Ushering in the American Millennium

Often apprehended primarily as a philosophical and literary phenomenon, Transcendentalism was also part of the aforementioned religious flowering of the early nineteenth century. Though the doomsaying Millerites were obviously disappointed, they were only the most literal manifestation of a widespread belief among many nineteenth-century Protestants that the end of days was approaching. Grounded in both the Book of Revelation and a progressive theory of human development, millennialism was the belief "that civilization was steadily heading toward a new age characterized by enlightenment, improvement, and the elimination of all worldly ills." This philosophy fired religious and political action across sectarian lines as

---

[23] Claudia Stokes, "Hymns by the Fireside: Religious Verse and the Rise and Fall of the Fireside Poets," in Bush and Yothers, *Above the American Renaissance*, 195–210, 197.
[24] Stokes, "Hymns by the Fireside," 198.

Protestant believers sought to "chang[e] the very course and vector of human civilization."²⁵

Millennial fervor proved particularly motivating to mid-century women writers, who were adept at crafting textual tools for evangelization and conversion. Largely barred from the pulpit, the seminary, and the theological journal, women writers found willing and eager audiences for tales that advocated both individual self-improvement and societal reform. Susan Warner's 1850 bestseller *The Wide, Wide World* represented both the apotheosis of the genre identified by Nina Baym as "woman's fiction" and a guide for forming democratic character, whether in women or men.²⁶ Young Ellen Montgomery learns self-denial by reading both the Bible and Mason Weems's hagiographic *History of the Life and Death, Virtues and Exploits of General George Washington*; when she is shipped away to Europe, she patriotically defends Washington's honor to her Scottish relatives. Two years later, in 1852, Harriet Beecher Stowe would definitively refute the oft-uttered claim that women were too delicate or preoccupied with home and family to take an interest in politics. *Uncle Tom's Cabin*, though it may not have "started this great war," as Lincoln supposedly claimed, undoubtedly shifted the political conversation around slavery and the Fugitive Slave Law in particular.²⁷ While the novel's most anthologized chapters (Eliza's flight across the Ohio River, Little Eva's death, and Uncle Tom's martyrdom) are its most emotionally evocative, the novel is rife with political polemic – as when the fugitive George Harris uses the Founding Fathers' words to justify escape and revolt – and transformation – as when Senator Bird alters his convictions after meeting Eliza and her hunted child. The sentimentalism that infused these mid-century bestsellers was long dismissed by critics as a flight from the difficulties and complexities of the real world – the "political sense obfuscated or gone rancid," as Ann Douglas famously asserted.²⁸ But in fact, as Julie Ellison has shown, sentimentalism was an inherently political mode of discourse based in eighteenth-century Whig sociability. In adopting this cultural mode, nineteenth-century women authors fused an existing political strategy with a rhetoric of religious sensibility to address cultural and

---

²⁵ Claudia Stokes, *The Altar at Home: Sentimental Literature and Nineteenth-Century American Religion* (University of Pennsylvania Press, 2014), 106.
²⁶ Nina Baym, *Woman's Fiction: A Guide to Novels by and about Women in America, 1820–1870* (Cornell University Press, 1978).
²⁷ Joan Hedrick, *Harriet Beecher Stowe: A Life* (Oxford University Press, 1994), xvii.
²⁸ Ann Douglas, *The Feminization of American Culture* (Knopf, 1977), 254.

social inequality by appealing to the millennial fervor of their largely Christian readership.[29]

Identifying the sentimental novel as a "political enterprise," Jane Tompkins placed it "halfway between sermon and social theory." And indeed, the oral form of the sermon echoes through nineteenth-century American literature.[30] As David S. Reynolds has demonstrated, tract literature's narrative impulse – tracts asked readers to identify with fictional characters rather than assent to specific doctrines – came to dominate both revival preaching and pulpit homiletics as the century progressed.[31] But the channels of influence flowed in both directions, with the sermon shaping the development of fiction – particularly the novel – in numerous ways. In the late 1830s, at the request of the Unitarian minister Henry Ware, Jr., Catharine Sedgwick shifted from writing historical romances and novels of manners to producing didactic novellas that modeled domestic virtues for a rising middle class; reviewers often explicitly called these texts "sermons."[32] Harriet Beecher Stowe, daughter and sister to famous ministers, populated her novels and short stories with preachers both white and black; her own narrative voice, as Dawn Coleman has shown, could range from comforting and domestic to thundering and hortatory. Coleman has highlighted the unstable relationship between fiction and sermonizing in nineteenth-century literature: "[w]hile resisting preaching through mockery, irony, and satire," she argues, authors of fiction "also envied it, identified with it, and appropriated it as a distinctive and authoritative mode of addressing audiences."[33] Nathaniel Hawthorne's hypocritical Arthur Dimmesdale, Herman Melville's charismatic Father Mapple, and Stowe's inspired insurrectionist Dred emblematize this love–hate relationship with the figure of the minister and the mode of the sermon among nineteenth-century writers.

The minister and the sermon were central to African American religious, political, and literary activity since individual survival and communal cohesion often hinged on the oral transmission of knowledge and belief.

---

[29] Julie Ellison, *Cato's Tears and the Making of Anglo-American Emotion* (University of Chicago Press, 1999).

[30] Jane P. Tompkins, *Sensational Designs: The Cultural Work of American Fiction, 1790–1860* (Oxford University Press, 1985), 126.

[31] David S. Reynolds, "From Doctrine to Narrative: The Rise of Pulpit Storytelling in America," *American Quarterly* 32:5 (1980), 479–498.

[32] Ware's request that Sedgwick contribute to his series of tale-tracts appears in Sedgwick, *Life and Letters*, 238–240. For the claim that critics identified these texts as sermons, see Douglas, *Feminization*, 109.

[33] Dawn Coleman, *Preaching and the Rise of the American Novel* (Ohio State University Press, 2013), 4.

Hortense Spillers has argued that "the sermon, as the African-American's proto-typical public speaking, locates the primary instrument of moral and political change within the community."[34] Early activists including David Walker and Maria Stewart patterned their political speeches and pamphlets after the model of the sermon, while fugitive slave narratives took on the form of the spiritual autobiography. In slave narratives, which often originated in oral form on the abolitionist lecture circuit, African American speakers and writers employed sentimental appeals alongside Christian soteriological tropes of captivity, redemption, and resurrection to "transfor[m] their status from spiritual outcasts," ostensible descendants of Cain and Ham, "to chosen people."[35] Henry "Box" Brown's spectacular stage performances included scenes in which he was symbolically buried and then "resurrected" from the wooden crate in which he had mailed himself from Richmond to Philadelphia, his ingenious method for escaping slavery.[36] Harriet Jacobs, one of the few women to publish a complete narrative of her life under and escape from slavery before the Civil War, painted her enslaver – and sexual abuser – "Dr. Flint" as a devil masquerading as a god: "if you deceive me," he told her, "you shall feel the fires of hell." Jacobs credited her literacy and her grandmother's piety for helping her see through her master's mask: "Truly," she writes, "Satan had no difficulty in distinguishing the color of his soul!"[37] William Wells Brown, who escaped enslavement by boat on the Mississippi River, renamed himself after a Quaker benefactor and reflected in his narrative on his ironic desire to go to Canada:

> An American citizen was fleeing from a Democratic, Republican, Christian government, to receive protection under the monarchy of Great Britain. While the people of the United States boast of their freedom, they at the same time keep three millions of their own citizens in chains; and while I am seated here in sight of Bunker Hill Monument, writing this narrative, I am a slave.[38]

---

[34] Hortense Spillers, "Moving On Down the Line," *American Quarterly* 40:1 (1988), 83–109, 86.
[35] Gregory S. Jackson, *The Word and Its Witness: The Spiritualization of American Realism* (University of Chicago Press, 2009), 124. On the relationship between the spiritual autobiography and the fugitive slave narrative, see Yolanda Pierce, "Redeeming Bondage: The Captivity Narrative and the Spiritual Autobiography in the African American Slave Narrative Tradition," in Audrey A. Fisch, ed., *The Cambridge Companion to the African American Slave Narrative* (Cambridge University Press, 2007), 83–98.
[36] On Henry Brown's escape, see Daphne Brooks, *Bodies in Dissent: Spectacular Performances of Race and Freedom, 1850–1910* (Duke University Press, 2006).
[37] Harriet Jacobs, *Incidents in the Life of a Slave Girl, Written by Herself*, ed. Nell Irvin Painter (Penguin Books, 2000), 65, 38.
[38] William Wells Brown, *Narrative of William W. Brown, a Fugitive Slave. Written by Himself* (Published at the Anti-slavery Office, No. 25 Cornhill, 1847), *Documenting the American South* (DocSouth), https://docsouth.unc.edu/neh/brown47/brown47.html.

Fugitive slave narratives combined a Christian typological tradition with sentimental appeals to white sensibility, shared humanity, and democratic values to produce a compelling and effective religio-political discourse.

The questions of slavery, emancipation, and black self-determination shaped the Protestant denominational landscape throughout the nineteenth century. The earliest black-led Protestant denominations were the African Methodist Episcopal Church and African Methodist Episcopal Church Zion, which formed in 1816 and 1820, respectively, when free blacks in Philadelphia and New York tired of discriminatory practices in white Methodist congregations and withdrew to form their own institutions. Beyond these formal structures, black Christians throughout the North and South built vital faith communities by combining biblical exegesis, Arminian free will theology, African folk beliefs, and shared oral and musical traditions. Though southern slaveholders had introduced Christianity to enslaved people as "[a]n agency of social control," black Americans transformed it into "a source of economic cooperation, an arena for political activity, a sponsor of education, and a refuge in a hostile white world."[39] Black Christianity was – and remains – a powerful religious counter-discourse that could prompt both rhetorical action and armed uprising. The poet and novelist Frances Ellen Watkins Harper gained a national reputation on the antislavery lecture circuit, becoming successful enough to provide financial support to the Underground Railroad. David Walker's *Appeal to the Colored Citizens of the World* (1829) and Frederick Douglass's *Narrative of the Life of Frederick Douglass, an American Slave, Written by Himself* (1845) drew a bright line between the hypocrisy of white slaveholding Christianity and the truer faith of the black church, and the enslaved preacher and revolutionary Nat Turner claimed the title of prophet, searching both the Bible and the stars for signs that the day of God's judgment against slaveholders was at hand.

Looking Beyond

The search for signs and wonders was a common one in the nineteenth-century United States as the rapid pace of scientific and technological progress called nearly every form of established knowledge into question. In the early part of the century, Franz Anton Mesmer's new technique of manipulating subjects' "animal magnetism" drew Ben Franklin's

---

[39] Albert J. Raboteau, *Slave Religion: The Invisible Institution in the Antebellum South* (Oxford University Press, 1978), ix.

skepticism and, later, Margaret Fuller's approbation. In 1848, two otherwise unremarkable little girls in Hydesville, New York, suddenly began receiving communications from the spirit of a peddler who had died in their home. This discovery sparked a nationwide movement among Americans of every gender, race, and religious tradition, millions of whom began enthusiastically attempting to communicate with the dead. Referring to such communication as the "spiritual telegraph" and presenting it as an empirical science – one that could be tested through controlled experiment – Spiritualist seekers joined neighborhood séance circles, attended trance lectures and demonstrations, and held intimate sessions with the automatic writing device known as the planchette.[40] Since nineteenth-century gender ideology figured men as active or "positive" and women as passive and receptive, women often found more success as mediums, leading to a paradoxical situation in which the most outwardly demure woman could appear on stage and endorse the most politically radical positions – including abolitionism, temperance, free love, and woman's suffrage – so long as the spirits seemed to be speaking through her.[41]

While all communal religious experience is discursive, Spiritualism was especially so. Self-appointed leaders including Thomas Lake Harris and Andrew Jackson Davis produced stacks of books, and Spiritualist circles published magazines and newspapers from the long-lived (the Boston-based *Banner of Light* stayed in print for fifty years) to the barely there (the Milwaukee *Anthropologist* lasted 5 months in 1851). As a religiously unsettling and often politically radical movement, Spiritualism drew the ire of established Christian clergy and the ridicule of skeptical authors, including Nathaniel Hawthorne (whose *Blithedale Romance* centers on a diabolical mesmerist and a frail female medium) and Mark Twain (who lampoons mediums in both *Life on the Mississippi* and the Mysterious Stranger narratives). But it also produced a blockbuster bestseller, Elizabeth Stuart Phelps's *The Gates Ajar* (1868). Though Phelps denied that she or her text endorsed Spiritualism, the novel's repeated insistence that the dead retain the physical and personal characteristics they

---

[40] On the history of Spiritualism in the mid-nineteenth-century United States, see Cathy Gutierrez, *Plato's Ghost: Spiritualism in the American Renaissance* (Oxford University Press, 2009) and Bret E. Carroll, *Spiritualism in Antebellum America* (Indiana University Press, 1997).
[41] Ann Braude, *Radical Spirits: Spiritualism and Women's Rights in Nineteenth-Century America* (Beacon Press, 1989). Spiritualism was so closely aligned with the women's rights movement that the first woman to run a campaign for the US presidency, Victoria Woodhull, was both a woman's rights advocate and a vocal Spiritualist.

displayed on earth was the theological foundation for all Spiritualist practice, and bereaved readers found comfort in its (and its sequels') vivid descriptions of a comfortable and familiar domestic afterlife.

As Robert S. Cox and Molly McGarry have noted, Spiritualism's cultural dynamics shifted significantly over the first few decades of the movement. The "spirit guides" who greeted séance-goers in the 1850s were most often dead family members, but during and after the Civil War these otherworldly interlocutors were replaced by Native American figures. Spiritualist seekers and the mediums who catered to them increasingly "rel[ied] on a cultural understanding of Native Americans as highly spiritual, and mapp[ed] onto the spirit world the colonial relationship of the Indian as a guide for the white man."[42] White settlers in North America had always been suspicious of Indigenous spiritual traditions, often interpreting Indigenous practices as self-evidently diabolical.[43] Cultural and literary discourse of the early nineteenth century, however, offered up fictional Native American characters, including Lydia Maria Child's Hobomok (*Hobomok*, 1824) and Catharine Maria Sedgwick's Magawisca (*Hope Leslie*, 1827) as benevolent nature worshippers who educated the novels' white settler characters – and their readers – in the Great Spirit's wisdom.[44] As Grant Shreve has argued, the early national historical novel promoted intra-Protestant unity by appropriating Indigenous religion's most attractive aspects (Native Americans' purported closeness to nature, for instance), folding them into a pluralistic and domestic vision of Protestant national life, and then evacuating Indigenous Americans themselves from the landscape.[45]

Even as white authors were busily disappearing them, however, Indigenous speakers and writers such as the Pequot clergyman and activist William Apess and the Cherokee novelist John Rollin Ridge maintained a continuing presence in the public sphere.[46] Over the course of the

---

[42] Molly McGarry, *Ghosts of Futures Past: Spiritualism and the Cultural Politics of Nineteenth-Century America* (University of California Press, 2008), 66. See also Robert S. Cox, *Body and Soul: A Sympathetic History of American Spiritualism* (University of Virginia Press, 2003), 189–192.

[43] See Ronald Niezen, *Spirit Wars: Native North American Religions in the Age of Nation Building* (University of California Press, 2000).

[44] While it is simplistic to lump all Indigenous North American spiritual practices together, Vine Deloria offers a useful overview of some of their shared characteristics, with particular attention to spirituality as a source of political power. See Vine Deloria, *God Is Red: A Native View of Religion* (Fulcrum, 2003).

[45] Grant Shreve, "Fragile Belief: Lydia Maria Child's *Hobomok* and the Scene of American Secularity," *American Literature* 86:4 (2014), 655–682. See also Ashley Reed, "*Hope Leslie* and the Grounds of Secularism," *ESQ: A Journal of Nineteenth-Century American Literature and Culture* 66:1 (2020), 88–131.

[46] See William Apess, *On Our Own Ground: The Complete Writings of William Apess, a Pequot*, ed. Barry O'Connell (University of Massachusetts Press, 1992). On Ridge, see Lori Merish, "Print,

nineteenth century, westward expansion and white settlers' repeated encounters with spiritually and militarily formidable Indigenous peoples continually disrupted white efforts to locate native peoples and their non-Christian cosmologies safely in the past. The poet Jane Johnston Schoolcraft recorded the Ojibwa songs and legends told to her by her mother, translating some into English and recording others in the Ojibwe language. Sarah Winnemucca Hopkins's *Life Among the Paiutes: Their Wrongs and Claims* (1884) offered a scathing indictment of the US government's and Christian missionaries' treatment of her people. And Yankton Dakota writer Zitkála-Šá's autobiographical essays in the *Atlantic Monthly* in 1900, which detail her removal from the Yankton Indian Reservation to a residential school in Indiana, were and remain some of the most powerful English-language writing by a Native American author, while her "Why I Am a Pagan" opposes Indigenous spiritualities to the colonizing Christianity that she labeled "the new superstition."[47]

The final decades of the nineteenth century saw a reorganization of the relationship between literature, religion, and politics in the United States. The Civil War, as Mark Noll has argued, indexed a "theological crisis" in American life, as competing visions of America's providential destiny – often promulgated in literary form – came into violent conflict.[48] On the eve of the war, the publication of Charles Darwin's *On the Origin of Species* (1859) undermined the millennia-old Christian belief in an ordered universe in which man, formed in God's own image, held dominion over creation. Darwin's assertion that the natural world had come to be not through divine design but through random chance threw Christian cosmology into disarray. Not merely the content of Christian belief but its vehicle of transmission came into doubt in the later decades of the nineteenth century as scholars and theologians in the United States grappled with the "higher criticism" of the Bible. Initiated by German theologians in the mid-eighteenth century, the higher criticism approached biblical texts in historical perspective; rather than the stable and unchanging word of God, the books of the Old and New Testaments were historically situated documents that could be subjected to the types of critique applied to secular texts. Such study revealed biblical texts

---

Cultural Memory, and John Rollin Ridge's *The Life and Adventures of Joaquín Murieta, the Celebrated California Bandit*," *Arizona Quarterly: A Journal of American Literature, Culture, and Theory* 59:4 (2003), 31–70.

[47] Zitkála-Šá [Gertrude Bonnin], "Why I Am a Pagan," *Atlantic Monthly* 90:542 (1902), 801–803, 803. For a recent and compelling discussion of Indigenous thought and writing produced mostly, though not entirely, in what is now North America, see Daniel Heath Justice, *Why Indigenous Literatures Matter* (Wilfrid Laurier University Press, 2018).

[48] Mark A. Noll, *The Civil War As a Theological Crisis* (University of North Carolina Press, 2006).

to be unstable, historically contingent, and internally contradictory. Before the Civil War, the radical ideas promulgated by the higher critics influenced the British Romantics and, through them, the American Transcendentalists; by the late nineteenth century they had become impossible to ignore.[49]

Amid these religious and political upheavals, literary realism came to occupy a central place in American literary life. Realism's rise has sometimes been described as a secularizing process, but it is more accurate to say that realist authors embraced a moderate liberal Protestantism evacuated of the theological, conversionary, and reform impulses of prewar romanticism and sentimentalism. If realist literature had political ambitions, they were, according to Nancy Glazener, to solidify New England middle-class cultural hegemony and to "insulat[e] bourgeois men from the 'private griefs' of women and tempe[r] white people's awareness of African Americans' oppression with an emphasis on the pathos of the white people's perceptions of it."[50] Gregory Jackson, however, has traced a counter-strain of late nineteenth-century "homiletic realism" that included works by Stowe, Louisa May Alcott, and especially Charles Sheldon and Walter Wyckoff. Homiletic novels including Sheldon's *In His Steps: What Would Jesus Do?* (1897) "aimed to facilitate private devotion, strengthen moral autonomy, and foster social engagement through particular acts of reading. It was to a nation of like-minded Christians what the sermon had been to smaller, regional communities."[51] Rather than allowing middle-class audiences to stand aloof from the suffering caused by industrialization and unrestrained capitalism,[52] homiletic realism encouraged readers to approach social ills as opportunities for concerted religious and political action. Meanwhile, literary naturalists, frustrated with "the drama of a broken teacup," as Frank Norris famously described high realism, absorbed some of prewar sentimentalism's crusading spirit.[53] In its (sometimes voyeuristic) concern with those cast out, cut down, or left

---

[49] On the higher criticism and its influence on American literature, see Jerry Wayne Brown, *The Rise of Biblical Criticism in America, 1800–1870: The New England Scholars* (Wesleyan University Press, 1969); Richard A. Grusin, *Transcendentalist Hermeneutics: Institutional Authority and the Higher Criticism of the Bible* (Duke University Press, 1991); and Gail K. Smith, "Higher Reading: *Uncle Tom's Cabin* and Biblical Higher Criticism," in Bush and Yothers, *Above the American Renaissance*, 107–124.

[50] Nancy Glazener, *Reading for Realism: The History of a US Literary Institution, 1850–1910* (Duke University Press, 1997), 43.

[51] Jackson, *The Word*, 158–159.

[52] On the "realist disposition" to construct literary and cultural prestige through class difference, see Phillip Barrish, *American Literary Realism, Critical Theory, and Intellectual Prestige, 1880–1995* (Cambridge University Press, 2001).

[53] Frank Norris, "A Plea for Romantic Fiction," *Boston Evening Transcript* (December 18, 1901).

behind, naturalism was capacious enough to admit the existence of non-Christian Americans who, though they had been in the country for decades or even centuries, had been all but invisible in literature. Works like Abraham Cahan's *Yekl: A Tale of the New York Ghetto* (1896) and Sui Sin Far's (Edith Maude Eaton's) "Mrs. Spring Fragrance" and other stories and essays revealed the spiritual lives of Eastern European and Chinese immigrants. In doing so, they shone a bright light on the exclusions produced by the assumption that to be American is to be a Protestant Christian of Northern European descent.

The nineteenth century, then, saw many transformations in the relationship between religion and politics – transformations that can be traced through, but not reduced to, their literary manifestations. Literature could be a venue for theological debate, a vehicle for conversion, a passionate plea for abused humanity, or an imaginative space for envisioning social reform. In each of these modes, authors of literature intervened not only in religious discourses but in the vital political life of the nation. To apprehend truly the role of religion and politics in nineteenth-century American life and literature, readers must recognize the interpenetration of these discourses and the inextricability of these terms.

Further Reading

Audi, Robert. "Religion and Politics." In David Estlund, ed., *The Oxford Handbook of Political Philosophy*. Oxford University Press, 2012, 223–240.

Brooks, Joanna. *American Lazarus: Religion and the Rise of African-American and Native American Literatures*. Oxford University Press, 2003.

Brown, Candy Gunther. *The Word in the World: Evangelical Writing, Publishing, and Reading in America, 1789–1880*. University of North Carolina Press, 2004.

Bush, Harold K. and Brian Yothers, eds. *Above the American Renaissance: David S. Reynolds and the Spiritual Imagination in American Literary Studies*. University of Massachusetts Press, 2018.

Butler, Jon. *Awash in a Sea of Faith*. Harvard University Press, 1990.

Fenton, Elizabeth. *Religious Liberties: Anti-Catholicism and Liberal Democracy in Nineteenth-Century US Literature and Culture*. Oxford University Press, 2011.

Fessenden, Tracy. *Culture and Redemption: Religion, the Secular, and American Literature*. Princeton University Press, 2007.

Franchot, Jenny. *Roads to Rome: The Antebellum Protestant Encounter with Catholicism*. University of California Press, 1994.

Johnson, Sylvester. *African American Religions, 1500–2000: Colonialism, Democracy, and Freedom*. Taylor & Francis, 2016.

Loebel, Thomas. *The Letter and the Spirit of Nineteenth-Century American Literature: Justice, Politics, Theology*. McGill-Queen's University Press, 2005.

McGarry, Molly. *Ghosts of Futures Past: Spiritualism and the Cultural Politics of Nineteenth-Century America*. University of California Press, 2008.

McKanan, Dan. *Identifying the Image of God: Radical Christians and Nonviolent Power in the Antebellum United States*. Oxford University Press, 2002.

Murison, Justine S. *Faith in Exposure: Privacy and Secularism in the Nineteenth-Century United States*. University of Pennsylvania Press, 2023.

Murphy, Gretchen. *New England Women Writers, Secularity, and the Federalist Politics of Church and State*. Oxford University Press, 2021.

Noll, Mark A. and Luke E. Harlow, eds. *Religion and American Politics: From the Colonial Period to the Present*. Oxford University Press, 2007.

Whitehead, Deborah. "Beyond Belief: Religion, Law, and Popular Culture." In Nan Goodman and Simon Stern, eds., *The Routledge Research Companion to Law and Humanities in Nineteenth-Century America*. Taylor & Francis, 2017, 340–355.

CHAPTER 8

Competing Views of Partisanship and Factionalism

Sandra M. Gustafson

The denouement of Henry Adams's *Democracy: An American Novel* (1880) exposes the partisan dealings of Senator Silas P. Ratcliffe. Hailing from Illinois, which developed a reputation for electoral fraud even before it became a state, the aptly named Ratcliffe displays his partisan tendencies early in the novel when he relates the story of his participation in voter fraud during the Civil War. Ostensibly he involved himself in the scheme to keep the presidency from falling to the "peace party," saving the Union as a more or less direct consequence – or so he claims.[1] In another scene he expresses contempt for civil service reform, being himself a prolific dispenser of offices to his fellow party members. These episodes diminish his stature somewhat in the eyes of Madeleine Lee, the woman he wishes to marry because he believes that she can help him win the White House, but they do not turn her completely against him. Wealthy, cultured, and educated, she remains unable to exercise direct political power through so much as a vote, and her ambition draws her to this man of dubious ethics who can make her one of the most powerful women in the world.

Ratcliffe's ultimate downfall comes in the form of a letter that Madeleine receives from John Carrington, a romantic rival to Ratcliffe, relating an occasion when Ratcliffe gave the appearance of having accepted a bribe to pass a bill that subsidized a steamship company to expand its service. Confronted with the letter, Ratcliffe does not deny the charge, but he does reframe it, seeking to justify his actions as less financial corruption than party loyalty and, ultimately, patriotism. The company, he tells Madeleine, did not pay a bribe directly to the Senator himself but rather to his party's National Central Committee, which had accumulated a large

---

[1] Henry Adams, *Democracy: An American Novel*, in *Novels, Mont Saint Michel, The Education* (Library of America), 54. Ratcliffe's unnamed party corresponds to the Republican Party, while the "peace party" refers to the Democrats. I provide a longer discussion of the background to the novel in Sandra M. Gustafson, "Henry Adams, Political Reform, and the Legacy of the Republican Roman Senate," *Classical Receptions Journal* 7:1 (2015), 97–112.

campaign debt in the effort to retain the presidency and prevent the South from reclaiming the dominance it once held over national politics. Adams adds a further layer to the story of the bribe through the narrator, who presents the events described from a different perspective, that of "Mr. Ratcliffe's associates," who might have offered the following story if Madeleine had consulted them: "that Ratcliffe had dragged them [that is, the party organization] into an enormous expenditure to carry his own State, and with it his own reelection to the Senate; that they had tried to hold him responsible, and he had tried to shirk the responsibility"; and that ultimately Ratcliffe forced their hand and "compelled them, in order to save their own credit, to receive the money" (175). In other words, Ratcliffe needed financial support from his party in order to secure votes for both the presidency and his own office, and the best way he found to repay the investment was through a corrupt bargain with a corporate interest. Adams suggests that beneath a surface commitment to the Union cause, personal and partisan benefit are tangled up in a dubious relationship to industry. Through the device of competing stories, Adams suggests that Ratcliffe's party and Ratcliffe himself have used the preservation of the Union as a screen for political corruption, each applying the partisan logic that anything is allowed in a Manichean battle between good and evil.

Adams's presentation of Ratcliffe's downfall amounts to a critique of partisanship that was rooted in his youthful experiences in Washington during the "Secession Winter" of 1860–1861, when he watched his father and other Republican leaders try to avert war in the months following Abraham Lincoln's election. Adams held the sharply divided Senate responsible for exacerbating the conflict rather than resolving it. His abiding dislike of the institution comes through when the narrator describes Ratcliffe's tense relation with Lord Skye, tracing the Senator's hostility to the fear that the British Minister may fail to understand that "democracy ... is the government of the people, by the people, for the benefit of Senators" (17). The novel's ironic tone divides the reader's political sympathies between Madeleine, who arrives in the seat of national power determined to learn if "America is right or wrong" (39), and Baron Jacobi, the Bulgarian minister and member of Madeleine's salon, whose worldliness and cynicism pose a sharp challenge to the notion of American exceptionalism. Taking aim at Ratcliffe, Jacobi proclaims that if the United States is exceptional, it is so only in the degree of the thoroughness with which its citizens and their government have embraced financial gain as a motivating force, which is how Jacobi defines "corruption." The republican form of mixed government that Henry Adams's great-grandfather, President John Adams, had hoped would improve on previous ruling systems was doomed, in Baron Jacobi's view, to fall instead even lower on the scale of abuse of power.

The two-party system emerges in Henry Adams's *Democracy: An American Novel* as a principal source of the corruption that he and others – collectively described as "Mugwumps" – battled against, in Adams's case through his work supporting civil service reform. In 1780 John Adams had warned that "a Division of the Republick into two great Parties ... is to be dreaded as the greatest political Evil."[2] His fears were quickly put to the test. The first party system arose during the debates over the Constitution, between supporters of that document (the Federalists) and its opponents (the Anti-Federalists); in time the Anti-Federalists evolved into the Democratic-Republicans, led by James Madison and Thomas Jefferson, while the Federalists, who were associated with the legacy of Alexander Hamilton, collapsed in 1824. The brief absence of party divisions in the 1824 presidential election did not have the effect of eliminating political malfeasance. Instead, the single-party election produced four top candidates who all identified as Democratic-Republicans. The failure of any candidate to achieve a clear majority of electoral votes led the US House of Representatives to select John Quincy Adams (Henry's grandfather), a choice that his rival Andrew Jackson labelled a "corrupt bargain." Jackson, who had won the most popular and electoral votes (though not a majority), responded to what he believed to have been the collusion between Clay and Adams that kept him from office by collaborating with Martin Van Buren to restore the two-party system. Their Jacksonian Democrats became the nation's first modern political party, possessed of a more robust organizational apparatus than their predecessors; Henry Clay led the rival Whig Party that formed in response. This "second party system" launched an enduring feature of the political landscape in the United States: two dominant parties, occasionally supplemented by minor parties such as the Anti-Masonic Party or the American Party, which after a brief period of influence were either absorbed into one or the other dominant party or simply disbanded, leaving their members to find a political home elsewhere. By the time that Henry Adams wrote *Democracy*, then, John Adams's fears about the "Division of the Republick into two great Parties ... each arranged under its Leader, and concerting Measures in opposition to each other" had been realized. These

---

[2] Letter from John Adams to Jonathan Jackson, October 2, 1780, Founders Online, National Archives, https://founders.archives.gov/documents/Adams/06-10-02-0113. For additional context, see Gustafson, "Henry Adams," 101–103.

considerations influenced Henry Adams's Mugwump turn in the 1880s: he elevated character over ideology, embraced an independent political identity, and rejected party ties.

Partisanship was not viewed as a political evil by every member of the founding generation. In *Federalist* No. 10, James Madison described factional conflict as inescapably rooted in the diversity of human interests, abilities, and beliefs, and he warned – in a passage that calls to mind Silas Ratcliffe – that "it is in vain to say that enlightened statesmen will be able to adjust these clashing interests, and render them all subservient to the public good. Enlightened statesmen will not always be at the helm."[3] Even if enlightened leadership could somehow be guaranteed, there would be other complicating factors, including the inevitable tension between the immediate situation and long-term outcomes. Madison celebrated two aspects of the Constitution that he believed would mitigate the dangers of faction: the representative nature of the government, which he contrasted favorably with direct democracy, and the large and increasing size of the United States. "Extend the sphere" of the republic, Madison wrote,

> and you take in a greater variety of parties and interests; you make it less probable that a majority of the whole will have a common motive to invade the rights of other citizens; or if such a common motive exists, it will be more difficult for all who feel it to discover their own strength, and to act in unison with each other.

An extensive republic with numerous competing interest groups would produce shifting coalitions and protect minority interests.

The writer Hugh Henry Brackenridge, who had been Madison's classmate at Princeton, offered a different view of political parties in his novel *Modern Chivalry*. Two volumes of this picaresque tale modeled on *Don Quixote* appeared in 1792; the full four-volume edition of the novel was published in 1815. A vast, eclectic work about the political culture of the early United States, *Modern Chivalry* varies in voice, stance, and tone, including lengthy pronouncements on a range of topics, sometimes in the voice of the elite protagonist Captain Farrago, and sometimes in the voice of the narrator, who is not sharply distinguished from Brackenridge himself.[4] In one of these discursive sections, the narrator comments on

---

[3] *Federalist* No. 10, *The Federalist Papers*, Avalon Project, https://avalon.law.yale.edu/18th_century/fed10.asp.

[4] John Engell, "Brackenridge, 'Modern Chivalry,' and American Humor," *Early American Literature* 22:1 (1987), 43–62, www.jstor.org/stable/25056646. I have consulted the 1819 edition: Hugh Henry Brackenridge, *Modern Chivalry: Containing the Adventures of a Captain, and Teague O'Regan, His Servant* (R. Patterson & Lambdin, 1819).

"the reason of the fluctuations of parties in republics" – a topic related to Madison's theory of shifting alliances. One explanation offered is "the unskilful driving of the state carriage" (347), which Brackenridge compares to Phaeton losing control of the sun god's carriage and falling to his death. "All depends upon the wisdom, and integrity of those that lead," he writes, and then asks rhetorically, "What ruined the federal administration, but the intemperance of driving" (347)? Shifting his focus from the role of parties to the place of individual representatives, he stresses that "an honest man in a deliberate body" should trust "his own judgment" and nothing else: "let him think humbly, diligently, extensively, distrusting preconceived opinions, and laying his mind open to the light of truth" (348). He should consult colleagues who have expertise in a particular field, as well as those who manifest genuine concern for the public good. Pivoting back to the question of parties, Brackenridge concludes the section with the statement that "no party in a republic will retain power always, because they will abuse it" (348); still, the longer a party correctly identifies the moderate policy and sticks to it, the longer that party will retain its hold on the reins of government. Moderation wins out over "vigour" (348). Brackenridge's emphasis on moderate policy and the common good draws on the classical republican tradition.[5]

To sum up, four ways of considering partisanship and factionalism dominated the political landscape of the nineteenth-century United States. The first way involved the residual anti-party views of classical republicans, who were often drawn to a traditional politics of deference involving voluntary allegiance to leaders of a higher class who would advance the "common good" (Madison's "Enlightened statesmen" and Brackenridge's Captain Farrago). The Madisonian alternative – given that "Enlightened statesmen will not always be at the helm" – involved multiple factions, in shifting configurations extending across a large geographic expanse, that could prevent majorities from dominating minorities. A third approach reflected the stance of those like Andrew Jackson who believed that parties harnessed the power of the people, whose interests would otherwise suffer neglect or worse from elite leaders. Finally, the fear of a polarizing, two-party system expressed by John Adams evolved in the

---

[5] On the transformation of classical republican thought in the early nineteenth century, see Sandra M. Gustafson, "Daniel Webster and the Making of Modern Liberty in the Atlantic World," in Caroline Fuller Sloat, ed., *Liberty! Égalité! Independencia! Print Culture, Enlightenment, and Revolution in the Americas, 1776–1838* (American Antiquarian Society, 2007), 175–192, and Gustafson, *Imagining Deliberative Democracy in the Early American Republic* (University of Chicago Press, 2011).

views of a Mugwump like Henry Adams, who held himself apart from partisan corruption without aspiring to restore the elite politics of deference.[6]

A variant of Henry Adams's position can be found in *The American Democrat* (1838), James Fenimore Cooper's response to Alexis de Tocqueville, written as the effects of Jacksonian Democracy were coming into focus. Cooper had moved to Europe in 1826 during John Quincy Adams's presidency, and he returned to the United States in 1833 at the beginning of Jackson's second term. Despite his long-standing support for Jackson, Cooper was appalled at the partisanship that had, under the second party system, overtaken the United States during his absence. His evolving attitudes toward partisan behavior become apparent through a comparison of his treatment of the subject in *The Prairie* (1827), which he began in the United States and completed in France, and in *The American Democrat* eleven years later. *The Prairie* is the third Leatherstocking Tale in order of composition and the final one in the life story of Natty Bumppo, the hero of this five-novel series. The plot features the Pawnee chief Hard-Heart, who is repeatedly designated as "the Partizan" (alternatively spelled Partisan), a term that Cooper explains in a note is "derived from the French."[7] He treats Hard-Heart and the Pawnees favorably, allying them with Natty Bumppo, and emphasizing their peaceful relations with white Americans. The Teton leader Mahtoree is also a partisan, but he is characterized as a demagogue, and Cooper links him to the excesses of the French Revolution. Vicious and deceptive, Mahtoree leads his people against the settlers. The seeds of Cooper's later critique of partisanship are present in Mahtoree's character.

In *The Prairie*, Cooper portrays positive and negative forms of partisanship, but by the time he wrote *The American Democrat* his attitude had hardened into the hostility that is clearly present in the section on "Party."[8] Here Cooper claims that political parties "control the people" and writes that "when party rules, the people do not rule, but merely such a portion of the people as can manage to get control of party" (181) – a passage that reads like a sketch of Ratcliffe's character. Party, Cooper continues, operates by passion and personal interest, not dispassionate disinterest; it

---

[6] J. G. A. Pocock, "The Classical Theory of Deference," *The American Historical Review* 81:3 (1976), 516–523, www.jstor.org/stable/1852422.
[7] James Fenimore Cooper, *The Prairie; A Tale*, in The Leatherstocking Tales, Vol. 1 (Library of America, 1985), 1297.
[8] James Fenimore Cooper, *The American Democrat: Or, Hints on the Social and Civic Relations of the United States of America* (H. & E. Phinney, 1838), 179–182.

"overshadows truth, justice, patriotism, and every other publick virtue, completely reversing the order of democracy, by putting unworthy motives in the place of reason" (181). Evoking and amplifying prejudices, parties cloud the individual's perceptions of political issues and aims. The section closes with a skeptical response to faction. The "freeman" could in good conscience "act in concert" with those who shared his views, but he should never become "a mere party man" or let his mind be clouded by the "prejudices, frauds, and tyrranny [sic] of factions" (182). Where Madison had seen the potential for shifting coalitions to enhance republican self-governance, Cooper saw distortion and conflict. The distinction that Cooper draws in this section is between coordinated action informed by individual knowledge and reflection, and party associations that are so strong that they become a form of enthusiasm.

In the same year that Cooper published *The American Democrat*, the Unitarian minister William Ellery Channing touched on similar themes in "Self-Culture," which he delivered as a lecture at Boston in September 1838; the text was subsequently published on both sides of the Atlantic, with new editions appearing into the twentieth century. Like Cooper, Channing stresses the importance of independent thought and consequently advises holding lightly to party affiliations. The "first and grand condition of mental progress" is "to receive the truth, no matter how it bears on myself," he emphasizes. "I must follow it, no matter where it leads, what interests it opposes, to what persecution or loss it lays me open, from what party it severs me, or to what party it allies."[9] Channing describes this stance as "fairness of mind" or "disinterested love of truth" (19), and he makes a sharp distinction between this quality, which he views as the animating spirit of self-culture, and partisan behavior. He describes party spirit as a distorting force that warps the senses and the intellect, undermines "moral independence," and produces "passionate partizans" (53) who surrender their freedom of thought and action to a political organization. Channing particularly stresses the division of the parties along class lines, which he sees as threatening to create hardened distinctions that are, in practice, more diffuse and labile than party rhetoric allows. "The vast and ever-growing property of this country, where is it?" he asked. "It is diffused like the atmosphere, and almost as variable, changing hands with the seasons, shifting from rich to poor, not by the violence but by the industry and skill of the latter class" (54). By pointing to

---

[9] William Ellery Channing, *Self-Culture: An Address Introductory to the Franklin Lectures, Delivered at Boston, September, 1838* (Dutton and Wentworth, 1838), 19.

property becoming less concentrated and more widely distributed, Channing suggests that the stark divisions of party are not tied to class divisions and thus are rooted in ideas and rhetoric rather than a material inequality.

Channing was a guiding figure for the Transcendentalists, and echoes of his thought appear in the essays of Ralph Waldo Emerson, who writes in a similar vein about the love of truth and its distance from party politics. In "The Conservative" (1841) Emerson asserts that "the reformer, the partisan loses himself in driving to the utmost some specialty of right conduct, until his own nature and all nature resist him."[10] He develops a more refined sense of partisanship and factionalism in "Politics" (1844), where he distinguishes between parties based in the inescapable conflict of interests (planters versus merchants, or capitalists versus industrialists) and "parties of principle" (religious sectarianism, abolitionism, support for free trade, opposition to capital punishment) that "degenerate into personalities, or would inspire enthusiasm."[11] Building on a fundamental contrast that he drew in "The Conservative" between the "party of Conservatism and that of Innovation," in "Politics" he stresses the appeal of the democratic values espoused by one of the two main parties of his day (the Democrats) and the superior merit of the men associated with the other party (the Whigs). Summing up his opposition to the dominant party system, Emerson writes:

> [T]he spirit of our American radicalism is destructive and aimless: it is not loving; it has no ulterior and divine ends; but is destructive only out of hatred and selfishness. On the other side, the conservative party, composed of the most moderate, able, and cultivated part of the population, is timid, and merely defensive of property ... From neither party, when in power, has the world any benefit to expect in science, art, or humanity, at all commensurate with the resources of the nation.

Elements of these debates over the nature and value of partisanship figure in Nathaniel Hawthorne's *The House of the Seven Gables* (1851). One scene in particular evokes the kind of mindless absorption in party that Cooper and Channing feared. In a chapter called "The Arched Window," Clifford Pyncheon looks down upon a political procession and has to be restrained from throwing himself out of the window to merge with the

---

[10] Ralph Waldo Emerson, "The Conservative," lecture delivered at the Masonic Temple, Boston, December 9, 1841, *American Transcendentalism Web*, https://archive.vcu.edu/english/engweb/transcendentalism/authors/emerson/essays/conservative.html.

[11] Ralph Waldo Emerson, "The Essays," Second Series (1844), *American Transcendentalism Web*, https://archive.vcu.edu/english/engweb/transcendentalism/authors/emerson/essays/politics.html.

crowd, dead or alive. Hawthorne's characteristic ambiguity – his presentation of alternatives – is exceptionally pointed in this scene. As a young man, Clifford was framed by his cousin for his uncle's murder. After years of imprisonment, he has returned to the house where his uncle died, now in a frail and somewhat unbalanced state. He suffers from enduring social ostracism due to his alleged crime, which is further exacerbated by his evident oddity. The narrator observes that the lure of party that the procession represents for Clifford may be the result of "terror" propelling him toward the crowd that he fears. Alternatively, it may be "a natural magnetism, tending toward the great centre of humanity"; or it may have elements of both impulses.[12] The loss of self in the crowd reflects a desire to unite with others that can be healthy, but it can also be deadly – in both a literal sense and, more figuratively, through the obliteration of individual thought.

Clifford is prevented from throwing himself out of the arched window into the political procession, and the novel pursues its theme of political reconciliation through the marriage between Phoebe Pyncheon and Holgrave, the descendant of the Pyncheons' ancient class enemy Matthew Maule. Mapping onto this relationship his era's political conflict between Jacksonian Democrats, who were champions of the "common man," and their "aristocratic" Whig antagonists, Hawthorne resolves a generations-long dispute through the coupling of Phoebe and Holgrave, who unite in a comfortable middle-class vision of stability, cheerfulness, and good housekeeping. There is more of a connection to national politics than this "romance of reconciliation" ending might suggest. *The House of the Seven Gables* appeared the year before Hawthorne's longtime friend Franklin Pierce became the successful Democratic candidate for president – an effort that Hawthorne supported by publishing a campaign biography of Pierce in 1852. This narrative imagining the end of class-based conflict registers the waning relevance of the Whig Party, which failed to recover from the loss to Pierce. A strong economy made the Whig economic program irrelevant, while the passage of the Kansas–Nebraska Act in 1854 decisively elevated slavery – supported by both Whigs and Democrats – as the central political issue dividing the country. Opposed to slavery, the Republican Party emerged that same year as the main alternative to the Democrats. Hawthorne's support for Pierce, and his notoriously ambiguous commitment to the Union cause in "Chiefly about War Matters, by a Peaceable Man" (1862), signaled his

---

[12] Nathaniel Hawthorne, *The House of the Seven Gables* (Penguin Classics, 1986), 166.

continued focus on harmonizing the interests of white Americans across class divides – and later, sectional divides – even as the political field had shifted from common-man Democrats opposing elite Whigs to proslavery Democrats opposing abolitionist Republicans. *The House of the Seven Gables* highlighted the potential to ameliorate partisan class conflicts at the moment when race and slavery were eclipsing class as the hottest flashpoints in American politics.

The way party affiliation warped the prospects for the abolition of slavery figures in Harriet Beecher Stowe's major antislavery novels. In *Uncle Tom's Cabin* (1852), Stowe presents the transformation of Senator Bird, who supports the Fugitive Slave Act of 1850 until he meets actual fugitives, Eliza Harris and her son, Harry, and is schooled by his wife, Mary Bird, in the difference between human and divine law. Mr. Bird ends up breaking the law that he had defended so ardently when he assists Eliza and Harry on their journey to freedom. In *Dred: A Tale of the Great Dismal Swamp* (1856), Stowe explores the role of party as a constraint on ethical political action in the chapter "Frank Russel's Opinions." Russel is a minor character, most noteworthy as a foil and interlocutor for the hero, Edward Clayton. In this chapter, Clayton presses Russel on his candidacy for the state legislature and the role he might play in passing legislation mandating gradual emancipation. Russel acknowledges without hesitation that "there never was anything under heaven so atrocious as our slave-code. It's a bottomless pit of oppression."[13] Still, he denies having the ability to make ending slavery a campaign issue because "I have to represent my party, and, of course, I can't afford to do anything that will compromise them" (464).

Clayton tries to provoke his friend by calling him "the bond-slave of a party," but Russel claims that his compliance with party interests is a tactic to gain control of the party himself – not with a view to end slavery, or to achieve any other common good, but in order to enable himself to "rise in the world" (464). Russel has no faith that party politics can be a vehicle for achieving justice; for him, the system is a contest between those who have power and intend to keep it, and those who want power and conspire to get it. Russel is firmly in the latter camp, and this commitment to his own interests ties him to the "policy of the leaders of this generation": they must spread the slave system "over the whole territory" and "get the balance of power in the country, to build themselves up against the public opinion of mankind." Russel predicts that they will be

---

[13] Harriet Beecher Stowe, *Dred: A Tale of the Great Dismal Swamp* (Penguin, 2000), 463.

successful in this effort, and "the fuss of anti-slavery will die out in the world" (466). On this point Russel miscalculates, but his view of party power as both an end in itself and a vehicle for individual ambition became even more pronounced in the years following the Civil War.

Albion Tourgée shows how partisanship warped the politics of Reconstruction in his bestselling novels *A Fool's Errand* (1879) and *Bricks without Straw* (1880). In the former novel, the chapter titled "Wisdom Crieth in the Streets" (from Proverbs 1:20) presents a letter written by one of the "Wise Men who had framed those laws under which the greatest political experiment of modern civilization was to be made" to Comfort Servosse, the semi-autobiographic hero who has recently been elected to the Constitutional Convention charged with revising the North Carolina state constitution in order for the state to reenter the Union.[14] The letter is dated December 16, 1867, and addressed from the US Senate Chamber by a longtime Senator from "the Commonwealth of —" (presumably Massachusetts, whose senators at the time were the Radical Republicans Charles Sumner and Henry Wilson; Wilson was Ulysses S. Grant's vice president from 1873 until Wilson's death in late 1875 and may be the imagined author of the letter). After criticizing President Andrew Johnson for dividing the Republican Party and throwing the 1868 election into question, the letter presents a set of goals that Servosse, as a Republican activist, should help his party achieve. These include reconstructing and restoring his state as quickly as possible, so that voters there can support the Republican candidate in the upcoming presidential contest and help secure the adoption of the Constitutional Amendments securing citizenship rights for formerly enslaved people. In order to accomplish all this, the letter instructs Servosse, he must pursue limited revisions to the state Constitution so that the process can come to a rapid conclusion. A different course of action would undermine the party's plan, leading to a situation where "the colored people and white Unionists of the South would have no protection, and the nation no guaranties against future rebellion" (163). The narrator comments about this letter that the now-dead author had hoped through these measures "to smooth somewhat his pathway to the highest place in the nation" (164); that is, the presidency.

Servosse rejects the writer's instructions in his response on two grounds: He refuses to view the circumstances in his state "from a purely partisan

---

[14] Albion W. Tourgée, *A Fool's Errand*, ed. John Hope Franklin (The Belknap Press of Harvard University Press, 1961), 161.

stand-point" (165) and he rejects the implication that "present success" at maintaining political power is "highest policy" (166). He goes on to detail what he understands to be "the true object and purpose of Reconstruction" (166), and he challenges the assumption that the party will benefit from the proposed course of action, noting that "a party builded upon ignorance, inexperience, and poverty, and mainly composed of a race of pariahs, who are marked and distinguished by their color, can not stand against intelligence, wealth, the pride of a conquered nation, and race-prejudice whose intensity laughs to shame the exclusive haughtiness of the Brahmins" (167). The underlying social structure of the South, with the wealthy white planter class set against poor whites and freedmen, required transformation before the nation could achieve "homogeneous development" anchored in "individual action, freedom of opinion, diversity of industry, and general education" (168). Servosse presents as the vehicle for this transformation the northern township system, the "nursery of democratic freedom" that must be introduced in the South. His correspondent's plan would not benefit the Republican Party in the ways described, but more importantly, the good of the country would suffer. Exemplifying the values of individual action and freedom of opinion that he has just celebrated, Servosse closes the letter by asserting that "as I was a citizen before I was a Republican, and as I fought for the country and not for the party, you must excuse me if I follow my convictions rather than your counsel" (168). The succeeding chapter jumps ahead to the end of Reconstruction, ironically proclaiming that "the Republican party had accomplished a great mission" and "Yankee-land could now bend its undivided energies to its industries and commerce," leaving the South to "look after its own interests" (169). The remainder of the novel illustrates the resurgence of white supremacy that follows this rushed process, which has been driven by partisan interests.

Tourgée returns to these themes at the end of *Bricks without Straw*, where he describes with additional specificity how party politics shaped the undoing of the township system and the rollback of protections for the freed people, represented by the destruction of the black town of Red Wing by the Ku Klux Klan. The restoration of an oligarchical system where political appointees replace elected officials ensures an "entire harmony throughout the state."[15] A not-so-subtle irony marks the narrator's comments on these changes, signaled by the use of exclamation points to mark

---

[15] Albion W. Tourgée, *Bricks without Straw: A Novel*, ed. Carolyn Karcher (Duke University Press, 2009), 395.

the most outrageous misrepresentations, followed by a statement of the logic underlying the partisan power grab:

> Of course, in this counter-revolution there was not any idea of propagating or confirming the power of the political party instituting it! It was done simply to protect the State against incompetent officials! The people were not wise enough to govern themselves, and could only become so by being wisely and beneficently governed by others, as in the ante-bellum era. (392)

Tourgée criticizes partisanship for the way it warps politics from the true democracy of the township system, where citizens meet face to face to deliberate together and make informed judgments about concrete problems affecting their community. He returns to this theme in the penultimate chapter of the novel. There, the southern aristocrat-turned-Unionist Hesden Le Moyne cites Alexis de Tocqueville (author of *Democracy in America*) and Horace Greeley (editor of the *New-York Tribune*), both champions of the New England township system, as he tries to persuade a northern congressman that this system is the root cause of the North's economic and political success, and that an autochthonous form of this same type of local self-government is essential for advancing the post-slavery South toward greater equality and prosperity.[16]

How accurate was this image of the New England town meeting as a school for democracy, which Tourgée found in Tocqueville and shared with notable contemporaries, including Greeley and John Dewey? A story by Sarah Orne Jewett published in 1881 suggests a different reality. "From a Mournful Villager" celebrates the old customs of small-town New England, particularly the front yards that were once the semi-public domain of otherwise isolated women. As women's opportunities expanded, these yards had fallen out of favor, since "the whole world is their front yard nowadays."[17] Even as her narrator paints a seemingly fond picture, Jewett describes the "restricted and narrowly limited life in the old days" that prompted religious sectarianism and "more bigotry in every cause and question – a fiercer partisanship" involving "a whole-souled concentration of energy that was as efficient as it was sometimes narrow and short-sighted" (587) – the very passion and prejudice that Cooper had

---

[16] Tourgée had been closely involved with introducing the township system and the town meeting into North Carolina's postwar Constitution. Daniel Farbman highlights Tourgée's role in "Reconstructing Local Government," *Vanderbilt Law Review* 70:2 (2017), 413–497. Tourgée's literary career is the focus of Sandra M. Gustafson and Robert S. Levine, eds., *Reimagining the Republic: Race, Citizenship, and Nation in the Literary Work of Albion W. Tourgée* (Fordham University Press, 2023).
[17] Sarah Orne Jewett, *Novels and Stories* (Library of America, 1994), 587.

lamented in *The American Democrat*. Though not explicitly about town politics, the story describes the confined world of the village as stimulating partisan conflict, not the thoughtful, well-informed, independent decision-making that Tourgée and other advocates of the town meeting envisioned.

Partisanship took other forms, as Mark Twain humorously captured in *Pudd'nhead Wilson and Those Extraordinary Twins* (1894). The twins of the title, Angelo and Luigi Capello, are recruited to be members of a "rum party" that opposes an "anti-rum party" – a reference to the temperance cause. Luigi gladly accepts an invitation to "a mass-meeting of [the rum-drinking] faction," and Angelo is carried along to the event despite his "teetotaler" leanings. (Twain originally conceived of the men as conjoined twins, which heightens the humor of the scene.) The gathering resembles many such mass assemblies, including the parade in *House of the Seven Gables*: "In the distance one could see a long wavering line of torches drifting down the main street, and could hear the throbbing of the bass drum, the clash of cymbals, the squeaking of a fife or two, and the faint roar of remote hurrahs." The twins enter a hall that is "full of people, torches, smoke, noise, and enthusiasm." They are immediately and unanimously elected members and offered glasses of whiskey, which Luigi gladly quaffs, while Angelo sets his glass down without drinking. Realizing their mistake, the group promises to repeal Angelo's membership, but the bylaws of the organization prevent them from acting until the next regular meeting. He is temporarily forced to remain a member of the "rum party."[18]

There is a serious point behind Twain's humor. Resistance to temperance legislation was a wedge issue that the influential liquor lobby held over the heads of the major parties, restricting the parties' ability to advance legal restrictions on liquor sales. The Potawatomi author Simon Pokagon offered a solution to this problem in the temperance-themed closing section of *Ogimawkwe Mitigwaki (Queen of the Woods: A Novel)* (1899). The novel's central plot features numerous tragic deaths related to alcohol, and temperance emerges in the final pages as an urgent moral cause that Pokagon explicitly links to abolitionism. "The great cause of temperance ought never to have been 'abinoji' (an offspring) of one political party more than another," he writes, incorporating Algonquin phrases as he has done throughout the novel. "It would be just as reasonable to make 'botadowin gaie meno' (vice and virtue) a party issue as the cause of temperance." The

---

[18] Mark Twain, *Pudd'nhead Wilson and Those Extraordinary Twins*, ed. Langston Hughes (Bantam Books, 1922), 66–67.

parties should adopt a common plank in their platforms, "declaring it to be their determination to crush out the deadly plague." They could then develop distinctive policies on contested aspects of the solution and let the voters choose among them. If this is done, "the great fear of the liquor ballot, which so long has hung over the two great political parties like a funeral pall, will vanish as 'tchbawi' (a phantom) of a nightly dream."[19]

To sum up, much nineteenth-century literary writing on partisanship and factionalism emphasizes the value of independent reflection and rejects groupthink, either through irony (as in Adams, Hawthorne, and Twain) or through direct statement. As many historians have documented, the rise of popular politics involved the creation of strong partisan identifications that organized the world for members. Exuberant partisanship shaped American politics from the late 1820s through the 1890s, but the emphasis on party rivalries inhibited legislative accomplishment and enabled corruption. The strength of party-based loyalties diminished during the early twentieth-century Progressive movement as voters increasingly turned away from conflict-based politics and embraced the role of government in solving many of the social problems created by industrialization and urbanization.[20]

Further Reading

Altschuler, Glenn C. and Stuart M. Blumin. *Rude Republic: Americans and Their Politics in the Nineteenth Century*. Princeton University Press, 2000.

Baker, Jean H. *Affairs of Party: The Political Culture of Northern Democrats in the Mid-Nineteenth Century*. Fordham University Press, 1998.

Funchion, John. "Partisan." In D. Berton Emerson and Gregory Laski, eds., *Democracies in America: Keywords for the Nineteenth Century and Today*. Oxford University Press, 2023, 163–173.

Grinspan, Jon. *The Age of Acrimony: How Americans Fought to Fix Their Democracy*. Bloomsbury, 2021.

Gustafson, Sandra M. *Imagining Deliberative Democracy in the Early American Republic*. University of Chicago Press, 2011.

McCormick, Richard L. *The Party Period and Public Policy: American Politics from the Age of Jackson to the Progressive Era*. Oxford University Press, 1986.

McGerr, Michael E. *The Decline of Popular Politics: The American North, 1865–1928*. Oxford University Press, 1986.

---

[19] Simon Pokagon, *Ogimawkwe Mitigwaki (Queen of the Woods: A Novel)* (Michigan State University Press, 2011), 188.

[20] Jon Grinspan traces the rise of Progressive ideas in the late nineteenth century in *The Age of Acrimony: How Americans Fought to Fix Their Democracy* (Bloomsbury, 2021).

Ryan, Mary P. *Civic Wars: Democracy and Public Life in the American City during the Nineteenth Century*. University of California Press, 1997.

Silbey, Joel H. *The American Party Battle: Election Campaign Pamphlets, 1828–1876*. Harvard University Press, 1999.

Wolff, Nathan. *Not Quite Hope and Other Political Emotions in the Gilded Age*. Oxford University Press, 2019.

PART II
Issues

CHAPTER 9

Slavery: African American Vigilance in Slave Narratives of the 1820s and 1830s
Kelly Ross

The 1820s and 1830s have often been neglected in histories of US abolition that prioritize white-dominated antislavery institutions.[1] Situated between the waning of the first wave of local, gradualist, often religiously affiliated abolition societies and the second wave of national, immediatist abolition organizations, these decades have seemed to signify an ebb in US antislavery. By extension, slave narratives of the 1820s and 1830s have been understudied, perhaps because their themes and literary conventions differ from the widely circulated and well-known slave narratives of the 1840s and 1850s, which were shaped by the agenda of the institutional abolition movement dominated by whites. Attending to African American antislavery activism of the 1820s and 1830s, however, reveals that these were in fact dynamic and transformative decades, particularly regarding the issues of colonization, immediate abolition, and kidnapping. These themes, which arose from and reflected the specific political concerns of an often-overshadowed constituency, African Americans themselves, shaped the literary conventions of slave narratives published in these earlier two decades.

In particular, ex-slave narrators and their white amanuenses of the 1820s and 1830s echo black abolitionist rhetoric regarding the need for relentless vigilance to prevent the widespread, insidious practice of kidnapping free black people resident in the United States. While these idiosyncratic narratives did not reach the large audiences of the later antebellum slave narratives, they are nevertheless valuable for the insight they provide into the dynamics of surveillance in the slave system. Ex-slave narrators feature in their texts an active practice of vigilant watchfulness that anticipates and

---

[1] See Manisha Sinha, *The Slave's Cause: A History of Abolition* (Yale University Press, 2016), especially chap. 6, "The Neglected Period of Antislavery," and Richard S. Newman's *The Transformation of American Abolitionism: Fighting Slavery in the Early Republic* (University of North Carolina Press, 2002).

counters the threat of surveillance through sousveillance (watching from below). Sousveillance is thus a specific narrative manifestation of the vigilance urged by black political activists. Later slave narratives, shaped by the priorities of white-dominated institutional abolition, downplay the agency of African American sousveillants in favor of a more passive story of victimization.

If, as Manisha Sinha declares, "[s]lave narratives were the movement literature of abolition," the narratives of the 1820s and 1830s reveal the priorities of the black abolitionists who kept the movement alive in the period before the rise of institutional abolition and its attendant print culture set the more familiar rhetorical parameters of the movement.[2] Competing ideas among white and black abolitionists about how to make the slave narrative as a genre more politically effective exerted pressures on the form itself. We can discern the effects of these pressures in particular texts through the various topics they address and formal strategies they employ. Broadly speaking, the genre shifts from an eighteenth-century religious strategy focused on opposing the international slave trade to a vigilance strategy emphasizing African American agency in the 1820s and 1830s to an evidentiary strategy of empirically documenting US slavery's atrocities from the 1840s onward. The changing literary conventions of the slave narrative genre that this chapter analyzes testify to the broader political effort to use the genre to express the concerns and priorities of various constituencies and influence the views of multiple groups of readers. Attending to the transformation of the slave narrative genre over time thus offers a broader lesson in literature's relation to politics.

Black Abolitionism in the 1820s and 1830s

The most pressing issues for black abolitionists in the 1820s and 1830s were the colonization movement and the widespread practice of kidnapping free black people and selling them into slavery. Black activists took the lead on both of these issues, developing a militant rhetoric of critique that initiated the shift toward immediate abolition. Black abolitionists challenged the American Colonization Society (ACS, founded in 1816), arguing that the colonization movement denigrated the character of free black people and

---

[2] Sinha, *The Slave's Cause*, 421.

undermined efforts to attain black citizenship in the United States.³ Supporters of the ACS claimed that colonization would eventually bring about the end of slavery by relocating free blacks to African colonies. The General Colored Association (GCA), a black abolitionist organization founded in 1826, denounced this approach. David Walker, one of the GCA's founding members, published a resounding condemnation of colonization in his *Appeal, in Four Articles; Together with a Preamble, to the Coloured Citizens of the World* (1829). Walker fervently refutes colonizationists' professions of benevolence and declares, "This country is as much ours as it is the whites['], whether they will admit it now or not, they will see and believe it by and by."⁴ *Freedom's Journal*, the first African American newspaper, founded in 1827, initially critiqued the colonization movement and instead promoted emancipation, education, and citizenship for black people.⁵ Black abolitionists from 1816 onward almost uniformly opposed colonization, insisting that they were part of the nation and their emancipation must include their equal citizenship.

Black protest against colonization inspired white antislavery activists including William Lloyd Garrison to reject the ACS and instead put their energy toward immediate emancipation. Immediate abolition was a departure from the gradualist approach to ending slavery, which had characterized abolition's first wave, and the movement's tactics shifted to emphasize mass mobilization through print and material culture as well as traveling agents and lecturers.⁶ According to Richard Newman, a "new generation of immediatist organizations ... formed in the early 1830s ... where black and white activists formed crucial ties."⁷ Among the most prominent of these associations were the New England Anti-Slavery Society, founded in 1832 and reorganized in 1835 as the Massachusetts Anti-Slavery Society, and the American Anti-Slavery Society (AASS), founded in 1833. As Teresa Goddu argues regarding the AASS, through its "centralized bureaucracy and alternative publishing system ... the 1830s AASS established the foundation upon which future forms of abolition would

---

³ See Ousmane K. Power-Greene, *Against Wind and Tide: The African American Struggle against the Colonization Movement* (New York University Press, 2014).
⁴ David Walker, *Walker's Appeal*, 1st ed. (David Walker, 1829), 55.
⁵ John Russwurm, who became editor in September 1827, eventually came to support colonization and printed a defense of the ACS; Russwurm's pro-colonization position received a great deal of criticism from his readers, and the paper ceased publication the following month. See Jacqueline Bacon, *Freedom's Journal: The First African-American Newspaper* (Lexington Books, 2007).
⁶ See Trish Loughran, "Abolitionist Nation," in *The Republic in Print: Print Culture in the Age of U.S. Nation Building, 1770–1870* (Columbia University Press, 2007).
⁷ Newman, *The Transformation of American Abolitionism*, 3.

build."[8] While the "interracial but white-dominated" AASS successfully disseminated its message of immediate abolition, it did not fully integrate black abolitionists or their concerns into its organization.[9] Thus, through the 1830s, black activists continued their tradition of protest and reform in state and national Colored Conventions as well as local organizations that focused on educational uplift, antiracism, and anti-kidnapping work.[10]

Preventing the kidnapping of free black people was a primary goal for black abolitionists, as well as for first-wave white abolitionists. Sinha notes that "Between 1813 and 1820 nearly all free states bordering the slave South passed antikidnapping laws ... Even so, the explosive growth of slavery led to hundreds, if not thousands of free blacks being kidnapped and sold into Deep South slavery, a development that galvanized border state abolitionism."[11] The earliest white antislavery societies in the new nation explicitly emphasized protection against kidnapping in their titles – for example, the society that eventually became known as the Pennsylvania Society for the Abolition of Slavery was founded in 1775 as the Society for the Relief of Free Negroes Unlawfully Held in Bondage. These societies funded the legal defense of kidnapped free blacks and litigated against enslavers. Moreover, as Carol Wilson observes, they petitioned state and federal governments "to enact stronger antikidnapping laws and to enforce those already on the books."[12] However, Wilson asserts that "[a]fter the 1820s, the [white] abolitionists' resistance to kidnapping declined noticeably" (96).

Black antislavery activists, on the other hand, never slackened their efforts to fight kidnapping. Like the white antislavery societies, black antislavery activists petitioned state and national legislatures and provided assistance to kidnapped free blacks, but they went further in their fight against kidnapping. As Wilson argues, most black resistance to kidnapping occurred in ad hoc groups that formed spontaneously in response to specific incidents: "since members of the community lived so closely

---

[8] Teresa A. Goddu, *Selling Antislavery: Abolition and Mass Media in Antebellum America (Material Texts)*, 1st ed. (University of Pennsylvania Press, 2020), 10–11.

[9] Leslie M. Harris, *In the Shadow of Slavery: African Americans in New York City, 1626–1863* (University of Chicago Press, 2004), 176.

[10] Goddu, *Selling Antislavery*, 12. See also Jim Casey, P. Gabrielle Foreman, and Sarah Lynn Patterson, eds., *The Colored Conventions Movement: Black Organizing in the Nineteenth Century* (University of North Carolina Press, 2021); and the Colored Conventions Project, https://coloredconventions.org/.

[11] Sinha, *The Slave's Cause*, 176–177.

[12] Carol Wilson, *Freedom at Risk: The Kidnapping of Free Blacks in America, 1780–1865* (University Press of Kentucky, 2009), 87. All subsequent references are cited parenthetically.

together and maintained daily contact with each other, they could immediately regroup and take action when threatened" (104). In Baltimore, this informal resistance coalesced in 1819 into a relief society for persons threatened with enslavement, followed in 1827 by the Baltimore Society for the Protection of Free People of Color. Black-led vigilance committees were established in other northern cities in the 1830s, including the New York Committee of Vigilance (founded in 1835).[13] The emphasis on watchfulness in the titles of these vigilance committees indicates the need to be on the lookout for kidnappers and share information via what Richard Bell calls "de facto neighborhood-watch networks."[14] These early vigilance organizations, both informal and official, provided the infrastructure of what would become known as the Underground Railroad.[15]

Kidnapping in Slave Narratives of the 1820s and 1830s

Fugitive slave narratives of the 1820s and 1830s reflect black abolitionists' emphasis on vigilance, presenting ex-slave narrators as informants who could provide valuable intelligence to prevent kidnappings, rather than as eyewitnesses for the prosecution of slavery on trial. Thanks to the 2013 Steve McQueen film *Twelve Years a Slave*, Solomon Northup's story of the same title (on which the film is based) is the most well-known example of a free man kidnapped and sold in slavery. However, more than twenty years before Northup's 1853 narrative, slave narratives of the 1820s and 1830s underscored this issue, reflecting its urgency among African Americans. These earlier narratives have been overlooked in the study of the genre because they were published in the transitional decades as the gradualist first wave of abolition, embodied in numerous local religiously affiliated societies, was superseded by the immediatist second wave, which was highly centralized and efficiently managed by national antislavery institutions like the AASS.

From 1825 to 1838, when the AASS published its first book-length slave narrative, *Narrative of James Williams*, slave narratives were highly idiosyncratic in their antislavery messages and their depictions of the ex-slave

---

[13] Leonard P. Curry, *The Free Black in Urban America, 1800–1850: The Shadow of the Dream* (University of Chicago Press, 1981), 229.
[14] Richard Bell, "Counterfeit Kin: Kidnappers of Color, the Reverse Underground Railroad, and the Origins of Practical Abolition," *Journal of the Early Republic* 38:2 (2018), 199–230, 224.
[15] See Eric Foner, *Gateway to Freedom: The Hidden History of the Underground Railroad* (W. W. Norton & Company, 2015).

narrator. The fugitive slave narratives of the 1820s and 1830s differ markedly from white-authenticated fugitive slave narratives of the 1840s onward, familiarized by Frederick Douglass's 1845 *Narrative*. Since John Sekora's influential description of antebellum slave narratives as "a black message ... sealed within a white envelope," numerous scholars have detailed the conventions that white-dominated abolitionist institutions such as the AASS used to shape black testimony, including letters of authentication prefacing the narrative, catalogues of brutal punishments suffered by enslaved people, and an insistence on facticity.[16] The white abolitionist movement's political goal was to convince white, northern readers that the institution of slavery was unremittingly cruel and must be eradicated. Goddu has recently argued that we should understand the post-1838 slave narrative as a "factual compendium" akin to the AASS's antislavery almanacs and documentary compilations, such as Theodore Weld's *American Slavery As It Is* (1839). Indeed, Goddu contends, the aggregated clippings from southern newspapers and white testimony of "*American Slavery As It Is*, not the *Narrative of James Williams*, served as the origin text for the antebellum slave narrative."[17] The authenticity crisis over the *Narrative of James Williams*, which was challenged by southern enslavers and subsequently withdrawn from circulation by the AASS, entrenched the AASS's insistence on empiricism at the expense of black individualism and agency. As I will show, the *Narrative of James Williams* uniquely documents the genre's shift from a focus on vigilance to abuse, as Williams sousveilled the AASS agents with whom he was negotiating the publication of his story and detected their preference for a more passive story of victimization. Williams then cannily omitted the portions of his story that were of little interest to the AASS agents, portions that foregrounded his own active watchfulness.

I return to Williams's narrative at the conclusion of this chapter to elaborate further this point that the evolving political goals of the abolition movement exerted pressure on the form of the slave narrative, which changed accordingly. Whereas eighteenth-century slave narratives were "published, read, reviewed, and reprinted as much for their religious as racial experiences," nineteenth-century slave narratives, particularly those

---

[16] John Sekora, "Black Message/White Envelope: Genre, Authenticity, and Authority in the Antebellum Slave Narrative," *Callaloo* 32 (1987), 482–515, 502.

[17] Goddu, *Selling Antislavery*, 56–57. See also Jeannine DeLombard, *Slavery on Trial: Law, Abolitionism, and Print Culture* (University of North Carolina Press, 2007), and Charles Olney, "'I Was Born': Slave Narratives, Their Status as Autobiography and as Literature," in Charles. T. Davis and Henry Louis Gates, Jr., eds., *The Slave's Narrative* (Oxford University Press, 1985), 148–175.

published from the 1830s onward, focused on the abolition of slavery (rather than the abolition of the slave trade, the primary concern of eighteenth-century slave narratives).[18] Just as the AASS's political goal to convert white readers to the abolition movement shaped the genre, earlier antislavery activists' political aims resulted in different formal manifestations of enslaved persons' autobiographies. The narratives of the 1820s and 1830s represent a middle period between two better-known political strategies of religious opposition to the international slave trade and empirical evidence of US slavery's atrocities. As the religious impetus for the genre waned, but before institutional abolition set a new agenda for the genre, slave narratives came to focus on the ingenuity of fugitive enslaved people rather than on their spiritual autobiographies. In the 1820s and 1830s, reflecting black abolitionists' concern with the threat posed by surveillance and kidnapping, narrators and editors urged a strategy of vigilant watchfulness. Many of the narratives in these two decades dwell on instances of kidnapping. Solomon Bayley, for example, in *A Narrative of Some Remarkable Incidents, in the Life of Solomon Bayley* (1825), reports that he was in the midst of a freedom suit against his Delaware enslaver, since the enslaver had taken Bayley from Delaware into Virginia, and "the laws of Delaware did say, that slaves carried out of that state should be free."[19] Two days before the court was to hear his case, Bayley was kidnapped and transported to Richmond to be sold. The enslaver of Bayley's parents and younger siblings had also used deceit to evade a legal process that entitled them to freedom: "My father and mother they pretended to set free, to stop a trial in court, and after they had been free about eleven months, they came upon them unawares; [they] were taken in the night, and carried to Long Island, one of the West India Islands, and sold" (39). As I discuss later in this chapter, Bayley's pious 1825 narrative combines the religious model of first-wave antislavery with the emphasis on vigilance of the 1820s and 1830s, marking the beginning of the genre's transitionary period.

Similarly, Robert Voorhis, in *Life and Adventures of Robert, the Hermit of Massachusetts* (1829), describes the villainy of James Bevens, "the author of as great an act of cruelty and injustice, as ever was recorded in the catalogue

---

[18] Philip Gould, "The Rise, Development, and Circulation of the Slave Narrative," in Audrey A. Fisch, ed., *The Cambridge Companion to the African American Slave Narrative* (Cambridge University Press, 2007), 11–27, 12. See also Frances Smith Foster, *Witnessing Slavery: The Development of Ante-Bellum Slave Narratives* (Greenwood Press, 1979), especially chap. 3, "The Development of Slave Narratives," and William Andrews, *To Tell a Free Story: The First Century of Afro-American Autobiography, 1760–1865* (University of Illinois Press, 1988).

[19] Solomon Bayley, *A Narrative of Some Remarkable Incidents in the Life of Solomon Bayley* (Harvey and Darton, 1825), 2. All subsequent references are cited parenthetically.

of human depravity." Voorhis and Bevens had agreed that Bevens would purchase Voorhis from his enslaver for fifty pounds with the understanding that Voorhis would thenceforth be free, albeit indebted to Bevens for this same amount. Voorhis made payments to Bevens, keeping up his end of the bargain, but he did not retain receipts of these payments. Without warning one night, Bevens and another man burst into Voorhis's house, "seized and pinioned" him, and "in the most secret manner, at eleven at night" put him in irons on board a schooner bound for Charleston, South Carolina, where Voorhis was sold at auction.[20] Though Voorhis was legally Bevens's property and could be seized and sold at will, he presents his story as an account of kidnapping. By describing Bevens as a "ruffian" (12) and a "monster in human shape" (13), Voorhis condemns Bevens's acts as criminal, though they have the sanction of the law. Voorhis's narrative demonstrates that, like other militant critics of slavery, he did not draw fine distinctions between the illegal practice of kidnapping free blacks and the legal buying and selling of enslaved people. As Wilson notes, radical abolitionists operated from the premise that all enslaved people were kidnapped since "slaves had originally been taken against their will from Africa[;] . . . they and their descendants . . . were, therefore, illegally held in bondage" (5). In keeping with this sweeping definition, ex-slave narrators imply that breaches of promise and deception intended to evade proper legal procedures also constituted kidnapping. By rendering what are, in effect, legal (albeit immoral) sales as illegitimate captures, these narratives engage rhetorically with an issue of genuine and urgent concern to their producers and their intended audience: the issue of kidnapping.

Charles Ball, in *Slavery in the United States* (1836), also discusses several instances of kidnapping or illegal sales. Outside Baltimore, Ball's second wife and their children, who are legally free, are kidnapped and sold into slavery by white men in blackface. Ball indicates the efficacy of anti-kidnapping activists by noting that the kidnappers, upon finding another free black woman in the house, become anxious that she will "give intelligence of what [she] had seen . . . [to] members of the abolition society, . . . [and the kidnappers] would certainly be detected and punished, for the crimes they were committing." They therefore leave the free black woman bound and gagged in the house and make their escape.[21] Earlier in the text, Ball reports the story of a mulatto boy on a neighboring plantation in

---

[20] Robert Voorhis and Henry Trumbull, *Life and Adventures of Robert, the Hermit of Massachusetts* (Henry Trumbull, 1829), 12–13.
[21] Charles Ball and Isaac Fisher, *Slavery in the United States* (J. W. Shugert, 1836), 399–400. All subsequent references are cited parenthetically.

Georgia whose white mother travels there with the sheriff to claim the boy as her freeborn son; her father had illegally sold the boy into slavery (276–280). Later in the text, during Ball's first escape, he meets another runaway whose enslaver's will had provided for his manumission when he turned twenty-five but who was instead sold to a cotton planter in South Carolina (339), an event that the text suggests amounts to an instance of kidnapping. Ball also describes being followed and attacked by a mulatto man outside of Richmond, Virginia, who was "undoubtedly one of those wretches, who are employed by white men to kidknap [sic] and betray such unfortunate people of colour as may chance to fall into their hands; but for once the deceiver was deceived, and he who intended to make prey of me, had well nigh fallen a sacrifice himself" (356–357).[22] Ball knocks the man down with his stick and beats him until the man begs for mercy. These instances, spread throughout Ball's text, demonstrate his persistent vigilance regarding the threat of kidnapping.

Ball himself is the victim of kidnapping when he is captured and taken back to Georgia by the brother of his enslaver. Ball notes that the brother has claimed him as his own slave, "without the colour of legal right" (375): Since Ball in fact belongs to the man's sister, "my present master had no right whatso ever to me, in either law, or justice" (376). Ball attempts to obtain his freedom through the Georgia courts, paying a lawyer to file a writ on his behalf even though the lawyer advises him that it will be difficult to prove his case since he had no witnesses to testify on his behalf. The judge rules against Ball, "declar[ing] that the law was well settled in Georgia, that every negro was presumed to be a slave, until he proved his freedom by the clearest evidence" (378). Ball's narrative demonstrates the numerous assaults on black freedom, many perpetuated by deceit and upheld by the legal system, with which anti-kidnapping activists had to contend. As all of these examples show, slave narratives of the 1820s and 1830s align with the priorities of black abolitionists, namely the prevention of kidnapping through constant vigilance, a vigilance both thematized in the text (and performed by black agents in those texts) and promoted in those texts as a political practice to be enacted by their readers. The political imperatives of the abolition movement in this period between the two major waves of US antislavery shaped the characteristics of the slave narrative genre, representing black fugitive slaves as active agents

---

[22] See Bell, "Counterfeit Kin," for more on this practice of hiring or bribing African Americans to lure free blacks to kidnappers.

within the text just as black antislavery activists took the lead in anti-colonization debates and societies for the protection of people of color.

Surveillance and Sousveillance in Slave Narratives of the 1820s and 1830s

In the slave narratives of the 1820s and 1830s, this emphasis on vigilance translates into an attention to practices of surveillance in the slave South as well as the North. As Simone Browne argues, enslaved people resisted the top-down surveillance system of enslavers through "dark sousveillance": "the tactics employed to render one's self out of sight, and strategies used in the flight to freedom from slavery."[23] Fugitive slave narratives of the 1820s and 1830s devote more attention to the dynamics of surveillance and sousveillance than narratives produced within the constraints of the "abolitionist culture industry" of the late 1830s onward.[24] Whereas later slave narratives emphasize the cruelty of enslavers, narratives from the 1820s and 1830s elucidate the complex ways in which African Americans evade enslavers' oversight and practice vigilance to protect and defend themselves.[25] In contrast to the more passive role of sufferer that abolitionist institutions later assign to fugitive enslaved people, narrators of the 1820s and 1830s highlight their own agency as watchers and frame their narratives as inside accounts, providing politically damning intelligence on the slave system (but not quite militant resistance of the kind feared and enacted by imaginary and real insurrections).

The genre's shift in purpose from proselytizing to abolition had significant consequences for its depiction of surveillance. In eighteenth- and early nineteenth-century slave narratives, with their religious focus, the eye of God was the ultimate surveillant. As the genre shifted away from the spiritual narrative as a model and became more engaged in the sociopolitical circumstances of US slavery in the 1820s, narratives turned to the methods of secular surveillance, with the vigilance of human agents replacing that of the divine. Appearing at the outset of this transition, Bayley's 1825 *Narrative* offers a striking example of sousveillance that indexes this move from religious-focused slave narratives before the 1820s

---

[23] Simone Browne, *Dark Matters: On the Surveillance of Blackness* (Duke University Press, 2015), 22, 21.
[24] Loughran, *The Republic in Print*, 238.
[25] Summarizing the generic conventions of the form after the publication of *Slavery As It Is*, Goddu states, "Nearly all antebellum slave narratives foreground punishments and cruelty and include in their appendices an array of corroborating evidence and supporting documents to verify their testimony" (*Selling Antislavery*, 79).

to abolitionist slave narratives of the 1830s onward. Combining piety with a robust attention to the dynamics of watching from above and below, Bayley's narrative demonstrates the pressures that new political aims, such as combatting the kidnapping of free black people, put on the genre's older religious model.

The first nine pages of Bayley's narrative focus on his flight from his kidnappers; the prominent themes are Bayley's concealment and deception and his pursuers' efforts at tracking him. By hiding in some bushes, he escapes from the wagon caravan that was taking him west to be sold; after the slave traders search for him for forty-five minutes, he states, "that was the last I ever saw or heard of them" (3). This escape from his immediate captors is incomplete, however, as he finds himself under totalizing surveillance by slave society as a whole. Lamenting that he and his fellow fugitive were "hunted like partridges" (6), Bayley highlights the three times he is chased by dogs, as well as the three times he is "examined" by suspicious whites. He also describes his betrayal by a black man, who leads white men to Bayley's hiding place to capture him; luckily Bayley has had a premonition about the betrayal and has moved to a different hiding place and covered himself with branches, so the men do not find him. In this section of Bayley's narrative, he figures himself as the prey of ubiquitous slave hunters: not only his own enslaver, who is specifically seeking to recapture him, but all of white society, who are disposed to suspect and examine any black person they encounter. Bayley demonstrates how southern whites have been deputized by the slave system to act as detectives at all times, presuming the guilt of any black person they encounter.

Bayley's narrative amalgamates his knowledge of the slave system's surveillance practices with his faith, resulting in an episode of miraculous sousveillance. The strangeness of the episode is explained when we understand the historical context of shifting political imperatives served by the slave narratives in these decades, a context that involves pressure exerted by prior religious models as well as resistance to these models as writers and producers adapt to new political aims such as opposing particular aspects of slavery and racism in the United States, including kidnapping free blacks. Bayley's immersion into the pervasive surveillance of slave society leads him to begin practicing sousveillance. Worried that a white man who "examined" him about his reason for being in the neighborhood is now coming after him, he tries to evade detection by going the opposite direction to the route he had inquired about and hiding in a counterintuitive place. Despite Bayley's sousveillant maneuvers, the man and a companion whom Bayley calls "the old conjuror" manage to track him down. Yet, though they walk within inches of Bayley and "look[] right into [his] eyes" (12), they cannot see him because God has created a magical circle, demarcated by birds, within which Bayley is protected.

Bayley explicitly figures this dramatic scene as a conflict between surveillance and sousveillance, but he in fact supplements his own watching from below with divine oversight, thereby elevating his subordinated vision to meet the surveillance of enslavers eye to eye. Throughout the passage, Bayley repeats the language of sight, both literal and metaphorical. When he awakes in his hiding place he observes two birds: "seeing the little strange looking birds, it roused up all my senses . . . I saw the birds went all round me" (10). At first, he is not sure what this sight means, but he realizes that God has sent the birds to protect him; as he reflects on this impression, "a sight of my faults came before me, and a scanty sight of the highness and holiness of the great Creator of all things" (10). Recalling the biblical trope of the scales falling from Saul's eyes (as well as the reminder in Luke that God's eye is on the sparrow), Bayley's religious faith grants him sharpened sight. Moreover, it makes him invisible to the surveillance of the two white men, who are using a stick as a divining rod to dowse for Bayley. Their superstitious belief in the divining rod is trumped by Bayley's true faith, as God tells Bayley to "Stand still and see the salvation of the Lord" (12). Obeying this dictate, Bayley watches the men from his hiding place: "I opened my eyes and saw them right before me . . . I sat there, and looked right at them" (11). Ultimately, surveillance (technologically enhanced via the divining rod) and sousveillance come eye to eye:

> [T]he young man stopped and looked right down on me, as I thought, and I looked right up into his eyes; and then he stood and looked right into my eyes, and when he turned away, he ran after the old man, and I thought he saw me; but when he overtook the old man, he kept on, and then I knew he had not seen me. (12–13)

Bayley's emphasis on the antagonists' looking "right down," "right up," and finally "right into [one another's] eyes" indexes the way in which the vigilance urged by African American antislavery activists aimed to undermine the visual superiority of white surveillance. Conflating literal and metaphorical sight at the conclusion of the passage, Bayley gives thanks to God for his supernaturally aided sousveillance: "Then I said, bless the Lord, he that gave sight to man's eyes, hath kept him from seeing me this day" (13). This divine oversight lifts Bayley from his disadvantaged position, protecting him from white surveillance. Bayley's narrative thus participates in the older, religiously inflected mode of divinely enacted uplift associated with the slave narrative's earlier phase. Though Bayley attributes his sousveillance to divine power, this passage also anticipates the secularized analyses of the conflict between surveillance and sousveillance in subsequent slave narratives of the 1820s and 1830s.

As I have argued elsewhere, this attention to the dialectic of racialized surveillance and sousveillance is most pronounced in Ball's *Slavery in the United States*. Presenting himself as a spy for northern white readers who do not have access to the hidden operations of the slave system, "Ball frames his narrative not as legal testimony but as a document of sousveillance that provides intelligence on the slave system."[26] The other slave narratives published between 1825 and 1838, with the exception of *Narrative of James Williams* (which I discuss later in this section), also depict the dynamics of surveillance, often emphasizing the ways in which the ex-slave narrator parlays intelligence gained from shrewd sousveillance to negotiate better conditions or to facilitate escape. For example, in *Life of William Grimes, the Runaway Slave* (1825), Grimes describes manipulating an overseer named Bennet by threatening him with the disclosure of incriminating information that Grimes has discovered. When Bennet whips Grimes, Grimes forces him to stop by threatening to inform the master, Colonel Thornton, that Bennet and his mother "secretly bought things from the negroes which they had stolen from my master."

> [Bennet] promised me that if I would hold my tongue, and say nothing about this, he would see that I should not be whipped. He knew that it was for his interest to keep me from exposing their buying things which they knew the slaves had stolen. My master, however, heard something about this scrape, and was going to whip me, but Mr. Bennet interfered, and told him that I was drunk, as I said, and that he had whipped me enough.[27]

Grimes's sousveillance provides him information about his overseers, which he can then strategically deploy to avoid or curtail a whipping.

Whereas the slave narratives published outside (because prior to) the institutional apparatus of the AASS detail the operations of surveillance as well as the ways enslaved people continuously challenged and negotiated that surveillance through their own vigilant sousveillance, in *Narrative of James Williams*, published by the AASS in 1838, there is almost no attention

---

[26] Kelly Ross, "Watching from Below: Racialized Surveillance and Vulnerable Sousveillance," *PMLA* 135:2 (2020), 299–314, 304.
[27] William Grimes, *Life of William Grimes, the Runaway Slave*, ed. William L. Andrews and Regina E. Mason (Oxford University Press, 2008), 46–47.

paid to sousveillance. Instead, the narrative is essentially a catalogue of gruesome punishments and profound sufferings of the enslaved. Williams details how he is forced into complicity with enslavers' surveillance and policing system when he is coerced by the overseer to whip and torture his fellow enslaved people or risk his own whipping or death. The narrative dwells on the occasions when fugitive slaves were captured and brutalized by bloodhounds, but it gives almost no account of enslaved people's subversive actions or sousveillant practices. The ex-slave narrator's gaze has transformed from Ball's covert spying to pained spectatorship as it is now compelled to bear witness to the "routine display of the slave's ravaged body," as Saidiya Hartman has argued.[28] Williams and the enslaved people he depicts in his narrative appear in the passive role of victim rather than the active role of sousveillant evident in the other fugitive slave narratives of the 1820s and 1830s, an emphasis on scenes of subjection characteristic of an emergent antislavery discourse reflecting the political strategy of predominantly white abolitionist institutions like the AASS (whose amanuensis for *The Narrative of James Williams*, the poet John Greenleaf Whittier, would go on to write popular antislavery poetry employing this same rhetorical method of depicting passive slaves atrociously mistreated).[29]

Significantly for my argument, however, recent investigative scholarship by Hank Trent has revealed Williams's agency in shaping the narrative by omission. Williams's sousveillance of Whittier and other AASS leaders prompted him to detect that they did not want to hear the aspects of his story that foregrounded his own agency but rather preferred for him to give a more passive account of his experiences as an enslaved man.[30] Williams thus deliberately excluded from the narrative portions of his life that presented him as an active agent, such as his first escape. After Williams's narrative appeared in print, an Alabama newspaper editor named John B. Rittenhouse published several articles discrediting Williams's story by pointing out several "falsehood[s]."[31] Eventually, the AASS concluded that

---

[28] Saidiya Hartman, *Scenes of Subjection: Terror, Slavery, and Self-Making in Nineteenth-Century America* (Oxford University Press, 1997), 3.

[29] See Goddu, *Selling Antislavery*, chap. 3, "The African American Slave Narrative as Factual Compendium," and Goddu, "The African American Slave Narrative and the Gothic," in Charles L. Crow, ed., *A Companion to American Gothic* (Wiley Blackwell, 2014), 71–83, 74–75.

[30] Hank Trent notes that while Williams gave Whittier and other white abolitionists a "crafted story," he shared the "full secret truth of how he had spent the last two years" with his sister in a letter he sent in the midst of his interviews with Whittier. See Trent's "Introduction," in *Narrative of James Williams, an American Slave*, ed. Hank Trent (Louisiana State University Press, 2013), ix–xlviii, xvi–xvii. All subsequent references will be cited parenthetically.

[31] Quoted in Trent, "Introduction," xix.

Rittenhouse's evidence was accurate and Williams's narrative was not true; they discontinued the sale of the *Narrative*.[32] Though scholars long accepted the AASS's position that Williams's narrative was fraudulent, Trent has painstakingly documented the veracity of portions of Williams's story and filled in details of his life that Williams left out of his narrative.

Williams was indeed a fugitive slave who had grown up in Virginia and was then taken to Alabama where he worked on a cotton plantation and eventually escaped to the North. Yet contrary to the story he tells in his narrative, in which he claims he was tricked into going to Alabama by his enslaver, he was in fact sold down south after he was accused of (but not prosecuted for) complicity in a plot to poison neighboring enslavers. Furthermore, his escape was much more complicated than the brief account he presents in the narrative, in which he emphasizes the role of luck rather than sousveillance. In fact, Williams escaped by collaborating with James B. White, a con man, who pretended to sell Williams to a local farmer and then secretly helped him run away. The two men repeated this swindle as they progressed northward until they reached Baltimore, where White ended his participation in the scheme, selling Williams to a slave trader who prepared to send Williams back to the Deep South for sale. To prevent this calamity, Williams told the slave trader about the scam White had been perpetrating with him, and the trader informed the police, who arrested White. Williams spent a few weeks in the Baltimore jail waiting for his enslaver to come from Alabama to claim him. His enslaver sold him to a slave trader, who eventually sent Williams to New Orleans where he was sold to a hotel owner. Williams soon escaped by stowing away on board a Mississippi steamboat and then masquerading as a waiter on board. Eventually arriving in Cincinnati, Williams then traveled to Carlisle, Pennsylvania, where, as Trent states, he "found the Quaker-run Underground Railroad that led him to the American Anti-Slavery Society, John Greenleaf Whittier, and a chance to trade his story for freedom."[33]

Williams, that is, left out the parts of his story that evidence sousveillance: his involvement in a plot to poison a white couple, his participation in a slave-stealing scam, and the details of his daring escape. As Williams negotiated with the AASS about their publication of his story, he detected what they did and did not want to hear, and he provided them with what they wanted, rather than the entire truth, in order to accomplish his own goal, which was to obtain passage out of the country and thus to safety

[32] Trent, "Introduction," xxiv.   [33] Trent, "Introduction," xxxvii–xxxviii.

abroad. Trent argues that "Williams watched the abolitionists' reactions, concentrating on the parts that seemed to interest them most, such as descriptions of his overseer's brutality, and omitting the parts that reflected badly on him or on abolitionists in general."[34] Shortly after Williams arrived in New York and met with AASS leaders, they heard that three men were in the city to recapture him. Williams was terrified of being recaptured, and Trent suggests that the AASS "made their offer, implicitly if not explicitly: after he had dictated all the information to . . . Whittier, they would conduct him to safety by providing him passage to Liverpool, England."[35] After Williams reached England, the AASS never heard from him again, despite their efforts to contact him to disprove Rittenhouse's attacks on the narrative. Though the details of racialized surveillance and sousveillance are absent in the narrative he and Whittier produced, Williams's long and complex flight to freedom, including his strategic negotiations with the AASS, demonstrates his own sousveillance, something the changing politics of abolition led him to suppress in favor of giving white abolitionists what their distinct political strategy sought thereafter to emphasize: passive black victimization rather than active back vigilance. Changing political imperatives thus directly altered the genre's form.

Attending to the concerns of fugitive slave narratives published in the 1820s and 1830s, particularly their emphasis on vigilance regarding the dynamics of surveillance, offers a more nuanced view of the genre's development. The constraints placed on slave narratives by the institutional abolitionist movement of the late 1830s onward are more familiar to us, but the instances of the genre published in the 1820s and 1830s reflect the priorities of black abolitionists in this period. Studying this period of the slave narrative genre, therefore, leads us closer to understanding black opponents of slavery and advocates for abolition on their own terms, rather than through the lens of white institutional agendas.

Further Reading

Ball, Charles. *Slavery in the United States*. Published by John S. Taylor, 1837. https://docsouth.unc.edu/neh/ballslavery/ball.html.

Bayley, Solomon. *A Narrative of Some Remarkable Incidents in the Life of Solomon Bayley, Formerly a Slave in the State of Delaware, North America; Written by Himself, and Published for His Benefit; to Which Are Prefixed, a Few Remarks by*

---

[34] Trent, "Introduction," xvi. [35] Trent, "Introduction," xvi.

Robert Hurnard. 1825. *Documenting the American South* (DocSouth). http://docsouth.unc.edu/neh/bayley/bayley.html.

Fournier, Jake. "Phillis Wheatley's Abolition Rhetoric and Nineteenth-Century Lyricization," *ESQ: A Journal of Nineteenth-Century American Literature and Culture* 68:2 (2022), 223–259.

Garvey, T. Gregory. *Creating the Culture of Reform in Antebellum America*. University of Georgia Press, 2006.

Grant, David. *Political Antislavery Discourse and American Literature of the 1850s*. University of Delaware Press, 2012.

Roberts, Neil, ed. *A Political Companion to Frederick Douglass*. University Press of Kentucky, 2018.

Sánchez-Eppler, Karen. *Touching Liberty: Abolition, Feminism, and the Politics of the Body*. University of California Press, 1993.

Sinha, Manisha. *The Slave's Cause: A History of Abolition*. Yale University Press, 2016.

Voorhis, Robert and Henry Trumbull. *Life and Adventures of Robert, the Hermit of Massachusetts: Who Has Lived 14 Years in a Cave, Secluded from Human Society: Comprising, an Account of His Birth, Parentage, Sufferings, and Providential Escape from Unjust and Cruel Bondage in Early Life, and His Reasons for Becoming a Recluse*. Henry Trumbull, 1829. *Documenting the American South* (DocSouth). http://docsouth.unc.edu/neh/robert/menu.html.

Williams, James. *Narrative of James Williams, an American Slave*, ed. Hank Trent. Annotated edition. Louisiana State University Press, 2013.

Wilson, Carol. *Freedom at Risk: The Kidnapping of Free Blacks in America, 1780–1865*. University Press of Kentucky, 2009.

CHAPTER 10

Disfranchisement, Segregation, and the Rise of African American Literature

Kenneth W. Warren

Toward the end of Sutton E. Grigg's 1905 novel, *The Hindered Hand*, the ill-fated Eunice Seabright, who by virtue of a highly publicized court case has been exposed as having African American ancestry, finds herself suddenly subject to the strictures and prohibitions that the Jim Crow South imposed on black Americans as a group. Well-mannered, well-spoken, well-dressed, and attractive, Eunice has, up to that moment, taken for granted the respect accorded to her in public and on public conveyances as a woman of means and graceful bearing. But now, as she walks the streets and attempts to hire a cab, ride a streetcar, and reenter the hotel room she had rented earlier, she finds that being identified as a black woman has tumbled her into a world that at every turn seems organized to impress on her the inferior social status to which she and those like her are relegated. Demoralized, she decides to leave town by train and tries to secure a berth in the sleeper car, only to be "told that all the berths were taken." Of course, this is a lie, which Eunice learns upon leaving the ticket window when a white woman steps to the window and secures a sleeping berth on the same train. Outraged, Eunice returns to the clerk to protest what has happened, but to no avail. Yet while the clerk has no intention of acceding to Eunice's appeal for fairness, he seems less intent on insulting her than in enlightening her, explaining that he can't help her because "You belong to a voteless race and I can't give you a berth." When Eunice responds by asking, "What has voting to do with my getting a suitable place to ride on a train?," the agent explains the politics and political economy of segregation as he understands them. Being voteless, he affirms, has "Everything" to do with segregation.

> "You see it is this way," he continued. "The Governor of this state, who sprang from a class of whites, who never had much love for the Negro, happened to take a sleeper that was occupied by a few Negroes who did not conduct themselves properly. Though the great body of Negroes who were

able and disposed to occupy berths were genteel and well-behaved, this governor, to properly bolster his dignity resolved upon a course that would work discomfort for thousands. He threatened to recommend to the legislature that a law be passed demanding separate sleeping cars for the two races unless Negroes were kept out of sleepers. We lose less by keeping Negroes out than we would by being compelled to operate two sets of cars. If you people had voting power and could stand by us we could stand by you. It is a matter of business with us."[1]

The white ticket agent's account of segregation, in what it gets right and in what it gets wrong about the politics of the moment, illuminates a great deal about the relation of American literature to the rise and consolidation of Jim Crow, a political, social, and economic order that used disfranchisement, violence, legislation, the judiciary, and racial segregation to establish and maintain several decades of rule by southern plantation and industrial elites. On the one hand, the agent is right in noting the political roots of segregation. As observed by the historian Judith Stein, "Disfranchisement permitted the passage of Jim Crow laws."[2] In the 1880s, the political rule of southern elites had been challenged by interracial Populism, the late nineteenth-century labor movement that brought together agricultural, mining, and lumber laborers, along with some small farmers in the South and the West to try to enact a new industrial and economic order. The political success of Populism had depended on the possession of the right to vote by black men. What enabled white and black workers to stand with each other was the possibility of winning elections. Defeating Populism required disfranchising blacks and many poor whites and interdicting the possibility of social interaction among black and white laborers. As indicated by Stein and by Griggs's ticket agent, the imposition of racial subordination was a matter of class rule. But this agreement between the historian on one side and the novelist and his character on the other goes only so far. Stein makes it clear that to look for the source of the laws that demoralize Eunice Seabright one must look more to the power of the South's planters and industrialists than to the attitudes of poor whites. Jim Crow segregation furthered the interests of those at the top.

---

[1] Sutton E. Griggs, *The Hindered Hand, or the Reign of the Repressionist* (1905), ed. John Cullen Gruesser and Hanna Walllinger (West Virginia University Press, 2017), 171–172.
[2] Judith Stein, "'Of Mr. Booker T. Washington and Others': The Political Economy of Racism in the United States," in Adolph L. Reed Jr. and Kenneth W. Warren, eds., *Renewing Black Intellectual History: The Ideological and Material Foundations of African American Thought* (Paradigm Press, 2010), 19–50, 42.

However, what Griggs's characters, along with Griggs himself, and many of the authors I mention in this chapter, believed they saw when they looked to the statehouses and state legislatures was primarily the tyranny of a new order defined by the ascendance of a lower class of whites "who never had much love for the Negro," and who, with the reins of government in hand were now allowing their antiblack passions to gallop across the South. These were the "tree-toad" and "fish-belly" whites whom Mark Twain had satirized in the figure of Pap Finn in *The Adventures of Huckleberry Finn* – people who were outraged by black electoral participation, especially when black voters displayed the graces of genteel breeding. Pap's complaint about this "wonderful govment" is illustrative:

> Why, looky here. There was a free nigger there, from Ohio; a mulatter, most as white as a white man. He had the whitest shirt on you ever see, too, and the shiniest hat; and there ain't a man in that town that's got as fine clothes as what he had; and he had a gold watch and chain, and a silver-headed cane – the awfulest old gray-headed nabob in the State. And what do you think? They said he was a p'fessor in a college, and could talk all kinds of languages, and knowed everything. And that ain't the wust. They said he could *vote*, when he was at home. Well, that let me out. Thinks I, what is the country a-coming to? It was 'lection day, and I was just about to go and vote, myself, if I warn't too drunk to get there; but when they told me there was a State in this country where they'd let that nigger vote, I drawed out. I says I'll never vote agin.[3]

With few apparent qualms about the target of its satire, Twain's novel anchors the sentiments for disfranchisement in the undernourished breasts of those deemed incapable and unworthy of exercising it themselves, and who are unaware that their disgusted withdrawal from the franchise might be celebrated rather than lamented. To be sure, poor southern whites harbored more than their share of racist sentiments. In his *The Strange Career of Jim Crow*, the historian C. Vann Woodward notes the "phobias and fanaticisms" of "the depressed lower economic classes" of whites played a significant role in imposing segregation.[4] But Huck's understanding that his "infernal" decision to help an escaping slave placed him outside of respectable southern society (notwithstanding Aunt Polly's deathbed renunciation of her decision to sell Jim downriver) also locates the

---

[3] Mark Twain, *The Adventures of Huckleberry Finn*, ed. Thomas Cooley (W. W. Norton, 1999), 39. Although Twain's novel is set in the antebellum south, Pap's fulminations about voting are one of the story's many features attesting to the novel's status as a post-emancipation text.

[4] C. Vann Woodward, *The Strange Career of Jim Crow: A Commemorative Edition* (Oxford University Press, 2002), 62.

responsibility for the exploitation and enslavement of black Americans with the respectable southerners who wielded power in their states, people who had been slaveowners and were at the time of the writing of *Huckleberry Finn* the owners of land, property, and commerce in the South. And while, as Woodward further notes, however deeply seated were the racist sentiments of poor whites, many from this group were also capable of recognizing that they shared with southern blacks a status of victimization by the wealthy and powerful and as a consequence were able to embrace "an equalitarianism of want and poverty, the kinship of common grievance and a common oppressor."[5]

Determining just who was most responsible for the rise of Jim Crow shaped the representation of segregation in much of the literature emerging from the South at the turn of the twentieth century: Was the desire to segregate blacks from whites rooted in the racial animus of poor whites, resentful of their own lowly status? Or was segregation primarily a tool deployed by plantation and extraction elites in the South to weaken and rout working-class insurgency? Although Pap Finn in 1885 fulminated against a "govment" that protected the civil and political rights of black Americans, it would take a little more than a decade for Pap's hated government, through the US Supreme Court's "separate but equal" ruling in *Plessy* v. *Ferguson* (with only one justice, Louis Harlan, in dissent) to sanction the invidious treatment of black and white Americans. In fact, a year before *Plessy*, Booker T. Washington had declared that the social separation of blacks and whites was in harmony with the industrial and economic progress of the nation. Speaking to whites and blacks at the Atlanta Cotton States Exposition, Washington, who had founded Tuskegee Institute (now Tuskegee University) in Alabama in 1881, assured southern planters and industrialists that in exchange for a secure place in the modernizing New South, black Americans would accept a role as virtual apprentices to white southerners in the civic and economic demands of modernization. Driving home his point dramatically, Washington raised his hand and declared, "In all things that are purely social we can be as separate as the fingers, yet one as the hand in all things essential to mutual progress."[6]

To be sure racial segregation and its representation in literature were common on the social and literary scenes earlier in the nineteenth century. Writing about his experiences in Rhode Island while working as an

---

[5] Vann Woodward, *Strange Career*, 61.
[6] Booker T. Washington, *Up from Slavery*, ed. William L. Andrews (W. W. Norton, 1995), 100.

abolitionist in the 1840s, Frederick Douglass recalled that he "suffered much rough usage within her borders" because the state "was like all the northern States at that time, under the influence of slave power, and often showed a proscription and persecuting spirit, especially upon its railways, steamboats, and public houses."[7] Decrying the "mean, dirty, and uncomfortable car set apart for colored travelers, called the 'Jim Crow'" car, which he frequently encountered on the "Eastern Railroad, from Boston to Portland," Douglass was inclined to describe the practice of segregation in the northern states as "the fruit of slaveholding prejudice" and "the spirit of slavery" rather than as an integral feature of northern economic and social relations. Sometimes he even went so far as to attribute the practice of discrimination in the North to a regrettable tendency on the part of black citizens to acquiesce in, rather than defy, social subordination. Douglass observed that when faced with the expectation or demand that he move to the Jim Crow car, he "resolved to avoid this car, though it sometimes required courage to do so," in contrast to the response of his black fellow citizens, who, he says, "generally accepted the situation, and complained of me as making matters worse rather than better by refusing to submit to this proscription."[8] But while Douglass's views of his fellow African Americans might have been unusually harsh, he was not alone in describing racism in the North as capitulation to the mores of southern slavery. Through its lengthy subtitle, Harriet Wilson's 1859 novel, *Our Nig, or Sketches from the Life of a Free Black, in a Two-Story White House, North, Showing That Slavery's Shadows Fall, Even There*, which is set in New Hampshire, makes the same point.

Although the terrors and indignities visited upon Wilson's protagonist, Frado, are made possible by proximity to rather than distance from her oppressors, Wilson's depiction of the North, like Douglass's, reflects the fact that prior to the war against the treasonous insurrection of the slave-owning states, "[r]acial discrimination in political and civil rights was the rule in the free states and any relaxation the exception."[9] Indeed, it would only be after the war that a significant number of lawmakers and reformers would begin to see that moving toward racial equality within the United States would be required to secure the social gains that abolition and the defeat of the Confederacy had made possible. These views led to the passage of the Fourteenth and Fifteenth Amendments to the US Constitution, and the

---

[7] Frederick Douglass, *The Life and Times of Frederick Douglass: His Early Life As a Slave, His Escape from Bondage, and His Complete History* (Citadel Press, 1983), 225.
[8] Douglass, *Life and Times*, 227.   [9] Woodward, *Strange Career*, 20.

passage of the 1875 Civil Rights Act, which though often indifferently enforced, prohibited racial discrimination in public places including restaurants and public transportation. For some political actors, advocating for egalitarian policies was more a matter of political pragmaticism than moral commitment. Nonetheless, for a time the effects were real. As Judith Stein has written, to "prevent the resurgence of the planter class, Northern capitalists were willing to endorse elements of the Radical program – the ballot, property rights, wage labor, and education – during" the period of Radical Reconstruction from 1867 to 1872.[10] Then in the late 1880s, a decade after the defeat of the radical phase of Reconstruction, the Southern Farmers' Alliance and the Colored Farmers' Alliance began channeling their interests and efforts into what became Populism, which according to Stein, had by 1895 become "the most effective means to struggle against discriminatory practices, disfranchisement and racism, all of which affected prosperous black Southerners as well as the poor."[11] But Populism's apex was also the moment it began to tumble into defeat. Disfranchisement across the South, the rise of Booker T. Washington's regime of "race relations," and the *Plessy* decision marked the onset of the "era of stiff conformity and fanatical rigidity" that we know as the Jim Crow South.[12]

However, as black writers began self-consciously to construct African American literature in the 1890s, they usually did not represent the social reality of the South in relation to the defeat of labor insurgency. Rare were such depictions of budding solidarity, like that in the twenty-seventh chapter of J. McHenry Jones's 1895 novel, *Hearts of Gold*, which exposes the "leasing" of the labor of black convicts to black mine owners as tool of labor exploitation. In this chapter, two fleeing black inmates successfully plead for sanctuary among a town of Welsh immigrant miners. Moved by the story of abuse told by the two men, the white miners refuse the demands of the mine captain to turn over the escaped inmates, asserting:

> There is a higher law – a law that existed previous to the legislature that legalized this damnable tool of cheap labor. We refuse by the law of common humanity, by the statutes of self preservation, to allow these men, to longer compete with us in the struggle of existence. If we had no hearts, if our sympathies did not go out to the poor, ill-treated, half-starved wretches, an enlightened self interest would no longer permit oppressive capitalists to use these victims of a misdirected and ruinous state economy,

[10] Stein, "Of Mr. Booker T. Washington," 427. [11] Stein, "Of Mr. Booker T. Washington," 445.
[12] Woodward, *Strange Career*, 44.

to glut the markets with their cheap products to the injury of free labor. This convict system is a piece of short-sighted retrenchment; it may be a saving to the state, but it means poor work at starvation wages for the miners.[13]

This brief recognition that solidarity might emerge from acknowledging the common humanity of exploited workers regardless of race, coupled with a realization that the point of convict leasing was to lower the cost of labor across the board, is rare within the literature of the period. More frequently black writers portrayed worker militancy as either misguided or antithetical to the nature and interest of black workers. For example, Booker T. Washington derided workers who had the temerity to "strike" against their employers, observing that this "was something which, it seemed, usually occurred whenever the men got two or three months ahead in the savings. During the strike, of course, they spent all that they had saved, and would often return to work in debt at the same wages, or would move to another mine at considerable expense," leaving "them worse off at the end of a strike."[14] In a similar vein, one of the heroic black characters in Frances Ellen Watkins Harper's 1892 novel *Iola Leroy, or Shadows Uplifted*, Dr. Henry Latimer, asserts the Americanness of "the negro" by distancing black Americans from political militancy, declaring, "the negro is not plotting in beer-saloons against the peace and order of society. His fingers are not dripping with dynamite, neither is he spitting upon your flag, nor flaunting the red banner of anarchy in your face."[15] Anna Julia Cooper's *A Voice from the South* similarly adduces innate racial qualities to commend black workers to their white fellow citizens, remarking of "the Negro" that

> his instinct for law and order, his inborn respect for authority, his inaptitude for rioting and anarchy, his gentleness and cheerfulness as a laborer, and his deep-rooted faith in God will prove indispensable and invaluable elements in a nation menaced as America is by anarchy, socialism, communism, and skepticism poured in with all the jail birds from the continents of Europe and Asia.[16]

In an attempt to fashion a bulwark against the rise of the segregation order, writers like Harper, Cooper, and Washington, and later, Griggs, Pauline Hopkins, and Charles Chesnutt, sought to appeal to the class interests of

---

[13] J. McHenry Jones, *Hearts of Gold* (Daily Intelligencer Job Press, 1896), 130.
[14] Washington, *Up from Slavery*, 35.
[15] Frances Ellen Watkins Harper, *Iola Leroy, or Shadows Uplifted*, in *The African-American Novel in the Age of Reaction: Three Classics*, ed. William L. Andrews (Mentor, 1992), 167.
[16] Anna Julia Cooper, *A Voice from the South* (1892) (Oxford University Press, 1988), 173.

white southern elites, whose place atop the social-political order would be threatened by the widespread dissemination of the ideas and beliefs that Cooper disparages.

The texts produced by these writers sometimes oscillated between decrying the demoralizing effects of segregation on the ambitions and sensibilities of the better educated and better situated black (and white) Americans and noting the perhaps inadvertent opportunities for racial uplift created by imposing racial separation on American society. For example, in *The Souls of Black Folk*, Du Bois complained that segregation exacerbated racial animus, writing:

> All this segregation by color is largely independent of that natural clustering by social grades common to all communities. A Negro slum may be in dangerous proximity to a white residence quarter, while it is quite common to find a white slum planted in the heart of a respectable Negro district. One thing, however, seldom occurs: the best of the whites and the best of the Negroes almost never live in anything like close proximity. It thus happens that in nearly every Southern town and city, both whites and blacks see commonly the worst of each other.[17]

On this view, segregation interdicted a social order that reflected "natural" distinctions based on achievement and comportment. In making this observation, Du Bois agreed with the condemnation of segregation put forward by the white, southern liberal writer George Washington Cable, who in his lengthy essay "The Freedman's Case in Equity," remarked that segregation "spurns" the black American's "ambition, tramples upon his languishing self-respect, and indignantly refuses to let him either buy with money, or earn by any excellence of inner life or outward behavior, the most momentary immunity from these public indignities even for his wife and daughters."[18] But black writers sometimes also asserted, pragmatically, that the imposition of racial affinity by law and practice had, perhaps inadvertently, created the social basis for racial solidarity and the possibility of moral and educational uplift. "How many of us today," asked Professor Langhorne, one of the accomplished black characters in Harper's *Iola Leroy*,

---

[17] W. E. B. Du Bois, *The Souls of Black Folk*, in *Writings*, ed. Nathan Huggins (Library of America Press, 1986), 477.
[18] George Washington Cable, "The Freedman's Case in Equity" (1889), in *The Silent South: Together with "The Freedman's Case in Equity" and "The Convict-Lease System"* (Charles Scribner's Sons, 1907), 18.

would be teaching in the South, if every field of labor in the North was as accessible to us as to the whites? It has been estimated that a million young white men have left the South since the war, and, had our chances been equal to theirs, would we have been any more willing to stay in the South with those who need us than they? But this prejudice, by impacting us together, gives us a common cause and brings our intellect in contact with the less favored of our race.[19]

Professor Langhorne's account of racial solidarity positions the educated, well-off black individual not as a peer of their fellow blacks but as benefactor to their race as a whole.

This attempt to embrace racial identity as a mission did not, however, always come without any second thoughts and difficulties. When Charles Chesnutt depicted the plight of the accomplished Dr. William Miller in his 1901 novel *The Marrow of Tradition*, which fictionalizes the Wilmington Massacre in Wilmington, North Carolina in 1898, he dramatized the difficulty of reconciling democratic principle with social distaste. Forced to leave the first-class car where he has been riding with a white fellow physician, Miller takes up a seat in the Jim Crow car, where he is soon joined by a "noisy, loquacious, happy, dirty, and malodorous" group of black laborers. Although Miller is initially "amused and pleased" because these "were his people, and he felt a certain expansive warmth toward them in spite of their obvious shortcomings," his magnanimous sentiments soon change. The narrator continues:

> By and by, however, the air became too close, and he went out upon the platform. For the sake of the democratic ideal, which means so much to his race, he might have endured the affliction. He could easily imagine that people of refinement, with the power in their hands, might be tempted to strain the democratic ideal in order to avoid such contact; but personally, and apart from the mere matter of racial sympathy, these people were just as offensive to him as to the whites in the other end of the train. Surely, if a classification of passengers on trains was at all desirable, it might be made upon some more logical and considerate basis than a mere arbitrary, tactless, and, by the very nature of things, brutal drawing of a color line.[20]

And by the end of Chesnutt's bleak novel, the fragile bridge to a possible social future does not rest on the piers supporting the idea of racial solidarity across the class differences that offend Dr. Miller's sensibilities but rather on the possibly too-tardy recognition by genteel white

---

[19] Harper, *Iola Leroy*, 186.
[20] Charles W. Chesnutt, *The Marrow of Tradition*, ed. Werner Sollors (W. W. Norton, 2012), 40–41.

professionals that they share a class-interest with their counterparts across the color line.

The black writers who took up their pens against the imposition of segregation across the South in the 1890s were not merely objecting to the separation of blacks and whites in social and civic life but to the political, social, and economic subordination that Jim Crow sought to enforce on black Americans across the board. Throughout this period, black Americans had opposed these laws and practices in a variety of ways – indeed, the devastating *Plessy* decision was the outcome of one such challenge. But the rewriting of southern state constitutions to circumvent the Fourteenth and Fifteenth Amendments and secure the defeat of Populism had eroded the social and institutional basis upon which white supremacy could be directly challenged in the South. In response, the political activities of literate black Americans were amplified and channeled into "appeals to the ruling elements of society" on behalf of blacks as a group.[21] Novels, poems, short stories, and belletristic essays were part and parcel of such appeals. Accordingly, rather than having emerged as the collective political project of African Americans across all walks of life, the idea that the interests of the race as a whole required establishing an African American literature reflected the common sense of relatively elite blacks in the wake of disfranchisement and Jim Crow. The words of Belton Piedmont, the protagonist of Sutton E. Griggs's first novel, *Imperium in Imperio*, were representative. Acknowledging that blacks were increasingly unable to use the "sword (and spear) and the ballot" to right the wrongs that were being perpetrated against them, Piedmont asserts: "There is a weapon mightier than either of these. I speak of the pen. If denied the use of the ballot let us devote our attention to that mightier weapon, the pen." Carried away by the spirit of his exhortation, Piedmont adds:

> [I]t would be a worthy theme for the songs of the Holy Angels, if every Negro, away from the land of his nativity, can by means of the pen, force an acknowledgment of equality from the proud lips of the fierce, all conquering Anglo-Saxon, thus eclipsing the record of all other races of men, who without exception have had to wade through blood to achieve their freedom.[22]

---

[21] Stein, "Of Mr. Booker T. Washington," 42.
[22] Sutton E. Griggs, *Imperium in Imperio*, ed. Tess Chakkalakal and Kenneth W. Warren (West Virginia University Press, 2022), 127.

Challenging segregation, then, was not merely a theme or preoccupation of many African American literary texts but, in many ways, a mission that would become that literature's *raison d'être*.

"[T]he problem of the Twentieth Century is the problem of the color-line," W. E. B. Du Bois thundered in *The Souls of Black Folk*, in words betokening how the situation of black literature in the 1890s would shape black American literary activity for the next seven decades and beyond.[23] For despite the heterogeneity of literary writing by twentieth-century black authors, their works, individually and collectively, have come to be regarded as evidence of collective black achievement or as the communal voice of a politically silenced race. Indeed, even after the civil rights movement of the 1950s and 1960s successfully toppled the legal pillars of Jim Crow and returned black Americans en masse, if imperfectly, to the nation's political life, the idea that positive political outcomes for black Americans depend on the ongoing production of a distinctive literature remains a compelling belief among many writers and scholars.

Further Reading

Bruce, Dixon D. *Black American Writing from the Nadir: The Evolution of a Literary Tradition, 1877–1915*. Louisiana State University Press, 1989.

Castronovo, Russ. "Beauty along the Color Line: Lynching, Form, and Aesthetics." In *Beautiful Democracy: Aesthetics and Anarchy in a Global Era*. University of Chicago Press, 2007, 106–135.

Chakkalakal, Tess. "Disfranchisement." In D. Berton Emerson and Gregory Laski, eds., *Democracies in America: Keywords for the Nineteenth Century and Today*. Oxford University Press, 2023, 242–251.

Fields, Karen. E. and Barbara J. Fields. *Racecraft: The Soul of Inequality in American Life*. Verso, 2012.

Gates, Henry Louis, Jr. *Stony the Road: Reconstruction, White Supremacy, and the Rise of Jim Crow*. Penguin, 2019.

Laski, Gregory. *Untimely Democracy: The Politics of Progress after Slavery*. Oxford University Press, 2018.

Miller, Vivien. "Race, Crime, and Segregation." In Jonathan Daniel Wells, ed., *The Routledge History of Nineteenth-Century America*. Taylor & Francis, 2017, 292–306.

Moses, Wilson J. *Afrotopia: The Roots of African American Popular History*. Cambridge University Press, 1998.

Reed, Adolph L., Jr. *W. E. B. Du Bois and American Political Thought: Fabianism and the Color Line*. Oxford University Press, 1999.

---

[23] Du Bois, *Souls*, 359.

Seay-Howard, Ariel Elizabeth, "Anti-Black Violence." In D. Berton Emerson and Gregory Laski, eds., *Democracies in America: Keywords for the Nineteenth Century and Today*. Oxford University Press, 2023, 94–103.

Thomas, Brook. *The Literature of Reconstruction: Not in Plain Black and White*. Johns Hopkins University Press, 2017.

Warren, Kenneth W. *What Was African American Literature?* Harvard University Press, 2011.

West, Michael R. *The Education of Booker T. Washington: American Democracy and the Idea of Race Relations*. Columbia University Press, 2006.

Wilson, Ivy. "The Color Line: James Monroe Whitfield and Albery Allson Whitman." In Kerry Larson, ed., *The Cambridge Companion to Nineteenth-Century American Poetry*. Cambridge University Press, 2011, 208–224.

CHAPTER 11

Immigration: "The Chinese Question" in Economics, Law, and Literature
Spencer Tricker

The politics of immigration in the nineteenth-century United States is best understood in relation to historically divergent patterns of racialization, or race making, with which it was tightly intertwined. The Naturalization Act of 1790, passed by the first Congress, signals the earliest use of immigration law to build the nation according to white supremacist principles. This act allowed only "free white person[s]" to become US citizens.[1] While it has been conventional in historical scholarship to view US policies regulating and restricting immigration as having begun only in the late nineteenth century, Aristide Zolberg argues that US leaders were engaged with immigration concerns from the time of the nation's founding. The relative "absence of federal legislation [in the early decades of the nation's history]," he observes, "Does not reflect a lack of interest in regulating entry, but was attributable to the overriding of immigration policy by what was then [in the antebellum period] the central issue of national politics, the matter of states' rights in relation to slavery."[2] Thus, while it is true that federal laws constraining immigration began to proliferate only in the late nineteenth century, immigration was nonetheless a long-simmering, if not always preeminent, political issue that inflected American literature and culture throughout the century.

The bulk of immigration to the United States during this period came from Europe. Among other groups, the Irish represent an important bellwether indexing the relationship between European immigration patterns and the historical process of racial formation in America.[3] They arrived in huge numbers after a series of potato blights in the 1840s.

---

[1] US Congress, *Statutes at Large*, First Congress, Second Session, 1790, *American Memory*, Library of Congress, https://memory.loc.gov/cgi-bin/ampage?collId=llsl&fileName=001/lls l001.db&recNum=226.
[2] Aristide R. Zolberg, *A Nation by Design* (Harvard University Press, 2006), 3.
[3] For more on the concept of racial formation, see Michael Omi and Howard Winant, *Racial Formation in the United States*, 3rd ed. (Routledge, 2015), 105–136.

From 1847 to 1857, around 1.5 million Irish immigrated to the United States. Initially, the European-descended, Protestant majority did not view these newcomers as fellow whites. Indeed, in New York City and other urban centers, "No Irish Need Apply" signs were a common sight for much of the century. Anti-Catholic sentiment was a driving force behind this prejudice, which spawned the "Know Nothing" party of the mid-1850s and persisted to some degree until the election of John F. Kennedy in 1960. Nevertheless, from as early as the 1840s, the Democratic Party courted Irish voters by appealing to them as members of the white race. As Noel Ignatiev notes, "The need to gain the loyalty of the Irish explains why the Democratic Party, on the whole, rejected nativism."[4] Importantly, however, Irish Americans did not support the party "out of sentimental attachment to those who gave them the vote." Rather, "The Democratic Party eased their assimilation as whites, and more than any other institution, it taught them the meaning of whiteness."[5]

The trajectory of the Irish toward whiteness finds its most significant contrast in the contemporaneous situation faced by the Chinese, who, despite arriving in smaller numbers and being largely concentrated in California and the West, were at the center of immigration restriction laws that took shape after mid-century. Underscoring this outsized and transformative role, the following pages focus on this group and its representation in American literature. In the first section, I address the history of the Chinese in America, focusing on key economic issues and laws related to immigration. In the second section, I track the widely known figure of the "Heathen Chinee" through works of the 1870s and 1880s, highlighting how this literary trope directly mediated political and economic issues of the period, while also illustrating its shaping role in English-language writings by early Chinese immigrants. Some of this latter work, I conclude, anticipates the later emergence of Asian American politics and the contemporary racialization of Asians as America's model minority.

The History of Chinese Immigration and Exclusion

The Chinese first arrived in significant numbers shortly after the 1848 discovery of gold at Sutter's Mill in California.[6] Even before their arrival,

---

[4] Noel Ignatiev, *How the Irish Became White* (Routledge, 1995), 69.   [5] Ignatiev, *Irish*, 76.
[6] For a global history of Chinese immigrants in nineteenth-century gold rushes, see Mae Ngai, *The Chinese Question: The Gold Rushes and Global Politics* (Norton, 2021).

the prospect of Chinese immigration elicited the rage of white miners, who were concerned that Chinese labor would facilitate large-scale mining operations and undercut small claims. By 1854, the California Supreme Court ruled in *The People* v. *Hall* that a Chinese person could not legally testify against a white man in court. That same year, the author John Rollin Ridge published *The Life and Adventures of Joaquín Murieta: The Celebrated California Bandit*. Ridge's popular novel repeatedly stages brutal scenes of anti-Chinese violence. At one point, the narrator notes that "it was a politic stroke" for a Mexican bandit "to kill Chinamen in preference to Americans, for no one cared for so alien a class, and they were left to shift for themselves."[7] The fact that Ridge, also known as Yellow Bird, was half Cherokee illustrates tensions between marginalized communities in California during this period, although Daniel Liestman has noted that Chinese and American Indian relations were heterogeneous and "ranged from mass murder to matrimony."[8] Soon subject to an onerous foreign miner's tax, while being forcibly driven off claims and out of many towns throughout the West, Chinese migrants, who were predominantly male, opened laundries and restaurants. They would also play a pivotal role in railroad construction.

Leland Stanford, who was both governor of California and co-owner of the Central Pacific Railroad company, played to popular Sinophobic sentiment in his first gubernatorial address, stating, "To my mind it is clear, that the settlement among us of an inferior race is to be discouraged by every legitimate means" and that "it will afford me great pleasure to concur with the Legislature in any constitutional action, having for its object the repression of the immigration of the Asiatic races."[9] By 1865, however, the Central Pacific began hiring Chinese workers en masse to fill construction jobs that Caucasian workers quickly and routinely abandoned. Chinese immigrants, many of whom hailed from the mountainous Pearl River Delta in Guangdong province, comprised roughly 80 percent of the workforce. These laborers undertook one of the most significant engineering feats of the nineteenth century: blasting through the Sierra Nevada Mountains to lay track for the transcontinental railroad. To facilitate the flow of cheap Chinese labor, despised by California's working

---

[7] John Rollin Ridge, *The Life and Adventures of Joaquín Murieta: The Celebrated California Bandit*, ed. Hsuan L. Hsu (Penguin, 2018), 85.
[8] Daniel Liestman, "Horizontal Inter-ethnic Relations: Chinese and American Indians in the Nineteenth-Century American West," *Western Historical Quarterly* 30:3 (1999), 327–349, 328.
[9] Leland Stanford, "Inaugural Address," delivered January 10, 1862, *The Governors' Gallery*, California State Library, https://governors.library.ca.gov/addresses/08-Stanford.html.

class but beloved by its capitalists, the Qing dynasty representative Anson Burlingame and Secretary of State William Henry Seward signed an 1868 treaty "with labor procurement as its central concern." Ratified by Congress in 1871, it nonetheless "specified that the right of entry should not be construed to entail the right to acquire citizenship by naturalization." As Zolberg explains, this combination of concerns – cheap labor and exclusion from citizenship – "indicates that the design [of the US government] assumed Chinese workers would not be incorporated into American society, and hence envisioned, at least tacitly, the formation of an institutional limbo, populated by a mass of permanently segregated noncitizen workers, neither slave nor free."[10]

After the Central Pacific and Union Pacific railroad lines were joined at Promontory Point (1869), many Chinese workers returned to California and other parts of the West, prompting a new upsurge of anti-Chinese sentiment and violence. Among the most disturbing of these were the Los Angeles lynchings of October 24, 1871, during which nineteen Chinese were murdered by "a mob of five hundred Mexican and Anglo men, [or] nearly 10 percent of the population of Los Angeles" at that time.[11] Broadly, Jean Pfaelzer notes that "the brutality and the roundups of Chinese people in the 1870s exposed the inchoate state of California as a place of multiple and disputed borderlands and clashing cultures."[12] The Panic of 1873 further intensified tensions and, in 1877, the Workingmen's Party was formed in California. Led by the labor organizer and populist orator Denis Kearney, this group effectively took control of the California Democratic Party and became a powerful anti-Chinese voice lobbying the national legislature. At the core of its animosity was what Colleen Lye terms the "racial economism of Asiatic racial form," or "a form in which economic interests are not masked but are the primary medium of race's historical expression."[13] More recently, Iyko Day has observed how this economism fits into a broader historical "logic of romantic anticapitalism," or "the misperception of the *appearance* of capitalist relations for their essence."[14] This ideology "*glorifie[d]* the concrete dimension" of labor, racialized as white, "while casting as evil the abstract domination of

---

[10] Zolberg, *Nation*, 180–181.
[11] Jean Pfaelzer, *Driven Out: The Forgotten War against Chinese Americans* (University of California Press, 2008), 48.
[12] Pfaelzer, *Driven Out*, 56.
[13] Colleen Lye, *America's Asia: Racial Form and American Literature, 1893–1945* (Princeton University Press, 2005), 102.
[14] Iyko Day, *Alien Capital: Asian Racialization and the Logic of Settler Colonial Capitalism* (Duke University Press, 2016), 8 (emphasis in original).

capitalism," racially figured in the image of the Chinese worker or "coolie" figure.[15]

If racial economism represented the main theme of anti-Chinese immigration discourse, a critically important variation was its anxiety over Chinese gender and sexuality. The preponderance of Chinese men over Chinese women (who comprised between 3.6 and 7.2 percent of the Chinese immigrant population between 1870 and 1890) was key to this anxiety.[16] On the one hand, there emerged a tendency to both emasculate and hypersexualize Chinese men. Many white observers considered them "sexless" and "feminine."[17] This view contributed to a long-standing tradition of representation "in which the Asian American male is both materially and psychically feminized within the context of a larger U.S. cultural imaginary."[18] However, Chinese men were also figured as lecherous and predatory, as both literature and popular cartoons of the period make clear.[19] On the other hand, there was a "widely held view that all Chinese women were prostitutes."[20] In fact, during the early stages of Chinese immigration, human traffickers did import women – often against their will – for sex work. It has been estimated that, in 1870, there were between 1,000 and 1,600 Chinese women sex workers in San Francisco. The presence of these women stoked widespread fears about the corruption of white American families. "By the mid-1870s," Pfaelzer explains, "Physicians were making dire claims about the inevitable transmission of syphilis from Chinese prostitutes to white males and, with quiet implication, to white wives, as though contagion flowed in only one direction."[21] In 1875, Congress passed the Page Act, which, as Zolberg observes, represented "the first national measure to control immigration by direct means since the prohibition on slave imports." Most significantly for Chinese immigration, it specifically targeted the importation of "women for the purposes of prostitution," which, in combination with popular discourse that framed Chinese women as sex workers, "plac[ed]

---

[15] Day, *Alien Capital*, 11 (emphasis in original).
[16] Sucheng Chan, "The Exclusion of Chinese Women, 1870–1943," in Sucheng Chan, ed., *Entry Denied: Exclusion and the Chinese Community in America, 1882–1943* (Temple University Press, 1991), 94–146, 94.
[17] Eric Hayot, "Coolie," in Rachel C. Lee, ed., *The Routledge Companion to Asian American and Pacific Islander Literature* (Routledge, 2014), 81–90, 86.
[18] David L. Eng, *Racial Castration: Managing Masculinity in Asian America* (Duke University Press, 2001), 2.
[19] Hsuan L. Hsu, "Introduction," in Sui Sin Far, *Mrs. Spring Fragrance*, ed. Hsuan L. Hsu (Broadview, 2011), 9–23, 17.
[20] Chan, "Exclusion," 95. [21] Pfaelzer, *Driven Out*, 96–97.

every incoming Chinese female under suspicion, ... reinforcing the exclusively male composition of the Chinese population and thereby, in combination with anti-miscegenation laws, of minimizing [that population's] natural reproduction."[22]

The Page Act set the stage for the broader Chinese Exclusion Act of 1882, which prohibited the immigration of all Chinese laborers. This federal law was the first to deny entry to members of a specific ethnic or national group and – despite its allowance for a small quota of "teachers, students, and merchants," as well as "a remarkable number of Chinese [who] challenged [its] application" – it would dramatically curtail the Chinese immigrant population for more than half a century.[23] The Geary Act of 1892 extended the exclusion period for another decade (the original duration had been ten years) and forced Chinese immigrants to carry identification papers, banned them from serving as witnesses in court, and disqualified them from receiving bail. Chinese exclusion was extended indefinitely in 1902 and not repealed until the 1943 Magnuson Act, which established a quota of 105 immigrants per year, largely as a gesture of diplomatic respect to China, which became an ally of the United States during World War II. Importantly, Chinese exclusion also provided a foretaste of broader, anti-Asian immigration restriction in the early twentieth century. In 1917, another law created an Asiatic Barred Zone preventing individuals from most areas of Asia (with the important exception of the Philippines, which became an American colony in 1898) from legally entering the country. In 1924, the Johnson–Reed Act solidified unequal immigration quotas based on the 1890 census, effectively privileging European countries of origin. It would remain in effect until the Hart–Celler Act of 1965, which opened the door to large numbers of Asian immigrants.

Importantly, Gordon H. Chang has noted a tendency among historians to consider the Chinese Exclusion Act as something of "a foregone conclusion" or "inevitability," whereas, in fact, there was a considerable subset of the US government, as well as many businesspeople, who actively promoted Chinese immigration and friendly ties between the United States and China, generally.[24] As I have already mentioned, a key representative of this faction was William Henry Seward, the author of

---

[22] Zolberg, *Nation*, 188.
[23] Bill Ong Hing, *Making and Remaking Asian America through Immigration Policy, 1850–1990* (Stanford University Press, 1993), 24, 240.
[24] Gordon H. Chang, "China and the Pursuit of America's Destiny: Nineteenth-Century Imagining and Why Immigration Restriction Took So Long," *Journal of Asian American Studies* 15:2 (2012), 145–169, 146.

the Burlingame–Seward Treaty of 1868. Another important figure was the capitalist Asa Whitney who, in a similar vein to Seward's messianic conception of American commercial empire, championed the transcontinental railroad, in 1849, as the catalyst for a new cosmopolitan world order centered on the Pacific:

> We see that the commerce of Asia, with civilization, has marched west. Each nation, from the Phoenicians to proud England, when supplanted, or forced to relinquish it, has declined, and dwindled into almost nothingness, and a new nation, west, risen up, with vigor and life, to control all. When this road shall have been completed, that commerce, with civilization, will have encircled the globe. It can go no further. Here, then, would be the consummation of all things; and here it would be as fixed, as fast, as time and earth itself. Here we should stand forever, reaching out one hand to all Asia and the other to all Europe, willing that all may enjoy the great blessing which we possess, claiming free intercourse and exchange of commodities with all, and seeking not to subjugate any; but all, the entire, the whole, tributary, and, at our will, subject to us.[25]

Whitney's convoluted language illustrates a budding nineteenth-century discourse, which I term *Pacific imminence*, that substantially revised and supplemented preexisting notions of civilization's westward trajectory by forecasting a novel, Pacific-oriented vision of cosmopolitan futurity.[26] In this vision, the United States would occupy the position of first among equals: the benevolent power to which all others would inevitably become "tributary" and "subject." However, the colonialist undertones of Whitney's ostensibly pluralist vision would soon find material corollaries as the United States overthrew the Hawaiian monarchy and assumed control of Cuba, Puerto Rico, the Philippines, and Guam after the Spanish-American War (1898). In short, it is important to recognize that many politicians and capitalists who vigorously promoted friendly relations with China were also firmly committed to a broader vision of American geopolitical dominance in transpacific affairs.

"The Heathen Chinee" in Literature by White Authors

Although the Chinese are not as commonly represented in nineteenth-century Anglo-American literature as members of other racial minority groups, there are quite a few texts, particularly toward the end of the

---

[25] Asa Whitney, *A Project for a Railroad to the Pacific* (George W. Wood, 1849), 40.
[26] I elaborate the literary, cultural, and historical contours of this discourse in a forthcoming manuscript under revision.

century, that feature Chinese characters and subjects. These include works such as (the aforementioned) Ridge's *Life and Adventures of Joaquín Murieta* (1854), Ambrose Bierce's short story "The Haunted Valley" (1871), Mark Twain and Bret Harte's play *Ah Sin* (1877), Horatio Alger's *The Young Miner* (1879), Adeline Knapp's "The Ways That Are Dark" (1895), and Frank Norris's *Moran of the Lady Letty* (1898). Caricatures of the pidgin-speaking "Chinaman" recur in many of these texts, which, as in the unfortunate case of Twain and Harte's play, "affirm[ed] and reproduc[ed] a racist vision of the Chinese character that would persist for much of the twentieth century and beyond using the antiblack theatrical form of minstrelsy."[27] Later in the century, the Chinese occupied an important role in the development of naturalist fiction. "If," as Colleen Lye notes, the movement known as "naturalism provides examples of American literature's most relentless effort at figuring the unseen power of social abstraction," such as the material and psychological effects of capitalism on the working and middle classes, the Chinese were represented, in the works of California-based naturalist writers like Frank Norris and Jack London, as a menacing and multitudinous "yellow peril" who represent a "variant of naturalism's degenerationist imagination, in which [racial] hierarchies are always reversible."[28]

Against this backdrop, the single most significant work of literature to represent the Chinese was Bret Harte's "Plain Language from Truthful James" (1870), better known to most nineteenth-century readers as "The Heathen Chinee." "One of the most popular poems ever published," it "made Bret Harte a household name" within days of its appearance in the *Overland Monthly*. Soon thereafter, it was reprinted around the country.[29] Importantly, Harte intended the poem as a satire of Sinophobic racism in California. It was not, however, interpreted that way by most readers, who took its racial caricature at face value. In Harte's defense, the title "Plain Language from Truthful James" places marked emphasis on the speaker, whose opening lines suggest buffoonery:

> Which I wish to remark,
> And my language is plain,
> That for ways that are dark
> And for tricks that are vain,

---

[27] Caroline H. Yang, *The Peculiar Afterlife of Slavery: The Chinese Worker and the Minstrel Form* (Stanford University Press, 2020), 101.
[28] Lye, *America's Asia*, 7–8.
[29] Gary Scharnhorst, "'Ways That Are Dark': Appropriations of Bret Harte's 'Plain Language from Truthful James'," *Nineteenth-Century Literature* 51:3 (1996), 377–399, 377–378.

> The heathen Chinee is peculiar,
> Which the same I would rise to explain.[30]

James then goes on to "explain" these "peculiar" behaviors by describing a game of euchre in which a white man, Bill Nye, attempts to swindle a Chinese man, Ah Sin, who claims not to understand the rules. When it is revealed that Ah Sin has been cheating, himself, Nye cries out "we are ruined by Chinese cheap labor!" and proceeds to attack Ah Sin, sending cards flying around the room. Truthful James's unmusical repetition of Nye's phrase is an overt non sequitur underscoring the dubiousness of arguments blaming the Chinese, rather than monopoly capitalism, for the economic struggles of the white working class. However, in the titular shift from "Truthful James" to "The Heathen Chinee" we can easily see where readers finally located the object of satirical humor. Notably, phrases like "Heathen Chinee" and "Chinese cheap labor" were recycled throughout the 1870s in published news items pertaining to Chinese immigration, and the poem was also cited on the floor of Congress during immigration debates. "The heathen Chinee" was therefore more than a common nineteenth-century phrase; it became the key cultural lens through which many Americans (especially those outside of the West) viewed and imagined the Chinese immigrant population.[31]

Among popular reprintings of Harte's poem is an unauthorized pamphlet edition advertising the Chicago, Rock Island, and Pacific Railroad line. Complete with eleven illustrations, it follows a trend among other illustrated versions of the poem, which tended to embellish it "by portraying overt violence against the Chinese."[32] In the final illustration, Bill Nye grasps Ah Sin by his queue (the long, braided pigtail worn by subjects of the Qing dynasty in this period), kicks him into the air, and brandishes a large knife – presumably to cut Ah Sin's hair. The caption beneath the image reads "the language that was plain," while an advertisement at the top of the page states, "Take the Rock Island Route, the only first class road in the West."[33] Violent acts focusing on Ah Sin's queue were a regular feature of the poem's illustrations, which some interpret as an act of figurative emasculation.[34] Stephen J. Mexal has argued that the poem's use by the railroad company serves to "promot[e] the American West as

---

[30] Bret Harte, "Plain Language from Truthful James," *The Overland Monthly* (September 1870), 287.
[31] Scharnhorst, "Appropriations," 383–386. [32] Scharnhorst, "Appropriations," 381.
[33] Bret Harte, "The Heathen Chinee" in the pamphlet *Heathen Chinee* (Chicago, Rock Island, and Pacific Railroad, 1872).
[34] Scharnhorst, "Appropriations," 381.

a space amenable to the reproduction of liberal republican modernity" in an effort to "constitute a western public."[35] I would add that by co-opting a poem about the Chinese, who served so pivotal a role in the construction of the transcontinental railroad's western segments, it also dramatizes how organized capital in the Reconstruction era exploited Chinese immigrants both materially – as sources of low-wage, high-risk labor – and culturally, as popular objects of racist abuse mobilized to advance settler colonialism and white supremacy in the American West.

Early Chinese American Literature: Wong Chin Foo and Yan Phou Lee

The increasing digitization of periodicals makes clear that, during the latter decades of the nineteenth century, there were several highly active writers of Chinese ancestry publishing English-language literature in North America. Today, the best known of these is Edith Maude Eaton, who usually published under the pen name Sui Sin Far. As Mary Chapman observes, Far's known catalogue of works now stands at "over 260 texts," representing a tenfold increase in widely available materials since scholars first began to rediscover her work in the early 1980s.[36] Her sister, Winnifred Eaton, who passed as a mixed-race Japanese woman and wrote under the pseudonym Onoto Watanna, was actually a far more successful author in her day.[37] Yet, while the careers of the Eaton sisters have started to become familiar to scholars of American literature, that of Wong Chin Foo, an equally important Chinese American writer in this era, has only recently begun to reemerge.

As Hsuan L. Hsu notes, Wong "was one of the most eloquent nineteenth-century Chinese authors to publish in English," whose work appeared alongside that of some of the leading writers of the period in the *Atlantic Monthly*, *Harper's Monthly*, and the *Cosmopolitan*.[38] Wong is

---

[35] Stephen J. Mexal, *Reading for Liberalism: The Overland Monthly and the Writing of the Modern American West* (University of Nebraska Press, 2013), 62.
[36] Mary Chapman, "Introduction," in *Becoming Sui Sin Far*, ed. Mary Chapman (McGill-Queen's University Press, 2016), xiii–lxxvi, xix–xxi. Sui Sin Far's most well-known work, originally published in 1912, is *Mrs. Spring Fragrance*.
[37] See the *Winnifred Eaton Archive* for a growing collection of her previously out-of-print writings: Mary Chapman, Jean Lee Cole, and Joey Takeda, "About," The Winnifred Eaton Archive, edited by Mary Chapman and Jean Lee Cole, v. 1.0, August 16, 2020, https://winnifredeatonarchive.org/about.html.
[38] Hsuan L. Hsu, "Wong Chin Foo's Periodical Writing and Chinese Exclusion," *Genre* 39:3 (2006), 83–105, 84.

also difficult to place within the longer history of Asian American literature, since his works "range in tone from self-commodifying 'goodwill' to bitter political criticism" and illustrate how "he could confront and challenge as much as he entertained his audiences."[39] Wong was also an unusual Chinese immigrant in that he hailed from Shandong province in the northeastern part of China (as opposed to the southeastern provinces of Guangdong and Fujian) and, brought to the United States for training as a Christian missionary in 1867, spent part of his early twenties studying at Columbian College preparatory school and the Lewisburg Academy (forerunners of George Washington University and Bucknell University, respectively). Shortly after returning to China, he took part in subversive activities and was forced to flee. He then made his way back to the United States and managed to be naturalized as a citizen in Grand Rapids, Michigan (1874), less than a decade before national anti-Chinese legislation rendered such naturalization impossible. He took up a career on the lyceum circuit, delivering lectures throughout the East, Midwest, and South (regions where anti-Chinese racism was not so fervent as in the West) on a wide range of Chinese topics throughout the next three decades. In the 1880s, he edited Chinese-language newspapers in New York City and Chicago and became the first writer to use the term "Chinese American" to describe American residents of Chinese origin.[40] He also won a public debate with Denis Kearney, the exclusionist leader of the California Workingman's Party, in 1887, after first challenging him to a duel (Kearney declined).

Wong's most overtly provocative piece of writing is "Why Am I a Heathen?," an August 1887 essay that excoriates Christianity and hyperbolically celebrates the superiority of Chinese culture. Published in the *North American Review* as part of a nearly four-year-long series of articles (often beginning with the phrase "Why Am I") showcasing various religious perspectives, "Why Am I a Heathen?" finds Wong diverging from the relatively staid affirmations of previous contributors. At the start of the essay, Wong describes his adolescent experiences with Christianity, which he encountered through missionaries in China. As a young man, he notes that he "seriously contemplated becoming the bearer of heavenly tidings to my 'benighted' heathen people."[41] Having sampled a variety of Christian sects, however, he becomes "disgusted" and decides to "tur[n] to a simple

---

[39] Hsu, "Wong Chin Foo," 84.
[40] Scott Seligman, *The First Chinese American: The Remarkable Life of Wong Chin Foo* (Hong Kong University Press, 2013), xii.
[41] Wong Chin Foo, "Why Am I a Heathen?," *The North American Review* 145:369 (1887), 169.

study of the 'inspired Bible' for enlightenment." Once he learns of the "New Dispensation," however, "with its sin-forgiving business," he decides to give up on Christianity. If everyone is entitled to forgiveness, he muses, what would stop Denis Kearney from sneaking into heaven, resurrecting his favorite slogan ("The Chinese must go!"), and "organiz[ing] a heavenly crusade to have me and others immediately cast out into the other place?"[42] He then unfolds a litany of Christian hypocrisies, eventually transitioning to a secular critique of Western capitalism, stating,

> Business men are lauded as great financiers who actually conspire to buy laws, place judges, control senates, corner and regulate at will the price of natural products; and, in fact, act as if the whole political and social machinery should be a lever to them to operate against the interests of the nation and people. In a heathen country such conspirators against social order and the general welfare would have short shrift.[43]

Such passages illuminate the fact that Wong tends to invert, rather than deconstruct, Orientalist binaries that valorized Western modernity over Eastern barbarism. At the same time, however, they demonstrate that – despite a willingness to conciliate and entertain white readers in some of his other works – he may have been the most openly combative Chinese immigrant writing in the United States at a time when sympathy for the Chinese was at its lowest ebb.

"Why Am I a Heathen?" makes several exaggerated claims, as when Wong states, "We [Chinese] are so far heathenish as to no longer persecute men simply on account of race, color, or previous condition of servitude." Such moments evoke a utopian image of China free from any form of prejudice, despite long histories of interethnic conflict. Even so, it is important to contextualize the essay as a pointed literary response to the culture of racist caricature and Sinophobic thinking emblematized by Harte's wildly popular "Heathen Chinee." His nationalist rhetoric, which lashed out against missionary condescension and imperialist domination of the Chinese people in the decades following the Opium Wars (1839–1842 and 1856–1860), must also be understood in relation to his personal history of multidirectional dissent and activism, which he directed against both the Qing dynasty and the US government. Indeed, Wong's activist spirit marks the text as perhaps the most significant literary expression of Chinese resistance to American racism in the nineteenth century. By embracing the epithet "heathen," he both anticipates the political

---

[42] Wong, "Why Am I a Heathen?," 171.   [43] Wong, Why Am I a Heathen?," 177.

reclamation of slurs by marginalized groups in the twenty-first century (as in the case of the word "queer" by gay, lesbian, bisexual, and trans communities) and discursively confronts Christian ideals with exploitative material practices carried out in their name. Yet, despite the evident sincerity of Wong's criticisms (which he reinforced with regular petitions and legal efforts into the 1890s), his sardonic tone also indexes his career as a public contrarian with a "lifelong penchant for the sensational."[44] It is difficult to read his closing sentences without picturing a wry smile: "This is what keeps me the heathen I am! And I earnestly invite the Christians of America to come to Confucius."[45]

If one of Wong's chief aims with "Why Am I a Heathen?" was to stir controversy, he certainly succeeded. The article was taken up by other journals around the country and created "a veritable firestorm of reaction, most of it highly critical and defensive."[46] However, among these textual responses, the most interesting was written by Yan Phou Lee, who, one month after the appearance of Wong's essay, published "Why I Am Not a Heathen: A Rejoinder to Wong Chin Foo" in the *North American Review*. Lee's essay is significant for at least two reasons. The first stems from Lee's hard distinction between essences and appearances, or what he designates as the divide between "religion," which "pertains to the heart," and "ethics," which "deals more with outward conduct."[47] According to this dynamic, Lee chastises Wong for misidentifying hypocrites as Christians proper. His insistent reassertion of this binary betrays one of the radical aspects of Wong's argument: that Christianity is what it does, and what Christians have done to the Chinese – often in the form of capitalist and imperialist exploitation – is immoral and unjust. At stake between Lee and Wong's differing conceptions is the issue of whether missionary activities are necessarily imperialist enterprises (be they of settler or commercial varieties). Wong's assertion is that they exist on the same continuum, a conclusion borne out by the imminent overthrow of Hawaii's monarchy by descendants of Protestant missionaries who arrived just decades earlier, in 1820. The second important point about "Why I Am Not a Heathen" is that it exhibits how civility politics and cosmopolitanism – understood, here, as an ecumenical invocation of world community – were harnessed to stifle immigrant acts of resistance. By publishing a rebuttal to Wong, something the *North American Review* had never

[44] Seligman, *The First Chinese American*, 20.   [45] Wong, Why Am I a Heathen?," 179.
[46] Seligman, *The First Chinese American*, 140.
[47] Yan Phou Lee, "Why I Am Not a Heathen: A Rejoinder to Wong Chin Foo," *The North American Review* 143:370 (1887), 306.

done in the "Why Am I" series, the journal attempted to reestablish a tone of liberal tolerance and neutralize Chinese vituperation with Chinese docility. Without condemning Wong outright, Yan Phou Lee nonetheless endeavors to show the superiority of his "cosmopolitan views" and Christian faith, which "gives him the requisite strength to act the good citizen and true husband."[48] However, this blithe allusion to citizenship, which Lee seems not to intend in a legal or political sense (since he was unable to obtain US citizenship for himself), ironically underscores Wong's grievance about the hypocrisy of Western missionaries, namely that their expressions of Christian brotherhood were, fundamentally, bad-faith articulations of cosmopolitanism that obscured bitter, material realities of the Chinese Exclusion era.[49]

Tracing the trope of the "Heathen Chinee" from Harte to Wong to Lee reveals much about how nineteenth-century American literature mediated a key anti-Asian trend in the evolution of the nation's immigration policy. By overtly connecting the "Heathen" Chinese with the threat of "cheap labor," Harte's poem epitomizes the "economism of Asiatic racial form" that Lye, as we have seen, locates at the heart of "yellow peril" discourse. Within this context, Wong's passionate "Why Am I a Heathen?" and Lee's dispassionate "Why I Am Not a Heathen," showcase, in miniature, the beginnings of a pronounced fissure cutting across diasporic Asian communities in North America. By this I mean the distinction between a resistant, activist contingent – prefigured here by Wong and taken up more fully by student activists of the late 1960s – and an assimilationist contingent, anticipated by Lee, more inclined to embrace the racial myth of the "model minority": that is, the idea that Asian Americans constitute an exceptional social group who prove the rule of America's colorblind meritocracy.[50] However, if Wong and Lee's exchange in 1887 sketches the contours of still-resonant conflicts within Asian American communities, it is worth concluding with the point that their experiences as highly educated Chinese men living and publishing in Gilded Age America made them quite unusual. We would be remiss, therefore, to consider them spokespeople for the larger Chinese immigrant population but can

---

[48] Lee, "Why I Am Not a Heathen," 310, 309.
[49] For Lee's biography and legal status, see Richard V. Lee's "Introduction," in Yan Phou Lee, *When I Was a Boy in China*, ed. Richard V. Lee (Xlibris, 2003), 11–20, and Mark Alden Branch, "Neither Here Nor There," *Yale Alumni Magazine* (May/June 2021), https://yalealumnimagazine.com/articles/5324-yan-phou-lee.
[50] For more on this division and the model minority as racial fiction, see Ellen D. Wu, *The Color of Success* (Princeton University Press, 2014), 242–258.

nonetheless see in their work that a heterogeneous Chinese American literary culture had already started to take shape in the nineteenth century.

Further Reading

Cheung, Floyd, "The Origins of Chinese American Autobiography." In Rajini Srikanth and Min Hyoung Song, eds., *The Cambridge History of Asian American Literature*. Cambridge University Press, 2015, 39–54.

Far, Sui Sin. "In the Land of the Free." In *Mrs. Spring Fragrance*, ed. Hsuan L. Hsu. Broadview, 2011, 120–129.

Higham, John. *Strangers in the Land: Patterns of American Nativism, 1860–1925*, rev. ed. Rutgers University Press, 2002.

Honig, Bonnie. "Democracy and Foreignness: Democratic Cosmopolitanism and the Myth of an Immigrant America." In Anthony Simon Laden and David Owen, eds., *Multiculturalism and Political Theory*. Cambridge University Press, 2007, 373–407.

Lew-Williams, Beth. *The Chinese Must Go: Violence, Exclusion, and the Making of the Alien in America*. Harvard University Press, 2018.

Ngai, Mae. *Impossible Subjects: Illegal Aliens and the Making of Modern America*. Princeton University Press, 2014.

Pfaelzer, Jean. *Driven Out: The Forgotten War against Chinese Americans*. University of California Press, 2008.

Tchen, John Kuo Wei, *New York before Chinatown: Orientalism and the Shaping of American Culture, 1776–1882*. Johns Hopkins University Press, 1999.

Wong, Edlie L. "A Gatekeeping Nation: Asian Invasion and the Rise of Xenophobic Immigration Law." In Nan Goodman and Simon Stern, eds., *The Routledge Research Companion to Law and Humanities in Nineteenth-Century America*. Routledge, 2017, 274–289.

Wong, Edlie L. *Racial Reconstruction: Black Inclusion, Chinese Exclusion, and the Fictions of Citizenship*. New York University Press, 2015.

CHAPTER 12

Territoriality: The Possessive Logics of American Placemaking

Kathryn Walkiewicz

Territory, as understood in a nineteenth-century US context, encompassed far more than was cartographically renderable – it was as much about *what could be* as about *what was*. Throughout the nineteenth century, especially in literature, territoriality expressed desired imperial occupations just as much as it did concrete political boundaries. For example, "America" itself evokes this slippage, as the name of both a hemisphere and a nation-state. In short, territory described a geographic imaginary that was central to a nationalist project of turning land into a thing that could be owned and regulated, thereby enabling the rationalization of genocide, colonization, slavery, and racial capitalism.

In this chapter, I linger on the very notion of territory itself as a spatial imaginary, a literary trope, and a political crucible for competing ideas of sovereignty. In particular, I examine how territory, or perhaps more precisely, territoriality (by which I mean the ideological maintenance of a territory), did not simply work at the behest of US empire but also served as an essential spatial register for working alongside and even against US territorial annexation, occupation, and colonization. Throughout the nineteenth century, the United States asserted an understanding of sovereignty that foregrounded dominance over a territory and its inhabitants. At the broadest scale, territory denoted the sovereign's property (the United States), and sovereignty denoted control over territory. Settler-colonial notions of sovereignty and territory stood in conflict with Indigenous understandings of sovereignty that often foreground *responsibility* to human and other-than-human relatives within a shared space or territory rather than *possession* of property. Critical for US territorial expansion was the promulgation of a particular understanding of territory that delegitimized Indigenous belonging and foregrounded what the Geonpul scholar Aileen Moreton-Robinson terms the "possessive logics" of "patriarchal white sovereignty," "an excessive desire to invest in reproducing and reaffirming the nation-state's ownership, control, and domination."[1]

Territorial expansion was also not simply about physical occupation. It was an epistemological paradigm attached to the *idea* of a place, and nineteenth-century US writers repeatedly took up this spatial imagining. Even the shapes of internal US borders were themselves a fiction. By this, I mean continental US states and territories did not always have "organic" borders informed by ecological and topographic variance, such as rivers and mountain ranges. Even when borders were organic, people shaped them through policy and violent projects of genocidal conquest. Conquest was not about being in tune with the land; it was about a desire for accumulation and dominance that no amount of land could adequately satiate. We get a sense of the ways territorial expansion was less about a particular object and more about affective desire in Walt Whitman's 1860 poem "Facing West from California's Shores." As the poem's speaker looks out across the Pacific, they acknowledge being "inquiring, tireless, seeking what is yet unfound," yet their situation of "long having wander'd" prompts the following final questions (whose critical implications breach the parentheses that seek to enclose them): "(But where is what I started for, so long ago? / And why is it yet unfound?)."[2] Whitman's poem expresses a restlessness that traversing a continent fails to quench. However, even as it (parenthetically) interrogates that restlessness, it also evokes a naivete or willful forgetfulness about how warfare, violence, and extraction (here euphemized as merely "having wander'd") enable the speaker to perch wistfully over the Pacific in the first place.

By the end of the century, a distinct set of questions about territorial expansion emerged but invoked the same possessive logics as those that undergirded territorial expansion throughout the nineteenth century. Following the illegal overthrow of the Hawaiian Kingdom (1893) and the end of the Spanish-American War (1898), the United States seized Hawaii, Puerto Rico, Guam, the Philippines, and, to some extent, Cuba. Questions about how these territories would function led to a series of Supreme Court decisions in 1901 called the Insular Cases that ostensibly created a classification

---

[1] Aileen Moreton-Robinson, *The White Possessive: Property, Power, and Indigenous Sovereignty* (University of Minnesota Press, 2015), xii.
[2] Walt Whitman, "Facing West from California's Shores," in *Leaves of Grass* (1867), 116, *The Walt Whitman Archive*, ed. Matt Cohen, Ed Folsom, and Kenneth M. Price, https://whitmanarchive.org/published/LG/1867/poems/14.

system for US territories.[3] The cases distinguished "incorporated" and "unincorporated" territories, and the court debated whether or not all US territories must eventually become states. Instead of clarifying forms of US territorial expansion, the cases instituted a flexible form of territoriality. The court decided that territories deemed "unincorporated" were "foreign in a domestic sense" and therefore could be occupied without the promise of full incorporation.[4] While the cases led to public debates about whether or not the United States had become an empire (I argue it already was), the United States has continued to use the slippery categories that emerged. Importantly, debates about whether or not a territory was "fit" for statehood redeployed anti-Indigenous and racialized rhetoric expressed through fears that these territories' inhabitants, predominantly comprised of non-white people, posed an insurmountable challenge to the growth of patriarchal white sovereignty.

Essential to geopolitical modes of statecraft were literary and cultural expressions of placemaking that reinforced (and naturalized) a settler-colonial map of occupation that was dependent on slavery and racial capitalism. Literature framed readers' expectations about the "frontier" and often made the boundary between fiction and reality indiscernible. Throughout the century, fictional depictions of a territory routinely preceded physical conquest there; just as significantly, fiction often shaped what US settlers imagined they would find in these "new" territories. In the nineteenth century, entire genres of US literary production were instrumental in imaginatively shaping readers' understandings of space, most explicitly the frontier romance, the western, and the captivity narrative.

This chapter is divided into three sections, each taking up a concept of territoriality that profoundly influenced US colonial expansion at the expense of other narratives of placemaking: "Terra Nullius," "Indian Territory," and "Black Territorialities." By territoriality, I mean a sense of spatial identity, especially the cultural, discursive, and ideological work of making place, as well as making home. In these sections, I detail how narratives of territoriality, including the doctrine of discovery, state rights, filibusterism, and American exceptionalism, profoundly influenced US politics and culture, but I also describe competing notions of placemaking

---

[3] For more on the Insular Cases, see Christina Duffy Burnett and Burke Marshall, eds., *Foreign in a Domestic Sense: Puerto Rico, American Expansion, and the Constitution* (Duke University Press, 2001).

[4] See Christina Duffy Burnett and Burke Marshall, "Between the Foreign and the Domestic: The Doctrine of Territorial Incorporation, Invented and Reinvented," in Burnett and Marshall, *Foreign in a Domestic Sense*, 1–36.

that disrupt this dominant narrative. Detailing this disruption requires paying close attention not only to westward expansion and Manifest Destiny but also to understandings of territory that challenged US-dominant modes of placemaking – for example, the Underground Railroad, marronage, and Indigenous sovereignty, all of which posed a challenge to a unified understanding of what territory meant for those living in North America. Despite sustained efforts to colonize and either eliminate or control them, proponents of other territorialities continued to override, undermine, and disturb the insistent spatialities of US empire. I use "empire" here intentionally to describe US settler colonialism (colonizing land with the intent to stay) *and* US colonial, neocolonial, and military interventions, especially those that were not necessarily about increasing the physical size of the United States but about expanding its power and control.[5]

Terra Nullius

The Peace Treaty of Westphalia (1648) ushered in a political order that would have global ramifications for hundreds of years to come, shaping European understandings of "territory." The treaty defined sovereign states as having authority over everything within their fixed territorial borders. It argued that states could not intervene in one another's affairs but instead must negotiate as self-determining entities. As European powers stretched their colonial interests across the globe, colonizers weaponized the Westphalian notion of a state as the supreme form of governance to disregard Indigenous peoples' sovereignty, assert European superiority, and justify global projects of occupation and extraction.[6]

Native Hawaiian scholar J. Kēhaulani Kauanui emphasizes how a Westphalian model foregrounded private property as "central for the 'achievement' of statehood" and was crucial in framing the US nation.[7]

---

[5] For Maile Arvin, settler colonialism "usually operates simultaneously through economy (the turning of land and natural resources into profit), law (the imposition of the legal-political apparatus of a settler nation-state, rather than an Indigenous form of governance), and ideology (culturally and morally defined ways of being and knowing resulting from European post-Enlightenment thought)." Maile Arvin, *Possessing Polynesians: The Science of Settler Colonial Whiteness in Hawai'i and Polynesia* (Duke University Press, 2019), 15.

[6] Moon-Kie Jung argues that the United States has always been an "empire-state" rather than a nation-state. See Moon-Kie Jung, "The Racial Constitution of the U.S. Empire State," in *Beneath the Surface of White Supremacy: Denaturalizing U.S. Racism's Past and Present* (Stanford University Press, 2015), 58–59.

[7] J. Kēhaulani Kauanui, *Paradoxes of Hawaiian Sovereignty: Land, Sex, and the Colonial Politics of State Nationalism* (Duke University Press, 2018), 38.

The assurance that if colonies joined the new nation they would retain, as US states, the right to sell their lands without needing authorization to do so from a sovereign national government had been necessary to persuade the earliest states, the original thirteen colonies, to join the United States. In the Americas, the Westphalian model served as a justification for delegitimizing Indigenous peoples' rights to land because Indigenous communities did not organize themselves along the lines of Westphalian states that prioritize property and possession. However, as the example of the Cherokee Nation made evident in the 1820s and 1830s, even when Indigenous nations did emulate a Westphalian model, Indigenous polities were still not recognized by the federal government as autonomous but at best as "domestic dependent nations."[8]

Terra nullius, or "nobody's land," was itself a fiction that imagined the entire North American continent as empty and ready for the taking, a tale that disregarded the diversity and abundance of Indigenous communities, tribal alliances, and trade routes already well established long before European contact. Literature often coupled terra nullius thinking with a fantasy of Indigenous erasure, either through the figure of the "vanishing Indian," as depicted in the work of James Fenimore Cooper (particularly his Leatherstocking Tales [1823–1841]) and Lydia Maria Child (particularly *Hobomok* [1824]), or through "Indian killer" novels like Robert Montgomery Bird's disturbingly violent *Nick of the Woods; or The Jibbenainesay* (1837). At the same time that many fictional characters popularized and crystallized a sense of national identity attached to territorial expansion, numerous writers participated in the actual projects of territorial taxonomy, including the apparently anti-expansionist Henry David Thoreau, who worked as a land surveyor.

In his writing, Thoreau obscures his work laying property lines and how he benefits from both the work itself (economically, via his salary) and the lines that result (nationally, as a US citizen). Such an omission conceals his complicity in one effective tool of expansion (surveying) while utilizing another (writing). Walking is an integral part of surveying, as the surveyor uses rudimentary tools to map out the terrain on foot. In the essay "Walking," however, Thoreau suggests that "at present, in this vicinity, the best part of the land is not private property; no one owns the landscape, and the walker enjoys comparative freedom," thus omitting his role in enabling the land to be "partitioned off" in preparation for the very

---

[8] *Cherokee Nation v. Georgia*, 5 Pet. 1 (1831).

"fences" he considers both dreadful and inevitable.⁹ By lamenting how private property and development have impacted the natural world, Thoreau appears to oppose US westward expansion and posits literary walking as an alternative that situates the walker metaphysically in a "terra nullius" outside the constraints of political order: "eastward I go only by force; but westward I go free."¹⁰ Like the speaker who has "wander'd" in Whitman's "Facing West from California's Shores," Thoreau walks unencumbered in ways that – through an ableist logic – suggest a spatial fantasy of expanse and openness itself made possible precisely by possession through whiteness, that is, the sense that he belongs everywhere. For Thoreau, the wilderness provides a model of territory that he reveres because he imagines it as distinct from society. However, this imagined wilderness where he is free from settler-colonial involvement is paradoxically only made possible through the settler occupation and modernization he participates in *both* ideologically, as a published writer, and procedurally, as a surveyor. His discursive disavowal of this dual complicity in producing the terra nullius he purports to describe obscures the genocidal logics of terra nullius that make his outsider fantasy of freedom from his society, enabling his resistance to it, possible in the first place.

Thoreau's territorial logic in "Walking" operates similarly to that of Frederick Jackson Turner's 1893 frontier thesis, which became the dominant historical narrative of territory and territorial expansion until the second half of the twentieth century. For Turner, the "frontier" provided a liminal space for revitalizing "Americaness" until its supposed closing in the 1890s created a US crisis of identity. What Thoreau describes in literary and embodied terms Turner narrates as history. Turner stages the US frontier as physical space necessary for the exceptionalist project of white expansion and Manifest Destiny – the frontier is where territoriality and national identity are forged.¹¹ He patriotically viewed expansion as an inherent and democratic good that regrettably necessitated violence, oppression, genocide, and slavery, and he deemphasized the fact that the frontier was as conceptual as it was material.¹² The affinity we find between

---

⁹ Henry David Thoreau, "Walking," *Henry David Thoreau Online*, www.thoreau-online.org/walking-page6.html.
¹⁰ Thoreau, "Walking." See Patrick Chura, *Thoreau the Land Surveyor* (University Press of Florida, 2010).
¹¹ Frederick Jackson Turner, "The Significance of the Frontier in American History," in *Annual Report of the American Historical Association for the Year 1893* (Government Printing Office, 1894), 197–227, *The Internet Archive*, https://archive.org/details/1893annualreport00ameruoft/page/226/mode/2up.
¹² In a recent challenge to Turner, Jodi A. Byrd argues it is the figure of the Indian, not the frontier, that serves to mediate, narrate, and trouble US empire. See Jodi A. Byrd, "Is and Was: Poststructural

Thoreau and Turner reveals the interrelationship of literature, history, geography, and surveying in narrating the possessive logics of US settler colonialism. This terra nullius fantasy of US territorial expansion – which continues to be influential – was intellectually and politically dominant well into the twentieth century before there were robust, field-shifting critiques of its white patriarchal vision of freedom through colonial occupation and Indigenous dispossession.

While land surveying may appear on the surface to be – perhaps unlike literature, history, and geography – an apolitical scientific pursuit, it was in fact deeply imbued with the possessive logics of US power. As presidents, both George Washington and Thomas Jefferson, each of whom had surveyed land, helped develop a national strategy for land surveying that, following the Northwest Ordinance of 1787, established a Surveyor General and General Land Office.[13] The survey was a powerful weapon in presuming property. Surveying was often an early step in securing territorial possession, establishing eligibility for statehood formation, extending plantation boundaries, and incorporating Indigenous, Mexican, and Spanish land. Later in the century, such logics would back the project of allotment, or the assignment of discrete parcels of tribal lands to individual tribal members as their private property, which resulted in the systematic theft of millions of acres of Indigenous land (approximately 90 million) in an effort that also systematically sought to destroy Indigenous communities.[14]

Meeting the strong demand for surveyable land required increasing its supply, and the primary nineteenth-century means for doing so was waging war and extracting territorial concessions. The Treaty of Guadalupe Hidalgo (1848), for instance, resulted in Mexico ceding a massive territory to the United States following the US-Mexico War, and by excluding Indigenous leaders in treaty negotiations (even though the agreement explicitly acknowledged Indigenous resistance to *both* Mexican and US occupation), the US expropriated land from both Mexicans and Indigenous peoples at once. The US land acquisitions from this treaty were the largest since the Louisiana Purchase, affirming a territorial expansion project and exacerbating national

---

Indians without Ancestry," in *The Transit of Empire: Indigenous Critiques of Colonialism* (University of Minnesota Press, 2011), 1–38.

[13] For more on the role of the survey in US statehood and territorial expansion, see Hildegard Binder Johnson, *Order upon the Land: The U.S. Rectangular Land Survey and the Upper Mississippi Country* (Oxford University Press, 1976).

[14] See David A. Chang, *The Color of the Land: Race, Nation, and the Politics of Landownership in Oklahoma, 1832–1929* (University of North Carolina Press, 2010); C. Joseph Genetin-Pilawa, *Crooked Paths to Allotment: The Fight over Federal Indian Policy after the Civil War* (University of North Carolina Press, 2012).

debates surrounding slavery. The US-Mexico War was part of a larger expansionist ethos that drove filibusterism in the Caribbean and Latin America and an increasing US presence in the Pacific. With the acquisition of ports along the Pacific coast, the United States emerged from the US-Mexico War with greater accessibility via railroad and ship to a global market.[15]

The US-Mexico War also marked a pivotal moment of Latinx racial formation in which Mexicanness became racialized rather than nationalized. While Mexicans, Tejanxs, Californixs, Latin American exiles, and others did not necessarily subscribe to this interpellation themselves, there were legal and cultural efforts to codify "Mexicanness" within the borders of the United States, even as individuals thus racially-nationally designated continued to understand belonging in other ways.[16] As one example, Mexican landowners faced a confounding position. Once landowning gentry whose wealth benefited from Indigenous dispossession and a hacienda system not dissimilar from that of the plantation, after the US-Mexico War many Californio lost their landholdings under the California Land Act of 1851. This emerging race-based legislation also shaped notions of gender and class. For example, while (affluent) women could own land under Mexican law, they could not do so under the US legal system.[17]

The Spanish mission system and Mexican occupation informed the US territorial occupation of California, but the new state also organized belonging and exclusion in ways distinctive to the United States. The Anti-Vagrancy Act of 1855 all but legalized anti-Mexican violence in California. The Foreign Miners' Tax (1850) and numerous anti-immigration policies throughout the 1850s attempted to codify state inclusion and exclusion in terms of race. California statehood, the gold rush, and the building of the transcontinental railroad brought a new set of questions about geographic and racial inclusion that shifted away from Indigenous, Spanish, and

---

[15] Here again, we might return to Whitman's poem and how the speaker's longing gaze out onto "my" Pacific gestures toward a fantasy of global US imperialism: "Look off the shores of *my* Western Sea – the circle almost circled" (my italics). Whitman, "Facing West from California's Shores," *The Walt Whitman Archive*, https://whitmanarchive.org/published/LG/1867/poems/14.

[16] Carmen E. Lamas convincingly argues for a "Latino/a continuum" that she applies to the nineteenth century in "Raimundo Cabrera, the Latin American Archive, and the Latina/o Continuum," in Rodrigo Lazo and Jesse Alemán, eds., *The Latino Nineteenth Century* (New York University Press, 2016), 210–229.

[17] In their introduction to *The Squatter and the Don*, Sánchez and Pita discuss the seizure of hacienda land under California law following US statehood. See Rosaura Sánchez and Beatrice Pita, "Introduction," in María Amparo Ruiz de Burton, *The Squatter and the Don*, ed. Rosaura Sánchez and Beatrice Pita (Arte Publico Press, 1997), 7–47.

Mexican systems of belonging and toward Anglo whiteness. These questions of racialization and exclusion influenced the work of many California writers, including María Amparo Ruiz de Burton, Jennie Carter, Edith Maude Eaton/Sui Sin Far, John Rollin Ridge/Yellow Bird, Pablo Tac, Thocmetony/Sarah Winnemucca [Hopkins], James Monroe Whitfield, as well as the many unnamed, pseudonymous, and collective authors who published work in territorial, state, and national periodicals.

Indian Territory

The root for territory in English is not terra (land) but terror. This confusion of the two – land and terror – aptly describes the experiences of many Indigenous peoples and others who faced brutal projects of US colonization, genocide, and land theft. The United States took more than 1.5 billion acres of land from Indigenous peoples during its first hundred years, but land was not all the United States seized and occupied. Along with the sweeping occupation of lands came the promulgation of slavery, forced assimilation of the colonized and enslaved, and attempts to eradicate other lifeways and cultures. As I demonstrated earlier in the chapter, territorial expansion was as much a cultural project as anything else, and it had dramatic effects on understandings of race, class, gender, and belonging.[18] The hyphenated nation-state is critical to settler articulations of territory, which are as much about cultural and narrative forms of identity (the nation) as they are about legal jurisdiction (the state).[19]

A Royal Proclamation of 1763 established a boundary line between British "civilization" and Indian Territory. The proclamation defined Indian Territory as "any lands beyon[d] the heads or sources of any of the rivers which fall into the Atlantic Ocean from the West & North

---

[18] Mishuana Goeman (Tonawanda Band of Seneca) reminds us that the settler logic of territory "extends beyond legal court systems that set in place political authority and borders, and relies on narrations and mythmaking." Mishuana Goeman, *Mark My Words: Native Women Mapping Our Nations* (University of Minnesota Press, 2013), 34.

[19] "Nation-state" did not come into use until the end of the nineteenth century. However, I use it strategically in this chapter to gesture toward how the state (juridico-political order) became associated with the nation (shared cultural identity). An interdependency between state and nation was especially true of US federalism. For a very general history of the emergence of the nation and the state, see Jörg Fisch, "Peoples and Nations," in Bardo Fassbender and Anne Peters, eds., *The Oxford Handbook of the History of International Law* (Oxford University Press, 2012), 27–48. For more on federalism and the nation-state, see Gregory Ablavsky, "Empire States: The Coming of Dual Federalism," *Yale Law Journal* 128:7 (2019), 1792–1868.

West."[20] However, as the United States took on continental expansion, this logic no longer held. The nation could not ignore the hundreds of Indigenous tribal nations that already inhabited the continent and had their own conceptions of territory, governance, and diplomacy. Through its rulings in *Johnson* v. *McIntosh* (1823), *Cherokee Nation* v. *Georgia* (1831), and *Worcester* v. *Georgia* (1832) (sometimes termed the Marshall trilogy), the Supreme Court laid out a contradictory definition of Indigenous sovereignty. Joanne Barker (Lenape) explains that "the [Supreme Court's] ideologies made for some incredibly incoherent legal actions that at once affirmed and undermined tribal rights to self-government and territorial integrity."[21] For instance, the court expressed contradictory beliefs that "Indian tribes" were "savage, barbarian, violent, heathen, immoral, backward" but somehow also "timeless, noble, and proud."[22] Infamously, in *Cherokee Nation* v. *Georgia*, the court ruled that Indigenous "nations" are paradoxically "domestically dependent" on the United States. Despite US efforts to justify the contradictory nature of federal Indian policy, Native people continued to call out its hypocrisy and challenge attempts to displace and disenfranchise their communities. Later in the century, the US government demanded that many Native communities allot their lands and forcibly send their children to boarding schools, removing Native children from their homes and attempting to strip them of their languages and cultures in the name of assimilation.

The westward expansion of US settler colonialism not only demanded a US-centered map but also insisted on the supremacy of a US notion of territory, one founded in Westphalian logics, terra nullius, and the doctrine of discovery (the idea that European "discovery" of the Americas gave them rights to the lands they conquered, rights that subsequently extended, it was assumed, to the sovereign United States). However, Indigenous territorialities persisted, and Indigenous people continued to have their own ways of being in relation to the land and the other-than-human world, including networks of roads, highways, trails, and other long-standing geographies of trade, mobility, and diplomacy. Indigenous

---

[20] Quoted in James Madison, "Report on Instructions on Peace Negotiations (7 January 1782)," in *The Papers of James Madison*, Vol. 4, ed. William T. Hutchinson and William M. E. Rachal (University of Chicago Press, 1965), 4–17, *Founders Online*, National Archives, https://founders.archives.gov/documents/Madison/01-04-02-0002.

[21] Joanne Barker, *Native Acts: Law, Recognition, and Cultural Authenticity* (Duke University Press, 2011), 29.

[22] Barker, *Native Acts*, 29.

people also had systems of writing and documentation that predated colonization.²³

Also critical to US settler colonialism was a systematic attempt to destroy Indigenous kinship networks and understandings of gender. The Niimiipuu scholar Beth Piatote terms this process "national domestication."²⁴ She argues that, in response, the Indigenous home became a symbolic site of resistance to US colonization and one through which Native writers could construct an "anticolonial imaginary."²⁵ There were many Native writers in the last decades of the nineteenth century, especially women, who challenged settler-colonial territoriality and advocated for Indigenous self-determination in their writings, including Laura Cornelius Kellogg (Oneida), Susette La Flesche [Tibbles]/ Inshata Theumba (Omaha), Zitkála-Šá/Gertrude Simmons Bonin (Yankton Sioux), and Sarah Winnemucca [Hopkins]/ Thocmetony (Northern Paiute). Throughout the nineteenth century, numerous Native writers vocalized emphatic critiques of the genocidal project of colonization both on the pages of their own newspapers, magazines, and books and in non-Native publications.

For example, William Apess famously used his adept rhetorical skills in his writing and oration to right the wrongs narrated in colonizer histories of the northeast. He lobbied on behalf of Indigenous communities facing increased encroachment by whites, most famously through his involvement in the Mashpee Revolt of 1833, a nonviolent protest of white territorial and political encroachment on Mashpee autonomy. Meanwhile, Jane Johnston Schoolcraft/Bamewawagezhikaquay (Ojibwe), one of the best-known Native literary writers of the first decades of the nineteenth century, wrote poetry and translated songs and stories in both English and Anishinaabemowin. In these, she detailed a shifting Indigenous world profoundly shaped by US territorial occupation and expansion. She grew up in the Great Lakes region, in what the United States called Michigan Territory, and she and her family experienced numerous political and cultural upheavals in a relatively short time as Indigenous–colonial relations shifted.

However, in works like her poem "Invocation" (written 1823, published 1860), Schoolcraft wrote about the constancy of Indigenous life

---

[23] See Birgit Brander Rasmussen, *Queequeg's Coffin: Indigenous Literacies and Early American Literature* (Duke University Press, 2012), 29.
[24] Beth H. Piatote, *Domestic Subjects: Gender, Citizenship, and Law in Native American Literature* (Yale University Press, 2013), 5.
[25] Piatote, *Domestic Subjects*, 9.

rather than the changes brought on by US settler colonialism. The poem is addressed "To my Maternal Grand-father on hearing his descent from Chippewa ancestors misrepresented" and challenges the belief that he was Sioux and not Anishinaabe. She also reworks the "vanishing Indian" myth that came to prominence in the first decades of the nineteenth century. She celebrates her grandfather's enduring legacy and assures him that not only will people remember him but his relatives will continue to carry his name and his life with them. In writing "Thy deeds and thy name, / Thy child's child shall proclaim," she insists on Indigenous futurity. Through his family, through her love for him, and (enlisting the persistence of the literary) through the writing down of this poem, his legacy will continue to shape his family and his people long after his passing. The two final lines of the poem reaffirm this emphasis on Indigenous futurity: "Yet thy name shall be held in my heart's warmest core, / And cherish'd till valour and love be no more."[26] The ode utilizes European rhyme schemes and poetic conventions to eternalize her grandfather. While the poem is seemingly about discrediting rumors of personal family lineage, its world is an unapologetically Anishinaabe one that depicts a fully Indigenous cosmology centered on tribal differences, disagreements, and histories.

"Invocation" is not unique among Schoolcraft's body of work in this regard, and her poetry and the work of many of the other Indigenous writers mentioned in this chapter not only challenge but also reject US colonial logics by celebrating enduring Indigenous lifeways. Thus, while settler literature was profoundly influential in shaping perceptions of Indigenous people that promulgated stereotyping in ways so significant that they continue to shape genocidal perceptions of Native people as savage "Indians" or a "dying race," many nineteenth-century Native writers used the same forms, genres, and tropes to disrupt stereotypes and fight for the continued vitality of their communities. Not all Indigenous communities embraced writing, print, or the literary, but those that did so extended the existing means of expressing the vibrancy of Indigenous life, supplementing an established multiplicity of strategies for protecting, nourishing, and carrying forward Indigenous story.

---

[26] Jane Johnston Schoolcraft, "Invocation," in Robert Dale Parker, ed., *Changing Is Not Vanishing: A Collection of Early American Indian Poetry to 1930* (University of Pennsylvania Press, 2011), 54–55.

Black Territorialities

Discussions of territory and territorial expansion often preclude black spatialities, in no small part due to US antiblack spatial logics that attempt to fix blackness in space (for example, the 1850 Fugitive Slave Act and Jim Crow laws) while simultaneously attempting to make blackness placeless (for example, the way transatlantic slavery attempted to strip enslaved people of attachments to specific African homelands). However, Katherine McKittrick reminds us that black spatialities, especially black women's geographies, "open up a meaningful way to approach both the power and possibilities of geographic inquiry."[27] Therefore, it is essential to acknowledge the many ways those in the African diaspora made space for themselves throughout the nineteenth century.

Slavery and segregation inarguably shaped political debates (like territorial expansion, statehood, and states' rights), legislation (like the Missouri Compromise [1820] and the Fugitive Slave Act [1850]), and court rulings (like the *Dred Scott* decision [1857] and *Plessy* v. *Ferguson* [1896]), but I am less interested here in narrating the ways US territorial formations excluded black political participation via enslavement, segregation, and antiblackness and more interested in detailing some of the ways black communities shaped territorialities beyond the state. The Underground Railroad, as both a material and an ideological form of transportation, is one example. While the transcontinental railroad was the physical manifestation of total US access, the Underground Railroad undermined that total physical access by rejecting the spatial violence of slavery in a manner that intentionally obscured itself from the gaze of a white supremacist landscape. As such, it served as a relational network intended to be visible and accessible only to those invested in geographies of freedom beyond the white supremacist nation-state. Similarly, maroon communities, some of which predated the United States, often operated geopolitically outside the United States and asserted a black sovereignty oppositional to a Westphalian logic. Unlike US states, whose borders were inorganic, maroon communities understood territoriality in direct relation to the land akin to Indigenous territorialities. Utilizing the terrain of swamps, dense forests, and other difficult-to-survey environments aided maroon communities' ability to evade US interference.

---

[27] Katherine McKittrick, *Demonic Grounds: Black Women and the Cartographies of Struggle* (University of Minnesota, 2006), xii.

Many black writers, orators, and activists challenged dominant formulations of territoriality precisely *because* of how such a logic of property-owning subjects often excluded black participation. Sometimes these challenges worked alongside the aims of US Manifest Destiny but rarely with the same orientation toward domination, supremacy, and control as white settler projects. Throughout the first half of the nineteenth century, colonization organizations like the American Colonization Society justified black emigration from the United States "back" to Africa using the segregationist logic that black people would never be fully assimilable into the United States. By the 1850s, however, prominent black leaders like Martin Delany argued in favor of emigration to Africa given their belief not that they were unassimilable but that the United States was intractable: It would never abolish slavery and eradicate antiblack racism.

Mary Ann Shadd's pamphlet *A Plea for Emigration* aimed at persuading African Americans to migrate to western Canada for better opportunities. Black participation in territorial expansion provided black communities some autonomy over civic and economic life, but homesteading was not necessarily as utopic as *A Plea for Emigration* suggests, especially in the United States. State and territorial laws placed constraints on black homesteading; an 1844 exclusion law in Oregon Territory ostensibly banned black homesteading entirely.[28] One reason "all-black" communities emerged, especially in Indian and Oklahoma Territories at the end of the century, was because they provided some refuge from lynching and other forms of white supremacist violence and provided social welfare and consolidated capital and resources.

Some black writers used their writing to imagine spatial possibilities for black freedom explicitly outside modes of US territoriality. For instance, in "Bury Me in a Free Land" (1858), Frances Ellen Watkins Harper lyrically ruminates on spatial possibilities beyond US territoriality and refuses to be held captive by it. Harper interrogates how what Katherine McKittrick calls "geographies of domination" aim to organize race, gender, life, and death in the poem, and she rejects their totality.[29] Through direct address, the speaker begins by explaining that they do not care whether or not they are buried "in a lowly vale or a lofty hill," but they refuse burial anyplace

---

[28] Cognizant of this, recent Black studies scholars imagine spatialities outside or in spite of the regime of US territoriality. See Tiffany Lethabo King, *The Black Shoals: Offshore Formations of Black and Native Studies* (Duke University Press, 2019); Fred Moten, "The Case of Blackness," *Criticism* 50:2 (2008), 177–218, https://doi.org/10.1353/crt.0.0062; and Neil Roberts, *Freedom As Marronage* (University of Chicago Press, 2015).

[29] McKittrick, *Demonic Grounds*, xv.

where they would still bear witness to enslavement.[30] By sensorially evoking sounds and sights of chains, whips, attack dogs, and family separation, the speaker demonstrates how slavery's violence saturates the ecosystem, infecting the air, the ground, the embodied, the human, and the other-than-human. The speaker's inability to "rest" or "sleep" in such a landscape subverts an individualistic, property-based relationship to territory.[31] In its stead, the speaker foregrounds one of collective care and reciprocity across space and time. The refusal to rest in the midst of suffering serves as a form of haunting, an unwillingness to be at peace or be at home. The speaker is ultimately concerned less about resting within specific coordinates than they are about expressing an unwillingness to be spatially comfortable in a geography predicated on racial and sexual violence: "All that my spirit yearning craves, / Is – bury me not in the land of slaves."[32]

Conclusion

In *Culture and Imperialism*, Edward Said (Palestine) asserts that "none of us is completely free from the struggle of geography," but perhaps in a US context we could revise his assertion and claim that no one is free from the struggle of territory.[33] Making territory out of geography was central to the ideological project of nineteenth-century US empire. With this came attempts to make other ways of being, other territorialities, unimaginable. Black, Indigenous, of-color, and migrant narratives of place and belonging not only challenge the universality of this notion of territory but also continue to be enormously influential in formulating alternative spatialities of being and belonging that shape life and territorial thinking in the twenty-first century. Literature played a decisive part in shaping a national imaginary explicitly tied to spatial fantasies of conquest, property, and capital. However, as I have demonstrated, other spatialities and mapping continued to endure, to take hold, and to make place otherwise, alongside, and in refusal of a singular notion of territoriality dependent on Westphalian models of sovereignty and governance. Literature played a critical role in such placemaking. In a future-oriented country, literature of the nineteenth century expressed possibility and potentiality, inviting lived experience to impact national identity, then and now.

---

[30] Frances Ellen Watkins Harper, "Bury Me in a Free Land," *The Anti-slavery Bugle*, November 20, 1858, *Chronicling America: Historic American Newspapers*, Library of Congress, https://chroniclingamerica.loc.gov/lccn/sn83035487/1858-11-20/ed-1/seq-3/.
[31] Harper, "Bury Me in a Free Land."   [32] Harper, "Bury Me in a Free Land."
[33] Edward Said, *Culture and Imperialism* (Vintage, 1994), 7.

Further Reading

Alyosha Goldstein, ed. *Formations of United States Colonialism.* Duke University Press, 2014.

Byrd, Jodi A. *The Transit of Empire.* University of Minnesota Press, 2011.

Goeman, Mishuana. *Mark My Words: Native Women Mapping Our Nations.* University of Minnesota Press, 2013.

Harris, Cheryl I. "Whiteness As Property." *Harvard Law Review* 106:8 (1993), 1707–1791. https://doi.org/10.2307/1341787.

Justice, Daniel Heath and Jean M. O'Brien, eds. *Allotment Stories: Indigenous Land Relations Under Siege.* University of Minnesota Press, 2021.

King, Tiffany Lethabo. *The Black Shoals: Offshore Formations of Black and Native Studies.* Duke University Press, 2019.

McKittrick, Katherine. *Demonic Grounds: Black Women and the Cartographies of Struggle.* University of Minnesota Press, 2006.

Miller, Robert J., Jacinta Ruru, Larissa Behrendt, and Tracey Lindberg, eds. *Discovering Indigenous Lands: The Doctrine of Discovery in the English Colonies.* Oxford University Press, 2010.

Moreton-Robinson, Aileen. *The White Possessive: Property, Power, and Indigenous Sovereignty.* University of Minnesota Press, 2015.

Piatote, Beth H. *Domestic Subjects: Gender, Citizenship, and Law in Native American Literature.* Yale University Press, 2013.

Saranillio, Dean Itsuji. *Unsustainable Empire: Alternative Histories of Hawai'i Statehood.* Duke University Press, 2018.

Tawil, Ezra. *The Making of Racial Sentiment: Slavery and the Birth of the Frontier Romance.* Cambridge University Press, 2006.

Tsai, Robert L. "Legal Language: Expansion, Consolidation, Resistance." In Nan Goodman and Simon Stern, eds., *The Routledge Research Companion to Law and Humanities in Nineteenth-Century America.* Taylor & Francis, 2017, 150–162.

Watts, Edward. *Colonizing the Past: Mythmaking and Pre-Columbian Whites in Nineteenth-Century American Writing.* University of Virginia Press, 2020.

Wesling, Meg. *Empire's Proxy: American Literature and U.S. Imperialism in the Philippines.* New York University Press, 2011.

CHAPTER 13

Voting Rights: "The Most Salient and Peculiar Point in Our Social Life"

Leslie Petty

In 1883, Henry James recorded in his notebook plans for a new novel about the "so called 'woman's movement.'" James describes the characters as the "radical reforming type" who are working for "the emancipation of women, giving them the suffrage, releasing them from bondage, co-educating them with men, etc."[1] He goes on to say, "the subject is very national, very typical. I wished to write a very *American* tale, a tale very characteristic of our social conditions, and I asked myself what was the most salient and peculiar point in our social life. The answer was: the situation of women, the decline of the sentiment of sex, the agitation on their behalf."[2] James is outlining what would become *The Bostonians* (1886), arguably the best-known work of literature on the American women's suffrage movement. James is right that the effort to expand voting rights – not just for white women but for African American men and women as well – was a core element of national life throughout the nineteenth century. However, there is a disconnect between the centrality of suffrage activism in American politics and the paucity of its representation in the nation's literature. In fact, James's novel is one of only a handful of well-known literary texts that depict suffrage activism. Nevertheless, the key questions in the political debate over expanding the suffrage – how to interpret the nation's founding documents, what qualities of character make one fit to vote, and whether a gendered and/or racial integration of the public sphere is warranted – broadly inform and animate the nineteenth-century American literary landscape. What follows is a brief history of the nineteenth-century efforts to expand voting and other political rights, interspersed with analysis of key literary texts in which the question of voting rights is a palpable concern, even though it is sometimes not

---

[1] Henry James, *The Complete Notebooks of Henry James*, ed. Leon Edel and Lyall H. Powers (Oxford University Press, 1987), 18.
[2] James, *Notebooks*, 20.

overtly addressed. This history and analysis demonstrate how the rhetoric and stakes of women's suffrage and black suffrage evolved throughout the nineteenth century and how it became deeply implicated in questions of race, gender, and ultimately, in national belonging.

Antebellum Reform Movements

At the beginning of the nineteenth century, property ownership was a prerequisite for suffrage in virtually all US states. This requirement stemmed from a prevalent eighteenth-century belief that owning land was proof of one's investment in the community as well as one's autonomy and independence. Such a requirement, however, also meant that it was quite literally unthinkable that white women or people of color would ever vote. To begin, American domestic law was based on the British concept of *coverture*, in which a married woman's legal identity was "covered" by that of her husband, meaning that she had no legal or civic presence; this resulted in, among other things, the vast majority of white women not being allowed to own property. Furthermore, most black men and women were enslaved, and those who were not often did not have the financial means to buy land. Things changed, however, in the early 1800s, when according to Jacob Katz Cogan, widespread belief about what made an ideal voter shifted from the "external view" of land ownership to an "internal view" or "look within," which stressed that "virtue and intelligence" were the most important attributes for suffrage, and these qualities could be found "within each and every [white] man."[3] Thus, according to Cogan, most states revised their constitutions in the early years of the century to eliminate the property requirement so that by "the 1840s, white manhood suffrage became the norm."[4] The elimination of the property requirement meant that white women and at least unenslaved black men and women could imagine a path to suffrage for themselves, but it also meant that they had to embark on this path within a social context that held many preconceived ideas and mythologies about the nature of *their* characters that would seem to exclude them from the franchise.

Suffrage, however, was not the only, or even the main, goal of reformers in the 1820s–1850s. The desire for the vote by the disenfranchised was intertwined with even more pressing concerns, like overturning the

---

[3] Jacob Katz Cogan, "The Look Within: Property, Capacity, and Suffrage in Nineteenth-Century America," *The Yale Law Journal* 107:2 (1997), 473–498, 484.
[4] Cogan, "The Look Within," 484.

coverture system writ large and, even more urgently, abolishing slavery. Many activists were devoted to both efforts, as the women's rights movement in many ways grew directly out of the abolitionist movement. It is the case, moreover, that these various reform efforts hinged on the same broad question of "character" central to efforts to extend voting rights. Therefore, when novels, essays, and bibliographic narratives about women's rights and abolition became part of the nation's literature, they were most often an interrogation of character, and specifically of the notion that "virtue and intelligence" should be attributed primarily to white men.

Both white women and African American men and women had to contend with a legal history that oppressed them in the name of their "nature" or "character." The founding legal documents of America, the Declaration of Independence and later the Constitution, seem to be clean breaks from the British governing system, asserting the individual rights of all men and the sovereignty of the citizens. However, many contradictions existed in these ostensibly radical documents. One was that America adopted British domestic laws almost wholesale, and these were based on *coverture*, as mentioned. These laws meant that not only could married women not own property but they also could not keep their own wages, sign legal contracts, divorce, or have a legal right to their children. Husbands were even allowed to punish their wives physically (within limits). In practice, it also meant women did not have any real access to professional work or higher education. This legal "death" was idealized and romanticized by an ideology that arose in the 1820s and 1830s, which asserted that men and women should occupy separate spaces or "spheres" corresponding to the innate qualities and distinct capacities ascribed to each: nurturing the family within the home or competing in the marketplace outside of it. While scholars have for years debunked the idea that, in practice, women and men stayed within these spheres – or that the spheres were really separate at all – the *rhetoric* of separate spheres was quite powerful and was used to justify middle- and upper-class women's relegation to the home.

This rhetoric also insisted that women were not suited for political rights, especially the vote. The ostensibly masculine qualities of "virtue and intelligence" suggest a rational, ethical mind capable of dispassionate, deliberate choices. Women, because they were emotional, passive, and other-centered, were not suited to make such important decisions, even though they were considered the moral authority of the family. Furthermore, for a woman to venture into politics would usurp the masculine prerogative of the public sphere and threaten the husband's leadership role in the family. It caused quite a commotion, then, when women decided not only to wade into political water but also to give public lectures. When abolitionists like Abby Kelley or Angelina Grimké spoke before "promiscuous," or mixed-gender audiences, they were reviled in the press and sometimes heckled and threatened by audience members. Clergymen railed against the practice in the pulpit and in print. Indeed, it was this intense backlash that made some white women become aware of the hypocrisy of their world. They believed it was their duty as moral authorities to weigh in on the *immorality* of enslaving people, but when their efforts were met with such hostility, some, like Elizabeth Cady Stanton and Lucretia Mott, decided to focus on their own oppression.

Given the powerful hold separate spheres rhetoric had on early nineteenth-century America, it is not surprising that the first novels depicting women as political reformers are organized around the public/private split and treat the heroine who ventures into the public eye as transgressive and in danger. In moving beyond the bounds of their "sphere," activist heroines often meet a tragic end typically reserved for women who commit other unpardonable social sins like adultery. In Sarah Josepha Hale's 1839 novel *The Lecturess*, the first novel about a women's rights activist, Marian Forrester dies alone, rejected by her husband and having lost her child because, despite her husband's objections/disapproval, she has repeatedly lectured for women's rights and abolitionism. On her deathbed, she regrets these actions and sends word to her husband that her impending death has taught her that "true independence in a woman, is to fill the place which her God assigns her; ... and to yield her will to [her husband's] in all things." In staying within her sphere and submitting herself to others, "a woman [will] attain her *rights* – the affection of her husband, the respect of her children and the world, and the approval of heaven."[5] While Hale's novel does place some blame on the husband for not being quicker to forgive, the sins lie squarely with Marian, not only for speaking publicly but also for daring to have desires that contradict her spouse's.

Even antebellum novels that are less hostile toward women's rights and abolitionism depict the dangers and potential tragedy of advocating for them. Nathaniel Hawthorne's *The Blithedale Romance* (1852) is based on the author's time at Brook Farm, a utopian commune started by Transcendentalists. One of the four main characters is Zenobia, a beautiful, brilliant woman who advocates for women's rights. A superficial interpretation of the novel suggests that Zenobia gives up all claims to independence by falling madly in love with

---

[5] Sarah Josepha Hale, *The Lecturess* (Whipple and Damrell, 1839), 120.

Hollingsworth and committing suicide by drowning when he rejects her for Priscilla, her younger sister who is the ideal "clinging vine," a character of pure passivity and dependence. Although there is critical debate about Zenobia's motivations at the end, there is no doubt that her story ends tragically. When the narrator, Coverdale, finds her body, it is contorted as if "she struggled against Providence in never-ending hostility."[6] Coverdale suggests that Zenobia's death stems from her inability to remain within her God-ordained role and for daring to defy her feminine nature. The eponymous heroine of Laura Bullard's *Christine, or Woman's Trials and Triumphs* (1856) – one of the only pro-women's rights novels in the antebellum period – suffers for daring to be a political activist and public advocate, but her punishment is inflicted not by God but by her family, who want to confine her to the domestic realm. To this end, they commit her to an asylum for almost a year, a time during which Christine wonders if "she might not indeed become mad."[7] Bullard, however, was a women's rights activist herself and wrote her novel to sway readers to support her cause. Thus her narrative, while pointing out how dangerous it can be to go against the conventional grain of gendered roles, allows her heroine to escape such a tragic fate: Christine is released from confinement and goes on to have a successful marriage and career as a reformer.

While most literary representations of separate spheres depict them spatially, as the public domain of politics and the domestic confines of the home, some essayists and speech writers treated them using different metaphors. One of the most original attacks on the conventional notions of spheres came from Margaret Fuller, the inspiration for Hawthorne's Zenobia in *The Blithedale Romance*. Writing from a feminist Transcendentalist perspective, Fuller turns the metaphor of separate spheres on its head in *Woman in the Nineteenth Century* (1845). As a Transcendentalist, Fuller believed that God was within each human and was immanent in Nature but that the only way for humans to commune with the Divine within and around them was to shut out social convention and use their intuition to hear the divine Voice within. Unlike her male counterparts, however, Fuller believed that the current state of gender norms was – far from keeping order – keeping both men and women from this ideal state. Fuller's solution is to "have every arbitrary barrier thrown down ... [and] have every path

---

[6] Nathaniel Hawthorne, *The Blithedale Romance* (1852), ed. Richard H. Millington (W. W. Norton & Company, 2011), 161.
[7] Laura Curtis Bullard, *Christine, or, Woman's Trials and Triumphs* (1856), ed. Denise M. Kohn (University of Nebraska Press, 2010), 222.

laid open to woman as freely as to man." If such unqualified freedom were granted, Fuller "believe[d] the divine energy would pervade nature to a degree unknown in the history of former ages, and that no discordant collision, but a ravishing harmony of the spheres, would ensue."[8] Here, Fuller replaces the prosaic idea of separate gendered spheres with the cosmic idea of celestial spheres, suggesting that what is needed to set the universe aright is unqualified freedom for all humans.

While Fuller was not an activist, her interpretation of spheres influenced the rhetoric around women's suffrage, especially that of Elizabeth Cady Stanton, who as a young woman attended Fuller's "Conversations," small group discussions on intellectual topics for women. Stanton is widely regarded as having launched the women's rights movement when she and Lucretia Mott organized the Seneca Falls Convention in 1848, eight years after they had been denied seats on the floor of the World Anti-Slavery Convention in London. In her first public speech, Stanton adapts Fuller's emphasis on souls to foreground the essential sameness of all humans. Stanton states that as the world progresses, "the sphere of woman gradually becomes wider," but that not even in the United States, which Stanton takes to be the most civilized country in the world, "is [woman's sphere] what God designed it to be." Instead, "in every country and clime does man assume the responsibility of marking out the path for her to tread."[9] Unsurprisingly, Stanton rejects men's right to dictate her path and instead claims that women possess the same natural rights as citizens that men have, including the right to suffrage. But she also makes a more philosophical plea: "Let woman live as she should. Let her feel her accountability to her Maker. Let her know that her spirit is fitted for as high a sphere as man's, and that her soul requires food as pure and exalted as his."[10] For Stanton, like Fuller, access to concrete opportunities like education and suffrage matters because it is through these means that all humans achieve their potential, not just spiritual but moral, intellectual, and physical as well. This perspective was extreme for its day, and although the speech was well received by those in attendance, Stanton, Mott, and other participants were met with the same derision and castigation that

---

[8] Margaret Fuller, *Woman in the Nineteenth Century* (1845), ed. Larry J. Reynolds (W. W. Norton & Company, 1998), 20.
[9] Elizabeth Cady Stanton, "Address Delivered at Seneca Falls, July 19, 1848," in *Elizabeth Cady Stanton and Susan B. Anthony: Correspondence, Writings, Speeches*, ed. Ellen Carol DuBois (Schocken Books, 1987), 28.
[10] Stanton, "Address Delivered at Seneca Falls," 33.

abolitionist women had met before them, being dismissed in the press as "heretics, radicals, and old maids."[11]

If the state of *coverture* was one of the hypocrisies of the American democratic experiment, then the institution of slavery and its negation of enslaved people's humanity was an even graver one. The Constitution infamously registered non-free people as three-fifths of a person when counting state inhabitants for proportional representation. This codification of inferior status led to a widespread belief that even unenslaved African Americans were not citizens of the United States, a sentiment eventually written into law by the US Supreme Court's 1857 Dred Scott decision. Thus, while the abolition of slavery was the most urgent reform sought by and for people of color in antebellum America, the rights to citizenship and the franchise were related goals for many northern black men who, while unenslaved, were disenfranchised. According to Derrick R. Spires, Black State Conventions held in the 1840s throughout the northeast were focused primarily on "activism for political rights, especially the suffrage," and these conventions "created a public black civic presence, demonstrating that black citizens could and did conduct themselves as people fully capable of self-determination in a republican government."[12] Spires argues that both the form and the content of these conventions were designed to showcase black men as rational, civic-minded beings who were intelligent and virtuous, as capable as their white counterparts of engaging in calm debate and intellectual arguments. Thus, the men showed how they could take part in "the deliberative politics that opponents claimed were beyond black citizens' mental capacities or social conditions."[13] Interestingly, the attendees of the Pennsylvania convention of 1848 based their appeal for suffrage on their status as "free men," contrasting themselves with enslaved men whose circumstances made it impossible for them to achieve, as these "free men" had done, the self-respect and educational level needed for citizenship and the franchise: "The Slaves have but learned to lick the dust, and stifle the voice of free inquiry; but we are not slaves – our right to natural liberty and qualified citizenship is guaranteed to us by the Constitution."[14] For these African American men seeking full citizenship rights, humanity – and masculinity in particular – is antithetical to

---

[11] Penny A. Weiss, *Canon Fodder: Historical Women Political Thinkers* (Pennsylvania State University Press, 2009), 118.
[12] Derrick R. Spires, "Imagining a State of Fellow Citizens: Early African American Politics of Publicity in the Black State Conventions," in Lara Langer Cohen and Jordan Alexander Stein, eds., *Early African American Print Culture* (University of Pennsylvania Press, 2012), 274–289, 274.
[13] Spires, "Imagining," 283. [14] Quoted in Spires, "Imagining," 288.

enslavement. It is the training that enslaved people receive, and not their race, that makes them unfit for the free exercise of their faculties; enslavement affects not only their rationality but also their self-respect, and in this way it disqualifies them from citizenship and, thus, voting.

Similar assertions about how enslavement affects masculinity and, by extension, one's fitness for citizenship and the franchise are at the heart of one of the best-known firsthand accounts of enslavement, the *Narrative of the Life of Frederick Douglass, an American Slave, Written by Himself* (1845). The milestones that Douglass identifies in his quest for freedom mark his becoming not just a strong person but a strong *man*, and thus worthy of being a fully integrated citizen. Under threat of punishment from his "master," Douglass teaches himself to read and write, and his literacy makes it possible for him to learn about abolitionism. This knowledge creates a great longing in him for freedom, which is briefly quelled when he is under the control of Edward Covey. The turning point of the narrative comes at Douglass's lowest point, when his life resembles what the black conventioneers describe as the typical experience of enslavement: "[B]roken in body, soul, and spirit" after months of abuse from Covey, Douglass finds himself with no interest in pursuits of the mind. He says his "intellect languished" and his "disposition to read departed." Indeed, he spends his small amount of leisure time in a "beastlike stupor," but this state does not last.[15] Douglass describes the climactic moment of his narrative using a chiasmus: "You have seen how a man was made a slave; you shall see how a slave was made a man."[16] Douglass achieves this transition by standing up to Covey in a fight, a mano a mano physical confrontation in which Douglass is victorious. After his defeat of Covey, he resolves, "however long I might remain a slave in form, the day had passed forever when I could be a slave in fact."[17] Like those at the Black Conventions, Douglass sees the state of enslavement as mutually exclusive from that of manhood, but for him, enslavement is as much a state of mind as bodily circumstance. Not just his escape but also his restoration to manhood, his physical strength, his intelligence, as well as his narrative's rationality and eloquence together prove him worthy of freedom, citizenship, and ultimately, the vote.

The obvious gap in both the activism for and the literature about voting and other political rights is a consideration of black women as political

---

[15] Frederick Douglass, *Narrative of the Life of Frederick Douglass* (1845), ed. Henry Louis Gates, Jr. (Dell Publishing, 1997), 64.
[16] Douglass, *Life*, 66.   [17] Douglass, *Life*, 72.

agents. While there are many representations of women of color in reform literature, most often they are presented as tragic victims of racism and enslavement; they are rarely acknowledged as needing or wanting an active role in politics. For perhaps obvious reasons, African American women faced a more problematic and more dire situation than did either white women or black men. As black women, they did not fit into the separate spheres paradigm, which was implicitly a white, middle-class phenomenon, so they did not receive its benefits – security in their own domestic space, respect as mothers and moral agents, exemption from difficult physical labor, relative security from physical and sexual violence – even as they suffered the same gendered oppression. *Incidents in the Life of a Slave Girl*, written by Harriet Jacobs on the cusp of the Civil War, ends with the lament, "Reader, my story ends with freedom; not in the usual way, with marriage ... The dream of my life is not yet realized. I do not sit with my children in a home of my own."[18] Implicitly, Jacobs reminds her white readers – some who are actively working to escape the private sphere – what a privilege it is to approach the world with the stability of a home. Furthermore, even though black women suffered under slavery and racist oppression just like their black male counterparts, they did not have the same status or opportunities. There was, nevertheless, a cadre of prominent black women reformers, such as Maria Stewart, and later Sojourner Truth and Frances Ellen Watkins Harper, who all identified as both abolitionists and women's rights activists.

Postbellum Voting Rights Reform

This question of black women's rights was briefly visible in reform circles after the Civil War, when the still-nascent women's rights movement and the recently victorious antislavery movement joined forces in the American Equal Rights Association (AERA), with the stated goal of universal suffrage. While the history of this short-lived organization (1866–1869) is fraught and complex, the upshot is that tensions were always high within it, as members disagreed over a series of amendments to the US Constitution – in particular the Fourteenth and Fifteenth – that would, by inserting the word "male" into the Constitution for the first time with regard to citizenship and suffrage, ostensibly secure citizenship and voting rights for black men but at the same time make achieving women's suffrage

---

[18] Harriet Jacobs, *Incidents in the Life of a Slave Girl* (1861), ed. Nellie McKay and Frances Smith Foster (W. W. Norton & Company, 2001), 156.

more difficult. When Frederick Douglass spoke in favor of the amendments, calling the need for black male suffrage "a question of life and death" because of the violent conditions and imminent danger for black communities in the South, he was asked if these conditions were "not all true about black women" too. Douglass insisted that they were, but because they were "black," not "women."[19] While Stanton and her activist partner and best friend, Susan B. Anthony, were adamantly opposed to the amendments, African American women activists were conflicted. Sojourner Truth worried that if the Fourteenth Amendment passed, "the colored men will be masters over the women, and it will be just as bad as it was before."[20] Frances Ellen Watkins Harper, meanwhile, asserted that "when it was a question of race, she let the lesser question of sex go."[21]

Noteworthy literature from around this time makes clear the difficult, complex position of black women, especially as citizens and voters. For example, in 1869, the year the AERA collapsed, Harper makes a more explicit plea for black women's rights in her novella *Minnie's Sacrifice*. Recalling the common refrain at the AERA that it was "the Negro's hour," Minnie asks, "is it not the negro woman's hour also? Has she not as many rights and claims as the negro man?"[22] Minnie articulates the utopian goals that motivated the AERA in the first place: "I think ... that basing our rights on the ground of our common humanity is the only true foundation for national peace and durability."[23] The novella, however, ends with Minnie's death at the hands of the Ku Klux Klan, underscoring the extreme vulnerability of black women's bodies. C. C. O'Brien notes that, in this way, Harper impresses upon her reader "black women's compelling need to defend themselves with the vote."[24]

Ellen Carol DuBois asserts that the AERA will primarily be remembered for the "rancor into which it dissolved," causing in some ways a deep division between the movements for racial equality and those for women's suffrage, with African American women continuing to be caught in the middle but often lost in the conversation.[25] The AERA did, however, elevate the status of the women's rights movement, bringing it into the national conversation. On the heels of the AERA's dissolution, two

---

[19] Ellen Carol DuBois, *Suffrage: Women's Long Battle for the Vote* (Simon & Schuster, 2020), 76.
[20] DuBois, *Suffrage*, 65.   [21] DuBois, *Suffrage*, 77.
[22] Frances Ellen Watkins Harper, *Minnie's Sacrifice, Sowing and Reaping, Trial and Triumphs*, ed. Frances Smith Foster (Beacon Press, 1994), 78.
[23] Harper, *Minnie's Sacrifice*, 79.
[24] C. C. O'Brien, "'The White Women All Go for Sex': Frances Harper on Suffrage, Citizenship, and the Reconstruction South," *African American Review* 43:4 (2009), 605–620, 611.
[25] DuBois, *Suffrage*, 78.

competing national organizations, the National Woman Suffrage Association (NWSA) and the American Woman Suffrage Association (AWSA), were founded, divided by some of the same questions that dissolved the AERA. Nevertheless, both were devoted to women's rights, and their presence and influence grew exponentially in the second half of the nineteenth century. They were joined in their fight for suffrage by the Women's Christian Temperance Union (WCTU), under the leadership of Frances Willard, and this organization, more conservative in nature but broader in appeal, helped bring the cause into the mainstream, so that by the early 1880s there were standing committees on the question of women's suffrage in both houses of Congress. While the vote remained elusive, these activists succeeded at chipping away at other aspects of *coverture*. By the 1880s, married women could own their own property and wages and could enter legal contracts. By 1890, women were approximately 40 percent of the total college graduates – including public and private schools, coeducational institutions, and women's colleges. The natural result of so many women attending college and gaining some independence was that professional opportunities opened up for them in fields such as law, medicine, business, and the academy. The term "New Woman" was coined in the early 1890s to describe the pervasive change in women's opportunities, rights, and attitudes. These opportunities were more widely available to white, elite women; however, the New Woman ideal also influenced African American women, including Mrs. Booker T. Washington, who gave the speech "The New Negro Woman" in 1895. The attendant interest in women's careers created a broader and more receptive audience for women advocating for themselves, whether they sought to improve the working conditions of their low-paying, high-risk jobs or, increasingly, to extend their political rights, including the right to vote.

It is this momentum that Henry James registers when he notes that women's rights reform was the most "salient and peculiar point in [America's] social life." Even so, mainstream American writers rarely chose women's voting rights as their overt subject matter; however, the zeitgeist of the New Woman certainly informed much canonical literature. While novels continued to focus primarily on the heterosexual romance plot, works such as Constance Fenimore Woolson's "Miss Grief" (1880), James's *Portrait of a Lady* (1881), Mary Wilkins Freeman's "A New England Nun" (1891), and Kate Chopin's *The Awakening* (1899) took a closer look than ever before at the costs and difficulties of women asserting their autonomy, desires, and voice in a patriarchal world, an interrogation that would not have been possible without the ongoing campaign for women's suffrage. James's *The Bostonians* (1886), which anomalously deals directly with women's suffrage activism, seems to be conservative, telling the story of Olive Chancellor, intrepid suffragist and single woman, losing her best friend and brilliant lecturess, Verena Tarrant, to marriage with an avowed reactionary, Basil Ransom. The novel, however, is more ambiguous than this synopsis suggests.[26] At the end, Verena's marriage is depicted forebodingly. The narrator notes that Verena is crying as she leaves with Basil and fears that "these were not the last [tears] she was destined to shed."[27] Meanwhile, painfully shy Olive ascends the stage to give the speech that Verena was to have made. Even though she expects to be "hissed, and hooted and insulted," the "hush" that greets her "is respectful."[28] At least one suffragist, Celia B. Whitehead, saw the latent potential for women's rights in this ending. She published "Another Chapter of 'The Bostonians'" under the pseudonym Henrietta James in 1887. In this addendum, Basil abandons Verena and their child, and Verena and Olive reunite and renew their efforts to expand women's rights.[29]

While many writers in this era were increasingly skeptical about gendered expectations, in some corners of the suffrage movement itself some activists strategically embraced these expectations, arguing that their femininity would make women good voters. Although they still claimed to have "intelligence and virtue," they doubled down on the idea of gender difference and claimed that their inherent capacities for nurturing, self-abnegation, and domesticity would bring a new element to politics that would improve the nation. In part, this shift came from the influence of women like Willard, who coined the term "Home Protection" as a euphemism for suffrage, arguing that "the changeless instincts of her nature" granted to women by God have made her "the born conservator of home," and that only by receiving the vote will these women be able to do their feminine duty of protecting their sons and husbands from liquor interests and other evils.[30] The second half of the nineteenth century saw a marked increase of feminist activists writing novels to support their cause,

---

[26] See Leslie Petty, *Romancing the Vote: Feminist Activism in American Fiction, 1870–1920* (University of Georgia Press, 2006), chap. 4, for an analysis of James's ambivalent representation of feminist activism.

[27] Henry James, *The Bostonians* (1886), ed. Richard Lansdown (Penguin, 2000), 350.

[28] James, *Bostonians*, 349.

[29] Henrietta James (Celia B. Whitehead), "Another Chapter of 'The Bostonians,' (1887)," in *Treacherous Texts: U.S. Suffrage Literature, 1846–1946*, ed. Mary Chapman and Angela Mills (Rutgers University Press, 2011), 100–107.

[30] Frances Williard, "Home Protection (1876)," in *Let Something Good Be Said: Speeches and Writings of Frances E. Willard*, ed. Carolyn Gifford and Amy Slagell (University of Illinois Press, 2007), 20.

and often they created narratives in which femininity per se was not challenged but was instead the source of the heroine's strength. For example, Elizabeth Boynton Harbert's *Out of Her Sphere* (1871) is about a heroine, Marjory, in whom "intense love and intense womanliness, could be united with self-reliance and consecration to the public good."[31] A less conventional example that nevertheless hinges on women's particular perspective is *Pray You Sir, Whose Daughter?*, written by Helen Hamilton Gardener in 1892. Gardener, angry about the double standard regarding promiscuity and infidelity, the prevalence of prostitution, and the efforts by many state governments to lower the age of consent to protect men who hired underage sex workers, wrote the novel to demonstrate that if women had the vote, these kinds of legal atrocities and sexual abuses would not happen because women would vote to protect other vulnerable women from selfishly motivated, lascivious men.

While these texts about women's rights often depict interclass relations, the characters are almost exclusively white. Although a growing number of African American women worked tirelessly for suffrage, including Ida B. Wells, Mary Church Terrell, Josephine Ruffin, Anna Julia Cooper, and the now-elderly Frances Ellen Watkins Harper, these efforts were increasingly segregated. The fracturing of the AERA had created a schism between the women's suffrage and black suffrage movements that only widened after Reconstruction. Even though African American men had nominally been assured the rights to citizenship and to vote in the Fourteenth and Fifteenth Amendments, ensuing Jim Crow laws such as literacy tests and poll taxes disenfranchised them in practice. Meanwhile, as I have noted, the women's suffrage movement was picking up steam, in part because many in the mainstream movement had embraced the more conservative tactic of touting women's moral superiority and sexual purity, qualities that were tacitly assumed to apply only to white, middle-class women. Tactics to quell African Americans' increased political and social power did not end, however, with legal strategies like Jim Crow laws. Lynchings – especially of black men and boys – were widespread, and they were often justified by the mythology that black men were instinctively prone/driven to raping white women.

Maegan Parker explores the political implications of this racist mythology by analyzing a public feud between Willard and Ida B. Wells. In 1891, Willard gave an interview in which she "attributed the South's racial

---

[31] Elizabeth Boynton Harbert, *Out of Her Sphere* (Mills & Co., 1871), 118. See chapter 1 of Petty, *Romancing the Vote*, for an analysis of Harbert's feminist appropriation of separate spheres ideology.

problems to one categorial culprit: the drunken black beast rapist."[32] In this way, Willard was able to gain support from white southerners for the temperance movement. Wells publicly refuted Willard's characterization, in part by claiming that white women desired and engaged in consensual sex with African American men. Parker points out the broader political implications of this disagreement:

> In Willard's case, she could not concede to Wells that white women willfully participated in acts of miscegenation without threatening the premise that women's moral superiority formed the basis for their right to vote. For Wells, on the other hand, the argument that white women were consensually involved with black men supported her contention that the lynch-for-rape mythology, which effectively barred black men from political assertion, was a subterfuge masking Southern white men's efforts to retain exclusive rights of full citizenship.[33]

This seeming impasse makes clear how irreconcilable the rhetoric of the two movements had become and also exposes how African American women are once again left out of the rhetorical equation, even though in reality African American women were increasingly advocating for racial *and* gendered justice.

American literature played a role in disenfranchising African American men, but not necessarily by depicting them as violent or aggressive. In fact, one of the most effective literary tools for restoring white supremacy after the Civil War was Reconciliation literature, which idealized hierarchical race relations in the antebellum South. Thomas Nelson Page, a famous Reconciliationist, wrote stories in stereotypical "black dialect," narrated by formerly enslaved men who are nostalgic for their lives "befo the war," when they were well taken care of by their "master." Joel Chandler Harris's internationally popular Uncle Remus stories took a similar approach, depicting a wizened formerly enslaved man who lives on his former master's plantation and tends to his employer's young son, telling him animal tales for amusement and instruction in a heavy, stereotypical dialect. Page's and Harris's stories assured northern readers that the efforts to restore the racial status quo in the South were warranted for everyone's happiness. Jeremy Wells observes, "In terms of representation developed by ... [Harris] and Page, African Americans came to seem more like

---

[32] Maegan Parker, "Desiring Citizenship: An Analysis of the Wells/Willard Controversy," *Women's Studies in Communication* 31:1 (2008), 56–78, 56.
[33] Parker, "Desiring Citizenship," 57.

dependencies" over whom "white American men [needed] to assume responsibility."³⁴

African American authors and activists had to refute, then, a wide range of dehumanizing stereotypes that cropped up in postbellum America – bestial and hypersexual on one end and childlike and dependent on the other – designed to justify the increasing political suppression of black men, a suppression based on spurious claims that they were neither virtuous nor intelligent enough to vote. In his prolific career, Charles Chesnutt addressed many of these stereotypes head-on. Chesnutt first had literary success with the "conjure tales" he published in the *Atlantic Monthly*, beginning with "The Goophered Grapevine" in 1887. On the surface, Chesnutt's stories seemed a lot like an Uncle Remus story, or even a Thomas Nelson Page story, but a closer investigation reveals how subversive they are. Uncle Julius, the formerly enslaved narrator, tells his white northern employers fantastical stories that are allegories of the real horrors of slavery, so far from being a childlike, docile employee, Uncle Julius proves to be a trickster figure who manipulates his employers for personal gain. As his career advanced, Chesnutt's work became more overtly critical of racism. His late novel *The Marrow of Tradition* (1901) is a fictionalized account of a massacre that took place in Wilmington, North Carolina in 1898, in which white leaders incited mob violence against the African American community because it had gained too much political representation. Chesnutt's novel deconstructs the "lynch-for-rape" myth, much as Wells's speeches do, and it also shows the power of the white press in promulgating racial stereotypes that justified the kind of violence that happened in Wilmington. A central couple, Dr. and Mrs. Miller, are leaders in the African American community and embody the respectable gendered character traits of the moment: Dr. Miller is a thoughtful, intelligent, accomplished physician and a good father, while Mrs. Miller – half-sister to Mrs. Carteret, the central white woman in the story – emerges as the most moral, maternal figure in the book. In these representations, Chesnutt makes a case against the current disenfranchisement of African Americans and posits (as Wells had before him) that whites are the violent, immoral force in American social and political life. It is worth noting that Chesnutt must make the same case that Frederick Douglass had made almost sixty years earlier about the humanity, masculinity, and civility of black men, while Chesnutt also advances the

---

³⁴ Jeremy Wells, *Romances of the White Man's Burdens: Race, Empire, and the Plantation in American Literature, 1880–1936* (Vanderbilt University Press, 2011), 81 (emphasis in original).

argument that African American women are more virtuous and honorable than their white counterparts.

Conclusion

At the dawn of the twentieth century, voting rights looked at once very different and eerily similar to the way they looked in 1800. African American men had been constitutionally enfranchised for more than thirty years, but the country's refusal to take federal control of voting laws (as well as intractable institutional racism) meant that black men had much less political power in 1900 than they did in 1870, as Jim Crow laws and extralegal violence had taken their toll on the substantial progress African Americans experienced immediately after the Civil War. White women, similarly, were still decades away from being granted suffrage at the national level; however, they had made lasting and significant political and social in-roads in areas such as education and professional work, and they had gained a great deal of political influence through women's clubs and activist organizations.[35] In practice, white men still controlled the franchise at all levels at the end of the nineteenth century, but white women were gaining power. In 1920, the Nineteenth Amendment gave women the right to vote; however, because of the endurance of Jim Crow at the state level, many black women were still disenfranchised until the Voting Rights Act of 1965 put an end to many discriminatory practices. Well into the twenty-first century, however, voting rights, especially for people of color, are still vulnerable to discriminatory state laws and a lack of protection at the federal level.

Further Reading

Chapman, Mary. *Making Noise, Making News: U.S. Suffrage Print Culture and Literary Modernism*. Oxford University Press, 2014.

Chapman, Mary. "US Suffrage Literature." In Dale M. Bauer, ed., *The Cambridge History of American Women's Literature*. Cambridge University Press, 2012, 326–351.

Davidson, Cathy and Jessamyn Hatchers, eds. *No More Separate Spheres! A Next Wave American Studies Reader*. Duke University Press, 2002.

DuPlessis, Rachel B. *Writing beyond the Ending: Narrative Strategies of Twentieth-Century Women Writers*. Indiana University Press, 1985.

---

[35] See chapter 3 of Petty, *Romancing the Vote*, for further discussion of suffrage literature in the early twentieth century.

Elbert, Monika, ed. *Separate Spheres No More: Gender Convergence in American Literature, 1830–1930*. University of Alabama Press, 2000.

Gaines, Kevin. *Uplifting the Race: Black Leadership, Politics, and Culture in the Twentieth Century*. University of North Carolina Press, 1996.

Gold, David. "Women's Suffrage." In D. Berton Emerson and Gregory Laski, eds., *Democracies in America: Keywords for the Nineteenth Century and Today*. Oxford University Press, 2023, 104–114.

Hyde, Carrie. *Civic Longing: The Speculative Origins of U.S. Citizenship*. Harvard University Press, 2018.

Laughlin-Schultz, Bonnie. "Women's Rights and Gender Ideology, 1848–1890." In Jonathan Daniel Wells, ed., *The Routledge History of Nineteenth-Century America*. Taylor & Francis, 2017, 275–291.

Pitts, Yvonne. "Civic Capacity and Participatory Citizenship." In Nan Goodman and Simon Stern, eds., *The Routledge Research Companion to Law and Humanities in Nineteenth-Century America*. Taylor & Francis, 2017, 311–322.

Tate, Claudia. *Domestic Allegories of Political Desire: The Black Heroine's Text at the Turn of the Century*. Oxford University Press, 1992.

Tetrault, Lisa. *The Myth of Seneca Falls: Memory and the Women's Suffrage Movement 1848–1898*. University of North Carolina Press, 2014.

Wilson, Ivy G. *Specters of Democracy: Blackness and the Aesthetics of Politics in the Antebellum U.S.* Oxford University Press, 2011.

Wong, Edlie L. *Racial Reconstruction: Black Inclusion, Chinese Exclusion, and the Fictions of Citizenship*. New York University Press, 2015.

CHAPTER 14

Defining and Defying a Woman's Sphere
Monika M. Elbert

> [I]f charity begins at home, it must not end there ... no home can be healthful in which are not cherished seeds of good for the world at large.
>
> Margaret Fuller[1]

> We would have every path laid open to woman as freely as to man ... We believe ... that no discordant collision, but a ravishing harmony of the spheres would ensue.
>
> Margaret Fuller[2]

Nineteenth-century American women writers, thinkers, and reformers knew that they needed to approach their female audiences cautiously with their fervent desires to join the male marketplace of ideas. The safest way to these women's hearts and minds often was through the sentimentality of True Womanhood discourse. Long before twentieth-century second-wave feminists, Fuller recognized in her *Woman of the Nineteenth Century* (1845) that the personal is truly political. When the image of the New Woman emerged, feminists remained anxious about abandoning the maternal. Their writings showed the dangers posed by independent-thinking women to relationships and feminine identity. In this chapter, I illustrate how women at the forefront of activism for disenfranchised women and African Americans favored modalities of womanhood recognizable by middle-class woman drawn to maternal rhetoric.

Late twentieth-century feminism inspired studies of nineteenth-century womanhood focused on the middle class and motherhood, celebrating what Barbara Welter in 1966 termed "the cult of true womanhood" that

---

[1] Margaret Fuller, "Thanksgiving," *New-York Tribune*, December 12, 1844, in *Margaret Fuller's New York Journalism: A Biographical Essay and Key Writings*, ed. Catherine C. Mitchell (University of Tennessee Press, 1995), 177.
[2] Margaret Fuller, *Woman in the Nineteenth Century* (1845), in *The Essential Margaret Fuller*, ed. Jeffrey Steele (Rutgers University Press, 1995), 260.

Defining and Defying a Woman's Sphere   239

privileged the middle class.³ Mary Ryan, in her 1985 study *The Empire of the Mother: American Writing about Domesticity, 1830–1860*, continued in the claustrophobic vein highlighting women's domesticity, but in *Women in Public: Between Romance and Ballots, 1835–1880* (1990), Ryan revealed a more liberating image of women working in the public eye.⁴ This scholarly shift toward women's public engagement surfaced in Barbara Leslie Epstein's 1981 study of the "politics of domesticity," which presented women leveraging religion to participate in the public sphere. Literary critics like Joyce Warren and Mary Kelley likewise showed the expansive public influence of women steeped in communal values exceeding the masculinist model of individualist expression.⁵

More radical studies at the turn of the twentieth century saw less separation between the male marketplace and the female homestead and recognized that the queen of the household effected change in politics and education. Volumes edited by me and by Cathy Davidson optimistically anticipated critical evaluations merging the separate spheres and showing more agency for women than previously acknowledged. A sense of hopefulness permeates these studies extending a focus beyond the middle class to reveal women active in political and religious realms. However, the collision of female experience with the politics of poverty on the street, in the factory, in the fields, or in prison ushered in a different kind of turmoil. Motherhood persisted as a defining characteristic of feminine identity from guidebooks to radical manifestos: Lydia Maria Child's handbook to mothering (1831) offers a down-to-earth approach in contradistinction to Lydia Sigourney's euphoric rendering of motherhood in 1838 as the "climax of [one's] happiness";⁶ Beecher and Stowe's vision of a home regulated by domestic science (1869) stands in contrast to Gilman's idea of a perfect (but

---

³ See Barbara Welter, "The Cult of True Womanhood: 1820–1860," *American Quarterly* 18:2 (Summer 1966), 151–174.
⁴ See Mary P. Ryan, *The Empire of the Mother: American Writing about American Domesticity, 1830–1860* (Harrington Park Press, 1985); and *Women in Public: Between Romance and Ballots, 1835–1880* (Johns Hopkins University Press, 1990).
⁵ See Barbara Leslie Epstein, *The Politics of Domesticity: Women, Evangelism, and Temperance in Nineteenth-Century America* (Wesleyan University Press, 1981); Joyce W. Warren, "Introduction: Canons and Canon Fodder," in Joyce W. Warren, ed., *The (Other) American Traditions: Nineteenth-Century Women Writers* (Rutgers University Press, 1993), 1–28; and Mary Kelley, *Private Woman, Public Stage: Literary Domesticity in Nineteenth-Century America* (Oxford University Press, 1984). On changing views of the domestic and public woman, see Frances B. Cogan, *All-American Girl: The Idea of Real Womanhood in Mid-Nineteenth Century America* (University of Georgia Press, 1989); and Susan M. Cruea, "Changing Ideals of Womanhood during the Nineteenth-Century Woman Movement," *ATQ* 19:3 (2005), 187–204.
⁶ See Lydia Maria Child, *The Mother's Book* (1831) (Applewood Books, 1989); and Lydia H. Sigourney, *Letters to Mothers* (1838) (Harper and Brothers, 1845), 9.

unnatural) harmonious society based on motherhood in the all-female dystopia *Herland* (1915), where only the privileged few can physically reproduce.[7] For good or ill, historians and literary critics acknowledged the ubiquity of romanticized narratives of motherhood in women's writing with varying political implications. Lydia Maria Child, in keeping with a Protestant work ethic, cautioned against materialist indulgence, warning mothers not to "bestow upon their children, the accursed inheritance of indolent and extravagant habits."[8] Nina Baym's criticism has represented such maternal thinking positively: "If worldly values could dominate the home, perhaps the direction of influence could be reversed so that home values dominated the world."[9]

The Spectacle of the City and the Drama of Public Charity

The chapter epigraphs from Fuller illuminate my ideas about Child's and others' insistence on transporting homespun charity to urban centers. Fuller clearly insists in her *New-York Tribune* essays on bringing the Cult of True Womanhood to the street as a means to understand incarcerated or otherwise disenfranchised women, abandoned or unemployed. Her New York journalism dramatizes the need to support the unhoused and impoverished in order to foment activism among women reformers. Lydia Maria Child, during her 1840s New York sojourn, employs melodrama and sentimentality to render poignant scenes of suffering. In Letter XIV (February 17, 1842) from her *Letters from New York*, Child dramatically imagines a child's future in prison for lack of "a mother's voice."[10] She creates a disturbing scenario of a young newspaper boy turning criminal due to a void of parental affection. Favoring the maternal impulse behind charity, Child asserts she is haunted by "hungry eyes, that look as if they had pleaded long for sympathy and at last gone mute in still despair."[11] She calls for maternal or angelic voices (often synonymous), "But watchmen and constables were around him, and they have small fellowship with

---

[7] See Catharine E. Beecher and Harriet Beecher Stowe, *The American Woman's Home, Or Principles of Domestic Science* (1869), ed. Joseph Van Why (Stowe-Day Foundation, 1994); and Charlotte Perkins Gilman, *Herland, The Yellow Wall-Paper, and Selected Writings*, ed. Denise D. Knight (Penguin, 1999).
[8] Lydia Maria Child, *The American Frugal Housewife, Dedicated to Those Who Are Not Ashamed of Economy* (Carter, Hendee, and Co., 1833), 113.
[9] Nina Baym, *American Women Writers and the Work of History, 1790–1860* (Rutgers University Press, 1995), 48.
[10] Lydia Maria Child, *Letters from New York, 1st and 2nd Series, 1841–1844* (F. Pitman, 1879), 83.
[11] Child, *Letters from New York*, 65.

angels."[12] Another scene shows an encounter with two immigrant boys fighting – their mother, despondent, emaciated, and ragged. Child gives alms to the mother, "though political economy reprove the deed."[13] She witnesses "two ragged little boys, asleep in each other's arms" and recalls a newspaper article about two vagabond motherless children.[14] In a third scenario, Child encounters a drunk woman whose "garments were all draggled in New York gutters."[15] Another woman is apprehended by a watchman advising the unfortunate to go home. Her response: "Thank you kindly, Sir, I should like to go home."[16] Home and urban homelessness culminate as a theme in Child's visits to the burial ground of the immigrant poor: "On one upright shingle was painted only 'Mutter' ... On another was scrawled ... 'So ruhe wohl, Du unser liebes Kind'" (Rest well, our beloved child).[17] Any condescension in *Letters From New York* gives way to authentic charity in Child's personal letter to Ann Loring on December 26, 1843, in which she describes helping an orphan on Christmas. The boy was "in the Tombs, not because he committed any crime, but he had nowhere to go."[18] Five dollars and a pair of new boots from the asylum ladies enabled Child to remove the boy from the Tombs and eventually find him a "good place in the country."[19]

Besides street poverty, Child is concerned in *Letters from New York* with the dearth of women in public spectacles and activist empowerment. In witnessing militaristic parades and pageants of men from all trades and classes, she notes the obvious absence: "I missed the women and the children; for without something to represent the genial influence of domestic life, the circle of joy and hope is ever incomplete."[20] Child's visits to New York's almshouses and prisons are impactful, as they are also for Fuller, Alcott, and Fanny Fern. On visiting the prison at Blackwell's Island, Child laments the inequities wrought by commercial capitalism: "Society, with its unequal distribution, its perverted education, its manifold injustice, its cold neglect, its biting mockery, has taken from them the gifts of God."[21] (She also attacks sensational journalism for reporting salacious crimes without seeking remedy of the ill.) Child concludes: "The poor need houses of encouragement, and society gives them houses

---

[12] Child, *Letters from New York*, 67.   [13] Child, *Letters from New York*, 66.
[14] Child, *Letters from New York*, 85.   [15] Child, *Letters from New York*, 67.
[16] Child, *Letters from New York*, 68.   [17] Child, *Letters from New York*, 69.
[18] Lydia Maria Child, *Letters of Lydia Maria Child*, ed. John G. Whittier (Houghton and Mifflin, 1882), 53.
[19] Child, *Letters of Lydia Maria Child*, 54.   [20] Child, *Letters from New York*, 9.
[21] Child, *Letters from New York*, 150.

of correction."[22] The superintendent of Blackwell Penitentiary believes that "the whole system tended to increase crime," prompting her to ask, "If society is the criminal, were it not well to reform society?"[23]

Child's visit to Long Island Farms is more hopeful. Children there are provided with "wholesome food, comfortable clothing, and the common rudiments of education," but maternal love is missing: "The oppressive feeling is that there are no mothers there. Everything moves by machinery, as it always must with masses of children, never subdivided into families."[24] The boys were "daily drilled to military exercises, as a useful means of forming habits of order, as well as fitting for the future service of the State."[25] When visiting the hospital for these children on Blackwell's Island, her lament becomes more pronounced, as the living conditions of the sick orphans is appalling: "Here the absence of maternal love was most agonizing; not even the patience and gentleness of a saint could supply its place, and saints are rarely hired by the public."[26]

In Child's visit to Sing-Sing in Volume 2 (December 8, 1844) of *Letters from New York*, she observes the women's department of the prison and bemoans the fact that there still is corporal punishment in the prison. But she commends the improvements made by the head administrator, Mrs. Farnham. And she recounts the story of how the president of Sing-Sing, on the previous Fourth of July, "sent each of the 73 women prisoners a beautiful bouquet, with a note, asking them to receive the flowers as a testimonial of his approbation for their good conduct."[27] In Child's eyes, this display of commendation softened the demeanor of even the most hardened or difficult prisoners. She also describes a holiday where a matron plays a piano as reward for prisoners' good behavior, so that "tunes of praise were mingled with friendly exhortations"; as a result, the inmates "wept like children."[28] Wary of criticism, Child, asserts, "I am well aware that this will sound very sentimental to many readers. Very likely some may jestingly describe these suggestions as 'a new transcendental mode of curing crime by music and flowers.'"[29] Child invokes the maternal as remedy: "[I]f she were thy own daughter, dependent on the kindness and forbearance of strangers, is it *thus* you would have them treat her? If she once had a mother, who watched her cradle tenderly, and folded her warmly to a loving heart, treat her gently for that mother's sake."[30] Thus, she invokes

[22] Child, *Letters from New York*, 153.
[23] Child, *Letters from New York*, 152, 154.
[24] Child, *Letters from New York*, 156.
[25] Child, *Letters from New York*, 156.
[26] Child, *Letters from New York*, 157.
[27] Child, *Letters from New York*, 409.
[28] Child, *Letters from New York*, 410.
[29] Child, *Letters from New York*, 410.
[30] Child, *Letters from New York*, 413.

the principles of her domestic treatise in her application to improvement for the working-class and poverty-stricken woman.

Christmas as a season of giving is prominent throughout both versions of Child's *Letters from New York* (first and second series), and the second series/volume actually begins with Christmas 1843 and ends with New Year's Eve, 1844. Child feels that Christmastime is when "the principle of Love – that feminine principle of the universe, the inmost centre of Christianity prevails."[31] Writing twenty-four years later, Louisa May Alcott makes a similar spectacle of charity in *Little Women* (1868), when the daughters are forced early in the work to see (through their mother's eyes) the true meaning of Christmas and later in the narrative to see the meaning of charity by giving to the poor German immigrant family. Here, too, the intensity of emotion is heightened by the spectacle of giving. In a book that shows Alcott's love of drama (inscribed on Jo's personality), it is not surprising that this first scene of holiday giving will set the tone for the rest of the book: "Not far away from here," Marmee tells her four daughters, "lives a poor woman with a little newborn baby. Six children are huddled into one bed to keep from freezing, for they have no fire. There is nothing to eat over there, and the oldest boy came to tell me they were suffering hunger and cold. My girls, will you give them your breakfast as a Christmas present?"[32] The girls agree to "The morning charities and ceremonies" for the Hummel family.[33] Men, however, can be charitable, too. Old Mr. Laurence sends a spread of ice cream, cake, fruit, and flowers to the Marches. Giving, for Child and Alcott, should be shared by both genders. Child describes the generosity of a male friend giving to the poor at Christmas: "He filled a large basket full of cakes, and went forth into our most miserable streets, to distribute them among hungry children."[34] Children's eyes sparkle and mothers are overwhelmed by his generosity as domestic values of maternal care transferred to public domains prove beneficial.

Both Child and Alcott reaffirmed their commitment to Christian giving after the eye-opening experiences of New York. Fuller, after relocating to New York to report for the *Tribune* (1844–1846), writes passionately about poor women in her Christmas and Thanksgiving editorials. No longer content with merely lecturing, she is moved to action to help the poor. As I have stated elsewhere,

---

[31] Child, *Letters from New York*, 15.
[32] Louisa May Alcott, *Little Women*, ed. Anne K. Phillips and Gregory Eiselein (Norton, 2004), 21.
[33] Alcott, *Little Women*, 23.   [34] Child, *Letters from New York*, 223.

[Fuller] was able to join political activism (the traditionally male, public sphere) with compassionate feeling (the traditionally female, private sphere). This raising of her consciousness (an interesting androgynous merging of the spheres she had recommended in *Woman*) in a political context paved the way for her political radicalism in Italy, when she became actively involved in the struggle for the rights of the disenfranchised.[35]

Nonetheless she did not recant the message of her earlier "Conversations" in Boston regarding the empowerment of middle- and upper-class women who ultimately chose motherhood and marriage over self-reliance. Even in that earlier period, Fuller advocated for empowered Transcendentalist women by utilizing strong goddess images, like Minerva or Diana, in *Woman of the Nineteenth Century*. Her depiction of the Virgin Mary as a figure reconciliatory of self-reliance and maternal nurturing even before her New York ventures establishes the importance of motherhood for her feminist beliefs.

When Fuller witnesses the suffering of women who are incarcerated or institutionalized, her reaction is similar to that of Lydia Maria Child – a deep sense of shock and a radical desire to effect change in terms of maternal values. When she visits the Bellevue Almshouse, the Farm School, the Asylum for the Insane, and the penitentiary on Blackwell's Island, Fuller is astounded by horrible conditions and lack of privacy for inmates enduring the confines of a panopticon environment: "We are sorry to see mothers with their newborn infants exposed to the careless scrutiny of male visitors. In the hospital, those who had children scarce a day old were not secure from the gaze of the stranger."[36] She observes joyless orphans in ill health: "The terrible scourge, ophthalmia, disfigured many among them. This disease, from some cause not yet detected, has been prevalent here for many years ... There is not enough water here to give the children decent advantages as to bathing."[37] Fuller contended that personal, Transcendental consciousness-raising would effect more change than laws.

Fanny Fern, whom Hawthorne admired and rightly observed wrote as if she had "the devil ... in her," learned to be an independent mother

---

[35] Monika Elbert, "Urban Reform and the Plight of the Poor in Women's Journalistic Writing," in Frank Q. Christianson and Leslee Thorne-Murphy, eds., *Philanthropic Discourse in Anglo-American Literature, 1850–1920* (Indiana University Press, 2017), 84–113, 93.
[36] Fuller, *Margaret Fuller's New York Journalism*, 89.
[37] Fuller, *Margaret Fuller's New York Journalism*, 90 (March 19, 1845).

throughout her several marriages.[38] (Indeed, Fern's character Ruth Hall is much like the independent Hester Prynne.) In her visits to Blackwell's Island, Fern demanded that the inmates, often "fallen women," be treated with dignity and compassion. She saw incarcerated women as victims of a masculinized legal system and marketplace that robbed women of a proud worker's identity: "Women lead, most of them, lives of unbroken monotony, and have much more need of exhilarating influences than men, whose life is out of doors in the breathing, active world."[39] Fern insists that the monotony or boredom of the housewife/mother causes a sense of desperation not inflicted on men: "[I]f home is not sufficient for him, why should it suffice for her? whose work is never done – who can literally have *no* such thing as system (and here's where a mother's discouragement comes in), while her babies are in their infancy."[40] Fern describes the fatigue of maternal and domestic duties:

> [The mother] often says to herself at night, though she would not for words part with one of them, "I can't tell what I have actually accomplished to-day, and yet, I have not been idle a minute," and day after day passes on in this way, and perhaps for weeks she does not pass a threshold for a breath of fresh air, and yet men talk of "monotony!" and being "differently constituted," and needing amusement and exhilaration; and "business" is the broad mantle which it is not always safe for a wife to lift.[41]

Despite the recognition of the hardships of mothering by Romantic writers such as Child, Fuller, Fern, and Alcott, the problem of defining female identity apart from maternal subjectivity remained unresolved.

Although the image of a maternal benefactor is most obvious and celebrated in Alcott's *Little Women* (1868–1869), Alcott refused the "happy" ending of Laurie and Jo's marriage demanded by her audience. Indeed, Jo was to remain single; in compromise, Alcott marries her to an intellectual peer, Professor Bhaer, to parent male children of the next generation suitable for emancipated women. Alcott does not give in to an ending that eclipses Jo's personality, whose tomboyish streak and originality put her in good stead as a mother. As mothers, strong characters

---

[38] Nathaniel Hawthorne, "Letter of 2 February, 1855," in *The Centenary Edition of the Works of Nathaniel Hawthorne, Vol. 17: The Letters, 1853–1856*, ed. Thomas Woodson, L. Neal Smith, Norman Holmes Pearson, Fredson Bowers, and James A. Rubino (Ohio State University Press, 1987), 308.
[39] Fanny Fern, "Blackwell's Island, Number 3," *New York Ledger*, in *Ruth Hall and Other Writings*, ed. Joyce W. Warren (Rutgers University Press, 1988), 308.
[40] Fern, "Blackwell's Island, Number 3," 308. [41] Fern, "Blackwell's Island, Number 3," 308.

like Jo extend for reformers the utility of the Cult of True Womanhood into the late nineteenth century.

At the heart of the feminist argument against slavery is the demand to respect the independence of enslaved black mothers and their children – and the call for making the sanctity of marriage a God-given right to African American families. Thus, one of Harriet Beecher Stowe's most poignant moments in *Uncle Tom's Cabin* is Mrs. Bird's reaching out to the escaped slave Eliza through the common bond of motherhood.[42] Mrs. Bird, like many nineteenth-century women, mourns a dead child, creating an altar of mementos and clothes that she will donate to Eliza, who is in danger of likewise losing her child. Mrs. Bird tests her love for her husband and questions whether, in his decision to uphold the laws of the state house and ignore the plight of mother and child denied a safe home, he is a genuine father and a Christian. Similarly, in Harriet Jacobs's account of her life in slavery, she elucidates for the northern sympathetic reader her respectability as a mother:

> Oh, ye happy women, whose purity has been sheltered from childhood, who have been free to choose the objects of your affection, whose homes are protected by law, do not judge the poor desolate girl too severely. If slavery had been abolished, I also could have married the man of my own choice; I could have had a home shielded by the laws.[43]

---

[42] In *Domestic Individualism: Imagining Self in Nineteenth-Century America* (University of California Press, 1990), Gillian Brown refers in her chapter on "domestic politics" to the empowerment of the maternal in Stowe's novel: "*Uncle Tom's Cabin* reinterprets domesticity as a double agentry in which women simultaneously act within as its exemplars (Mrs. Shelby, Eva) and at the boundaries of society as its critics and revolutionaries (Rachel, Mrs. Bird, Cassy)" (37). Thus, Brown envisions the radical power of the domestic sphere, as domestic women can become activists: "In immediate political terms this means the enlistment of mothers in the abolitionist movement" (37). On a more global level, according to Brown, Stowe imagines "a feminized world and domestic economy" (37) that would transform world politics.

[43] Harriet A. Jacobs, *Incidents in the Life of a Slave Girl, Written by Herself*, ed. Jean Fagan Yellin (Harvard University Press, 1987), 54. Jacobs refers to the centrality of motherhood in her audience's response, but she makes clear the different perils of motherhood under slavery. Recently, critics have pointed to the lack of attention to the plight of black women in key studies about white middle-class women, such as Ann Douglas's *The Feminization of American Culture* (1977), a privileged attitude that Jane Tompkins critiqued in her book, *Sensational Designs* (1985); see Kevin Pelletier, Claudia Stokes, and Abram Van Engen, "The Last Cleric: Ann Douglas, Intellectual Authority, and the Legacy of *Feminization*," *J19: The Journal of Nineteenth-Century Americanists* 7:1 (Spring 2019), 185–208. For a recent study showing how a white feminist political agenda sometimes perpetuated the marginalization of some women in its focus on white women's liberation (e.g. Elizabeth Cady Stanton) and neglected or downplayed the works of black feminists like Frances Ellen Watkins Harper or Harriet Jacobs, see Kyla Schuller, *The Trouble with White Women: A Counterhistory of Feminism* (Bold Type Books, 2021).

Jacobs situates her motherhood as foreign to a white, middle-class readership, who would not understand her desperate predicament of being unable to marry. Jacobs must remain in an unsatisfactory domestic arrangement to protect herself from Dr. Flint and her children born out of wedlock: "I would ten thousand times rather that my children should be the half-starved paupers of Ireland than to be the most pampered among the slaves of America."[44]

Though Margaret Fuller created an unequal comparison by collapsing the plight of the slaves with that of the American woman (in *Woman in the Nineteenth Century*), she drew on the strength of the enslaved woman to create metaphors of the empowered woman in critique of hypocritical men in power: "Those who think the physical circumstances of women should make a part in the national government unsuitable, are by no means those who think it impossible for the negresses to endure field work, even during pregnancy, or the sempstresses [*sic*] to go through their killing labors."[45] Though the comparison appropriates for middle-class white women the plight of the slave and sweatshop worker, its reference ("even during pregnancy") to the motherhood that these diverse women share demonstrates how maternity provided a persistent rhetorical and political resource for women activists of this period.

Becoming the New Woman: Reconceptualizing the Home, Deposing/Redefining the Mother

The late-century "New Woman" emerges from discontent with the limitation of the "True Woman." Perhaps a more accurate way of redefining the concept of True Womanhood would be, as Frances Cogan has pointed out, to replace it with "Real Womanhood," as actual nineteenth-century women, associated with "True Womanhood," were in fact more active and self-reliant than previously understood.[46] Indeed, an interim account of womanhood preceding the New Woman emerged from women's Civil War traumas (managing the home alone; acting as nurses; widowed mothers needing to support children) that were both liberating and horrifying. But the "New Woman" who grows out of the discontent of the "True Woman" still finds herself limited by gender roles.

---

[44] Jacobs, *Incidents in the Life*, 31.
[45] Fuller, *Woman in the Nineteenth Century*, 259.
[46] Frances B. Cogan, *All-American Girl: The Idea of Real Womanhood in Mid-Nineteenth Century America* (University of Georgia Press, 1989), 197–256.

Fanny Fern acts as foremother to the likes of Charlotte Perkins Gilman, who continues the idolization of children but who will demand her own rights as an individual. In *Ruth Hall* (1854), Fanny Fern's autobiographical protagonist does not settle for motherhood, as her widowhood forces her to earn wages as a teacher and writer. However, the daughter she allows to be raised by her in-laws (due to financial hardship) becomes more dependent and fearful than the daughter she raises herself, suggesting that nurturing one's biological children oneself is somewhat superior to having an outsider raise them. Although Gilman showed the Gothic implications of postpartum depression in "The Yellow Wall-Paper" (1892), she herself tries to reinvent the institution of marriage and motherhood, and children remain at the forefront of her writings, even in her later stories, as she offers alternative and radical ways to mother, as in "Turned" (1911), "Making a Change" (1911), "His Mother" (1914), and "The Unnatural Mother" (1916). Gilman's poems sometimes romanticize motherhood (as in "The Purpose" [1904], where the child is seen as more significant than a woman's husband or lover), but more strident poems seek a maternal order to undo male catastrophic thinking, as in "Matriatism" (1914), where she imagines maternal ecological harmony resistant to a "Fatherland": "From a war-stained past to a world of peace, / Our fair, sweet Mother Earth."[47]

Gilman, despite her novel ways of mothering (giving her own child an alternative by divorcing her husband, allowing their daughter to be raised by his new wife, a friend of Gilman's), still seems obsessed with motherhood as a means for righting the wrongs of patriarchy. Although recent feminist critics have challenged her ideal form of privileged motherhood as upper-middle-class and white, Gilman nevertheless believes that progress for the human race will come through mothers – when, that is, those mothers exercise a kind of utopian communal or extended motherhood and domestic science. In *The Home: Its Work and Influence* (1903), she laments the fact that women have been bound to the home and affirms their need to escape their domestic confinement for their own sake and the sake of their children: "Our mothers are beginning to come out of their isolation into human contact; to take that first step toward wisdom – the acknowledgement of ignorance; and to study what little is known of this new science, Child-Culture."[48] In *Women and Economics* (1898), she

---

[47] Charlotte Perkins Gilman, *Herland, The Yellow Wall-Paper, and Selected Writings*, ed. Denise D. Knight (Penguin, 1999), 343.
[48] Charlotte Perkins Gilman, *The Home: Its Work and Influence* (1903), ed. Michael S. Kimmel (AltaMira Press, 2002), 243.

likewise asked women to step out of the domestic sphere and become producers in the marketplace rather than just consumers at home.[49] In a later work, *Our Androcentric Culture, or the Man-Made World* (1911), Gilman calls for women coming together in "Women's Clubs" movements: "In 'village improvements,' in traveling libraries, in lecture courses and exhibitions, in promoting good legislation; in many a line of noble effort our Women's Clubs show what women want to do."[50] Even as Gilman applauds the new proactive woman, she nevertheless admits that, through their earlier domestic values, women brought substantial improvements to the public arena: "Even in their crippled, smothered past, they have made valiant efforts – not always wise – in charity and philanthropy."[51] She ends this treatise by calling for "full equal citizenship": "The great woman's movement and labor movement of to-day are parts of the same pressure, the same world-progress. An economic democracy must rest on a free womanhood; and a free womanhood leads to an economic democracy."[52]

Like Gilman, Julia Ward Howe tries to transform domesticity. After all, it was Howe who tried to initiate a Mother's Day holiday back in 1870, which was a reaction to the carnage wrought by men's wars ("We will not have great questions decided by irrelevant agencies, and our husbands shall not come to us, reeking with carnage, for caresses and appeals"), and expressed her desire to "protect their sons, who have been taught the virtues of charity, mercy, and patience" by their mothers: "We women of one country will be too tender of those of another country to allow our sons to be trained to injure theirs."[53] Howe internationalizes her constituency and her appeal, so that the fight of nation against nation must itself confront the cooperative tone among mothers of all nations: "In the name of womanhood and of humanity, I earnestly ask that a general congress of women without limit of nationality may be appointed and of the earliest period consistent with its objects, to promote the alliance of the different nationalities, the amicable settlement of international questions, the great and general ideas of peace."[54] This very radical idea of superseding national affiliation with a coalition of mothers goes against what Amy

---

[49] Charlotte Perkins Gilman, *Women and Economics* (1898) (Dover Publications, 1997).
[50] Charlotte Perkins Gilman, *Our Androcentric Culture, or the Man-Made World* (1911) (Humanity Books, 2001), 133.
[51] Gilman, *Our Androcentric Culture*, 133. [52] Gilman, *Our Androcentric Culture*, 134.
[53] Julia Ward Howe, "Mother's Day Proclamation" (1870) in "The Original Mother's Day Proclamation by Julia Ward Howe," *Plough* (May 7, 2014), www.plough.com/en/topics/culture/holidays/mothers-day/the-original-mother-s-day-proclamation.
[54] Howe, "Mother's Day Proclamation."

Kaplan sees as "manifest domesticity," an American form of domesticity making American male and female realms complicit in Manifest Destiny thinking that privileged American national interests over those of separate nations or cultures. Kaplan aligns nineteenth-century domesticity with "nationalism and imperialism," but Howe clearly shows how her vision of domesticity resists those agendas.[55]

Although Howe's "Mother's Day Proclamation" is a liberating political manifesto, she still sees motherhood as woman's prime purpose. Woman "must be the moral and spiritual equivalent of man" because, otherwise, woman could not be "entrusted with the awful and inevitable responsibilities of maternity."[56] In her 1896 address, "Why Are Women the Natural Guardians of Social Morals?," Howe, like Fuller, idealizes the self-reliant goddess Minerva, but rather than celebrating triumphant single womanhood, Howe sounds more like Child when she laments the spectacular plight of "The neglected child, wandering about the streets to learn the lessons of meanness and of crime."[57] She admonishes women to follow their natural maternal impulses: "At the sight of him, oh! Women, let your woman's heart be touched. Let your blessed motherhood put itself at interest, multiply itself so as to embrace him, the homeless, the friendless."[58] Once again, the maternal instinct survives transposed from the home to the street.

Certainly the "recovered" novels authored by nineteenth-century women that I read most enthusiastically as a graduate student in the 1980s, books that were supposed to redefine women outside of motherhood, likewise offer no escape from that biological role or revered institution. The first-person protagonist in Gilman's "The Yellow-Wallpaper" (1892) suffers from postpartum depression but is denied, through a type of rest cure prescribed by the likes of S. Weir Mitchell, her writing tablet and her pen to make sense of her experience, and so she finds solace in madness. Edna Pontellier, the protagonist in Chopin's *The Awakening* (1899), tries to escape her role as mother but commits suicide after she is horrified witnessing her best friend, Madame Ratignolle, birthing a (fourth) child: "With an inward agony, with as flaming, outspoken revolt against the ways

---

[55] Amy Kaplan, "Manifest Domesticity," in Cathy Davidson and Jessamyn Hatcher, eds., *No More Separate Spheres! A Next Wave American Studies Reader* (Duke University Press, 2002), 183–208, 184.
[56] Julia Ward Howe and Florence Howe Hall, *Julia Ward Howe and the Woman Suffrage Movement: A Selection from Her Speeches and Essays* (Dana, Estes, and Co., 1913), 13.
[57] Julia Ward Howe, "Why Are Women the Natural Guardians of Social Morals?," in Howe and Hall, *Julia Ward Howe and the Woman Suffrage Movement*, 101.
[58] Howe, "Why Are Women the Natural Guardians of Social Morals?," 102.

of Nature, she witnessed the scene of torture."[59] Adele's admonishment to "Think of the children. Edna. Oh, think of the children! Remember them!" sends Edna to her suicide a few pages later.[60] One of the most promising books I read, Elizabeth Stuart Phelps's *The Story of Avis* (1877), allows a gifted woman to dream of her future as an artist only to have those dreams dashed when she gives in to sympathy for a former injured beau returning from the Civil War. Later, because of her husband's ineptitude as a provider and father, Avis must care for both of her children on her own while her impaired/invalid husband goes on a kind of rest cure permitted to males with neurasthenia (traveling to Europe), and she is left in the unhappy and exhausting role of father and mother to both her son and daughter. Her son and husband later suffer an untimely death, and she is left dreaming of a future, but not her own, of a woman carving out her destiny without a male; she passes on her dream of becoming an artist to her daughter named (aptly but somewhat heavy-handedly) Wait.

It would seem that the nineteenth century refused to let women forget their procreative powers, although it did allow the displacement of the maternal role to a public sphere that granted women a degree of political influence beyond the domestic realm. But that "ravishing harmony of the spheres" cited in this chapter's epigraph that Margaret Fuller dreamt about at mid-century would still remain a dream at century's end.

Further Reading

Alcott, Louisa May. *The Journals of Louisa May Alcott*, ed. Joel Myerson and Daniel Shealy. Little, Brown, 1989.

Baker, Jean Harvey. "Public Women and Partisan Politics, 1840–1860." In Gary W. Gallagher and Rachel A. Shelden, eds., *A Political Nation: New Directions in Mid-Nineteenth-Century American Political History*. University of Virginia Press, 2012, 64–81.

Bauer, Dale M., ed. *The Cambridge History of American Women's Literature*. Cambridge University Press, 2012.

Cott, Nancy F. *The Grounding of Modern Feminism*. Yale University Press, 1987.

Davidson, Cathy and Jessamyn Hatchers, eds. *No More Separate Spheres! A Next Wave American Studies Reader*. Duke University Press, 2002.

Elbert, Monika, ed. *Separate Spheres No More: Gender Convergence in American Literature, 1830–1930*. University of Alabama Press, 2000.

---

[59] Kate Chopin, *The Awakening*, *The Awakening and Selected Stories*, ed. Sandra M. Gilbert (Penguin, 1983), 170.
[60] Chopin, *The Awakening*, 170.

Romero, Lora. "Vanishing Americans: Gender, Empire, and New Historicism." In Michael Moon and Cathy N. Davidson, eds., *Subjects and Citizens: Nation, Race, and Gender from Oroonoko to Anita Hill.* Duke University Press, 1995, 86–105.

Ryan, Mary P. *Women in Public: Between Banners and Ballots, 1825–1880.* Johns Hopkins University Press, 1992.

Sizer, Lyde Cullen. *The Political Work of Northern Women Writers and the Civil War, 1850–1872.* University of North Carolina Press, 2000.

Warren, Joyce W. "Women: Politics, Culture, and the Law." In Nan Goodman and Simon Stern, eds., *The Routledge Research Companion to Law and Humanities in Nineteenth-Century America.* Taylor & Francis, 2017, 5–19.

Welter, Barbara. *Dimity Convictions: The American Woman in the Nineteenth Century.* Ohio University Press, 1976.

CHAPTER 15

Beyond the City and the Country: Rural Scarcity and Indigenous Survivance

John Funchion

Since the late eighteenth century, divisions associated with the country and the city have powerfully framed conflicts in US politics and culture. Shortly after Pennsylvania ratified the Constitution, an anti-Federalist riot broke out in Carlisle. Those who participated in this 1788 fracas, which followed Shays' Rebellion and presaged the Whiskey Rebellion, cast their struggle as one that upheld the backcountry "nobility and dignity of simple farmers and artisans" in opposition to the Federalist "gentlemen of wealth and education."[1] Population density thus became a surrogate for class conflict. The rural figured as the domain of disempowered laborers and farmers while the urban represented the locus of intellectual and financial authority. Historians largely "reinforced the marginality" of "the backcountry" by placing writing by "seaport intellectuals" at the center of their scholarship.[2] A different but related dynamic unfolded among those who study late nineteenth-century local-color or regionalist writing. June Howard incisively avers that debates about these literary works fixate on whether they are "written by insiders or outsiders, nationalist or subversive, empathetic or exploitive, and so on."[3] Lurking behind what Howard views as these unhelpful binaries lies the country and city diode whereby power only flows toward the urban, which either produces or gets challenged by the region.

The assumptions scholars make about country and city and local and national writing predispose us to read for regional antagonism. Structurally, the US apportioning of congressional representation based on states and population rather than along ideological lines contributes to

---

[1] Saul Cornell, "Aristocracy Assailed: The Ideology of Backcountry Anti-Federalism," *The Journal of American History* 76 (1990), 1148–1172, 1155.
[2] Ed White, *The Backcountry and the City: Colonization and Conflict in Early America* (University of Minnesota Press, 2005), 12–13.
[3] June Howard, *The Center of the World: Regional Writing and the Puzzles of Place-Time* (Oxford University Press, 2018), 22.

the tendency to conflate political interest with geographical location. Assumed cultural divisions between country and city have proven resilient throughout the nation's history, so that even in the twenty-first century the *New York Times* and similar news outlets will incessantly profile rural counties to make sense of an impending or recent national election.

But as intellectually and politically satisfying as these reports can be for the answers they seemingly offer, this city and country binary works in concert with what Daniel Immerwahr aptly identifies as "one of the truly distinctive features of the United States' empire": It is "persistently ignored" and hidden.[4] Country and city thus often get enlisted as proxies for political, racial, and cultural positions. The provincial operates as the custodian of the "real America," which gets imagined as white, masculine, traditionalist, and working class. The city, meanwhile, teems with the elite and the cosmopolitan. Such gestures conjure away any trace of Indigenous peoples, migrant farmers and ranchers, urban–rural labor alliances, black agrarian Populists, and the city's intersectional working class. Even as we must acknowledge the generative role country-and-city scholarship has played in US literary criticism, this chapter ultimately calls for rethinking this binary by turning to texts that provide a different account of the rural – a narrative that *the country* as a concept so effectively obfuscates. Focusing specifically on Hamlin Garland and Zitkála-Šá, two turn-of-the-century authors whose work conventionally gets categorized as local-color or regional writing, I argue that scarcity and survivance rather than city and country shaped the cultural politics of rural spaces in the nineteenth century. To grasp how Garland's representation of scarcity and Zitkála-Šá's practice of survivance challenge pastoral ideations of the country, I first attend to the roles that *frontier* and *region* play in shaping US perceptions of the country.

Naming Possessions and Disaffected Literatures

Within nineteenth-century US literary studies, political tensions and continuities between rural and urban spaces get pinned to two principal terms: frontier and region. The frontier and the region operate as conceptual terminuses connected via a process of territorialization, described by Andy Doolen as the Anglo-American expansionist effort "to interpret and define the intricate network of rivers, mountains, and valleys as a seemingly

---

[4] Daniel Immerwahr, *How to Hide an Empire: A History of the Greater United States* (Farrar, Straus and Giroux, 2019), 18.

obvious and natural cartographic logic for occupying and possessing contiguous territories."⁵ Put simply, when we conceptualize backcountry or country culture and politics in terms of frontier and region, we remain inextricably bound to empire's "cartographic logic" and its process of colonial settlement and Indigenous displacement. While the frontier evokes fluid notions of an anarchic yet-to-be incorporated terra incognita, the region fixes a set of cultural characteristics to a particular place, determining what places offer in service to the empire. Both frontier and regional writing typically imagine their addressees as urban readers, bolstering the mythology of the rural as a site of rugged individualism and production aimed at sating metropolitan material and cultural consumer desires.

In this chapter, I shift emphasis away from frontier and region, which foreground how power flows from imperial metropoles outward to extend territorial frontiers and regionalize rural spaces. While the processes of territorialization and regionalization assist in explaining the cultural machinery that propels US imperialism, they can conceal the political dynamics that unfold within these spaces. Indigenous and black struggles are figured predominantly as empire's obstacles while frontiersmen and the settlers who followed them are cast as mutable avatars representing US values like individualism and determination. This imperialist framework revolves around a city and country binary shaped by decades of scholarship itself influenced by nineteenth-century writing. In *The Country and the City*, for instance, Raymond Williams asserts that "a whole reality is admitted in the industrial districts" in England, but "a selected reality in the rural" predominates as one of "natural country ease."⁶ The English understanding of the countryside is one that is at once both pastoral and aristocratic; it teems with a traditionalist investment of conservative values that denied rural labor's presence.

While for Williams capitalism permeated the countryside from its inception, Myth and Symbol critics, such as Leo Marx, frame industrialization as an intruding force that imperiled the bucolic landscape. Even though Marx cast the pastoral as an ideal, he still cast it as becoming interrupted by, rather than working concomitantly with, "the forces of industrialism."⁷ He imagines an unpopulated North American wilderness

---

⁵ Andy Doolen, *Territories of Empire: U.S. Writing from the Louisiana Purchase to Mexican Independence* (Oxford University Press, 2014), 9.
⁶ Raymond Williams, *The Country and the City* (Oxford University Press, 1973), 180.
⁷ Leo Marx, *The Machine in the Garden: Technology and the Pastoral Ideal in America* (Oxford University Press, 1964), 26.

that either offered pastoral refuge or consisted of "unimproved land" going to "waste."[8] The first of these, the pastoral refuge for aristocracy that Williams identifies as the English model, had already been imported into nineteenth-century US regionalism, as embodied in work by writers such as Thomas Nelson Page who depicted the Old South as one that "brooded a softness and beauty, the joint product of Chivalry and Christianity."[9] Such traditionalist mythology, which brushes aside Reconstruction as an era that sullied a genteel region, later gained support from the Dunning school of Civil War historiography and still finds its echo in contemporary depictions of the Midwest as "the Heartland." This "Nowheresville," as Patricia Hampl succinctly opines in her memoir, is "where the American imagination has decided to archive innocence."[10]

The alternative to this regionalism – to being imagined in terms of Williams's pastoral aristocratic refuge – was to construe North American lands as the frontier, an unimproved waste that Ed White calls the North American backcountry. White establishes that often British North America and subsequently the early United States, despite being predominantly rural in the eighteenth and nineteenth centuries, cast "agrarian culture in negative terms, as a cultural absence or backwardness."[11] What both Williams's and White's approaches share is a sense that urban cultural centers set the terms of rural representation. White, however, instructively points to a set of other dynamics at play in the backcountry: a litany of "insurrections that occurred from the late seventeenth century to the end of the eighteenth."[12] The nineteenth century inherited this insurrectionist spirit, so that rural spaces appeared at the time less bucolic than bellicose. Frequently, settlers and Indigenous peoples alike expressed deep dissatisfaction with the federal government and its institutions. Despite their long history as frontier antagonists, European-derived settlers and Native Americans appeared to share a common political foe: urban finance

---

[8] Marx, *Machine in the Garden*, 156. Later Myth and Symbol scholars would expose the masculinist violence lurking beneath accounts of the country in Marx's *The Machine and the Garden* (1964) and Henry Nash Smith's *Virgin Land: The American West As Symbol and Myth* (1950). See Richard Slotkin, *Regeneration through Violence: The Mythology of the American Frontier, 1600–1860* (Wesleyan University Press, 1973); and Annette Kolodny, *The Lay of the Land: Metaphor As Experience and History in American Life and Letters* (University of North Carolina Press, 1975).

[9] Thomas Nelson Page, "The Old South," in *The Old South: Essays Social and Political* (Charles Scribner's Sons, 1892), 5.

[10] Patricia Hampl, *The Florist's Daughter* (Harcourt, 2007), 125. See also Sherwood Anderson's *Winesburg, Ohio* or Garrison Keillor's *Prairie Home Companion* radio series as examples of where the rural is figured as isolated and as innocent. Jane Smiley's *A Thousand Acres*, by contrast, takes aim at such characterizations by setting her retelling of *King Lear* on an Iowan farm.

[11] White, *Backcountry and the City*, 15.   [12] White, *Backcountry and the City*, 1.

capitalism. Here my aim is not to dispute the constitutive roles territorial expansionism and its many accompanying banners – Manifest Destiny, the Monroe Doctrine, and the Wild West – played in US culture and politics but to grapple more effectively with how pitting rural interests against urban ones sabotaged many potential intersectional political movements among rural white people, black people, and First Nations.[13]

As the agitators behind the early frontier insurrections, white settlers saw themselves as the exploited tools of urban interests rather than as the agents of empire. They perceived themselves as less politically favored than their black and Indigenous neighbors. To grapple with this false consciousness, I organize the remainder of this chapter not around the terms of representation favored by urban centers – region and frontier – but instead around two distinct responses to finance capitalism's threat to rural settler-colonists and Indigenous people: The fear of scarcity in the case of the former and the practice of survivance with the latter. Lacking pastoral abundance, agrarian movements in the United States rallied around narratives of scarcity. Such perceptions promoted economic populism and white supremacist ideology; they saw themselves as locked into a zero-sum contest with First Nations and corporate trusts alike. In contrast to scarcity's animating place in white rural regional politics, many Indigenous writers rallied around what the Chippewa scholar Gerald Vizenor calls survivance, defined as "an active sense of presence over absence, deracination, and oblivion; survivance is the continuance of stories, not a mere reaction, however pertinent."[14] Zitkála-Šá enacts survivance by challenging positivist historicity and reanimating the mode of Indigenous storytelling that rejects what Lloyd Pratt describes as literary regionalism's "spatialization of time," which separates the nation into different historical time zones in contrast to the cosmopolitan progressive present.[15] Understanding the dividing lines between country and city in nineteenth-century US culture, I argue, requires coming to terms with these two different reactions to the harms wrought by finance capitalism that both culminated in resistance and are contrastingly spurred by white resentment on the one hand and Indigenous persistence on the other.

---

[13] For a fuller account of how nineteenth-century literature represented finance capitalism, the economic panics it incited, and its political consequences, see David A. Zimmerman, *Panic! Markets, Crises, and Crowds in American Fiction* (University of North Carolina Press, 2006).
[14] Gerald Vizenor, "Aesthetics of Survivance: Literary Theory and Practice," in *Survivance: Narratives of Native Presence*, ed. Gerald Vizenor (University of Nebraska Press, 2008), 1–25, 1.
[15] Lloyd Pratt, *Archives of American Time: Literature and Modernity in the Nineteenth Century* (University of Pennsylvania Press, 2010), 129.

Scarcity and Battling the Foreclosure of Hope

In an essay written for B. O. Flowers's *Arena* magazine, Hamlin Garland declared that "there is no real scarcity of land – we have only twenty people to the square mile as a nation; but the *artificial* scarcity of land is already to the danger point."[16] Land speculation and monopolization of industry suppressed wages and kept consumer prices high, foisting economic blight upon rural communities. These conditions prompted farmers and rural neighbors to form voluntary associations such as the Grange and the Farmers' Alliance, which eventually coalesced into an insurgent political movement, the People's Party, that sought centralized political reforms despite its grassroots origins.[17] Garland contended that scarcity did more than just deprive these people of essential goods; it also constricted art, privileging the tastes of the wealthy metropolitan readers and the authors who catered to them.[18] This aesthetic oligarchy posed a threat to the nation, and Garland concluded that only local-color writing coupled with greater economic equality could repair democracy's essential cultural cornerstone.[19] Scarcity, in other words, promotes monopolistic dominance of what Nancy Glazener referred to as the *Atlantic*-group's cultural hegemony over the literary marketplace.[20]

Even though the Populist movement and Garland deemed scarcity unnecessary and wastefully destructive, it became central to nineteenth-century economic thought. Ute Tellmann explains that "the link between population, land, and scarcity provided the new science of political economy with a unifying and systematizing core that it would have otherwise lacked: the nexus between population and scarcity organized the causal

---

[16] Hamlin Garland, "The Land Question, and Its Relation to Art and Literature," in *Hamlin Garland, Prairie Radical: Writings from the 1890s*, ed. Donald Pizer (University of Illinois Press, 2010), 108. These observations coincided with Frederick Jackson Turner's frontier thesis, which argued that the frontier that had previously molded US culture and its citizens had closed.

[17] For more information on the People's Party and agrarian and labor organizations that contributed to its rise and eventual fall, see Charles Postel, *The Populist Vision* (Oxford University Press, 2007).

[18] See Garland, "The Land Question," 112.

[19] For Garland, local color means "something more than a forced study of the picturesque"; it must possess "such quality of texture and back-ground that it could not have been written in any other place" and that only someone from this place could have written it. Hamlin Garland, *Crumbling Idols: Twelve Essays on Art Dealing Chiefly with Literature, Painting, and the Drama* (Harvard University Press, 1960), 53–54. He defines local color in opposition to the touristic writing pitched for urban readers that critics such as Judith Fetterley and Marjorie Pryse would associate with local color writing in contrast to what they call regionalism.

[20] Nancy Glazener, *Reading for Realism: The History of a U.S. Literary Institution, 1850–1910* (Duke University Press, 1997), 11, 31.

relations between rent, capital, labor, and wealth."[21] Whether discussed in the context of Thomas Malthus's overpopulation thesis or in Marx's crisis theory, scarcity – perceived as either natural or manufactured – powered capitalism. Yet scarcity did not preclude abundance; it just confined it to a select minority who practiced what Thorstein Veblen came to call "conspicuous consumption" whose scale, despite being practiced by very few, still resulted in ecological devastation. Garland, faulting a lack of competition for creating concentrated wealth, did not subscribe to Karl Marx's critique of private property. Like many involved in the Populist movement, he embraced Henry George's belief that private property ownership constituted a natural right: "the denial of the equal right to the use of land is necessarily," George asserted, "the denial of the right of labor to its own produce."[22] Both George and Garland felt that, if left unchecked, monopolistic capitalism would destroy society by exacerbating economic disparity. Garland for this reason endorsed George's single tax scheme, a specific property tax on unearned increases in land value not tied to improvements, which was designed to combat land speculation and monopolization.

But Garland also recognized that scarcity could animate a political and cultural movement. It could conjure a people – a political subject. Radical artists like himself sought to recast "old forms of government into new shapes, catching from earth and sea and air, new songs to sing, new thoughts to frame, new deeds to dare."[23] Garland's short stories, by depicting the hardships of farmers and returning war veterans, fuel an antipastoral aesthetics that paints the rural as a site of ceaseless toil constantly enveloped within a cycle of scarce resources and crushing debt.

For decades, Garland has held on to his place as a minor canonical figure, but he stands out as one of the few authors to dramatize the late nineteenth-century US Populist movement in his work. Populist themes also appear in several novels by Ignatius Donnelly, who served as a political organizer as well. But Donnelly's writing displays a conspiratorial flavor, and he never enjoyed the literary accolades bestowed upon Garland. Literary critics have thoroughly attended to how Garland's collection of short stories, *Main-Travelled Roads*, depicts the challenges that farmers confronted, especially when industrial power became increasingly

---

[21] Ute Tellmann, *Life and Money: The Genealogy of the Liberal Economy and the Displacement of Politics* (Columbia University Press, 2017), 65.
[22] Henry George, *Progress and Poverty: An Inquiry into the Cause of Industrial Depressions, and of Increase of Want with Increase of Wealth* (D. Appleton and Company, 1886), 306.
[23] Garland, *Crumbling Idols*, 124.

monopolistic after the US Civil War, a conflict whose toll in human life and trauma likewise harmed rural areas. Far less attention, on the other hand, has been paid to Garland's explicitly political novel, *A Spoil of Office*.

This novel throws the usual regionalist plot into a hard reverse. Instead of sending the urban cosmopolite into the rural unknown, Garland dispatches a small-town Iowan to Washington. While *Main-Travelled Roads* presents readers with a series of stories that implicitly provide the rationale for the "Populist revolt" of the 1890s, it does so without representing the grassroots and electoral dynamics behind this major third-party movement.[24] *A Spoil of Office*, by contrast, belonged to a burgeoning genre of political novels that emerged in the 1890s and continued to appear in the opening decades of the twentieth century.[25] Although Garland's sympathies clearly lie with the agrarian movements of the West, from the Grange to the Farmers' Alliance, he hardly casts the country as a provincial site of unsullied virtue.

Reviewers took exception, however, not to his account of the country but to his rendition of the capitol. By having a newly elected congressperson from Iowa, Bradley Talcott, serve as the reader's interlocutor, Garland effectively provincializes the nation's seat of power as a city that "may be said to die, when Congress adjourns."[26] While Talcott arrives with a romantic reverence for Washington, he eventually determines that Congress is packed with "great, bloated, swaggering, unscrupulous, treacherous tricksters" (*Spoil* 299). These characterizations underscore the perceived distance between DC and the Midwest – a place of depravity in contrast to one of deprivation. What makes Garland's novel an instructive departure from many other narratives depicting tensions between the country and the city is its commitment to institutions despite their failures. *A Spoil of Office* provides readers with neither an unqualified positive celebration of DC nor a caustic populist takedown of the political elites. As Nathan Wolff explains, the nineteenth-century US fostered "a political public sphere that both attracts and repels," prompting him to argue that "the shocking intensity of partisan disagreement, the unseemly appetites of the politically ambitious, and the surprising emotional toll of the election

---

[24] John D. Hicks, *The Populist Revolt: A History of the Farmers' Alliance and People's Party* (University of Minnesota Press, 1931), 2.
[25] For more on this broader radical context, see Walter B. Rideout, *The Radical Novel in the United States, 1900–1954: Some Interrelations of Literature and Society* (Harvard University Press, 1956); and Holly Jackson, *American Radicals: How Nineteenth-Century Protest Shaped the Nation* (Crown Books, 2019).
[26] Hamlin Garland, *A Spoil of Office: A Story of the Modern West* (D. Appleton, 1897), 275. Hereafter, all page citations appear parenthetically as *Spoil*.

season" created the "national anxiety" scholars have seen as characteristic of the post–Civil War era.[27] In this respect, *A Spoil of Office* is an answer to the nostalgic politics exhibited in the short stories of *Main-Travelled Roads*, which usually end in anti-institutional resignation.[28]

A Spoil of Office, however, gets messier than his short fiction in politically productive ways. At times, it very much anticipates Garland's later turn to conservativism by replicating sentiments expressed in Henry Adams's *Democracy*, which expresses a "mugwump worldview": "a disbelief in utopian schemes and a distrust of government."[29] Yet every time Talcott believes he has escaped, he gets pulled back into electoral politics. Expressing dismay at the "type of legislator whose idea of legislation was to have a good time and look out for re-election," he nevertheless decides he must remain in Congress to fight for his community (*Spoil* 316). Rural scarcity and metropolitan abundance shape both Bradley's disaffection with legislative institutions and his community's steady commitment to reforming them. Scarcity can breed disaffection and narcissistic sectarian politics, but it also has the capacity to forge communal solidarity and inspire Bradley to embrace civic disinterestedness.[30] It traces the lines of antagonism that emerge in the text, so that Bradley and his supporters come to realize "there is no war between the town and the country" but instead "between the people and the monopolist wherever he is, whether he is in the country or in the town" (*Spoil* 192). This decidedly populist logic generates an affect not fully aligned with despair or hope but one that approximates the sublimity of what Bradley's love interest and future wife, Ida Wilber, calls "a new religion" that helps those fighting for equality "to forget mud and rain and cold and monotony" (*Spoil* 198).

Garland does not depict the rural as "an ideal land of abundance and joy," as Marx claimed previous agrarian and travel writers depicted the North American wilderness, but instead as one where Bradley and his community struggle to make ends meet.[31] Even though Bradley reflects upon the beauty of the "low swells of the prairies between Chicago and the

---

[27] Nathan Wolff, *Not Quite Hope and Other Political Emotions in the Gilded Age* (Oxford University Press, 2019), 9.
[28] Hamlin Garland, *Main-Travelled Roads* (University of Nebraska Press, 1995), 87. For my reading of how nostalgia animated the populist aesthetics found in Garland's short stories, see John Funchion, *Novel Nostalgias: The Aesthetics of Antagonism in Nineteenth-Century U.S. Literature* (Ohio State University Press, 2015), 96–121.
[29] Wolff, *Not Quite Hope*, 53, 52.
[30] Here Garland taps into classical and Atlantic republican discourse, which pays obeisance to the virtue of putting the interests of one's state above self-interest in all political matters.
[31] Marx, *Machine in the Garden*, 61.

Mississippi," he recognizes that the rural serves as a site of resource extraction and of labor exploitation (*Spoil* 317–318). As Cargill, a fellow reformer in Washington, informs him, "the corporations in this country are eating the life out of it" (*Spoil* 210). Bradley had already discovered in his early experiences that this exploitation is not solely economic but also affective in character. The corporate assault on farmers and rural communities produces both shame and helplessness. As Garland declares at the beginning of the novel, "the farmer had been oppressed," and "he had been helpless and would continue helpless till he asked and demanded his rights" (*Spoil* 8). Consistently, Garland reveals that the cruel optimism associated with homesteading's promise became punctured by simple cruelty and cynical resignation.[32] When Bradley returns to the Midwest as a congressperson and encounters "poverty which he now saw everywhere" (*Spoil* 335), his rage fuels his political commitment rather than leaving him hopeless.

Scarcity creates the basis for drawing the lines of antagonism that typically shape populist political movements.[33] But instead of calling for revolution, Bradley embraces the grassroots organizations that he believes can reform the US government. His faith in these organizations rests with how they rally against the corporate power that manufactures scarcity. Under Ida's guidance, he builds upon the foundation laid by fledgling organizations such as the Grange by bringing rural farmers and urban laborers together under the banner of a third political party capable of rejecting monopolistic power and the scarcity it generates. Even his newfound political optimism, however, exhibits clear limits. Despite recognizing that "poverty has few distinctions among its victims" and that black men "stood close beside [their] white brother in adversity," Garland can only envision a white working-class alliance, relegating his black characters to the margins as barely visible service workers (*Spoil* 340). No Indigenous person ever appears in *A Spoil of Office* either, even though the Meskwaki and Sauk once occupied most of Iowa until the United States forcibly pushed them west and almost completely out of the state during the nineteenth century. Garland only twice describes someone as an "Indian": his white protagonist, Bradley Talcott (*Spoil* 76). The Populist Party that emerges in the final pages of Garland's political novel proves to

---

[32] While the Homestead Act of 1862 wound up enriching large landholders and corporations, for some time it sustained a "good-life fantasy" that drove many small farmers to accept and even defend their precarious lives in a manner that embodies what Lauren Berlant means by "cruel optimism." Berlant, *Cruel Optimism* (Duke University Press, 2011), 21.

[33] See Ernesto Laclau, *On Populist Reason* (Verso, 2005).

be yet another in a series of US settler revolts that confine their demands for equality and equity to white labor.

Ditching Country Time: The Agency of Indigenous Aesthetics

If the political and cultural grievances exemplified in Garland's fiction amplify what drove rural white resentment in the United States, then the work by Zitkála-Šá, an Ihanktonwan writer and activist, shifts our attention away from white victimization to focus instead on the land grabs and colonial violence that made regional writing possible. Late twentieth-century readers most likely became introduced to Zitkála-Šá as a regional writer alongside northeastern white women authors such as Mary Wilkins Freeman and Sarah Orne Jewett, but this grouping risks reaffirming the very imperial logic that such researchers wished to challenge.[34] When examining Laura Ingalls Wilder's Little House series, the Crow Creek Dakota scholar Elizabeth Cook-Lynn establishes how regional fiction valorizes "stalwart, self-sustaining, and rugged antigovernment individuals" and overlooks "the criminal settlement of the midwestern states" often by failing to acknowledge the presence of Indigenous peoples altogether.[35] Far from embracing the aims of her local-color writing contemporaries, Zitkála-Šá resists regionalism's transformation of settler into native.

Situating Standing Rock and the 2016–2017 fight against the Dakota Access Pipeline within the long history of Indigenous resistance, Nick Estes underscores how "*traditions* of Indigenous resistance" do not remain static; instead, "by drawing upon earlier struggles and incorporating elements of them into their own experience, each generation continues to build dynamic and vital traditions of resistance."[36] These traditions do not restrict themselves to a single locality but extend into a broader world. Zitkála-Šá, for a Kul Wicasa scholar such as Estes, stands out as someone who "advocated Indigenous cultural renewal and a radical form of political self-determination."[37] Zitkála-Šá's writing unsettles settler-colonial agrarianism, which contrasts sharply with Garland's brand of local-color, a mode

---

[34] See Judith Fetterley and Marjorie Pryse, eds., *American Women Regionalists: 1850–1910* (W. W. Norton, 1992).
[35] Elizabeth Cook-Lynn, *A Separate Country: Postcoloniality and American Indian Nations* (Texas Tech University, 2012), 148–149.
[36] Nick Estes, *Our History Is the Future: Standing Rock versus the Dakota Access Pipeline, and the Long Tradition of Indigenous Resistance* (Verso Books, 2019), 21 (emphasis in original).
[37] Estes, *Our History*, 208.

in which he rebuked the imperial metropole's cultural authority by characterizing writing by rural white authors as "indigenous as the plant growth."[38] These claims to authenticity rest upon Garland's participation in "the performative tradition of aboriginal American identity" that the Dakota scholar Philip J. Deloria describes as "playing Indian."[39] Zitkála-Šá forcefully rebuts this appropriated autochthony, which legitimized settler claims to occupied land.[40] Enacting a politics too radical for regionalism, Zitkála-Šá's was smeared as the "rankest Bolshevekist" for her work with the Society of American Indians in the twentieth century.[41]

Zitkála-Šá wrote in a variety of different forms, including memoirs, folktales, poetry, essays, and an opera. Throughout this work, time becomes interwoven rather than abiding by the "chronological boundary between past and present" associated with the positivism that "dominated Western scholarship" even "among historians and philosophers who did not necessarily see themselves as positivists."[42] As a precocious child forced to attend a series of boarding schools charged with forcibly assimilating Indigenous children, Zitkála-Šá eventually attended Earlham College where she delivered a speech, "Side by Side," in 1895. She opens by recasting the British country as one of "bloody conquest" perpetrated by the "war-like Saxon."[43] Williams underscores how the British pastoral associated "the idea of a happier past" with the rural through a "suppression of work in the countryside," but Zitkála-Šá articulates how the property disparities examined by Williams's trenchant critique were first forged through imperial conquest.[44]

The scarcity pervading the economic struggles exposed by Williams and Garland therefore hides what Aileen Moreton-Robinson calls the long history of white possession that, in the mode of a palimpsest, writes "on and yet over the sovereign ground of Native Americans and Indigenous

---

[38] Garland, *Crumbling Idols*, 54.
[39] Philip J. Deloria, *Playing Indian* (Yale University Press, 1998), 8.
[40] For an account of Garland's turn away from populist local-color writing toward the western romance and its relationship to Native American administration, see Andrew Hebard, *The Poetics of Sovereignty in American Literature, 1885–1910* (Cambridge University Press, 2013), 103–132. Hebard also sets Zitkála-Šá in opposition to Garland but is principally concerned with her use of literary impressionism.
[41] Editorial, "Editorial Sanctum: The Sioux Number of Our Magazine," *American Indian*, January to March 1918, quoted in Estes, *Our History*, 217.
[42] Michel-Rolph Trouillot, *Silencing the Past: Power and the Production of History* (Beacon Press, 1995), 5.
[43] Zitkála-Šá, "Side by Side," in *American Indian Stories, Legends, and Other Writings*, ed. Cathy N. Davidson and Ada Norris (Penguin Books, 2003), 222. Hereafter cited parenthetically as "Side."
[44] Williams, *The Country and the City*, 46.

people."[45] By locating this history not on the eastern shores of North America but along the Northern Sea of the British coast, Zitkála-Šá turns against the conquerors the tropes used by European contact literature writers to describe what they perceived as violent behavior inherent to Indigenous culture.

"Side by Side," however, is not just "aimed directly at the forehead of colonialism," as the Oglala Lakota poet Layli Long Soldier puts it, but also pushes European imperialism to the periphery of an Indigenous center.[46] "At the bidding of the thought," Zitkála-Šá declares, "the tide of time rolls back four hundred years" and returns all the colonists and explorers to Europe, so that "America is one great wilderness again" ("Side" 223). Here the Indigenous subject exerts cosmic and affirmative agency over time and space, stripping away what Yellowknives Dene scholar Glen Sean Coulthard describes as those "interrelated discursive and nondiscursive facets of economic, gendered, racial, and state power" that are "structured into a relatively secure sedimented set of hierarchical social relations that continue to facilitate the *dispossession* of Indigenous peoples of their lands and self-determining authority."[47] This moment expands under "the benign influence of the Great Spirit" whereupon Indigenous peoples still struggled with "famine and disease" and experienced war and peace but survived these to enjoy the kind of sovereignty associated with "the common lot of mankind" rather than a sovereignty contingent upon individual property ownership ("Side" 223). Zitkála-Šá then returns her auditors to their present by imploring them to consider what European invasion wrought, castigating the "White Man's bullet" for heralding the forced migration of Indigenous peoples and environmental destructiveness ("Side" 224). She cites an excerpt from Lydia Huntley Sigourney's poem "Indian Names," which laments the vanishing Indian, only to dispense with this myth by demanding equality and equity for the Indigenous peoples who still inhabit a common land "side by side" with their colonizers ("Side" 226).

Having just turned twenty years old, Zitkála-Šá had crafted her own version of an aesthetics of survivance. Tonally, it reads as neither historically pessimistic nor futurist; it instead folds time out of sequence to demand sovereignty in the present. The speech's invoked temporal regression to

---

[45] Aileen Moreton-Robinson, *The White Possessive: Property, Power, and Indigenous Sovereignty* (University of Minnesota Press, 2015), 61.
[46] Layli Long Soldier, "Introduction," in *American Indian Stories* (Modern Library, 2019), xi.
[47] Glen Sean Coulthard, *Red Skin, White Masks: Rejecting the Colonial Politics of Recognition* (University of Minnesota Press, 2014), 6–7 (emphasis in original).

a time when "America is one great wilderness again" reveals a palimpsest overwritten with colonial text that cannot erase a prior Indigenous narrative in which it hardly matters whether it be through "constitutional law or imperial decree" that white colonists have "girdled the globe with their possessions" ("Side" 222). References to law, decree, and possession reveal this piece employing rhetorically crafted concessions to US values aimed at persuading those listening to her.

Zitkála-Šá later revisited her oratorical speech in her autobiographical impressions to demonstrate how her Indian boarding school failed to deracinate her from her people. While Andrew Hebard astutely notes how she "deliberately resists transforming impressions into narrative" in "Impressions of an Indian Childhood," Zitkála-Šá crafts a linear narrative associated with the conventional *Bildungsroman* in "The School Days of an Indian Girl."[48] She formally reproduces the intended aims of her involuntary reeducation as structured pedagogical sequence but depicts herself as a subject who will not assimilate to the disciplinary structure that the narrative performs. When reflecting upon delivering her speech "Side by Side," she draws attention to the hostility she confronted from some members of the audience to underscore how she learned to resist rather than to accept the imperial gaze. She recalled how one of them "threw out a large white flag" with a racist drawing on it.[49] Zitkála-Šá stresses that she "gleamed fiercely upon the throngs of palefaces" after witnessing this act only to watch the flag abruptly disappear after she learned she received one of only two prizes in oratory ("School" 103). Even though she earned the colonizers' prize for "Side by Side," she now retrospectively celebrates her own Indigenous rebellion more so than this imperial recognition.

Just as her memoirs recontextualized her prize-winning oratorical piece, so too did Zitkála-Šá's "Old Indian Legends" recontextualize those memoirs. Much in the same way that she abandons linear historicity when centering Indigeneity against the backdrop of colonial contact, her writing functions as a web of interconnections that constantly invite the reader to reevaluate their interpretation of any one text in relation to the rest. In her preface to "Legends," she explains that "Iktomi, the snare weaver, Iya, the Eater, and Old Double-Face are not wholly fanciful creatures," as these "personified elements and other spirits played in a vast world right around

---

[48] Hebard, *Poetics of Sovereignty*, 131.
[49] Zitkála-Šá, "The School Days of an Indian Girl," in Zitkála-Šá, *American Indian Stories, Legends, and Other Writings*, 102. Hereafter cited parenthetically as "School."

the center fire of the wigwam."⁵⁰ Zitkála-Šá dismantles the empiricist enclosures that separate the fantastic from the factual and the human from the nonhuman. When refracted through her memoirs, this preface bears witness to a woman whose education transformed the palimpsest, marking her with imperial traces that ultimately fail to inhume her Indigenous traditions. Her memory of the Iktomi legends instead overwrites this early trauma, enabling her to join those storytellers who "in both Dakotas, North and South" tell "the same story" again and again. These legends remain actively present as much as Zitkála-Šá acknowledges they might also be perceived as "relics of our country's once virgin soil."⁵¹ Here "our country" implies a colonialist trope intimately tied to customary views of "America" having "once" been "one great wilderness" of "virgin soil." But her "country" is not a virginal fallow field violated by the "machine image" and its "sudden appearance in the landscape"; it is instead preseeded with what are not dead relics but living memories, defying the imperial violence cloaked by the promise of "rural peace and simplicity," a promise that wound up being so scarcely realized by the settlers who imposed their pastoral tropes on the Indigenous landscape.⁵² If those in the city must insist on finding ethnic authenticity in the country, then Zitkála-Šá reminds us that it is she and her people, not Garland's farmers, who are the "real Dakotas."⁵³ Such assertions speak to an aesthetics of survivance antithetical to regionalism – a literary rebuke of the city and state that treated Indigenous peoples "as wards and not as citizens of their own freedom loving land."⁵⁴

Garland and Zitkála-Šá both hailed from the same general area of the United States, and both of them designed literary fictions that contested the repressive politics associated with viewing the country as a simple pastoral refuge from urban industry and labor unrest. In different ways, they also challenged the bureaucratic state, characterizing it as an entity that protected the interests of capital by subjecting settlers to constant precarity and violently seeking to dispossess Indigenous peoples of their own land, liberty, and literature. Later, when writing *The Book of the American Indian*, Garland would attend to grievances voiced by Indigenous peoples, but this work still

---

⁵⁰ Zitkála-Šá, "Old Indian Legends," in Zitkála-Šá, *American Indian Stories, Legends, and Other Writings*, 5.
⁵¹ Zitkála-Šá, "Old Indian Legends," 5.   ⁵² Marx, *Machine in the Garden*, 16, 19.
⁵³ Zitkála-Šá, "Impressions of an Indian Childhood," in Zitkála-Šá, *American Indian Stories, Legends, and Other Writings*, 85.
⁵⁴ Zitkála-Šá, "America's Indian Problem," in Zitkála-Šá, *American Indian Stories, Legends, and Other Writings*, 155.

figures as an example of salvage ethnography aimed at archiving vanishing cultures for a white settler audience. Zitkála-Šá, however, increasingly saw the expansive potential of Indigenous resistance, aligning her activism with the same radical activism that fueled the Paris Commune of 1871 and the labor and anarchist movements in the United States inspired by those events.[55] Her calls for Indigenous sovereignty thus ultimately rejected the pastoral and industrial appropriations of the country to dream of a global community unfettered by capital.

Further Reading

Ali, Omar H. *In the Lion's Mouth: Black Populism in the New South, 1886–1900*. University of Mississippi Press, 2010.

Dunbar-Ortiz, Roxanne. *Not A Nation of Immigrants: Settler Colonialism, White Supremacy, and a History of Erasure and Exclusion*. Beacon Press, 2021.

Foote, Stephanie. *Regional Fictions: Culture and Identity in Nineteenth-Century American Literature*. University of Wisconsin Press, 2001.

Howard, June. *The Center of the World: Regional Writing and the Puzzles of Place-Time*. Oxford University Press, 2018.

King, Tiffany Lethabo. *The Black Shoals: Offshore Formations of Black and Native Studies*. Duke University Press, 2019.

Simpson, Leanne Betasamosake. *As We Have Always Done: Indigenous Freedom through Radical Resistance*. University of Minnesota Press, 2017.

Stein, Judith. "'Of Mr. Booker T. Washington and Others': The Political Economy of Racism in the United States," *Science & Society* 38:4 (1974–1975), 422–463.

Watts, Edward. *An American Colony: Regionalism and the Roots of Midwestern Culture*. Ohio University Press, 2002.

White, Ed. *The Backcountry and the City: Colonization and Conflict in Early America*. University of Minnesota Press, 2005.

Woertendyke, Gretchen J. *Hemispheric Regionalism: Romance and the Geography of Genre*. Oxford University Press, 2016.

---

[55] For more on the transformative effect the Paris Commune had upon US politics and culture, see J. Michelle Coghlan, *Sensational Internationalism: The Paris Commune and the Remapping of American Memory in the Long Nineteenth Century* (Edinburgh University Press, 2016).

PART III
Genres

CHAPTER 16

Political Poetics: Intercrossing Discourses and American Belonging

Shira Wolosky

There is a striking change in American poetry following the turn of the nineteenth century, with considerable significance not only for poetics but as a phenomenon of American history, politics, and religion. Most agree that there are strong links between the First Great Awakening of the 1740s and the revolutionary period; but disagreement continues about just what that relationship was. In vivid contrast to the hostility in France between Church and Revolution, the "black regiment" of American clergy supported the rebellion. Sermons throughout the revolutionary period spoke for the American cause. Yet the American Revolution was itself closely identified with Enlightenment philosophies and political theories. Then, in the aftermath of the Revolution and the start of the next century, a Second Great Awakening swept America. Religion, far from being displaced by reason, became entangled with it, variously called civil millennialism, civil religion, or, in Lincoln's terms, political religion.[1]

This strange mixture between religious and Enlightenment discourses strongly marks the politics of the nineteenth century, as well as the poetics. These public discourses appear as textual mixtures and mismatches between Enlightenment and religious poetic discourses, intercrossing with other public issues: elite rule as against democratizing tendencies, each of which could mobilize both religious and republican discourses; the pull toward private interests through the unfolding market economy and industrial urban reorganization of labor and life; and whether or to what

---

[1] On civil millennialism, see Nathan O. Hatch, "The Origins of Civil Millennialism in America: New England Clergymen, War with France, and the Revolution," *The William and Mary Quarterly* 31:3 (1974), 407–430. On civil religion, see Robert Neelly Bellah, "Civil Religion in America," *Daedalus: Journal of the American Academy of Arts and Sciences* 96:1 (Winter 1967), 1–21. For Abraham Lincoln's exhortation "Let reverence for the laws ... become the *political religion* of the nation," see "The Perpetuation Address, January 27, 1838," in *The Mind and Art of Abraham Lincoln, Philosopher Statesman: Texts and Interpretations of Twenty Great Speeches*, ed. David Lowenthal (Lexington Books, 2012), 12 (emphasis in original).

extent the American polity represented an abstract set of principles to which individuals could pledge themselves or, going back to covenant theology, claimed solidarity with the specific destiny of a people. There thus emerged in America two types of belonging, abstract principles and particular nationality – both in tension with the possessive individualism that defines the self through its own self-interest.[2]

Each of these trends made competing but also intercrossing claims as to what, how, and through what institutions and discourses the American "nation" was to take shape. How was participation in and belonging to that "nation" to be brought about, and on what principles? Solidarity was challenged by the centrifugal forces unleashed as the Revolution replaced British rule; followed by disestablishment, democratization, industrialization, and sectional conflict; and not least the economic individualism where the public sphere becomes the arena not for belonging but for the advancement of private interests. How are the different "factions," as Madison calls them in *Federalist* No. 10, as well as the different states and regions, individuals, classes, religious, ethnic, and racial groups to address each other as also belonging to a common polity, society, culture, or "nation"? Is belonging itself a coercive and exclusive structure or a mode of participation? Who and how can we belong in ways at once committed to a society that is neither atomistically individual nor intolerantly collective?

It is no longer necessary to argue for the participation of poetry in public discourse. This has been a prominent note of the scholarship of the last decades, for both the eighteenth and nineteenth centuries.[3] Poetry widely circulated in the newspapers, periodicals, and magazines in which public discourse was conducted, often directed to the very social, political, and religious issues to which other print culture was devoted and which it

---

[2] For one of many discussions of this, see John Higham, *Send These to Me: Immigrants in Urban America* (Johns Hopkins University Press, 1984): there is on the one hand the claim that Americans "are a truly cosmopolitan people" creating a "universalistic and eclectic sense of national identity" (20). But these "cosmopolitan principles of the Enlightenment" resided alongside a sense of the "white Protestant northern European culture that had produced those ideals" (32). Compare with Sacvan Bercovitch's "How the Puritans Won the American Revolution," *The Massachusetts Review* 17:4 (Winter 1976), 597–630, where Bercovitch writes that "the *American Way*, of all modern ideologies, managed to circumvent the paradoxes inherent in these approaches. Of all symbols of identity, only *American* united nationality and universality, civic and spiritual selfhood, sacred and profane history, the country's past and paradise to be, in a single transcendent ideal" (616) (emphasis in original).

[3] For a fuller discussion of poetry as public discourse, see Shira Wolosky, *Poetry and Public Discourse in Nineteenth-Century America* (Palgrave Macmillan, 2010) and Shira Wolosky, *The Bible in American Poetic Culture* (Palgrave Macmillan, 2023).

actively impelled.[4] New technologies in mechanized presses and transportation increased the volume and pace of publication and distribution exponentially, carrying poetry with it. Women, newly educated through the opening of secondary schools and then seminaries and colleges in the early republic, made up new writers and new readers, with literature one of the only acceptable modes of public address: women could not be lawyers, judges, or politicians; professors or journalists; lecturers, preachers, or ministers. The notion that women only wrote about domesticity has also been confounded through various studies, although, again, not usually tied to the immense participation and activism of women in church voluntary associations.[5] Many groups crafted, sustained themselves on, and circulated newsletters, pamphlets, and periodicals, including political parties, ethnic groups as they arrived and organized reform movements, and the emerging voices of African Americans. Yet outnumbering them all were religious tracts and biblical publications, which dwarfed all other literary enterprises in the new nation up until and through the Civil War, when the American Bible Society itself distributed more than three million Bibles to the North's combatants and the South pledged to put a Bible in each soldier's hands.

The focus and method in this chapter is to track the sorts of language that poetic texts deployed, considering what cultural contexts they draw on and are drawn from and how language and culture then reside together within the textual frame. This does not close off text from context, nor readers from writers, but rather charts exactly how these positions encounter each other through the languages each recognizes, at times sharing discourses to different degrees and in different ways, at times missing each other's meanings quite starkly.

Discussion of the lyric, especially in Romantic terms, tends to focus on the self. Here the emphasis will be on public languages, as they appear in verse as in other public discourses.[6] Poetry of the period joins with other forms of public discourse in both posing questions and shaping answers to

---

[4] Higham, *Send These to Me*, 26.
[5] See Shira Wolosky, "Civic Feminism and Religious Association," in *Feminist Theory across Disciplines: Feminist Community in American Women's Poetry* (Routledge, 2013), 116–139.
[6] Aesthetic theory suffers from an ongoing split between formalist and ahistorical analysis on the one hand, as against historicist, political, social analysis on the other. In my view this is a false opposition. For discussion of "historical poetics," see Shira Wolosky, "The Claims of Rhetoric: Towards an Historical Poetics," *American Literary History* 15:1 (Spring 2003), 14–22; and Shira Wolosky, "Formal, New, and Relational Aesthetics: Dickinson's Multitexts," in Branka Arsic, ed., *American Impersonal* (Bloomsbury, 2014), 255–280. The course of these trends can be followed in *The Lyric Theory Reader: A Critical Anthology*, ed. Virginia Jackson and Yopie Prins (Johns Hopkins University Press, 2014).

them. Appearing widely in newspapers and periodicals, poetry offered an accessible, timely, and interactive medium for addressing, exchanging, and debating positions, circulating the very discourses whose claims are being argued. Like the pulpit and published political speeches, poetry could reach a wide public. "Poet's Corners" in journals allowed poetic responses in ongoing exchanges, each text taking its place in the unfolding print arena. When poems were songs, they had a greater power to enlist and inspire joint public experience than perhaps any other medium. Poetry itself became a participant in liberty as free speech as well as deploying the multiple senses of liberty and other key terms of both accord and dispute.[7]

There are many groups, causes, and politics circulating in poetry in the nineteenth century, and here I can only look, still briefly, at a few: the poetry of abolition in the work of John Greenleaf Whittier and Frances Ellen Watkins Harper; the poetry of war in Herman Melville and Emily Dickinson; ethnic voices, including Jewish and African American ones; Gilman's civic feminism; and the poetry of participation in Walt Whitman. In these cases, through its deployment and circulation of public discourses, poetry took part in and also refracted, in especially intense and focal ways, the drama, questions, and terms of belonging crucial to, and conflictual in, the unfolding of America.

John Greenleaf Whittier's poetry resides alongside his pamphlets, prose writings, newspaper editing, lobbying, and political activism, specifically in the antislavery cause he helped organize and conduct. Whittier particularly draws on the hymnal tradition, in poems he calls hymns but also in the pacing, phrasing, and diction of his poems generally. Hymns are the ultimate popular poetry, shared across generations and populations, whose spirituality conjoined with nationalism at the birth of the republic.[8] A poem called "Hymn," which Whittier wrote for the meeting of the Anti-Slavery Society in 1834, strikingly illustrates his interweaving of distinct discourses in ways that make them seamlessly strengthen and support each other.[9] Opening with allusion to the Exodus, "Hymn" takes the Old Testament typologically to foretell America, as had been the case from the first Puritan landing:

> O THOU, whose presence went before
> Our fathers in their weary way,

---

[7] Michael Cohen, *The Social Lives of Poems in Nineteenth-Century America* (University of Pennsylvania Press, 2016), 72.
[8] Nathan Hatch, *The Democratization of American Christianity* (Yale University Press, 1989), 125–154.
[9] John Greenleaf Whittier, "Hymn," in *Anti-Slavery Poems: Songs of Labor and Reform* (Houghton, Mifflin & Co., 1888), 29–30, University of Michigan Humanities Text Initiative, *American Verse Project*, https://quod.lib.umich.edu/a/amverse/BAE0044.0001.001/1:4.5?rgn=div2;view=fulltext.

Political Poetics: Discourses of Belonging

> As with Thy chosen moved of yore
> The fire by night, the cloud by day!¹⁰

Thus far, America correlates with and indeed inherits the destiny as "chosen," prefigured in Israel in the Old Testament but now translated to the American people. The next stanza adds a further dimension: expressly republican and enlightened as an appeal to freedom: "When from each temple of the free." The temple here is a site of freedom as translocated to America. America in turn offers prayers to the divine:

> A nation's song ascends to Heaven,
> Most Holy Father! unto Thee
> May not our humble prayer be given?¹¹

"Our" is here highly performative: it creates the inclusion it speaks for. What follows makes explicit who precisely is to be included and on what principles:

> Thy children all, though hue and form
> Are varied in Thine own good will,
> With Thy own holy breathings warm,
> And fashioned in Thine image still.¹²

"Our" embraces "Thy children all," with whatever variation of "hue and form." Black and white, woman and man, all are fashioned in "Thine image" – a liberal reading of the Bible that marks the intersection between religious and Enlightenment senses of the absolute value of each individual. That this Enlightened religious declaration is contradicted by actual American religion and politics does not escape Whittier:

> For those who, under Freedom's wing,
> Are bound in Slavery's fetters still:
> For those to whom Thy written word
> Of light and love is never given.¹³

Slavery contradicts Enlightenment freedom but also biblical injunction. "Thy written word" invokes both revolutionary documents and biblical text, both denied to slaves in the draconian laws against reading, writing, assembly, and the condition of enslavement itself.

---

[10] Whittier, "Hymn," 29.   [11] Whittier, "Hymn," 29.   [12] Whittier, "Hymn," 29.
[13] Whittier, "Hymn," 30.

Abolition was a foray into liberal religion, marshalling religious terms toward equality in which the image of God conjoined with Enlightenment claims for men [sic] of reason. This is a religious republicanism found in Frances Ellen Watkins Harper's poetry, one which chastises America's own failure to fulfill its pledge to its own commitments. Harper's "Bury Me in a Free Land" (1858) challenges "The Star-Spangled Banner's" claim that America is "the land of the free" in her demand not to be buried "in a land of slaves."[14] "The Freedom Bell" (1871) echoes "My Country 'Tis of Thee," which was written in 1831 by a Baptist minister, recalling the concluding line "Let Freedom ring." "The Freedom Bell" is at once more overtly sacral and more sadly ironic than the national hymn:

> Ring, aye, ring the freedom bell,
> And let its tones be loud and clear;
> With glad hosannas let it swell
> Until it reach the Bondman's ear.
>
> Through pain that wrings the life apart,
> And spasms full of deadly strife,
> And throes that shake the nation's heart,
> The fainting land renews her life.[15]

"[G]lad hosannas" celebrate freedom with prayer. However, "Until it reach the Bondman's ear" is both invitation and irony. Harper, a free black woman born in Baltimore in 1825, was active in the Underground Railroad before the Civil War and in advocating for black civil rights as well as women's suffrage after it. As she well knew, freedom had not yet come to African Americans despite the "pain" and "spasms of deadly strife" of war. Yet she casts the "nation" itself in the terms of a Christian conversion experience, "the fainting land renews her life," suggesting a nation that, through the travails of war and of slavery, itself will be reborn.

Or will it? In another characteristic Harper poetic strategy, time sequences are unclear in this 1871 text. In something like a stream of time running opposite to prophecy, Harper projects what should be present time but is not. It is after the war, and yet it is only in an unattained future that "the ransom'd slave shall kneel in prayer," in a fulfilment in freedom that has not yet arrived. This unfulfilled future that should be past marks the time grammars of the remaining stanzas. The "Freeman's joyful song" "shall

---

[14] Frances Ellen Watkins Harper, "Bury Me in a Free Land" (1858), in *Major Voices: 19th Century American Women's Poetry*, ed. Shira Wolosky (Toby Press, 2003), 164.
[15] Frances Ellen Watkins Harper, "The Freedom Bell" (1871), in *Major Voices*, ed. Wolosky, 187.

rise" but has not yet done so. As to the freedom bell, it is unclear just when the poem's "then" is meant to take place:

> Then ring, aye, ring the freedom bell,
> Proclaiming all the nation free;
> Let earth with sweet thanksgiving swell
> And heaven catch up the melody.[16]

Alas, "all" the nation is not yet "free." The republican promise should join with the religious "thanksgiving" but has not yet done so. "Ring" is an imperative directed at a future state, the present not yet fulfilling what should already have come to pass.

"Freedom" is one of the pivotal terms that stretches across both political and religious discourses. In this, it plays on ambiguities that allow it to bridge the two discourses, while at the same time carrying and indeed concealing different senses that may augment each other but may also clash.[17] The concluding lines of "The Freedom Bell" pose one form of equivocality: Is freedom an inner spiritual liberty or outward, concrete political rights? This text seems to summon the Lord's Prayer – "on earth as it is in heaven" – in the name of both sorts of freedom. The slave spirituals, first published after the war as "Songs of the Contraband" slaves who escaped to Union army lines, stretch back into the experience of slavery from long before. There, the equivocation of spiritual or political freedom served less as choice than as code. Appeals to freedom could be disguised as exclusively spiritual for white overseers assigned to monitor black religious assemblies lest they take religious, biblical discourses too concretely. Yet, as Thomas Wentworth Higginson already remarked in his notes on the war while colonel of the first black Union regiment, the lyrics of the songs had double meanings, one to fool the overseers, one to inspire African Americans – a point Frederick Douglass also makes. In code, religious freedoms are deployed against the forces of constraint imposed by political and economic orders. "Let my people go" is not merely biblical quotation or spiritual plea but a bid for political freedom from an America here cast as Pharaoh's Egypt.

This equivocation marks the slave spirituals Harper invokes as the "Freeman's joyful song," and which she more fully reenacts in her poem "Deliverance" (1901):[18]

---

[16] Harper, "The Freedom Bell," 188.
[17] See J. G. A. Pocock, *Politics, Language, Time: Essays on Political Thought and History* (University of Chicago Press, 1960), 17, 19–20, 23; and Ruth Bloch, *Visionary Republic: Millennial Themes in American Thought, 1756–1800* (Cambridge University Press, 1985), 44–46.
[18] Compare with Whittier's very popular "The Jubilee Singers" (1880): "VOICE of a people suffering long, / ... Their cry like that which Israel gave" (*Anti-Slavery Poems*, 268); University of Michigan Humanities Text Initiative, *American Verse Project*, https://quod.lib.umich.edu/a/amverse/BA

> The sons of Abraham no more
> Shall crouch 'neath Pharaoh's hand,
> Trembling with agony and dread
> He'll thrust you from the land.[19]

As in the slave spirituals, the Exodus story is reassigned in all its roles and locations. The slaves are "the sons of Abraham," white Christians are Pharaoh, and America is Egypt. The promise of redemption is claimed by African Americans – whose prophet, here, is Harper as woman poet in Moses's role. In one sense the poem marks failure. Although written in 1871, it is cast into an as-yet unaccomplished future. True emancipation is yet to come. Equality remains unfulfilled prophecy. In another sense, Harper and the slave spirituals themselves are participating in the American discourses of Exodus and redemption, claiming them as their own in an act that is profoundly American, even as dispute.[20]

The tradition of coded disguise in which political freedom is summoned through discourses of religious freedom is reenacted at the end of the nineteenth century in Paul Laurence Dunbar's "An Ante-bellum Sermon" (1896). Drawing on both slave spirituals and African American preaching, the poem is spoken in the dialect voice of a slave preacher to his congregation, as surveilled by white overseers: which is to say it is spoken in two voices, with multiple meanings to many different audiences – the slaves addressed in the text and their overseers but also the African American and white readers of Dunbar's Jim Crow time:

> An' de lan' shall hyeah his thundah,
> Lak a blas' f'om Gab'el's ho'n,
> Fu' de Lawd of hosts is mighty
> When he girds his ahmor on.
> But fu' feah some one mistakes me,
> I will pause right hyeah to say,
> Dat I'm still a-preachin' ancient,
> I ain't talkin' 'bout to-day.[21]

E0044.0001.001/1:4.65.6?rgn=div3;view=fulltext. See also his "New Exodus" (1856), in *Anti-Slavery Poems*, 348–50, University of Michigan Humanities Text Initiative, *American Verse Project*, https://quod.lib.umich.edu/a/amverse/BAE0044.0001.001/1:5.23?rgn=div2;view=fulltext.

[19] Frances Ellen Watkins Harper, "Deliverance" (1901), in *Major Voices*, ed. Wolosky, 212.
[20] Werner Sollors, *Beyond Ethnicity: Consent and Descent in American Culture* (Oxford University Press, 1986), 42–58.
[21] Paul Laurence Dunbar, *Lyrics of Lowly Life* (Chapman & Hall, 1897), 27, University of Michigan Humanities Text Initiative, *American Verse Project*, https://quod.lib.umich.edu/a/amverse/BAC5659.0001.001/1:21?rgn=div1;view=fulltext;q1=lyrics+of+lowly+life.

Dunbar's antebellum preacher brings biblical promise to his immediate present, not however as fulfilment but as prophecy of deliverance still awaiting its future. Its message splits between the white overseers who would control the biblical message to a frozen past they can claim under their own authority – "I'm still a-preachin' ancient / I ain't talkin' 'bout to-day" – and the black congregation who share the speaker's dialect and his counterclaim – "Fu' de Lawd of hosts is mighty" – opening biblical language to its multiplicity of meanings as itself investing each self with value and agency.

Religion in these cases joins with democratic equality against its abuse. But religious discourses can go the other way. Religious discourses can be mobilized in defense of freedom, but they also opposed freedom in the interests of power in both church and state. It is a telling part of Civil War history that the churches broke apart before the Union did. The same denominations professing the same doctrines and church principles each defended or opposed slavery through how each interpreted the same religious terms and biblical texts. Whittier targets the churches' defense of slavery in "Clerical Oppressors" (1836). Whittier speaks out against the men who claim biblical typology – "Men who their hands with prayer and blessing lay / On Israel's Ark of light!" – but who then "preach, and kidnap men."[22] Harper's "Bible Defence of Slavery" (1854) denounces the false, oppressive use of religion in the name of true religion:

> A reverend man, whose light should be
> The guide of age and youth,
> Brings to the shrine of slavery
> The sacrifice of truth![23]

In the reversals that characterize Harper's poetic craft, "light" is made into darkness in the (white) reverend, who should be a "guide" but is not. Slavery is the altar on which truth is "sacrificed," not served. She, however, knows what "the direst wrong of man" (165) in truth is. She knows the true "word of life" with which she contests "to give your God the lie" (165). There is no doubt in the existence of religious truth, just the distortion or recognition of it.

Harper's poem opposes against each other two competing approaches to religion and the Bible: a liberal one that saw the image of God as investing each person with equal value in ways that matched Enlightenment republicanism

---

[22] Whittier, "Clerical Oppressors," in *Anti-Slavery Poems*, 38, University of Michigan Humanities Text Initiative, *American Verse Project*, https://quod.lib.umich.edu/a/amverse/BAE0044.0001.001/1:4.9?rgn=div2;view=fulltext.
[23] Frances Ellen Watkins Harper, "Bible Defence of Slavery" (1854), in *Major Voices*, ed. Wolosky, 164–165.

and a conservative one presenting God as the ultimate authoritarian, sanctioning hierarchy in which both ministers and civil rulers alone have the power to interpret in the name of sustaining their own authority.[24] In this second, conservative reading, both church and state claim "reverence" (recalling Harper's "reverend man") for what Drew Gilpin Faust calls "authoritarian hierarchy," urging "social and political deference" through submission and obedience to God and government. "Evangelism and republicanism" as "the two touchstones of 19th century America" could be either "reactionary or progressive, elitist or democratic." The South made reactionary readings "part of Confederate identity" in the churches' support of slavery.[25]

These are the strands Henry Timrod's verse interweaves. Considered the poet laureate of the South, he redeploys the revolutionary call "To fall and crush the tyrants and the slaves" against the North ("Spring" [1862]).[26] "Ethnogenesis" (1861), hailed as the anthem of the new southern nation, projects a society that, unlike the North, would "scorn sordid gain" and instead uphold

> Unblemished honor, truth without a stain,
> Faith, justice, reverence, charitable wealth,
> And, for the poor and humble, laws which give,
> Not the mean right to buy the right to live,
> But life, and home, and health![27]

"Truth" here is aligned with the "honor" and "reverence" for hierarchy. "Charitable wealth ... for the poor and humble" signals superiority and deference, in an appeal to traditional "life and home and health" that evades the economic and racial subordination they rested on. This civic passage then merges into a religious confirmation with full biblical invocation:

> To doubt the end were want of trust in God,
> Who, if he has decreed
> That we must pass a redder sea
> Than that which rang to Miriam's holy glee,
> Will surely raise at need
> A Moses with his rod![28]

---

[24] Shira Wolosky, "Women's Bibles," in Wolosky, *Poetry and Public Discourse*, 97–113.
[25] Drew Gilpin Faust, *The Creation of Confederate Nationalism: Ideology and Identity in the Civil War South* (Louisiana State University, 1988), 32–33.
[26] Henry Timrod, "Spring" (1862), in *The Poems of Henry Timrod* (E. J. Hale & Son, 1872), 131, University of North Carolina at Chapel Hill, *Documenting the American South* (DocSouth), https://docsouth.unc.edu/southlit/timrod/timrod.html#timr131.
[27] Henry Timrod, "Ethnogenesis" (1861), in *The Poems of Henry Timrod*, 103.
[28] Timrod, "Ethnogenesis," 103.

The biblical Red Sea becomes a Civil War sea of blood as apocalyptic image, his own song like Miriam's, with "trust in God" that a new Moses like Christ will part the sea with his rod.

In the North, too, there were poets who trumpeted martial tones, urging political consolidation under the banner of the republic:

> You whom the fathers made free and defended,
> Stain not the scroll that emblazons their fame!
> You whose fair heritage spotless descended,
> Leave not your children a birthright of shame!²⁹

Like Timrod, Oliver Wendell Holmes Sr., doctor, poet, and Harvard alumnus, appeals to a "fair heritage spotless descended" that "the fathers made free and defended." His are the New England Puritan fathers, whose birthright he as a Boston Brahmin inherits, certainly in the name of freedom but one slanted toward elite privilege. The call here is secular and civic, but the poem, "Never or Now" (1862), continues with hints of millennial horizon, albeit in a sort of generalized, half-secular gesture:

> Now is the day and the hour of salvation, –
> Never or now! peals the trumpet of doom!³⁰

Much popular poetry veered between political and religious poetics. However, two unpopular mid-century poets, Emily Dickinson and Herman Melville, resisted these dominant discourses. What is piecemeal in Melville's *Battle-Pieces and Aspects of the War* (1866) is the rhetoric, both civic and religious, of the war the volume tracks. *The Rebellion Record*, his main historical and rhetorical source, was a remarkable collection of public notices and speeches from both North and South during the war. It made plain how the warring sections shared the same American discourses, each claiming to represent and embody them authentically against the other. At once a parody and a reflection of the newspaper culture and newspaper power that was mobilized as part of both war efforts, and the war poetry circulating in the press, *Battle-Pieces* breaks apart the language webs out of which events and representation were both

---

[29] Oliver Wendell Holmes, "Never or Now" (1862), in *The Poetical Works of Oliver Wendell Holmes* (Houghton Mifflin, 1975), 193, *Project Gutenberg*, www.gutenberg.org/cache/epub/7400/pg7400.html.
[30] Holmes, "Never or Now," 193.

woven.[31] Consider the first poem from *Battle-Pieces*, "The Portent" (1859):

> Hanging from the beam,
> Slowly swaying (such the law),
> Gaunt the shadow on your green,
>   Shenandoah!
> The cut is on the crown
> (Lo, John Brown),
> And the stabs shall heal no more.
>
> Hidden in the cap
>   Is the anguish none can draw;
> So your future veils its face,
>   Shenandoah!
> But the streaming beard is shown
> (Weird John Brown),
> The meteor of the war.[32]

John Brown's attack on Harpers Ferry in 1859 realized the most aggressive antislavery activism and the South's worst fears of incitement to slave rebellion. The ensuing trial sharply divided even the antislavery community, with Emerson calling Brown "a pure idealist" whose "martyrdom ... will make the gallows glorious like the cross," in response to which Hawthorne wrote in "Chiefly about War Matters" (1862): "Nobody was ever more justly hanged."[33] Even Horace Greeley and William Lloyd Garrison were severe.[34] Melville found the Civil War vortex uninterpretable. The unmetrical, unrhymable "Shenandoah" registers the lack of alignment between event and consequence, the world's unreadability as to how experiences fit into meaningful pattern. The future is veiled, all is in shadow, stabs will not heal. All that is certain is "The meteor of the war," which John Brown's body unknowingly launched. Raised in the strictly Calvinist Dutch Reformed Church, Melville grew up with predestinarian theologies of preestablished total designs. This comes to the surface, or rather, is hidden here, in the Christic hanging and crown of John Brown.

---

[31] Shira Wolosky, "Fragmented Rhetoric in *Battle-Pieces*," in Wolosky, *Poetry and Public Discourse*, 113–125.
[32] Herman Melville, "The Portent" (1859), in *Selected Poems of Herman Melville*, ed. Hennig Cohen (Fordham University Press, 1991), 2.
[33] Emerson and Hawthorne are each quoted in John J. McDonald's "Emerson and John Brown," *The New England Quarterly* 44:3 (1971), 377–396, Emerson on 386 and 387n27, and Hawthorne on 387n29.
[34] John Stauffer and Zoe Trodd's *Meteor of War: The John Brown Story* (Brandywine Press, 2004) offers an anthology of additional responses.

But Brown does not bring healing or revelation. The intersection between time and eternity, event and meaning, is severed. Melville in this way challenges what were the central modes of interpreting, justifying, and indeed fighting the Civil War.

Emily Dickinson, not unlike Melville, lived the war in sequestered distance.[35] But, as Hawthorne remarked (also from his remote consulship in England), there was no place the war did not penetrate. In Dickinson, the paradoxes of American discourses become the center of attention. America treasured individual rights and individual enterprise, both as Enlightenment commitment to the equality of all and the increasingly market values that interpreted pursuit of happiness as the way to wealth. But how then could civic virtue in republican senses mobilize participation in a joint national life? Religious discourses also proclaimed equality, grounded in the image of God, yet with different implications from the individualist rights carrier of natural law. Religion remained a call to solidarity, a commitment to others as sharing divine blessings as well as chastisements. But across all arenas – political, religious, and economic – solidarity remained in tension with individual freedoms and enterprise.

Dickinson's poetic eye and word are trained on just these splits in American nationality:

> Robbed by Death – but that was easy –
> To the failing Eye
> I could hold the latest Glowing –
> Robbed by Liberty
>
> For Her Jugular Defences –
> This, too, I endured –
> Hint of Glory – it afforded –
> For the Brave Beloved –
>
> Fraud of Distance – Fraud of Danger,
> Fraud of Death – to bear –
> It is Bounty – to Suspense's
> Vague Calamity –
>
> Stalking our entire Possession
> On a Hair's result –
> Then – seesawing – coolly – on it –
> Trying if it split –[36]

---

[35] Shira Wolosky, *Emily Dickinson: A Voice of War* (Yale University Press, 1984), 33, 62.
[36] *Emily Dickinson's Poems As She Preserved Them*, ed. Cristanne Miller (Harvard University Press, 2016), 413. This edition supersedes earlier ones.

To be "Robbed by Death" is easy: that is what death does. To be "Robbed by Liberty," however, poses an oxymoron. Liberty is what protects life. Both rights are promised in the Declaration. But when life is called – demanded? – for "Defences" of liberty itself, the terms contradict each other. "Glory" as "afforded" likewise veers toward contradiction. It introduces the economic language that Dickinson habitually and always ironically sneaks into her verse. Economic reductions of the self in industrializing America are also intrinsic to the independent individual of self-owning possessive individualism, which Locke suggests in equating liberty with property.[37] But to defend independence here requires its sacrifice for a "Glory" that the poem suspects to be a "Fraud of Distance – Fraud of Danger." The "Brave" remain "Beloved." But the "Bounty" is not theirs. In another economic term – "Possession" – Dickinson's text finally splits between these paradoxes of liberty, in which defending the state in the name of liberty requires losing one's own.

Melville mistakenly thought he was writing the sort of war verse that had gained wide circulation. Dickinson turned her back on that sort of publicity ("I'm nobody," she declared, disdaining to be "public like a frog"), although she did see herself as writing a "Letter to the World." In her verse she certainly contended with the variety of American domains she lived through, ensnaring their rhetorics in her own poetic traps.[38] Most poetry, however, both before and after the war, did so less as critique of American discourses than as investment in them: attempting to proclaim either a particular discourse as the true American one or to harmonize differences. And a majority of nineteenth-century verse, surprisingly from the viewpoint of twentieth-century aestheticism, was fully intentioned as public and often political address.

The coercions and exclusions that accompany religious belonging led some to abandon religious discourses, except in order to expose them. Charlotte Gilman at the end of the century writes poetry as a form of feminist polemic, in which, in a poem like "The Holy Stove" (1893), the sacralization of domesticity is parodied. In the poem "Homes: A Sestina" (1893), domesticity itself speaks in ironic reversal of what Gilman's feminism would say:

> And are we not the woman's perfect world,
> Prescribed by nature and ordained of God,
> Beyond which she can have no right desires,
> No need for service other than in homes?[39]

---

[37] C. B. MacPherson, *The Political Theory of Possessive Individualism: Hobbes to Locke* (Oxford University Press, 1966).
[38] Shira Wolosky, "Modest Selves: Dickinson's Critique of American Identity," in Gudrun Grabher and Martina Antretter, eds., *Emily Dickinson at Home* (Wissenschaftlicher Verlag Trier, 2001), 1–12.
[39] Charlotte Gilman, "Homes: A Sestina" (1893), in *Major Voices*, ed. Wolosky, 515.

Gilman draws her discourse resources from a civic republicanism that she specifically distances from the economic individualism increasingly dominant and driving America from any sort of commonwealth to a battleground of privatized competition. Her poem "Nationalism" (1893) declares common labor for common good:

> The nation is a unit. That which makes
> You an American of our to-day,
> Requires the nation and its history,
> Requires the sum of all our citizens,
> Requires the product of our common toil,
> Requires the freedom of our common laws,
> The common heart of our humanity.[40]

Gilman is in her own way speaking for a mode of belonging, equal between all genders and citizens who share the burden of freedom – the poem lists requirements – in common laws and common toil. Hers is a vision at once national and enlightened, with principles all can embrace. This is not a freedom of atomized individuals or balkanized groups. Gilman speaks in the performative "our" that brings people to share a common language each in his and her own way.

I will turn next to what is an icon of public, civic poetry in America, Emma Lazarus's Statue of Liberty poem "The New Colossus" (1883):

> "Keep, ancient lands, your storied pomp!" cries she
> With silent lips. "Give me your tired, your poor,
> Your huddled masses yearning to breathe free,
> The wretched refuse of your teeming shore.
> Send these, the homeless, tempest-tost to me,
> I lift my lamp beside the golden door!"[41]

Lazarus is one of the first declaredly "ethnic" voices in America, reflecting directly on her status as both a minority and an American. Wealthy and privately educated, she first saw herself as belonging to the elite intellectual class of New England, writing decorous poetry softly gendered. Both voice and membership were more or less radically transformed by a visit to Ward Island with her rabbi, where she witnessed the mass immigration of Jews from pogroms in Russia in 1882. She then plunged into polemical essays and prophetic poems proclaiming newly emerging modes of Jewish peoplehood, both in America and in a restored Jewish homeland. This sonnet, written to

---

[40] Charlotte Gilman, "Nationalism" (1893), in *Major Voices*, ed. Wolosky, 559.
[41] Emma Lazarus, "The New Colossus" (1883), in *Major Voices*, ed. Wolosky, 451.

help raise funds for the pedestal of the Statue of Liberty, transformed it from a French gift celebrating French and American friendship to a vision of America as the home for all, welcoming diverse peoples who could together share both liberty and solidarity. The poem is very specifically gendered, according to the norms of the nineteenth century. Against the very male "brazen Giant of Greek fame" (450) she counters a feminized America, casting the country in the image of American women who took on the work of community in what was called benevolence: charity, hospital care, orphan care, teaching – education itself was in the hands of women. The poem has then civic and moral, feminized and historical dimensions. Interestingly and importantly for the portrait of America as inclusive yet respecting and supporting differences, also encoded is a Jewish dimension. Rachel as "Mother of Exiles" and Deborah as "A mighty woman with a torch, whose flame / Is the imprisoned lightning" are stitched into the poem. The lamp lifted beside the golden door appears in many Lazarus poems as a Hanukkah menorah, standing for Jewish cultural life and survival.[42] The lamp that welcomes refugees and immigrants to America is thus both Jewish and American, dedicated to the thriving of both difference and solidarity.

But the greatest performative poet of individual belonging is surely Walt Whitman. He concludes his "Song of Myself" (1891), by which he means each self:

> Failing to fetch me at first keep encouraged,
> Missing me one place search another,
> I stop somewhere waiting for you.[43]

His invitation is to take part in shaping America where citizenship and poetic creativity are images and models for each other. As he writes in his 1855 "Preface" to *Leaves of Grass*, "The United States themselves are essentially the greatest poem."[44] But that is precisely his invitation: to create an America of intertwining voices, an America he is acutely aware does not yet exist. "I Sing the Body Electric" (1891) makes this summons out of the depths of what Melville, in the poem "Misgivings" (1860), calls "the world's fairest hope linked with man's foulest crime"[45]:

---

[42] Shira Wolosky, "Emma Lazarus's American-Jewish Prophetics," in Wolosky, *Poetry and Public Discourse*, 139–152.
[43] Walt Whitman, "Song of Myself" (1891), in *Walt Whitman: Poetry and Prose*, ed. Justin Kaplan (Library of America, 1996), 247.
[44] Walt Whitman, "Preface" (1855), in *Poetry and Prose*, ed. Kaplan, 5.
[45] Herman Melville, "Misgivings" (1860), in *Selected Poems*, ed. Cohen, 3.

> A man's body at auction,
> (For before the war I often go to the slave-mart and watch the sale,)
>
> I help the auctioneer, the sloven does not half know his business.
>
> Gentlemen look on this wonder.
> Whatever the bids of the bidders they cannot be high enough for it . . .
>
> In this head the all-baffling brain,
> In it and below it the makings of heroes . . .
>
> This is not only one man, this the father of those who shall be fathers in their turns,
> In him the start of populous states and rich republics,
> Of him countless immortal lives with countless embodiments and enjoyments.[46]

Whitman's text is a direct address and a direct summons to witness the slave auction. But he commandeers the very language of the auction, which would reduce human being to inert thinghood, sheer commodity, and transforms it into a declaration of illimitable and infinite value. He does so through reference to the public language of civic republicanism, the equality and value of each person: "Of him countless immortal lives with countless embodiments and enjoyments." These are the citizens who will make up "populous states and rich republics," emphatically including the African Americans now excluded from citizenship as chattel to be sold. He also invokes traditions of religious individualism with the person as created "wonder," meaning miracle, the person in the image of God. In a stunning rhetorical inversion, the poem converts the auction scene of utmost degradation to the revelation of the incalculable value of the individual, transforming economic language itself, as each one, in public language, is declared "the makings of heroes."

Further Reading

Barrett, Faith. *To Fight Aloud Is Very Brave: American Poetry and the Civil War*. University of Massachusetts Press, 2012.

Cohen, Michael. *The Social Lives of Poems in Nineteenth-Century America*. University of Pennsylvania Press, 2015.

Erkkila, Betsy. *Whitman the Political Poet*. Oxford University Press, 1989.

Erkkila, Betsy. *The Whitman Revolution: Sex, Poetry, and Politics*. University of Iowa Press, 2020.

---

[46] Walt Whitman, "I Sing the Body Electric" (1891), in *Walt Whitman: Poetry and Prose*, ed. Justin Kaplan (Library of America, 1996), 123.

Folsom, Ed. "Walt Whitman's Invention of a Democratic Poetry." In Alfred Bendixen and Stephen Burt, eds., *The Cambridge History of American Poetry*. Cambridge University Press, 2014, 329–359.

Hoffman, Tyler. "Political Poets and Naturalism." In Alfred Bendixen and Stephen Burt, eds., *The Cambridge History of American Poetry*. Cambridge University Press, 2014, 472–494.

Jackson, Virginia. *Before Modernism: Inventing American Lyric*. Princeton University Press, 2023.

Kete, Mary Louise. "The Reception of Nineteenth-Century American Poetry." In Kerry Larson, ed., *The Cambridge Companion to Nineteenth-Century American Poetry*. Cambridge University Press, 2011, 13–35.

Loeffelholz, Mary. *From School to Salon: Reading Nineteenth-Century American Women's Poetry*. Princeton University Press, 2004.

Loeffelholtz, Mary. "Other Voices, Other Verses: Cultures of American Poetry at Midcentury." In Alfred Bendixen and Stephen Burt, eds., *The Cambridge History of American Poetry*. Cambridge University Press, 2014, 282–305.

Lootens, Tricia. *The Political Poetess: Victorian Femininity, Race, and the Legacy of Separate Spheres*. Princeton University Press, 2017.

Renker, Elizabeth. "Nineteenth-Century American Women's Poetry: Past and Prospects." In Dale M. Bauer, ed., *The Cambridge History of American Women's Literature*. Cambridge University Press, 2012, 232–255.

Seery, John E., ed. *A Political Companion to Walt Whitman*. University Press of Kentucky, 2011.

Wolosky, Shira. *Poetry and Public Discourse in Nineteenth-Century America*. Palgrave Macmillan, 2010.

CHAPTER 17

Staging Debate in American Drama: Cheeses and Politics and Pigs

Heather S. Nathans

Searching for the word "politics" in the Chadwyck-Healey "American Drama 1714–1915" database of plays nets hundreds of hits among a century's worth of dramatic texts from 1800 to 1899.[1] In 1815, the playwright David Humphreys's comedy *The Yankey in England* acknowledged the rapidly shifting political landscape of the time: "The revolutions in taste as well as in politics, succeed each other with such unprecedented rapidity, that you, who are so much in vogue, and possess so much power today, instead of giving, may be under the necessity of receiving protection to-morrow."[2] Humphreys highlights *power* as a key theme in understanding political sway, and "revolutions" suggests a constant state of upheaval in US society. This chapter explores the oscillations of political power and the "revolutions" – both violent and subtle – that appeared on the US stage throughout the nineteenth century. I begin with a brief contextual overview of the expansion of nineteenth-century US theater. I then turn to a discussion of some the noisy "revolutions" (riots) in US theaters, followed by an exploration of some of the "quieter" revolutions visible in both familiar and unfamiliar play texts.

After a brief banishment during the Revolution, theater companies rapidly reasserted themselves in the postwar world. Rising urban elite groups imported British stars and repertoires of British, French, and German plays.[3] Touring companies traveled circuits from Georgia to Maine, and their frequent stops in impromptu performance sites between

---

[1] Unless otherwise noted, all play citations come from the Chadwyck-Healey database, available on ProQuest. Please note that page numbers from the Chadwyck-Healey database may not necessarily reflect page numbers in original printed versions of the plays. When available, I have also included act and scene numbers for the citations.
[2] David Humphreys, *The Yankey in England* (publisher unknown, 1815), 4, www.proquest.com/books/yankey-england-1815/docview/2138580618/se-2?accountid=14434.
[3] See Heather S. Nathans, *Early American Theatre from the Revolution to Thomas Jefferson: Into the Hands of the People* (Cambridge University Press, 2003), 71–90.

major cities fostered a widespread taste for theatergoing.[4] As white settlers migrated beyond the East Coast, expanding systems of slavery across the South and forcing Indigenous peoples further westward, theatrical entertainments followed them.[5] Some white American playwrights created Native American characters framed as the "last" of their tribes, thus burying Indigenous futurity and tacitly acknowledging the US government's policy of genocide.[6] Others crafted stereotypically childish, sly, or subservient enslaved black characters.[7] And still others trafficked in ethnic stereotypes, simultaneously mocking Irish, Asian, Jewish, and other non-Anglo-European figures and blaming them for problems including labor issues and urban crime. By animating these fantasy figures, the theater fueled white Americans' colonizing mission. However, it also debated the thorny political questions about settler-colonial expansion westward and the country's reliance on enslaved and immigrant labor.

Steamboat and railroad systems brought theatrical entertainments to more audiences, creating new national conversations about plays such as *Uncle Tom's Cabin* (1852). Both before and after the Civil War, black Americans developed their own theater companies, frequently encountering ridicule and persecution from white audiences who imagined such performances as incursions into white privilege.[8] Growing numbers of Irish and Jewish immigrants shifted the issues and the characters represented on the stage, inviting audiences into domestic spheres that challenged normative white middle-class identity.[9] Asian communities

---

[4] See Rosemarie K. Bank, *Theatre Culture in America, 1825–1860* (Cambridge University Press, 1997), 27–59; and Bruce McConachie, *Melodramatic Formations: American Theatre and Society, 1820–1870* (University of Iowa Press, 1992), 5–29.

[5] See Joshua Bellin, *Medicine Bundle: Indian Sacred Performance and American Literature, 1824–1932* (University of Pennsylvania Press, 2008), 78–133.

[6] See Bellin, *Medicine Bundle*, 78–133; Matthew Rebhorn, *Pioneer Performances: Staging the Frontier* (Oxford University Press, 2012), 1–24; and Jill Lepore, *The Name of War: King Philip's War and the Origins of American Identity* (Vintage Books, 1999), 191–226.

[7] See Sarah Meer, *Uncle Tom Mania: Slavery, Minstrelsy, and Transatlantic Culture in the 1850s* (University of Georgia Press, 2005), 19–72; John L. Brooke, *"There Is a North": Fugitive Slaves, Political Crisis, and Cultural Transformation in the Coming of the Civil War* (University of Massachusetts Press, 2019), 116–158; and Amy E. Hughes, *Spectacles of Reform: Theatre and Activism in Nineteenth-Century America* (University of Michigan Press, 2012), 86–117.

[8] See Douglas A. Jones, Jr., *The Captive Stage: Performance and the Pro-Slavery Imagination of the Antebellum North* (University of Michigan Press, 2014), 50–74; Marvin McAllister, *Whiting Up: Whiteface Minstrels and Stage Europeans in African American Performance* (University of North Carolina Press, 2011), 50–72; and Heather S. Nathans, *Slavery and Sentiment on the American Stage, 1787–1861* (Cambridge University Press, 2009), 133–169.

[9] See Michelle Granshaw, *Irish on the Move: Performing Mobility in American Variety Theatre* (University of Iowa Press, 2019), 31–70; Nahma Sandrow, "Yiddish Theatre in America," in Hana Wirth-Nesher, ed., *The Cambridge History of Jewish American Literature* (Cambridge University Press, 2015), 224–241; Edna Nahshon, *New York's Yiddish Theatre from the Bowery to Broadway* (Columbia University Press,

established their own theaters offering refuges from the minstrel, vaudeville, and burlesque stages that routinely presented degrading images of Asian identities.[10]

Political controversies inevitably have roots entangled in many causes, and I hope this chapter illuminates the ways that political issues manifested onstage in both expected *and* unexpected ways, suggesting ways to situate dramatic literature and theatrical entertainments alongside each other in an *everyday* political discourse. For example, plays such as *Rural Felicity* (1801), *The Essex Junto* (1802), *Whigs and Democrats* (1839), *A Glance at New York* (1848), *The Mulligan Guard Ball* (1879), and *Shenandoah* (1897) rely on scenes of daily life, rather than lavish spectacle, to trace political conflicts such as the Federalist/Republican schisms in the early 1800s, antebellum nativism, postwar reconciliations, and anti-immigration policies.[11] By contrast, comedies, tragedies, and pageants such as *She Would Be a Soldier* (1819), *Metamora* (1829), *The Octoroon* (1859), and Buffalo Bill's Wild West Show (1883) showcase Indigenous peoples as symbols of the unspoiled frontier *and* as threats to white civilization. In many of these more extravagant works, the heightened representations emphasize the "alien" quality of Native Americans, implicitly distancing them from the "reality" of white American life.

Popular melodramas such as *The Drunkard* (1844), *Under the Gaslight* (1867), and *Bertha the Sewing Machine Girl* (1871) trace shifting representations of women from domestic "angels in the house" to factory girls inspiring revolts as part of burgeoning labor movements. Their struggles highlight the gap between middle-class visions of white female domestic bliss and the social, political, and economic reality encountered by so many women, particularly in the post–Civil War era.

Works including *Uncle Tom's Cabin* (1852), *The Escape* (1858), and *Clorindy: The Origin of the Cakewalk* (1898; the first all-black show on Broadway) reveal the struggle of black Americans to combat the systemic racism that permeated every aspect of American society. Black Americans

---

2016), 8–49; and Alison Kibler, *Censoring Racial Ridicule: Irish, Jewish, and African American Struggles over Race and Representation, 1890–1930* (University of North Carolina Press, 2015), 21–50.

[10] See Shannon Steen, *Racial Geometries of the Black Atlantic, Asian Pacific and American Theatre* (Palgrave Macmillan, 2010), 33–62.

[11] In the prologue to *Whigs and Democrats*, James Ewell Heath contends that "Dramatic interest may be sustained by the delineation of simple, natural, everyday circumstances, without the aid of wild and extravagant incidents"; see Heath 's *Whigs and Democrats; or Love of No Politics* (Richmond: 1839), 5, www.proquest.com/books/whigs-democrats-1839/docview/2138581820/se-2?accountid=14434.

fought to see their own stories represented, rather than the humiliating minstrel shows that glorified plantation life and demeaned black culture.

Indeed, many of the "revolutions" on nineteenth-century US stages document standoffs between largely white, middle- or upper-class Gentile consumers versus those who seemed to threaten their claims to authority (blacks, Native Americans, non-Gentiles, immigrants, white working-class men, women, etc.). While the revolutionary groups shifted over the century, struggles for cultural, economic, political, and social dominance remained at the core of their conflicts, and dramatic works drew upon these conflicts as a source of plots and characters.

Cheeses and Politics and Pigs

The subtitle of this chapter, "Cheeses, and Politics and Pigs," comes from a Thomas Morton comedy, *The School of Reform* (1805).[12] The line emphasizes the "ordinariness" (and perhaps even unavoidability) of political discourse. Morton's "ordinary" play prompted one Philadelphia newspaper to describe it as a hackneyed piece, trading in characters "too well-known ... Everyone moralizes, weeps, and melts, until the patience of the reader is quite dissolved."[13] As the scornful reviewer suggests, audiences expected certain tropes in their comedies, and authors struggled to inject novelty into familiar settings. Nevertheless, Morton's play ran for more than fifty performances during the 1805 London season, and when it debuted on the US stage in 1806, a New York paper assured audiences that they might "reasonably anticipate much delight and edification."[14] Intriguingly, the paper's praise implies expectations about the "proper" role of theater in US culture – that it should entertain and educate, rather than rile spectators. It also suggests expectations for audience behavior, important in an era in which party adherents regularly acted out political rivalries in the playhouse. Only a decade before Morton's comedy debuted, a theatrical prologue at Boston's Federal Street Theatre had implored fractious audiences to "Let austere politics one hour flee / And join in free democracy of glee!"[15] Did the trite plot of *The School of Reform* (a tale of a son lost and miraculously recovered after many misadventures and misunderstandings) offer an escape, calming a fraught political

---

[12] Thomas Morton, *The School of Reform* (London, 1805), Act I, sc. ii, 22. www.proquest.com/books/school-reform-1805/docview/2138582462/se-2?accountid=14434.
[13] "Literary Selections," *United States' Gazette* (Philadelphia) 29:4109 (October 24, 1805), 2.
[14] "Communication. Theatrical," *American Citizen* (New York) 6:1883 (April 16, 1806), 2.
[15] Prologue quoted in Nathans, *Early American Theatre*, 71.

environment both within and beyond the playhouse? Or, as Jay Fliegelman argues, did such tales of filial reconciliation echo postwar political themes and invite audiences to perform as better political actors?[16]

The question of what constituted "education" in the playhouse raises question about the *kind* of education on offer, from whom, to whom, and for what ends. Theater founders often envisioned dramatic performances as providing an ennobling classical discourse to elevate political debate. Audiences routinely exercised their free will in interpreting or ignoring these pacifying lessons and acting out, sometimes violently, their responses to the plays *and* to their would-be instructors. Could serving up a menu of "cheeses, politics, and pigs" strike a balance between extremes?

For instance, in the 1859 drama *Ossawattomie Brown*, Kate Edwards Swayze reframes the Harpers Ferry uprising in an improbable love story. This incongruously domestic drama debuted two weeks after John Brown's execution for his raid on the federal armory at Harpers Ferry. And the play's title references Brown's role in 1856's "Bleeding Kansas" turmoil. Yet, in apparent indifference to these bloody events, Swayze's play opens with Brown's female servant, Jeptha, bringing in a wedding cake for Brown's son, Frederick, while joking about their neighbors' resemblance to various farm animals. The audience next learns that Brown's daughter, Alice, is also engaged; she plans to marry a man named Ralph Dearborn, who once saved Brown's life. However, Ralph's father wants him to marry his wealthy cousin, Lucy, and objects to his son's association with the daughter of "an outlaw and a murderer."[17] As Jeptha observes, "the queer shines the old man's been cutting up" have thwarted Alice's romance, but thankfully Alice and Ralph are reconciled – *after* Brown's execution and the revelation that she was not his daughter.[18] Hearing Brown's armed insurrections described as "queer shines" and seeing Swayze's play swerve away from Brown's final moments in prison to Alice and Ralph's reunion may strike a modern reader as bizarre. Weeping for his sons who died in the abolitionist cause, Brown proclaims:

> Whatever is represented to the contrary, believe me, our sole object was to free the slaves, from motives of philanthropy. We look upon ourselves as

---

[16] Jay Fliegelman, *Prodigals and Pilgrims: The American Revolution against Patriarchal Authority, 1750–1800* (Cambridge University Press, 1982), 197–226.
[17] Kate Edwards Swayze, *Ossawattomie Brown* (Samuel French, 1859), Act II, sc. iii, 14, www.proquest.com/books/ossawattomie-brown-1859/docview/2138582532/se-2?accountid=14434. Authorship is often attributed to Swayze's husband (J. C. Swayze).
[18] Swayze, *Ossawattomie Brown*, Act III, sc. ii, 19, www.proquest.com/books/ossawattomie-brown-1859/docview/2138582532/se-2?accountid=14434.

workers in a great and good cause, to which we have sacrificed our lives. I would have wished it otherwise, but being so, we lay them down freely, and trust that the future will beam on more successful efforts.[19]

The scene shifts abruptly from Brown's political prophecy, and the play closes with Alice and Ralph clasping hands to receive his father's blessing. Cheeses and politics and pigs indeed.

Despite the jarring switch in tone, Swayze's romantic framework may have served a larger political purpose. The theater scholar Elizabeth Reitz Mullenix suggests that Kate Edwards Swayze (whose husband was a political journalist) enveloped Brown's rebellion – politics – in a domestic drama – cheeses and pigs – to "recoup John Brown for an embryonic Republican Party bent on spinning Brown's life and works so as to avoid associations with fanaticism."[20] Locating him amidst homely concerns about wedding cakes and livestock could make Brown more relatable as a father and husband. Mullenix also contends that Jeptha, the rustic character, was in fact "deliberately constructed [as a] Republican *raisonneur*" (the spokesperson for the playwright's Republican views).[21]

Plays like Swayze's that appeared during fraught political times prompt numerous questions: How did nineteenth-century American audiences engage with politics in the playhouse? Did they come anticipating debate and riot over political schisms, abolition, immigration, and so on? Did they come for escapist entertainment – a "free democracy of glee"? How did nineteenth-century American playwrights infuse their works with political content – choosing between the familiar and the spectacular to convey their messages? And how did theater managers and actors navigate choppy political waters in live performance?

"Do You Come Here to Breed a Riot in Our Camp?"

Painful firsthand experience taught many theater managers to shy away from openly expressing political opinions or allegiances.[22] Throughout the 1790s, hapless performers and musicians found themselves showered with

---

[19] Swayze, *Ossawattomie Brown*, Act III, sc. vi, 25, www.proquest.com/books/ossawattomie-brown-1859/docview/2138582532/se-2?accountid=14434.

[20] Elizabeth Reitz Mullenix, "Dion Boucicault's *The Octoroon* and the Work of Republicanism," in Beth Osborne and Christine Woodworth, eds., *Working in the Wings: New Perspectives on Theatre History and Labor* (Southern Illinois University Press, 2015), 141–155, 150.

[21] Mullenix, "Dion Boucicault," 153n22.

[22] The quote "Do you come here to breed a riot in our camp?" in the section title is from Mordecai Noah, *She Would Be a Soldier, or The Plains of Chippewa* (Longworth, 1819), www.proquest.com/books/she-would-be-soldier-1819/docview/2138581842/se-2?accountid=14434.

broken glass and other missiles if plays or songs antagonized competing parties.²³ New York's Bowery Theatre erupted in a riot on July 9, 1834, because theater manager George Farren expressed sympathy for the abolitionist cause. As the *Newark Daily Advertiser* reported, "There is no withstanding popular feeling in this country. Once excited, like a rushing torrent it sweeps everything before it."²⁴ A furor arose in Philadelphia's Chestnut Street Theatre during the contested 1844 election season when the actor Thomas "Daddy" Rice, famous for his racist blackface "Jim Crow" character, brought a raccoon onstage during a burlesque version of *Othello*. Many assumed the animal represented the Whig candidate Henry Clay. The theater historian Aaron Tobiason observes that Rice's ill-judged move "instantly drew the ire of Democrats in the audience, who demanded that their cherished mascot, the rooster, be brought onstage to answer the raccoon's implicit challenge."²⁵ Perhaps the best-known, bloodiest, and most politicized theater-related incident occurred on May 10, 1849, with the Astor Place Riot. Factions from the city's elite and working classes faced off over two productions of *Macbeth* in a clash that left roughly thirty Americans dead and a nation aghast at the carnage.²⁶

Politically driven theater riots persisted into the second half of the nineteenth century, suggesting that far from offering a refuge from violence, theatrical entertainments often became fluid extensions of political debates.²⁷ After the Civil War, a Pennsylvania newspaper reported a *threatened* riot at Washington DC's National Theatre on June 10, 1869, as a result of a new law admitting black spectators. The article suggested that a fear of "negro gangs" rampaging in the city kept white audiences away from the theater and "five thousand white registered voters ... away from the polls."²⁸

Throughout the 1870s, white policemen harassed Chinese theatergoers in San Francisco, staging ambushes, invading theaters on the pretext of

---

²³ See Nathans, *Early American Theatre*, 71–90.   ²⁴ *Newark Daily Advertiser* (July 10, 1834), 2.
²⁵ Aaron Tobiason, "An Extraordinary Power: Journalist Playwrights, The Free Press, and The Politics of the American Stage, 1794–1844" (PhD dissertation, University of Maryland, 2013), 9.
²⁶ For more on the riot see, McConachie, *Melodramatic Formations*, 144–154; and Nigel Cliff, *The Shakespeare Riots: Revenge, Drama, and Death in Nineteenth-Century America* (Random House, 2007).
²⁷ For example, April 12, 1860, witnessed an attack on Bowery Theatre manager J. H. Allen by the Irish American "Dead Rabbits" gang of Five Points. "The Riot in the Bowery Theatre to the Editor of the Herald Bowery Theatre, April 13, 1860," *New York Herald*, no. 8620 (April 14, 1860), 7. Violence involving Irish immigrant labor resurfaced with the Draft Riots of 1863.
²⁸ "The Washington Riot! Partial Development of the Great Radical Plot Against Democracy," *Patriot* (Harrisburg, Pennsylvania), no. 1 (June 10, 1869) 1.

"disarming" audience members or enforcing curfews, beating actors and spectators alike, and marching them to prison by tying their queues of hair together.[29] These riots paralleled a growing anti-Asian movement in the United States, fueled by white-led labor unions *and* widespread racist rhetoric characterizing the Chinese as carriers of disease, and which culminated in the 1882 Chinese Exclusion Act.[30]

Yet, while violent incidents like these loom large in histories of US theater, they can mask the *daily* power struggles being negotiated in the playhouse and the ways in which some of the most seemingly innocuous content – like the domestic scenes in *Ossawattomie Brown* – reflects political discourse throughout the nineteenth century. Looking only for the *overtly* political content in nineteenth-century US playhouses elides the world of "cheeses and politics and pigs" that most Americans inhabited, in which the political represented the *ordinary* rather than the extraordinary, and in which theater makers strove to find a balance between delight and edification, partisanship and peace.

Pearls before Swine?

While cautious theater managers shied away from overtly political content that might provoke riots, that seldom stopped would-be playwrights from infusing political commentary into their work. Like the writers for twenty-first-century sitcoms, nineteenth-century playwrights peppered their plays with political references that might prompt laughter or discussion rather than uproar. I trace some of these political themes in what follows.

Mordecai Noah, a Tammany Democrat, pro-Jewish, antiblack newspaper editor, theater critic, sheriff, and playwright, often embedded political content in his work, including the issue of territorial sovereignty.[31] His most popular comedy, *She Would Be a Soldier* (1819), centers on Christine, who is in love with Captain Lenox but betrothed against her will to the clownish Jerry Mayflower. To escape, she disguises herself as a soldier and follows Lenox to the Battle of Chippewa. The play also features an Indigenous character known simply as the Indian Chief. Through the

---

[29] See "Threatened Riot," *San Francisco Bulletin* 30:14 (April 23, 1870), 3; and Morgan Gerard Boyd, "The Gold Mountain Theater Riots: A Social History of Chinese Theater Riots in San Francisco during the 1870s and 1880s" (MA thesis, San Jose State University, 2012), 35–36.

[30] Joan B. Trauner, "The Chinese As Medical Scapegoats in San Francisco, 1870–1905," *California History* 57:1 (1978), 70–87.

[31] See Heather S. Nathans, *Hideous Characters and Beautiful Pagans: Performing Jewish Identity on the Antebellum American Stage* (University of Michigan Press, 2017), 39–44.

"Indian" character, Noah showcases pro-US patriotism in the wake of the War of 1812, while also slipping in coded references to the forced exodus of both Native Americans and European Jews. As the Chief proclaims: "Were you not satisfied with taking our land from us ... Think you I would be your enemy unless urged by powerful wrongs? No, white man, no!" Despite the Chief's challenging political message, the play ends with the promise of "domestic peace and happiness."[32] Predicated as it is on the marginalization of Indigenous rights, this "happy" ending again demonstrates an effort to envelop political debate within a larger context of patriotic consensus, thus tempering potentially fraught political provocation with entertainment.

In 1828, the abolitionist and amateur author Robert Montgomery Bird's play *The City Looking Glass* tackled slavery and secession through a love story between a northerner and southerner whose fathers clash over their conflicting political views. It never received theatrical production – perhaps because it contained explicit abolitionist statements, such as "I think it [slavery] a system abhorrent to the general principles of morality and justice, and disgraceful to the character of our country," and it described the "doctrine of States' Rights" as "ridiculous."[33] Somewhat surprisingly, Bird's even more openly revolutionary drama of a slave uprising, *The Gladiator* (1831), written for star performer Edwin Forrest, became a hit that played for decades. It includes the oft-cited lines of Spartacus, "Ho, slaves, arise! it is your hour to kill! / Kill and spare not – For wrath and liberty! – / Freedom for bondmen – freedom and revenge!"[34] Bird himself, and later Walt Whitman, queried why audiences seemed oblivious to the play's antislavery message – particularly in the context of Nat Turner's rebellion that same year.[35] However, as the scholars Karl Kippola, Matthew Rebhorn, and Peter Reed have argued, Forrest played Spartacus not as a "Negro" slave but as a white working-class hero, sidestepping the slavery question and tapping into the country's growing class rivalries and the

---

[32] Mordecai Noah, *She Would Be a Soldier, or The Plains of Chippewa* (1819), Act III, sc. i, 65, www.proquest.com/books/she-would-be-soldier-1819/docview/2138581842/se-2?accountid=14434.
[33] Robert Montgomery Bird, *The City Looking Glass* (Benjamin Blom, 1972), Act IV, sc. vi, 108, www.proquest.com.books/city-looking-glass/docview/2138580964/se-2?accountid=14434.
[34] Robert Montgomery Bird, *The Gladiator*, in *The Life and Dramatic Works of Robert Montgomery Bird* (Knickerbocker Press, 1919), Act II, sc. iii, 355, www.proquest.com/books/gladiator/docview/2163037026/se-2?accountid=14434.
[35] Walt Whitman, *The Gathering of the Forces*, ed. Cleveland Rogers and John Black (G. P. Putnam, 1920), 331.

populist rhetoric of white Jacksonian masculinity.[36] That "heroic" white masculinity resurfaced in the casual violence of the Bowery B'hoys on display in *A Glance at New York* in 1848, and it sowed the seeds of insurrection at the 1849 Astor Place Riot.

Other pre–Civil War playwrights such as Anna Cora Mowatt or H. J. Conway had a firsthand sense of what made a commercial hit without causing a scandal. They tamped down on divisive political content, but their works still engaged with contemporary political debates. For example, Mowatt's comedy *Fashion* (1845) reveals the precarity of women's social and economic power in mid-century America. The heroine, Gertrude, works as a governess for a *nouveau riche* family the Tiffanys, declaring that she has a "love of independence!"[37] Much of the humor centers on the family's absurd social climbing and the con men who exploit them. Yet the play offers a more serious message. When one of the con men accuses Gertrude of planning an illicit assignation, the Tiffanys fire her, and she finds herself "ruined" financially and socially. While she eventually clears her name, the play makes a political point when it acknowledges that the threat of ruin would have forced her out of "respectable" society and into a life of poverty, menial labor, and perhaps even prostitution.

The theme of independent women in peril recurs throughout nineteenth-century US dramatic literature, paralleling larger political debates on women's rights. Augustin Daly's melodrama *Under the Gaslight* (1867) features the heroine, Laura Cortland, struggling out of poverty and urban crime, and it introduces one of the most famous scenes in US theater history: the railroad-track rescue. This original rescue scene was *not* the now-clichéd image of the helpless maiden tied to the rails awaiting her gallant savior. At the moment of peril, Laura is locked in a shack alongside the track. It is a one-armed Confederate war veteran named Snorkey who lies tied to the rails. Laura grabs an axe and chops her way out of the shed, freeing Snorkey just in time. As the scene closes, Snorkey exclaims, "And these are the women that ain't to have a vote!"[38] The theater scholar Amy Hughes observes that

---

[36] See Karl Kippola, *Acts of Manhood: The Performance of Masculinity on the American Stage, 1828–1865* (Palgrave, 2012), 111–113; Matthew Rebhorn, *Pioneer Performances: Staging the Frontier* (Oxford University Press, 2012), 38–40; Peter P. Reed, *Rogue Performances: Staging the Underclasses in American Theatre* (Palgrave, 2009), 151–174.

[37] Anna Cora Mowatt, *Fashion* (Ticknor and Fields, 1855), Act II, sc. ii, 20, www.proquest.com/books/fashion-1855/docview/2138590514/se-2?accountid=14434.

[38] Augustin Daly, *Under the Gaslight* (printed for the author, 1867), Act IV, sc. iii, 86, www.proquest.com/books/under-gaslight-1867/docview/2138583734/se-2?accountid=14434.

Snorkey's comment marks a pivotal moment on the US stage and in US culture:

> *Gaslight* premiered at a time of tremendous political ferment [1867]: one year after Elizabeth Cady Stanton and Susan B. Anthony founded the American Equal Rights Association, which advocated voting rights for women; and a year before the full ratification of the Fourteenth Amendment, which laid the foundation for the enfranchisement of African American men but in the process excluded all women.[39]

Similarly, the 1871 factory-girl drama *Bertha, the Sewing Machine Girl* makes a brief foray into women's rights and issues of labor exploitation (before revealing that Bertha is an heiress).[40] The play highlights the abusive labor practices thousands of working women encountered in industrial centers across the United States, but by making Bertha rich, it couples this edification with a dose of delight in seeing Bertha's happy ending. While *Bertha* invokes familiar melodrama tropes, it also boasts a "ripped from the headlines" quality, as newspapers targeted exploitative bosses, working women's poverty, and the need for labor reform.[41]

Following the fates of Gertrude, Laura, and Bertha, three "independent" female characters on the mainstream US stage, suggests how sensitive audiences were to questions of reputation, women's labor, and women's suffrage. By the 1880s, playwrights increasingly incorporated references to the women's rights movement into their works (in both pro- and anti-suffrage plays). Pro-suffrage plays envisioned futures that took women beyond domestic joys. In Ella Thayer Cheever's *Lords of Creation* (1883), the heroine, Kate Grovenor, steps in to run her family's business, pay off its debts, and facilitate the marriages of everyone around her. In the final line of the play she declares, "I wish to every woman in the land might come equal rights, independence, and last, but not least, love."[42]

If plays treating women's rights had to tread lightly among American audiences, those confronting slavery faced even greater challenges in creating conversations rather than riots. The compromises in white-authored antislavery plays reveal prevailing political conditions. For example, in 1859, H. J. Conway produced one of the innumerable stage adaptations of Harriet Beecher Stowe's *Uncle Tom's Cabin*. Conway downplayed the

---

[39] Hughes, *Spectacles of Reform*, 119.
[40] Charles Foster, *Bertha the Sewing Machine Girl; or Death at the Wheel* (publisher unknown, 1871).
[41] For more on *Bertha*'s history, see Heather S. Nathans, "Defying 'Death at the Wheel': The Unexpectedly Long Life and Far Reach of *Bertha the Sewing Machine Girl*," *TDR* 65:2 (2021), 29–44.
[42] Ella Cheever Thayer, *Lords of Creation* (Walter H. Baker, 1883), 38, www.proquest.com/books/lords-creation/docview/2138582677/se-2?accountid=14434.

"cruder points" and "objectionable features" of Stowe's work, creating what became known as the "Compromise Uncle Tom."[43] In a letter, Conway describes the strategic cuts he planned. He recommends eliminating Emmeline (the beautiful octoroon woman whom Simon Legree buys to replace his enslaved mistress, Cassy) and cutting references to Cassy as Eliza's mother. Even these few changes reveal a significant erasure of the sexual violence against black women depicted in the novel and vital in mobilizing certain antislavery factions before the war.[44] Conway's "compromises" render the content more palatable to a majority white audience.

Unlike Conway, William Wells Brown, the orator, novelist, playwright, and abolitionist, refused to compromise his politics for his audience's comfort. Brown escaped from slavery and spent much of his career sharing the dehumanizing and brutal experiences he had endured. Brown understood that no speech, play, poem, or novel could ever truly capture the horrors of slavery, stating, "Slavery never has been represented. Slavery never can be represented."[45] This was particularly true when stories of enslaved people were written by white authors and performed by white actors in blackface (the custom in nineteenth-century US theatre). Thus Brown took on the revolutionary role of performer as well as playwright (playing all the roles in staged readings of his work – a bold choice in an era that traditionally denied black performers visibility onstage). His drama *The Escape* focuses on three enslaved black characters, Glen, Melinda, and Cato. Glen and Melinda hope to marry, but Melinda's white enslaver, Dr. Gaines, wants her as his concubine. Mrs. Gaines, jealous of Melinda's beauty, tries to poison her. Glen rescues her, and they flee for Canada. Cato, who initially seems to represent the comical stage slave, jettisons that role to make his escape with them. Brown's work, which combines comedy, melodrama, and even subversive nods to blackface minstrelsy, vaunts moral law over political bickering. The black characters reject the "Eagle" (US) for a more just system, proclaiming, "The Eagle ... she's a bird of spoil / Like worships like! for each devours / The earnings of another's toil."[46] Both the text and Wells Brown's embodied performance of *The Escape* challenge political and social norms of the slave system, acknowledging the capitalist-driven concerns that kept it operating.

---

[43] John W. Frick, *Uncle Tom's Cabin on the American Stage and Screen* (Palgrave Macmillan, 2012), 71.
[44] See Nathans, *Slavery and Sentiment on the American Stage*, 212–246.
[45] William Wells Brown, quoted in John Ernest's introduction to *The Escape; or a Leap for Freedom*, 1st ed. (University of Tennessee Press, 2001), xxxi.
[46] William Wells Brown, *The Escape* (R. F. Wallcut, 1858), Act V, sc. ii, 42, www.proquest.com/books/escape/docview/2138585547/se-2?accountid=14434

In contrast to Brown's *The Escape*, post–Civil War plays by white authors skirted the political minefields presented by the collapse of Reconstruction, the rise of Jim Crow, and racial violence across the United States. Bronson Howard's popular drama *Shenandoah* (1889) stages a romance during the Civil War (with the lovers on warring sides). The stage directions call for music so politicized that it might have ignited a riot even ten years earlier: "Dixie," "When This Cruel War Is Over," "John Brown's Body," "Glory, Glory, Hallelujah!," and "Johnnie Comes Marching Home."[47] As the play opens on the eve of the attack on Fort Sumter, best friends Kerchival West and Robert Ellingham muse that war seems "inevitable," but they promise, "Whatever else comes, our friendship shall be unbroken!"[48] Yet despite the play's failure to mention slavery as the cause of the war or to include any black characters, critics hailed it as an "authentic" representation of the conflict.[49] It certainly matched the political tone of the day, focusing on reconciliation rather than states' rights or abolishing slavery.

"The Melting Pot Where Nothing Melted"

As I have noted, the post–Civil War era ushered in a host of professional playwrights, expanded theatrical circuits, and complicated debates on US politics.[50] The US government clamped down on immigration, fueling anti-immigrant rhetoric and demeaning ethnic representations. Reconstruction-era stages teemed with minstrel shows that conjured an ersatz nostalgia for vanished plantation life, expunging the horrors of slavery.

In response to these increasing restrictions and distorted representations, the vaudeville stage launched new genres of political humor that educated and delighted audiences much in the manner of contemporary *Saturday Night Live* skits. Duo acts such as Harrigan and Hart and Weber and Fields depicted Irish and "Dutch" (German/Jewish) immigrants navigating white American power structures. Harrigan and Hart sang about the "Babies on Our Block," celebrating the newborn "American" infants among immigrant communities. Weber and Fields's comedy traded in comic malapropisms, but it also riffed

---

[47] All the orchestra music is listed at the beginning of the script. See Bronson Howard, *Shenandoah* (Samuel French, 1897), 8, www.proquest.com/books/shenandoah/docview/2138586221/se-2?accountid=14434.
[48] Howard, *Shenandoah*, Act I, sc. i, 10, www.proquest.com/books/shenandoah/docview/2138586221/se-2?accountid=14434.
[49] See "Incidents of the Stage," *New York Tribune* (February 9, 1889), 7.
[50] The quote "The melting pot where nothing melted" in the section title is from Tony Kushner, *Angels in America: A Gay Fantasia on National Themes*, revised and complete ed. (Theatre Communications Group, 2013), part I, 10.

on immigrants' perpetual sense of displacement.[51] Vaudeville acts also addressed domestic migration – a particularly resonant theme for black performers and audiences. George Walker and Bert Williams, two of the most successful black artists of the late 1890s and early 1900s, created shows about ongoing transformations in the black community during the Great Migration. The characters in Williams and Walker's works try to figure out whom they can and cannot trust, and how to avoid exploitation.[52] They also seem perpetually in search of a place to call *home* in a nation denying black citizens opportunities to vote, purchase property, secure higher education, or enjoy dignified employment.

The postbellum expansion of different types of theatrical venues eased some of the burden of mixing audiences of all classes, races, and political allegiances in one playhouse. Yet, while black, Jewish, or Irish audiences might have relished escaping white middle-class spectators, the proliferation of performance sites underscored the seemingly irreconcilable schisms between many factions of US society. These schisms were papered over by the late-century rise of the Theatrical Syndicate – an organization that supplied entertainments to theaters across the nation but that also controlled the content of those productions, tailoring them toward a largely white, middle-class audience.

However, the rise of performers like Harrigan and Hart, Weber and Fields, Williams and Walker, and others, along with the launch of the Little Theatre movement, helped to bring more local and less hegemonic political questions to the stage. As David Humphreys prophesied in 1815, "The revolutions in taste as well as in politics, succeed each other with such unprecedented rapidity," and the power dynamics of the playhouse continued to transform as well.

Further Reading

Bellin, Joshua. *Medicine Bundle: Indian Sacred Performance and American Literature, 1824–1932*. University of Pennsylvania Press, 2008.

Brooke, John L. *"There Is a North": Fugitive Slaves, Political Crisis, and Cultural Transformation in the Coming of the Civil War*. University of Massachusetts Press, 2019.

---

[51] To hear Weber and Fields's slapstick comedy routine "The Hypnotist," a recording of which was made in 1904, see "'I'm A Gizzard': The Vaudeville Comedy of Weber and Fields," *History Matters: The U.S. Survey Course on the Web*, http://historymatters.gmu.edu/d/5764/.

[52] See David Krasner, *Resistance, Parody, and Double-Consciousness in African American Theatre, 1895–1910* (Palgrave Macmillan, 1997), 99–116.

Hughes, Amy E. *Spectacles of Reform: Theatre and Activism in Nineteenth-Century America*. University of Michigan Press, 2012.
Jones, Douglas A. Jr. *The Captive Stage: Performance and the Pro-Slavery Imagination of the Antebellum North*. University of Michigan Press, 2014.
Kibler, Alison. *Censoring Racial Ridicule: Irish, Jewish, and African American Struggles over Race and Representation, 1890–1930*. University of North Carolina Press, 2015.
McConachie, Bruce. *Melodramatic Formations: American Theatre and Society, 1820–1870*. University of Iowa Press, 1992.
Neely, Mark E. Jr. *The Boundaries of American Political Culture in the Civil War Era*. University of North Carolina Press, 2005.

CHAPTER 18

The Evolving Modalities of Fiction and Politics

D. Berton Emerson

In the opening paragraph of Mark Twain's *Adventures of Huckleberry Finn* (1885), the eponymous narrator declares, "You don't know about me without you have read a book by the name of The Adventures of Tom Sawyer; but that ain't no matter. That book was made by Mr. Mark Twain, and he told the truth, mainly. There was things which he stretched, but mainly he told the truth."[1] A comic opening from the indelible voice of one of US literature's best-known characters, the self-reflexive reference to the book's author and his tendencies to tell both truth as well as "stretchers" (3) illustrates not only age-old tensions of producing truth in writing but also decades-old concerns regarding the composition of truth in the made-up worlds of fiction. Three decades prior, in one of the most widely read works of US fiction in the century – Harriet Beecher Stowe's *Uncle Tom's Cabin* (1852) – readers encountered a preface that valorized writers at mid-century who would "seek out and embellish the common and gentler humanities of life, and, under the allurements of fiction, breathe a humanizing and subduing influence, favorable to the development of the great principles of Christian brotherhood."[2] Whereas Stowe understands fiction's "allurements" to provide an ideal vehicle by which truth ("great principles") could be relayed and political change thereby effected, Twain's comedy operates on the assumption that since audiences know that they are reading a work of fiction, distinctions among truth or stretchers or all-out lies are thus comically irrelevant to this thoroughly fabricated mode. That said, like Stowe's novel, Twain's aims at political work, in this case a less explicit if also searing critique of contemporary politics that have abandoned the project of reconstructing the nation with justice toward formerly enslaved people.

Despite their very different tonal registers (Stowe's high moral seriousness and Twain's low comic irony), both novelists demonstrate a persistent

---

[1] Mark Twain, *The Adventures of Huckleberry Finn* (1885) (Penguin Classics, 2003), 9.
[2] Harriet Beecher Stowe, *Uncle Tom's Cabin; or, Life among the Lowly* (1852) (Norton, 2018), 3.

nineteenth-century commitment to viewing fiction as a credible purveyor of truth and thus as a potent political tool. They thus stand together in contrast to their influential European contemporary, Friedrich Nietzsche, whose "On Truth and Lies in a Nonmoral Sense" (1873) would urge radical skepticism about the ability not just of fiction but of all linguistic mediation to convey truths about the world.[3] While Nietzsche's denunciation of all language as lies has exerted an enduring influence on twentieth- and twenty-first-century understandings of fiction's relation to truth and its consequent role in politics, neither Stowe nor Twain is a Nietzschean. Stowe's defense of truth and political efficacy in fiction and Twain's willingness (voiced through Huck) to forgive occasional stretchers from someone who "tells the truth, mainly" each demonstrate an enduring optimism about mediation, a trust in language further demonstrated by Stowe's frequent authorial intrusions and Twain's assurance of authentic dialect and unaffected slang. Lies, then, are not endemic to the institution of language for Stowe and Twain but are particular to specific uses of it and, as such, should impugn not, for them, the essentially trustworthy medium of language but, instead, the virtue of the author or the character perpetrating a given lie. This conviction that language's users, and not language itself, are responsible for lies, underwrites a nineteenth-century understanding that even fiction, when in the hands of a truth-teller, can convey the "truth" of "great principles" and thus do political work.

To demonstrate these nineteenth-century understandings of the intersections of fiction and politics, I will divide the century into different periods consistent with the history of the book and print culture. This vantage points reveals that, at century's dawn, printers and readers existed far apart in localized and decentralized networks that extended across the Atlantic Ocean (evidenced by the speed with which US printers reproduced the work of a famous European author soon after it arrived from across the ocean). These conditions changed dramatically with the arrival in the second quarter of the century of transportation and communications revolutions that not only added urgency to long-existent calls for a distinctive US literary culture but also augmented the facility with which there might emerge a centralized book trade. The Civil War disrupted this consolidation, but it also spurred material technologies and nationalist ideologies that connected far-flung locations and accelerated

---

[3] Friedrich Nietzsche, "On Truth and Lies in a Nonmoral Sense," (1873), in David Wood and José Medina, eds., *Truth: Engagements across Philosophical Traditions* (Wiley, 2005), 14–24.

the mass consumption of fiction, prompting new uses for artwork and enabling the mass production of literary texts.[4]

With this print-historical framework in mind, one can see early US fiction providing a subtle and not-so-subtle site for the expressions of political concerns, most commonly about the negative consequences that would come from citizens wasting time by reading fiction, time that would be better used for nation-building. A few decades into the nineteenth century, however, amidst the general retreat from incendiary revolutionary language and during the consolidation of liberalism and market capitalism in the adolescent nation, US literary culture saw the rise of "aesthetic autonomy" that was becoming commonplace at home and abroad. This rise proved a development across the nineteenth century, one in which cultural advocates for fiction fashioned, to borrow the words of Nancy Glazener, "a space for imaginative experimentation under governments wary of revolution – and among citizens weary of polarization – [which] seemed to require stipulating that the aesthetic subject was completely separate from the citizen capable of rabble-rousing."[5] From the perspective of authors, this form of aesthetic autonomy could be seen as securing some protection from charges of libel or treason, with the only costs coming in the form of blunted political efficacy. From another cultural angle, key shifts in the relationship between fiction and politics came with changes resulting from clerical disestablishment (completed by 1833) and the rising influence of feminine sensibilities in the literary marketplace, which, according to Ann Douglas, likewise resulted in authorial investments and consumer preferences for expressions of "influence" rather than explicit political work.[6] By mid-century, both now-canonical and more popular writers tended to eschew politics explicitly, often with some appreciation of aesthetic autonomy for themselves and, increasingly, their works, even as they took up politics indirectly. Around 1880, near the end of the period that book historians have dubbed the era of the "Industrial Book," fiction had secured an esteemed and well-understood place in culture, and many authors continued to use fiction to voice their political concerns: sometimes subtly, sometimes more earnestly, but consistently from a perspective that took for granted the political efficacy of fictive truth. As the century closed, emerging investments in the modernist concern for art as autonomous entity – combined with a growing consensus around

---

[4] This periodization is best captured in the five volumes of the History of the Book in America series published by the University of North Carolina Press.
[5] Nancy Glazener, *Literature in the Making: A History of US Literary Culture in the Long Nineteenth Century* (Oxford University Press, 2016), 63.
[6] Ann Douglas, *The Feminization of American Culture* (Avon, 1977), 7–8.

critiques like Nietzsche's – meant that authorial convictions like those shared by Stowe and Twain were on their way out. Such changes in cultural conceptions of art thus loom large in any discussion of fiction and politics, paralleling simultaneous material transformations associated with political history and the history of the book and print culture.[7]

***

The conventional story about the literary culture of the new nation runs something like this: While leaders were able to declare independence, secure the new nation through war, revise a weaker constitution into a stronger one, and do some delicate tap dancing through potential civil strife, literary culture had done very little to establish itself in any distinguished way in the world republic of letters. Cathy Davidson was one of the first scholars to challenge this assessment in her groundbreaking study *Revolution and the Word* (1986), and Thomas Koenigs's more recent *Founded in Fiction* (2021) has extended Davidson's arguments by elucidating the tendencies for scholars of fiction to presume – problematically more often than not – the novel as the default modality of fiction writing. (Such scholars regularly note how Nathaniel Hawthorne made a careful distinction between novels and romances as a "form of composition" in his preface to *The House of the Seven Gables* (1851); there Hawthorne characterizes the novel as having "very minute fidelity, not merely to the possible, but the probable and ordinary course of man's experience" and declared his preference for a different compositional form or mode, the romance, which allows the author "to present that truth under circumstances, to a great extent, of the writer's own choosing or creation.")[8] While Hawthorne's novel/romance distinction conveys his own modal preference, Koenigs demonstrates that early American writers – ones lesser known today than Hawthorne but quite popular and influential in their own eras – understood that fiction could work across a range of modalities:

> In the [early] republic fictions ... could invoke widely divergent conceptions of fictional "truth," a term that might refer to a narrative's moral vision, its mimetic accuracy, or its aesthetic impact. Counterintuitively, the

---

[7] Jacques Rancière offers a different way of thinking about art and politics in the nineteenth century, one that is tied less to book history and more to a structuralist model of identifying synchronic "regimes" or systems of cognitive competency that succeed each other diachronically and provide variant enabling conditions for those who can claim that competency to render the world of sensation intelligible to themselves according to socially shared perceptible categories. For examples of Rancière's structuralist approach to nineteenth-century literary history, see *Aisthesis: Scenes from the Aesthetic Regime of Art*, trans. Zakir Paul (Verso, 2011).
[8] Nathaniel Hawthorne, *The House of the Seven Gables* (1851) (Norton, 2006), 3.

prevailing skepticism about fiction's ability to serve as a source of knowledge about "the world as it is" made early American writers especially attuned to the unique kinds of speculative and suppositional knowledge that fiction *could* impart.[9]

Koenigs's idea of "speculative and suppositional knowledge" evokes various grammatical modes, emphasizing the subjunctive or hypothetical over other ones like the indicative, the imperative, or the interrogative. If the indicative is the mode of journalistic truth-telling, early US fiction explored alternative modes resembling not just the subjunctive but also the imperative, the interrogative, and even the hortatory as vehicles for engagement with the contemporary world of politics.

An early US writer whose fictional modality blended the interrogative and the imperative was Charles Brockden Brown. Largely understood as drawing upon emerging conventions of the Gothic, Brown's fiction tested the limits of the Enlightenment in politics, taking up a slew of classical republican questions (i.e. the interrogative), ranging from slander in the press and the separation of church and state to the proper balance between liberty and authority. *Wieland, or the Transformation* (1798), for instance, juxtaposes two men, the first a man of faith and the second a man of reason, and the ways that exclusive affinity for either was a recipe for disaster in collective life. While the two leading characters can spend their genteel days debating the merits of their worldviews, they are hardly prepared for a mischief-maker named Carwin who has ventriloquistic abilities that enable him both to imitate voices and to project them in ways that operate free from an embodied person. Midway through the novel, the titular character hears what he believes to be the voice of God demanding (i.e. the imperative) the sacrifice of his wife and children and follows through with their murders. Struggling to identify the ultimate agent of these deaths, the narrative ends up casting some measure of blame on the victims: "That virtue should become the victim of treachery is, no doubt, a mournful consideration; but the evils of which Carwin [was] the author, owed their existence to the errors of the sufferers."[10] This final pronouncement – a didactic overture that goes beyond journalistic facts and offers a more conditional non-truth that nevertheless gestures toward truth – registers political efficacy by charging sensitive readers with questions regarding

---

[9] Thomas Koenigs, *Founded in Fiction: The Uses of Fiction in the Early United States* (Princeton University Press, 2021), 3 (emphasis in original).
[10] Charles Brockden Brown, *Wieland; or, The Transformation: An American Tale* (1798) (Norton, 2011), 181.

whether their nation's new form of representative democracy might turn final responsibility back on those who bear the greatest risk of being harmed.

Two decades later, a fiction writer who took a very different approach to politics found extensive appreciation on both sides of the Atlantic. Washington Irving produced a number of comical sketches, largely obscuring the lines that later critics would draw between fiction and nonfiction, historical writing and imaginative mythmaking. Whether taking up the pen name of Geoffrey Crayon or claiming that he drew from official histories, Irving took advantage of emerging notions of aesthetic autonomy, or the appearance of purpose combined with an absence of actual utility. As one telling example, the title character of "Rip Van Winkle" (1819) was no political rabble-rouser. To the contrary, his accidental and complete evasion of political revolution confirms his role as disinterested and autonomous subject, not only making him an excellent figure for the role of storyteller by story's end but also offering a strong rebuttal to any presumption about the centrality of political controversies in the public lives of everyday citizens. The story imagines a rural character who, fleeing the slings and arrows of a tyrannical, henpecking wife at home, ventures into the mountains and sleeps for twenty years, right through the presumably transformative period of the American Revolution. For old Rip and his surviving companions (his wife not among them), the revolutionary changes are more superficial than essential. While US citizens (formerly British subjects) continue to debate contemporary political issues, Rip is liberated from subjection to private and domestic tyranny, enabling him to adopt a public and social role that (similar to Irving's) involves the aesthetic autonomy of telling the folk – or old wives' – tales that his now-dead wife cannot. Had the story appeared in the more politically polarizing times of the 1790s, Irving might have been criticized for his character's political apathy. But by 1819 the developing norms around fiction and aesthetic autonomy enabled his fiction to do a new kind of political work: challenging social norms around gender and domestic spaces to present storytelling as a public and social practice rather than a domestic and private one and to promote men like Rip (and, by extension, Irving himself) as legitimate sources of those fictional tales.

If Irving's comedic sketches disavow politics in favor of an aesthetic autonomy disengaged from public debate of social issues, we see nominal political engagement in the popular genre of historical romances that dominated the later years of this early period. James Fenimore Cooper's *The Pioneers* (1823) and *The Last of the Mohicans* (1826), Lydia Maria

Child's *Hobomok* (1824), Catharine Maria Sedgwick's *Hope Leslie* (1827), and William Gilmore Simms's *The Yemasee* (1835) variously address the removal of Indigenous peoples from eastern states. These fictive narratives most certainly followed the lead and popularity of Sir Walter Scott, whose historical romances were wildly popular on both sides of the Atlantic. Cooper and perhaps Simms came as close as any US author to challenge Scott's marketplace supremacy in the sales of fiction, and their works largely normalized the trope of the "vanishing Indian." Sedgwick's and Child's fictions prove more complicated. Both authors register moments of opposition to racist and imperialist presumptions undergirding arguments for Indian Removal, but their fictions offered mixed results. Whereas a religious or political or even a fictional appeal might employ a hortatory command, the rising principle of aesthetic autonomy yielded a deeper sense of the hypothetical. In other words, rather than offering the admonition "let us act," as the political would require, these romances more indelibly presented a directive to "let us imagine." Reading these books might have raised awareness of the moral or ethical shortcomings of national policies like Indian Removal, but they also – and perhaps more powerfully – promoted a disinterested civic virtue that deflected attention away from the urgent and immediate concerns of politics.

***

By the 1830s, fiction had gained higher cultural esteem, partly due to the popularity of historical romances, and partly due to the efforts of advocates like the theologian William Ellery Channing, who explicitly tied the fortunes of the nation with the development of its literary culture. Channing embraced the classical republican idea that the young nation depended upon the cultivation of "superior men" and rejoiced that he saw "the influence of literature ... perpetually increasing" as "[r]eading, once the privilege of a few, is now the occupation of multitudes."[11] Celebrating this new status quo, Channing envisions a new cultural world freed from a concern that fiction readers would be poorer democratic citizens, and others followed his lead. While Channing appreciated fiction that delivered instructional lessons via hortatory rhetoric in a spirit of moral reform, many authors untethered their writings from such didactic ends, an approach most indelibly articulated by Edgar Allan Poe's criticism in

---

[11] William Ellery Channing, "Remarks on National Literature," in *The Works of William E. Channing, D.D.* (American Unitarian Association, 1890), 126.

the 1830s and 1840s.[12] Literary productions of this period appeared on a continuum between explicit political advocacy – most often tied to moral reform – and more aestheticized alternatives, whose politics were less overt and thus often complicit in normalizing a shift from civic republican accounts of virtuous individuals disinterestedly promoting the public good to a liberal-capitalist program committed to self-interested individuals pursuing private gain at the expense of others.

The most famous of nineteenth-century US fictions have tended to be heralded for their aesthetic innovation, meaning that their politics emerge more subtly through allegory. Novels like Nathaniel Hawthorne's *The Scarlet Letter* (1850) and Herman Melville's *Moby-Dick* (1851) took such approaches. The former borrowed from the firmly established reputation of historical romance and built a lightly discernible connection between moral life and political concerns. Set in the seventeenth century and depicting the lives of colonial Puritans, the narrative depicts that moment's failed theocracy in order to challenge Hawthorne's contemporaries, abolitionists who believe the law's letter and spirit – Hester Prynne and Arthur Dimmesdale, respectively – can be brought together, and demonstrating instead that the letter of the law alone, the US Constitution ("A" for America), should guide political life in the nation. Hester Prynne might suffer the indignities of communal shame due to the sins of private desire made public, but the larger moral conveyed in the novel's conclusion targets Dimmesdale rather than Hester and associates his falsity with an illegibility not applicable to the letter-bearing Hester: "Among many morals which press upon us from the poor minister's miserable experience, we put only this into a sentence: – 'Be true! Be true! Be true! Show freely to the world, if not your worst, yet some trait whereby the worst may be inferred!'"[13] Writing, as Hester's letter attests, is the vehicle of truth and the antidote to Dimmesdale's seeming spiritual purity but ultimate social falsity, so the imperative to live by the publicly legible letter rather than the invisible spirit – even if it means obeying the Fugitive Slave Law of 1850 passed later that year – aligns truth with legibility through the itself legible and truth-telling medium of Hawthorne's fiction. Melville's *Moby-Dick*, loosely drawn from a historical event, has often been appreciated for its indictment of Enlightenment epistemology that had fostered the imperialistic ambitions of many Americans and had made them crassly devoted to

---

[12] For instance, see "The Poetic Principle," which resists "the heresy of *The Didactic*" in favor of viewing a poem as an end in itself, "this poem written solely for the poem's sake" (*Home Journal* 36 [August 31, 1850], 1).

[13] Nathaniel Hawthorne, *The Scarlet Letter* (1850) (Penguin, 2015), 246.

a mode of conquest – of "Manifest Destiny" – that could very well lead to self-destruction of persons and nations. The novel employs the interrogatory mode to engage political concerns through its depiction of a tyrannical Captain Ahab, whose monomaniacal vendetta subordinates the freedom of individual sailors to his dictatorial policies on this allegorical ship of state – a ship containing as many people as there were then states in the Union. Not unlike Hawthorne's, Melville's narrative suggests that the nation was then imperiled by domineering and monomaniacal political agendas – whether abolishing or entrenching slavery – whose Ahab-like promoters misconstrued their politics and wills to be indomitable natural forces.

Stowe's *Uncle Tom's Cabin* presents, on one hand, more of a head-on attempt at political reform but also stands as the premier example of politics vis-à-vis influence or moral suasion. Along with her affirmation of fiction quoted earlier in the chapter, Stowe's preface acknowledges that plenty of books had taken up slavery in a more indicative, journalistic mode depicting its horrors. One of the most famous, *Slavery As It Is* (1839), had essentially cut and pasted descriptions of slavery from the news stories and advertisements published in the non-fictive periodical press. While *Slavery As It Is* had tremendous influence in the political movement of antislavery, it did not produce the public outcry achieved by Stowe, who summoned all the "allurements" that fiction could provide – for a reading public that was ready to take the words of fiction potentially as "truth" – to ignite a more mainstream current of antislavery activism. Not only did this sentimental approach in the imperative mode adapt fiction to the political purposes of "searching into abuses, righting wrongs, alleviating distresses, and bringing to the knowledge and sympathies of the world the lowly, the oppressed, and the forgotten."[14] It also presents politically charged events, such as the Ohio state Senator Bird casting his vote in support of fugitive slave laws in the morning before meeting targets of that enforcement, Eliza Harris and her young son, that evening. These fictive episodes distill aggregate policy debates into transformative individual dilemmas: The Senator, corrupted by rationality in the state house, is redeemed by emotion in his personal home, helps the fugitives, and thus demonstrates in himself the political potential Stowe identifies in each of her readers in the imperative mode of her novel's "Concluding Remarks": "There is one thing that every individual can do, – they can see to it that *they feel right* . . . See, then, to your sympathies in this matter! Are they in harmony with the sympathies of Christ? or are they swayed and perverted by the sophistries of

---

[14] Stowe, *Uncle Tom's Cabin*, 3.

worldly policy?"[15] Stowe's fictional recasting of legally abstract legislative debates as morally urgent individual choices makes systemic political change, wherever the individual reader might stand on a given issue, seem achievable.

Stowe's fiction had political influence, evidenced not only by widespread praise for and objections against it in the press but also by the reactionary fiction produced to correct her "false" depiction. Fighting fiction with fiction, authors like Simms (*The Sword and the Distaff* in 1852), Sarah Josepha Hale (*Liberia; or, Mr. Peyton's Experiments* in 1853), and Caroline Lee Hentz (*The Planter's Northern Bride* in 1854) promoted politics opposed to Stowe's abolitionism. Each sought to refute (hypothetically) the incendiary description of slavery that Stowe had (hypothetically) wrought. Stowe's fiction also inspired different tactics from other antislavery authors, most obviously Frederick Douglass, who took his one turn at fiction in *The Heroic Slave* (1852). Like others who seized upon an historical event – in this case, the 1840 rebellion led by Madison Washington – Douglass understood fictive conventions and deployed them to demonstrate ways that a morally intuitive black man could recognize the injustice of his enslaved condition and take courageous action against it. Likewise demonstrating the plausibility of cross-racial alliance, Douglass made the case for abolition through political coalitions of the like-minded. William Wells Brown's *Clotel, or the President's Daughter* (1853), reputedly the first African American novel, appeared soon after, assembling a variety of figures to speculate on the rumor of Thomas Jefferson's and Sally Hemings's offspring in order to align the anecdotal and incidental concerns of fiction with the political goal of exposing the illogic and hypocrisy of slavery.

While these politically censorious modes of fiction have attracted a great deal of attention from contemporary scholars, many lesser-known authors from this period similarly employed fiction as a vehicle for issuing political indictments. Authors found substantial material in electoral politics, often in the mode of satire. John Beauchamp Jones's *The Adventures of Col. Gracchus Vanderbomb* (1854) imagines one man's quixotic quest for the office of president. On a more local scale, Johnson Jones Hooper's mock-campaign biography titled *Adventures of Captain Simon Suggs* (1845) portrays a comical swindler making a morally questionable run for the post of local sheriff. Both narratives take aim at the weakest spots of electoral politics, readily demonstrating the ways that con artists like Vanderbomb

---

[15] Stowe, *Uncle Tom's Cabin*, 414–415.

and Suggs can manipulate political processes through chicanery and rhetorical manipulation of the press. Together, such fictions suggest a corrupt facet of the so-called golden era of democratic political participation.[16]

Perhaps the pinnacle of this satiric mode of fictional truth-telling about politics is John Rollin Ridge's *The Adventures of Joaquín Murieta* (1854). This novel – acknowledged as the first published by a Native American author – depicts a Mexican migrant moving north to pursue opportunities in the mines of California at the height of the Gold Rush. Joaquín arrives with many from all over the world, much to the frustration of his white American counterparts, who persecute him viciously. After his wife is raped, his brother lynched, and he himself is publicly whipped, he vows vengeance and then proceeds to wreak havoc across the California landscape for the next year plus. Different antagonists take their shot at stopping Joaquín and his seemingly ubiquitous band of marauders, but only when a group of white citizens lobbies the recently established state government do all property owners gain relief: Joaquín is captured by a state-authorized posse. But the narrative closes with a note of ambivalence, offering a trite moral in the closing paragraphs: "that there is nothing so dangerous in its consequences as *injustice* to *individuals*."[17] On the one hand, the protagonist's fate implies a final deference to the liberal ideal of protecting property and esteeming individual rights in order to bring relief to the community. On the other, the moral reminds readers that the story of the once-virtuous Joaquín demonstrates a clear complaint against the white supremacy that promotes mistreatment – and thereby incites acts of vengeance.

Such ambiguities show fiction operating in the subjunctive, wrestling with important concerns about the political identity of the now-continental nation. As these diverse examples demonstrate, the most prominent works of this era's fiction should be understood as expressing what Nina Baym has described as a "consensus critique of the consensus."[18] However critical a fiction writer's political aims might be, very few risked alienating consensus political norms. For instance, one of the most popular writers of the 1850s, Fanny Fern, challenged gender norms and the

---

[16] The period earns this label largely through the expansion of voting rights to all white men and to the nearly 80 percent participation rate among eligible voters in the 1840 presidential election. Glenn C. Altschuler and Stuart M. Blumin have complicated this account with their book *Rude Republic: Americans and Their Politics in the Nineteenth Century* (Princeton University Press, 2000).

[17] John Rollin Ridge, *The Life and Adventures of Joaquín Murieta, the Celebrated California Bandit* (1854) (University of Oklahoma Press, 1955), 158 (emphasis in original).

[18] Nina Baym, "Melodramas of Beset Manhood: How Theories of American Fiction Exclude Women Authors," *American Quarterly* 33:2 (1981), 123–139.

opportunities for women in publishing, most indelibly in her semi-autobiographical novel *Ruth Hall* (1854). While Fern's narrative aims at making space for women writers in the literary marketplace, it defers to the idea that a woman most urgently needs money to find her security, thereby critiquing gender norms but affirming the capitalist economy of the day.

Although authors in this era frequently appraised political norms of their day, just how radical they were remains questionable. More tellingly, these middle decades were a period that saw the expansion of the nation and technological changes that facilitated a new mass culture industry, which yielded a wider range of fiction that met the eyes of a growing reading public, impacted political opinions in both coherent and inconsistent ways, and often failed to maintain that attention beyond more ephemeral moments. As much as the well-known literary figures like Melville, Hawthorne, Stowe, and Douglass might have found fiction an ideal form with which to address, criticize, support, or adjudicate various political issues, this era also included writers like Jones and Hooper, Fern and Ridge, whose less-celebrated works coupled political resistance with affirmations of the predominantly self-interested, liberal-individualistic nature of American literature and US politics.

***

Following the Civil War, literary culture in some ways became even more consolidated and in others even more diversified. The era saw the rise of the artful novel, exemplified by early modernist fictions crafted by the likes of Henry James and Edith Wharton. While certainly making comments about politics, these works offered a new variety of aesthetic autonomy and sought distinction as high literary art.[19] The ambition for artistic success came with the rise of opportunity and wealth heralded by the Gilded Age, with people of many different stripes eager to draw the line between the elites and the rest. Also connected with this elite reading culture came a more diverse set of authors whose work captured the attention of fiction readers thanks in large part to the leading editor of the time, William Dean Howells, who not only championed writers like James, Wharton, and Twain, but also fostered the careers of non-male and non-white authors like Mary Murfree, Sarah Orne Jewett, and Charles Chesnutt, who came to be appreciated for their local color. Through one lens, these latter authors rose to success thanks to an elite reading public of prestigious magazines like the *Atlantic Monthly* and *Harper's New Monthly*

---

[19] Mark McGurl chronicles the implications of changes like these in *The Novel Art: Elevations of American Fiction after Henry James* (Princeton University Press, 2001).

Magazine, who indulged in the fantasy that the more unrefined types were distributed in a manageable fashion, oddities fit for a tourist's transient gaze.[20] Complicating this presumption of elites determining late-century's culture of fiction, scholars like Judith Fetterley and Marjorie Pryse have made a strong case about the potent feminism of regionalist writing, and Kenneth Warren has done much of the same concerning African American writing as Jim Crow segregation took hold after Reconstruction's defeat in 1877.[21] Late-century fiction presents an even more complex political mix when we include the wildly popular Beadle's Dime Novels, inexpensive formulaic works that were typically anchored to bootstraps narratives, patriarchal and white supremacy, and capitalist boosterism measured against its discontents.[22] Somewhere between the elite and the masses, the pursuit of literary achievement and popular appeal generated the call for the Great American Novel, an ambition coined in an 1868 essay by John W. De Forest that aimed at identifying the highest literary achievement that could, at the same time, be critically lauded as both exceptional and exemplary.[23]

As way of conclusion, I return once again to *Huckleberry Finn* and its consideration of "truth," "lies," and "stretchers." In these transitional decades, this novel wrestles with the decades-old convictions about truth and lies, storytelling and politics that both facilitated and curtailed the impact of fiction on politics, largely holding true to faith in an author's aims, while also registering a mode of exasperation that casts more nihilistic doubts on the political efficacy of fiction. In the novel's final chapters, having fled from Tom Sawyer's false adventures derived from books in order to have true adventures of his own (including the sinking of the steamboat *Walter Scott* – a clear blow at early-century romances), Huck eventually finds Tom once again, agrees to switch identities and fool everyone (except readers), and thus collapses fact back onto fiction in the ruse of their reunited but inverted characters. Interesting here is the politics of the choices made by the author. After stopping work on the novel in 1876, right about the time of Reconstruction's defeat, Twain later finished

---

[20] See Richard H. Brodhead, *Cultures of Letters: Scenes of Reading and Writing in Nineteenth-Century America* (University of Chicago Press, 1993).

[21] Judith Fetterley and Marjorie Pryse, *Writing Out of Place: Regionalism, Women, and American Culture* (University of Illinois Press, 2005); Kenneth Warren, *What Was African-American Literature?* (Harvard University Press, 2011).

[22] See Albert Johannsen, *The House of Beadle & Adams and Its Dime and Nickel Novels: The Story of a Vanished Literature* (University of Oklahoma Press, 1950) and Michael Denning, *Mechanic Accents: Dime Novels and Working-Class Culture in America* (Verso, 1987).

[23] Lawrence Buell, *The Dream of the Great American Novel* (Harvard University Press, 2014).

the novel by having Huck, who at an earlier moment had heroically committed to betraying his "conscience" and freeing Jim (famously declaring, "All right then, I'll go to hell!"), succumb to the allure of Tom's "style" as a way of achieving this mutual end.[24] What follows is an elaborate fiction that unnecessarily prolongs Jim's unjust captivity, an ending that has diminished this novel's merits in the eyes of many critics.[25]

What is the political message here, if any? In allowing Tom, whose aunt is a plantation owner and Jim's captor, to be in charge of freeing Jim, Twain allegorizes the defeat of Reconstruction. In doing so he indirectly addresses a topic that another author, Albion Tourgée, had explicitly chronicled in his six-novel series on the Civil War and Reconstruction, the final volume of which, *Hot Plowshares* (1883), was published the year before Twain finally completed *Huckleberry Finn*. Tourgée's "Preface" to *Hot Plowshares* opens with the assertion, "Fiction is the handmaid of Truth," continuing that "Fiction … vivifies the past of which History only furnishes the record."[26] While Tourgée's political message is overt, his very title's reference to the medieval ordeal of walking across red-hot iron exhorts postbellum Americans to emulate the antebellum abolitionists in pursuing the courage of their convictions even to the point of civil war, Twain's is so subtle that most entirely miss it: Huck, initially Twain's figure of the antebellum North's gradual arrival at a commitment to freeing slaves in the war, later defers to Tom, the figure for the South and its political deal (the Hayes–Tilden compromise) to have federal troops withdrawn from the South, a withdrawal that enables a southern "style" of effecting emancipation. This set of moves, however, leads to the opposite of intentions: Klan violence and Jim Crow segregation popularly labeled Redemption. This collapse of Tom onto Huck, of the South's program onto the North's, and of abolitionist truth back onto Redemption lies allegorically suggests that a naive Huck (the North) has been duped by a sly Tom (the South) to cooperate in an effort to set an enslaved man "free that was already free before," as a bewildered Huck later describes Tom's incoherent project.[27]

Tom's allegorical Redemption, in which Jim's being freed is no different from his being imprisoned, returns us to the question of fiction's relation to the kind of truth that politics promises and fiction's identity with the kind of lies that politics perpetrates. Such a caustically exasperated ending no

---

[24] Twain, *The Adventures of Huckleberry Finn*, 227.
[25] A sample of such takes can be found in Buell, *The Dream of the Great American Novel*, 185.
[26] Albion W. Tourgée, *Hot Plowshares. A Novel* (Fords, Howard, and Hulbert, 1883), v.
[27] Twain, *The Adventures of Huckleberry Finn*, 306.

doubt offers a prescient anticipation of the more widespread commitment, following Nietzsche's skeptical lead, to the inherent falsity of all mediation and thus to the pervasiveness of fiction in the subsequent century and our own. But also, not yet.

Further Reading

Armstrong, Nancy and Leonard Tennenhouse. *Novels in the Time of Democratic Writing: The American Example.* University of Pennsylvania Press, 2018.

Buell, Lawrence. *The Dream of the Great American Novel.* Harvard University Press, 2014.

Cohen, Lara Langer. *The Fabrication of American Literature: Fraudulence in Antebellum Print Culture.* University of Pennsylvania Press, 2011.

Emerson, D. Berton and Gregory Laski, eds. *Democracies in America: Keywords for the Nineteenth-Century and Today.* Oxford University Press, 2023.

Glazener, Nancy. *Literature in the Making: A History of U.S. Literary Culture in the Long Nineteenth Century.* Oxford University Press, 2016.

Howe, Daniel Walker. *What Hath God Wrought: The Transformation of America, 1815–1848.* Oxford University Press, 2007.

Koenigs, Thomas. *Founded in Fiction: The Uses of Fiction in the Early United States.* Princeton University Press, 2021.

Loughran, Trish. *The Republic in Print: Print Culture in the Age of US Nation Building, 1770–1870.* Columbia University Press, 2007.

Nelson, Dana D. *Commons Democracy: Reading the Politics of Participation in the Early United States.* Fordham University Press, 2015.

Spires, Derrick R. *The Practice of Citizenship: Black Politics and Print Culture in the Early United States.* University of Pennsylvania Press, 2019.

CHAPTER 19

Oratory: Persuasion in Performance

Angela G. Ray

"O the orator's joys!" wrote Walt Whitman in the 1860 edition of *Leaves of Grass*. "To inflate the chest – to roll the thunder of the voice out from the ribs and throat, / To make the people rage, weep, hate, desire, with yourself, / To lead America – to quell America with a great tongue."[1] This stanza not only celebrates the physicality, emotionality, and presumptive political power of an ephemeral, sonic art but in its own expansive oratorical style also illustrates the intertwining of literature and oratory. Indeed, for many in the nineteenth century the crafted spoken word was a type of literature. In 1871, for instance, the elocutionist Helen Potter categorized the lecture, sermon, address, and oration as forms of prose literary composition, alongside the letter, essay, tract, treatise, story, fable, parable, and allegory.[2] While the US academy's early twentieth-century separation of literature from performance (speech, theater, oral interpretation) continues to affect our retrospective impressions, in seeking to understand oratory's relation to nineteenth-century US literature and politics we might productively historicize our own categories.[3] How did literature and politics blend in nineteenth-century oratory? The admixture was always particular. This chapter thus begins with an exercise in historical listening through an imaginative visit to 1855 Philadelphia and then elucidates critical themes pertinent to nineteenth-century oratory broadly. Let's listen.

Oratory and Politics in the Keystone State

In January 1855 the new Whig governor of Pennsylvania, James Pollock, delivered his inaugural address at Harrisburg, reiterating policy claims from the campaign. Pollock identified education – especially learning

---

[1] Walt Whitman, *Leaves of Grass* (Thayer and Eldridge, 1860), 268.
[2] Helen Potter, *Manual of Reading, in Four Parts: Orthophony, Class Methods, Gesture, and Elocution* (Harper and Brothers, 1871), 90.
[3] Pat J. Gehrke and William M. Keith, eds., *A Century of Communication Studies: The Unfinished Conversation* (Routledge, 2015); Gerald Graff, *Professing Literature: An Institutional History* (University of Chicago Press, 1987), 36–51.

"that recognizes the Bible as the foundation of true knowledge" – as the bedrock of a republic. He spoke of supporting school funding, maintaining a cautious banking policy, promoting agriculture and trade, and selling transportation infrastructure to reduce state debt. Turning to national issues, Pollock said that the federal government had "violat[ed] the plighted faith and honor of the country" by the recent repeal of the Missouri Compromise in the Kansas–Nebraska Act, which made possible the extension of slavery into previously free territory. Like many other northern Whig and new Republican politicians – including the Illinois lawyer Abraham Lincoln, with whom he had shared a Washington boarding house when they were both US congressmen – Pollock opposed the extension of slavery but did not take an abolitionist stance. Without irony, Pollock concluded with a paean to American freedom: "The fundamental principles of freedom and human rights," he pronounced,

> are neither new nor startling. They were taught by patriotic fathers at the watch-fires of our country's defenders; and learned amid the bloody snows of Valley Forge ... They were stamped with indelible impress upon the great charter of our rights, ... and fell burning from the lips of orators and statesmen ... They have been the watch-word and the hope of millions.[4]

Pollock's inaugural address – thoroughly responsive to the expectations of the occasion – signaled his policy commitments, affirmed his allegiances, and recalled core values forged in war that continued to inspire.

Four months later Pollock was in the audience for a different speech. Having visited several schools for white students, on May 24 he came to Philadelphia's Institute for Colored Youth (ICY), the city's first high school for black girls and boys. A thin, tall eighteen-year-old named Jacob C. White Jr. was chosen to deliver a short address to the governor before his fellow students, his teachers, and visitors. Already an enthusiastic advocate of abolitionism, White would later teach boys' preparatory classes at the ICY and then become principal of a city primary school. White's speech, presented in a collective "we" voice, demonstrates the ICY students' political awareness: "We do not forget the noble sentiments uttered by you previous to your election, on the subject of Common School Education." Yet White invites the governor to reimagine his commitments: "We see in you one who believes in the duty of impartial

---

[4] James Pollock, *Inaugural Address of Governor Pollock, of Pennsylvania: Delivered at Harrisburg, on Tuesday, the 16th Day of January, 1855*, broadside (A. Boyd Hamilton, 1855), American Antiquarian Society, Worcester, MA. On the shared boarding house, see Ida M. Tarbell, "The Life of Abraham Lincoln: Lincoln in Congress," *McClure's Magazine* (May 1896), 538.

Education." Can you and I, even now, hear the stress on the word *impartial*? Likely so. For White makes the critique clear: He says that students, when reading of Pollock's visits to other schools, "have not failed to ask ourselves . . . 'Will the Governor visit our School?'"[5]

The question is plaintive but not naive. The state consistently taught its own lessons, not of freedom but of differential value: "For you see us, Sir, a little family by ourselves, set off from the other youth of this great commonwealth, and in this fact we are constantly reminded that Pennsylvania does not yet acknowledge the common brotherhood of her children." The argument is for integration and collaboration. While reporting pleasure in the governor's visit, White does not imply awe at the interaction. Instead, he says, students welcome the chance to communicate their ambitions. They have lessons of their own to teach. "We are glad therefore that in the midst of your numerous engagements," White continues, "your excellency has given us an opportunity to present ourselves before you, that you may see that though not recognized in the political arrangements of the commonwealth we are nevertheless preparing ourselves usefully for a future day when citizenship in our country will be based on manhood and not on color." This powerful statement claims the integrity of young men like White as they prepared themselves to contribute conscientiously to the state and nation.[6] At the same time, it falls short of recognizing White's female classmates and teachers as citizens; although the term *manhood* was sometimes read as pertaining to humankind, it often signaled male persons exclusively.

Aware of "restrictions" on their opportunities, the students, White says, believe that "we may yet, by means of this, and other schools, by aid of the mechanic arts and agriculture, and the strength of good characters, and a love for the right, make ourselves useful, worthy and respected citizens."[7] White thus situates the young black students shoulder to shoulder with the Pennsylvania governor in a shared belief in the value of education as a bulwark of the republic. At the same time, he uncovers the prejudicial premises of politicians' paeans: The freedom and rights they heralded in

---

[5] Jacob C. White Jr., "Address Read on the Reception of Governor Pollock at the Institute for Col'd Youth," May 24, 1855, 1, Leon Gardiner Collection of American Negro Historical Society Records, Historical Society of Pennsylvania, Philadelphia. On the ICY, see Jelani M. Favors, *Shelter in a Time of Storm: How Black Colleges Fostered Generations of Leadership and Activism* (University of North Carolina Press, 2019), 18–48.
[6] White, "Address," 1. See Darlene Clark Hine and Earnestine Jenkins, "Black Men's History: Toward a Gendered Perspective," in Darlene Clark Hine and Earnestine Jenkins, eds., *A Question of Manhood: A Reader in U.S. Black Men's History and Masculinity*, Vol. 1 (Indiana University Press, 1999), 1–58.
[7] White, "Address," 2.

their perfervid prose were designed only for white men. What determines a person's eligibility for freedom and its attendant rights?

White offers another lesson for the governor, who earlier in the week had presided over a meeting promoting colonization of black Americans in Africa. White not only uses the term "our country" and the even more pointed phrase "the country of our birth and affection" but also says that the students want to "prove" to the governor "that we may advance without an alienation from the land of our nativity." This is anticolonization language, framing the students' abilities as evidence in the ongoing public controversy. White concludes in a full-throated Pennsylvanian's voice, even while reminding the governor of his obligations to hear the pleas of disenfranchised petitioners: ICY students, he says, appreciate the chance "to express in your hearing our hope that as Governor of Pennsylvania you will support and defend though approached by its humblest inhabitant, its glorious motto '*Virtue Liberty* and *Independence*.'"[8] White asks Pollock to understand the grand abstractions capaciously. What is virtue? Whose liberty? Whose independence? The young man's oratorical performance dramatically personalizes the racial politics of citizenship.

White's speech so impressed visitor William Still – best known today for his coordination of the Underground Railroad – that Still supplied the full text for Mary Ann Shadd's *Provincial Freeman*, then published in Toronto, alongside his report of the "*vile schemes*" of the colonization meeting and an account of an antislavery lecture by the Boston minister Theodore Parker, who had mentioned covertly sending rifles to Kansas abolitionists. While Still blasted the "sophistry, subterfuge, and hypocrisy" of the colonizationists and lauded Parker's "admirable lecture," he gave primary attention to the "talented pupil" of teachers Charles Reason and Grace Mapps, providing White's statement and characterizing Pollock's response, which complimented the school but "said nothing" of the political and social rights "of which we have been so long robbed."[9]

For her part, Shadd would be in Philadelphia in October, attending the Colored National Convention of 1855. Although her participation as a woman sparked controversy, she was voted in as a corresponding member. Shadd, born in Delaware and educated in Pennsylvania, had moved to Canada West (Ontario) after the Fugitive Slave Act of 1850 significantly increased the danger to black Americans of being abducted into slavery. In

---

[8] White, "Address," 1–2.
[9] W[illiam] S[till], "From Our Philadelphia Correspondent," *[Toronto] Provincial Freeman*, June 9, 1855.

the *Provincial Freeman* she urged others to take a hard look at the United States and determine to make a better life outside its borders, and in 1852 she published *A Plea for Emigration; or, Notes of Canada West*, supplying details of agriculture, trades, land prices, currency, laws, churches, schools, climate, and customs. At the 1855 convention she delivered a forceful speech promoting emigration to Canada, which William J. Watkins, writing in *Frederick Douglass' Paper*, described as "her masterly exposition of our present condition, and the advantages Canada opens to colored men of enterprise."[10] Shadd herself, however, identified the convention as a "great failure" that revealed unpleasant truths about her opponents. While in Philadelphia she contested a local black abolitionist, Isaac Wears, in a well-attended public debate on emigration, and although three judges declared her the winner and she heightened her reputation as a political speaker and public advocate, she was pressing a case that met little support.[11] Later in her life, now with the surname Cary and living in Washington, she summoned foundational US political principles to argue that black women must be "invested with the right to vote as do men, that thus as in all Republics *indeed*, they may in future, be governed by their own consent."[12] Shadd Cary's emphasis – "all Republics *indeed*" – highlights a key question in American human rights advocacy: How might US political life become consistent with the accepted definition of *republic*?

Performing Politics

In addition to their common emphasis on freedom, these instances illuminate themes germane to nineteenth-century oratory broadly. First is its sheer ubiquity: Oratory occurred in government, education, religion, and reform, as assertion, argument, and activism. Preachers sermonized in a variety of registers, grave or impassioned; legislators spoke to each other and to constituents; attorneys appealed to juries and judges. Children were taught to stand and speak, uttering their own crafted prose or reciting the words of others.[13] In literary and debating societies, members read compositions, spoke in extemporaneous debate, or delivered prepared

---

[10] [William J. Watkins], "From Our Brooklyn Correspondent," *Frederick Douglass' Paper*, November 9, 1855.
[11] Jane Rhodes, *Mary Ann Shadd Cary: The Black Press and Protest in the Nineteenth Century* (Indiana University Press, 1998), 108–112.
[12] Philip S. Foner and Robert James Branham, eds., *Lift Every Voice: African American Oratory, 1787–1900* (University of Alabama Press, 1998), 514–517.
[13] Carolyn Eastman, *A Nation of Speechifiers: Making an American Public after the Revolution* (University of Chicago Press, 2009).

orations.[14] Even in the earliest years of the century, itinerant lecturers attracted audiences: The peripatetic, toga-clad Scottish immigrant James Ogilvie held forth on suicide, female education, or oratory itself, and entrepreneurial women schoolteachers like Anne Laura Clarke lectured on grammar, global clothing styles, or US history.[15] Later, popular lecturers traveled the lyceum circuits, especially in the Northeast and Midwest, supplying popular science, literature, inspiration, or tales of travel, celebrating or critiquing social and political systems, and interpreting the world and its peoples.[16]

Whereas the phrase "the golden age of American oratory" arose in 1857 as the title of a book by the attorney Edward G. Parker and, often quoted, paints the century in nostalgic, sepia tones, it is important to recognize that "golden" is in the eye of the beholder. Parker's evaluation pertained to the previous hundred years, supported a narrative of decline, and identified past oratorical excellence narrowly with the young nation's "unrivalled martial and civic glory," coincident with an "Anglo-Saxon longing for new lands."[17] Laments about the poor quality of oratory – compared to classical models, European antecedents, or just earlier decades – occurred throughout the period.[18] In turn, later pundits would point wistfully to nineteenth-century events like the Lincoln–Douglas senatorial debates of 1858 as

---

[14] Elizabeth McHenry, *Forgotten Readers: Recovering the Lost History of African American Literary Societies* (Duke University Press, 2002); Thomas Augst, *The Clerk's Tale: Young Men and Moral Life in Nineteenth-Century America* (University of Chicago Press, 2003); Angela G. Ray, "Warriors and Statesmen: Debate Education among Free African American Men in Antebellum Charleston," in J. Michael Hogan, Jessica A. Kurr, Michael J. Bergmaier, and Jeremy D. Johnson, eds., *Speech and Debate As Civic Education* (Pennsylvania State University Press, 2017), 25–35; Carly S. Woods, *Debating Women: Gender, Education, and Spaces for Argument, 1835–1945* (Michigan State University Press, 2018).

[15] Carolyn Eastman, *The Strange Genius of Mr. O: The World of the United States' First Forgotten Celebrity* (University of North Carolina Press, 2020); Granville Ganter, "Women's Entrepreneurial Lecturing in the Early National Period," in Angela G. Ray and Paul Stob, eds., *Thinking Together: Lecturing, Learning, and Difference in the Long Nineteenth Century* (Pennsylvania State University Press, 2018), 41–55.

[16] Carl Bode, *The American Lyceum: Town Meeting of the Mind* (Southern Illinois University Press, 1956); Donald M. Scott, "The Popular Lecture and the Creation of a Public in Mid-Nineteenth-Century America," *Journal of American History* 66:4 (1980), 791–809; Angela G. Ray, *The Lyceum and Public Culture in the Nineteenth-Century United States* (Michigan State University Press, 2005); Tom F. Wright, ed., *The Cosmopolitan Lyceum: Lecture Culture and the Globe in Nineteenth-Century America* (University of Massachusetts Press, 2013); Tom F. Wright, *Lecturing the Atlantic: Speech, Print, and an Anglo-American Commons, 1830–1870* (Oxford University Press, 2017); Ray and Stob, *Thinking Together*.

[17] Edward G. Parker, *The Golden Age of American Oratory* (Whittemore, Niles, and Hall, 1857), 1, 2.

[18] Carolyn Eastman, "Oratory and Platform Culture in Britain and North America, 1740–1900," in *Oxford Handbook Topics in Literature*, online ed. (Oxford Academic, 2016), https://doi.org/10.1093/oxfordhb/9780199935338.013.33.

models of political eloquence, undoubtedly without reading their long, convoluted texts.[19] While commentators and scholars of the nineteenth and twentieth centuries often examined or celebrated oratorical masterworks, scholars today are likely to comprehend oratory as a communicative medium generated through personal and institutional networks that channeled an array of perspectives. Identifying and critiquing "great speeches" remains of interest in pedagogical settings, but this activity is typically accompanied with an interrogation of the contested definitions of greatness. Quotidian examples of oratory – such as a gubernatorial inaugural, a school oration, or a convention speech – would rarely make it to a great speeches list, but they powerfully illuminate the sociopolitical cultures of specific moments: expectations of the occasion, presentations of the self, common topics and common appeals.

In addition to oratory's sheer ubiquity, the instances described in this chapter demonstrate a second theme: the intertwining of nineteenth-century oratory and print. Not only has evidence of these events come down to us in writing, but Pollock's inaugural and White's reception speech also circulated in their own time as printed texts, with Pollock's lengthy address published in broadside form by the state printer and White's short speech shared by Still in the black Canadian press. Contemporary scholars of nineteenth-century oratory show how speaker-writers like Ralph Waldo Emerson or William James honed ideas in public performance, affecting their later presentation in print, or explore the tight links between the media forms.[20] The press advertised speaking events and reported oratory as news, sometimes supplying texts provided by speakers or offering stenographic accounts. It is important, however, to remember the character of newspaper reports as persuasive documents, not transparent chronicles of events. Still's accounts of the colonization meeting, Parker's address, and the encounter between White and Pollock show this attribute clearly, as does the report of Shadd's convention speech, written by an auditor captivated with her oratorical abilities though not her argument.

The rhetorical character of newspaper texts and the malleability of oral performance are dramatically confirmed by variant press reports of events

---

[19] For a critical analysis of the debates, see David Zarefsky, *Lincoln, Douglas, and Slavery: In the Crucible of Public Debate* (University of Chicago Press, 1990).

[20] See, for example, Wright, *Lecturing the Atlantic*; Paul Stob, *William James and the Art of Popular Statement* (Michigan State University Press, 2013); Ray, *Lyceum and Public Culture*; Shirley Wilson Logan, *Liberating Language: Sites of Rhetorical Education in Nineteenth-Century Black America* (Southern Illinois University Press, 2008); Cheryl A. Wall, *On Freedom and the Will to Adorn: The Art of the African American Essay* (University of North Carolina Press, 2018); Eastman, *Strange Genius*.

like President Andrew Johnson's infamous "swing around the circle" of 1866, a disastrous speaking tour opposing congressional Reconstruction that impeachment proceedings later characterized as "utterances, declarations, threats, and harangues" that were "peculiarly indecent and unbecoming in the Chief Magistrate of the United States." For instance, reporters in Cleveland agreed on the basic facts of a key exchange: Johnson responds to a voice from the crowd that calls for the execution of the former Confederate president ("Hang Jeff Davis"); the Democrat Johnson, in a bellicose tone, points out his lack of judicial power and launches an attack on a perfidious Republican Congress. Differences in the stenographic accounts, however, create disparate impressions of the scene. Even punctuation signals variation in emotional intensity: Whereas the centrist *Cleveland Herald* depicts an excitable president ("I am not the jury"), the Johnson figure of the Radical Republican *Cleveland Leader* breathes fire: "I am not the Chief Justice! I am not the Attorney General! I am no jury!" The two papers also differentially report the crowd's attitude. When Johnson says, "I called upon your Congress, that is trying to break up the government," the *Herald*'s crowd offers "immense applause." The *Leader*'s crowd, in contrast, responds contentiously: "[Hisses and cries of 'A lie!' Great confusion. Voice, 'Don't get mad!'] I am not mad. [Hisses.]"[21] Such accounts call instructive attention to the rhetorical functions of all press reports, not just those recounting high-profile events. Further, by illuminating the specific case, they suggest how Johnson ceded control of the tour's meaning to the partisan press, as he ineptly followed conventions of a personal, interactive, combative stump speaking style when advances in telegraphy had made nationwide press coverage possible. Far from a frivolous indictment, the article of impeachment castigating Johnson's "harangues" elucidates an important intersection of oratorical practice, the politics of Reconstruction, expectations of presidential behavior, and evolving journalistic routines.

Johnson's obstreperous interactions with crowds also point to a third key element evident in the examples of Pollock, White, and Shadd: Oratory is addressed to an identifiable, delimited audience, and audiences affect the meaning of the oratorical event, whether they endorse or refute, attend or ignore, or, in Whitman's words, "rage, weep, hate, desire."[22] Consider, for instance, the audience of White's speech: Although the governor was the narrow audience invoked by White's words – "Governor of Pennsylvania,"

---

[21] *Trial of Andrew Johnson, President of the United States, before the Senate of the United States, on Impeachment by the House of Representatives for High Crimes and Misdemeanors*, Vol. 1 (US Government Publishing Office, 1868), 9, 326, 333.

[22] Whitman, *Leaves of Grass*, 268.

he began, and he continued with the specific "you," "your excellency," and "you the Chief Magistrate of this commonwealth"[23] – his speech was also crafted for his peers and teachers and for others like Still who were present for the occasion. Effectively representing his classmates and his community was a clear goal, to be achieved by demonstrating his knowledge of oratorical conventions and by making an assertive political statement. Further, while White's text issued a challenge to the governor from young black Philadelphians that was likely supported by most people in attendance, Shadd's convention speech on emigration was delivered primarily to opponents – to black delegates, almost all men, who were hostile to her message and a significant subset of whom questioned the suitability of a woman participating at all. Dynamics of audiences, to the extent they are accessible, are critical in understanding an oratorical event.

Like other attributes of nineteenth-century oratory, audiences are difficult to generalize. Religious revivalists generated emotional fervor, contrasting with sober responses to solemn ministerial fare. Parrying with hecklers was a skill that political stump speakers learned early, and auditors hectored popular lecturers as well; in 1831, for instance, a lyceum in Eastport, Maine, discussed rescinding its rules allowing audience interruption.[24] Whereas some audiences, like Johnson's, could be raucous, others, like one encountered by Ogilvie in Kentucky in 1811, indicated their approbation by remaining silent, with "*no clapping of hands.*"[25] Published accounts of the speeches of Sojourner Truth, interspersed with audience response, exhibit both the racism and the sexism of her auditors and Truth's skill at reframing comments to suit her own persuasive purposes.[26] In Philadelphia in 1838, the antislavery advocate Angelina Grimké enfolded threats from a violent mob outside the building into her speech, as evidence of the spirit of slavery.[27]

Whereas speakers framed their oratory for specific audiences or responded to situational exigencies, audience members also evaluated and commented on oratorical performances. Like Still and Watkins, auditors produced texts for publication, commenting on the features of the event, the speaker, and the spoken word; such commentaries in turn

---

[23] White, "Address," 1–2.   [24] Bode, *American Lyceum*, 57–58.
[25] Eastman, *Strange Genius*, 162 (emphasis in original).
[26] Suzanne Pullon Fitch and Roseann M. Mandziuk, *Sojourner Truth As Orator: Wit, Story, and Song* (Greenwood Press, 1997), 111–114; see Carla Peterson, *Doers of the Word: African-American Women Speakers and Writers in the North (1830–1880)* (Oxford University Press, 1995).
[27] Stephen Howard Browne, *Angelina Grimké: Rhetoric, Identity, and the Radical Imagination* (Michigan State University Press, 1999).

built the reputations of speakers and sponsoring institutions and, with enough repetition in enough publications inspiring enough word of mouth, generated celebrity.[28] Audiences not only produced published text but also talked to family and friends about the speeches they had heard, transforming them through circulation, and in letters and diaries they recorded their attendance at speaking events and commented on content and quality.[29] Ronald J. Zboray and Mary Saracino Zboray have found that, far from accepting passively what they heard, women diarists and letter writers in antebellum New England critically evaluated orators' claims. During the Civil War, Emilie Davis, a black seamstress in Philadelphia, recorded her attendance at many oratorical events, including four lectures by Frederick Douglass, Frances Ellen Watkins Harper's "The Cause and Effects of War," and a speech by Jacob C. White Sr., the Sunday school superintendent at her church and the father of the young ICY student who had challenged the governor a few years before.[30] Davis would later marry George B. White, and Jacob Jr. became her brother-in-law.[31] Mingling with reading and conversation among friends and family, the experience of public speech supplied fodder for developing understandings of self and other, politics and religion, literature and history.

The most critical attribute for understanding nineteenth-century oratory and its connections to US social and political life is obvious and yet easily overlooked: Oratory was an embodied performance. Whitman highlighted this dimension: "To inflate the chest – to roll the thunder of the voice out from the ribs and throat."[32] Although, like scholars of theater history, we study oratorical performance via the surrogates of published texts and accounts or handwritten letters, diaries, and speeches, we are far removed from the odors and sounds, the press of bodies, the noise or silence, the excitement or boredom in a nineteenth-century legislative chamber, courtroom, schoolroom, revival campground, church, or lecture

---

[28] See, for example, Eastman, *Strange Genius*; Wright, *Lecturing the Atlantic*; Ray, *Lyceum and Public Culture*.
[29] Ronald J. Zboray and Mary Saracino Zboray, *Everyday Ideas: Socioliterary Experience among Antebellum New Englanders* (University of Tennessee Press, 2006), 197–220.
[30] Ronald J. Zboray and Mary Saracino Zboray, "Women Thinking: The International Popular Lecture and Its Audience in Antebellum New England," in Wright, *Cosmopolitan Lyceum*, 42–66; Ronald J. Zboray and Mary Saracino Zboray, "The Portable Lyceum in the Civil War," in Ray and Stob, *Thinking Together*, 30.
[31] Karsonya Wise Whitehead, *Notes from a Colored Girl: The Civil War Pocket Diaries of Emilie Frances Davis* (University of South Carolina Press, 2014), 216.
[32] Whitman, *Leaves of Grass*, 268.

hall. Yet considering such features reminds us that a speech text is a performance script, which may not have been read verbatim.

Choose an extant speech text and read it aloud. You must make decisions of emphases and pauses and quickly assess the appropriate pronunciation of homographic terms like *tear* or *read*. Be alert for *read* in Lincoln's Second Inaugural, for instance, and note the shift in tense and the introduction of religion at that point. What does oral reading of this text illuminate? Other means of apprehending oratory in performance include seeking descriptive commentary, like Helen Potter's guidance for impersonating Susan B. Anthony in her courtroom speech of 1873: "Take short steps upon entering and retiring from the platform . . . sit down, but never lean back. Intense natures like hers sit forward. Make few gestures, and those of the emphatic sort only."[33] We might develop our own vocal skills, or we might take note of sweat stains on a speech text that a lecturer gripped as she stood on the platform.[34] Because printed texts were sometimes crafted for oral reading, we can gather performative cues from typography.[35] We can also investigate oratorical education, with its classical and elocutionary emphases.[36] We cannot travel back to attend events of the past, but recognizing them as ephemeral and performative is a significant step toward understanding their political and cultural significance. This recognition prompts us to wonder: How did Jacob C. White Jr. stand to deliver his speech? How did he gesture? What did the visual impression – of a tall, young, black man addressing a white governor and former congressman in his mid-forties – signify to the assembled auditors, even before White began to speak? How did Pollock deliver his complimentary but tepid response? When Watkins referred to the "charm and potency" of Shadd's convention speech and noted that her eyes "fairly flash when she is speaking," what cultural norms of oratory and gender did he invoke?[37] Questions like these press us to consider politics as performance.

---

[33] Helen Potter, *Helen Potter's Impersonations* (Edgar S. Werner, 1891), 16; Angela G. Ray, "Caricatures versus Character Studies: Helen Potter's Mimetic Advocacy for Women's Rights," in Patricia Bizzell and Lisa Zimmerelli, eds., *Nineteenth-Century American Activist Rhetorics* (Modern Language Association, 2021), 179–191.
[34] Judith Pascoe, *The Sarah Siddons Audio Files: Romanticism and the Lost Voice* (University of Michigan Press, 2011); Timothy H. Scherman, "Looking for Liz," *The Researcher: Journal of the Carteret County Historical Society* (Spring–Summer 1998), 4–17, 9.
[35] Marcy J. Dinius, "'Look!! Look!!! at This!!!!': The Radical Typography of David Walker's 'Appeal,'" *PMLA* 126:1 (2011), 55–72.
[36] Eastman, *Nation of Speechifiers*; Eastman, *Strange Genius*.
[37] [Watkins], "From Our Brooklyn Correspondent."

Finally, the examples that introduce this chapter signal the complex interactions of oratory, argument, and the politics of unity and difference. Orators, Whitman wrote, could "lead America," and cultural norms closely associated oratory, leadership, and democratic life.[38] Speakers commonly pointed to the founding ideal of equality, whether they were celebrating achievement, criticizing failures to live up to principles, or reflecting on future hope. Set beside White's oration, Pollock's paeans to freedom ring far more hollow than they would if compared to a proslavery sermon or to a speech of Stephen Douglas on popular sovereignty. White's assertive strength, when juxtaposed to Shadd's appeal for emigration, vividly illuminates an investment in the goals of racial uplift and in the unfulfilled promises of US democracy among black Philadelphians living under threats of violence and abduction. Nineteenth-century US oratory – such as that produced by Indigenous people, by Irish or Chinese immigrants, by black Americans, by women of various racial and ethnic identities, by religious minorities, by the working class – highlights limitations of national belonging as well as inventive efforts at sustenance and community building. The public speech of elite white men, certainly the best documented, also exhibits variation, contradiction, and rhetorical possibility. Oratory in the nineteenth-century United States supplies an avenue into culture, voice, and lived experience that helps explain trajectories to our own time.

Further Reading

Benson, Thomas W., ed. *Rhetoric and Political Culture in Nineteenth-Century America*. Michigan State University Press, 1997.
Eastman, Carolyn. *A Nation of Speechifiers: Making an American Public after the Revolution*. University of Chicago Press, 2009.
Eastman, Carolyn. "Oratory and Platform Culture in Britain and North America, 1740–1900." In *Oxford Handbook Topics in Literature*, online ed. Oxford Academic, 2016. https://doi.org/10.1093/oxfordhb/9780199935338.013.33.
Eastman, Carolyn. *The Strange Genius of Mr. O: The World of the United States' First Forgotten Celebrity*. University of North Carolina Press. 2020.
Foner, Philip S. and Robert James Branham, eds. *Lift Every Voice: African American Oratory, 1787–1900*. University of Alabama Press, 1998.
Gustafson, Sandra. *Eloquence Is Power: Oratory and Performance in Early America*. University of North Carolina Press, 2000.

---

[38] Whitman, *Leaves of Grass*, 268.

Peterson, Carla. *Doers of the Word: African-American Women Speakers and Writers in the North (1830–1880)*. Oxford University Press, 1995.

Ray, Angela G. *The Lyceum and Public Culture in the Nineteenth-Century United States*. Michigan State University Press, 2005.

Ray, Angela G. and Paul Stob, eds. *Thinking Together: Lecturing, Learning, and Difference in the Long Nineteenth Century*. Pennsylvania State University Press, 2018.

Wright, Tom F., ed. *The Cosmopolitan Lyceum: Lecture Culture and the Globe in Nineteenth-Century America*. University of Massachusetts Press, 2013.

Wright, Tom F. *Lecturing the Atlantic: Speech, Print, and an Anglo-American Commons, 1830–1870*. Oxford University Press, 2017.

Zarefsky, David. *Lincoln, Douglas, and Slavery: In the Crucible of Public Debate*. University of Chicago Press, 1990.

Zboray, Ronald J. and Mary Saracino Zboray. *Everyday Ideas: Socioliterary Experience among Antebellum New Englanders*. University of Tennessee Press, 2006.

CHAPTER 20

Authors on the Campaign Trail: "We Are Politicians Now"

John Hay

In September of 1861, the twenty-four-year-old William Dean Howells sat in a corridor of the White House, awaiting his fate. A door swung open and out stepped the man himself. Howells briefly met the gaze of those "melancholy eyes" but continued sitting silently as President Lincoln "walked up to the water-cooler that stood in the corner, and drew himself a full goblet from it, which he poured down his throat with a backward tilt of his head, and then went wearily within doors."[1] No words passed between the two.

Howells would go on to become one of the nation's foremost novelists and literary critics, but back then the young newspaperman's reputation rested upon a few well-received poems and a slim campaign biography of the man at the water cooler. Hoping to benefit from the spoils system upon Lincoln's election, Howells had written to John Nicolay, the president's secretary, asking for a diplomatic appointment in Munich. His petition included signatures from prominent Ohio politicians and editors, who recommended him for office by pointing to his poetic contributions to the *Atlantic Monthly* and his potential to promote "the growth and influence of American literature."[2] When Nicolay informed him that he could have a position in Rome, Howells promptly traveled to Washington to learn the details of his assignment. Finding that the Rome job paid poorly, he arranged a meeting with Nicolay and John Hay, Lincoln's other personal secretary, to see if he could secure something better. "I learned that as young Western men they were interested in me because I was a young Western man who had done something in literature, and they were willing to help me for that reason, and for no other that I ever knew," reflected Howells many years later. "They proposed my going to Venice; the salary

---

[1] William Dean Howells, *Literary Friends and Acquaintance: A Personal Retrospect of American Authorship*, ed. David F. Hiatt and Edwin H. Cady (Indiana University Press, 1968), 73.

[2] Quoted in Susan Goodman and Carl Dawson, *William Dean Howells: A Writer's Life* (University of California Press, 2005), 69.

was then seven hundred and fifty, but they thought they could get it put up to a thousand. In the end they got it put up to fifteen hundred, and so I went to Venice."³

Serving as US Consul to Venice from 1861 to 1865, Howells avoided military service during the Civil War and devoted much of his time to literature. In January 1862, not long after arriving in Venice, he wrote in his diary, "I must interest myself deeply in study, if I can, and enter upon the fulfillment of my purpose to write an American romance."⁴ Having "almost no official duties to distract him," he read copiously, wrote his first major book, *Venetian Life* (1866), and embarked upon one of the most celebrated careers in American literary history.⁵ The significance of his Lincoln campaign biography and the consular appointment it secured should not be overlooked. They were essential to his future success.

Howells's experience was not exceptional. In the nineteenth century, authors and artists were frequently employed in the diplomatic service; unlike career bureaucrats, writers brought cultural cachet and even fame to their positions, and politicians characterized such undemanding foreign assignments as a form of patronage for the arts. Whereas today's poets and novelists might spend countless hours applying for grants and fellowships from foundations both public and private (the National Endowment for the Humanities, the Fulbright Program, the Guggenheim Foundation, etc.), nineteenth-century authors sought plum political appointments with comfortable salaries and scant duties. As Amanda Claybaugh has observed in an essential essay on this topic, a remarkable number of American authors served as either a US Minister or Consul prior to civil service reform at the turn of the century.⁶ Joel Barlow, James Fenimore Cooper, Washington Irving, John Howard Payne, John Lloyd Stephens, Nathaniel Hawthorne, William Dean Howells, Donald Grant Mitchell, James Russell Lowell, Bret Harte, Bayard Taylor, Frederick Douglass, Lew Wallace, Albion Tourgée, and James Weldon Johnson all held such diplomatic positions overseas.⁷ Quite a few more – including Walt Whitman and Samuel Clemens – received similar

---

³ Howells, *Literary Friends*, 72.
⁴ William Dean Howells, Diary: Venice, 1861–1862 (January 24, 1862), 25. Howells Family Papers, Houghton Library, Harvard University. MS Am 1784.3(4), Box 24, Folder 4.
⁵ Kenneth S. Lynn, *William Dean Howells: An American Life* (Harcourt Brace Jovanovich, 1971), 110.
⁶ Amanda Claybaugh, "The Consular Service and US Literature: Nathaniel Hawthorne Abroad," *Novel* 42:2 (2009), 284–289.
⁷ This was also a period when diplomats might express a serious interest in literature – as when the US chargé d'affaires to the Netherlands was also the author of a substantial essay on the history of the novel. See Auguste Davezac, "The Literature of Fiction," *United States Magazine and Democratic Review* 16 (March 1845), 268–282.

sinecules at home, and many others pursued them unsuccessfully. As the eminent critic Brander Matthews noted in 1896, "A foreign appointment is almost the only honor a republic can bestow upon its foremost authors."[8]

In exchange for diplomatic largess, authors often wrote nonfiction narratives – sometimes in advance, to emphasize their suitability for appointment (e.g. Howells's *Life of Abraham Lincoln*), and sometimes afterward, to display the benefits they had received (e.g. Howells's *Venetian Life*). Such nonfiction narratives included histories, memoirs, and travel narratives. But perhaps the most curious and overlooked genre is the campaign biography, a form taken up by many notable nineteenth-century American authors.

The Campaign Biography

Campaign biographies date to 1824, when Andrew Jackson authorized the publication of his life story as part of his narrowly unsuccessful bid against John Quincy Adams for the US presidency.[9] They quickly became a regular feature of the nation's political cycles (and were later replaced by their modern descendants, ghostwritten autobiographies). The genre is not only especially powerful, designed to sway the election of the nation's highest official; it is also exceptionally American in its origins. "What we term 'Campaign literature,'" observed the bestselling nineteenth-century biographer James Parton, is "a peculiar product of the United States," a feature of the media environment surrounding democratic elections.[10]

"Campaign literature is dreadful stuff," Parton added. In an era when self-promotion was seen as vulgar (a candidate would stand for office instead of running for it), presidential hopefuls needed others to tell their stories. Campaign biographies were thus necessary tools for disseminating information about a candidate's background and personality, his accomplishments and qualifications. The genre was extremely formulaic; nearly

---

[8] Brander Matthews, *An Introduction to the Study of American Literature* (American Book Company, 1896), 52.
[9] John C. Calhoun was also the subject of a campaign biography in 1824, but Jill Lepore identifies John Eaton's 1824 revised edition of *The Life of Andrew Jackson* as the title that established "the genre's enduring conventions." Lepore, *The Story of America: Essays on Origins* (Princeton University Press, 2012), 149. On the history of the campaign biography, see also William Burlie Brown, *The People's Choice: The Presidential Image in the Campaign Biography* (Louisiana State University Press, 1960), xii–xiv, and M. J. Heale, *The Presidential Quest: Candidates and Images in American Political Culture, 1787–1852* (Longman, 1982), 157–162.
[10] James Parton, *Life of Andrew Jackson*, 3 vols. (Mason Brothers, 1860), 1: vi. In "They All Were Born in Log Cabins," *American Heritage* 7:5 (1956), 32–34, 102–105, the scholar James D. Hart would similarly conclude that the campaign biography "is an American institution" (105).

every title begins with a chapter curiously combining an impressive family genealogy with the candidate's humble origins (e.g. born in a log cabin) and includes snippets of speeches, testimonies from colleagues, and anecdotes illustrating character and integrity. In his *Life of Abraham Lincoln* (1860), for example, William Dean Howells depicted a young Abe defeating a gang of rowdy backwoodsmen in a wrestling match.

These well-worn conventions could make the genre seem subliterary, as Howells self-deprecatingly suggested in his short preface:

> A work which seeks only to acquaint people with the personal history of a man for whom they are asked to cast their votes – and whose past ceases to concern them in proportion as his present employs them – will not be numbered with those immortal books which survive the year of their publication. It does not challenge criticism; it fulfills the end of its being if it presents facts and incidents in a manner not altogether barren of interest.[11]

Why read a campaign biography after the campaign has ended? Why read the story of a US president that ends before he becomes president?

The twenty-three-year-old Howells may have considered his book to be propaganda rather than literature, but in her brief cultural history of the campaign biography, Jill Lepore concludes that Howells's *Life of Abraham Lincoln* is "the best example of the genre."[12] It was an astounding success for Howells; not only did his candidate prove victorious (he later joked to Mark Twain that his book got Lincoln elected)[13] but his well-funded residence in Venice during the war was tremendous compensation for a quickly written biography.

Nor was this an early anomaly in Howells's career. In 1876, several years into Howells's prominent position as editor of the *Atlantic Monthly*, Ohio Governor Rutherford B. Hayes, a cousin of Howells's mother-in-law, accepted the Republican nomination for president. Howells's publisher, Henry Houghton, wrote to him asking if he would pen the campaign biography. Houghton suspected that the book could score a hit in the literary marketplace: "Who knows but that it might recuperate the waning

---

[11] William Dean Howells, *Life of Abraham Lincoln* (1860) (Indiana University Press, 1960), xi. In the rough draft manuscript of his preface, Howells more succinctly observed that his work "does not belong to the class of literature which requires careful reading." Robert Price, "Young Howells Drafts a 'Life' for Lincoln," *Ohio History Journal* 76:4 (1967), 232–246, 242.

[12] Lepore, *The Story of America*, 155.

[13] *Selected Mark Twain–Howells Letters, 1872–1910*, ed. Frederick Anderson, William M. Gibson, and Henry Nash Smith (Harvard University Press, 1967), 74. Lincoln was supported by sixteen different campaign biographies in 1860, far more than those of his rivals. See Thomas A. Horrocks, *Lincoln's Campaign Biographies* (Southern Illinois University Press, 2014), 71.

fortunes of both of us? 70,000 copies sold of the miserable life of Fremont, when he was candidate for President."[14] Campaign biographies were not just vehicles for authors to secure political patronage; they were also potential profit generators for publishers. Howells accepted the assignment and quickly wrote *A Sketch of the Life and Character of Rutherford B. Hayes* (1876). The book, to Houghton's disappointment, only sold a couple of thousand copies, but Hayes won the election. For his efforts, Howells was considered for the position of US Minister to Switzerland, though he used his influence instead to help his father become Consul to Toronto, James Russell Lowell Minister to Spain, and Bret Harte Consul to Krefeld, Germany.[15]

As an older man, Howells expressed the belief that literature and politics were fundamentally separate endeavors. Claiming to have always remained aloof from "practical politics," a seventy-nine-year-old Howells implausibly declared that he had "never yet heard a political speech to the end."[16] But this sentiment reflects the turn that Howells took a few years after he composed the Hayes biography. In 1881, Howells resigned his editorship of the *Atlantic* (which was commonly perceived as sympathetic to the Republican Party) and focused his literary output on novels. His authorial practice and critical theorization of literary realism in the following years suggested a commitment to the aesthetics of fiction rather than to party politics. But in the 1870s, politically motivated fiction and nonfiction had often gone hand in hand. Christine Holbo has suggested that, in that era, the campaign biography was related to the genre of the "political roman-à-clef," which included works such as Albion Tourgée's *A Fool's Errand* (1879) and Henry Adams's *Democracy* (1880).[17]

Rather than characterizing the campaign biography as an inartistic work of propaganda written merely to secure a political appointment, we should understand it as a node in a wider network of literary and political narrative genres. During the mid-century rise of realism, novels could exert tremendous political influence by accurately representing national issues. The chief example is *Uncle Tom's Cabin* (1852) – and it should come as no surprise that Harriet Beecher Stowe herself penned a brief narrative of the life of Ulysses S. Grant that appeared just in time for his 1868 presidential

---

[14] Quoted in Lyon N. Richardson, "Men of Letters and the Hayes Administration," *New England Quarterly* 15:1 (1942), 110–141, 118.
[15] Richardson, "Men of Letters," 123.
[16] William Dean Howells, *Years of My Youth* (Harper and Brothers, 1916), 159, 160.
[17] Christine Holbo, *Legal Realisms: The American Novel under Reconstruction* (Oxford University Press, 2019), 299.

campaign.[18] Many other novelists also took up such work. Perhaps most notably, Lew Wallace, author of the bestselling 1880 novel *Ben-Hur*, wrote a campaign biography for his friend Benjamin Harrison in 1888.[19] Other examples abound. Richard Hildreth, author of the antislavery novel *The Slave; or, Memoirs of Archy Moore* (1836), wrote the life of William Henry Harrison in 1840.[20] Epes Sargent, a prolific and versatile writer with several novels to his name, penned a life of his friend Henry Clay for the 1844 election.[21] William M. Thayer, famous as a writer of juvenile literature, produced an extremely popular Lincoln biography titled *The Pioneer Boy, and How He Became President* (1863). William Taylor Adams, who similarly published dozens of children's titles under the pseudonym Oliver Optic, authored (as Optic) *Our Standard-Bearer; or, The Life of General Ulysses S. Grant* (1868). James R. Gilmore, who wrote popular novels under the pen name "Edmund Kirke," also wrote the influential *Life of James A. Garfield* (1880), which was published by the leading literary firm Harper and Brothers. And Charles Wolcot Balestier, the author of several late-century novels (and a friend of Henry James), was responsible for *James G. Blaine: A Sketch of His Life*, a contribution to Blaine's unsuccessful bid for the US presidency in 1884.[22]

Hawthorne's Political Positioning

The most famous campaign biography is undoubtedly Nathaniel Hawthorne's *Life of Franklin Pierce* (1852), an odd case in which the celebrity of the biographer far exceeded that of his subject. Hawthorne's support of the victorious dark horse Democratic candidate, his old Bowdoin College chum, in turn secured him the role of US Consul at Liverpool, generally considered the most lucrative and desirable position in the diplomatic service. Hawthorne helped to set the stage for future literary aspirants; Howells, for example, later claimed to believe that there was

---

[18] Harriet Beecher Stowe, "Ulysses S. Grant," in *Men of Our Times; or, Leading Patriots of the Day* (Hartford Publishing Company, 1868), 111–151. Stowe explained to her readers that Grant was "plainly needed as next President" (149). Her work was used as the basis for the biography in *For President, Ulysses S. Grant, of Illinois* (Bulletin Office, 1868), which was promoted by a committee of Connecticut Republicans prior to the party's national convention that year.

[19] Lew Wallace, *Life of Gen. Ben. Harrison* (Hubbard Brothers, 1888).

[20] Richard Hildreth, *The People's Presidential Candidate; or, The Life of William Henry Harrison, of Ohio* (Weeks, Jordan and Company, 1840).

[21] Epes Sargent, *The Life and Public Services of Henry Clay* (Greeley and McElrath, 1844).

[22] In his preface, Balestier acknowledged his admiration for Howells's Rutherford B. Hayes biography. Charles Wolcott Balestier, *James G. Blaine: A Sketch of His Life* (John W. Lovell Company, 1884), iv.

a "universal feeling, after the election of Lincoln, that I who had written his life ought to have a consulate, as had happened with Hawthorne, who had written the life of Franklin Pierce."[23] A reviewer for the *Literary World*, praising the *Life of Franklin Pierce*, expressed a hope that more writers of Hawthorne's caliber would take up campaign biographies. "The best writers should frankly and faithfully serve the public in this way," he opined, arguing for the social and cultural significance of the genre. "It is a species of work for the people, in which the author who leaves for it his more inviting individual occupations, should receive a cordial support."[24]

The genre was not entirely new for Hawthorne, who had relied on the Democratic Party to secure him Custom House positions that provided an income while he worked on less remunerative short stories. His 1839 appointment as a measurer at the Boston Custom House was arranged through the help of Pierce, then a US senator, and George Bancroft, a historian then serving as the Collector of the Port of Boston. In order to hire Hawthorne, Bancroft had written to the Secretary of the Treasury and described the young author as the "biographer of Cilley" – a reference to an 1838 biographical sketch Hawthorne had written of the murdered Maine congressman Jonathan Cilley, another Bowdoin College classmate.[25] So it was arguably through political biography that Hawthorne enjoyed his first government appointment.

The Pierce biography continued in this vein, though it was a much more prominent publication by a much more prominent writer and thus would become a curiosity for scholars. Why had Hawthorne volunteered to write a presidential campaign biography just as his reputation and his income were growing from the success of his new novels? The *Life of Franklin Pierce* (which he wrote over the course of just a few weeks) earned him $300 – and cost him, he claimed, "hundreds of friends."[26] His Massachusetts neighbors, mostly Whigs and Free Soilers and many of them abolitionists, couldn't understand his support for a Democratic politician who sympathized with slaveholders. Hawthorne's campaign biography explicitly promoted a view that "looks upon Slavery as one of those evils, which Divine Providence does

---

[23] Howells, *Years of My Youth*, 236.
[24] "Hawthorne's Life of Franklin Pierce," *The Literary World* (September 25, 1852), 195.
[25] Bancroft quoted in Robert S. Levine, "'The Honor of New England': Nathaniel Hawthorne and the Cilley–Graves Duel of 1838," in *The Field of Honor: Essays on Southern Character and American Identity*, ed. John Mayfield and Todd Hagstette (University of South Carolina Press, 2017), 147–162, 159.
[26] Nathaniel Hawthorne, *The Centenary Edition of the Works of Nathaniel Hawthorne, Vol. 16: The Letters, 1843–1853*, ed. Thomas Woodson, L. Neal Smith, and Norman Holmes Pearson (Ohio State University Press, 1985), 605.

not leave to be remedied by human contrivances, but which, in its own good time, by some means impossible to be anticipated, but of the simplest and easiest operation, when all its uses shall have been fulfilled, it causes to vanish like a dream."[27] His faith in a politics of inaction regarding the central issue of the time angered and dismayed many of his acquaintances in the North.

Of those offended by Hawthorne's campaign biography, two especially famous friends, Henry Thoreau and Herman Melville, publicly hinted at their disapproval. In *Walden* (1854), Thoreau gestures to his former neighbor by suggesting, "If your trade is with the Celestial Empire, then some small counting house on the coast, in some Salem harbor, will be fixture enough."[28] Referencing both Hawthorne's 1843 short story "The Celestial Rail-Road" (which gently satirized the Concord Transcendentalists) and his surveyorship in the Salem Custom House in the later 1840s, Thoreau implies that a fancy consulate is unnecessary; if Hawthorne's aims were truly "celestial," or transcendental (as were Thoreau's at Walden Pond), then he would not need to prostitute his talents in exchange for a lucrative foreign appointment. Thoreau sarcastically describes his own disappointment that his "townsmen would not after all admit me into the list of town officers, nor make my place a sinecure with a moderate allowance."[29] But his irony betrays a very serious political sentiment. Thoreau neither voted nor paid taxes, declining to participate in a system that recognized slavery. For the same reason, he, like many other Garrisonian abolitionists, absolutely refused to hold government office.[30]

Melville, who had himself hoped for a consular appointment in the Pierce administration, grumbled against Hawthorne's success. His brother Allan had written to Hawthorne in 1853 to see if he could persuade Pierce to offer Herman the position in Honolulu, but nothing came of it.[31] Melville's reaction appears in the dedicatory preface to his 1855 *Israel Potter: His Fifty Years of Exile*, which might be considered an anti-campaign biography. Based on a true story, the book offers the life of a pauper, an inglorious soldier from the Revolutionary War, concluding with his unsuccessful bid for a veteran's pension. (When Franklin Pierce

---

[27] Nathaniel Hawthorne, *The Life of Franklin Pierce*, in *The Centenary Edition of the Works of Nathaniel Hawthorne, Vol. 23: Miscellaneous Prose and Verse*, ed. Thomas Woodson, Claude M. Simpson, and L. Neal Smith (Ohio State University Press, 1994), 273–376, 352.
[28] Henry David Thoreau, *Walden and Civil Disobedience* (Penguin, 2017), 16.
[29] Thoreau, *Walden and Civil Disobedience*, 15.
[30] Laura Dassow Walls, *Henry David Thoreau: A Life* (University of Chicago Press, 2017), 139.
[31] Hershel Parker, *Herman Melville: A Biography*, 2 vols. (Johns Hopkins University Press, 2002), 2: 154.

was a US senator, he distinguished himself by investigating fraudulent claims and denying requests for military pensions – something Hawthorne specifically mentions in his Pierce biography.)[32] Melville begins his book with a gesture to genre:

> Biography, in its purer form, confined to the ended lives of the true and brave, may be held the fairest meed of human virtue – one given and received in entire disinterestedness – since neither can the biographer hope for acknowledgment from the subject, nor the subject at all avail himself of the biographical distinction conferred.[33]

Hawthorne's *Life of Franklin Pierce* was accordingly an *impure* biography, written of an ongoing life and acknowledged by a subject who most certainly did "avail himself of the biographical distinction conferred." Despite this implicit criticism, Melville would later, unlike Thoreau but just like Hawthorne, be happy to receive a government post (in 1866 taking on a stable position in the New York Custom House, which he held for nearly two decades), but he found such campaigning distasteful, and his own reputation as a customs officer was marked by his refusal to accept bribes and trade favors.[34]

Whatever the opinions of his contemporaries, Hawthorne had entered the campaign arena with eyes wide open. A few years earlier, in 1849, he had complained about his ouster from the Salem Custom House in a letter to a friend, insisting that, with the sole exception of his biographical sketch of Cilley, "I have never, in all my life, written one word that had reference to politics."[35] Yet three years later, upon finishing the manuscript for the Pierce biography, he conveyed a newfound ardor to his publisher, William Ticknor: "We are politicians now; and you must not expect to conduct yourself like a gentlemanly publisher."[36]

This transformation is perhaps best explained by "The Custom-House," Hawthorne's own account of his political appointment and dismissal, included with *The Scarlet Letter* (1850) as a long introductory essay. Here Hawthorne suggests that his acceptance of the Custom House position was a mistake; it sapped his imagination and effectively put a stop to his literary

---

[32] Hawthorne, *Life of Franklin Pierce*, 295–297.
[33] Herman Melville, *Israel Potter: His Fifty Years of Exile* (Penguin, 2008), 1.
[34] Andrew Delbanco, *Melville: His World and Work* (Knopf, 2005), 291.
[35] Hawthorne, *The Letters, 1843–1853*, 278.
[36] Hawthorne, *The Letters, 1843–1853*, 588. Ticknor, Reed, and Fields printed more copies of Hawthorne's *Life of Franklin Pierce* than of any previous book in the firm's history. See Scott E. Casper, *Constructing American Lives: Biography and Culture in Nineteenth-Century America* (University of North Carolina Press, 1999), 195.

labors. While insisting that he "was not a politician," he nevertheless concludes that his removal from the office rendered him "a politically dead man" – a symbolic process that allows for his rebirth into literary life.[37] This conclusion has long served as an affirmation of the divide between Hawthorne's politics and his literature. Yet Hawthorne himself reversed this position in his brief preface to the second edition of *The Scarlet Letter*, where he playfully expresses surprise and amusement regarding the "unprecedented excitement" caused by the publication of "The Custom-House." The publicity generated by Hawthorne's snarky (and quasi-scandalous) account of his removal seems to have emboldened the author; rather than retract such political statements from his historical romance's second edition, Hawthorne decided "to republish his introductory sketch without the change of a word."[38] He heartily acknowledges here that politics boosted the book's popularity, so it should come as little surprise that just two years later he would find attractive the prospect of promoting a campaign biography.

Yet even though the success of *The Scarlet Letter* was spurred by the notoriety of "The Custom-House," Hawthorne's impressive posthumous reputation rested largely upon his imaginative fiction alone. His campaign biography was ignored – indeed, nearly treated as apocryphal – for well over a century. But then suddenly, in the mid-1980s, the *Life of Franklin Pierce* became essential for understanding the "political unconscious" of Hawthorne's major romances. If one single book signaled the arrival of New Historicist criticism into studies of nineteenth-century American literature, it was Hawthorne's slim campaign biography, which briefly became required reading for budding Americanists. Following Jane Tompkins's insistence that "a literary reputation" – Hawthorne's in particular – "could never be anything but a political matter," scholars were no longer willing to suggest that literature and politics occupied two separate realms.[39]

Jonathan Arac was one of the first to direct attention to the *Life of Franklin Pierce*. In his 1986 essay "The Politics of *The Scarlet Letter*," Arac argued that the classroom staple about Puritanical adultery was inseparable from the political scene of the 1850s. Writing against generations of critics who had privileged Hawthorne's works for their apolitical aesthetics, Arac instead maintained that the separation of "art" and "politics" into necessarily separate

---

[37] Nathaniel Hawthorne, *The Centenary Edition of the Works of Nathaniel Hawthorne, Vol. 1: The Scarlet Letter*, ed. Fredson Bowers (Ohio State University Press, 1962), 13, 43.
[38] Hawthorne, *The Scarlet Letter*, 1, 2.
[39] Jane P. Tompkins, *Sensational Designs: The Cultural Work of American Fiction, 1790–1860* (Oxford University Press, 1985), 4.

spheres was a partisan act favoring a conservative agenda (i.e. opposing progressive change). He thus classified *The Scarlet Letter* as a conservative political allegory about privileging character over action, a literary construction of "a world in which action is not to be taken" – a fiction that worked to maintain the status quo of a slaveholding society.[40] Sacvan Bercovitch echoed Arac in 1988 by pointing to Hawthorne's support of Pierce's defense of the Compromise of 1850 (with its notorious Fugitive Slave Law) and suggesting that the ending of *The Scarlet Letter* celebrates Hester Prynne's "heroism of compromise."[41] Following Arac and Bercovitch, an impressive number of scholars trotted out the *Life of Franklin Pierce* in the late 1980s and early 1990s to cast Hawthorne's works in light of his objectionable politics.[42]

The degree to which Hawthorne's campaign biography was used by scholars as a tool for critiquing his novels was unusual, and more recent reconsiderations have softened the significance of the *Life of Franklin Pierce*. Examining the author's relationships with Horatio Bridge and Charles Sumner, Robert Levine concludes that "Hawthorne's Democratic politics are far more complicated than his Franklin Pierce campaign biography would suggest."[43] More extensively, Larry Reynolds takes issue with Bercovitch's suggestion that Hawthorne was personally endorsing Pierce's positions, especially regarding the Compromise of 1850: "While Hawthorne indeed tried to make the best case he could for Pierce's politics, they were not his own, and he identified with the Pierce he created no more than he did with the admirable characters in his fiction, whose motives and perspectives he illuminated for his readers."[44] Sometimes a campaign biography is just a campaign biography.

---

[40] Jonathan Arac, "The Politics of *The Scarlet Letter*," in Sacvan Bercovitch and Myra Jehlen, eds., *Ideology and Classic American Literature* (Cambridge University Press, 1986), 247–266, 261.

[41] Sacvan Bercovitch, "Hawthorne's A-Morality of Compromise," *Representations* 24 (1988), 1–27, 2. See also Bercovitch, *The Office of The Scarlet Letter* (Johns Hopkins University Press, 1991).

[42] Notable examples building upon Arac's and Bercovitch's criticisms include Richard Boyd, "The Politics of Exclusion: Hawthorne's *Life of Franklin Pierce*," *ATQ* 3:4 (1989), 337–351; Jean Fagan Yellin, "Hawthorne and the American National Sin," in H. Daniel Peck, ed., *The Green American Tradition: Essays and Poems for Sherman Paul* (Louisiana State University Press, 1989); Lauren Berlant, *The Anatomy of National Fantasy: Hawthorne, Utopia, and Everyday Life* (University of Chicago Press, 1991); Jennifer Fleischner, "Hawthorne and the Politics of Slavery," *Studies in the Novel* 23:1 (1991), 96–106; Scott E. Casper, "The Two Lives of Franklin Pierce: Hawthorne, Political Culture, and the Literary Market," *American Literary History* 5:2 (Summer 1993), 203–230; and Eric Cheyfitz, "The Irresistibleness of Great Literature: Reconstructing Hawthorne's Politics," *American Literary History* 6:3 (1994), 539–558.

[43] Robert S. Levine, *Dislocating Race and Nation: Episodes in Nineteenth-Century American Literary Nationalism* (University of North Carolina Press, 2008), 177.

[44] Larry J. Reynolds, *Devils and Rebels: The Making of Hawthorne's Damned Politics* (University of Michigan Press, 2008), 188. Other notable reconsiderations include Michael T. Gilmore, "Hawthorne and Politics (Again): Words and Deeds in the 1850s," in Millicent Bell, ed.,

What the New Historicist focus on Hawthorne's politics ultimately revealed was not this canonical author's crass commercialism or crypto-conservatism but rather the unexamined network in which creative writers relied on political patronage to pay the bills. And while the New Historicists saw themselves responding to an older generation of Cold War critics, the mid-century blind spot most forcefully exposed was perhaps the implicit privileging of poetry and fiction over the many genres of literary nonfiction that were popular and prominent throughout the nineteenth century.[45] "Politics" becomes a much more obvious feature of nineteenth-century literature when, instead of seeking an unconscious element in novels and poems, we look at the vast array of nonfiction works that were accorded the highest literary reputations of their time.

Historians, Travelers, and Reporters

When considering the connections between American literature and political patronage, we should recall that "nonfiction" was highly esteemed in the nineteenth century – as sermons, lectures, essays, memoirs, histories, biographies, travel narratives, scientific treatises, devotional reflections, and self-help manuals. In 1917, the august *Cambridge History of American Literature* devoted entire chapters to "Travelers and Observers," "Early Essayists," "Later Essayists," "Transcendentalism," "Publicists and Orators," "Writers on American History," "Early Humorists," "Divines and Moralists," "Newspapers," "Education," "Economists," and "Scholars." (And Daniel Webster and Abraham Lincoln each received entire chapters of their own.) Vernon Louis

---

Hawthorne and the Real: Bicentennial Essays (Ohio State University Press, 2005), 22–39; and Donald E. Pease, "Hawthorne in the Custom-House: The Metapolitics, Postpolitics, and Politics of *The Scarlet Letter*," boundary 2 32:1 (2005), 53–70. After the fall of the Soviet Union, Jonathan Arac changed his mind about Hawthorne's politics; see Bradley J. Fest, "An Interview with Jonathan Arac," boundary 2 43:2 (2016), 27–57.

[45] The academic privileging of poetry and fiction arguably dates back to the 1880s, when college English programs (still relatively new at that time) began to shift their focus from the philological study of language to the humanistic study of literature. Prior to that moment, publishers played a more prominent role than professors in determining what might be considered "literature." See Gerald Graff, *Professing Literature: An Institutional History* (University of Chicago, 1987), 77–80. The canon of texts that had been established by academic philologists leaned heavily toward poetry, and the late nineteenth-century rise in the popularity of the novel helped to bring fiction into the university fold – resulting in the widespread use of textbooks such as Cleanth Brooks and Robert Penn Warren's *Understanding Poetry* (1938) and *Understanding Fiction* (1943). "Nonfiction" was thereafter generally perceived as lacking the ambiguity and complexity that provided the richness of a genuinely "literary" text.

Parrington's influential *Main Currents in American Thought* (1927) similarly privileged the writings of statesmen and philosophers.

Indeed, nonfiction has always sat at the core of the canon of American literary history. The formation of American literature as a scholarly field in the early twentieth century owed much to Harvard's creation of an American Studies doctoral program in 1937 (under the name History of American Civilization). Whereas the study of English literature generally privileged poetry, fiction, and drama, the study of American culture privileged nonfiction texts – from Puritan sermons to Enlightenment pamphlets to abolitionist speeches. It was no surprise, in other words, that Ralph Waldo Emerson and Henry David Thoreau were among the five authors whom the Harvard professor F. O. Matthiessen enshrined in his field-defining *American Renaissance* (1941). But across the country, the study of American literature specifically within departments of English has often contended with the notion that poetry and fiction were the real aims of the literary tradition (a view particularly reinforced with the rise of creative writing MFA programs).[46]

A look beyond novelists reveals many prominent nineteenth-century American authors churning out nonfiction narratives in the hopes of receiving political spoils. Histories, for example, were a good way to curry favor with politicians. George Bancroft, who had been appointed by Martin Van Buren as Collector of Customs of the Port of Boston, was best known for his massive *History of the United States of America*, the first volume of which was published in 1834. A well-connected Democrat who enjoyed several enviable political appointments, Bancroft served as Secretary of the Navy under Polk and as US Minister to Prussia under Andrew Johnson. He too tried his hand at campaign biography, composing a life of Van Buren in 1844 that was withheld from publication for decades when the latter failed to receive the Democratic nomination that year.[47] Other historians similarly reaped the fruits of diplomatic service. John Lothrop Motley, for example, was Minister to the Austrian Empire during the Civil War (and thus William Dean Howells's immediate superior, as Venice was then controlled by the Austrians), while Henry

---

[46] For a nuanced analysis of how American literary studies succumbed to the New Critical program of analyzing apolitical poetry and fiction, see Graff, *Professing Literature*, especially 148–152 and 216–225. Graff concludes that "the failure of cultural history to become a centralizing context created a vacuum that was readily filled by an attenuated New Criticism of explication for explication's sake" (225).

[47] Brown, *The People's Choice*, 12; George Bancroft, *Martin Van Buren to the End of His Public Career* (Harper and Brothers, 1889).

Adams spent the war as private secretary to his father, whom Lincoln had designated Minister to Great Britain.[48]

Travel writers were also natural candidates for the consular service. John Lloyd Stephens, who made a name for himself with *Incidents of Travel in Egypt, Arabia Petraea, and the Holy Land* (1837), used his Democratic Party connections to become Minister to the Republic of Central America in 1839. Central America had fallen into civil war, rendering the ministry meaningless, but Stephens went there to explore Mayan ruins and to write his bestselling *Incidents of Travel in Central America, Chiapas, and Yucatán* (1841). The globetrotting Bayard Taylor, the most celebrated American travel writer of the century, held several different diplomatic appointments over the course of his career. He was the US Minister to Russia during the Civil War, and he died shortly after President Hayes named him Minister to Prussia in 1878.[49]

Newspapers provided the most obvious overlapping of literature and politics in the nineteenth century. A large number of nineteenth-century "men of letters," such as William Dean Howells, got their start in the newspaper business. Howells's friend Mark Twain is perhaps the most notable example. Long before he turned to novels, Twain found fame through his humorous travel narratives, especially *The Innocents Abroad* (1869) and *Roughing It* (1872). The latter reveals that Twain's career, just like Howells's, owed its origins to an Abraham Lincoln appointment. Twain's older brother Orion Clemens ran an Iowa newspaper and campaigned for Lincoln. After the election, the president appointed him Secretary of the Nevada Territory, and Orion took his younger brother Sam along as his personal assistant. It was while writing for Nevada newspapers that Sam Clemens became Mark Twain.

Nineteenth-century newspapers developed in tandem with political campaigns. As one historian has noted,

> Andrew Jackson's presidency marked a major turning point in the history of newspaper politics. Understanding exactly the role that newspaper editors played in his campaigns, Jackson amply expressed his gratitude to the network of editors that supported him, not only by doling out printing contracts but also by appointing at least seventy editors to federal offices and allowing several key editors to play crucial roles in his administration.[50]

---

[48] Adams himself would later, in 1882, decline an offer to become US Minister to Guatemala. Ernest Samuels, *Henry Adams: The Middle Years* (The Belknap Press of Harvard University Press, 1958), 158.
[49] For more on the nineteenth-century American travel narrative, see John Hay, *Postapocalyptic Fantasies in Antebellum American Literature* (Cambridge University Press, 2017), 143–223.
[50] Jeffrey L. Pasley, *"The Tyranny of Printers": Newspaper Politics in the Early American Republic* (University Press of Virginia, 2001), 392. Pasley further notes that "other than lawyers, partisan

As might be expected, journalists of the era occasionally sought political appointments by writing campaign biographies. Henry J. Raymond, the cofounder of the *New York Times*, wrote *The Life of Abraham Lincoln, of Illinois* (1864). And the notable muckraking journalist Jacob Riis, the author of the 1890 classic *How the Other Half Lives*, produced a campaign biography for his friend Theodore Roosevelt in 1904.

It is also worth noting that many of the celebrated works "recovered" in the last few decades have been nonfiction works – not forgotten but simply ignored by literary scholars focused on poetry and fiction. Slave narratives, for example, were once deemed "political" rather than "literary," though nineteenth-century readers would not necessarily have made the distinction.[51] "There is one portion of our permanent literature ... that could be written by none but Americans, and only here: I mean the Lives of Fugitive Slaves," observed Theodore Parker in 1849. "All the original romance of America is in them, not in the white man's novel."[52] To ignore such explicitly "political" nonfiction narratives would be to ignore a great deal of American literature.[53]

Conclusion

One of the friends dismayed by Hawthorne's published politics was the author and editor George William Curtis, who had first met Hawthorne in 1844 when they were both living in Concord.[54] Unable to understand his continuing support of Franklin Pierce through the years of the Civil War (Hawthorne dedicated his 1863 book *Our Old Home* to the ex-president, who was perceived as siding with the Confederacy), Curtis diagnosed Hawthorne with "a kind of moral blindness like color blindness."[55] In an essay published after Hawthorne's death in 1864, Curtis recalled his

---

journalists were probably the most disproportionately well-represented occupational group in Congress" (397).

[51] For much of the twentieth century, slave narratives were dismissed as mere historical documents or even as works of abolitionist propaganda. For an important work recovering slave narratives as a rich literary genre, see Charles T. Davis and Henry Louis Gates, Jr., eds., *The Slave's Narrative* (Oxford University Press, 1985).

[52] Theodore Parker, *Speeches, Addresses, and Occasional Sermons*, 3 vols. (Ticknor and Fields, 1861), 3: 391. Parker probably had Frederick Douglass in mind; Douglass would be named US Consul to Haiti in 1889.

[53] In her "Introduction" in *The Cambridge Companion to the African American Slave Narrative* (Cambridge University Press, 2007), Audrey A. Fisch describes the radical shift in recent decades that has established the slave narrative as a major genre in American literary history.

[54] Linda Dowling, *Galahad in the Gilded Age: A Life of George William Curtis* (Xlibris, 2021), 66–67.

[55] Quoted in Brenda Wineapple, *Hawthorne: A Life* (Random House, 2003), 358.

disbelief upon first hearing that the author had written "the 'campaign' Life of Franklin Pierce for the sake of getting an office": "That such a man should do such a work was possibly incomprehensible."[56]

Curtis, who first achieved fame as a travel writer, became the editor of *Harper's* and in the 1870s was (along with Howells) one of the most influential literary figures in the nation and a prominent spokesman for the Republican Party. But Curtis repeatedly turned down offers for diplomatic appointments and instead presided over the National Civil Service Reform League. His work led to the passage in 1883 of the Pendleton Civil Service Reform Act, designed to replace the spoils system with a merit system by instituting competitive exams.[57] This and other subsequent reforms – such as the Lodge Act of 1906 and the Stone–Flood Act of 1915 – professionalized diplomatic service and placed cushy consular positions outside the reach of writers hoping to attract the generosity of powerful politicians. Campaign literature could no longer secure a sinecure.

Further Reading

Brown, William Burlie. *The People's Choice: The Presidential Image in the Campaign Biography*. Louisiana State University Press, 1960.
Casper, Scott E. *Constructing American Lives: Biography and Culture in Nineteenth-Century America*. University of North Carolina Press, 1999.
Claybaugh, Amanda. "The Consular Service and US Literature: Nathaniel Hawthorne Abroad." *Novel* 42:2 (2009), 284–289.
Holbo, Christine. *Legal Realisms: The American Novel under Reconstruction*. Oxford University Press, 2019.
Horrocks, Thomas A. *Lincoln's Campaign Biographies*. Southern Illinois University Press, 2014.
Pasley, Jeffrey L. *"The Tyranny of Printers": Newspaper Politics in the Early American Republic*. University Press of Virginia, 2001.
Reynolds, Larry J. *Devils and Rebels: The Making of Hawthorne's Damned Politics*. University of Michigan Press, 2008.
Wolff, Nathan. *Not Quite Hope and Other Political Emotions in the Gilded Age*. Oxford University Press, 2019.

---

[56] George William Curtis, "The Works of Nathaniel Hawthorne," *North American Review* 99 (October 1864), 539–557, 556.
[57] Henry Adams was another significant American author publicly promoting civil service reform in this era. See Nathan Wolff, *Not Quite Hope and Other Political Emotions in the Gilded Age* (Oxford University Press, 2019), 64–68.

Index

14th and 15th Amendments, 229

abolitionism. *see also* Lincoln–Douglas senatorial debates, slavery, race and racism, fugitive slave narratives
  black abolitionists, 162–165
  black vigilance, 161, 164–165, 169
  colonization movement challenged, 162–163
  in "Declaration of Liberty," 120
  as foray into liberal religion, 276
  gender hierarchy as argument for, 43–44
  God's sovereignty as abolitionist argument, 121
  gradual approach to, in Hawthorne, 40–41, 311, 338
  immediate emancipation and abolition, turn toward, 163
  kidnapping fought, 164–165, 168, 169
  leading to questioning all American life, 58
  opposed in fiction, 313
  partisanship and, in Stowe, 152–153
  in plays, 297–298, 299–301
  radical abolition, conservative argument for, 38, 43, 44–45
  radical abolitionism, 59, 61–62, 131
  radical culture's regard for, 62, 63
  status hierarchy as argument for, in Stowe, 42–43
  temperance linked to, 156
  white goal of convincing white audiences, 166
  women's rights movement emerging from, 223
Adams, Henry, 143–145, 146, 261, 336, 345
Adams, John, 37, 145
Adams, John Quincy, 145
Adams, William Taylor (Oliver Optic), 337
The Adventures of Col. Gracchus Vanderbomb (Jones), 313
The Adventures of Huckleberry Finn (Twain), 180–181, 304–305, 316–317
Adventures of Captain Simon Suggs (Hooper), 313
"The Afro-American" (Du Bois), 86
The Agitator (Home settlement), 104

Ah Sin (Twain and Harte), 197
Alcott, Bronson, 131
Alcott, Louisa May, 140, 243, 245
Alger, Horatio, 197
Allen, John, 101
Allitt, Patrick, 37
American Anti-Slavery Society, 163, 165, 173–176
American Colonization Society, 162, 218
The American Democrat (Cooper), 148–149
American Equal Rights Association, 229, 230
American Renaissance (Matthiessen), 344
American Slavery As It Is (Weld), 166
American Woman Suffrage Association, 231
Ames, Lucia T., 55
"Another Chapter of 'The Bostonians'" (Whitehead/James), 232
"An Ante-bellum Sermon" (Dunbar), 278–279
Anthony, Susan B., 230, 329
antifoundationalism, 1–2, 14
antifoundationalist-theory-hope, 13–14
Anti-Vagrancy Act, 212
Apess, William, 138, 215
Appeal to the Colored Citizens of the World (Walker), 136
Appeal, in Four Articles (Walker), 163
Arac, Jonathan, 341
"Are We a Nation?" (Sumner), 69, 80
Asiatic Barred Zone, 195
Astor Place Riots, 295, 298
The Awakening (Chopin), 231, 250
Awful Disclosures of the Hotel Dieu Nunnery in Montreal (Monk), 128

Baldwin, James, 54
Ball, Charles, 168–169, 173
"The Ballads" (Lowell), 80
Baltimore Society for the Protection of Free People of Color, 165
Bamewawagezhikaquay (Jane Johnston Schoolcraft), 139, 215–216
Bancroft, George, 338, 344

Index

Baptist, Edward, 30
Barker, Joanne (Lenape), 214
Bass, Samuel, 26
Battle-Pieces and Aspects of the War (Melville), 281–283
Bayley, Solomon, 167, 170–173
Baym, Nina, 133, 240, 314
Beadle's Dime Novels, 316
Beecher, Catharine, 45, 239
Beecher, Lyman, 128
Bell, Richard, 165
Bellamy, Edward, 104
belonging and participation. *see also* nationalism, nation-states, religion
    citizenship and creativity, 286–287
    freedom as coded political and religious discourse, 276–279
    gender, religion, and immigration, 285–286
    oratory highlighting the limits of, 330
    overview, 272
    race and racism, 212–213
    slavery and, 275
    through common laws and common toil, 285
Ben-Hur (Wallace), 337
Bercovitch, Sacvan, 342
Berkman, Alexander, 104
Bertha the Sewing Machine Girl (Foster), 291, 299
Bestor, Arthur, 96
Bevens, James, 167–168
"Bible Defence of Slavery" (Harper), 279–280
Bierce, Ambrose, 197
bigotry. *see* Jim Crow and segregation, Chinese immigrants, settler colonialism, white supremacy, race and racism
Bird, Robert Montgomery, 209, 297–298
Black State Conventions, 227
Blackstone, William, 110
Bledsoe, Albert T., 29
The Blithedale Romance (Hawthorne), 53, 100, 137, 224
The Book of the American Indian (Garland), 267
The Bostonians (James)
    communitarianism, response to, 105
    dismissive tone toward activists, 58
    legacy of radical abolitionism and antebellum activism, 61–62
    E.P. Peabody and Miss Birdseye, 61–62
    portrayal of radicals, 55, 57, 62–63
    radical culture in, 54–55, 56
    regressive politics, 55–56
    women's movement in, 56, 57, 221, 232
Boucicault, Dion, 291
Brackenridge, Hugh Henry, 146–147
Bremer, Fredrika, 102
Bricks without Straw (Tourgée), 153, 154–155
Brisbane, Albert, 98, 101, 102

Bronstein, Michaela, 54
Brook Farm utopian community, 53, 99–101, *see also* communitarianism
Brother Jonathan, 72, 74
Brown, Candy Gunther, 129
Brown, Charles Brockden, 308–309
Brown, Henry "Box," 135
Brown, John, 114, 120–123, 282, 293–294
Brown, William Wells, 135, 291, 300, 313
Browne, Simone, 170
Brownson, Orestes, 131
Bryant, William Cullen, 132
Buckley, William F., Jr., 35, 37
Buffalo Bill's Wild West Show, 291
Bullard, Laura, 225
Burke, Edmund, 37, 39, 45, 48
Burlingame, Anson, 193
Burlingame–Seward Treaty, 196
"Bury Me in a Free Land" (Harper), 218–219, 276
Butler, Judith, 9

Cabet, Étienne, 100
Cable, George Washington, 185
Cahan, Abraham, 141
Calhoun, John C., 19, 37
California Land Act, 212
Cambridge History of American Literature, 343
Cameron, Sharon, 56
campaign biographies
    about, 334–335
    diplomatic and political appointments and, 333, 335, 336, 337, 344, 346–347
    Nathaniel Hawthorne's experiences with, 337–343, 346–347
    William Dean Howells's experiences with, 335–336
    as literary genre, 336–337
    newspapers and, 345–346
    political *roman-à-clef* and, 336
    as propaganda, 335
capitalism, 256–259, 267–268, *see also* communitarianism, labor, frontier, settler colonialism
Carlson, David, 108, 109, 111
Carlyle, Thomas, 100
"The Celestial Rail-Road" (Hawthorne), 339
Chang, Gordon H., 195
Channing, William Ellery, 130, 149–150, 310
character, 222–224, 227
charity, 240–243
Cheever, Ella Thayer, 299
Cherokee Nation. *see also* Indigenous peoples
    Constitution of 1827, 113–115, 120, 121
    as foreign state vs. dependent nation, 115
    lost tribes theory, 113, 115, 116–117

Cherokee Nation v. *Georgia*, 112–120, 214
Cherokee sovereignty. *see also* Cooper, James Fenimore
  articulating alternative relationship between Cherokee Nation and United States, 112, 115
  contested sovereignty, *Cherokee Nation* v. *Georgia*, 112–120
  Indian Removal advocates emboldened by, 113
  political autonomy divorced from territorial sovereignty, 116–117
  sovereignty and nationhood asserted, 112, 113–115, 209
  white recognition through collective departure, 116, 117
Chesnutt, Charles, 186, 235–236
"Chiefly about War Matters, by a Peaceable Man" (Hawthorne), 151, 282
Child, Lydia Maria. *see also* motherhood and domesticity, women's rights movement
  centrality of Indigenous sovereignty to writings of, 117
  charity and urban poverty, 240–243
  Indigenous people as spiritual guides for settlers, 138
  motherhood's importance, 239, 240–241, 242
  poverty, concern for, 240–243
  prison system and maternal values, 241–243
  vanishing Indian myth, 310
  women in public spectacles, dearth of, 241
  Hobomok, 138, 209, 310
  Letters from New-York, 240–243
Chinese Exclusion Act, 195, 296
Chinese immigrants
  as cheap labor, 193, 198
  economism and, 193, 203
  exploitation of, 199, 202
  gender and sexuality, anxiety over, 194
  "Heathen Chinee" as phrase, 198, 201
  "Heathen Chinee" in literature, 196–199, 201, 203
  immigration and exclusion, overview, 191–196
  immigration restriction laws, 191, 194–195
  naturalist fiction and, 197
  police harassment, 295
  Sinophobia, 192, 193, 197
Chopin, Kate, 231, 250
Christine, or Woman's Trials and Triumphs (Bullard), 225
Cilley, Jonathan, 338
citizenship, 320–322, *see also* 14th and 15th amendments, immigration
The City Looking Glass (Bird), 297
city-country binary, 253–254, 255, 256, *see also* region and regionalism, frontier
Civil Rights Act of 1875, 183

Clark, J. C. D., 108
Clarke, Anne Laura, 324
class and status. *see also* capitalism, race and racism, Stowe, Harriet Beecher, Hawthorne, Nathaniel
  ascendance of poor whites and disenfranchisement, 180
  black writers appealing to white southern elites, 183–185
  California Land Act and, 212
  capital–labor tensions, 96, 103
  class solidarity, 186–187, 262
  hierarchy as argument for abolition, 42–43
  Jim Crow furthering elite's interests, 179
  labor solidarity, 179, 183–185
  meritocratic progress for whites only, 47–49
  population density as surrogate for class conflict, 253
  Populism and, 179, 183
  victimization, status of, 181
Clay, Henry, 145, 295
Claybaugh, Amanda, 333
"Clerical Oppressors" (Whittier), 279
Clorindy: The Origin of the Cakewalk (Cook and Dunbar), 291
Clotel, or the President's Daughter (Brown), 313
Cogan, Frances, 247
Cogan, Jacob Katz, 222
Coleman, Dawn, 134
colonies, 107, 108
colonization movement, 162–163, 218, 322
Colored National Convention, 322
The Communist Manifesto (Marx and Engels), 93
communitarianism. *see also* James, Henry, Emerson, Ralph Waldo, Howells, William Dean, Melville, Herman, Hawthorne, Nathaniel
  amenable to socialism, 95
  Brook Farm, 53, 99–101
  capital-labor tensions and communitarian solutions, 96, 103
  during Civil War and Reconstruction, 102
  conservative and progressive views within, 96
  definition, 94
  dystopian risks of, 105
  Fourierism's (Associationism's) adoption and spread, 98–99, 101, 102
  C. Fourier's scientific communitarian philosophy, 97–98
  Home settlement, 104
  immigrant reformists and religious communes, 103
  literature and the arts, 93, 98–99, 104
  national audience for, 97, 98–99
  New Harmony Gazette, 97

Index

origins in America, 94–95
periodicals and journalism, 101–102, 103–104
promotional literature, 95
radicalism attractive aspect of, 97
reflections in mainstream literature, 104–106
Shaker Bible and vision of social reform, 95
shift toward American West, 103
as symbol of "American" tendencies, 96
unique forms of, 94
women and, 105
A Connecticut Yankee in King Arthur's Court (Twain), 105
conservatism. *see also The Bostonians* (James), Stowe, Harriet Beecher, Hawthorne, Nathaniel
   challenged, 38, 46, 49
   definitions of, 35
   humans inherently flawed, 36
   law of unintended consequences, 41
   more faith in history than political philosophy, 37
   origins, 35, 37
   politics of virtue, 46
   as practice of social control, 45
   proslavery policies and, 36–37
   right relations and inequality, 41
   The Scarlet Letter as conservative text, 39
   social change to be gradual, 36, 37, 41
   tradition the best means of governing people, 36, 37
   underlying assumptions, 35–36
   white supremacy and, 45–49
"The Conservative" (Emerson), 150
Consuelo (Sand), 102
Conway, H.J., 298, 299
Cook, Will Marion, 291
Cook-Lynn, Elizabeth, 263
Cooper Union Speech (Lincoln), 36
Cooper, Anna Julia, 184
Cooper, James Fenimore. *see also* territory and territoriality
   attitudes toward partisan behavior, 148–149
   centrality of Indigenous sovereignty to writings of, 117–120
   figure of the vanishing Indian, 209
   lost tribes theory of Indigenous peoples, 118–120
   recasting logic of *Cherokee Nation* v. *Georgia*, 119–120
   vanishing Indian myth, 309
   The American Democrat, 148–149
   The Last of the Mohicans, 309
   Leatherstocking Tales, 209
   Oak Openings, 117–120
   The Pioneers, 309

The Prairie, 148
"Cooperation vs. Competition" (Debs), 63
The Cooperative Commonwealth (Gronlund), 104
Coulthard, Glen Sean, 265
The Countess of Rudolstadt (Sand), 102
country. *see* city–country binary
Cox, Robert S., 138
Crane, Gregg, 46
The Cry for Justice (Sinclair), 65
Culler, Jonathan, 1
Culture and Imperialism (Said), 219
Curtis, George William, 346–347
"The Custom-House" (Hawthorne), 340–341

Dahl, Andrew, 111
Daly, Augustin, 291, 298–299
Dana, Charles, 101
Darwin, Charles, 139
Davidson, Cathy, 239, 307
Davis, Andrew Jackson, 137
Davis, David Brion, 20
Davis, Emilie, 328
Davis, Sara deSaussre, 56
Day, Iyko, 193
De Cleyre, Voltairine, 63
De Forest, John W., 69, 80–83, 316
Debs, Eugene V., 63
Declaration of Independence, 24–26
"Declaration of Liberty" (Brown), 120–121
Delany, Martin, 32, 120, 218
Delgado, Richard, 21
"Deliverance" (Harper), 277–278
Deloria, Philip J., 264
Democracy in America (Tocqueville), 155
Democracy: An American Novel (Adams), 143–145, 261, 336
Democratic Party, 191
Derrida, Jacques, 23
Dickinson, Emily, 283–284
Dillard, Angela D., 41
"Direct Action" (De Cleyre), 63
Discontent (Home settlement), 104
disenfranchisement. *see* Jim Crow and segregation, class and status, suffrage
domesticity. *see* motherhood and domesticity
Donnelly, Ignatius, 259
Doolen, Andy, 254
Douglas, Ann, 133, 306
Douglass, Frederick
   masculinity in *Narrative*, 228
   northern segregation and Jim Crow, 182
   slavery and personhood debate, 29
   support for 14th and 15th Amendments, 230
   The Heroic Slave, 313

Douglass, Frederick (cont.)
  Narrative of the Life of Frederick Douglass, 136, 166, 228
  "What to the Slave Is the Fourth of July," 80
drama. *see* theater and drama
Dred: A Tale of the Great Dismal Swamp (Stowe), 152–153
The Drunkard, 291
Du Bois, W. E. B.
  "Afro-American" term, 86–87
  double-consciousness, 87–88
  internationalism and Whitmans' American model, 88
  on segregation, 185, 188
  "The Afro-American," 86
  The Souls of Black Folk, 88, 185, 188
DuBois, Ellen Carol, 230
Dunbar, Paul Laurence, 278–279, 291
Dwight, John Sullivan, 101

"Earth's Holocaust" (Hawthorne), 35
Eaton, Edith Maude (Sui Sin Far), 141, 199
Eaton, Winnifred (Onoto Watanna), 199
economic class. *see* class and status
economism, 193, 203
Ellison, Julie, 133
Ellison, Ralph, 54
Emerson, Ralph Waldo
  Brook Farm and, 99–100
  characterizations of, 76, 131
  defense of John Brown, 122, 282
  literary implications of communitarianism, 99
  literature as expressions representing the national body, 79
  oratory and print, 325
  truth's distance from party politics, 150
  "The Conservative," 150
  Nature, 89
  "The Over-Soul," 89
  "Politics," 150
empire and imperialism. *see also* Du Bois, W. E. B., nation-states, territory and territoriality, sovereignty, settler colonialism, Emerson, Ralph Waldo, Whitman, Walt
  anti-imperialism through racial-continental segregation, 83
  assimilationism and, 83–86
  imperialism pushed to periphery of Indigenous center, 265–266
  imperialist ambition of US national character, 75–76
  Insular Cases and, 207
  missionary activities, 200, 202–203
  survivance challenging, 265–268
  territorialization and regionalization, 254–255
  Transcendentalism opposing, 90
  United States as imperial power, 69, 70
  US history inextricable from, 126
  US nature of, 208, 254
The Encantadas (Melville), 105
Engels, Friedrich, 93
Enlightenment, 39, 271, 275–276, 279
Epps, Edwin, 26
Epstein, Barbara Leslie, 239
equality. *see* Jim Crow and segregation, women's rights movement, suffrage, belonging and participation, abolitionism
The Escape (Brown), 291, 300
The Essex Junto, 291
Estes, Nick, 263
ethnicity. *see* Chinese immigrants, theater and drama, race and racism
"Ethnogenesis" (Timrod), 280–281

"Facing West from California's Shores" (Whitman), 206
Farren, George, 295
Fashion (Mowatt), 298
Faust, Drew Gilpin, 280
The Federalist Papers, 96
Fern, Fanny, 244, 248, 314
Fetterley, Judith, 316
fiction as genre
  aesthetic autonomy, 306
  artful novels, 315
  fictional modalities, 307–309
  fictional truth, 307, 312, 316–317
  frontier romance genre, 117–120
  historical romances, 309–310
  homiletic novels, 140
  local color writing, 258, 315
  novels vs. romances, 307
  politics and, 304–307, 308, 311
  storytelling as public, social practice, 309
Fish, Stanley, 12, 13–14
Fleissner, Jennifer, 56
Fliegelman, Jay, 293
A Fool's Errand (Tourgée), 11, 153–154, 336
Foreign Miners' Tax, 212
Forrest, Edwin, 297
Foster, Charles, 291, 299
Foucault, Michel, 9
foundationalism, 1–2, 14
Fourier, Charles, 97–98, 102
Fourierism and Associationism, 98–99, 101, 102
franchise. *see* suffrage
"The Freedman's Case in Equity" (Cable), 185
"The Freedom Bell" (Harper), 276–277
Freeman, Mary Wilkins, 231

"From a Mournful Villager" (Jewett), 155–156
frontier. *see also* territory and territoriality, region and regionalism, empire and imperialism
  anti-pastoral aesthetics of the rural, 259, 261
  frontier romance genre, 117–120
  frontier thesis, 210
  insurrections in, 256–257
  terra incognita evoked by, 255
  territorialization and empire, 254–255
  as unimproved waste and backcountry, 256
  urban finance capitalism as antagonist of, 256–259, 267–268
Fugitive Slave Act, 322
fugitive slave narratives
  as abolition's movement literature, 162, 165, 166, 171, 176
  genre shifts of, 162, 166–167, 170, 171, 176
  idiosyncrasies of 1820 and 1830s narratives, 165
  kidnapping, 167–170, 171
  political vs. literary, 346
  religio-political discourse of, 135–136, 171–173
  sousveillance, 162, 166, 170–176
  vigilant watchfulness in, 167, 169, 170
Fuller, Margaret. *see also* motherhood and domesticity, women's rights movement
  Cult of True Womanhood, 240
  influence on E. C. Stanton, 226
  motherhood's importance, 244, 247
  personal is political, 238
  prison system and maternal values, 244
  separate spheres metaphor, 225, 244
  urban poverty and charity, 240, 243
  women's equality, 131, 225–226, 247
  Woman in the Nineteenth Century, 225, 238, 244, 247
Funchion, John, 56, 60, 63

Gardener, Helen Hamilton, 233
The Garies and Their Friends (Webb), 38, 45–49
Garland, Hamlin, 258–263, 267–268
Garrison, William Lloyd, 163, 282
The Gates Ajar (Phelps), 137
Geary Act, 195
gender. *see also* motherhood and domesticity, women's rights movement
  California Land Act and, 212
  Chinese immigrants and, 194
  coverture and married women's legal identity, 222, 223, 231
  gender ideology, 137
  gender norms obstructing ideal state, 225
  hierarchy as argument for abolition, 43–44
  Indigenous gender understandings and settler colonialism, 215
  in Lazarus's "The New Colossus," 286

masculinity, 227–228, 235, 298
separate spheres ideology, 223–225, 229
General Colored Association, 163
Genovese, Eugene, 44
George, Henry, 259
Gilman, Charlotte Perkins. *see also* motherhood and domesticity, women's rights movement
  alternative ways of mothering, 248
  economic democracy requires free womanhood, 248–249
  motherhood and harmonious society, 239
  motherhood's inescapability, 250
  poetry as feminist polemic, 284–285
  women and communitarianism, 105
  Herland, 240
Gilmore, James R., 337
The Gladiator (Bird), 297–298
A Glance at New York, 291, 298
Glazener, Nancy, 140, 258, 306
Goddu, Teresa, 163, 166
Goldman, Emma, 51, 104
"The Goophered Grapevine" (Chesnutt), 235
"The Great American Novel" (De Forest), 69
Great American Novel, 316
Great Migration, 302
Greeley, Horace, 98, 155, 282
Green, Steven K., 127
Griggs, Sutton E., 178–179, 180, 187
Grimes, William, 173
Grimké, Angelina, 224, 327
Gronlund, Laurence, 104
Grossman, Allen, 6
Guarneri, Carl, 101
Guwi Sguwi (John Ross), 114–115

Hadley, Elaine, 49
Hale, Dorothy, 49
Hale, Sarah Josepha, 224, 313
Halker, Clark D., 64
Hamilton, Alexander, 145
Hampl, Patricia, 256
Hannah-Jones, Nikole, 30
Harbert, Elizabeth Boynton, 233
The Harbinger (Brook Farm), 101–102
Harper, Frances Ellen Watkins, 136, 184, 185–186, 218–219, 229, 230, 276–278, 279–280
Harper, William, 24
Harrigan and Hart, 301
Harrigan, Edward, 291
Harris, Joel Chandler, 234
Harris, Thomas Lake, 137
Hart, Tony, 291
Hart–Celler Act, 195
Harte, Bret, 197–199, 203
Hartman, Saidiya, 21, 174

Hartz, Louis, 19
"The Haunted Valley" (Bierce), 197
Havel, Hippolyte, 64
Hawthorne, Nathaniel. *see also* liberalism and slavery
  abolition and, 40–41, 311, 338
  on J. Brown, 282
  campaign biography of Pierce and fallout, 337–341, 346–347
  campaign biography of Pierce, scholarly interest in, 341–343
  conservatism of, 35, 37, 40, 342
  Custom House position, 338, 340
  diplomatic and political appointments, 337, 347
  engagement in personhood debate, 27, 28
  Enlightenment and, 39
  as liberal author, 28
  mode of sermon in literature, 134
  novels vs. romances, 307
  political agendas imperiling United States, 311
  radical utopian communities, 53, 100
  social change to be gradual, 37, 40–41
  Spiritualism ridiculed, 137
  tradition the best means of governing people, 38–39
  the Unpardonable Sin, 27
  The Blithedale Romance, 53, 100, 137, 224
  "The Celestial Rail-Road," 339
  "Chiefly About War Matters, By a Peaceable Man," 151, 282
  "The Custom-House," 341
  "Earth's Holocaust," 35
  The House of Seven Gables, 150–152, 307
  The Life of Franklin Pierce, 40, 151, 337–343
  Our Old Home, 346
  The Scarlet Letter, 37–39, 311, 342
Hay, John, 332
Hayes, Rutherford B., 335
A Hazard of New Fortunes (Howells), 54
Hearts of Gold (Jones), 183–184
Heath, James Ewell, 291
Heaton, Daniel, 61, 62
Hebard, Andrew, 266
Hentz, Caroline Lee, 313
Herland (Gilman), 240
The Heroic Slave (Douglass), 313
Hicks, Granville, 56
Higginson, Thomas Wentworth, 277
Hildreth, Richard, 337
The Hindered Hand (Griggs), 178–179
"His Mother" (Gilman), 248
history of political thought (political theory), 1, 5–6, 8
History of the United States of America (Bancroft), 344

Hobomok (Child), 138, 209, 310
Holbo, Christine, 336
Holland, Ben, 77
Holmes, Oliver Wendell, 132, 281
"The Holy Stove" (Gilman), 284
home and homelessness, 240–241
The Home: Its Work and Influence (Gilman), 248
Home settlement, 104
"Homes: A Sestina" (Gilman), 284–285
The Homes of the New World (Bremer), 102
homesteading, 218
homiletic novels, 140
Hooper, Johnson Jones, 313
Hope Leslie (Sedgwick), 138, 310
Hopkins, Sarah Winnemucca, 139
Hot Plowshares (Tourgée), 11, 317
Houghton, Henry, 335
The House of Seven Gables (Hawthorne), 150–152, 307
How the Other Half Lives (Riis), 105, 346
Howard, Bronson, 291, 301
Howard, June, 253
Howe, Julia Ward, 249–250
Howells, William Dean
  black bodies and American character, 83–85
  bodily identity in mixed bodies, 85
  campaign biographies, 335–336
  championing marginalized writers, 315
  communitarian politics, 104
  diplomatic appointments, 333, 335, 336, 337
  double-consciousness, 87
  imperialism and assimilationism in *An Imperative Duty*, 83–86
  literature and politics fundamentally separate, 336
  workers' strikes, 54
  A Hazard of New Fortunes, 54
  An Imperative Duty, 83–86
  Life of Abraham Lincoln, 335
  A Sketch of the Life and Character of Rutherford B. Hayes, 336
  A Traveler from Altruria, 105
  Venetian Life, 333
Hsu, Hsuan L., 199
Hughes, Amy, 298
Humphreys, David, 289, 302
Hutterites, 103
"Hymn" (Whittier), 274
hymns, 274

"I Sing the Body Electric" (Whitman), 286–287
Ignatiev, Noel, 191
Immerwahr, Daniel, 254
immigration, 103, 190–191, 195, 290, 296, 301, *see also* Chinese immigrants, citizenship

Index

Jewish immigrants, 290
  poetry and, 285–286
An Imperative Duty (Howells), 83–86
imperialism. *see* empire and imperialism
Imperium in Imperio (Griggs), 187
"Impressions of an Indian Childhood" (Zitkála-Šá), 266
In His Steps (Sheldon), 140
Incidents in the Life of a Slave Girl (Jacobs), 229
Incidents of Travel in Central America, Chiapas, and Yucatán (Stephens), 345
Incidents of Travel in Egypt, Arabia Petraea, and the Holy Land (Stephens), 345
"Indian Names" (Sigourney), 265
Indian Removal Act, 113
Indigenous peoples. *see also* Cherokee Nation
  appropriated in American literature while removed from landscape, 138
  assimilation efforts by US government, 214, 264, 266
  home, lifeways, and the anticolonial imaginary, 215–216
  Indigenous futurity, 216, 290
  Indigenous gender understandings and, 215
  Indigenous territorialities, 214
  land surveying, allotment, and land theft, 211
  national domestication, 215
  racialization of, 214
  resistance to erasure, 138–139
  in settler-colonial theater, 290, 291, 296
  Spiritualism and, 138
  survivance and Indigenous storytelling, 257
  terra nullius literature and erasure of, 209
  vanishing Indian myth and challenges to, 216, 265, 309–310
  westward expansion and white myths, 138
  whites playing Indian, 264
Indigenous sovereignty. *see also* Cherokee sovereignty
  centrality to frontier romance genre, 117–120
  criticized as dangerous political monstrosity, 112
  European imperialism pushed to periphery of Indigenous center, 265–266
  Indigenous peoples as dependent nations, 116, 209
  Marshall trilogy and, 214
  relationship between sovereign equals, 112
  territory and, 116–117, 205, 213–216
  time and, 265–266
  Treaty of Westphalia weaponized against, 208–209
  white recognition through collective departure, 119
  in Zitkála-Šá's writings, 263–268
industrialization, 255

inequality. *see* labor, Jim Crow and segregation, class and status, capitalism, motherhood and domesticity, women's rights movement, slavery, white supremacy, race and racism
The Innocents Abroad (Twain), 345
Institute for Colored Youth, 320–322
Insular Cases, 206
integration, 321
internationalism, 88–91
"Invocation" (Schoolcraft), 215–216
Iola Leroy, or Shadows Uplifted (Harper), 184, 185–186
Irish immigrants, 190, 191, 290
Irving, Washington, 309
Israel Potter (Melville), 339–340

Jackson, Andrew, 145, 334, 345
Jackson, Gregory, 140
Jackson, Holly, 58
Jacobs, Harriet, 135, 229
James, Henrietta, 232
James, Henry. *see also The Bostonians* (James)
  aesthetic autonomy, 315
  communitarianism in his writings, 105
  on Hawthrone's conservatism, 39
  E. P. Peabody, 61–62
  radical culture in his writings, 54, 57
  women's movement, 56, 57, 221, 231, 232
  Portrait of a Lady, 231
  The Princess Casamassima, 54
James, William, 15, 325
Jefferson, Thomas, 19, 126, 145, 211
Jewett, Sarah Orne, 155–156
Jews and Judaism, 286, 290
Jim Crow and segregation. *see also* white supremacy, race and racism
  African American literature as genre a response to, 187–188
  beginning of, 183
  black bodies possessing identity but not character, 83
  black writers appealing to white southern elites, 183–185
  black writers' opposition to subordination, 187–188
  demoralizing effects, 185
  disenfranchisement, 178–181, 233
  furthering class hierarchy, 179
  in northern states, 181–182
  opportunities for racial uplift, 185–186
  racial identity over class solidarity, 186–187, 262
  separate but equal, 181

Johnson v. McIntosh, 214
Johnson, Andrew, 326
Johnson, William, 116–117, 119
Johnson–Reed Act, 195
Jones, J. McHenry, 183–184
Jones, John Beauchamp, 313
Justice, Daniel Heath, 113, 114

Kaplan, Amy, 250
Kauanui, J. Kēhaulani, 208
Kearney, Denis, 193, 200
Kelley, Abby, 224
Kelley, D. G., 51
Kelley, Mary, 239
Kerr, Howard, 56
Kettner, James, 110
Kippola, Karl, 297
Kirk, Russell, 37, 40
Knapp, Adeline, 197
Koenigs, Thomas, 307–308
Konkle, Maureen, 109, 112

labor, 96, 103, 179, 183–185, 193, 198, *see also* class and status
The Last of the Mohicans (Cooper), 309
Lazarus, Emma, 285–286
Leatherstocking Tales (Cooper), 209
Leaves of Grass (Whitman), 70, 131, 286, 319
The Lecturess (Hale), 224
Lee, Yan Phou, 202–204
Lepore, Jill, 335
Letters from New-York (Child), 240–243
Levin, Yuval, 39
Levine, Herbert J., 131
Levine, Robert, 342
Lewis, Perry, 60
liberalism, 19, 22–23, 27–29, *see also* person and personhood
liberalism and slavery. *see also* Stowe, Harriet Beecher, Hawthorne, Nathaniel
  as the American Dilemma, 19–20
  binary opposition between liberty and slavery, 22
  "enslaved people" terminology, 30
  explanations for inherent contradiction between, 20–21, 23
  parsing Declaration of Independence, 24–26
  personhood debate, 26–29, 30
  personhood debate in modern academia, 29–32, 33
  racism and personhood, 31
  whose enslavement opposed and permitted, 22, 23–25
Liberia: or, Mr. Peyton's Experiments (Hale), 313
The Liberal Tradition in America (Hartz), 19

Liestman, Daniel, 192
Life among the Paiutes (Hopkins), 139
The Life and Adventures of Joaquín Murieta (Ridge), 192, 197, 314
Life and Adventures of Robert, the Hermit of Massachusetts (Voorhis), 167–168
Life of Abraham Lincoln (Howells), 335
The Life of Abraham Lincoln, of Illinois (Raymond), 346
The Life of Franklin Pierce (Hawthorne), 40, 151, 337–343
Life of James A. Garfield (Gilmore), 337
Life of William Grimes, the Runaway Slave (Grimes), 173
Life on the Mississippi (Twain), 137
Lincoln, Abraham, 22, 24, 32, 36–37, *see also* Lincoln–Douglas senatorial debates
Lincoln–Douglas senatorial debates, 2–4, 6–7, 8, 10–12
literarity, 7–8
Little House series (Wilder), 263
Little Women (Alcott), 243, 245
Living My Life (Goldman), 51
local-color writing, 258, 315
Locke, John, 19
Long Soldier, Layli, 265
Longfellow, Henry Wadsworth, 132
Looking Backward (Bellamy), 104
Lords of Creation (Cheever), 299
Losurdo, Dominick, 19
Lowell, James Russell, 70, 80, 132
Luciano, Dana, 59
Lye, Colleen, 193, 197, 203
lynching, 233–234, 235

MacIntyre, Alasdair, 94
MacMillan, Ken, 108, 110
Madison, James, 145, 146
Main Currents in American Thought (Parrington), 344
Main-Travelled Roads (Garland), 259
"Making a Change" (Gilman), 248
Manifest Destiny, 210, 218, 250, *see also* frontier, settler colonialism
Mapps, Grace, 322
maroon communities, 217
The Marrow of Tradition (Chesnutt), 186, 235
Marshall, John, 116, 119
Marx, Karl, 93, 99
Marx, Leo, 255, 261
Massachusetts Anti-Slavery Society, 163
"Matriatism" (Gilman), 248
Matthews, Brander, 334
Matthiessen, F. O., 344
Mays, R. B., 25

Index

McGarry, Molly, 138
McKittrick, Katherine, 217, 218
Melville, Herman
  J. Brown's execution and sovereignty, 122, 282–283
  challenging interpretations of Civil War, 281–283
  communitarianism in his writings, 105
  disapproval of Hawthorne's biography of Pierce, 339–340
  mode of sermon in literature, 134
  political agendas imperiling United States, 312
  Battle-Pieces and Aspects of the War, 281–283
  The Encantadas, 105
  Israel Potter, 339–340
  "Misgivings," 286
  Moby-Dick, 105, 311–312
  "The Portent," 122
Mesmer, Franz Anton, 136
Metamora, 291
Mexal, Stephen J., 198
millennialism, 132–134
Minnie's Sacrifice (Harper), 230
"Misgivings" (Melville), 286
Miss Ravenel's Conversion from Secession to Loyalty (De Forest), 80–83
Moby-Dick (Melville), 105, 311–312
Modern Chivalry (Brackenridge), 146–147
Monk, Maria, 128
Moran of the Lady Letty (Norris), 197
Moreton-Robinson, Aileen, 205, 264
Morton, Thomas, 292–293
Motely, John Lothrop, 344
motherhood and domesticity. *see also* Fuller, Margaret, Gilman, Charlotte Perkins, women's rights movement, Child, Lydia Maria, Stowe, Harriet Beecher
  alternative ways of mothering, 248
  as argument against slavery, 246–247
  female identity apart from, 245–246
  harmonious society and, 239
  importance of, to women writers, 240–241, 242, 244, 247, 250
  inescapability of, 250–251
  monotony leading to desperation, 245
  nationalism, imperialism, and, 249–250
  patriarchy challenged through, 247
  prison systems and, 241–243, 244
  raising independent daughters, 248
  romanticized narratives of, 239–240
  sacralization of, parodied, 284–285
  theater challenging images of, 291
  transformations of, 248–250
"Mother's Day Proclamation" (Howe), 249–250
Mott, Lucretia, 224, 226

Mowatt, Anna Cora, 298
"Miss Grief" (Woolson), 231
"Mrs. Spring Fragrance" (Sui Sin Far), 141
Mugwumps, 145, 146
Mullenix, Elizabeth Reitz, 294
The Mulligan Guard Ball (Harrigan and Hart), 291

The Narrative of James Williams (Williams), 165–166, 173–175
A Narrative of Some Remarkable Incidents (Bayley), 167, 170–173
Narrative of the Life of Frederick Douglass (Douglass), 136, 166, 228
National Woman Suffrage Association, 231
nationalism, 77, 78–79, 88–91, *see also* Cherokee Nation, empire and imperialism, sovereignty
"Nationalism" (Gilman), 285
nation-states. *see also* territory and territoriality, empire and imperialism, sovereignty, Indigenous peoples
  anthropomorphic model, 68, 70–72, 75–76, 77, 79
  as conjugal union, wife, and husband, 81, 83
  double-consciousness applied to, 87–88
  literary culture and, 79–80, 130
  motherhood superseding, 249
  national continuity, 80–82
  nationality as personhood, 88
  objects of affection proper for, 80
  remedy against imperialist threats, 77
  territorial articulations and, 213
  tokens of nationality, 80
  Treaty of Westphalia and, 208–209
  US national identity, character, and physicality, 74
Native Americans. *see* Indigenous peoples
naturalism, 140
Naturalization Act of 1790, 190
Nature (Emerson), 89
"Never or Now" (Holmes), 281
"The New Colossus" (Lazarus), 285–286
New England Anti-Slavery Society, 163
"A New England Nun" (Freeman), 231
A New England Tale (Sedgwick), 129
New Era (Home settlement), 104
New Harmony Gazette, 97
"The New Negro Woman" (Washington), 231
New York Committee of Vigilance, 165
The New York Tribune (Greeley), 98, 155
Newman, Richard, 163
newspapers overlapping literature and politics, 345–346
Nick of the Woods (Bird), 209

Nicolay, John, 332
Nietzsche, Friedrich, 305
Noah, Mordecai, 291, 296–297
Noll, Mark, 139
nonfiction, 343–346, *see also* campaign biographies
Norgren, Jill, 114
Norris, Frank, 140, 197
Northup, Solomon, 26, 165

O'Brien, C.C., 230
O'Hara, Kieron, 41
Oak Openings (Cooper), 117–120
The Octoroon (Boucicault), 291
Ogilvie, James, 324
Ogimawkwe Mitigwaki (Queen of the Woods: A Novel) (Pokagon), 156
"Old Indian Legends" (Zitkála-Šá), 266
On the Origin of Species (Darwin), 139
"On Truth and Lies in a Nonmoral Sense" (Nietzsche), 305
Onoto Watanna (Winnifred Eaton), 199
Optic, Oliver (William Taylor Adams), 337
oratory. *see also* Lincoln–Douglas senatorial debates, Douglass, Frederick, Emerson, Ralph Waldo, Whitman, Walt
  audience for, 326–327
  commentaries and evaluations by auditors, 327–328
  as embodied performance, 328
  limits of national belonging highlighted by, 330
  as literature, 319
  print intertwined with, 325–326
  studying oratorical performance, 328–330
  ubiquity of, 323–325
Ossawattomie Brown (Swayze), 293–294
Our Androcentric Culture, or the Man-Made World (Gilman), 249
Our Nig, or Sketches from the Life of a Free Black (Wilson), 182
Our Old Home (Hawthorne), 346
Our Standard-Bearer (Adams, pseud. Oliver), 337
Out of Her Sphere (Harbert), 233
"The Over-Soul" (Emerson), 89
Owen, Robert, 95, 97

Pacific imminence, 196
Page Act, 194
Page, Thomas Nelson, 234, 256
Parker, Edward G., 324
Parker, Maegan, 233–234
Parker, Theodore, 131, 322, 346
Parrington, Vernon Louis, 344
Parsons, Lucy, 51, 53

partisanship. *see also* James, Henry, Emerson, Ralph Waldo, Stowe, Harriet Beecher, Adams, Henry, Twain, Mark, Hawthorne, Nathaniel
  abolition prospects warped by, 152–153
  attempts to ameliorate, 150–152
  conflicts of interest vs. of principle, 150
  as distorting force, 149
  dominant views of factionalism and, 145–148
  as inescapable, 146
  Jacksonian Democrats, 145, 151
  loss of self and, 150–151
  opposition to, 143–145, 261
  partisan behavior, 148–149
  Reconstruction and, 153–155
  Republican Party, 151
  rise of, 145, 155–156
  temperance movement and, 156–157
  truth's distance from, 150
  warping true democracy, 155
  Whig Party, 145, 151
Parton, James, 334
Peabody, Elizabeth Palmer, 61–62
Peace and Treaty of Westphalia, 78, 88, 110, 208–209, 214
Peirce, C.S., 15
Pels, Dick, 12–13
Pennsylvania Society for the Abolition of Slavery, 164
The People v. *Hall*, 192
The People's Party, 258
person and personhood. *see also* liberalism and slavery
  center of liberal thought, 22–23, 26, 28–29
  dehistoricized and decontextualized, 29–30
  essentialist ideas constituting, 32
  as historically contestable identity, 29
  nationality as personhood, 88
  not socially constructed, 27–28
  peoples anthropomorphized as a person, 78
  as political category, 25, 26
  racism and, 31–32
Pfaelzer, Jean, 193, 194
The Phalanx (Brisbane), 101
Phelps, Elizabeth Stuart, 137, 251
Philpott, Daniel, 110
Piatote, Beth, 215
The Pioneer Boy, and How He Became President (Thayer), 337
The Pioneers (Cooper), 309
"Plain Language from Truthful James" (Harte), 197–199, 203
The Planter's Northern Bride (Hentz), 313
"A Plea for Captain John Brown" (Thoreau), 122

A Plea for Emigration (Shadd), 218, 323
Plessy v. Ferguson, 181, 183
poetry in public discourse
  America foretold, 274–275
  belonging and participation in America, 275
  challenging interpretations of Civil War, 281–283
  freedom as coded political and religious discourse, 276–279
  immigration, 285–286
  individualism, freedom, and religious discourse, 131–132, 271, 275–276, 279, 283–284
  northern elitism and freedom, 281
  overview, 272–274
  poetry as feminist polemic, 284–285
  reactionary readings in South, 280–281
Pokagon, Simon, 156
political appointments for authors, 333, 335, 336, 337, 344–347
political philosophy, 1, 4–5
political science, 1, 4–5
political theory (history of political thought), 1, 5–6, 8
"Politics" (Emerson), 150
Pollock, James, 319–322, 325
Populism, 179, 183, 258, 259, 261
"The Portent" (Melville), 122, 282–283
Portrait of a Lady (James), 231
Potter, Helen, 319, 329
poverty, 240–243
pragmatism, 1–2, 14
The Prairie (Cooper), 148
Pratt, Lloyd, 257
Pray You Sir, Whose Daughter? (Gardener), 233
The Princess Casamassima (James)
  importance for American radicals, 54
  radical culture in, 54
prison systems, 241–243, 244
Provincial Freeman (Shadd), 322, 323
Pryse, Marjorie, 316
Pudd'nhead Wilson and Those Extraordinary Twins (Twain), 156
"The Purpose" (Gilman), 248

race and racism. *see also* person and personhood, Jim Crow and segregation, class and status, immigration, Indigenous peoples, slavery, white supremacy, Whitman, Walt
  anti-imperialism through racial-continental segregation, 83
  belonging, exclusion, and identity, 212–213
  citizenship and, 320–322
  Civil Rights Act of 1875, 183
  debates over territories' fitness for statehood, 207
  economism and, 193, 203
  internalized race relations of double-consciousness, 87
  interracial marriage vs. chain of subordination, 47–48
  labor racialized as white, 193
  lynching, 233–234, 235
  meritocratic progress for whites only, 47–49
  Mexicanness racialized, 212
  in northern states, 181–182
  Populism in opposition to, 183
  racial equality, need for recognized, 182
  racial exclusion and immigration, 191, 194–195
  racial hierarchy, 46–48, 234
  racial identity over class solidarity, 186–187, 262
  racial subordination and class rule, 179
  racialization of Indigenous peoples, 214
  slavery explained through, 31–33
Radical Abolitionism (Lewis), 61
Radical Reconstruction, 183
radicalism. *see also The Princess Casamassima* (James), communitarianism, abolitionism
  abolitionist movement, regard for, 62, 63
  antebellum vs. postbellum activism, 59–61
  Brook Farm utopian community, 53
  print culture of, as literature, 52, 59, 64–65
  questioning all of American life, 58
  relationship to the past, 62–64
  satire and, 53
Rancière, Jacques, 7–9, 10
Raymond, Henry J., 346
realism, 140–141
Reason, Charles, 322
The Rebellion Record, 281
Rebhorn, Matthew, 297
Reconciliation literature, 234
Reconstruction, 70, 102, 153–155, 316–317
Reed, Peter, 297
Reflections on the Revolution in France (Burke), 39
region and regionalism. *see also* territory and territoriality, frontier
  colonial violence enabling regional writing, 263
  country as unpopulated pastoral refuge, 255–256
  empire and, 254–255
  survivance antithetical to, 267
  transforming settler into native, 263
religion
  abolition as foray into liberal religion, 276
  anti-Catholic rhetoric and literature, 128
  black Christians and churches, 136
  centrality to cultural and political life, 127
  Christianity excoriated, 200–201

religion (cont.)
　disestablishing state-supported churches, 127–129
　Enlightenment discourses, 271
　ethics vs., 202
　fiction as tool for religious and social reform, 129
　Fireside Poets uniting Protestant values with American virtues, 132
　freedom and, 276–281, 283–284
　growth of religious movements, 128–129
　literary realism, 140
　millennialism, 132–134
　missionary activities and imperialism, 200, 202–203
　in poetry, 131–132, 271, 275–276, 279, 283–284
　print culture increasing religious adherence, 129
　reciprocal influence on literature, 130, 134
　Second Great Awakening, 129
　sentimentalism, 133–134
　slavery shaping Protestant denominational landscape, 136
　sovereignty's interplay between law and, 108, 115, 116–117, 121
　Spiritualism, 136–138
　theological crisis in American life, 139–140
　Transcendentalist movement, 130–131
"Resistance to Civil Government" (Thoreau), 123
Reynolds, David S., 134
Reynolds, Larry, 342
Rice, Thomas "Daddy," 295
Ridge, John Rollin, 138, 192, 197, 314
Riis, Jacob, 105, 346
"Rip Van Winkle" (Irving), 309
Ripley, George, 99, 101
Rittenhouse, John B., 174
Robin, Corey, 45, 46
Rockhill, Gabriel, 7–9
Ronda, Bruce A., 62
Ross, John (Guwi Sguwi), 114–115
Rossiter, Clinton, 37
Rowlandson, Mary, 107–108
rural. *see* city–country binary, region and regionalism
Rural Felicity, 291
Ruth Hall (Fern), 248, 315
Ryan, Mary, 239

Said, Edward, 219
Sand, George, 102
Sargent, Epes, 337
satire, 53, 313–314
Saussure, Ferdinand de, 1, 8
scarcity, 254, 257, 258–263, 264

The Scarlet Letter (Hawthorne), 37–39, 311, 342
"The School Days of an Indian Girl" (Zitkála-Šá), 266
The School of Reform (Morton), 292–293
Schoolcraft, Jane Johnston (Bamewawagezhikaquay), 139, 215–216
Schwab, Justus, 52
Scott, Walter, 130
Scudder, Horace E., 55
Sedgwick, Catharine Maria, 117, 125–126, 129, 134, 138, 310
Sedgwick, Pamela, 125
Sedgwick, Theodore, 125–126
segregation. *see* Jim Crow and segregation
Sekora, John, 166
"Self-Culture" (Channing), 149–150
Seneca Falls Convention, 226–227
sentimentalism, 133–134
Sergeant, John, 115
sermons, 134–136
settler colonialism. *see also* territory and territoriality, region and regionalism, empire and imperialism, sovereignty, Indigenous peoples
　Chinese immigrants exploited for, 199
　contested sovereignty, *Cherokee Nation v. Georgia*, 112–120
　frontier and, 255, 256
　Indigenous gender understandings and, 215
　Indigenous people as spiritual guides for settlers, 138
　Indigenous portrayal in theater, 290, 291, 296
　land surveying, allotment, and land theft, 211
　Manifest Destiny, 210, 218, 250
　reinforced through literature, 207
　scarcity and finance capitalism, 257
　terra incognita, 255
　terra nullius literature and erasure of Indigenous peoples, 209–211
　in theaters and dramas, 290
　US history inextricable from, 126
　vanishing Indian myth and challenges to, 216, 265, 309–310
　whites playing Indian, 264
Seward, William Henry, 193, 195
sexism. *see* motherhood and domesticity, women's rights movement
Shadd, Mary Ann, 218, 322–323, 329
Shakers, 94, 95
She Would Be a Soldier (Noah), 291, 296–297
Sheldon, Charles, 140
Shenandoah (Howard), 291, 301
Shklar, Judith, 20
Shreve, Grant, 138

"Side by Side" (Zitkála-Šá), 264–266
Sigourney, Lydia, 239, 265
Simms, William Gilmore, 310, 313
Sinclair, Upton, 65
Sinha, Manisha, 162, 164
A Sketch of the Life and Character of Rutherford B. Hayes (Howells), 336
The Slave; or, Memoirs of Archy Moore (Hildreth), 337
slavery. *see also* liberalism and slavery, partisanship, Jim Crow and segregation, Douglass, Frederick, race and racism, Stowe, Harriet Beecher, abolitionism, fugitive slave narratives
  belonging and participation, 275
  conservatism and proslavery policies, 36–37
  contradicting Enlightenment freedom and biblical injunction, 275
  explained through race, 31–33
  freedom coded as political and religious discourse, 276–279
  humanity antithetical to enslavement, 227
  illogic and hypocrisy of, exposed in fiction, 313
  masculinity and, 227–228, 298
  motherhood and sanctity of marriage, 246–247
  "personhood" debates, 23–25, 29
  in plays, 297–298, 299–301
  Protestant denominational landscape shaped by, 136
  slave spirituals and coded freedom, 277–278
  surveillance countered through sousveillance, 161
Slavery As It Is (Weld), 312
Slavery in the United States (Ball), 168–169, 173
Smith, Sydney, 79
Social Destiny of Man (Brisbane), 98, 102
The Social Reformer and Herald of Universal Health (Allen), 101
socialism, 95, *see also* communitarianism
Society for the Relief of Free Negroes Unlawfully Held in Bondage, 164
Society of American Indians, 264
"Song of Myself" (Whitman), 131
"Songs of the Contraband," 277
The Souls of Black Folk (Du Bois), 88, 185, 188
The Soveraignty and Goodness of God (Rowlandson), 107–108
sovereignty. *see also* Cherokee sovereignty, nation-states, territory and territoriality, Indigenous sovereignty
  black sovereignty, 217
  colonies and derivation of, 107–108
  control over territory, 205
  execution of J. Brown and, 122, 282–283
  God and, 107, 121
  overview, 109–112
  in plays, 296–297
  reconfiguration attempts, 121–122
  religion and law, interplay between, 108, 115, 116–117, 121
  resonance of term in colonies, 107, 108
  state, definition, 115
  Treaty of Westphalia and, 208–209
Spillers, Hortense, 135
Spires, Derrick R., 227
Spiritualism, 136–138
A Spoil of Office (Garland), 260–263
standpoint epistemology, 1, 10–13, 15
Stanford, Leland, 192
Stanton, Elizabeth Cady, 224, 226–227, 230
status. *see* class and status
Stein, Judith, 179, 183
Stephens, John Lloyd, 345
Stewart, Maria, 135, 229
Still, William, 322, 325
Stokes, Claudia, 132
The Story of Avis (Phelps), 251
Stowe, Harriet Beecher. *see also* liberalism and slavery, motherhood and domesticity, women's rights movement, *Uncle Tom's Cabin* (Stowe)
  campaign biography of Ulysses S. Grant, 336
  conservative argument for radical abolition, 38, 41–42, 43
  domesticity, 239
  on fiction and politics, 304–305
  homiletic realism, 140
  as liberal author, 28
  literary reactions to, 313
  partisanship and abolition, 152–153
  race, slavery, and personhood, 32
  sermons and narrative voice, 134
  social hierarchy used to advocate for abolition, 43
  Dred: A Tale of the Great Dismal Swamp, 152–153
Streeby, Shelley, 52
suffrage. *see also* Jim Crow and segregation, class and status, women's rights movement
  14th and 15th Amendments, 229–230
  black men and, 227–228, 321–322
  black women and, 230
  core to national life, 221
  enslavement disqualifying, 227
  femininity making for good voters, 232–233
  gaining national attention, 231
  Home Protection, 232
  ideal voter image shifting, 222

suffrage (cont.)
  literature and black disenfranchisement, 234–235
  paucity of representation in literature, 221
  property ownership as barrier to, 222
  pro-suffrage plays, 299
  universal suffrage, 229
Sui Sin Far (Edith Maude Eaton), 141, 199
Sumner, Charles, 69, 76, 80
survivance, 254, 257, 265–268
Swayze, Kate Edwards, 293–294
The Sword and the Distaff (Simms), 313

Taney, Roger B., 25
Taylor, Bayard, 345
Tellmann, Ute, 258
territory and territoriality. *see also* nation-states, region and regionalism, Indigenous sovereignty, frontier, empire and imperialism, sovereignty
  belonging, exclusion, and identity, 212–213
  black territorialities, 217–219
  debates over fitness for statehood, 207
  definition, 207
  definition of territoriality, 205
  doctrine of discovery, 214
  empire and, 254–255
  expansion, 206, 210, 211–212
  as geographical imaginary, 205, 206
  imperial occupations expressed, 205
  Indian territory, 213–216
  within Indigenous ideas of sovereignty, 205
  Indigenous sovereignty, 116–117
  Insular Cases and, 206
  land surveying, 209–211
  Manifest Destiny, 210
  Maroon communities, 217
  nation-states and articulations of, 213
  settler colonialism reinforced through literature, 207
  as sovereign's property, 205
  terra nullius, 209–211, 214
  Treaty of Westphalia and, 208–209, 214
  Underground Railroad, 217
  westward expansion's logic, 214
The Testimony of Christ's Second Appearing, 95
Thayer, William M., 337
theater and drama
  Asian theater companies, 290
  audiences, 292–293, 294, 302
  black theater companies, 290
  J. Brown recast in domestic drama, 293–294
  education in the playhouse, 293
  Great Migration, 302
  Irish immigrants, 290
  overview, 289–292
  political conflicts on the stage, 291
  politically driven riots, 294–296
  proper role of, 292
  settler colonialism of, 290, 291, 296
  slavery and abolition, 297–298, 299–301
  systemic racism challenged, 291
  territorial sovereignty in plays, 296–297
  vaudeville, 301
  women's representation in, 291
  women's rights, 298–299
Theatrical Syndicate, 302
Thoreau, Henry David, 122–123, 131, 209–210, 339
Ticknor, William, 340
Timrod, Henry, 280–281
Tobiason, Aaron, 295
Tocqueville, Alexis de, 155
Tompkins, Jane, 134, 341
Toulouse, Teresa, 107
Tourgée, Albion, 11, 153–155, 317, 336
Towers, Frank, 6
tract literature, 134
Transcendentalist movement, 90, 130–131, 150, 225
A Traveler from Altruria (Howells), 105
A Treatise on Domestic Economy (Beecher), 45
Treaty of Guadalupe Hidalgo, 211
Trent, Hank, 174–175, 176
True Womanhood, 238, 240, 246, 247
Truth, Sojourner, 229, 230, 327
Tuchinsky, Adam-Max, 98
"Turned" (Gilman), 248
Turner, Frederick Jackson, 210
Turner, Nat, 136
Twain, Mark
  allegory of Reconstruction and fictional truth, 316–317
  ascendance of lower class whites and disenfranchisement, 180–181
  communitarianism's dystopian risks, 105
  early career, 345
  on fiction and politics, 304–305, 316–317
  partisanship and temperance movement, 156
  Spiritualism ridiculed, 137
  The Adventures of Huckleberry Finn, 180–181, 304–305, 316–317
  Ah Sin, 197
  A Connecticut Yankee in King Arthur's Court, 105
  The Innocents Abroad, 345
  Life on the Mississippi, 137
  Pudd'nhead Wilson and Those Extraordinary Twins, 156
  Roughing It, 345
Twelve Years a Slave (Northup), 165

Uncle Remus stories, 234
Uncle Tom's Cabin (Stowe)
  conservative argument for radical abolition, 38, 41–42, 44–45
  on fiction and politics, 304–305
  gender hierarchy as argument for abolition, 43–44
  motherhood and domesticity, 246–247
  partisanship and abolition, 152
  political polemic in, 133
  politics via moral suasion, 312–313
  right relations and inequality, 41–45
  slaves as persons, 26, 28
Uncle Tom's Cabin (play) (Conway), 290, 291, 299
Under the Gaslight (Daly), 291, 298–299
Underground Railroad, 165, 175, 217
Unitarianism, 130
United States. *see* nation-states, empire and imperialism, sovereignty, belonging and participation
"The Unnatural Mother" (Gilman), 248
urban. *see* city–country binary, scarcity, capitalism
US-Mexico War, 211–212
utopianism, 103, *see also* communitarianism

Van Anglen, K. P., 130
Veblen, Thorstein, 259
Venetian Life (Howells), 333
Vizenor, Gerald, 257
Voegelin, Eric, 21
A Voice from the South (Cooper), 184
Voorhis, Robert, 167–168
voting. *see* suffrage
Voyage en Icarie (Cabet), 100

Walden (Thoreau), 339
Waldron, Jeremy, 22
Walker, David, 24, 135, 136, 163
Walker, George, 302
"Walking" (Thoreau), 209–210
Wallace, Lew, 337
Walzer, Michael, 93
Ware, Henry, Jr., 134
Warner, Michael, 127
Warner, Susan, 133
Warren, Joyce, 239
Warren, Kenneth, 316
Washington, Booker T., 181, 183, 184
Washington, Mrs. Booker T., 231
Washington, George, 211
Watkins, William J., 323, 329
Watts, Edward, 118
"The Ways That Are Dark" (Knapp), 197

Wears, Isaac, 323
Webb, Frank J., 38, 45–49
Weber and Fields, 301
Weld, Theodore, 166, 312
Wells, Ida B., 233–234
Wells, Jeremy, 234
Welter, Barbara, 238
West, Stephen, 125
Wharton, Edith, 315
"What to the Slave Is the Fourth of July" (Douglass), 80
Whatmore, Richard, 5–6
Whigs and Democrats (Heath), 291
white supremacy. *see also* Jim Crow and segregation, empire and imperialism, settler colonialism, race and racism
  Chinese immigrants exploited for, 199
  conservatism and, 45–49
  inciting violence, 314
  means to challenge undermined, 187
  Reconciliation literature, 234
  scarcity and, 257
White, Ed, 256
White, George W., 78
White, Jacob C., Jr., 320–322, 325, 326, 329
White, James B., 175
Whitehead, Celia B., 232
Whitman, Walt
  anthropomorphizing American continent, 70, 72
  on belonging, 286–287
  on Emerson as imperial Master of transcendentalist Over-Soul, 76
  literature as expressions representing the national body, 79
  on oratory, 319, 328, 330
  religion and *Leaves of Grass*, 131
  supremacy of Individuality, 71, 74, 75, 77, 82, 86, 89
  US ethnogenesis, 74
  US imperialism, 75–76
  US national character, 68, 70–72, 74, 75–76, 88
  "Facing West from California's Shores," 206
  "I Sing the Body Electric," 286
  Leaves of Grass, 70, 131, 286, 319
  "Song of Myself," 131
Whitney, Asa, 196
Whittier, John Greenleaf, 132, 174, 175, 274, 279
"Why Am I a Heathen?" (Wong), 200–202, 203
"Why Are Women the Natural Guardians of Social Morals?" (Howe), 250
"Why I Am a Pagan" (Zitkála-Šá), 139
"Why I Am Not a Heathen" (Lee), 202–204
The Wide, Wide World (Warner), 133

Wieland, or the Transformation (Brown), 308–309
Wilder, Laura Ingalls, 263
Willard, Frances, 231, 232, 233–234
Williams, Bert, 302
Williams, James, 165–166, 173–176
Williams, Raymond, 255, 264
Wilson, Carol, 164–165, 168
Wilson, Harriet, 182
Wilson, Ivy, 59
Wirt, William, 115
Wolff, Nathan, 260
Woman in the Nineteenth Century (Fuller), 225, 238, 244, 247
Women and Economics (Gilman), 105, 248
Women's Christian Temperance Union, 231
women's rights movement. *see also* Fuller, Margaret, Gilman, Charlotte Perkins, motherhood and domesticity, gender, Child, Lydia Maria, James, Henry, suffrage, Stowe, Harriet Beecher
    14th and 15th Amendments, 229–230
    black women and, 228–229, 230, 234, 235
    coverture and, 222, 223, 231
    Cult of True Womanhood, 240, 246, 247
    economic democracy requires free womanhood, 248–249
    emerging from abolitionism, 223
    essential sameness of all humans, 226
    literature predominantly white, 233
    motherhood and, 238, 239–240
    in national conversation, 230–231
    New Woman, 231–232, 238, 247
    oppression justified by character of, 223–224
    in plays, 298–299
    representations in literature, hostile, 224–225
    representations in literature, positive, 225–226, 231–233
    schism between white and black women, 233–234
    separate spheres ideology, 223–224
    women's equality, 131, 225–226, 247
    women's moral superiority and sexual purity, 232–234
Wong Chin Foo, 199–204
Woodward, C. Vann, 180
Woolson, Constance Fenimore, 231
Worcester v. *Georgia*, 214
Workingmen's Party, 193
Wright, Richard, 54
Wyckoff, Walter, 140

Yack, Bernard, 78
The Yankey in England (Humphreys), 289
Yekl (Cahan), 141
"The Yellow Wall-Paper" (Gilman), 248, 250
The Yemassee (Simms), 310
The Young Miner (Alger), 197

Zboray, Mary Saracino, 328
Zboray, Ronald J., 328
Zitkála-Šá, 139, 257, 263–268
Zolberg, Aristide, 190, 193, 194

CAMBRIDGE COMPANIONS TO ...

AUTHORS

Edward Albee edited by Stephen J. Bottoms
Margaret Atwood edited by Coral Ann Howells (second edition)
W. H. Auden edited by Stan Smith
Jane Austen edited by Edward Copeland and Juliet McMaster (second edition)
James Baldwin edited by Michele Elam
Balzac edited by Owen Heathcote and Andrew Watts
Beckett edited by John Pilling
Bede edited by Scott DeGregorio
Aphra Behn edited by Derek Hughes and Janet Todd
Saul Bellow edited by Victoria Aarons
Walter Benjamin edited by David S. Ferris
William Blake edited by Morris Eaves
Boccaccio edited by Guyda Armstrong, Rhiannon Daniels, and Stephen J. Milner
Jorge Luis Borges edited by Edwin Williamson
Brecht edited by Peter Thomson and Glendyr Sacks (second edition)
The Brontës edited by Heather Glen
Bunyan edited by Anne Dunan-Page
Frances Burney edited by Peter Sabor
Byron edited by Drummond Bone (second edition)
Albert Camus edited by Edward J. Hughes
Willa Cather edited by Marilee Lindemann
Catullus edited by Ian Du Quesnay and Tony Woodman
Cervantes edited by Anthony J. Cascardi
Chaucer edited by Piero Boitani and Jill Mann (second edition)
Chekhov edited by Vera Gottlieb and Paul Allain
Kate Chopin edited by Janet Beer
Caryl Churchill edited by Elaine Aston and Elin Diamond
Cicero edited by Catherine Steel
John Clare edited by Sarah Houghton-Walker
J. M. Coetzee edited by Jarad Zimbler
Coleridge edited by Lucy Newlyn
Coleridge edited by Tim Fulford (new edition)
Wilkie Collins edited by Jenny Bourne Taylor
Joseph Conrad edited by J. H. Stape
H. D. edited by Nephie J. Christodoulides and Polina Mackay
Dante edited by Rachel Jacoff (second edition)
Daniel Defoe edited by John Richetti
Don DeLillo edited by John N. Duvall
Charles Dickens edited by John O. Jordan
Emily Dickinson edited by Wendy Martin
John Donne edited by Achsah Guibbory

Dostoevskii edited by W. J. Leatherbarrow
Theodore Dreiser edited by Leonard Cassuto and Claire Virginia Eby
John Dryden edited by Steven N. Zwicker
W. E. B. Du Bois edited by Shamoon Zamir
George Eliot edited by George Levine and Nancy Henry (second edition)
T. S. Eliot edited by A. David Moody
Ralph Ellison edited by Ross Posnock
Ralph Waldo Emerson edited by Joel Porte and Saundra Morris
William Faulkner edited by Philip M. Weinstein
Henry Fielding edited by Claude Rawson
F. Scott Fitzgerald edited by Ruth Prigozy
F. Scott Fitzgerald edited by Michael Nowlin (second edition)
Flaubert edited by Timothy Unwin
E. M. Forster edited by David Bradshaw
Benjamin Franklin edited by Carla Mulford
Brian Friel edited by Anthony Roche
Robert Frost edited by Robert Faggen
Gabriel García Márquez edited by Philip Swanson
Elizabeth Gaskell edited by Jill L. Matus
Edward Gibbon edited by Karen O'Brien and Brian Young
Goethe edited by Lesley Sharpe
Günter Grass edited by Stuart Taberner
Thomas Hardy edited by Dale Kramer
David Hare edited by Richard Boon
Nathaniel Hawthorne edited by Richard Millington
Seamus Heaney edited by Bernard O'Donoghue
Ernest Hemingway edited by Scott Donaldson
Hildegard of Bingen edited by Jennifer Bain
Homer edited by Robert Fowler
Horace edited by Stephen Harrison
Ted Hughes edited by Terry Gifford
Ibsen edited by James McFarlane
Kazuo Ishiguro edited by Andrew Bennett
Henry James edited by Jonathan Freedman
Samuel Johnson edited by Greg Clingham
Ben Jonson edited by Richard Harp and Stanley Stewart
James Joyce edited by Derek Attridge (second edition)
Kafka edited by Julian Preece
Keats edited by Susan J. Wolfson
Rudyard Kipling edited by Howard J. Booth
Lacan edited by Jean-Michel Rabaté
D. H. Lawrence edited by Anne Fernihough
Primo Levi edited by Robert Gordon
Lucretius edited by Stuart Gillespie and Philip Hardie
Machiavelli edited by John M. Najemy

David Mamet edited by Christopher Bigsby
Thomas Mann edited by Ritchie Robertson
Christopher Marlowe edited by Patrick Cheney
Andrew Marvell edited by Derek Hirst and Steven N. Zwicker
Ian McEwan edited by Dominic Head
Herman Melville edited by Robert S. Levine
Arthur Miller edited by Christopher Bigsby (second edition)
Milton edited by Dennis Danielson (second edition)
Molière edited by David Bradby and Andrew Calder
William Morris edited by Marcus Waithe
Toni Morrison edited by Justine Tally
Alice Munro edited by David Staines
Nabokov edited by Julian W. Connolly
Eugene O'Neill edited by Michael Manheim
George Orwell edited by John Rodden
Ovid edited by Philip Hardie
Petrarch edited by Albert Russell Ascoli and Unn Falkeid
Harold Pinter edited by Peter Raby (second edition)
Sylvia Plath edited by Jo Gill
Plutarch edited by Frances B. Titchener and Alexei Zadorojnyi
Edgar Allan Poe edited by Kevin J. Hayes
Alexander Pope edited by Pat Rogers
Ezra Pound edited by Ira B. Nadel
Proust edited by Richard Bales
Pushkin edited by Andrew Kahn
Thomas Pynchon edited by Inger H. Dalsgaard, Luc Herman and Brian McHale
Rabelais edited by John O'Brien
Rilke edited by Karen Leeder and Robert Vilain
Philip Roth edited by Timothy Parrish
Salman Rushdie edited by Abdulrazak Gurnah
John Ruskin edited by Francis O'Gorman
Sappho edited by P. J. Finglass and Adrian Kelly
Seneca edited by Shadi Bartsch and Alessandro Schiesaro
Shakespeare edited by Margareta de Grazia and Stanley Wells (second edition)
George Bernard Shaw edited by Christopher Innes
Shelley edited by Timothy Morton
Mary Shelley edited by Esther Schor
Sam Shepard edited by Matthew C. Roudané
Spenser edited by Andrew Hadfield
Laurence Sterne edited by Thomas Keymer
Wallace Stevens edited by John N. Serio
Tom Stoppard edited by Katherine E. Kelly
Harriet Beecher Stowe edited by Cindy Weinstein
August Strindberg edited by Michael Robinson
Jonathan Swift edited by Christopher Fox

J. M. Synge edited by P. J. Mathews
Tacitus edited by A. J. Woodman
Henry David Thoreau edited by Joel Myerson
Thucydides edited by Polly Low
Tolstoy edited by Donna Tussing Orwin
Anthony Trollope edited by Carolyn Dever and Lisa Niles
Mark Twain edited by Forrest G. Robinson
John Updike edited by Stacey Olster
Mario Vargas Llosa edited by Efrain Kristal and John King
Virgil edited by Fiachra Mac Góráin and Charles Martindale (second edition)
Voltaire edited by Nicholas Cronk
David Foster Wallace edited by Ralph Clare
Edith Wharton edited by Millicent Bell
Walt Whitman edited by Ezra Greenspan
Oscar Wilde edited by Peter Raby
Tennessee Williams edited by Matthew C. Roudané
William Carlos Williams edited by Christopher MacGowan
August Wilson edited by Christopher Bigsby
Mary Wollstonecraft edited by Claudia L. Johnson
Virginia Woolf edited by Susan Sellers (second edition)
Wordsworth edited by Stephen Gill
Richard Wright edited by Glenda R. Carpio
W. B. Yeats edited by Marjorie Howes and John Kelly
Xenophon edited by Michael A. Flower
Zola edited by Brian Nelson

TOPICS

The Actress edited by Maggie B. Gale and John Stokes
The African American Novel edited by Maryemma Graham
The African American Slave Narrative edited by Audrey A. Fisch
African American Theatre edited by Harvey Young
Allegory edited by Rita Copeland and Peter Struck
American Crime Fiction edited by Catherine Ross Nickerson
American Gothic edited by Jeffrey Andrew Weinstock
The American Graphic Novel edited by Jan Baetens, Hugo Frey and Fabrice Leroy
American Horror edited by Stephen Shapiro and Mark Storey
American Literature and the Body edited by Travis M. Foster
American Literature and the Environment edited by Sarah Ensor and Susan Scott Parrish
American Literature of the 1930s edited by William Solomon
American Modernism edited by Walter Kalaidjian
American Poetry since 1945 edited by Jennifer Ashton
American Realism and Naturalism edited by Donald Pizer
American Short Story edited by Michael J. Collins and Gavin Jones

American Travel Writing edited by Alfred Bendixen and Judith Hamera
American Women Playwrights edited by Brenda Murphy
Ancient Rhetoric edited by Erik Gunderson
Arthurian Legend edited by Elizabeth Archibald and Ad Putter
Australian Literature edited by Elizabeth Webby
The Australian Novel edited by Nicholas Birns and Louis Klee
The Beats edited by Stephen Belletto
The Black Body in American Literature edited by Cherene Sherrard-Johnson
Boxing edited by Gerald Early
British Black and Asian Literature (1945–2010) edited by Deirdre Osborne
British Fiction: 1980–2018 edited by Peter Boxall
British Fiction since 1945 edited by David James
British Literature of the 1930s edited by James Smith
British Literature of the French Revolution edited by Pamela Clemit
British Romantic Poetry edited by James Chandler and Maureen N. McLane
British Romanticism edited by Stuart Curran (second edition)
British Romanticism and Religion edited by Jeffrey Barbeau
British Theatre, 1730–1830 edited by Jane Moody and Daniel O'Quinn
Canadian Literature edited by Eva-Marie Kröller (second edition)
The Canterbury Tales edited by Frank Grady
Children's Literature edited by M. O. Grenby and Andrea Immel
The City in World Literature edited by Ato Quayson and Jini Kim Watson
The Classic Russian Novel edited by Malcolm V. Jones and Robin Feuer Miller
Comics edited by Maaheen Ahmed
Contemporary African American Literature edited by Yogita Goyal
Contemporary Irish Poetry edited by Matthew Campbell
Creative Writing edited by David Morley and Philip Neilsen
Crime Fiction edited by Martin Priestman
Dante's "Commedia" edited by Zygmunt G. Barański and Simon Gilson
Dracula edited by Roger Luckhurst
Early American Literature edited by Bryce Traister
Early Modern Women's Writing edited by Laura Lunger Knoppers
The Eighteenth-Century Novel edited by John Richetti
Eighteenth-Century Poetry edited by John Sitter
Eighteenth-Century Thought edited by Frans De Bruyn
Emma edited by Peter Sabor
English Dictionaries edited by Sarah Ogilvie
English Literature, 1500–1600 edited by Arthur F. Kinney
English Literature, 1650–1740 edited by Steven N. Zwicker
English Literature, 1740–1830 edited by Thomas Keymer and Jon Mee
English Literature, 1830–1914 edited by Joanne Shattock
English Melodrama edited by Carolyn Williams
English Novelists edited by Adrian Poole
English Poetry, Donne to Marvell edited by Thomas N. Corns
English Poets edited by Claude Rawson

English Renaissance Drama edited by A. R. Braunmuller and Michael Hattaway (second edition)
English Renaissance Tragedy edited by Emma Smith and Garrett A. Sullivan Jr.
English Restoration Theatre edited by Deborah C. Payne Fisk
Environmental Humanities edited by Jeffrey Cohen and Stephanie Foote
The Epic edited by Catherine Bates
Erotic Literature edited by Bradford Mudge
The Essay edited by Kara Wittman and Evan Kindley
European Modernism edited by Pericles Lewis
European Novelists edited by Michael Bell
Fairy Tales edited by Maria Tatar
Fantasy Literature edited by Edward James and Farah Mendlesohn
Feminist Literary Theory edited by Ellen Rooney
Fiction in the Romantic Period edited by Richard Maxwell and Katie Trumpener
The Fin de Siècle edited by Gail Marshall
Frankenstein edited by Andrew Smith
The French Enlightenment edited by Daniel Brewer
French Literature edited by John D. Lyons
The French Novel: from 1800 to the Present edited by Timothy Unwin
Gay and Lesbian Writing edited by Hugh Stevens
German Romanticism edited by Nicholas Saul
Global Literature and Slavery edited by Laura T. Murphy
Gothic Fiction edited by Jerrold E. Hogle
The Graphic Novel edited by Stephen Tabachnick
The Greek and Roman Novel edited by Tim Whitmarsh
Greek and Roman Theatre edited by Marianne McDonald and J. Michael Walton
Greek Comedy edited by Martin Revermann
Greek Lyric edited by Felix Budelmann
Greek Mythology edited by Roger D. Woodard
Greek Tragedy edited by P. E. Easterling
The Harlem Renaissance edited by George Hutchinson
The History of the Book edited by Leslie Howsam
Human Rights and Literature edited by Crystal Parikh
The Irish Novel edited by John Wilson Foster
Irish Poets edited by Gerald Dawe
The Italian Novel edited by Peter Bondanella and Andrea Ciccarelli
The Italian Renaissance edited by Michael Wyatt
Jewish American Literature edited by Hana Wirth-Nesher and Michael P. Kramer
The Latin American Novel edited by Efraín Kristal
Latin American Poetry edited by Stephen Hart
Latina/o American Literature edited by John Morán González
Latin Love Elegy edited by Thea S. Thorsen
Literature and Animals edited by Derek Ryan
Literature and the Anthropocene edited by John Parham
Literature and Climate edited by Adeline Johns-Putra and Kelly Sultzbach

Literature and Disability edited by Clare Barker and Stuart Murray
Literature and Food edited by J. Michelle Coghlan
Literature and the Posthuman edited by Bruce Clarke and Manuela Rossini
Literature and Religion edited by Susan M. Felch
Literature and Science edited by Steven Meyer
The Literature of the American Civil War and Reconstruction edited by Kathleen Diffley and Coleman Hutchison
The Literature of the American Renaissance edited by Christopher N. Phillips
The Literature of Berlin edited by Andrew J. Webber
The Literature of the Crusades edited by Anthony Bale
The Literature of the First World War edited by Vincent Sherry
The Literature of London edited by Lawrence Manley
The Literature of Los Angeles edited by Kevin R. McNamara
The Literature of New York edited by Cyrus Patell and Bryan Waterman
The Literature of Paris edited by Anna-Louise Milne
The Literature of World War II edited by Marina MacKay
Literature on Screen edited by Deborah Cartmell and Imelda Whelehan
Lyrical Ballads edited by Sally Bushell
Medieval British Manuscripts edited by Orietta Da Rold and Elaine Treharne
Medieval English Culture edited by Andrew Galloway
Medieval English Law and Literature edited by Candace Barrington and Sebastian Sobecki
Medieval English Literature edited by Larry Scanlon
Medieval English Mysticism edited by Samuel Fanous and Vincent Gillespie
Medieval English Theatre edited by Richard Beadle and Alan J. Fletcher (second edition)
Medieval French Literature edited by Simon Gaunt and Sarah Kay
Medieval Romance edited by Roberta L. Krueger
Medieval Romance edited by Roberta L. Krueger (new edition)
Medieval Women's Writing edited by Carolyn Dinshaw and David Wallace
Modern American Culture edited by Christopher Bigsby
Modern British Women Playwrights edited by Elaine Aston and Janelle Reinelt
Modern French Culture edited by Nicholas Hewitt
Modern German Culture edited by Eva Kolinsky and Wilfried van der Will
The Modern German Novel edited by Graham Bartram
The Modern Gothic edited by Jerrold E. Hogle
Modern Irish Culture edited by Joe Cleary and Claire Connolly
Modern Italian Culture edited by Zygmunt G. Baranski and Rebecca J. West
Modern Latin American Culture edited by John King
Modern Russian Culture edited by Nicholas Rzhevsky
Modern Spanish Culture edited by David T. Gies
Modernism edited by Michael Levenson (second edition)
The Modernist Novel edited by Morag Shiach
Modernist Poetry edited by Alex Davis and Lee M. Jenkins
Modernist Women Writers edited by Maren Tova Linett

Narrative edited by David Herman
Narrative Theory edited by Matthew Garrett
Native American Literature edited by Joy Porter and Kenneth M. Roemer
Nineteen Eighty-Four edited by Nathan Waddell
Nineteenth-Century American Literature and Politics edited by John Kerkering
Nineteenth-Century American Poetry edited by Kerry Larson
Nineteenth-Century American Women's Writing edited by Dale M. Bauer and Philip Gould
Nineteenth-Century Thought edited by Gregory Claeys
The Novel edited by Eric Bulson
Old English Literature edited by Malcolm Godden and Michael Lapidge (second edition)
Performance Studies edited by Tracy C. Davis
Piers Plowman edited by Andrew Cole and Andrew Galloway
The Poetry of the First World War edited by Santanu Das
Popular Fiction edited by David Glover and Scott McCracken
Postcolonial Literary Studies edited by Neil Lazarus
Postcolonial Poetry edited by Jahan Ramazani
Postcolonial Travel Writing edited by Robert Clarke
Postmodern American Fiction edited by Paula Geyh
Postmodernism edited by Steven Connor
Prose edited by Daniel Tyler
The Pre-Raphaelites edited by Elizabeth Prettejohn
Pride and Prejudice edited by Janet Todd
Queer Studies edited by Siobhan B. Somerville
Renaissance Humanism edited by Jill Kraye
Robinson Crusoe edited by John Richetti
Roman Comedy edited by Martin T. Dinter
The Roman Historians edited by Andrew Feldherr
Roman Satire edited by Kirk Freudenburg
The Romantic Sublime edited by Cian Duffy
Science Fiction edited by Edward James and Farah Mendlesohn
Scottish Literature edited by Gerald Carruthers and Liam McIlvanney
Sensation Fiction edited by Andrew Mangham
Shakespeare and Contemporary Dramatists edited by Ton Hoenselaars
Shakespeare and Popular Culture edited by Robert Shaughnessy
Shakespeare and Race edited by Ayanna Thompson
Shakespeare and Religion edited by Hannibal Hamlin
Shakespeare and War edited by David Loewenstein and Paul Stevens
Shakespeare on Film edited by Russell Jackson (second edition)
Shakespeare on Screen edited by Russell Jackson
Shakespeare on Stage edited by Stanley Wells and Sarah Stanton
Shakespearean Comedy edited by Alexander Leggatt
Shakespearean Tragedy edited by Claire McEachern (second edition)
Shakespeare's First Folio edited by Emma Smith

Shakespeare's History Plays edited by Michael Hattaway
Shakespeare's Language edited by Lynne Magnusson with David Schalkwyk
Shakespeare's Last Plays edited by Catherine M. S. Alexander
Shakespeare's Poetry edited by Patrick Cheney
Sherlock Holmes edited by Janice M. Allan and Christopher Pittard
The Sonnet edited by A. D. Cousins and Peter Howarth
The Spanish Novel: from 1600 to the Present edited by Harriet Turner and Adelaida López de Martínez
Textual Scholarship edited by Neil Fraistat and Julia Flanders
Theatre and Science edited by Kristen E. Shepherd-Barr
Theatre History edited by David Wiles and Christine Dymkowski
Transnational American Literature edited by Yogita Goyal
Travel Writing edited by Peter Hulme and Tim Youngs
The Twentieth-Century American Novel and Politics edited by Bryan Santin
Twentieth-Century American Poetry and Politics edited by Daniel Morris
Twentieth-Century British and Irish Women's Poetry edited by Jane Dowson
The Twentieth-Century English Novel edited by Robert L. Caserio
Twentieth-Century English Poetry edited by Neil Corcoran
Twentieth-Century Irish Drama edited by Shaun Richards
Twentieth-Century Literature and Politics edited by Christos Hadjiyiannis and Rachel Potter
Twentieth-Century Russian Literature edited by Marina Balina and Evgeny Dobrenko
Utopian Literature edited by Gregory Claeys
Victorian and Edwardian Theatre edited by Kerry Powell
The Victorian Novel edited by Deirdre David (second edition)
Victorian Poetry edited by Joseph Bristow
Victorian Women's Poetry edited by Linda K. Hughes
Victorian Women's Writing edited by Linda H. Peterson
War Writing edited by Kate McLoughlin
Women's Writing in Britain, 1660–1789 edited by Catherine Ingrassia
Women's Writing in the Romantic Period edited by Devoney Looser
World Literature edited by Ben Etherington and Jarad Zimbler
World Crime Fiction edited by Jesper Gulddal, Stewart King and Alistair Rolls
Writing of the English Revolution edited by N. H. Keeble
The Writings of Julius Caesar edited by Christopher Krebs and Luca Grillo

For EU product safety concerns, contact us at Calle de José Abascal, 56–1°, 28003 Madrid, Spain or eugpsr@cambridge.org.

www.ingramcontent.com/pod-product-compliance
Lightning Source LLC
LaVergne TN
LVHW040731250326
834688LV00031B/243